second edition

READING AND LEARNING DISABILITIES

GEORGE KALUGER

Professor of Psychology and Education
Shippensburg State College
Shippensburg, Pennsylvania

CLIFFORD J. KOLSON

Program Consultant
Chelsea School
Bethesda, Maryland

second edition

READING AND LEARNING DISABILITIES

CHARLES E. MERRILL PUBLISHING COMPANY
A Bell & Howell Company
Columbus   Toronto   London   Sydney

Published by
CHARLES E. MERRILL PUBLISHING COMPANY
A *Bell & Howell Company*
Columbus, Ohio 43216

This book was set in Electra.
The Production Editor was Cynthia Donaldson.
The cover was prepared by Will Chenoweth.

Library of Congress Catalog Card Number: 77–91651

International Standard Book Number: 0–675–08524–1

1   2   3   4   5   6   7   8   9   10—82   81   80   79   78

PRINTED IN THE UNITED STATES OF AMERICA

Preface

Our concern is with the individual who is having difficulty learning to read and the techniques by which to teach him so that he can become a more efficient and effective reader. We know that if such persons are to become better readers, they must be taught by a teacher who knows the fields of reading and learning. There is no question but that the way to reach an inefficient learner is through a knowledgeable, understanding teacher. Our intent in this text is to present content in reading and in learning, based on research findings and our observations in clinics and classrooms, that will be useful and that will provide insight to those who would teach others who have problems in developing reading skills.

As a result of our experiences, studies, and research, we have come to three conclusions concerning disabled readers. First, readers in need of remedial help differ greatly as to the cause(s) of their deficiencies in reading. Second, all remedial readers cannot be taught in the same way because of the vast diversity of factors responsible for their learning problems. Third, it is helpful, indeed essential, for the teacher to know something about (a) how a child learns how to learn; (b) how a child learns to read; and (c) the content of reading, the process of learning, and how the two must interact. Even if we cannot search the brain to know precisely how it functions for a particular child, we can at least assume that it is the brain that does the learning. A child's style and quality of learning are reflected in his attempts at reading. Frequently, we do see indications that some sensory-neural process is not functioning as it should and is restricting a child's ability in learning to read.

We chose to include learning disabilities in our text because there are many learning disabled children who are very poor readers. Although we recognize the questions being raised concerning the adequacy of the definition of learning disability, we do, at the same time, know that there are children who have difficulty in processing information for learning, not because of environmental or psychological reasons, but because of central nervous system dysfunctions involving the reading and language processes. We are not "sensory process-oriented" educators. We do, however, recognize that some processing, especially auditory and verbal, are highly related to efficient reading. We are basically committed to the task or skills approach because without the learning of specific skills of reading, there is no learning to read. We hope to present a reasonable blend of the fields of reading and of learning disabilities so that teachers seeking to help children to read can benefit from the best that both fields have to offer.

Our backgrounds are founded in the classroom with teachers and children who were learning to read. We owe the many children, teachers, and graduate students in the fields of reading and of learning disabilities with whom we have come in contact a sincere expression of gratitude for what they have taught us. We have special thanks and appreciation to Meriem Fair Kaluger for her invaluable assistance and for the materials that she provided in the preparation of this text. In addition, we would like to thank Margaret Baker and Norma Strassburger for their interest and careful attention in the typing of this manuscript.

G. K.
C. J. K.

Contents

second edition

READING AND LEARNING DISABILITIES

chapter 1

Reading and
Learning Disabilities

Educators, psychologists, and members of the various medical professions have become increasingly aware of the normal child who is not achieving on his learning expectancy level.* Since the middle 1950s, educators have been developing quality, subject-centered educational programs for the schools. Approximately 85% of all school children have been able to succeed in these programs. However, about 15% of the children have not been able to master fundamental reading skills and, so, have become educationally retarded in other subjects which are primarily dependent upon reading ability.

Attention is now being directed to this group of poor readers. Knowledge concerning learning and reading disabilities and how to work with children having these problems is more abundant and accessible than it was several years ago. Many techniques and procedures for helping this remedial group are still in experimental stages, but major breakthroughs in methodology have been made. Information and worthwhile ideas are being filtered down from the research and experimental levels to teachers and clinicians working with the moderate to severely disabled readers. However, even with this increased amount of information, there is still very little knowledge available about how to help the hard-core 1 to 2% of our children who have the mental capacity to learn but who are known as *nonreaders* or *nonlearners*.

As might be expected, the information and principles currently being developed for working with reading and learning disabilities cases are quite varied in terms of approaches and procedures. In many cases the techniques are unproven and, frequently, quite inadequate in terms of the total remedial reading problem. This observation does not imply that there are no worthwhile ideas available but that the teacher who wishes to work with children in need of remedial help must know enough about the processes of reading and learning to make quality judgments concerning remediating specific needs of a particular child. Since few ready-made answers are available for many types of reading problems, the

---

* For editorial purposes we will use the masculine pronoun to identify the child (unless otherwise specified) and alternate the feminine and masculine pronoun for the teacher. But we wish to point out that both girls and boys have reading and learning disabilities, and that there are both male and female teachers of reading and learning disabilities.

teacher will need to be knowledgeable enough to modify known diagnostic and remedial techniques to better serve the child who needs help. The conventional approaches to assessment and remediation of reading disabilities are to be retained and respected for they have been tested and found to be valuable. But there are some children who have reading disabilities which are so severe or are due to such uncommon causes that the traditional procedures prove inadequate in helping them overcome their problems.

Reading Disabilities and Learning Disabilities

Reading disabilities and *learning disabilities:* Is there a difference? An honest answer would be, "We don't know for sure." If we don't know for sure, why pursue the question? Simply because if we continue to exert our resources and energy in trying to answer the question in a meaningful way, we might learn something that will help some child or adult learn to read who might otherwise have remained an illiterate.

Experience with remedial readers has indicated that a general classification of remedial readers is inadequate. Teachers and clinicians have learned that there are some poor readers who can profit from remedial reading training while others make little or no progress. Some techniques seem effective with some children, while different techniques must be used with other children. Research studies in remedial reading invariably indicate that a certain percentage of the children do not improve. A serious question can be raised as to the advisability of grouping all disabled readers under the general heading of *remedial readers* and considering their problem to be one of a degree of severity of disability while overlooking the possibility that these children may be quite different from one another in the cause of reading retardation and may need remediation specifically designed for their special needs.

The Problem of Definition

The question whether there is a difference between reading disabilities and learning disabilities theoretically could be resolved by adequately defining each field. But that, in part, is where the problem lies—there is no truly adequate definition of learning disabilities. Definitions of learning disabilities range from very simplistic ones, such as "the child can't learn" or "he has trouble learning to read" (definitions that are used by far too many uninformed professionals and parents), to rather grandiose, complex theoretical definitions that attempt to cover every possibility of a learning disorder in very detailed, precise terminology. Of the definitions that exist between these two extremes, there is a remarkable degree of similarity, but they fall short of specifically pinpointing the learning disabled child. Maybe that's because this child refuses to be pigeonholed. The characteristics of these children are so diverse, so varied, and so extensive that it is difficult to put your finger on one major characteristic and say, "There, that identifies him as a learning disabled child." That approach can be taken to identify the blind, the deaf, the cerebral palsied, and even the mentally retarded, but not the learning disabled (LD).

The areas of agreement in the definitions of learning disabilities center around four dimensions:

1. Intellectual capacity is average or better.
2. There is a discrepancy between expected and actual achievement.
3. There is a disorder in one or more of the basic psychophysical processes involved in using spoken or written language.

4. The deficiencies are not primarily due to visual, hearing, or motor handicaps; to mental retardation; to emotional disturbance; or to environmental disadvantage.

By implication, the problem of the learning disabled child is due to central nervous system dysfunctions in perceptual and conceptual processing. The causes of the dysfunction may be organic or biochemical in nature.

There are earnest efforts being made to come up with a good definition of learning disabilities. Professionals dealing with special education want to know how to identify the LD child. Congress is asking for a definition because it does not want to appropriate money for special education programs for children who cannot be classified or defined in exclusive and inclusive categorical terms. The state of the art as it relates to learning disabilities, however, is too new and young to have had enough time to work out all the details. (Chalfant & King, 1976; Bryant, 1976; Artley & Hardin, 1976).

Definitions of reading and reading disabilities are more acceptable than definitions of learning disabilities because they generally refer to skills, skill deficits, or the functional manifestation of the act of reading. Typical is the definition of Harris and Sepay (1976), "Reading disability: reading is significantly below expectancy for both age and intelligence and is also disparate with the learner's cultural, linguistic, and educational experience." Yet, Spache and Spache (1969) suggest that a definition of reading cannot be a simple one because reading may be defined under a variety of headings, such as skill development, a visual act, a perceptual act, a thinking process, and relatedness to cultural background. Most professionals in the field do not feel it necessary to give extensive definitions, but they do not dismiss the point made by Spache and Spache. What is of interest is that Spache and Spache include some dimensions, especially the perceptual act and the thinking process, that are strongly emphasized by many specialists in learning disabilities.

Delineation of Reading and Learning Disabilities

There are several points to be recognized. First, there is a degree of overlapping of content to be taught between the fields of reading and learning disabilities. That area of common interest is in the development of specific reading skills. These two fields share that academic concern with those who teach the blind, deaf, emotionally disturbed, culturally different, and mentally retarded how to read. Just because teachers of different types of children all teach reading does not mean that they should all teach it in the same way. It certainly does not mean that all of these children learn in the same way; nor can all children be helped with the same kinds of procedures, techniques, and materials as used with normal children.

A second point, more minor in nature yet worthy of note, is that not all learning disabled children are poor readers. It is true that most LD children are deficient in reading skills, but there are some who read very well but do very poorly only in arithmetic. The nature of their academic problem is related to that part of the brain which is not functioning properly. Thus, not all learning disabled children are poor readers, nor are all poor readers learning disabled.

A third point, again minor but significant in nature, is a recognition of the degree of severity of a reading or learning problem. Mild or minor cases usually would be difficult to categorize as to cause. The more severe the cause of the learning problem, the more clearly it can be identified. Just because a mild to moderate case cannot be diagnosed is no reason to reject the concept of specific learning disabilities in reading.

A fourth point to be observed is that the approach to reading by teachers of reading and of learning disabilities differ. Basically, reading specialists emphasize developmental reading skills that must be learned. Many teachers in learning disabilities analyze central nervous system processing problems and learning modalities. Which is correct? We believe there is an element of truth in both positions and that neither should be ignored for what they have to offer us in terms of telling us how to do a better job of teaching children to solve their reading problems.

Being involved with many teachers and classes of learning disabled children, Kaluger observed that, in the past, teachers trained in the field of special education usually did a poor job of teaching LD children to read. They were great on perceptual and motor problems, but this emphasis did not teach a child skills in reading. As a reading specialist and supervisor of reading, Kolson noted that many of his teachers did a fairly good job of teaching reading to some pupils, but there were always certain children who did not benefit from their remedial instruction. We recognize that as LD teachers learn more about the teaching of reading and as remedial reading teachers learn more about the intricacies of learning disabilities, they become more successful in their work. We concur with that part of the International Reading Association (IRA) Resolutions Committee's report on learning disabilities and reading which recommends that teachers

> seek their (legislators') support to certify graduates of reading/language programs both as reading/language specialists and as learning disabilities specialists. (1975-76 IRA Annual Report)

Conversely, we believe specialists trained in learning disabilities should be trained reading specialists. The country of Denmark has required their reading specialists to be knowledgeable in learning disabilities for some years. As far as we can tell, this approach has been very successful in reaching the kind of children who, in the past, could not learn to be effective readers.

Can reading disabilities be delineated from learning disabilities? We believe so, eventually. Since 85 to 90% of all LD children have reading problems, it would appear that it would not be necessary to indicate a difference; but there are differences. There are learning disabled children with identifiable cerebral dysfunctions whose only problem is learning arithmetic. Others only have gross or fine motor problems that interfere with handwriting and motor skills. Many LD children have behavior characteristics, such as extensive distractibility or excessive restlessness, that make it difficult for them to function effectively in a regular classroom. Others have cognitive problems in perceptual processing and conceptualization. We know that LD children generally do not improve much in reading when taught with a traditional, developmental approach. Techniques and materials involving a multisensory approach or that combine a sensory modality skill with a reading skill do improve their reading skills. The characteristics and the significance for learning will be discussed in the ensuing chapters. We will present both developmental and special techniques. Our prime position is this: If you want a child to learn to read, you must teach him reading skills. We recognize the need for further understanding and knowledge of the field. We are sympathetic to the need. But skills must be taught. Not all children learn the same way, hence they should not all be taught the same way. Teachers have a primary responsibility to their children, not to their academic discipline. Philosophical, political, and prejudicial positions should take second place to the needs of children.

Of special interest is a symposium which appeared in the *Journal of Learning Disabilities* (Sartain et al., 1976). The question was "Who shall teach the learning disabled child?" A reading specialist, a learning disabilities specialist, and a speech pathologist present their points of view. A fourth paper pinpoints the crucial issues that must be dealt with in terms of interdisciplinary cooperation. Indeed, Act 94-142 demands that an interdisciplinary approach be taken with all children who have exceptionalities by providing services and by developing an individualized educational program (IEP) for each child. The concept of an IEP could well become a requirement for all children in our schools in the not too distant future.

The Extent of Disabled Readers

Reading disabilities are generally considered to be a major problem in our schools. Leary (1965) reports from research studies that about 25% of the failures in the elementary grades are attributed to reading disabilities. He also notes that at the end of the third grade, about 40% of the children could not read grade-level material successfully, while at the end of the sixth grade about one-third of the children had an achievement level one or more years below grade level.

Betts (1957) cites various authorities who estimate that 8 to 15% of the school population have various degrees of reading disability. Durrell (1940) states a percentage of 15.2, while Monroe (1938) indicates 12 to 15% have reading deficiencies. Harrower (1955) points out that 75% of delinquent children in New York City are poor readers. A study of 3,946 sixth graders by Newborough and Kelley (1962) indicated that 14% were two years or more below grade level in reading achievement. Critchley (1964) reviewed 15 pertinent studies and concluded that in terms of sex-incidence, a ratio of four males for every one female could be accepted as a reasonable figure. Most all sex-incidence studies showed more male than female reading disability cases, with the ratio ranging from 3 to 1 to as high as 20 to 1.

The Texas State Legislature appointed a committee to investigate the extent of reading disability labeled by a variety of terms, such as *perceptually handicapped, dyslectic minimally brain damaged,* and *neurologically dysfunctional.* After a thorough study the committee reported that from 10 to 20% of all school children could be classified in this inclusive classification (Barnes, 1968).

The National Conference on Dyslexia in 1966 published its proceedings and papers in a book edited by Keeney and Keeney entitled *Dyslexia: Diagnosis and Treatment of Reading Disorders* (1968). The incidence of severe reading disorders (dyslexia) was estimated in this book by various participants: Nicholls cited 15% and also indicated that about two-thirds could be adequately corrected with the proper help; Rabinovitch suggested that at least 10% of all children had reading incompetencies before they reached seventh grade and he estimated one-fourth to one-third of this group had some degree of dyslexia; Schiffman did not give incidence figures but he did say that when the diagnosis of dyslexia was made in the first two grades of school, nearly 82% could be brought up to normal grade classwork while only 46% of the third graders, 42% of the fourth graders, and only 10 to 15% of the fifth to seventh graders could be helped if the diagnosis of dyslexia was made at those grade levels; and Critchley spoke of the "greatest" incidence of dyslexia being in English-speaking cultures but noted dyslexia was also found to a lesser degree in Germany, the Scandinavian countries, Italy, Russia, Rumania, and Spain. Makita (1968) found in a study in Japan that out of 9,195 children, only 89, or slightly less than 1%, were reported by their teachers as having a reading disability. He questioned the importance of emotional problems, laterality, auditory discrimination, as causes of reading disability but did postulate that the cause may be related to the structure of the language that the child learns to read.

The extent of reading disabilities goes beyond a mere recitation of statistics. Remedial reading specialists need to be aware that reading disabilities are found among a great variety of children and that these are live people with individual differences. A reading deficiency is overlooked in some types of children simply because they have other disorders which are more outstanding or demanding. Some of the different types of children who have reading problems are (a) children of normal intelligence who have the capacity to learn but have never developed the skills needed for reading, (b) children of normal intelligence who have a deficit in learning ability due to an acuity or physical problem, (c) children who are perceptually handicapped, (d) children who have a neurological dysfunction which impairs their learning ability and may even cause cerebral palsy, aphasia, alexia, or some other disorder due to brain injury, (e) children who are marginal or slow learners who have become educationally retarded and often are not given the needed help in reading simply because they cannot keep up with the reading groups in the class, (f) mentally retarded children who may be neglected on the assumption that they will never be able to read, (g) children who are emotional and social deviates and may not be able to permit themselves to learn, and (h) culturally disadvantaged environmentally deprived children who may not have developed their potential for learning. It does not seem sensible to group all of these children under the one heading, *remedial readers*, and use approximately the same techniques in the remedial process.

Types of Achievers in Reading

The distinction among different types of achievers in reading is one of a degree of retardation as well as kind of disability. It is difficult to establish clear cut classifications, and the dividing lines must be somewhat arbitrary. However, there is desirability for having some criteria by which the varying degrees and types of reading retardation can be identified so that the appropriate kind of reading instruction can be given. One does not teach a normal achiever in reading as one would teach a disabled reader.

Much difficulty in classifying disabled readers arises because reading specialists and institutions training reading specialists fail to define their terms. What is considered a remedial reader at one institution is referred to as a *clinical reader* at a second institution. To help clarify this maze of terminology as used in various reading clinics and centers we have constructed Table 1-1 to illustrate how children with different degrees of reading disabilities are classified at various universities.

The Developmental Reader

The child who achieves in accordance with his capacity and exhibits no retardation when his performance is compared to his mental ability is termed a *developmental reader*. The comparison is with one's own capacity rather than with chronological age or grade placement. A child may be a fast learner, achieving far beyond the achievement level generally assigned to his grade placement, or he may be a slow learner reading below his grade placement but up to his mental ability level. Another child could be of average ability and be doing the reading expected of his particular grade. In each of these three cases, the child is achieving in line with his capabilities; hence, each is considered a developmental reader.

	Univ. A	Univ. B	Univ. C	Kolson-Kaluger
A child reading up to capacity	Developmental	Developmental	Developmental	Developmental
A child at or near capacity, yet with a deficiency	Corrective	Developmental	Corrective	Corrective
A child one or more years behind capacity level who can progress with special help. No specialized techniques needed	Remedial	Corrective	Remedial	Remedial, Secondary
A child one or more years behind capacity level who needs special help and specialized technique	Clinical	Remedial	Remedial	Remedial, Primary

TABLE 1-1. How children with varying degrees of reading disability are classified at different university reading clinics.

The Corrective Reader

The corrective reader is one who experiences some minor difficulty in reading. He is reading slightly below his mental age level, generally not more than one year. He may be having difficulty with a particular word attack skill or with comprehension. He may have one or more defects in an otherwise normal pattern of reading skills. He would be classified as a *corrective reader*. Corrective readers are not considered serious problems and can be helped by the classroom teacher. The teacher merely has to identify the child's specific weakness in reading and then select and apply the appropriate method and materials needed to provide corrective therapy. This is not "remedial reading" in the strictest sense of the word.

The Remedial Reader

The remedial reader is a seriously disabled reader, one who is reading at a level far below his capacity and who is experiencing difficulty in progressing under normal learning conditions. The remedial reader is one who can learn but is not learning. He could be a child who can comprehend material read to him which is at a higher level than he can read and understand for himself. This child is handicapped by severe reading defects. A child who is mentally retarded will not be reading on his chronological age level, but he cannot be listed as a remedial reader until he is reading significantly below his mental age.

A discrepancy must exist between mental ability and accomplishment for any child to be considered a remedial reader. This discrepancy must be more than one year. Most authorities insist on two years retardation. Bond and Tinker (1967) use a sliding scale to indicate the degree of retardation for various age levels. This scale differs slightly from the one we have found helpful since ours tends to be a little more narrow in span of retardedness. The measures of retardation in reading development which we consider indicative of possible need for remedial reading instruction are as follows:

Grades	Behind in Reading
1, 2	3—6 months
3, 4	6—9 months
5, 6	9 months—1 year
Junior High	1 year—2 years
Senior High	2 years—3 years

Differential Classification

Until recently, it was not unusual for reading teachers to consider all retarded readers simply as children who had not learned to read. If there were different types of remedial readers, they were different only in the nature and severity of their reading defect. A review of the research in the past on reading has frequently been aimed at finding the one characteristic common to all severely disabled reading cases. Remedial reading techniques of various types have been tried by those seeking to find a method which would be successful with all retarded readers. In every instance, there remained a small percentage of remedial readers who could not be helped and who had certain characteristics not found in the other cases. This observation has raised the question whether or not a differential classification of remedial readers is needed. Observations made during our clinical experiences indicate that drastically different types of remediation approaches must be used with certain types of remedial readers, and thus we believe such a differentation is needed.

Rationale for Differential Classification

It has long been accepted that there are individual differences in children. Not only do they differ in the types of reading skills they acquire or in which they are deficient, but also in such factors as motivation, interest, possession of certain fundamental skills, personality characteristics, and attitudes. More significantly, they also differ in the degree to which they can use their various sensory modalities for learning. Some children are visual-cognitive learners. These are children who, according to Birch (1962), have reached the highest level of intrasensory functioning and learning. Other children are basically auditory learners, such as the "word-callers," who can read beautifully orally, but who have no comprehension of what they have read. Some children can only learn through the tactile-kinesthetic senses. The best way for them to gain knowledge of an article or word is by touching or handling it. There are few children whose only ability is to use the visual modality in learning through which they see configurations but cannot break a word down into its letters and parts. Another group of children are conceptually handicapped. Their sensory modalities of vision, hearing, and touch are adequate for learning, but their thought processes do not operate effectively. Many have difficulty with memory, scanning, or attending. Some cannot control the flow of thoughts or reasoning and therefore, cannot process the stimuli taken in, nor can they program for a response. Every classroom will contain some of these different kinds of children. It would be wrong to assume that all of them would learn equally efficiently and effectively if taught by the same method, such as the visual, or look and say approach, for example. Fortunately, most basal reader series do provide and encourage teachers to use a variety of modalities for learning purposes.

When one considers remedial readers, not only do we find children who are strong in certain sensory modalities and weak in others, but we also find the perceptually handicapped, the culturally deprived, the child who has a deep emotional problem and may be autistic, an occasional hyperactive child with brain damage, and other types as well. They may all exhibit the same deficiencies in reading skills, but the cause of the deficiencies stems from different sources.

Clinical observations have long indicated that it is not desirable nor possible to teach these different children in the exact same way and expect similar results, even if the reading skill in which they are deficient is exactly the same.

Research studies dealing with remedial reading invariably report that a certain percentage of the children improve, while a certain percentage do not. For example, Birch (1950) conducted a two-year experiment in England with remedial readers which resulted in 84% making improvement under a remedial program and 16% not making satisfactory improvement under the same program. Birch, too, found two distinct groups: those who could learn with the usual type of remediation and those who could not.

A number of other writers in various fields have alluded to the existence of two types of remedial learners. Fernald (1943) refers to cases of reading disability as being divided into two groups: those in which the disability occurs after the subject has learned to read and those in which the subject has never learned to read. She groups the theories of causation under two headings. First, she presents "physiological theories" on the basis of which she suggests that there are children who have a congenital condition or some defect acquired early in life which interferes with the development of a particular skill. Second, she groups other theories of causation under "psychological causes" from which she deduces that an individual loses a skill that he had acquired.

A study by the psychologist Koppitz (1964) on the use of The Bender Gestalt Test for Young Children concludes that in regard to disability in reading, one group of her cases did poorly because of their poor social and emotional environment, while another group did poorly because of perceptual problems. She makes the statement "It appears that perceptual problems may be the single most important factor contributing to poor reading ability." Clement (1963) suggests that there is a false dichotomy in thinking that only psychogenesis or organicity could cause dyslexia in children.

In a work edited by Wolman, *Handbook of Clinical Psychology*, Heiser and Wolman (1965) cite several studies seeking to establish classifications for levels of mental deficiencies. They found classification systems set up according to mental ability, social criteria, and etiology. Tredgold (1908) established an etiological classification system which contained four main groups:

1. Primary amentia, in which the deficiency is due to germinal or endogenous factors or simply to heredity.
2. Secondary amentia, in which the deficiency is due to exogenous factors, to causes from the environment.
3. Amentia due to mixed or combined, or both heredity and environmental causes.
4. Amentia with unknown causes.

Other systems of classification closely related to Tredgold's list only two main causes: (1) organic, or causes which operate though the direct impairment of the physical organism and its physiology so that normal intellectual powers and efficiency do not develop, and (2) functional, or psychological or environmental causes which impair the proper functioning of the organism. Many sources can be cited which contend that the causes of reading disability can be grouped under (1) organic causes, which are primary causes, and (2) functional causes, which are secondary causes of disability.

Although many agree there are different categories of reading deficiencies, it still remains to be shown through research that different types of remediation are needed for each category.

Reading Disability: Functional Deficits

The disabled reader whose learning mechanism is intact and who has the mental ability to learn but has a severe educational deficiency in reading skills, is a secondary reading case. This is due to functional deficits or limitations. Secondary reading disability is an acquired reading disability in the sense that the disability was incurred because the child failed to learn the necessary reading skills, even though he had the potential, organically and intellectually, to learn. Environmental or psychological factors restricted learning.

There is no specific syndrome which is applicable to all secondary reading cases. In many instances it is difficult to determine the cause, or causes, of disability. In fact, anomalies, deviations, or irregular characteristics existing in some secondary reading cases are also found to exist in a few very proficient readers. Research on this problem led Helen Robinson (1946) to formulate the Multiple-Causation Theory of reading difficulty. Briefly, this theory holds that a constellation of factors interplay within the child and his environment;

therefore, any number of combinations of factors can operate together to make a child a severely retarded reading case.

The source of the restriction in learning is to be found in environmental and emotional factors, rather than in inherent defects of those parts of the central nervous system concerned with learning. The environmental and emotional factors responsible for inferior or inadequate learning are numerous. They may be related to the home, school, teacher, peers, learning materials, teaching techniques, attitudes, emotional or intellectual atmosphere, or any number of other factors. Basically, the factors may be categorized as environmental causes, educational limitations, social or cultural restrictions, or psychological factors.

The type of reading disabilities that functional deficit cases have differ according to the combination of factors which caused the disability. Some of the reading difficulties which these children may have include disability of contextual clue skill, inadequate use of phonics, disability with syllabication, weakness in structural analysis, inadequate language, miscalling words, comprehension, vocabulary, study skills, location skills, and low rate of reading. To a lesser degree of severity, these same types of reading defects could also be found in corrective readers. However, recognize that it is not the type of reading disability that is important here but rather the fact that he is severely retarded in reading; there is nothing wrong with his learning capacity nor with his sensori-neural mechanism for learning.

Reading Disability: Primary Causes

There is the type of disabled reader who has at least average mental ability but whose learning mechanism is not intact or fully developed, and as a result he has a perceptual-conceptual handicap or a learning disorder. We refer to this type of remedial reader as a primary learning disability case. The physiological mechanism for learning is defective or not developed. The problem is organic and may be sensory, cognitive, or motor.

The following definition of learning disability has been suggested by the National Advisory Committee on Handicapped Children:

> Children with special learning disabilities exhibit a disorder in one or more of the basic psychological processes involved in understanding or in using spoken or written languages. These may be manifested in disorders of listening, thinking, talking, reading, writing, spelling, or arithmetic. They do not include learning problems which are due primarily to visual, hearing, or motor handicaps, to mental retardation, emotional disturbance, or to environmental disadvantaged.

Our concept of a primary learning disability is in keeping with this committee's (1968).

The causes of primary learning disability may be (1) a lack of neural organization or sensorimotor pattern for learning, (2) a subtle structural defect such as a lesion or inadequately developed synaptic knobs in the neurons, (3) a biochemical imbalance of a genetic condition producing neural inadequacy, possibly involving enzymes, DNA and RNA factors, or chromosomal aberrations, or (4) a developmental lag in the sensori-neural process.

The premise of primary learning disability is a hypothesis, as are the causes listed. We can not prove that these conditions produce perceptual-conceptual handicaps or learning disorders other than in those disorders found to be extreme. However, learning is fundamentally a cerebral process. The type of learning or skill involved, such as sensory, integrative, or motor, determines the neurological process which must function in order for that operation to take place. The efficiency with which the sensori-neural system operates determines the effectiveness of its attempts at learning.

We wish to call attention to the fact that we presented a duoclassification scheme based upon the thinking of Rabinovitch in *Clinical Aspects of Remedial Reading* (Kolson & Kaluger, 1963). In that book we defined "primary reading disability" as a congenital reading disability having a specific syndrome. We have learned since that the duoclassification idea is sound, but that the definition was inadequate inasmuch as primary reading disability need not be congenital. Also, we have not been able to substantiate the existence of a specific syndrome, especially the Gerstmann's syndrome supported by Herman (1959). Critchley also questions the validity of the Gerstmann syndrome (1968). It appears that the greater the severity of the learning disorder, the more symptoms a child has, but these symptoms do not spell out the same syndrome for all primary learning disability cases. Our clinical observations, however, reveal degrees of perceptual-conceptual handicaps and learning disorders. In general, the more severe the reading disability, the more likely it is to be a primary learning disability case.

An extreme primary learning disability case is the disabled reader who has detectable neurological defects and who may be a nonreader or severely retarded in spite of the fact that he has average mental ability. Some loss or impairment of the power to use words may be present. Technically, this condition is known as *aphasia* if it involves oral words, or *alexia* or *dyslexia* if it involves understanding printed words. Whether or not such a person can benefit from remedial reading instruction depends upon the location and the extent of the organic injury and upon the skill, knowledge, and patience of the reading teacher. The schools and public are becoming aware of the child with cerebral dysfunction and are seeking to provide better training for him. There is still much to be learned about how to help this type of child.

Some writers speak of *minimal brain damage,* but we avoid this label because we find it inadequate, meaningless, and inappropriate. Certain attitudes and facts should be recognized about the use of the term *brain damage.* First of all, there are not as many brain damaged children as may be implied by the current emphasis on "minimal cerebral dysfunctions," "minimal brain damage," and "learning disabilities" which imply to some people that brain damage is present. We prefer to use the term *cerebral dysfunction* because there are neurological and biochemical deviations other than brain damage that can cause limited ability to read. Second, there are varying degrees of cerebral dysfunction in those who do have these conditions and some of these individuals live perfectly normal lives with few handicaps. Some children with adequate intelligence can compensate for the handicaps they do have and become brilliant individuals, scholastically and otherwise, in spite of a cerebral dysfunction. Third, reading specialists and psychologists are not neurologists, and so they should not make any medical diagnosis or judgments. There are too many variables which must be considered before it is possible to conclude that cerebral dysfunction is present simply because a particular behavior is not adequate. Fourth, the term is so threatening to parents, to the child, and to some teachers that it should be avoided if at all possible.

Related Literature

For many years the term *word blindness* was used to describe the characteristics of a disabled reader who was similar to a primary reading disability case. The English physicians James Kerr (1897) and W. Pringle Morgan (1896) in separate reports drew attention to certain cases where children who seemed to be intellectually normal were having difficulty learning to read. Morgan spoke of a 14-year-old boy as being "a case of congenital word blindness." Since that time, others, mostly associated with the medical profession, have shown interest in word blindness. Rabinovitch (1959) presented a criteria which sought to group retarded readers under three categories: primary reading retardation, secondary reading retardation, and reading retardation associated with organic brain injury. Gradually, a variety of terms have come to be used in place of the somewhat misleading term *word blindness.*

THE WORK OF KNUD HERMAN. Knud Herman (1959) as chief physician of the neurological unit of the University Hospital in Copenhagen, Denmark, involved himself in the study of word blindness, and on the basis of his experience and research, made some observations concerning primary learning disability. He found that certain children attending his clinic were unlike other children and seemed to fall into a rather specific category in regard to reading disability. These children were severely retarded in reading, but they were all of at least average intelligence. The number of children so described amounted to about 10% of the total group. Herman consequently learned that similar ratios of 10 to 20% of "hard core" severely disabled readers were also noted in studies reported in England, Sweden, and Germany. He concluded that these children all had the same characteristics:

1. They all had a defective capacity for learning and could not read.
2. There were no apparent intellectual defects nor defects of sense organs, however.
3. The children had difficulty with symbols such as notes found in music, the Morse code, and numbers.
4. There was much evidence of a familial history and, as such, the defect seemed to imply that constitutional factors were responsible for its occurrence.
5. The disability persisted into adult life.

A review of the literature plus his own research convinced Herman of the existence of a group of disabled readers who had characteristics similar to each other but different from other disabled readers.

THE WORK OF HERMAN K. GOLDBERG. The American ophthalmologist Herman Krieger Goldberg (1959) reported on two electroencephalographic studies that he made with 125 children having reading difficulties. The results of his studies persuaded Goldberg to accept the existence of two different types of disabled readers. One of these groups was made up of poor achievers who had no demonstrable brain damage but who could not learn to read with remedial instruction offered. The other group seemed to have their learning mechanism intact and were without any constitutional disturbances.

Goldberg noted that most of his primary disability cases:

1. Had normal or superior intelligence.
2. Had a high incidence of left-handedness or ambidexterity.
3. Had indications of left–right disorientation.
4. Had difficulty recognizing a Gestalt figure as an entity.

Although stated differently, Goldberg found a group of disabled readers who had characteristics similar to those found by Herman and who fit the classification of Rabinovitch as primary disability cases.

Goldberg also noted a form of visual agnosia in the patients. Gestalt entities composed of dots were shown to the subjects. In most cases the subjects failed to achieve Gestalt Closure in order to recognize the form. Instead, the subjects saw only a series of dots as in Figure 1-1.

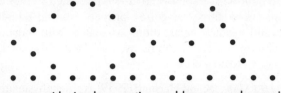

FIGURE 1-1. Some cases with visual perception problems see only a series of dots but not the figures. These cases lack closure ability to form gestalts.

THE WORK OF RALPH D.RABINOVITCH. Rabinovitch and his colleagues at the Hawthorne Center noted that many of the problem children being sent to their center for psychological therapy or psychiatric care were also severe reading disability cases. They embarked on a program to identify the nature of reading disability in these children because they came to believe that solving the reading problem was essential in many instances to overcoming the behavioral or emotional problem. As part of the investigation, Rabinovitch and Ingram (1962) reported a syndrome of primary retardation which they felt indicated levels of process disturbances. It is interesting to note how the various aspects of the syndrome which they developed can be related to characteristics in the Herman Syndrome. The Rabinovitch and Ingram disability characteristics are also five in number:

1. Retardation in School Achievement. There is a retardation in reading achievement which is usually severe. Occasionally the child has a small sight vocabulary which was learned by rote and some simple phonics skill, but not much else in reading functioning. Arithmetic competency is usually low but not always as low as the reading. Spelling may have the greatest impairment, especially when the child is attempting to write from dictation.

2. Reading Process Disturbance. The primary disability reader frequency has difficulties in certain visual and auditory recognition. Discrimination functioning seems to be adequate but the letter forms and sounds which they see or hear cannot be translated into meaningful concepts. This inability to make sense of the stimuli is further complicated by left-right directional confusion.

3. Indiscriminating Language Deficits. Usually the conversation of the primary disability reader is considered to be adequate. However, a close observation of his language pattern reveals certain minor disturbances in his expressive language. The most frequent difficulties are in finding the specific word which he wants to say, in imprecise articulation, and in the use of primitive syntax. Frequently a related but incorrect word will be spoken or a phrase will be used which has the right connotation but which is awkwardly put together. We believe that this type of deficiency in expressive control can be due to left-right directional disorientation resulting in inadequate symbolization.

4. Specific Concept-Symbolization Deficiency in Orientation. The symbolization defect can also be manifested in certain abstract conceptualizations which are related to such things as quantity, space, distance, and time. Such a child may say that the average man is ten feet tall and that the distance between Paris and New York is a great distance, maybe as great as two or three hundred miles,

5. Body Image. With the question of left-right disorientation also arises the question of body image. Many primary disability readers have a disturbance in personal-orientation or body image. They have difficulty knowing how much space their bodies take up or precisely where they are being touched on their body when they have their eyes closed. They may also have hesitances at the midpoint of their body when crossing from one side to the other.

Observation on Primary Learning Disability

As one reflects on the type of evidence existing for a primary reading disability group, the postulated causes, the Herman Syndrome, and the sociophysical characteristics of such readers, it becomes apparent that many of these factors seem to be both interrelated and interdependent. It is possible to combine any number of these characteristics and factors together to indicate their influence in producing primary disability readers. However, it is also noted that none of the factors mentioned thus far are adequate in themselves to identify primary disability cases. A number of the characteristics and situations found in PRD can also be found, to a degree, in normal achievers. Even to use the Herman Syndrome alone as a measuring stick would be inadequate because a person can learn to compensate for many of these deficiencies. At best, Herman's Syndrome and the sociophysical characteristics should be studied with the intent of gathering supportive evidence for the existence of primary reading disability. The final identification of PRD must come from the disturbances found within the reading process itself. Since the reading process involves recognition, language significance, and motor expression, it is here that we must search in order to identify the different types of primary disability readers.

Reading and the Exceptional Child

The emphasis today is on the fact that an exceptional child is first of all a child. The things that make him exceptional are just a matter of the degree of difference he exhibits. It is necessary to adjust the educational program in the classroom or school so that he may learn to the maximum of his capacity. The child with a low mental capacity is an exceptional child, but so is the so-called gifted child. The child who has hidden mental or physical disabilities is an exceptional child, but so is the child who has superior abilities in these areas.

Children Who Are Mentally Exceptional

Educators today try to avoid labeling children unless the label will aid in a better understanding of the child and his problems. Years ago the terms *feebleminded* and *moron* were used. Neither label contributed to a better understanding of the child. Today these terms have been replaced by labels more indicative of the educational prognosis. Children with I.Q.'s from 75 to 90 are classed as *slow learners*. It is unfair to expect them to achieve on the level of average children. It is also unfair to expect them to benefit from the same type of instruction given to average children.

In the area of reading, several adjustments must be made if the child who is a slow learner is to reach his capacity. First, his entrance into school should be delayed. Although a mental age of 6 is not necessary for one to learn to read, it is necessary under our present reading program and methods of teaching reading. The slow learner with an I.Q. of 90 has only a mental age of about 5 years 5 months when he enters school at chronological age 6. The slow learner with a 75 I.Q. has a mental age of only 4½. Neither is ready to profit from our present methods of teaching reading unless adjustments are made.

Secondly, the word *slow* indicates that more time and care must be spent with the slow learner in order for him to achieve. This implies a longer readiness period, more time spent learning a particular skill or knowledge, and more concretism since the ability to abstract is not as high as with more mentally endowed pupils.

Third, these children need a more thoroughly structured program. The so-called "discovery program" in arithmetic and other disciplines may be fine for the more mentally endowed, but with the slow learner, it is chaotic. He experiences difficulty learning facts let alone discerning finer subtleties and relationships.

Fourth, the reading program should have realistic objectives. Since the slow learner can function in an average society, the goals of instruction should be geared to give him the skills necessary to function adequately. Reading should aim at giving him the skills necessary to read the newspaper, some recreational reading ability, and special skills necessary for the performance of the kind of work which he will probably do. Instead of formal English in the high school, he should be given reading classes.

Children with I.Q.'s from 50 to 75 are now classified as *educably mentally retarded*. This label gives an educational prognosis which implies that there is some ability to profit from education but only in a limited degree. Much of what has been said about the slow learner can be restated concerning the reading program of the educably mentally retarded. As indicated earlier, exceptionality is merely a matter of degree. The educably mentally retarded child needs more realistic objectives, delayed entrance, a longer readiness period, more concretism, more time and care, and a more tightly structured program. In addition, although this is a debatable issue, this child needs a special class with a special teacher who is more highly trained than the average classroom teacher. This child needs more individual instruction. Hence, to have him in a regular classroom limits his chance for individualization of instruction. Small special classrooms are the only answer.

The child is considered trainable if his I.Q. is between 30 and 50. Since most schools exclude this child from the classroom, we will not discuss the problems here.

About all we can say for the other end of the mental continuum, the bright, gifted, and very gifted, is that at last there is at least much talk about it. There is little agreement or evidence as to what identifies a bright, gifted, or very gifted child, and what kind of program is best for him. There is sufficient evidence, however, to show that unless something is done for these mentally superior students, they are faced with adjustment problems and may become scholastically poor.

Children Who Are Physically Exceptional

Many children have visual defects which can be corrected through a refraction so that they may function adequately in the classroom. These children experience little difficulty when learning to read. There is, however, a small group of children with visual defects which cannot be refractively corrected. Many of the better schools have set up sight conservation classes in which the child may spend part or all of his time. Where no such program exists, the classroom teacher will be expected to handle the instruction of this child within the class.

The objective for the classroom teacher is to structure the learning situation and materials in order to facilitate the ease with which the visually deficient child can function. By making certain that the child sits as close to the material he is expected to see, the teacher can sometimes place the child in a more functional situation. When we cut the distance between eyes and material to be read, we cut the distance arithmetically, whereas we increase the acuity mathematically. One ophthalmologist claims that if a child can distinguish that there is a physical difference between a chair and a table, he has enough sight to read. The problem is just one of getting them close enough to the material.

If the classroom teacher will see that there is plenty of illumination and that the child is given books with large type, she will have gone far toward providing the kind of reading situation in which the child can be successful.

Children with hearing deficiencies can sometimes have near normal hearing by having a hearing aid. The job here for the teacher is to see that the child uses the aid. She can eliminate some of the child's self-consciousness by getting a hearing aid for the other children in the room to listen through so that they may have some idea about what the child with deficient hearing is experiencing.

Whether a child has an aid or not, the teacher should make certain the child is placed in a position so that he can always see the teacher's lips since many of these children become very proficient in lip reading. Besides, this will give them some idea about how to form their mouth in order to make certain sounds which they may be unable to hear. Some of the recently developed programmed materials for teaching word attack skills seem to offer possibilities for use with children who have a hearing problem. In all presentations the teacher should try to visualize what she wants to teach. Pictures illustrating sounds can help the deaf child make sounds he may not be able to hear. Generally, deaf or partially deaf children achieve somewhat below their capacities.

The physically handicapped child who has mild cerebral palsy, or physical defects due to polio, or some other physically devastating disease, must also have the environment controlled for him if he is to operate efficiently. The basic principle is what can be done to work around the physical defect. Children with defective legs should not be assigned to a teacher on the second floor, even if it means changing an entire class around.

Children Who Are Emotionally Handicapped

In every school there are children who are exceptional emotionally. The fact remains that these children must have specialized help, but if no help is available, then the classroom teacher is obligated to try to teach the child. Mandel Sherman said one of the best ways to relate to the child is to operate opposite the home. If the home environment is dictatorial, then the teacher should be permissive, and vice versa. Many times if the teacher attempts to restore self-confidence through praise and successes, she can go a long way toward eliminating emotional disability.

Many times the emotionally disturbed child is also a reading problem. A number of studies have shown that once the reading problem is overcome, the emotional problems seem to disappear.

Children with Speech Problems

The first step in assisting a child with a speech problem is to see that proper speech therapy is provided. Once speech therapy has been initiated, the speech therapist and the classroom teacher can cooperate to provide the child with the kind of program which will assist him in overcoming both his speech and reading problems, or at least enable him to cope with them.

Where no speech therapy is available, many times the teacher can help by placing the child with a group of slow learners needing guidance in phonics. By using the Phonovisual materials which have been designed for speech and reading, the teacher can contribute to the child's correct enunciation and pronunciation if these are his problems. As to whether or not the child should participate in oral reading, the answer is not a clear cut yes or no. The answer depends upon how the child himself views his problem. If the oral reading contributes toward feelings of inadequacy, the oral reading should be minimized. If, however, the child does not regard his speech impediment as serious, then he may read orally as much as he wishes.

Children with Brain Injury

This is a ticklish question since there is disagreement concerning the number of children with brain injury. An expert in this area once said that in a school of 1,000, at most there would be only one or two cases, whereas some authorities are acting on the principle that from 5 to 10% of the school population have brain injury. The surest course for the teacher is to avoid making medical diagnosis and to accept as brain injured only those children who have been medically diagnosed as such.

Brain-injured children are easily distracted, have a short attention span, and in most cases, are fidgety. This kind of child never has been known to contribute to the peace of mind of the teacher. Although the classroom teacher is working under extreme handicaps, there are certain things she can do to set the climate for some learning by the brain-injured child. One, she should cut out as much stimulation as possible. She should wear plain clothes (bright clothes and objects tend to distract these kids), refrain from the kinds of activities which overstimulate, and keep the learning situation as quiet as possible. Two, she can make sure she has a set and orderly routine which she follows religiously in order to give the brain-injured child the security of knowing where he is going. Three, she can have constructed a booth 4'x4'x4' in which the child can work since this will help to eliminate distractions. Fourth, she can consult the child's family physician concerning the possibility of using some type of tranquilizers in order to eliminate some of the distractability. Five, she should employ a multi-sensory technique in so far as is possible with the large numbers of children she has.

The Perceptually Handicapped Child

For years there have been recurring references in literature to children who seem to fit no known category of disability. These children have been referred to as *children with specific reading disability, dyslectics, neurologically disorganized, neurologically confused, mixed dominance, minimally brain damaged, primary disability,* and a host of other terms. The term *perceptually handicapped* has been frequently used to classify these children.

The perceptually handicapped child is a child who has no apparent inhibitory defects yet who is unable to learn to read to his capacity. He seems to defy the best kind of teaching available, and generally the defect in reading ability persists into adulthood. His behavior in reading is erratic since things taught and known for some time will seem to suddenly disappear from his store of knowledge and later will reappear just as suddenly. He is characterized by having an inadequate concept of left and right, and rotations and reversals run through his writing. His word attack seems to be handicapped by an inability to learn to blend. Sometimes his hearing seems defective even though thorough auditory checks fail to uncover a disability.

Regardless of the name given these children, it does appear that such a classification exists. It is also evident from the experiences of people who have worked with these children that they need special help in reading. If no such special help is available, the classroom teacher can get some results by following the suggestions made for dealing with the brain-injured child in this chapter.

Dissenting Opinion

There are a number of experts who maintain that the learning ability of the exceptional child is no different from that of the normal child. The only difference is in the rate of acquisition. To these people the teacher certainly must move much more slowly and may have to have more drill and repetitions, but in the final analysis, the basic method of acquisition remains the same. To these experts, the classroom teacher is equipped to handle these children since she has been trained in the observation of children, the diagnosis of their levels of development, and the adjustment of the program to fit the child's needs and level of development. We do not agree with this point of view which maintains that the same basic techniques are usable with all types of children nor do we agree that the average classroom teacher has been taught how to work with exceptional children.

chapter 2

Reading and
Reading Deficiencies

As a discipline, the field of reading is unique. At one and the same time, it seeks a theoretical basis, yet is emphasized from a pragmatic point of view. It is well structured in terms of skills, yet there is considerable debate as to the "what, how, when, and why" of the skills. There is a proliferation of strategies and systems of teaching reading, yet no one approach seems to be adequate for all children. No one seems to know exactly how a child learns to read, what developmental background is needed in order to learn to read, or how the brain functions in the learning-to-read process. Fortunately, most children learn to read by the procedures followed and the media employed by teachers. However, some children with average or above average intelligence cannot be taught to read by the procedures and media generally used. For this reason we must find ways to teach all children to read in keeping with their mental potential. If they have the capacity to learn, we must find the technique, the approach, and/or the material by which they can be reached. It may take a very different approach than the ones now being used. In order to work toward that goal, those interested in the discipline of reading would benefit from knowing as much as possible about the structure of reading as an element of language; the process of reading as a clue to teaching procedures; and the neurological mechanism of learning to read as the psychophysical basis of reading.

Basic Understandings

Definitions of Reading: Implications for
Models of Reading

There are almost as many definitions of reading as there are authors who wish to write a definition. As Jane Mackworth (1977) says "The word *reading* can only be defined in terms of who is reading *what,* in *what state,* and for *what reason".* Some authors say that we read to obtain information; others claim that reading is the ability to respond orally to printed symbols according to a learned system. The first part of the previous sentence emphasizes getting meaning from words, but not necessarily from every word read. The latter part of the sentence permits the possibility of word-calling, whereby every word could be said correctly but be devoid of meaning. If the rules of pronunciation were known, it would be possible to word-call a foreign language precisely, yet not understand a single word read. So knowledge of phonetic or structural analysis is not enough.

We take the position that obtaining meaning from what is read is an essential part of the reading process and, hence, of a definition of reading. This last statement has special meaning for learning disabled children, who frequently have conceptual and associative difficulties in giving meaning to words they can unlock, and for other types of LD children, who have difficulties in oral reading accuracy, yet have amazing comprehension of what has been read. Pat Rigg (1977) illustrates the difference between decoding the message and getting the message. She describes the approaches of two teachers who, through their way of teaching reading, indicate their definition of the term. One teacher taught reading as an exact oral reproduction of print but not stressing comprehension. The other teacher did not insist on exact reproduction of print but did emphasize comprehension of what was being read.

Generally, reading is defined by authors according to the model of the reading process being advocated. Models vary from those presenting a simple decoding process, to elaborate, complex processes involving all past experiences. Crosby and Liston (1968) define reading as translating graphic symbols into sound according to a recognized system that consists of three levels of skills: (a) decoding written signs into speech and understanding what was read only after hearing oneself saying it, (b) suppressing overt oral activity and going directly from sub-vocal speech to the sensory-speech area and to comprehension, and (c) going straight from visual perception to comprehension of meaning with no vocal involvement. Neisser (1967) says reading is a process on the sensory-vocal dimension whereby the sensory input is transformed, elaborated, stored, recovered and used, emphasizing the importance and use of memory. Mackworth (1973) stresses developmental aspects of reading by suggesting that, although reading is a visual-verbal process, it is actually the synthesis of (a) developing meaning (concept formation, a mental model), (b) the acquisition of language, a verbal spoken code with a synthesis taking place between certain sounds and meaning, and, finally, (c) a blending of the sounds of speech into a visual-verbal code of reading. She also considers the affective aspects of attention and motivation essential parts of the reading process.

Kenneth Goodman (1970) has defined reading from a psycholinguistic point of view. He states that reading is "a selective process that involves partial use of available language cues, selected from the perceptual input on the basis of the reader's expectation, and is an interaction between language and thought." In his definition Goodman stresses a neural model that reflects psychological factors such as expectancy, attention, and cognitive learning, together with other physiological changes that result in a heightened state of sensitivity to graphic language. Goodman also speaks of recode and recoding, implying going from one code to another, such as from a written code to an oral or spoken code. Decoding means going directly from code (print) to meaning; this procedure can be simultaneous with recoding if the reader has good comprehension of what he is reading. With difficult or unfamiliar material, the reader will revert to the recoding steps in order to get a better grasp of what is being read.

We offer no definition of reading. We do note the following aspects of the reading process as we view it:

  a. Reading relates symbols (printed or written) to meaningful sound combinations.
  b. Reading cues can be derived from the structure of language.
  c. Personal knowledge, concepts, and vocabulary contribute to an understanding of what is being read.
  d. Psychological factors of attention, motivation, working or short-term memory, and long-term memory are pertinent.
  e. Neural transmission, neural association, neural coding, and neural programming are vital to reading.
  f. Reading is an adaptive process permitting cognitive flexibility in processing, perceiving, remembering, and thinking.

At the present, we believe that no one definition of reading has been formulated that will sufficiently describe *the* reading process. A series of reading cases presented by Eleanor Gibson and Harry Levin in their book, *The Psychology of Reading* (1975) show the complexity of the problem of definition.

Historical Perspectives to Teaching Reading

Reading teachers in colonial times emphasized learning the letters of the alphabet and applying single letters and sounds to words. As such, the phonics approach was slowly developed. Under the influence of Horace Mann, the technique of sounding out words was dropped in favor of the whole word approach. Later in the century, phonics was reintroduced as a necessary tool in gaining proficiency in word recognition. The whole word approach and the phonics approach both have their strong advocates today, but most teachers make use of both approaches as the occasion demands. Thus, one could infer that both visual and auditory perceptual abilities are important to the reading act.

Around 1900, there was a heavy emphasis on mechanics of word recognition and fluency in oral reading. The 1920s saw the emphasis switch to teaching attitudes and skills concerned with clear and rapid comprehension in silent reading. By the middle 1930s, reading instructors believed that readers should learn to reflect their comprehension by interpreting what was read and by grasping implications.

Concepts of reading were further expanded by the end of the 1940s to include the idea that reading consisted of a large number of skills which varied in their application according to the purpose of reading, the kind of material read, and the values sought. Attitudes in pupil's interpretation of what was read and the role of reading in personality development were stressed in the 1950s. The 1960s and early 1970s were somewhat unsettled years in the field of reading because of growth in the area of learning disabilities, and the discovery that an extremely high percentage of LD children had severe reading problems. The question that finally emerged was—who should teach reading to LD children—the reading specialist or the special education instructor? The question is still being discussed. Reading today has a variety of approaches, any of which may be employed by a teacher in accordance with the needs of the individual child. In recent years the concept of reading has been extended by some to include every sensory impression one experiences, be it related to graphemes or not, such as in "reading" environmental signs or "body language."

According to Chall (1967), current methods of teaching to read fall roughly into two groups. First, there is the "meaning-emphasis" approach, which lays heavy stress on the immediate acquisition of meaning through learning whole words at sight, the development of a limited vocabulary of common but irregularly spelled words, the slow introduction of the alphabet and phonics, and the emphasis of story content based on a family. The second approach is the "code-emphasis" group, which stresses early acquisition of the alphabetic principles and greater individualization of instruction, and either asks for more imaginative content in stories or underplays content altogether. Chall believes that the "meaning-emphasis" approach prevails today in spite of the fact that the research in reading for the past fifty years supports the "code-emphasis" techniques.

Prereading Competencies Needed

To be able to read, the child must bring to the reading situation several competencies which will enable him to give meaning to the words. He must have an adequate vocabulary and language structure in speaking. He must have the ability to comprehend conversation and to use oral language appropriate to the level on which he wishes to read. The child must know that the symbols he sees on the printed page correspond in some way to his spoken language and that he must relate these symbols to words, sentences, and ideas. The implications are that the child must have (1) the perceptual maturity to detect likenesses and differences in both visual and auditory forms, (2) the memory to maintain these forms in a sequential order, (3) the capacity to relate the symbols to sounds, (4) the maturation to attend to and concentrate on the problem at hand, (5) the experiential background and concepts needed to bring meaning to the printed words, and (6) the mental capacity to deal with ideas and abstractions. Other competencies needed for adequacy in reading include social and emotional adjustment which imply self-control, self-reliance, and ability to follow directions, and a desire or motivation to read which reflects a curiosity and responsiveness to reading and books.

Rabinovitch (1968) considers the following processes of major import when academic learning is considered:

1. General intelligence   Verbal performance
2. Special senses   Vision including discrimination
                                    Hearing including discrimination
3. Neurologic status   Neurological readiness
                                    Neurological integration
4. Specific symbolization skills   Verbal comprehension and expression
                                    Visual memory and association
                                    Auditory memory and association
                                    Directionality
5. Emotional freedom to learn
6. Motivation
7. Opportunity to learn

In many ways, the above list coincides with observations presented on the elements of the reading process as well as with the prereading competencies needed for reading.

Laws of Perceptual Constancy

The term *perceptual handicap* refers to an impairment in the normal processes of perception, that is, in the basic ability of all human beings to make sense out of the environment in which they live. The child with a perceptual handicap misperceives. He may overlook important details or focus on them so strongly that he misses the whole. He may grasp isolated aspects of the whole but may not perceive their relationships to the whole itself. He may fail to attend to word structure. He may mishear word structures and so is misled in their meanings.

In the early years of preschool experience, a child perceives that an object has the same meaning or symbolic value regardless of changes in its directional orientation or rotation in space, and despite the addition, removal, translocation, or camouflage of component parts. A chair, for example, is always a chair, be it rotated sideways, right-to-left, backward, upside down, or on end, and even if it has rockers, soft cushions, missing arms or legs, or is taken apart. Similarly, a dog is a dog, no matter what position it assumes or whether it is large, small, spotted, hairless, or three-legged. This conceptual assumption is called the *Law of Object Constancy*.

This type of constancy does not apply to letters. In fact, the characters of the alphabet may greatly confuse the beginning reader if he applies this principle. No longer can objects, in this case letters, be rotated indiscriminately without changing their names, sounds, and meanings. Nor can fragments be added or removed without altering the form.

Two laws are necessary to amend the original concept of object constancy. These are the *Law of Directional Constancy* and the *Law of Form Constancy*.

The Law of Directional Constancy states that letters of the same shape have the same symbolic value only if their directional orientation is identical. A *b* is different from a *p*; a *b* and a *d* are different; a *b* and a *q* are not the same. Likewise a rotation is not allowed; so *N* and *Z* are different. The law also applies to the position of letters in words, so *was* is not *saw*, and *sacred god* is not the same as *scared dog*.

Learning the application of this law may be hindered by confusion arising from the fact that some letters such as *o* or *x* can be rotated in any direction without changing, while other letters such as *S*, *V*, *B*, and *H* can be rotated in some dimensions but not in others.

The second principle, the Law of Form Constancy, states that letters of similar shapes are identical in symbolic value only if all their parts are identical. Thus adding a line to a *c* changes it to an *e*, removing the hook from a *y* may make it a *v* or a *u*, and an *m* cannot be taken apart or it becomes *nn*. The law applies to words as well as letters: *scared* is neither *scarred* nor *cared*.

Conceptualization of these two laws is required for reading ability to develop and to move beyond the errors of letter and word orientation and form that characterize the beginning reader. In many instances, the child who fails to conceptualize these changes becomes the disabled reader who remains fixated at a primitive level.

Learning disability cases usually have visual, auditory, or tactile perceptual-motor deficits, resulting in poor discrimination and perceptual ability. A significant point, however, is that not all perceptual handicaps are due to organic causes. Poor perceptual ability will also result from severe emotional distress or emotional involvement. For that reason the causes of perceptual problems must be carefully studied. The teacher will need to know whether an organic or psychogenic problem is involved in order to provide the right kind of remediation.

Failure need not necessarily result because a perceptual handicap exists. Appropriate education given at the proper time can help a child to learn more normal ways of perceiving and thinking so that even if some deviations continue to be present, the gap between his faulty perceptions and normal ones can be reduced.

The child with a perceptual handicap can be helped to learn the basic academic tools in spite of his impairment by teaching methods which minimize the disturbing effects of his handicap or stimulate him to a more effective use of the impaired functions. He can learn to compensate for his deficiencies by recognizing them and working against them so that later he can return to the regular classroom to continue his schooling.

It is most important that he receive the specific and individualized help he needs when his learning and behavior problems first become apparent in order to prevent the emotional tensions which arise with repeated failure and the incorrect learning which results from distorted perceptions.

The Reading Process

There are several processes to be considered in analyzing the act of reading. First, there is the matter of the sensory processes by which the reader unlocks or recognizes the word or words. By some sensory means, such as visual, auditory, tactile (touch), or kinesthetic (muscle awareness), the reader does something to or with the word to bring it into his cerebral processes. This act involves the essence of word attack or word recognition skills. A second process stressed in reading is concept formation. Meaning is derived from one's mental storehouse of concepts and knowledge previously learned. Concepts, verbal mediation, and language are the vehicles for meaning. Sounds can only be comprehended within a language setting, so such a background must be available. A third element in the act of reading is comprehension for the purpose of communication. Without comprehension there is no meaning. Without meaning there is no communication between the author and the reader. Some reading specialists, however, claim that communication does not need to involve words because it is possible to "read" symptoms and expressions, as one can "read his face" or "read the clouds" and predict the weather.

The fact that the reader interprets and grasps implications from what is read suggests that reading is more than comprehension, as these activities involve abstract reasoning and comprehension always does not. This factor of interpretation is a fourth ingredient in the act of reading. A fifth consideration is the influence of the affective components (feelings) of the cerebral processes such as attitudes, values, and personality characteristics on performance in reading. A sixth factor is the action or behavior a person may undertake because of what he has read. The reader has been influenced to respond or behave intellectually, emotionally, or physically, in accordance with what—and how—he reads. Seventh, competent reading involves some degree of immediate evaluation of what was read to determine how valid or adequate the comprehension and interpretations are in terms of context and intent of the writer. Feedback will suggest where errors were made and where corrections are needed. Lastly, through reading the reader should gain some knowledge or an idea which he can add to his conceptual background of information and, thereby, can bring more "meaning" for the activities of comprehension and interpretation to his next reading experience. The elements in the reading process are summarized in Figure 2–1.

Hollander (1975) emphasizes the need to be aware of the many variables that are pertinent to the reading process. Since comprehension results from the reader's interaction with the graphic stimulus, both the reader and the text can be situational factors that may influence the process of reading. The reader brings physical, cognitive, and affective factors to the reading situation. The text combines the organization, style, and language systems used by the author with the format, typography, and visual aids used by the publisher. A third component exists which is the teaching-learning situation. These three major contributors of variables affect the reading process, which seeks to employ skills relating to semantic analysis, syntactic analysis, and graphophonic relationships. The matter does not stop there because there is a reading product involving recoding, decoding, interpretation of

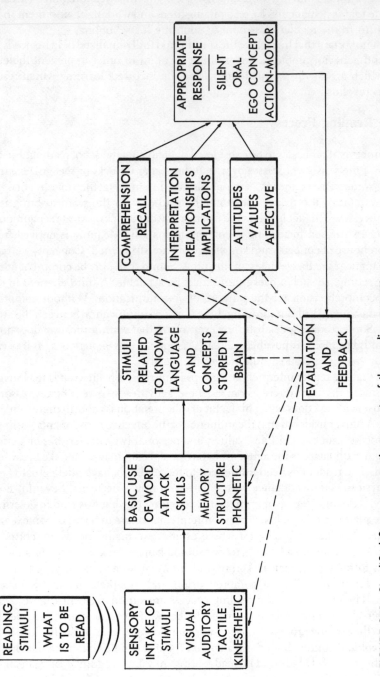

FIGURE 2–1. Simplified figure representing aspects of the reading process.

the message, and the formulation of meanings. The conclusion to be drawn from this recognition of variables is that each reading act takes place within a particular context to which individuals, because of their variabilities, respond in different ways. Therefore, each reader must be allowed to perform or respond in a manner congruent with his cognitive style, the characteristics of the text, and the needs of the moment. Each learner has his own learning style, which must be recognized if effective teaching is to take place. This is all the more reason to be aware of individual differences, no matter how structured and logical a model may seem.

Phonic Deprivation

Phonic deprivation theories hold that the only major and perhaps only task involved in reading is the association of a sound with a symbol and the integration of these associated sounds into words. The average 6-year-old child begins school with a minimal vocabulary of about 3,720 words and a maximal vocabulary of about 25,000 words. This child has an understanding and an oral recognition vocabulary far in excess of the vocabulary needed for reading first-grade books. If the child could be given the means by which he could transform the printed symbols into oral symbols, his understanding vocabulary could then take over and no reading problem would exist. Hence, phonic deprivation theorists hold that the cause of reading disability is the whole word approach to teaching reading. They claim that this method denies the child the opportunity to develop a reflex-like association between a printed symbol and its sound. The environment is sometimes blamed as not offering the necessary auditory stimulation so that a sound-symbol relationship can be developed.

A leading phonic deprivation theorist today is Charles C. Walcott (1963). His reading program, as presented in a series of readers, begins with isolated letter phonics. Drill is used to entrench the two meanings of a letter: (a) the sound the letter signals, and (b) the time sequence within a word when each sound is pronounced. Very little attempt is made to control the vocabulary in the Walcott and McCracken Readers since Walcott believes the child's understanding vocabulary to be large enough to handle meaning once pronunciation is unlocked.

The major defect in this theory as applied to all readers is that almost invariably the seriously disabled reader knows the sounds signaled by the letters of the alphabet, but he is not able to put the sounds together into words. For example, he will, in most cases, be able to identify the sound signaled by each of the following letters: *u, o, t, b, n*. Although most seriously disabled readers can give the sounds signaled by these letters in the preceding sentence, they can do little or nothing with them if they have to put them together into the word *button*.

Context of Reading

Stages in Developing Reading Skill

The actual stages in learning to read start at the time of conception. The infant passes through many stages, such as learning left and right, laterality, and eye-hand coordination. These all are necessary for learning to read. This section is more concerned with the stages which occur shortly before and while the child is learning to read.

Prerequisities for reading. The prerequisites for reading make up what is commonly called *reading readiness*. These prerequisites can be grouped into visual factors, auditory factors, and experience factors.

If a child has a vision handicap, he will have some difficulty learning to read because he expends so much energy trying to see properly. The child must have adequate acuity and adequate perceptual ability. A child must be able to discriminate between *o*, *c*, and *e*; *b*, *d*, *p*, and *q*; or *u*, *n*, and *m*, before he will be able to learn to read.

Most children entering our schools know how to speak. The words they know how to say are words that they have heard over and over again and learned to repeat. However, children must be taught to listen carefully and note differences in sounds. For example, a child may say "wiver" for "river" because he did not listen carefully for the beginning "sound." Reading Mother Goose rhymes over and over again to a child will help improve his auditory discrimination (Huus, 1965).

The most variable factor in reading readiness is experience. It is an undisputed fact that children with a rich background of experiences have fewer reading problems than those who lack them. This can easily be understood by comparing the differences in experiences of a boy who lives in a city and has never been out of the city and of the boy next door who spends two weeks every summer on a farm.

Concept building. Starting in kindergarten and moving into first grade, the concept of *home* is developed. During this first year many basic concepts must be formed. Concepts dealing with "what a thing is good for" must be taught. For example, a child must learn the purpose of a motor vehicle and the playground. Concept development continues throughout a person's entire life. As concepts broaden, a child's reading improves.

Word recognition. According to Tinker and McCullough (1968), before a child can actually begin to read, he must know somewhere between 40 and 100 sight words. These basic sight words are the basis for reading instruction. This is actually part of the reading readiness program. The child should be taught by the word method many of the words that he will encounter in his first reading book. A child can only learn so many sight words before he starts getting them confused. It is at this point that another stage in reading begins.

Structural analysis and phonetic analysis. Reading is improved for the next eight to ten years by structural and phonetic analysis. This process includes seeing the differences in printed words such as *work* and *works*, and *walk* and *walked*. At this time a child is introduced to compound words. Included in this stage is hearing different sounds. Vowel and consonant sounds are taught. The different sounds of a vowel are also taught. This stage gives the child his first real "word attack skill." For the next few years, the child is encouraged to use this skill.

Comprehension and interpretation. Comprehension is sometimes labeled *meaningful reading*. At first it is up to the teacher to give meaning to reading. He must give the children a reason to read. As this continues, the child gradually forms his own reasons for reading.

Comprehension is helped by pictures that represent something in the story. These pictures should be discussed and related to the story. Pictures also present excellent opportunities for practice in interpretation. *Why* questions should be used often. This type of question gives practice in interpretation and comprehension. Objective questions are also necessary for comprehension.

Oral reading to silent reading. Most children learn to read orally since language is initially an oral experience. From the beginning the teacher tries to get the child to read silently. This is hard for the child, and many times he will form every word that he reads with his mouth. A child must practice very hard to be able to think the words as he reads them. Some reading difficulties can be traced to the fact that the child could not make the transformation from oral reading to silent reading.

A critical part of any reading program is the teaching of skills underlying the reading process. Gross, Carr, Dornseif and Rouse (1974) worked with a Title III program and put together a set of behavioral objectives that relate the skill level of a task with an achievement grade level. The major categories of their skills program are (a) word recognition, (b) vocabulary development, (c) literal comprehension, (d) interpretive comprehension, (e) analytical comprehension, (f) study skills, (g) enriched reading, and (h) composition. This detailed program is worth looking up if you are interested in developing a program of individualized reading based on a skill level and achievement grade level approach.

Basic Reading Skills and Grade Levels

The research of psychologists with program development and teaching machines has made educators very conscious of the need to identify the basic units, elements, and sequential steps, if there be any, which make up skills and/or content material. The need for a "task analysis" of reading skills and for the grade placement for the teaching of these skills is paramount in importance for the remedial teacher. Not only can this information be used for diagnostic purposes, but it can also be used to determine the reading level of the child, where remediation must begin, and what must be taught. The material which follows was prepared by the staff of the General Brown Central School of Brownville and Dexter School District in New York in a series of workshop sessions under the direction of the reading consultants, Dr. Clifford J. Kolson and Dr. Winton H. Buddington, of the State University College of Potsdam, New York, and with the help of the "Prescriptive Teachers" of the school, Mrs. Persons and Mrs. Burke (1967).

I. First grade

  A. Pre-primer stage

    1. Word-study skills

      a. word meaning and concept building
      b. picture clues
      c. visual discrimination
        1.) left to right progression
        2.) word configuration
        3.) capital and small letter forms
      d. auditory perception
        1.) initial consonants—*b, c, d, f, g, h, l, m, p, r, s, t, w*
        2.) rhyming elements
      e. structural analysis—ex. plural nouns: adding *s*

    2. Comprehension skills

      a. associating text and pictures
      b. following oral directions
      c. main idea
      d. details
      e. sequence
      f. drawing conclusions
      g. seeing relationships

    B. Primer Stage

        1. Word-study skills

            a. review, reteach or teach all skills in Section A. Which child has not mastered
            b. expand vocabulary
                1.) context clues
                2.) phonetic analysis
                    a.) initial consonants
                    b.) rhymes
                    c.) learning letter names—*n, l, p, d, g, r, c*
                3.) Structural analysis

        2. Comprehension skills

            a. all those at Pre-primer level
            b. forming judgments
            c. making inferences
            d. classifying

    C. First reader

        1. Word-study skills

            a. all previous skills
            b. phonetic analysis
                 1.) final analysis—*n, d, k, m, t, p*
                2.) initial blends—*st, pl, bl, br, tr, dr, gr, fr*
            c. structural analysis
                 1.) verb forms
                    a.) adding *ed*
                    b.) adding *ing*
                2.) compound words

        2. Comprehension skills

            a. all previously taught skills
            b. recalling story facts
            c. predicting outcome
            d. following printed directions

  II. Second Grade

    A. Book one

        1. Word-study skills

            a. review and practice all first grade skills
            b. phonetic analysis
                 1.) rhyming words visually
                2.) consonants
                    a.) initial—*j*
                    b.) final—*x, r, l*
                    c.) blends—*cr, sn, sl, pr, cl*
                    d.) digraphs—*ai, oa*
            c. structural analysis
                 1.) plural of nouns—adding *s* and *es*
                2.) variant forms of verbs
                    a.) adding *es, ing*
                    b.) doubling consonants before adding *ing* or *ed*

      2. Comprehension skills

         a. all previously taught skills
         b. making generalizations
         c. seeing relationships
         d. interpreting pictures

  B. Book two

    1. Word-study skills

         a. all previously taught skills
         b. recognize words in alphabetical order
         c. phonetic analysis
            1.) consonant blends—*thr, gl, squ, apr, str*
            2.) phonograms—auditory and visual concepts of *ar, er, ir, ow, ick, ew, ay, own, uck, ed, ex, ouse, ark, oat, ound*
            3.) vowel differences
               a.) vowels lengthened by final *e*
               b.) long and short sounds of *y*
               c.) digraphs *ee, ea*
               d.) diphthongs—different sounds of *ow*
         d. structural analysis
            1.) contractions—*it's, I'm, I'll, that's, let's, don't, didn't, isn't*
            2.) variant forms of verbs—dropping *e* before adding *ing*
            3.) plural forms of nouns—changing *y* to *ies*

    2. Comprehension skills

         a. practice and use of all previously taught skills
         b. making inferences
         c. seeing cause and effect relationships

III. Third grade

  A. Book one

    1. Word-study skills

         a. all previously learned skills
         b. word-meaning
            1.) opposites
            2.) adding *er, est* to change form and meaning of words
            3.) words with multiple meanings
         c. phonetic analysis
            1.) consonants
               a.) hard and soft sounds *c, g*
               b.) recognizing consonants
               c.) digraphs
                  (1) *ck*
                  (2) vowels
                     (a) silent vowels
                     (b) digraphs—*ai, ea, ou, ee, ay, ui*
               d.) structural analysis
                  (1) contractions—*who's, we're, you're, aren't, that's, I'm, couldn't*
                  (2) possessive words
                  (3) suffixes—*en, est, ly*

           (4) variant forms of verbs
               (a) changing final *y* to *i* before adding *ed*
               (b) dropping *e* before adding *ing*
       e.) alphabetizing—first letter
       f.) syllabication—up to three syllable words

  2. Comprehension skills

    a. all skills previously learned
    b. detecting mood of situation
    c. relating story facts to own experiences
    d. reading pictorial maps
    e. skimming

B. Book two

  1. Word-study skills

    a. all previously learned skills
    b. word-meaning
      1.) homonyms
        a.) *dew, do*
        b.) *sea, see*
        c.) *whole, hole*
        d.) *made, maid*
        e.) *blew, blue*
        f.) *ewe, you*
        g.) *forth, fourth*
        h.) *thrown, throne*
      2.) synonyms
        a.) *throw, pitch*
        b.) *quiet, still*
        c.) *speak, say*
        d.) *lift, raise*
        e.) *tug, pull*
        f.) *large, big*
        g.) *swiftly, fast*
        h.) *believe, think*
        i.) *smart, clever*
        j.) *come, arrive*
        k.) *daybreak, dawn*
        l.) *fastened, tied*
    c. phonetic analysis
      1.) consonants—hard and soft sounds of *g, c*
        a.) *c* usually has a soft sound when it comes before *e* or *i*
        b.) *g* usually has a soft sound when it comes before *e* or *i*
      2.) vowels
        a.) diphthongs—*ou, ow, or, oy, aw, au*
        b.) sounds of vowels followed by *r*
    d. structural analysis
      1.) plurals—change *f* to *v* when adding *es*
      2.) contractions—*doesn't, you'll, they're*
      3.) suffixes
        a.) recognizing as syllables
        b.) adding *ly* and *ily*
        c.) positive, comparative, and superlative forms of adjectives

         4.) prefixes—*un* changes meaning of words to the opposite
    e. alphabetizing—using second letter
    f. syllabication
        1.) between double consonants
        2.) prefixes and suffixes as syllables
    g. accent—finding syllables said more heavily

  2. Comprehension skills

    a. all previously learned skills
    b. problem solving

IV. Fourth grade

  A. Word-study skills

    1. word meanings

      a. antonyms
      b. synonyms
      c. homonyms
      d. figures of speech
      e. sensory appeals in words

    2. word analysis

      a. phonetic analysis
        1.) consonants
          a.) silent
          b.) two sounds of *s*
          c.) hard and soft sounds of *c* and *g*
          d.) diacritical marks
            (1) long sound of vowels
            (2) short sound of vowels
            (3) *a* as in *care*
            (4) *a* as in *bars*
            (5) *u* as in *burn*
            (6) *a* as in *ask*
            (7) *e* as in *wet*
            (8) *e* as in *letter*
            (9) *oo* as in *moon*
            (10) *oo* as in *foot*
          e.) applying vowel principles
            (1) vowel in the middle of a word or syllable is usually *short*
            (2) vowel coming at the end of a one syllable word is usually *long*
            (3) when a one syllable word ends in *e*, the medial vowel in that word is usually *long*
            (4) when two vowels come together, the first vowel is usually *long* and the second vowel is *silent*
      b. structural analysis
        1.) hyphenated words—*good-by, thirty-one, rain-maker*
        2.) finding root words in word variants
        3.) prefixes—*dis, re, un, im*
        4.) suffixes—*ly, ness, ment, ful, ish, less*
        5.) syllabication
          a.) when a vowel sound is followed by one consonant, that consonant usually begins the next syllable

          b.) when a vowel sound in a word is followed by two consonants, this word is usually divided between the two consonants

          c.) prefixes and suffixes are usually syllables

          d.) compound words are usually divided between the word parts

          e.) in two-syllable words ending in *le* preceded by a consonant, the consonant joins the *le* and begins the final syllable

      6.) accent

B. Comprehension skills

  1. all previously learned skills

  2. reading for comprehension

  3. finding the main ideas

  4. finding details

  5. organizing and summarizing

  6. recalling story facts

  7. recognizing sequence

  8. reading for information

  9. creative reading

    a. classifying

    b. detecting the mood of a situation

    c. drawing conclusions

    d. forming judgments

    e. making inferences

    f. predicting outcomes

    g. seeing cause and effect relationships

    h. problem solving

  10. following printed directions

  11. skimming

V. Fifth grade

A. Word-study skills

  1. antonyms—review and give practice in using context clues

  2. expand vocabulary

  3. review figures of speech and introduce new ones to enrich vocabulary

  4. homonyms—review and introduce new ones

  5. synonyms—review and introduce new ones to expand vocabulary

  6. use of dictionary and glossary

    a. guide words

    b. accent marks

    c. diacritical marks

      1.) review â, ä, û, à, o͞o, ŏŏ, ëe

      2.) review long and short vowels

      3.) introduce schwa, half long ȯ

      4.) introduce italic ŭ, ĭ, ă, ĕ

      5.) introduce ' in omitted vowel

      6.) respellings

7. phonetic analysis
    a. review consonant sounds
    b. review pronunciation of diacritical marks
    c. review phonograms

8. structural analysis
    a. compound words
    b. words of similar configuration
    c. prefixes
        1.) review *un, im-, dis-, re-*
        2.) introduce *in-, anti-, inter-, mis-*
    d. suffixes
        1.) review *-en, -ment, -less, -ish, -ly, -ful, -y, -ed*
        2.) introduce *-sp, -or, -ours, -ness, -ward, -hood, -action, -al*
    e. principles of syllabication
        1.) review rules already taught
        2.) consonant blends and digraphs are treated as single sounds, and usually are not divided (*ma-chine*)
    f. application of word analysis in attacking words outside the basic vocabulary

B. Comprehension and study skills
    1. Continue development in following areas
        a. main idea
        b. sequence
        c. reading for details
        d. appreciating literary style
        e. drawing conclusions
        f. enriching information
        g. evaluating information
        h. forming opinions and generalizing
        i. interpreting ideas
        j. using alphabetical arrangement
        k. using dictionary or glossary skills
        l. interpreting maps and pictures
        m. skimming for purpose
        n. classifying ideas
        o. following directions
        p. outlining
        q. summarizing
        r. reading for accurate detail
        s. skimming

    2. Introduce and teach
        a. discrimination between fact and fiction
        b. perceiving related ideas
        c. strengthening power of recall
        d. using encyclopedias, atlas, almanac, and other references
        e. using charts and graphs
        f. using index and pronunciation keys
        g. reading to answer questions and for enjoyment of literary style.

VI. Sixth grade

    A. Word-study skills

        1. Word meaning

            a. antonyms—review and give practice in
            b. homonyms—develop ability to use correctly
            c. classify words of related meaning
            d. enrich word meaning
            e. review use of synonyms
            f. use context clues in attacking new words
            g. expand vocabulary
            h. become aware of expressions that refer to place and time and develop skill in interpreting such expressions
            i. use dictionary and glossary
                1.) further ability to use alphabetical order guide words and pronunciation key
                2.) review diacritical marks—introduce circumflex breve as in *sŏft*
                3.) review spelling

        2. Word analysis

            a. phonetic analysis
                1.) review consonant sounds
                2.) diacritical marks—interpreting pronunciation symbols
                3.) review vowel sounds principles
            b. structural analysis
                1.) review compound words
                2.) review hyphenated words
                3.) review prefixes
                    a.) review *un-, im-, dis-, re-, in-, anti-, inter-, mis-*
                    b.) introduce *trans-, pre-, fore-, ir-, non-*
                4.) review suffixes
                    a.) review *-en, -ment, -less, -ish, -ly, -ful, -y, -ed, -shy, -or, -er, -ous, -ness, -ward, -hood, -ation, -al*
                    b.) introduce *-able, -ance, -ence, -ate, -est, -ent, -ity, -ic, -ist, -like*
                5.) review principles of syllabication
                6.) review accented syllables
                7.) apply word analysis in attacking words outside the basic vocabulary

    B. Comprehension and study skills

        1. Continue development in the following areas:

            a. main ideas
            b. sequence
            c. reading for details
            d. appreciating literary style
            e. drawing conclusions
                1.) predicting outcomes
                2.) forming judgments
                3.) seeing relationships
            f. extending and enriching information
            g. interpreting pictures
            h. evaluating information
            i. interpreting ideas
            j. using facts to form opinions, generalizing

    2. Introduce the skills of

      a. enriching imagery
      b. discriminating between fact and fiction
      c. strengthening power of recall

    3. Locating and using information (study skills)

      a. review skills in the following
        1.) alphabetical arrangement
        2.) use of dictionary and glossary
        3.) use of encyclopedia, almanac and other references
        4.) interpreting maps and pictures
        5.) skimming for a purpose
        6.) classifying ideas
        7.) following directions
        8.) summarizing
        9.) outlining
        10.) reading for accurate detail
        11.) using index and pronunciation keys
        12.) using charts and graphs
        13.) reading to answer questions and for enjoyment of literary style
      b. introduce the following skills
        1.) use of facts and figures
        2.) use of headings and type style—especially use of italics
          a.) to give importance to a word or expression in a sentence
          b.) to show that a sentence has a special importance to the plot of the story
          c.) to set off a special title used in a sentence or a reference
        3.) use of an index
        4.) use of library
        5.) use of table of contents
        6.) taking notes
        7.) reading of information material
        8.) reading poetry

VII. Grades 7-12

  A. Recognition level

    1. Word analysis skills

      a. phonetic
        1.) identification of vowel sounds (short, long)
        2.) identification of consonant sounds
        3.) identification of blends
        4.) identification of other speech sounds
        5.) accent marks
      b. structural
        1.) identification of roots, prefixes, and suffixes
        2.) identification of compound words
        3.) syllabication

    2. Word meaning skills

      a. specific word meanings
        1.) use in context
        2.) use through modification by prefixes and suffixes

   3.) use through interpretation from roots
   4.) reference to dictionary
   5.) study of word origins
   6.) study of synonyms, antonyms, homonyms
  b. multiple word meanings
   1.) use in context
   2.) use through modification by suffixes and prefixes
   3.) use through interpretation from roots
   4.) use through reference to diction
   5.) use through study of word origins
   6.) use through study of synonyms, antonyms, and homonyms
  c. word evoking emotional moods
   1.) use in context (primarily)
   2.) through study of word origins
   3.) through reference to dictionary
   4.) *Roget's Thesaurus*

B. Comprehension level

 1. Reading the main idea

  a. identification of main idea in the topic sentence of a paragraph
  b. matching of a given set of main ideas with paragraph
  c. distinguishing between main idea and titles through paragraph analysis

 2. Reading for detail

  a. finding the main idea and major details
   1.) through underlining
   2.) use of block diagram
   3.) through outlining
  b. finding major and minor details in paragraphs
   1.) through use of block diagram
   2.) through outlining
   3.) through underlining

 3. Organizational skills

  a. classification
   1.) arrangement of related words or phrases into groups
   2.) sorting and arrangement of ideas into main and subtopics
  b. outlining
   1.) finding the main idea and subordinate ideas in a paragraph and placing these in modified outline structures
   2.) finding the main idea and subordinate ideas of a larger selection involving several paragraphs and arranging these in extended outline form
  c. reading to detect major patterns of paragraph organization
   1.) enumerative pattern (statement of facts)
   2.) comparison and contrast pattern
   3.) conclusion and proof pattern
   4.) classification pattern
   5.) time pattern

 4. Recall

  a. immediate recall (aided)
   1.) selection of facts
   2.) underlining of facts
   3.) note taking

           4.) diagramming
           5.) summarizing
           6.) outlining
           7.) expression of facts in oral or written form
      b. delayed recall (unaided)
           1.) review of previous notes, diagrams, outlines, etc.
           2.) expression of facts in oral or written form

5. Study skills

    a. SQ3R method
        1.) survey
        2.) question
        3.) read
        4.) review
        5.) recite
    b. reading to follow directions
    c. skimming
        1.) skimming to preview
        2.) skimming for main idea
        3.) skimming for details
        4.) skimming for key words
    d. location of information
        1.) use of table of contents
        2.) use of dictionary
        3.) use of index
        4.) use of *Reader's Guide*
        5.) use of almanacs
        6.) use of encyclopedia
        7.) use of biographical dictionaries
        8.) use of maps, charts, and graphs
    e. use of the library
        1.) card catalog
           a.) author cards
           b.) title or subject cards
        2.) Dewey decimal classification system or Library of Congress system
        3.) completing library call slips
    f. rate
        1.) use of reading material one or two reading levels below student's reading achievement level
        2.) grasping large word groups (span)
        3.) repressing physical movements
           a.) lips
           b.) head
           c.) finger pointing
           d.) eyes
              (1) fixation (pause)
              (2) regressing (re-reading)
              (3) left to right eye movements
        4.) constant application of time pressure
        5.) computation of effective reading rate
           a.) gross rate
           b.) per cent of accuracy in comprehension
           c.) formula: Effective rate = gross rate × % of accuracy
        6.) adaptability of rate to the type of reading material

C. Interpretation Level

    1. Reading to draw conclusions

        a. statements of the author
        b. statements of reader made on the basis of evaluation of the author's remarks

    2. Reading to distinguish between fact and opinion

        a. point of view of selection
        b. background of author
        c. known facts related to the topic (utilization of student experiences)
        d. designation by reader of fact or opinion

    3. Reading to detect propaganda

        a. name-calling
        b. glittering generalities
        c. testimonial
        d. transfer
        e. plain folks
        f. band wagon
        g. card stacking

    4. Reading to forecast results

        a. reading about an exciting situation
        b. identifying relationships of details in the situation
        c. predicting the outcome of that situation (a specific outcome)

    5. Reading to make generalizations

        a. reading statements made by the author
        b. general statements made by the reader on the basis of the author's remarks

    6. Reading to make comparisons

        a. reading statements made by the author
        b. comparison of these statements with other reading materials by same or different authors

    7. Reading to show contrast

        a. statements made by author
        b. contrast of these statements with other reading materials by the same or different authors.

    8. Reading to appraise or analyze

        a. reading and studying the author's statements
        b. identification of the problems
        c. reader's indication of his reaction to the author's remarks (a solution)

    9. Reading to elaborate

        a. reader is confronted with reading material which has incomplete endings or conclusions
        b. reader must complete the selection by addition of new material not mentioned in the original statements on the basis of his experience, background, or imagination

D. Recreational Reading

    1. Stimulating recreational reading

        a. book fairs
        b. book clubs
        c. preparation of attractive displays

      d. preparation of attractive bulletin boards
      e. use of mobiles
      f. group visits to the library
      g. use of community resources as book club speakers
      h. encouragement of classroom discussion about books read
      i. use of student book reports as classroom reference files
    2. Incorporating variety in recreational reading

  E. Use of various types of reading
    1. Short stories and novels
      a. reading to understand a character in a story
      b. reading to enjoy a description of a setting
      c. reading to follow plot of development
      d. reading to understand dialect
      e. reading to interpret figures of speech
    2. Drama
      a. reading to follow the plot through conversation
      b. reading to detect the printed format of a play
    3. Essay
      a. reading to detect the author's point of view on a subject
      b. reading to compare your point of view with that of the author
    4. Poetry
      a. reading to appreciate music in a poem
      b. reading to appreciate descriptions
      c. reading to appreciate humor
      d. reading to appreciate the format of a sonnet

  F. Motivation for reading improvement
    1. Understanding the importance of reading
      a. immediate objectives
        1.) a classroom situation
        2.) extra classroom situation
      b. long term objectives
        1.) preparation for higher learning
        2.) adjustment of community life
    2. Realizing the value of self-appraisal
      a. determining present reading status
        1.) reading level
        2.) skill deficiences
        3.) extent and frequency of reading
      b. planning reading improvement
      c. recording reading growth
        1.) interpretation of specific reading performances
        2.) use of appropriate charts for various types of reading
      d. importance of pacing in relation to reading tasks
    3. Use of reading devices
      a. mechanical devices
        1.) SRA accelerator
        2.) controlled reader

        3.) Rateometer
        4.) Tach-X device
        5.) Tachistoscope
        6.) Flash-X
        7.) Craig Reader
     b. Nonmechanical devices
        1.) grouping for unit work
          a.) choral reading
          b.) debating
          c.) dramatization
        2.) games
        3.) uses of community resources
        4.) use of pupil specialties
   4. Use of timely and interesting reading materials

Reading Deficits

Language and Reading

Those of us involved in the field of learning disabilities are well aware of the growing body of literature which suggests that problems with spoken language are characteristic of many students who are designated as learning disabled. For example, Wiig and Semel (1976) have found that LD children make an unusual number of phonological errors, including confusions in sound discrimination. As regards syntax, a considerable body of research indicates that LD children make a multitude of errors forming and understanding correct English sentences (Menyuk & Looney, 1972). Other reports indicate that semantic efficiency is also limited, particularly when verbal expressions consist of more than single words. Newcomer and Magee (1977) investigated the spoken language of reading disabled children to determine how significant a role spoken language deficits play in a "typical" group of reading disordered children. They concluded that the respective deficits appear to coexist, implying that, if a child doesn't use oral language as well as his peers, his chances of having reading problems are higher. They also note, however, that although some LD children in their study had oral language problems, many did not. They deemed it inappropriate to assume automatically that all LD or RD children have language problems.

Nevertheless, new research in the area of language-learning disabilities is lending experimental support to the hypothesis that the auditory-verbal language strategies of a number of learning disabled students are indeed different from those employed by normal children. A review of the current research on the topic by Wallach and Goldsmith (1977) found that qualitative differences as well as developmental delays in the language system of LD children do exist. They recognize the complexity of the question involving language, reading, and the LD child. The questions they still ask are (a) Is there a general comprehension problem shared by both visual and auditory language systems? (b) Is there a problem involving the inability of good auditory language to carry language signals over into the visual medium? (c) Are LD children more dependent than normal on things like inflectional cues which, when eliminated in reading, affect reading comprehension? and (d) Are the children unable to understand melody patterns in comprehending auditory language? as was found by Vogel (1974) in her study of dyslexics. Regardless of what the correct answers are, we continue to advocate to teachers what we have observed in our years of work with learning disabled children; that advice is, whatever you do in teaching an LD child, make certain that you emphasize language development.

Symptoms of Reading Disabilities

Anyone who is considering doing remedial work with disability cases must be aware of the symptoms of various disabilities in reading. These symptoms can be exhibited by both secondary and primary disability children. The following list was developed by Brueckner and Lewis (1947).

1. Slow rate of oral or silent reading.
2. Inability to answer questions about what is read, showing lack of comprehension.
3. Inability to state the main topic of a simple paragraph or story.
4. Inability to remember what is read.
5. Faulty study habits, such as failure to reread or summarize or outline.
6. Lack of skill in using tools to locate information such as index and table of contents.
7. Inability to follow simple printed or written instructions.
8. Reading word by word rather than in groups, indicating short perception span.
9. Lack of expression in oral reading.
10. Excessive lip movement in silent reading.
11. Vocalization in silent reading, whispering.
12. Lack of interest in reading in or out of school.
13. Excessive physical activity while reading, as squirming, head movements.
14. Mispronunciation of words.
    a. Gross mispronunciations, showing lack of phonetic ability.
    b. Minor mispronunciations, due to failure to discriminate beginnings and endings.
    c. Guessing and random substitutes.
    d. Stumbling over long, unfamiliar words; showing inability to attack unfamiliar words.
15. Omission of words and letters.
16. Insertion of words and letters.
    a. That spoil meaning.
    b. That do not spoil the meaning.
17. Substitution of words in oral reading.
    a. Meaningful.
    b. Meaningless.
18. Reversals of whole words or parts of words, largely faulty perception.
19. Repetition of words or groups of words when reading orally.
20. Character of eye movements.
    a. Excessive number of regressive eye movements.
    b. Faulty return sweep to beginning of next line.
    c. Short eye-voice span.
    d. Excessive number of eye fixations a line.
    e. Long pauses and periods of confusion, indicating difficulty in recognition.
    f. Inadequate muscular control of eye movements (imbalance).
    g. Inability to fuse vision of both eyes (often a cause of unclear imagery).

Specific Types of Reading Defects

The following is a list of reading defects which are most frequently encountered and evaluated in reading clinics:

1. Basic word attack skills.
   a. Structural analysis.
   b. Phonetic analysis.
      (1) Blendings.
      (2) Sound-symbol relationships.
   c. Contextual clue.
   d. Prefixes and suffixes.
   e. Syllabication.
2. Levels of comprehension and recall.
3. Level of vocabulary development.
4. Rate of reading.
5. Directional habit.
6. Study skills.
7. Location and reference skills.
8. Reading tastes and interests.
9. Needs of content fields.
10. Rate of learning.

Levin and Fuller (1972) did a rather comprehensive study of children with reading problems and arrived at the following conclusions:

1. Poor readers do poorly when confronted with inputs composed of many modalities, indicating that they have difficulty integrating separate sense modalities and also have intersensory problems.
2. Poor readers do better with individual sense modalities, especially the visual ones. Auditory modalities are less proficient.
3. Poor readers score higher on performance tasks than on verbal ones when dealing with the functions of intelligence. They do poorly on items dealing with the auditory-oral process.
4. In regard to cognitive style, poor readers process stimuli analytically but have trouble with the relational cognitive styles related to reading skills.
5. For the 9 and 10 year age group, conceptualization style is the most important factor. For the older 11 to 13 age group, emotional factors contribute more importantly to reading retardation.

The Complexity of Secondary School Reading

General and Specific Reading Skills

Reading skills can be divided into two classifications: Those skills which apply to anything which is read and therefore general skills, and those skills peculiar to a discipline and therefore specific.

The basic word attack skills are more or less examples of general skills which must be utilized by the reader regardless of the kind of material he is reading. At the other extreme is the skill of interpreting a mathematical formula, which is a skill specific to mathematics. In between these two extremes are various stages of gray. Vocabulary development is a general skill, yet each discipline has its own terminology requiring somewhat different methods of developing the concept to match the symbol. The use of the dictionary is a general skill which can be developed in the reading program, but the use of specialized dictionaries and glossaries are skills specific to each discipline and need to be taught.

In the elementary school where concepts and terms were simpler, the elementary teacher, because of her training, could develop both the general skills and the specific skills. Once the secondary school has been reached, the concepts become somewhat more complex, hence requiring someone with specialized training in the discipline to develop the concepts of the discipline. What is true of concepts and vocabulary is also true of the other specific reading skills. They too need someone specially trained in the discipline to handle the teaching of the skills.

Basic Differences

If we view the elementary teacher more as a generalist and the secondary teacher as a specialist, we find that the first basic difference between elementary and secondary reading is the depth of a discipline. The elementary teacher has a broad background of knowledge of the basic elements of many disciplines, but unless she or he has a deep interest in a discipline and a desire to learn more in the discipline seldom does the elementary teacher acquire the depth a teacher educated to teach the discipline has.

A second basic difference between elementary and secondary teachers is in the kind of training in reading they receive. Although it is true that the requirements for elementary teachers vary from state to state and the range of emphasis on reading varies widely, the fact remains that all elementary teachers receive some training in the teaching of reading. It may be merely a part of a course in the teaching of the language arts, or it may be a specific course in the teaching of reading. On the other side, however, it is the rare secondary teacher who has been given any training in the teaching of reading. A few states require a course in teaching secondary reading for secondary teachers or English teachers but most do not. The result is that most secondary teachers do not realize what a complex thing reading is and how many and varied are the problems associated with teaching reading. Because of years of training and experience with reading, the secondary teacher seems to read so easily that it is difficult for her to understand why the teaching of reading cannot be accomplished by the end of first grade.

The third basic difference between elementary and secondary teachers is in the area of domain. A good reading program utilizes four avenues for teaching children to read: basal, diagnostic, interest, and study. In the elementary school the teacher, in most cases, teaches all subjects and hence is responsible for all four avenues, including the study approach. When the secondary school is reached, suddenly one of these avenues, the study approach, is no longer within the reading teacher's domain, and she must begin to share the assessment approach with the content area teacher. In any endeavor, as soon as two or more people begin to share the responsibility for the same thing, there is a need for cooperation and joint planning.

The Widening Spread of Abilities: Quantitatively

It has long been recognized that children differ in their rates of growth and potential for assimilation of academic materials. The physical side of the differing rates can be seen in any first grade. The tallest child is half again the size of the smallest child. Although the same kinds of differences exist mentally, the evidences of the differences are more subtle, hence harder to realize. The formula, Learning Expectancy Level equals the Mental Age minus five, is generally accepted as being an indicator of the capacity level of a child at a given age. If we use this formula to determine the potentials of three children with different I.Q.'s, the mental difference of the children is obvious.

At the first-grade level, there is a spread of four years between the potential of the *brightest* and the potential of the *slowest*. By the sixth grade, this range has been increased by almost seven years. At seventh grade the range between the *average* child and the *dullest* child is now exactly the same as the range was in the first grade between the brightest and the dullest. The seventh-grade teacher is faced with a range of different tasks almost double that of the first-grade teacher. By the time this group reaches the high school level the range will be monumental.

The differences in potential can also be seen in the results of achievement tests. We are concerned with reading, but what holds for reading also holds for the other areas of the curriculum. The range in achievement is just as wide and continually widening as is the range of potential. The higher we go in the school system, the more complex the task becomes.

The Widening Spread of Abilities: Qualitatively

It is always so much easier to show changes quantitatively than qualitatively. All we have to do is administer a test, plot the scores, and say there it is. With the qualitative aspects it is a little more difficult. About the closest we can come to showing qualitative changes quantitatively is through the work done by Walter (1953, 1959) with brain waves. Walter's work shows that the child does not develop an adult brain wave pattern until he is somewhere between 12 and 14 years of age. This range indicates probably the normal range of ages in the development of adult brain wave patterns. There are undoubtedly those who develop earlier and those who develop later. This seems to indicate that there is a difference in the qualitative aspects of different children's mental processes.

Further evidence of difference can be seen if the theory of Hebb (1949) is validated. Hebb proposes that there are in reality two kinds of learning in all humans. Early learning is characterized by trial and error behavior and slow learning. Adult learning is characterized by the Gestalt principle of insight of rapid learning and best explained by the field theory of neural processes.

Coupling the theory of Hebb with the findings of Walter seems to give credibility to the idea that qualitative aspects of mental processes differ from child to child. Probably the differences widen as the children mature since this conforms to what we know concerning other kinds of development in children. To the classroom teacher in the secondary school this means having children still operating on the early learning of Hebb, children operating on the adult learning of Hebb, and children operating on various combinations in between. What a task!

Attitudes of Learners

Almost every child comes to school expecting to learn to read. Prior to his school entrance he has seen older children go off to school and learn to read. He has heard parents and friends tell him he will go to school and learn to read. It is safe assumption that all children enter school expecting to be *taught* to read. What is more important, both their parents and their teachers expect them to learn to read.

Those poor unfortunate children who run into difficulty in learning to read slowly develop an antagonistic or futile attitude toward reading until by the time they reach the secondary school, their attitude is one of expecting failure and avoidance of the unpleasant reading situation. The secondary teacher must now cope with a child who cannot read and who is against reading.

A further difference exists in the area of cooperativeness. Small children have a tendency to accept the leadership of adults out of respect or fear, hence they are cooperative. Teen-agers, on the other hand, are in a period of self-assertion and movement toward independence. Many times this behavior is directed against adult authority, hence some degree of uncooperativeness exists in every teen-ager. This uncooperativeness sometimes finds its expression in resisting the attempts of the teacher to teach the virtual nonreader to read.

Many of these youngsters have experienced a succession of reading teachers, tutors, and clinics and are still unable to read. What is worse, they have been "waltzed around again, Willie." It is a safe bet that a secondary student who has run the gauntlet of special help has been "phonicsized" again and again and even been subjected to the same materials many times without any positive results. More of the same is nonproductive.

Attitudes of Teachers

Although numerically the attitude we are about to discuss is relatively small, any degree of existence is catastrophic. Teachers sometimes through the lack of knowledge of the complexities of reading assume that any child who has failed to measure up to a standard is a "dummy" and therefore not worthy of too much attention or help. Or they may assume that the child is lazy and all that needs to be done is "to growl at 'em." Both these attitudes contribute nothing to the child who is experiencing difficulty. Too much research has shown that many of the children who find difficulty with reading are above average in intelligence, and too many clinicians are amazed at the amount of maneuvering poor readers have done to try to read to accept either of these propositions. All that these kinds of attitudes can do is further complicate the problem by increasing the child's antipathy toward reading and reading tasks.

Another attitude of some teachers which further complicates the problem is when the teacher teaches a discipline and not reading. Such a teacher shortsightedly has failed to realize that he is supposed to teach his discipline in such a manner that every child in his charge will reach his maximum potential. This means that if he must spend 20 minutes developing concepts or teaching the child to read a formula, then he is contributing to their fuller growth, and the activities, though reading, are part and parcel of his obligation. No one is better qualified to teach the specific reading skills than the discipline teacher himself.

We hold the position that secondary content teachers said on their application for their jobs "I want to teach social studies (or math, science, home ec, industrial arts." They did not say that they wanted to teach their content material to "kids who can read." Therefore, it is their responsibility to teach their content to all students, whether they can read or not. The most common reason given for a student failing a course is "He can't read the material." If the content is really vital, then all youngsters need it. If as a teacher I can dismiss a fourth of my class from gaining my content because they can't read, I am in essence saying that my content is unimportant and should be taken out of the curriculum. No child should be penalized from acquiring content because he cannot read. In the book, *Damn Reading*, Gibson (1969) claims that if Gutenberg had invented television, we would have remedial television teachers today. Because he invented the printing press, we are tied to the Gutenberg Syndrome which says "the only way one can learn is through print."

School Support System for Reading

Many times we have been asked to serve as consultants to a school which finds itself in trouble either because of poor test scores, parental and community dissatisfaction, or faculty turmoil. Almost without exception, we have found that the school has very good reading programs. If you will notice, we said "programs." We visit room after room and find each teacher is doing a good job of teaching reading. The problem is that what Teacher A is doing bears little relationship to what Teacher B is doing. A is using Ginn. B is using Holt. C is using language experience. D is using individualized reading. There is no totally coordinated school reading program.

In a study conducted to determine patterns in good schools and in poor schools, we found that poor schools had no consistency from grade to grade or across grade level. Good schools did. An analysis of the good schools showed that they:

1. Have a written philosophy.
2. Involve the principal, faculty, and parents in the development of a philosophy.
3. Make provisions for children's learning styles.
4. Have written goals and objectives.
5. Have principals who accept their role as instructional leaders.
6. Have an assessment program.
7. Have an adequate record keeping system.
8. Have a well-defined recruitment and selection process.
9. Have an organizational pattern.
10. Have media activities coordinated with classroom activities.
11. Have a basal reading series as a core of the reading program.
12. Have a reading teacher who works with the classroom teacher and with students.

Good schools are just as interested in providing services for the teaching and improvement of reading on the secondary level as they are on the elementary level.

chapter 3

Learning Process and Learning Disabilities

A baby is born. At birth the main considerations of the parents and obstetrician are how much does he weigh, what is his length, what color is his hair, and does he have the normal number of fingers and toes. Very little consideration is given to the baby's intellectual status except to ask the question "Is he all right?" What becomes important after the initial physical investigation, of course, is the stabilization of his organic functions and needs because we have here a little guy who is going to have to get all of his systems working properly if he is to survive. Once we know he is on the right pathway for survival, then we try to find the right formula and routine for continued growth and development. But our thinking and efforts are generally centered on physical growth or development without much thought or consideration to the fact that this baby is also beginning, from the very moment of birth, to develop those cognitive and perceptual functions that are so important to good intellectual development. Infants who are stifled in areas of mental development through denial or deficient application of sensory and language stimulating activities will become limited in cognitive development.

Basic Understandings

At birth, an infant's perceptual pattern and perceptual field are practically nonexistent. This neonate responds almost completely on the basis of maturational reactions and reflexes. Lawson (1967) states that the things that a newborn child does not have to learn are (a) a primitive figure on ground perception, as indicated by Hebb's theory, (b) various motor acts, such as flexing and extending limbs, turning the head, moving the eyes, and grasping objects, (c) the production of crying and of single noncrying vowel and consonant sounds, and (d) a certain degree of integration and coordination of behavior, which, according to Kaluger and Kaluger (1974), will further be developed through maturation. According to Hebb (1949) and Piaget (1952), the child must learn (a) to identify objects, people, and

49

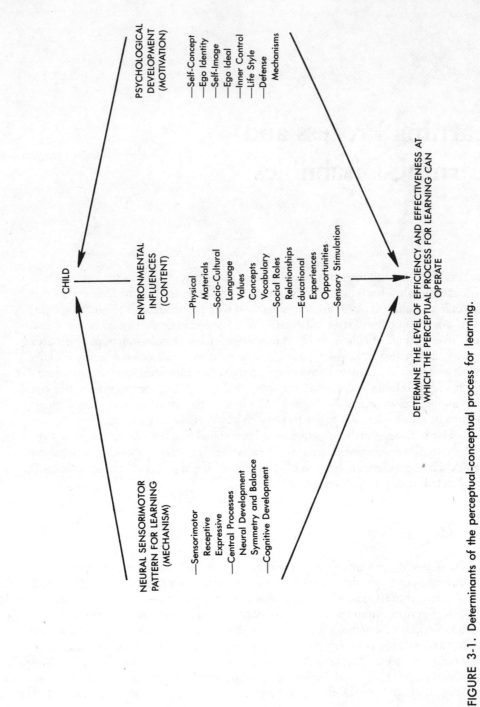

FIGURE 3-1. Determinants of the perceptual-conceptual process for learning.

symbols as existing independently in space and time, and (b) to coordinate his behavior with that of the objects and people in his environment.

The implication is, as we see it, that the child is born with a primitive but basic response pattern in visual, auditory, motor, and other sensory areas, upon which, or in addition to which, a perceptual-conceptual pattern must be developed through learning. It is aided in development by maturational growth. We theorize that there are three major determinants which are involved in the development of the perceptual-conceptual processes and, subsequently, the perceptual field. They are (1) the neural sensorimotor pattern which consists of the organic elements having to do with learning, (2) environmental influences which provide, among other things, the content or information of learning, and (3) psychogenetic development which has to do with the origin and development of behavior, personality, and mental or psychological processes such as motivation and self-concept. Figure 3–1 illustrates the relationship of the determinants to the effectiveness of the perceptual process.

Neural Determinants

At birth, the sensorimotor pattern and the neural pattern of the central nervous system are very primitive in terms of the operation of the cognitive process. The basic blueprint and the parts, all placed in their proper positions, are present, however, for the development of a "mental computer." Through maturation, sequential development, and learning, the neurological elements become organized for more efficient and effective adaptive responses. Neurologists and others interested in the study of neurological organization or neural circuit development are not in agreement as to how, or even if, neural processes and learning are related, but it is generally assumed that something resembling organized neural patterns or neural responses takes place organically or chemically and that these developments are instrumental in enabling an infant to respond cognitively, helping him to be more adaptive to his environment. We proceed upon this assumption, following the thinking of Gesell (1949), Piaget, and Hebb.

DEVELOPMENT OF THE CENTRAL PROCESSES. We postulate that there are several neural developments which must take place in order for an effective perceptual-conceptual process to be operative. First, the primitive sensorimotor patterns must develop through maturation and learning so that appropriate receptive (input or recognition) and expressive (output or response) duties can be carried out. The sensory pattern must develop such abilities as tactile, auditory, visual, and other types of sensory awareness, discrimination, and reminiscence which includes retention, recognition, recall, and sequentialization ability. The motor pattern must achieve the ability to program and perform speech, writing, muscular movements, and gross and fine sensorimotor skills.

The central processes must be organized to retain and to store information for further use, to develop concepts, and to process incoming impulses from the senses so that meanings and interpretations can be made. To explain what happens in the development of the central processes Gesell writes of the maturational sequential pattern, Piaget speaks of the interaction of the environment and sensorimotor responses in developing schemata, Hebb introduces a neurological explanation citing the development of cell assemblies and phases, and Kephart (1971) stresses the importance of motor balance, laterality, and directionality. The one idea that all of these writers have in common is that somehow motor development in the infant's early life is related to cognitive development and that this relationship is manifested in an organic (neurological) manner. Consideration must also be given to the ideas of Thurstone (1941) concerning the primary mental ability traits, and to the theories of Guilford (1967) pertaining to intellectual functions and how both of these aspects of intelligence are developed. The significance and the necessity of development of laterality and cerebral dominance are still being debated. We know that the rate of postnatal brain growth is at its peak during the tenth to eighteenth months. We postulate that the first three months of development are very critical, perhaps the most critical for development of balance and symmetry. The next six months are the next most critical. Readiness for learning how to learn begins very early.

It would be enlightening to know just a little more about the concepts of Thurstone and of Guilford on the nature of intelligence. The factor analysis conducted by Thurstone and his team of workers to determine exactly what is being measured by intelligence tests concluded that instead of an individual having one global intelligence function, and hence, one I.Q., each individual actually has eight separate and distinct IQs. They are known as factors.

V *Factor.*   Verbal Reasoning—Ability to get meaning from words, printed or spoken.

N *Factor.*   Numerical Reasoning—Ability to reason with numbers and quantities (not a computational process, but a reasoning process).

*I *Factor.*   Inductive Reasoning—Ability to do abstract reasoning that progresses from specifics or clues to a generalization or conclusion.

*D *Factor.*   Deductive Reasoning—Ability to do abstract reasoning that progresses from a generalization or conclusion to details or specifics.

M *Factor.*   Memory—Ability to retain and recall, short-term and/or long-term memory.

W *Factor.*   Word Fluency—Ability to think of a large number of pertinent words in a short span of time.

P *Factor.*   Perceptual Speed and Accuracy—Ability to recognize likenesses or differences in details quickly.

S *Factor.*   Spatial or Space Relations—Ability to be able to visualize and mentally manipulate objects or designs in space.

Guilford's concept of intellect basically refers to the mental manipulations and functions used by the intellect. His three faces of intellect refer to the operation, content, and product of cognitive processing. The mental operations that can be performed are (a) cognition, (b) memory, (c) divergent thinking, (d) convergent thinking, and (e) evaluation. The cognitive content can be transmitted in figural, symbolic, semantic, or behavioral forms. The product resulting from the structuring of these cognitive stimuli may be on the level of units, classes, relations, systems, transformations, or implications.

The ultimate implication of cognitive development is that not only is it important to know about the development of intelligence, but one must also be aware of the nature and function of intelligence. With learning disabled children, we frequently find a very bright youngster who cannot process intellectual functions in one or two areas of operations. Or we

---

* The I and D Factors are generally included under an A or R Factor, which stands for the ability to do abstract reasoning without the aid of printed or written material.

find the child very capable in some forms of intellect, such as word fluency, numerical reasoning, or spatial relations, but very inadequate in verbal reasoning. You must know the field of study in order to make proper assessments of the learning situation.

BIOCHEMICAL DEVELOPMENTAL NEEDS. The physiological structure and makeup of the organism itself must be considered. For example there are biochemical considerations which can affect synaptic transmission. The quality of memory may be dependent upon chemical factors. The part that DNA (deoxyribonucleic acid) and RNA (ribonucleic acid) play in the development of nerve cells and their relatedness to intelligence must be recognized. The functions of the nerve cells may be affected by such things as genetic factors, lesions, tumors, vascular damage, retarded development, inadequately developed synaptic knobs, and so-called "minimal brain damage." This is a gross listing of brain pathology, and it is not based on verified opinion as to whether or not the learning-reading process is hampered by the presence of such pathology, but there is reason (logic) to believe that some distortion in efficiency of learning can occur because of structural defects in the cortex and cerebrum of the brain.

The effect of chemical imbalance or trauma on prenatal, perinatal, or postnatal development must be considered. Chemical imbalance in the mother during the germinal and embryonic periods of pregnancy can produce several types of physical deviations resulting in mental retardation, perceptual handicaps, and organic dysfunctions. The rubella or German measles epidemic of the 1960s along the eastern seaboard of the United States produced many children with degrees of learning disabilities. These children are now trying to make their way through the schools and are having problems. Difficulties at birth also produce some learning disability cases. Asthma and allergies in early infancy indicate the potentiality for learning difficulties. A serious illness with a persistent high temperature, a physical trauma to the head area, and other such conditions are known to have affected some children. All of these conditions merely suggest, they do not prove, that a learning deficiency was caused by them.

MATURATIONAL LAG. A word should be said about maturational or developmental lag, sometimes referred to as delayed development. Children show a variety of rates of growth as they develop. Some develop neurologically much more quickly than others. Eustis (1947) describes an immaturity syndrome which he believes represents a delay in development. He cites a slow tempo of neuromuscular maturation, which is probably indicative of slow myelination of motor and associative nerve tracts. A maturational lag does not necessarily imply a structural defect, deficiency, or loss, however. Ilg and Ames (1965) and de Hirsch (1966) have developed readiness tests based at least in part on the maturational lag concept. No known studies indicate what percentage of children having reading difficulty in the primary grades are hindered by handicaps related to maturational lag and what percentage are affected by other factors.

Our clinical experiences suggest that by the time a child is 9 years old and in the third grade, enough neural development should have taken place to give him (1) visual and auditory discrimination ability, (2) awareness of sound-symbol relationships and blendings, (3) a right-left orientation or the ability to compensate so as to maintain this orientation, and (4) a working vocabulary and meaningful concepts. Early deficiencies in these areas may or may not be related to developmental lag. Another clinical observation is that the more intelligent the child, the more likely he is to find ways of circumventing a perceptual handicap, which again may or may not be due to a lag. Most children learn to compensate.

By the age of 14 or so, the myelin sheaths covering the neural pathways usually have reached a mature state of organic development and offer better insulation to the nerves to prevent accidental discharges of nerve impulses. This protection plus a higher cognitive development level gives the child of this age a better opportunity to learn some things he could not pick up earlier. However, by this time, the older child is usually emotionally upset by the frustration he has experienced in learning and so may not be amenable to learning.

We cannot say that maturational lag is the answer for all learning disability cases without obvious cerebral dysfunctions. Cerebral immaturity implies that the child with a developmental lag should eventually improve provided, of course, that attempts to learn are continued long enough. Some adolescents and adults whom we see in our clinical studies do not seem to be helped by the maturational process. Because not all children eventually "mature" and become ready to learn to read, we believe that remedial measures should be taken when a child first gets behind in learning without waiting to see if he will "grow out of it." In fact, we recommend that preventative measures be taken to eliminate as many reading problems as possible. We estimate that perhaps one-fourth to one-third of the disabled readers in primary grades have a maturational lag.

PREMATURE BIRTH. Rubin, Rosenblatt, and Barlow (1973) studied 241 premature infants, as defined by birth weight and gestation age. They learned that low birth weight was more highly correlated with education impairment than was gestation age. Low birth weight males had a higher incidence of school problems warranting special class placement than did full term weight males. These children also scored lower on all measures of intelligence, language development, school readiness, and academic achievement through 7 years of age. These males also had a higher incidence of school identified problems than did low birth weight females. Socioeconomic status showed no significant differences.

NUTRITIONAL NEEDS. The results of research are still somewhat inconclusive, but more and more studies are stressing the need for an adequate diet during the first three years of life in order for the brain to develop to its highest level of functional potential. Scientists at the 1967 International Conference on Malnutrition, Learning, and Behavior reported findings from South American and Central American countries which suggest very strongly that malnutrition can interact with infection, heredity, and social factors to bring about physical and mental impairment. Several studies showed a relationship between undernourishment and poor intersensory integration (Young & Scrimshaw, 1971).

The general implication that mental capacity and learning behavior are interrelated has long had acceptance, but scientific evidence to support the theory has been inconclusive. In recent years experiments show gross undernutrition and serious growth failure in very early periods of development are coincidental with retarded development and functioning. These findings led to the hypothesis (Martin, 1971) that severe undernutrition in late prenatal life and infancy may prevent children from achieving their full intellectual capacity. Prolonged deficiencies in early life also have a crippling effect on intellectual potential and learning behavior.

The period of rapid brain growth, therefore, is critical from the standpoint of the need for nutrient supplies and their effect on brain growth. Growth of the brain and other structures of the central nervous system is dependent on the supply of energy and nutrients and on the internal environment that will build these into highly specialized tissues. Any interruption or shortage in supplies may be reflected in retarded growth. In addition, it has been indicated that severe malnutrition can reduce the amount of deoxyribonucleic acid (DNA) and protein in the growing brain. DNA is the chemical element in the nucleus of a cell that determines the kind and amount of protein laid down to manufacture brain tissue. Currently, numerous studies are being carried out in which preschool children are given psychological testing and their progress followed over a period of several years. Preliminary results to date show that there is a definite lag in learning in malnourished children.

Environmental Component

The environment provides the "content" or "information bits" to be stored for use in the developing "mental computer." Maturation helps develop organic abilities such as reaching, walking, and speech production, but the environment will determine where the child will walk, what he will see and experience in his walking, what objects he will touch, what words and language he will hear, and what attitudes and values he will develop. The environment provides the *life space*. The child can only learn or develop what is available to him in his life space and only to the degree that his organic makeup and psychological self will permit him to respond.

SOCIAL ENVIRONMENT. Educators and psychologists have long recognized the importance of the social environment on the upbringing of the child. The influences of the parents and the child's peers are pertinent not only to his mental health and personality development, but also to his intellectual and conceptual growth. When parents care about the child's education and demonstrate this care with positive action, such as working with the schools, insisting that the schools do a good job, seeing that the child does the work he is supposed to do, and setting an example by attitude and response in the home that says "education is important," the child is more apt to respond favorably to learning. Demonstration projects in ghettos and slum areas have found that education can be improved and that children will respond more if their parents are involved in seeking and maintaining good educational practices and values. Parental acceptance or rejection of the child has also been shown to have a direct effect on the child's development and motivation for learning. Children who associate with other children who care about learning and who make an effort and do not belittle educational endeavors usually respond in the same manner as their friends. The ascribed and achieved roles that a child has to play will certainly have a positive or negative effect on learning, depending upon the nature of the role. The youngster well thought of and confident that others consider him worthwhile and capable will respond more readily to learning than the child regarded by others as a trouble-maker, retard, or clown.

Raphaela Best (in press), with the assistance of Jessie Bernard, traced the natural history or development of classroom structure between the first and the third grade. By the third grade Best found the formation of an "in-group" and a group of rejected boys, or "losers." Best concluded that the losers had been socialized into the out-group. The results on the losers, as far as reading was concerned, was devastating. Not only did they fail to make progress, but some even regressed. Best also found that this "socializing into the out-group" did not occur among girls. Best's hypothesis is that boys are subjected to more sex role pressure from adults than girls and, therefore, organize into groups to protect themselves. To quote Bernard, "In simplest form, it states that the imposition of rigorous 'macho' norms on small boys places them under a considerable amount of pressure. They must be 'instant men.' Individually, they are vulnerable. Together they can support one another."

CULTURAL ENVIRONMENT. The cultural environment has much to say about the language, vocabulary, concepts, and values which a child acquires. Katz and Deutch (1963) show the effects of cultural differences upon the learning-reading process. They note explicit auditory and visual modality deficiencies which seem to exist above and beyond socioeconomic and environmental dissimilarities which these children encounter. They hypothesize that the auditory deficiency may be a consequence of their environment. The constant hum and drone of noises encountered in large cities have been said by some investigators to contribute to a lack of sensitive auditory discrimination. Speech patterns in ghettos and slums, in rural and mountain sections, and in other areas of cultural isolation, often differ from standard English forms, producing characteristics of speech which are quite different from those found in reading material. Not only do the language and grammar structures differ, but so do the sounds (phonemes) representing the letters (graphemes). Some accents and dialects are so thick that outsiders find them difficult to understand. Residents of the Harlem area of New York City speak a language with characteristics quite different from "downtown English." The remedial reading teacher seeking to help a Harlem youngster learn phonics will encounter many difficulties if she does not recognize this fact. There is a tendency for some children to drop the sounds of some letters, such as *l* and *r* as in *mistah* and *be yo sef*. They may slur words such as *gimmedat* (give me that) or *beseeinya* (be seeing you). The "th" sound turns to "f" in *bofe* meaning *both*. Cultural forces in many black communities are currently seeking to resist efforts to change their culture and language form because these represent elements of identity. They do not want to lose that identity but to develop it. In some places attempts are being made to teach standard English as a "second language" for use "downtown" or on the job, while retaining the original or nonstandard language usage for other occasions.

There are still other verbal and concept deficiencies found among the culturally different that are not mentioned here. The significance of visual, auditory, tactile, and cognitive experiences in developing a background for learning should not be underestimated, however. The Head Start programs initiated by the government to help overcome some of these initial sensory and cultural deficiencies have been developed because educators recognize the importance of an early start in reading training.

Failure in reading has been a major educational problem of children from a variety of culturally different subgroups. Reference has been made to blacks and the special dialect and language structure that they use in conversation. Yet, even among blacks, there is a variety of dialects, word choices, and language patterns when regional areas of the country such as Philadelphia, Los Angeles, New Orleans, and the rural South are compared. Dialects differ among whites as well; compare the dialects of Bostonians with Midwesterners, and these with the desert West natives. One of the thickest Southern accents heard by one of the authors was spoken by a group of people who live in the mountain valleys of West Virginia, not more than 30 miles south of the Pennsylvania border. When we talk about Spanish-speaking populations, thoughts usually turn to Puerto Ricans living in Miami or New York, or the Mexican-Americans of Texas and the far West. Yet, in the Amish Dutch country of Lancaster County, Pennsylvania, there are some 60,000 Spanish-speaking people. In Maine, there are settlements of French-speaking people.

We believe that educators have an obligation to teach *all* of the children of *all* of the people in the country. If it takes special procedures and arrangements to reach those who are culturally different, then we must undertake that obligation, providing we do it in such a fashion as to permit them to maintain the self-respect and dignity to which they are entitled. Culturally different people have language facility, and they use language extensively. Their language must not be stifled, ridiculed, or criticized because it is different. We must build on what language facility is present and introduce language forms that are not found in their language but are needed for reading. Procedures for teaching necessary reading skills must be modified in order to develop reading. Perhaps more emphasis should be placed on learning to unlock words silently, making better use of context cues, and, above all else, stressing how to gain comprehension. Less emphasis should be placed on oral reading. Why should all children, of all backgrounds, be programmed into a pattern mold or a one-track channel that all learners of reading must follow? We do not insist on such rigidity for children who are not culturally different.

SENSORY STIMULATION. The importance of sensory stimulation for the development of sensory awareness and sensitivity has been learned by psychologists working with animals raised in darkness or otherwise deprived of stimulation. Bruner (1966) notes the cognitive consequences of sensory deprivation in children, especially those from poorer socioeconomic homes. Studies show a difference in the auditory-verbal awareness in favor of school-age children who at the age of two had mothers read to them as compared to children whose mothers did not read to them. Psychologists see vivid differences at the age of about one and a half between middle-class babies and those born into poor homes. By school age, most of the poor children are already remedial cases. The deficiencies may be due to either a lack of sensory stimulation or a lack of verbal and cognitive stimulation.

Hunt (1961) stresses the importance of very early sensory and verbal training of the child to good intellectual development. This importance is expressed by Piaget and Hebb as well. Gesell, however, can be interpreted as being somewhat committed to predetermined innate maturational growth, at least in motor development, although he does not seek to underestimate the importance of environmental factors. Pine (1967) states that the single most urgent need of preschool children today is for adequate day-care centers for the children of working mothers so that the children might receive sufficient intellectual stimulation and growth. In terms of intellectual development, some developmental psychologists are saying that sensory stimulation of the brain is more important than mother's love!

EDUCATIONAL ENVIRONMENT. The educational environment should not be overlooked when considering factors influencing the conceptual development of children. Children need opportunities to learn. Although many things will be learned outside the schools, the school is the formal agency given the responsibility for providing structured learning. The quality of the teaching, the curriculum materials, the techniques and methods used, the program of study, the physical facilities, and the personality of the teacher all affect the learning situation. There is no substitute for good teachers in good schools. Unfortunately, some children do receive poor instruction in some schools.

The Cooperative Research Studies reported by Bond and Dykstra (1967) lend credence to the tenet that the teacher is more important in the quality of instruction rather than the particular method used. The CRS project studied 29 published systems for teaching beginning reading. At the end of the study, no significant differences were found in the effectiveness of one program over another but there was a difference among teachers using the same system. Apparently the teacher was the key element.

Psychogenic Determinants

EMOTIONAL FACTORS. At one time much stress was placed on the idea that many children could not read because they were emotionally upset over failure to learn to read. As a result, most remedial recommendations specified the need to overcome emotional problems before the child could be helped with his reading. The emotional angle was overused and probably overemphasized. At least the trend lately has been to look elsewhere for causes and obstacles resulting in reading disabilities.

However, without underestimating the significance of emotional involvement, our clinical experiences do suggest that emotional difficulties in the primary grades are not too prevalent except in cases where the parents had made delay in learning to read an emotional issue at home. Still, by the time most disabled readers reach fifth grade or the age of 10 or 11, emotional signs due to reading failure can be detected. Emotional symptoms are quite evident in children of junior high school age. Defensive mechanisms are rather strongly entrenched in boys and girls 14 years of age and older who cannot read well. The principle appears to be that the older the child with a reading problem, the more likely it is that remediation will need to take emotional factors into account. Excessive anxieties and negative attitudes always make learning more difficult.

A study by Harris (1965) cites the following factors as causing emotional blocks to learning. First, the socioeconomic status of the home has some significance. The lower-class offspring usually lacks the motivation to learn for the sake of learning because of a lack of intellectual stimulation by the family and the family's low anxiety about the child's repeating a grade. Second, the emotional block created by family disorganization due to incompatibility of the marriage or the employment of the mother outside the home often gives a child a chronic feeling of anxious insecurity as to whether or not his home will stay intact.

Third, the personal self-seeking ambitiousness of the parents, especially of the mother, to gain status through the achievement of the child causes an emotional block to learning. Children with low average mental ability cannot gratify their mothers' need for vicarious achievement and assume defensive behaviors, such as resistance to the teacher, dawdling, or procrastination, for fear of being measured and found wanting. Harris listed birth order and expectations of maturity as a fourth area of emotional blockage. Apparently the last-born tends to be less serious and responsible than the first-born because parents have lower expectations of maturity for the younger child. Fifth, Harris found that nonlearners were either aggressively hostile or extremely submissive. Both extremes were associated with difficulties in reading. Sixth, the study seems to indicate that how consistently income comes into the family is more important than how much income the family earns. A steady low income seems to cause fewer problems than a high erratic income.

SELF-CONCEPT AND EGO DEVELOPMENT. Self-concept is a person's view of himself, a self-appraisal reflecting one's good and bad points. Remedial personnel must be acutely aware of the child's self-concept because it will affect his learning, and, in turn, learning experiences can influence the self-concept. The learning that a child does may be determined, influenced, and even distorted by his own self-image. Learning is accepted much more readily if the learner feels it is enhancing his self-concept, but learning is avoided if the learning situation is perceived as threatening.

Dimensions of self-concept seem to entail self-esteem, a level of anxiety-tension, independence or self-autonomy, emotional indifference, and body image. These factors have much to do with learning.

Anxious children usually have poorer self-concepts than confident children. Children with high self-esteem are more active in class discussions, are more enthusiastic about competition, and are less afraid of threatening situations. A degree of independence and emotional indifference permits one to operate with a degree of openness or "psychological safety," which makes it easier for that person to permit himself to learn. Body image and body identity are considered by some, such as Kephart, to be fundamental to the development of an ego structure which has stable reference points from whence the child can reach out into his environment and comprehend it.

Rappaport (1965) places great emphasis upon organic ego development and its relationship to the learning act, with the implication that brain damage interferes with ego development. He believes that it is often possible to establish skills and self-controls which have been deficient because of the damage, thus improving ego structure and self-concept.

Black (1974) states that emotional and behavioral problems are commonly reported concomitants of learning disabilities, being characterized both as primary causes of the learning problem and as secondary to the frustrations of repeated academic failures. He provides more substantive information on the relationship of self-concept and academic achievement through a study of elementary children who were all failing one or more subjects at the time of evaluation. The results of his study show that learning disabled children with reading retardation score significantly lower on the self-concept test than normal readers and learning disabled "achieving" readers. Significant negative correlations were obtained for self-concept scores in relation to chronological age and grade. Black suggests this finding is of importance to those children whose learning problems are not adequately identified and remedied in the early school career. He feels the difficulties in remediation of older learning disabled students and the subsequent drop-out rate among the learning disabled are directly related.

A facet of research in learning disabilities which is gaining more and more recognition is the correlation found between the delinquent youth and the learning disabled youth. We think this correlation alone has great implication toward showing a need for working through social and emotional problems with learning disabled youngsters. A study reported by Mauser (1974) points out that one of the most common descriptions associated with attitudes of the juvenile delinquent has been a dislike for schools and teachers. Specifically, the dislike centers around subjects requiring memory, persistent effort, and logical reasoning. These deficiencies characterize many children with learning disabilities. Mauser points out also that early detection and remediation of learning disabilities, and a system of reward and success, rather than punishment, are the definite route to follow in preventing learning disabled youngsters from resorting to delinquent behavior later on (Mauser, 1974). Developing a feeling of competency leads to confidence and a self-concept which says "I can do it."

INTEREST, ATTENTION, AND VOLITION. The psychologic factors of interest, attention, motivation, and level of aspiration are pertinent to the learning-reading process. The desire of the child to read will serve as a drive allowing him to be taught. The level of aspiration will set the practical limits of learning and will indicate how much the child really wants to learn. The importance of the child's interest in the reading material or in learning to read is well known. A child will attend better to what he likes than to what he dislikes.

An outgrowth of this emphasis on interest has been the development of "high interest-low reading level" books for retarded readers. A 14-year-old boy's effort to learn to read above a second-grade level was disastrously affected by some junior high school age boys teasing him because he was seen coming from a remedial reading class with a copy of *Uncle Funny Bunny* under his arm. The boy immediately lost interest in learning to read. Not until the teacher introduced some of the new high interest-low level books could she convince him to try again. She showed him a copy of *The Iron Duke* and explained that the other boys had been wanting to take the book out of the library but she reserved it for him.

Attention is a psychological phenomenon about which remedial teachers should be more familiar. The act of attention is the process whereby part of the field of awareness becomes clearer or more emphasized. It is maintenance of a perceptual set for one object or activity and disregard for others. Teachers speak of this phenomenon as concentration, and it is far more complicated than most contend. To illustrate, psychologists concerned with the psychology of consciousness make attention a central concept and then speak of duration of attention, fluctuation of attention, inertia of attention, primary attention, secondary attention, etc.

The significance of this topic is that concentration or attention is not a simple condition which a reader can willfully control "if he wants to." To say that "all he needs to do is to concentrate" is to reveal how little the teacher understands of the process. Physiological factors, environmental conditions, and psychogenic elements all enter into the picture to determine the degree of concentration which a child can apply to a task at any given time.

Learning How to Learn

If we are to understand what the nature of reading readiness means, we must begin with the process by which a child learns how to learn. Admittedly, in most children this concern is of no real consequence because the majority of children go through the growth and development stages of learning how to learn without much difficulty. This enables the teacher to begin the teaching of reading without any major regard for the level of readiness for the bulk of her children. Our concern is with the learning disabled reader, how he got that way, and what must be overcome in order to permit his learning processes to operate efficiently on grade level, enabling him to learn how to read. The determinants of the development of the central nervous system patterns of learning were discussed earlier. Those concepts will also have meaning here. Some type of perceptual-conceptual pattern or organization of neural circuits and processes for the purpose of learning is needed. The hows, whys, and wherefores by which the child's brain is developed for the purpose of responding adequately to his environment is referred to as the process of *learning how to learn*. We will indicate what factual information is available and refer to ideas of major theorists. The ultimate intent is to lay the groundwork for answering the questions (a) how does readiness for learning to read begin, and (b) what are the major components of that foundation? There is much that is not yet known or fully understood as to how a child develops his ability to learn, but the following information is presented as a starting point.

Developmental Research and Theories

How does a child develop a pattern for learning? There are several points of view. The classic theory of Piaget (1952, 1969, 1970) states that the construct of intellectual growth and readiness for different levels of learning emerges through a sequential development of four stages starting with sensorimotor perceptual development (ages 0–2 years). The second stage, including the preconceptual and intuitive thought phases, occurs when symbolic-representational insight is learned (ages 2–7 years), followed by the concrete-operational reasoning stage (ages 7–11 or 12 years), and the formal-operational stage of development (ages 11 to 16 years). Piaget's concepts will be presented in detail later in this section.

Hebb (1949) presents a neural organizational view with his concepts of Intelligence A, which is the basic genetic and neural potential of learning that a child is born with, and Intelligence B, which becomes the developed functional intellect of the individual as the child interacts with various aspects of the environment. He either develops or causes a deterioration of the potential of Intelligence A that he was born with. Learning takes place through the formation of cell assemblies that form the basis of bits of learned information. A phase sequence process is used to trigger or fire these bits of information in the proper order, such as firing the letters d - o - g in that order to get the word *dog*. A third theory is that of Gesell (1949). He states that physical maturational capabilities take place as the child goes through a motor stage of development; he interacts with the environment and develops language, cognitive, social, and personal skills. Certain organized patterns of growth of neural structure have to be present before environmental factors can be effective.

Kephart (1971) has been largely responsible for a proliferation of theories that stress the importance of developing a perceptual-motor match, perceptual-motor organization, and perceptual development. These learning processes are attained through motor and perceptual growth and development and by the emergence of laterality, directionality, and balance. The theory was well reasoned by Kephart, but not proven. Frostig (1964) emphasized visual perceptual development. She published a test based on her theory and research and developed remedial materials to go with the tests. The works of Ayres (1972) and Gibson (1969) have extended the theories of perceptual development to a much higher level of sophistication and understanding. Gibson makes use of much experimental research in visual perception to support her view that the perceptual systems emerge through learning experiences. Ayres mixes research and theory from the point of view of neurological development of the central nervous system. She refers to such behaviors as tonic neck reflexes and central nervous system (CNS) development to substantiate her views.

The entire area of language development has assumed major significance as it relates to reading and disabled learners. The importance of auditory-verbal and language development have been stressed by such notables as Helmer Myklebust (1964) and Joseph Wepman (1962). Receptive, inner, and expressive speech and language development have been stressed by many researchers, including Benjamin Whorf (1956) who is interested in linguistics. Norm Chomsky (1968), another linguist, assumes that language is innate and that a child learns by "maturing" into it by being exposed to various experiences. This view is somewhat supported by Carol Chomsky (1972), who has found empirical evidence that certain language patterns are not present before a given age. For example, a comprehensive task, such as the one devised by Otto et al. (1974), illustrates Chomsky's observation:

> Given two sentences that differ only in the use of the words *and* and *although*, a child would give different interpretations to "I would have done the same" in each sentence:
>
> 1. "Mike scolded Bill for eating it, *and* I would have done the same." (Meaning: I would have scolded Bill)
>
> 2. "Mike scolded Bill for eating it, *although* I would have done the same." (Meaning: I would have eaten it)

At the other extreme is the theory of Skinnerian behaviorists concerning language development. They believe that no learning—language, reading or otherwise—occurs without some form of reward. Learning, to behaviorists, is a habit system that must be taught in sequential, reinforceable steps emphasizing the teaching of small subskills to a great degree.

Birch (1962) refers to concepts from comparative psychology and the maturational sequence in developmental psychology which he believes may give some answers to causes of certain types of reading disabilities. One concept that he mentions relates to the ways in

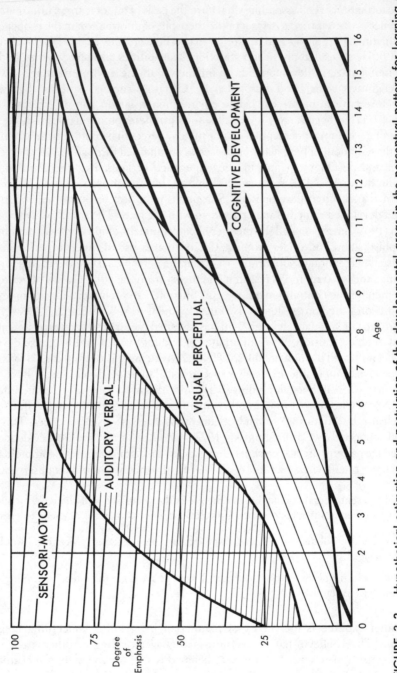

FIGURE 3-2. Hypothetical estimation and postulation of the developmental areas in the perceptual pattern for learning and the degree of emphasis the various areas receive at different ages.

62

which animals differ from one another in the hierarchical organization of their sensory systems. Human beings have the highest level of hierarchical organization. This view states that the developing child goes through a number of developmental sequences, in the course of which alterations in the nature of the hierarchical structuring of the avenues of senses occur. The child eventually develops a hierarchical organization which will produce a dominant visual system. A second concept which he reports suggests that the growth of perceptual behavior is related to the process of developing intersensory patterning. The central nervous system apparently seeks to integrate the functions of the existent major input systems. Reading, to be effective, requires the integration of visual information with other information such as verbal, auditory-spatial direction, and temporal sequence. A third concept, in part conceived by Birch, suggests that there are levels of perceptual development. The early level of perceptual discrimination is one of ability to recognize objects and to discriminate between identities and nonidentities, but only in their global aspects. The second level of perceptual analysis differentiates the elements or details of a gestalt. The highest level is that of perceptual synthesis wherein the elements of the gestalt are effectively recombined into a figural whole, giving the perceiver a higher and more complex level of visual perceptual function and understanding. Birch suggests that some reading disability cases will be found which will have markedly defective analytic and/or synthetic perceptual capacities.

The concept of *traducing* implies the ability to integrate the input of the various sensory modalities into an organized, meaningful whole. The child who cannot traduce the incoming stimuli may have some difficulty if taught by a multisensory approach. This child needs an approach that makes use of his strongest sensory modality. Of special significance, as pointed out by Vande Voort, Senf and Benton (1972), is the fact that although poor traducing (cross-modality association) is found in many children with deficient reading skills, the critical factors were not the sequencing of simultaneous matching of stimuli from different channels. Their research indicates that attention and encoding (conceptual) processes were more important to learning how to read than was the ability to traduce.

We postulate that the neural pattern of learning consists of four developmental areas which are (1) sensorimotor development with concomitant tactile-kinesthetic development, (2) auditory-verbal development, (3) visual perceptual development, and (4) cognitive development. These developmental areas are (a) hierarchical in complexity as far as levels of learning are concerned, (b) maturational in nature and somewhat sequential in development within each area, (c) all developing at one and the same time although with varying degrees of emphasis in the various areas at different age levels, and (4) dependent upon proper environmental interaction for adequate development and functioning in learning situations. Figure 3–2 illustrates the hypothesis of the four developmental areas and the degree of emphasis on the various areas at different age levels.

The Neural Pattern of Learning

The developmental concept of Kaluger and Kaluger (1974) states that each child develops a unique neural or neurological pattern of learning processes. This pattern involves the organization and an interfunctional relationship of the central nervous system in order to perform cerebral processes such as receiving and organizing perceptual or sensory inputs; associating and interpreting the stimuli recognized and registered by the brain; and programming and initiating motor responses or outputs. We cannot explain the neurological intricacies involved. But we do know that the brain functions in the process of learning, and it is there that we must look for factors that inhibit or promote the quality of learning abilities.

Our basic concept is that something involving the neural organism, probably biochemical in nature, occurs when learning takes place. This change enables the child to progress from an organism that initially responds only by the use of basic reactions and reflexes in global or primitive ways in the sensory, cognitive, and motor realms, to a conscious, attentive, conceptualizing, reflective, problem solving, purposefully responding individual. He does this by using a complex array of cerebral processes that integrate and interrelate in performing the input, decoding, encoding, and output functions. We believe that a neural organization structured around the adaptive processes of language, perception, socialization, and cognitive functions have their beginning in the innate, maturational process of development but are abetted, enhanced, and influenced by a variety of factors that are part of the child's life-space and environment.

SENSORIMOTOR DEVELOPMENT. During the first two years of life, the major portion of developmental emphasis is related to the sensorimotor area of the brain. The central processes of learning are being organized partly through the maturational process and partly through sensory experiences. The infant progresses from responding primarily on the basis of fundamental reactions and reflexes to being able to induce purposeful action. There is some question as to what kind of learning behavior actually structures the central processes for intellectual functions. Piaget (1952) and Osgood (1953) suggest that motor behavior and experiences are fundamental to the cognitive processes. Hebb (1949) argues that it is perceptual experience that is important in establishing the central processes which facilitate problem solving. No doubt both types of experiences are important.

The question of "sequential development" is pertinent at this point. Gesell (1941) and Shirley (1933) assume predetermined development, an unfolding of motor abilities in sequential order, only partly influenced by the environmental circumstances of development. Piaget, on the other hand, is mindful of the interaction of the environment and of its influence on assimilation and accommodation of new learnings. Dennis (1960) has shown that children who have lain unstimulated in cots in an orphanage in Teheran almost never creep and that between the ages of 3 and 5 months they "scoot" rather than creep before walking. The concept of a predetermined sequential pattern and a step-by-step emergence of motor development can be challenged, but the important question of whether or not a deviation in sequential motor development can result in the development of a less effective neural pattern for learning and reading remains unanswered.

Kagan (1973) recently completed a longitudinal study with children living in an isolated village in Guatemala that may upset a number of theories and beliefs concerning the need for sensory stimulation and motor development in order to attain good functional intelligence. It appears that the traditional culture of this secluded village is to keep infants up to the age of 2 years isolated from unnecessary human contact and, indeed, to keep the infants in a state of semidarkness with little activity to occupy them. When the children were tested at the ages of 5 and 6, they were found to be mentally retarded and developmentally delayed as compared to other children of their country. However, examining the same children when they became 12 years of age showed that they were functioning on the same mental and developmental levels as their counterparts. They improved in every respect. The study shows the resiliency of the central nervous system and its ability to overcome a poor developmental start. This last point has special significance for learning disabled children and their parents and teachers; that is: never give up!

Kephart (1966) does not emphasize specifics in initial motor development, but he does suggest that perceptual-motor skills sequentially develop from gross motor skills, to eye-hand coordination skills, to temporal-spatial translation, to form perception. He theorizes that an infant must develop body image and laterality to provide orientation and localization in space and to develop right-left orientation and directionality to provide temporal and spatial sequence. Thus, this development leads not only to a matching of motor output to visual input but also to a perceptual-motor matching which will enable the child to make sense out of symbols and sounds of which he becomes aware. Motor speech patterns as well as motor writing patterns must be developed. Ebersole, Kephart, and Ebersole (1968) consider six general stages of learning which they claim are hierarchical in nature. These developmental stages are (a) gross-motor, (b) motor-perceptual, (c) perceptual-motor, (d) perceptual, (e) perceptual-conceptual, and (f) the conceptual stage. The order of the stages is more important than when each occurs because the stages build upon themselves and are dependent upon the adequate development of the previous stages.

We believe that a perceptual system must be properly developed before the cognitive system can become effective. We contend that stimulation of the tactile, auditory, and visual senses is needed in addition to innate maturational growth in order for an adequate pattern of learning to be developed. We do not have research proof for these statements, but we base them upon our observations of the developmental histories of some of the severely disabled readers with whom we have worked and of some of the remedial techniques we have used and found to be at least correlative factors, if not causative factors, in the improvement of reading ability.

A fundamental question as yet to be answered is "At what stage of maturational motor development should we direct our attention and research toward the purpose of determining readiness to begin learning how to learn?" We believe that this stage may come quite early, much before the creeping and crawling stages. Some signs of abnormality can be detected at birth. An abnormal palm print has been found to exist in some types of mentally retarded children and in some children whose mothers had rubella during the first four months of pregnancy. Other signs, such as asymmetry and atypical tonic neck reflexes, are also suspect.

A problem we have with the motor-perceptual development theories is that not all cultures are affected the same way in spite of similar motor development. For example, Iroquois Indians do not appear to have perceptual problems, especially as they relate to height. These Indians are among the best of high-rise iron workers on bridges and buildings, supposedly because they have no fear of heights. On a test designed to determine how individuals see the size of automobiles from a fourth floor level, the Iroquois consistently outperform others in their perceptual capacity. A perceptual study was done with Zulu tribesmen living in South Africa. The research by Gregory (1966) reveals that they had no difficulty with perceptual illusions and distortions. The Zulus live in an artifact and mentifact culture that emphasizes roundness and curved lines rather than straight lines. It is believed by the researchers that their environment has much to do with the quality of their perceptual development.

AUDITORY-VERBAL DEVELOPMENT. At the age of 1½ to 2 years, the child not only can make, understand, and discriminate between some sounds, but he now attaches meanings to sounds and says and uses words to communicate. Between the ages of 2 and 4 or 5, talking develops at a rapid pace and words become very important. The child learns by listening to sounds and imitating spoken words. He develops concepts and builds a mental storehouse of meanings. Later, he will use these words and sound symbols to do verbal mediation (thinking). Eventually, the child learns that sounds can stand for printed symbols. He will need to make use of this concept of "sound-symbol relationships" to learn phonics.

Children who do not have adequate auditory and verbal stimulation during this developmental period may not develop an efficient auditory discrimination pattern. In fact, they may not even develop a sensitive auditory awareness for sounds. The studies of Wepman (1962) indicate that children with slower developing auditory perception, especially auditory discrimination, are slower to talk and slower to acquire speech accuracy. Some children do not develop adequate discrimination until the age of 8. Auditory memory, temporal discrimination, and lateralization must also be learned. Children who are not encouraged to relate their experiences or to talk to develop their communication skills, children who are not exposed to new words so they can develop an adequate understanding or speaking vocabulary, and children who learn to pronounce words incorrectly, will all be auditorially and verbally deprived when they begin to learn to read. The studies of Holmes and Singer (1961) indicate that one of the most significant substrata-factors accounting for differences in reading accomplishment is auding (listening).

We believe that auditory awareness, discrimination, recognition, and memory are of great significance and importance in the development of good readers. Our work with remedial readers leads us to the observation that more disabled readers are deficient in auditory perception than in visual perception. In our classrooms, we do more remedial work with the development of listening habits, auditory awareness and discrimination, and sound-symbol relationships than we do with visual discrimination, visual temporal sequence, and spatial orientation. We feel that although much of the literature is on visual perception and its relationship to reading, auditory perception must not be overlooked or underestimated as a major tool or skill in learning to read.

Table 3–1 illustrates normal language and motor development in children. The age levels can be used as guide-lines in assessing the development of children if some leeway is given to provide for a normal range of distribution of abilities.

VISUAL PERCEPTION. The infant begins to make visual differentiations in the first few days of life. In a very gross manner, the neonate can begin to separate figure from ground, especially with moving objects. Soon the baby learns to focus on an object for some period of time. Perceptual form is visualized in a primitive fashion at first, but with experience the child begins to differentiate and begins to detect details. Frostig (1964) states that a child emphasizes the development of visual perception between the ages of 3½ and 7½ years. We concur with this idea. This is the time when the child not only improves his visual-motor coordination but also begins to develop a dexterity which involves a more sensitive degree of visual interpretation. The child begins to control the crayon or the pencil and seeks to make it do what the mind wants it to do. In the cognitive realm, the child learns concepts such as *more* or *less, many* or *few, longer* or *shorter,* and the child must depend upon his visual input—as well as his understanding of the terms—to give the appropriate answer. Even "Point to the doggie in the picture," or "What is that?" requires the child to use visual understanding. Eventually the child will learn the visual skills of figure and ground, form and configuration, visual memory and recall, spatial and temporal relations, and perceptual constancy.

We believe that the development of visual perception serves several purposes. First, it aids in visual-motor coordination which eventually will be used in writing. Second, visual discrimination will be needed to differentiate like and unlike and to identify symbols in their

TABLE 3–1. Pattern of normal language development in expressive speech and comprehension of speech.*

AGE	EXPRESSION	COMPREHENSION
1 to 2 years	Uses 1 to 3 words at 12 months, 10 to 15 at 15 months, 15 to 20 at 18 months, about 100 to 200 by 2 years. Knows names of most objects he uses. Names few people, uses verbs but not correctly with subjects. Jargon and echolalia. Names 1 to 3 pictures.	Begins to relate symbol and object meaning. Adjusts to comments. Inhibits on command. Responds correctly to "give me that," "sit down," "stand up," with gestures. Puts watch to ear on command. Understands simple questions. Recognizes 120 to 275 words.
2 to 3 years	Vocabulary increases to 300 to 500 words. Says "where kitty," "ball all gone," "want cookie," "go bye bye car." Jargon mostly gone, vocalizing increases. Has fluency trouble. Speech not adequate for communication needs.	Rapid increase in comprehension vocabulary to 400 at 2½ years, 800 at 3 years. Responds to commands using "on," "under," "up," "down," "over there," "bye," "run," "walk," "jump up," "throw," "run fast," "be quiet," and commands containing two related actions.
3 to 4 years	Uses 600 to 1,000 words; becomes conscious of speech. Uses 3 to 4 words per speech response. Personal pronouns, some adjectives, adverbs, and prepositions appear. Mostly simple sentences, but some complex. Speech more useful.	Understands up to 1,500 words by age 4 years. Recognizes plurals, sex difference, pronouns, adjectives. Comprehends complex and compound sentences. Answers simple questions.
4 to 5 years	Increase in vocabulary to 1,100 to 1,600 words. More 3- to 4-syllable words, more adjectives, adverbs, prepositions, and conjunctions. Articles appear. Uses 4-, 5-, and 6-word sentences; syntax quite good. Uses plurals. Fluency improves. Proper nouns decrease, pronouns increase.	Comprehends from 1,500 to 2,000 words. Carries out more complex commands, with 2 to 3 actions. Understands dependent clause, "if," "because," "when," "why."
5 to 6 years	Increase in vocabulary to 1,500 to 2,100 words. Complete 5- to 6-word sentences, compound, complex, with some dependent clauses. Syntax near normal. Quite fluent. More multisyllable words.	Understands vocabulary of 2,500 to 2,800 words. Responds correctly to more complicated sentences but is still confused at times by involved sentences.

* Modified from Miller, G. A.: *Language and communication.* New York: McGraw-Hill, 1951, pp. 140–57.

proper spatial and temporal relationships. Third, visual scrutiny, awareness, and differentiation of details in the environment will be needed for cognitive development which will in turn have an effect upon reading performance. Therefore, the development of visual readiness for reading should emphasize several elements, not just visual-motor coordination.

Cognitive Development According to Piaget

Piaget's most famous work is his theory of cognitive development. In his theory of development, Piaget has postulated a series of distinct phases and subphases of development which he calls stages (1952).

The sensorimotor phase, extending from birth to about 2 years, is the first period of Piaget's developmental continuum. During this phase, the child depends mostly on sensori- and body-motor experience. In addition, he depends on his body for self-expression and communication.

The first stage is the Use of Reflexes. This stage covers the infant's first month of life. During this stage, the child is only able to exercise reflexes which are present at birth. Spontaneous repetition by internal and external stimuli provides experience which establishes rhythm and a quality of regularity and also furnishes the first traces of sequential use and sense of order. At this age, the infant initiates general organizational patterns of behavior which are basic to his unfolding life.

The Primary Circular Reactions stage spans from approximately the second to the fourth month of the child's life and involves the coordination of reflexes and responses. Hand movements become coordinated with eye movements. He looks at what he hears and reaches for and sucks objects. Piaget considers this schema to be an established pattern of behavior which can be repeated and coordinated with other behavioral events. He learns to incorporate new results of his behavior as part of his continuing behavior.

The Secondary Circular Reaction stage is present from about the fourth to the ninth month. The major aim of the infant's behavior is retention rather than repetition. Reflexive behavior is slowly being replaced by voluntary movements and he begins to anticipate responses that have produced interesting results.

The Coordination of Secondary Schemata and Its Application to New Situations stage shows the child beginning to differentiate means from ends, using established responses to attain goals. It covers the ages of 9 months to approximately 1 year. At this age, if a desirable toy is hidden, the child will actively search for it and will remove obstacles to get to it. This stage is marked by an increased experimentation and greater mobility which the infant uses to explore his environment beyond what he has previously known. When he becomes aware of the continued existence of an object, he is able to reason that, if it is beyond his immediate perception, it has been removed. He is now able to use trial-and-error experimentation to search for the missing object.

The Tertiary Circular Reactions stage, spanning the period of 12 to 18 months, is characterized by active experimentation, exploration, variation, and modification of behavior. It is common for the child to show much curiosity. He has developed an awareness of relationships between objects and this development forms the early traces of memory and retention. Discovery of objects as objects introduces awareness of their spatial relationships. The child recognizes that there are existing causes which are completely independent of his own activity. Play, which involves primarily the repetition of learned behavior as a self-satisfying occupation, becomes an increasingly important function of the individual.

The sixth stage is the Invention of New Means Through Mental Combinations. The infant now tends to act in set ways until his behavior patterns have become solidified. During this stage, which spans from eighteen to about twenty-four months, there is an emergence of the child's capacity to respond to, or think about, objects and events that are not immediately observable. The infant invents new means of accomplishing goals through "mental combinations" or imagination and ideas. Once he discovers that objects can endure in the passage of time, it is possible for newly-acquired mental images of objects to be retained beyond immediate sensory experience with them. He is able to see and remember as much of an object at any given time as he can understand at that time. Finally, some degree of problem solving, remembering, planning, imagining, and pretending are all possible. Sensorimotor patterns are slowly being replaced by semi-mental functionings, but he still depends on a sensorimotor approach.

PHASE II: PRECONCEPTUAL PHASE (AGES 2–4 YEARS)

This phase extends from about 2 years until about 4 years and marks emergence of real symbolic activity. The child investigates his environment and all the possibilities of his activity within it.

Because the child has a limited view of things, he believes that everyone thinks as he does and understands him; therefore, he does not have to work to convey his thoughts and feelings. He acquires more facility in language. This language serves as a vehicle of development as the child repeats words and connects them with visible objects or perceived actions.

He begins to engage in symbolic play such as pretending his tricycle is a racing car. This play occupies most of his waking time and becomes his primary tool for adaptation, as the child quickly turns his experiences of the world into play. Play has all the elements of reality for him, but appears to be sheer fantasy to the uninitiated bystander. Imitation of others and symbolic imitation are mostly spontaneous.

Thought and reason in the 2 year old are entirely egocentric, with a predominance of self-reference. He places his experiences in verbal proximity with the use of words. If one event follows another, they must have a causal relationship, or so it seems to the child. He begins to think in terms of relationships and establishes his own view of cause and effect. He judges events by their outward appearance, regardless of their objective logic. He tends to experience either the qualitative or the quantitative aspects, but not both at once with any connection between them.

During this phase, the child tends to identify with those individuals who satisfy his immediate needs and interests and chooses them as his models. He has a sense of awe and respect for the superior powers of parents, guardians, and other adults. He has expanded his original focus or interest from only his own body to his immediate environment. He takes orders literally as if the words were objects or actions and often finds himself quite confused as a result. For example, when told to "be good," he may end up in a dilemma since he does not know what to do in the absence of a demand for a specific behavior.

PHASE III: THE PHASE OF INTUITIVE THOUGHT (AGES 4–7 YEARS)

This developmental phase covers the years of 4 to 7 and marks a widening of the child's social interest in the world about him. He conceptualizes more and elaborates on these concepts. In addition, he constructs more complex thoughts and images. His organization of his expanding knowledge helps him gain the capacity to generalize his mental experience.

Egocentricity is reduced because of repeated contact with others. Social participation is increased, and he begins to use words in his thought. At first, his thinking and reasoning are still acted out. He now uses speech to express his thinking, but this thinking is still largely egocentric and he can think only of one idea at a time. His knowledge is specific, but he applies it universally. He can think only in terms of ongoing events.

The child will increasingly use appropriate language without fully understanding its meaning. In addition, he may know how to count even though he has no concept of numbers. He keeps his previous notion that his thoughts and body are one. In his basic pattern of relating all things, he now reflects an objective point of view. Increased accommodation allows added attention to events beyond him, and he begins to observe objects according to multiple properties of color, form, and utility.

Play reflects much of the evolutionary intellectual development in these years. Play becomes noticeably social, but underlying thinking processes are still egocentric. Genuine make-believe play appears and indicates that the child can now think in terms of others.

PHASE IV: THE PHASE OF CONCRETE OPERATIONS (AGES 7–11 OR 12 YEARS)

During this phase, which extends from approximately 7 to 11 years of age, the child begins to relate different aspects of situations and figures out an idea of conservation. Before, when two identical balls of clay were rolled into different shapes, the child would state that there were different amounts of clay in these balls. Now, however, he realizes that the amount of clay remains the same regardless of the shape it retains.

He has developed a concept of reversibility in which steps can be retraced and actions can be cancelled. He can restore things back to the original. He can explore several possible solutions to a problem without necessarily adopting any particular one, since he can always return to his original outlook.

The child uses logic and reasoning in an elementary way, but applies them only in the manipulation of concrete objects, not to verbal propositions. He can put dolls in order by height, but has trouble with the verbal problem, "Who is taller?" He can count, classify, and put into series events and objects. With his new level of thought, operational thought, he can relate and order an experience to an organized whole.

In his development of language, he adopts meanings for words without fully being aware of all they convey. Contacts with his physical environment become more meaningful because of his increased accommodation and more accurate perception. Objects become known for their internal parts and tend to be defined according to their use.

Cognitive thought tends to internalize all sense of morality, and he becomes interested in rules which will regulate activities with other children. Children examine rules for all their details and are concerned with equality in punishment so that they know exactly what punishment to expect. A sense of equality appears.

PHASE V: THE PHASE OF FORMAL OPERATIONS (AGES 11 OR 12–16 YEARS)

The period of formal operations extends from the age of about 11 to 16. The individual can now think scientifically and can imagine what might be possible. In addition he can speculate, this speculation being governed by logical rules. He is able to consider a hypothesis which may or may not be true and consider what would follow if it were true. He can follow the form of an argument while disregarding its concrete content.

He acquires the capacity to think and reason beyond his own realistic world and beliefs. He enters into a world of ideas. Cognition begins to rely upon pure symbolism rather than pure reality. He begins to understand questions dealing with proportions. A concept of relativity emerges. By the age of 16, he can use logical operations and formal logic in an adult manner in solving problems.

He has acquired new values which will eventually come into balance near the end of adolescence. Egocentricity has been dissolved, and a sense of equality supersedes submission to adult authority. According to Piaget, the child has reached the critical stage in intellectual development.

IMPLICATIONS FOR REMEDIAL READING. The first implication of the theory of cognitive development is that the first six years of the child's life are crucial in the development of a neural pattern for learning which can be used in the learning-reading process, with the first years being as significant as the latter. Further, several types of sensori-cerebral functions are being developed, all of which are necessary for the learning-reading process. A third implication is that both cerebral development and environmental stimulation are important, and each plays a significant part in preparing the child to read. Fourth, insufficient or inefficient development in any one of the developmental areas, either due to sensori-neurological or to environmental factors, will result in a deficiency in learning ability. Lastly, reading disability is a deficiency of a particular functional ability, and the disturbance may be due to a variety of etiologies which may be sensori-neurological, environmental, or psychogenic in origin. To consider reading disability as if it were merely a functional disturbance with varying degrees of severity and to apply remedial techniques simply on the basis of severity and lack of skills without first determining the cause of the deficiency is to ignore the learning and reading process with its implications of perceptual handicaps, cerebral dysfunctions, emotional disruptions, environmental limitations, and the necessity of using remedial techniques in keeping with the specific learning needs of the child. The reading specialist or psychologist who ignores neurological, environmental, and psychological factors while being concerned only with educational factors is ignoring modern concepts.

The Perceptual-Conceptual Process

Reading is more than a recognition, retention, and recall skill; it involves perceptual and conceptual processes. As such, reading is fundamentally a complex cerebral procedure. The learner must make a variety of cerebral responses to a reading situation. He does this by organizing sensory complexes (perceptual processes) into stable, meaningful, recognized patterns of perceptions (conceptual processes). In order for the reading teacher to understand how the learning of reading takes place, what might interfere with that learning and what to do about it, she must know something about how the central nervous system organizes its forces for the purpose of learning.

Perceptual Field, Life Space, and Perception

One's perceptual field consists of all those aspects of the external environment, such as sights, sounds, words, and events, to which the individual makes a discriminating response at any given time. How much one "sees," what he "sees," and how he "sees" it constitute the perceptual field. It is composed of what the individual perceives, not necessarily of what is actually there. The teacher may think that the child can "see" that a word is made up of letters, a sentence is made of words, and a paragraph consists of sentences, but this is an assumption on her part. If a child does not have auditory awareness, he will not be conscious of major, let alone subtle, differences in sounds. We may assume that anyone can "see" that the letters *d*, *b*, *q* are different, but a child with limited visual awareness in his perceptual field may say the letters are all alike because they are all made up of a ball, *o*, and a stick, *l*.

One's "lifespace" is composed of all the objects, experiences, factors, and forces which influence the development of the child. Life space provides the opportunities and possibilities which influence what one can learn and what attitudes he will adopt. Thus, life space determines what he has to work with and will set the boundaries of understanding and interpretation which one has to his perceptual field. In order to be able to communicate with a child or to be able to understand what abilities a child has to bring to a reading situation, the teacher must know the nature and boundaries of the child's perceptual field. The teacher must converse with the child on the child's perceptual level if that child is to gain any understanding. Of course, part of the job of the teacher is to expand the child's perceptual and conceptual horizons by extending and making more meaningful the life space. Thus, the child is enabled to gain more insights. The stifling effect of limited environments such as ghettos, backwoods areas, and culturally different homes is that the stimulating effects of the life space of the child are so limited or so contrary to what is needed for adequate development of the perceptual and conceptual processes that the child's perceptual field of understanding becomes extremely limited.

Perception is the awareness, or the process of becoming aware, of external or internal objects, symbols, events, or forces, by means of the sensory processes, under the influence of prior experiences (knowledge), orientation, expectation, or disposition (set). Perception is the means by which an individual makes contact with the environment and gives meaning to what he perceives. A child learns through perceptual experiences. He learns about symbols, objects, events that he encounters by using a combination of his senses and his brain. When he goes to school, he will hopefully possess a certain level of readiness (his perceptual field) made up of visual and auditory perceptual abilities which will enable him to learn to read, write, spell, speak, and do arithmetic or anything else that involves the recognition, retention, and recall of visual or aural symbols. The perceptual process is the total process of having awareness in differentiating a stimulus, giving meaning to that stimulus, and making an appropriate response to the stimulus. Involved in the process are (1) the sensory impression, (2) the cognitive background which a person has to deal with that sensory impression to give it meaning, and (3) a response pattern. The perceptual-conceptual process is the perceptual process with an added emphasis on concept forming, concept using, and cognition.

The Perceptual-Conceptual Process (Theories)

There are at least thirteen theories seeking to explain the perceptual-conceptual process. Most of these theories agree to five basic steps. These steps are included under three phases of the process: (1) sensory recognition, (2) cognitive processes, and (3) motor response. Figure 3–3 diagrams the elements of the perceptual-conceptual process.

STEP 1—*INPUT OR RECOGNITION.* Input is the process of becoming aware of a stimulus by the activation of nerve endings in those sense organs which are responding to the stimulus and triggering a nerve impulse if the threshold level is reached. The nerve impulse travels to the proper sensory projection areas of the brain where the effects of the impulse somehow radiate throughout the association areas of the cerebrum and to other pertinent neural areas. Compared to the operation of a mechanical computer, this is the phase in which the data or the questions are fed into the computer and a certain type of response is desired.

STEP 2—*DECODING OR INTEGRATION.* Decoding is the process by which the brain transforms the stimuli (signals) into meanings (messages). This step seeks to organize and to integrate all of the sensory inputs being received at that moment with the known and available data stored in the brain. The purpose is to come up with some kind of an "elaborated" meaning to attach to the stimuli. The mechanical computer, at this phase,

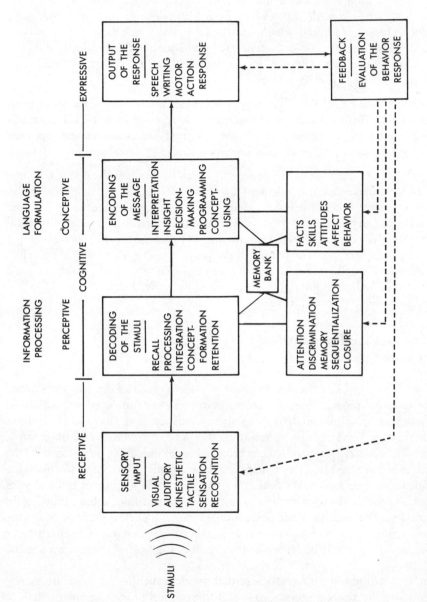

FIGURE 3-3. Reading and the perceptual-conceptual process.

scans its storage areas of information bits and programs for the purpose of collecting all of the facts or processes which are pertinent to the data just received in the input phase.

STEP 3—ENCODING OR FORMULATION. Encoding is the process whereby the "elaborated" message or meaning is translated into behavior which is deemed to be the appropriate response to the original stimuli. Interpretations and implications of the meaning are pursued and a decision is made as to what should be done next. Once the decision has been made, the appropriate neural response patterns are formulated and programmed for action. At this stage, a mechanical computer, having collected the necessary information or procedures, is preparing to divulge its answer.

STEP 4—OUTPUT OR RESPONSE. The response decided upon in the encoding stage is now put into effect. The brain has been programmed to respond internally or externally through the glands or muscles in the form of speech, writing, etc. A mechanical computer does likewise usually by typing its answers or sorting cards.

STEP 5—FEEDBACK. Feedback is the process by which the brain evaluates the outcome of the response and makes a value judgment about the adequacy of the behavior. It also makes a judgment as to where the error or fault in the perceptual process may be if the response was deemed not accurate or appropriate enough. That faulty part of the perceptual process is then reactivated to examine the performance at that stage with the hope of coming up with a better interpretation. The brain will not provide feedback unless the individual seeks to or can make use of this function. The mechanical computer, however, can only tell the operator that something is not right, but it cannot judge what went wrong unless it is programmed to evaluate its own procedures.

Reading and the Perceptual-Conceptual Process

The act of reading involves the development of skills in each of the five steps of the perceptual-conceptual process. Step 1 involves word recognition or word attack skills in terms of phonetic or structural analysis using visual, auditory, and, perhaps, tactile form discrimination. Step 2 reflects the background, the store of concepts and information related to the symbols that the individual can bring to bear in unlocking the meaning of the signals encountered in Step 1 in order to help provide comprehension. Step 3 interprets the comprehended meanings and makes decisions as to what to do with them or because of them. Step 4 puts the decision into action through speaking, writing, acting, thinking, or other appropriate action such as storage (retention). Finally, Step 5, if used, evaluates the adequacy and appropriateness of the response and makes suggestions as to what needs to be reconsidered in order to come up with a better response. Figure 3–4 relates learning and reading factors.

It is important for the teacher to recognize that the steps mentioned above are merely basic categories in the reading process, and that they do not provide enough details to explain or suggest what needs to be done to help a child. Basically, a teacher must know the details pertaining to "how" a child differentiates symbols by the visual, auditory, or tactile processes; "how" a child recognizes or is able to recall graphemes (printed symbols) and phonemes (units of sounds); "how" a child goes about applying meaning to what he perceives; "how" he decides what to do or say about the symbols; and "how" he programs or formulates neural patterns, if such are involved, to respond orally or otherwise.

PUPILS HAVE VARYING LEVELS OF READINESS IN:	EFFECTIVE READING REQUIRES EFFICIENT USE OF:
—MENTAL MATURITY	—WORD RECOGNITION
—PERCEPTUAL SKILLS	—COMPREHENSION ABILITY
—LANGUAGE ABILITY	—RETENTION & RECALL
—CONCEPT FORMATIONS	—WORD ATTACK SKILLS
—ATTENTION FACTORS	—LEFT-RIGHT ORIENTATION
—MEMORY FACTORS	—SEQUENTIAL ABILITY
—MOTIVATION & INTEREST	—VOCABULARY
—SOCIAL & EMOTIONAL ADJUSTMENT	—LISTENING AWARENESS
	—STRUCTURAL AWARENESS

THE TEACHER USES THE METHODS, MATERIALS, AND TECHNIQUES MOST APPROPRIATE FOR EACH CHILD IN TERMS OF WHAT LEARNING ABILITIES HE DOES HAVE IN ORDER TO DEVELOP THE READING SKILLS HE NEEDS TO BECOME A MORE EFFICIENT AND EFFECTIVE READER

THE IMPROVEMENT OF READING ABILITY

FIGURE 3–4. The use of learning abilities and reading skills to improve reading. Individual differences demand individual attention.

It is essential that the reading teacher or psychologist recognize that there are certain basic elements of the learning-reading process which must be considered when teaching a child to read. First, the child brings to the reading situation a certain perceptual capability made up of (1) sensory and neural structures, (2) conceptual background, and (3) affective (psychological) characteristics. Second, the reading process consists of certain skills and content which are independent of the child. Third, it is possible to teach the reading skills and content to the child only to the degree that the child's perceptual capability can receive, absorb, and interpret the material being taught. Table 3–2 illustrates how the perceptual-conceptual process is related to reading.

If a child has a perceptual handicap, such as poor auditory discrimination, he may make some initial gains in learning to read by the sight or whole word method, but he will have increasing difficulty learning to read because he will have trouble learning phonics and how to do phonetic analysis. He will not be able to use this tool effectively in unlocking new words. The teacher will need to take a different approach in teaching this child to read than she would with a child merely lacking in content skills. She may need to stimulate or develop the perceptual learning deficit, or she may seek to teach new words by emphasizing the use of a sensory-perceptual area in which the child is stronger. The task of working with the perceptually handicapped child is twofold: (1) recognizing and working with the perceptual problem and (2) teaching the reading skills in such a way that this particular child can best learn them. On the other hand, if a child's perceptual capabilities are intact and mature enough, more emphasis will be placed on teaching the reading skills per se. The

TABLE 3–2. The perceptual-conceptual process and reading.

Basic Elements of P-C Process	Observations in Classroom	Related to Reading
INPUT OF STIMULI Use of sensory modalities through which environmental stimuli enter the brain, namely, visual, auditory, kinesthetic, tactile (VAKT) (Receptive response)	Visual—Ability to see printed or written symbols adequately. Does the child squint; hold his book too close or too far; have red eyes; does he get headaches? Auditory—Ability to hear sounds, words or verbal commands adequately. Does he tilt his head to a side; cup his hand to his ear; not understand common words or directions? Kinesthetic and Tactile—Ability to identify objects through touch adequately. Does he have to look at an object while touching it in order to name it? Can he identify numbers, letters, or words written on the palm of his hand or on his back?	Visual acuity to be aware of details of letters. Auditory acuity to hear differences in spoken sounds and words. Tactile ability to identify shapes by touch and hand movement.
DECODE STIMULI Using perceptual skills to unscramble, reorganize, integrate and give meaning to incoming stimuli. (Perceptual response)	Ability to use discrimination, recall, sequentialization and other perceptual skills. How well can he do the following? (1) Copy from the board. (2) Repeat verbal and written directions. (3) Recall and recognize letters, numbers, words, facts, and events. (4) Discriminate between sounds, symbols, objects, or pictures. (5) Match words, symbols, or sounds. (6) Sequence details of stories, events, of pictures, letters, or numbers.	Discriminate between letters, words, or numbers. Remember sight words, prefixes, suffixes, phonics. Use word-attack skills by use of different sensory modalities. Sequencing letters and words in a left-to-right orientation.

ENCODE STIMULI

Gaining meaningful interpretation of stimuli so that concepts, skills, or affective responses are generated and used to program a response. (Conceptual response)

Can the child:

(1) Use the new information or skills in appropriate ways?

(2) Make inferences from the new learning?

(3) Make good judgments, good decisions, and solve problems related to the new material?

(4) Compare and contrast new information with old information?

(5) Classify and categorize new learning?

(6) Understand what has been read or said?

(7) Identify similarities and differences?

Grasp main idea of sentence, paragraph or story.

Group letters into words, words into phrases, and phrases into sentences.

Remember specific details to answer questions.

Gain meaning from reading.

Utilize cues to make inferences.

Use context cues for meaning.

Show comprehension of what was read.

OUTPUT OF STIMULI

Use of motor, verbal, or cognitive means by which appropriate oral, written, or cognitive responses are expressed. (Expressive response)

Can the child:

(1) Make an appropriate cognitive or intelligent response to the stimuli?

(2) Formulate appropriate language responses?

(3) Formulate appropriate written responses?

(4) Hold a pencil correctly to form letters and numbers?

(5) Form speech sounds correctly?

(6) Move in a left-to-right direction in reading and writing?

Do efficient oral reading with comprehension.

Do silent reading with comprehension.

Make appropriate responses to written material.

Point to the correct word, repeat the word, and copy the word.

Use appropriate speech socially and in academic situations.

Free from emotional involvement with reading.

FEEDBACK

Cognitive means by which the child evaluates his own performance and makes a value judgment of the adequacy of his response.

Does he catch his own errors?

Does he correct himself?

Does he realize whether his response was right, wrong, or incomplete?

Does he know how and where to look for his error to make a correction?

Will go back and re-read a word or part that did not sound right.

Can get more information from the part read after a second reading.

Will recognize discrepancy in sequencing.

Will correct error to fit contextual cues.

techniques used in teaching a nonperceptually handicapped child generally are not effective or efficient in working with a perceptually handicapped child. Experiences in clinics and classrooms with which we are familiar seem to bear out this observation although many reading specialists are not convinced of the validity of this statement. A moderate view concerning the need for special techniques for perceptually handicapped children is deemed by the authors to be the best approach for remediation. We believe that some but not all remedial readers will need special remedial techniques to overcome specific learning deficits. Although special techniques are needed for teaching certain remedial children, there is no reason to expect that all children—especially developmental readers—would benefit from the use of the same techniques.

Learning Deficits

The learning process in reading involves (a) recognition, (b) language significance, and (c) responses. The child must develop the mechanism by which all of this can be done. The developmental tasks related to learning to read are (1) motor development, (2) tactile development, (3) auditory discrimination, (4) language development, (5) visual discrimination, (6) various types of memory development, and (7) concept and cognitive development. Deficiencies in any of these areas may be due to either primary (organic) or secondary (functional) causes. The implication is that some perceptual handicaps can be due to nonorganic factors, such as emotional stress.

Primary Learning Deficits

Primary learning deficits include deficits in any of the following areas:

1. Auditory skills
   a. auditory comprehension or understanding, extracting meaning from sound patterns.
   b. auditory discrimination to differentiate and compare sounds.
   c. auditory memory to recall sounds.
   d. auditory temporal discrimination to hear sounds in their proper time sequence.
   e. auditory lateralization and localization to be able to tell direction and position from which sounds come.
   f. auditory awareness to be conscious of listening for sounds.
   g. sound-symbol relationships to know and understand that a particular sound goes with a particular letter or word and to be able to apply the sound to those letters.
   h. adequate auditory acuity to hear the difference between consonant sounds and to distinguish and be aware of high frequency sounds.
2. Visual Skills
   a. visual perception of spatial and temporal relations to view the letters in their proper shape and proper sequence within the word.
   b. visual perceptual form and configuration to be able to discriminate, recognize, and identify the letters or words.
   c. visual perceptual constancy to be able to recognize the letter in its various forms, such as capitals and small letters.

    d. visual memory and recall to be able to remember the letter form and to be able to revisualize or recall it without help.

    e. visual figure-ground perception so that the reader can concentrate on the letters or words without his attention shifting from one word to another or can shift attention from one stimulus (word) and not concentrate on it too long.

    f. visual acuity so the shapes of the letters and words stand out clearly.

    g. perception of the position of self in space as related to objects or symbols so that the proper position of the stimuli can be compared to the left and right of the body and thereby know that a letter goes in one direction, *d,* or the other, *b.*

3. Motor Skills

    a. perceptual motor coordination so that the child can move whatever muscles are involved, whether writing or speaking, in coordination with how he sees or hears.

    b. motor speech patterns properly developed so words are enunciated as they should be.

    c. motor writing patterns developed so he can write while reading, if necessary, and at other times.

4. Language Skills

    a. language awareness.

    b. language significance to give meaning.

    c. concept formation to gain knowledge.

    d. language formulation to be able to respond verbally.

5. Cognitive Skills

    a. to be able to associate.

    b. to be able to reason and do problem solving.

    c. to be able to imagine.

    d. to be able to think verbally.

Secondary Factors Affecting Learning

1. Educational retardation due to poor attendance, poor teaching, poor curriculum, poor materials, poor attitudes.

2. Emotional blocks due to a poor self-concept, lack of confidence, interest in social or affiliation needs rather than achievement needs, low level of aspiration, family disorganization, social-economic class factors, poor emotional adjustment.

3. Underachievement due to cultural deprivation, lack of perceptual skills, physical conditions.

4. Lack of study skills and not knowing how to learn.

5. A basic deficiency in reading skills or other fundamental educational skills.

6. Lack of background and knowledge in a content field.

chapter 4

The Learning Disabled Child

The child or adult who has a learning disability, implying that the ability to learn is made less effective because of a central nervous system involvement, is a unique individual when it comes to identifiable characteristics. There are two reasons for this. In the first place, specific characteristics differ from child to child so much that it is difficult to pinpoint the traits or behaviors that are typical of a group of learning disabled children. If that is true, what are the criteria that do classify children into the category *learning disabled*, or children with specific learning disabilities? There are three identifying characteristics that these children have in common: (a) All learning disabled children (and adults) have average or above average intelligence; (b) All learning disabled children will be substantially below their mental age or grade level in achievement in one or more of the basic academic skills, primarily reading or arithmetic; and (c) The cause of their lack of achievement will be due to central nervous system dysfunctions, primarily organic or biochemical in nature, and not to environmental or psychological factors.

In the second place, learning disabled children and adults are unique because their academic deficiency may exist only in one field such as reading; they may be performing on mental age or grade level in the other fields. Along with an academic inability, children within the LD group will vary as to (a) the severity of their deficiency, being mild, moderate, or severe to profound in nature, (b) their preference of learning styles and/or sensory modalities that they tend to use in learning, (c) the specific part of the learning process in which they have a weakness or deficit, such as the receptive, perceptual, associative, conceptual, or expressive areas, (d) the teaching approach and media that will work best with each child and will differ from individual to individual, and (e) the etiology or cause of their problem. Learning disabled children as a group are unique because, even though they are categorized under one umbrella, they differ tremendously from one another.

Causes of Learning Disabilities

Fifty years of research covering reading and the remedial reader have produced a number of studies of why children who are seemingly internally or externally unimpaired fail to learn to read. One cannot read the reviews of this research in *The Encyclopedia of Educational Research* without being struck by the recurrence of the word *inconclusive*. Do visual anomalies cause reading disability? The results are inconclusive. Do emotional problems cause reading disability? The results are inconclusive. Yet, the urgency of the problem continues to produce research designed to broaden the understanding of the problem. Seldom does a decade go by without a number of new theories being proposed on the basis of the latest research and the newest insights.

Each of the theories offers a limited explanation of the problem. In most cases, however, they raise more questions than are answered. Nevertheless, the theories make a definite contribution to the ultimate solution of the problem by serving as guideposts to subsequent research which, in turn, lead to the refinement of these and other theories. Some theories refer specifically to primary learning disabilities; other theories are related to the problem of reading deficiencies among children of normal intelligence. Bateman (1964) presents an excellent bibliography of theories pertaining to learning disabilities.

Familial Incidence

Herman (1959) had much to say about the importance of considering the hereditary factor as a cause of inhibited development of normal skills in working with printed and written symbols. He noted that Thomas (1905) and Hinshelwood (1917) both made the suggestion that congenital word blindness was a familial incidence, i.e., related or due to heredity. Skydsgaards (1944) wrote a dissertation containing a series of genealogical tables which illustrated the importance of heredity in this matter. Hallgren (1950) rather firmly established a hereditary transmission. However, Park (1952) raised some questions concerning the familial incidence in cases of word blindness. His studies seemed to indicate that not all primary disability readers were such because of heredity.

There may be predisposing conditions permitting primary reading disability to occur. One notion states that a certain pelvic formation is hereditary in the women of certain families. This pelvic condition makes the process of birth more difficult. Since boy babies generally have larger heads at birth than do female neonates, it can be expected that in the families with this particular pelvic formation, more boys would end up as primary reading disability readers than would girls. Statistics support the belief that more boys than girls are primary disability readers. Fuller (1964) states that the sex ratio has been reported from about four boys to one girl to as high as 20 to 1. In the Language Clinic at Hawthorne Center directed by Rabinovitch, girls with primary reading disability are extremely rare.

An analysis of close to 500 developmental history forms in our personal clinical records suggests that about 20% of our LD cases have a parent, uncle, or grandparent who had difficulty learning to read. Usually it was the father who exhibited the problem; only occasionally was it the mother. The specific problem that we identify in familial incidence is one of a maturational lag in development of the neurological organisms involved in the reading and language processes.

Neurological Anomaly

The larger size of the boys' heads increases the possibility of a more difficult birth for them. The more difficult births present more opportunity for anoxia to occur. An extreme case of anoxia is very evident in the form of cerebral palsy or some other neurological disorder. But could a lesser amount of anoxia cause some minimal damage? Rabinovitch (1959) feels it could. According to the proponents, this minimal amount of damage occurs in the association centers in the parietal lobes of the brain. The implication is that, although a primary disability reader may have symbol recognition and perceptual stability, he may not be able to associate the symbols with meaningful entities.

The minimal brain damage concept can be extended to include not only brain damage occurring at birth but also possibly during either the fetal period or the postnatal period as well. The brain damage may be nothing more than a lesion or scar tissue. It is possible for the defect to show some other type of neurological dysfunction such as the endocrine imbalance. There is also some consideration being given to the improper development of the neurological structure system itself.

Some researchers estimate that approximately 50% of the children with learning disabilities have some form of physical handicap, including such things as a lack of proper neurological development, glandular dysfunction, imbalance of chemical distribution, or brain damage.

Neural Transmission

The neural transmission theorists believe reading and learning disability to be caused by a defect in the transmission of neural impulses. The best known of these theories is the theory promulgated by Smith and Carrigan (1960) which attempts to explain the "why" of reading disability through improper synaptic transmission timing. Smith and Carrigan theorized that each person has a different synaptic transmission time due to the fact that each person has a different amount of the chemicals acetylcholine and cholinesterase found at the synapse.

An oversimplification of the theory states that acetylcholine is the agent which helps with the transmission or the crossing of a neural impulse over the synapse from one neuron to another. Cholinesterase is the agent which helps the neuron regain its electro-chemical balance so that it can be ready for the next firing of a neural impulse. If an improper ratio or balance exists between these two chemical substances, then the neural impulse is transmitted either too fast or too slow. Perceptual efficiency depends upon a proper neural transmission. If the impulse is transmitted too quickly, then the circuit is broken too quickly and there is not enough time to leave facilitation traces in the brain. In this case, no sooner does the person notice the stimuli than his attention shifts. This reader will be a rapid but inaccurate reader. If the transmission rate is too slow, a repetitive firing occurs and the reader cannot change his fixation. He sees the same thing over and over. He will be a slow methodical reader and will have little comprehension because of the slowness of reading. Smith and Carrigan estimate that about 30% of the children they tested had transmission difficulties.

At first glance, this theory seems to offer comprehensive answers; however, closer scrutiny finds that it too falls short of doing the complete job. For one thing, it does nothing to explain why so many disabled readers are tremendous auditory learners. The synapses between neurons are just as important in auditory transmission as in visual transmission.

Maturational or Developmental Lag

In the early sixties, the senior author made a presentation to a medical society consisting of pediatric neurologists and other medical professionals interested in the then emerging field of "learning disabilities." The discussion related to the conceptual processes, perceptual handicaps, and how the brain is involved and affected in the quality and ability of learning. The audience was receptive and all went well, as the ensuing years were to prove, but one question was asked that made me seriously search for an answer. The question was a simple one: "What percentage of your LD or perceptually handicapped cases are due to a maturational lag?" My initial, inner reaction was to infer that the question was seeking to be supportive of the answer frequently given by pediatricians to anxious mothers who wonder if their child is developing normally—that "he will grow out of it." I reflected on the question and reasoned it out loud with the group, using my clinical knowledge of the LD children with whom I was working; I estimated that about 30% of our cases had a maturational lag in neurological areas related to the learning processes.

Subsequent studies that we did of LD children showed that, indeed, at least one-third of the children did have a maturational or developmental lag. Furthermore, the younger the group of children (kindergarten or first graders), the higher the percentage having delayed neurological development. Most of these children outgrew their problems by the age of 9; a few children had such immaturity of neural development that they did not overcome their problem until about the age of 14. Studies being conducted at the Kennedy Institute at Johns Hopkins University on the myelinization process—that is, the development of the myelin sheath that encases nerve fibers—confirm that there are children with a developmental lag in the maturation of the myelin sheath, making learning less effective and efficient.

The biggest problem confronted by the teacher is to know how to help the child control and structure his mental and cognitive processes so that he can control, retain, and learn. Since the brain waves are inconsistent in ability to function properly, there is great variability in learning quality from day to day or from occasion to occasion. Another problem that the child and the school face is how to keep the youngster from getting too far behind academically. Once the child reaches the developmental point where he is able to control and learn, the question becomes one of how to help the child get caught up on his learning.

Similar observations of a maturational lag have been reported by Bender (1968) and Slingerland (1971) who suggest that the apparent immaturity of some children with learning disabilities may be related to a lag in the maturation of central nervous system components. Bateman (1966) points out that the immaturity does not necessarily imply a structural defect or the loss of potential. Bryant (1972) suggests that complications during pregnancy, early trauma, infections, or poor nutrition may result in a maturational lag. He also observes that children with a maturational lag tend to overcome this difficulty as they grow older.

Neurological Organization

The neurological organization theorists believe that reading disability is caused by a lack of proper neuro-psychological organization and development. Two of the chief proponents of this view are Glenn Doman and Carl H. Delacato. Delacato (1963) claims that the central nervous system of man is somewhat different from that of other animals in that there is a horizontal development as well as a vertical development in the nervous system. The sequence of development of the central nervous system for all animals is: spinal cord, medulla, pons, cerebellum, then cerebrum—a vertical development. Delacato points out that man has evolved one step further, whereby one of the hemispheres gains a hemispheric dominance of the cerebral cortex, and that this development is a horizontal one. First, the right hemisphere develops; then the left hemisphere develops. Delacato believes that the remedial reader fails to make an adequate horizontal development and so ends with a neurologically disorganized body. This neurological disunity is due to the improper development of some step or level of the crawling or creeping sequence in the pattern of development. The task, therefore, is to go back to the improperly developed phase of the sequence and to re-educate or develop it by retraining. This training should follow the developmental process normally pursued by the sensorimotor sequential pattern at the level where the inadequate development occurred. The ultimate aims are to establish a dominant cerebral hemisphere and good laterality.

The biggest shortcoming of this theory seems to be its lack of explanation of why both good and poor readers display the mixed laterality symptoms. The Delacato system has much to do with mixed laterality, but it does not explain its presence in good readers. The remedial techniques advocated in keeping with this theory have received very poor results in research. The study of Robbins (1966) was especially negative in its findings. One observation made, however, was that Robbins used normal children, while Delacato probably worked with brain damaged children.

At a national conference of the Association of Children with Learning Disabilities in Atlantic City in 1972, Delacato was asked to indicate what percentage of his cases seemed to improve with his training procedures involving creeping and crawling and a number of other techniques alleged to improve cerebral dominance. Delacato, in candid honesty, replied that his staff sees improvement in about one-third of their cases. In another third, they see something happening but they are not sure what or why. In the final third of their group, they see nothing happening at all. Improvement in the one-third of his cases could be attributed to maturational development, say some developmental psychologists and a number of physical therapists working with cerebral palsy children. At least, the variable of the maturational process has not been accounted for or ruled out. Isolated cases appear to make spectacular gains, in terms of expectations at the beginning; these cases tend to give parents and others hope which may not be warranted. Yet, who knows for certain. Chapter 9 contains additional information.

Basic Symmetry and Balance

An interesting theory is being evolved by Carolyn L. Heil, a physical therapist, who is finding that patterns of symmetry and balance which are present in normal infants 3 to 9 months old are either distorted or missing in children of school age who are learning disability cases. She postulates that the child who does not develop the early basic patterns of symmetry and balance, for any variety of reasons, will lack the neurological basis for developing normal motor patterns or the perceptual-motor match suggested by Kephart which will be involved in various acts of learning. When symmetry and balance are distorted or disturbed in the very young infant, motor development will also be retarded, thus adversely affecting the child's perceptual development. Motor acts allow the child to investigate his environment through his sensory systems. These sensory inputs and contacts with the stimuli of the environment result in integrated neural patterns by which the child learns to give meaning to his outside world. Lacking symmetry and having distorted sensory inputs only leads to lack of learning or at least inadequate learning (Kaluger & Heil, 1970).

Heil is primarily concerned with the maturational sequence of bodily development in its earliest stage. She considers the first three months to be most crucial to the proper neurological and motor development of the infant, followed in importance by the next six months. She considers the cephalocaudal and proximodistal sequential patterns of growth to be meaningful in terms of describing what is truly fundamental in motor development. She is concerned with body righting reflexes, extension patterns of neck and upper trunk, and the positive supporting mechanisms of the arms and shoulders. The normal child of 6 months, she observes, is truly symmetrical. Neither hand nor weight bearing surface of the leg is dominant at this time. The child is able to balance with compensatory weight shifting postural patterns when reaching. It is at this time that he is learning spatial relationships and eye-hand coordination. With normal motor development he is also gaining normal perceptual development.

Many professionals concerned with motor development and balance suggest therapeutic techniques based on ontological developments which occur later in the sequence of a child's motor development. Heil believes that the visual, motor, space, and body image perceptual mechanisms will be deprived of the necessary correct type of stimulation if a child misses the steps of positive support of the arms and shoulders which are part of the early development of the first three months. These steps are essential to body symmetry and balance. This deprivation will affect future balance, weight-bearing, and eye-hand coordination even though the child appears to be walking in a normal pattern. This theory implies that some importance must be given to the positioning of the neonate and young infant for its early sensory experience, and a need to avoid a damping effect of the righting mechanisms of the neck and body righting reactions. It also implies that lack of symmetry in the newborn is a reason for cautious handling and observation by the parents and attending physician.

Although Heil is still in the process of developing her theory and gathering data, she has made some tentative observations concerning the motor patterns of a number of children with learning disabilities. She evaluates these children of preschool and school age with a test consisting of some items of basic motor patterns found in children 0 to 12 months as well as motor and perceptual items as found at older age levels. In a study of 50 children with known learning disabilities but without apparent physical involvement, she noted a number of distorted reactions. For example:

a. The body symmetry is often abnormal, with frequent lateral flexion of the trunk and head.
b. The child is unable to turn over in a smooth coordinated manner; frequently the child can turn to one side only.
c. The child is asymmetrical when bearing weight on his elbows when lying prone or he has difficulty maintaining the pattern.
d. He has difficulty in raising the head and shoulders high enough from a prone position to be able to bring both arms through.
e. The child has difficulty in listening to the request to perform a certain motor act and then following through in doing the pattern.
f. He has difficulty raising head and shoulders with his elbows extended and weight on his hands; one arm is frequently unable to bear the shift of weight when reaching with the opposite hand; the eyes do not follow the hand and the head frequently drops and turns away from the hand.
g. He frequently sits with legs flexed and feet behind the buttocks (kneeling on the chair of his desk).

h. The child appears to listen and/or understand better when he is standing rather than sitting or lying.

The therapeutic tools Heil suggests seek to follow a more inclusive and fundamental program than is usually presented by others. She wonders if associative learning can take place when certain motor skills are drilled in an isolated context. She questions the helpfulness of learning to walk a balance beam until the feat is perfected or if any functional skill is enhanced from creeping or crawling around on the floor many times a day. Her approach is to inhibit the abnormal responses and to facilitate the normal ones by a variety of classroom and playground activities. She makes liberal use of ideas derived from her studies of Proprioceptive Neuromuscular Facilitation, The Bobath Method, and the sensory and motor stimulation techniques of Margaret Rood.

Perceptual-Motor Match

Kephart (1971) maintains children must become familiar with the basic realities of the universe which surrounds them. Essentially these realities are time and space. The child must first learn to make precise observations about the various dimensions of space and time and then combine these observations into a system or structure within which he can organize and integrate objects and events. It is through such a comprehensive and organized structure that events in the environment become comprehensible to the child and eventually he can begin to see the relationship between these events.

In order for a child to do this, he must have training in the sensorimotor functions necessary for development and learning which is essential to any educational program. By using Kephart's Survey Scale, the child's motor activities can be observed and evaluated. The child's strength, flexibility, balance, speed and agility, laterality, directionality, and fine and gross motor coordination are appraised, and the rhythm of his movements is observed.

For example, directionality, according to Kephart, begins within the body and is developed or projected outward into objective space. Therefore, we should begin this with activities involving the child's own body.

The directional sense is often associated with visual kinesthetic impressions, with audition playing a valuable role in certain aspects of training, especially since many children with this disturbance have more auditory than visual competence. The child may be asked to close his eyes, listen to the sound of a bell, and then turn his head toward the source of the sound. Then he opens his eyes to determine if his observation is correct.

The child can learn to coordinate visual and kinesthetic impressions by observing himself in a mirror, noting the position of the hand that is up, down, or over his head. Through verbal discussion and by watching himself in the mirror, he can learn to perceive right and left in others. Verbalizing directions also stabilizes the child's perceptions.

Kephart speaks here of matching perceptual information to earlier motor information which he calls the perceptual-motor match. If the match is not made, the child comes to live in two worlds: one a motor world in which he moves and responds, and the other a perceptual world in which he sees, hears, smells, and so on. Since the two worlds are not matched, they give information which cannot be collated. The resulting behavior is bizarre because his responses are based upon a different body of information than was the stimulation.

Developmental Central Nervous System Deficits

A review of Developmental History Forms filled out by parents when they bring their children in for a clinical evaluation reveals a wide variety of possible causes of central nervous system deficits that may affect the child's effective use of his learning potential. The learning disabilities of most children are related to prenatal, perinatal, and postnatal problems. A number of these children were born to mothers who had some type of illness or distress that may have upset the biochemical balance of her blood and indirectly affected the developing fetus during the first 8 to 10 weeks of pregnancy. We have a number of cases of mothers who had the flu or a virus in the first trimester; others were on certain kinds of medication or drugs. One mother reported taking diet pills so she wouldn't get fat. Prenatal conditions usually involved labor and delivery abnormalities. In postnatal development, a common condition was to learn that the child had a high fever brought on by a childhood disease, generally chickenpox or a severe case of the measles, sometime during the first 18 months after birth. A number of LD children were dehydrated during the first year of life and required hospital care. There were many other factors that showed up on the developmental history forms. We must stress, however, that we have not proven that these factors "caused" the child to develop a learning problem. We can only say these conditions existed in many of our cases.

Pasemanick and Knoblock (1973) did do a scientific study of factors associated with prenatal neurological damage and later learning problems. Among these factors were:

1. Maternal endocrine disorders
2. Maternal-fetal blood type incompatabilities (RH factor)
3. Maternal age, reproductive readiness and efficiency
4. Radiation
5. Drugs
6. Rubella (3 day measles)
7. Anoxia
8. Maternal cigarette smoking
9. Prematurity of fetal birth or low birth weight
10. Accidents

The "continuum of reproductive causality" theory of Kawi and Pasamanick (1958) contends that traumatic experiences occurring prenatally and at birth can give rise to a variety of physical, neuro-psychiatric and behavioral sequelae. The anomalies of cognition functioning, both minimal and severe, are considered to be a result of cerebral damage. Paul (1969) studied the relationships between relatively minor prenatal and perinatal stress and the degree to which certain cognitive processes were impaired. He found that children with two or more of the following variables in their developmental history manifested deficits of several aspects of cognitive functioning due to mild insult to the central nervous system: previous pregnancy by mother resulting in stillbirth or in miscarriage, mother aged below 15 years, no prenatal care of mother, preeclampsia, abnormal EEG obtained from mother, Rh negative factor in mother, prematurity, postmaturity, prolonged labor, precipitous labor, caesarean section, breech presentation, delayed respiration of one minute or more in neonate, umbilical cord looped around neck, birth weight less than 5 pounds, birth weight over 10 pounds, and apgar rating of 5 or lower.

Nutritional deficits are also a possible cause of learning disabilities. Cravioto (1973) believes that malnutrition may directly affect the development of the central nervous system and may modify the growth and biochemical maturation of the brain. Hallahan and Cruickshank (1973) hypothesize a relationship between malnutrition, particularly protein-calorie malnutrition, and learning disabilities. Reports have been made concerning developmental delays in intersensory integration with protein-calorie malnutrition. Cott (1972) and Wunderlich (1973) work on the premise that protein, vitamin, and mineral deficiencies may be major causes of learning and behavior problems. They claim that the use of megavitamin therapy (massive doses of certain vitamins) in their medical practices have been highly successful. The wide range of uniqueness in LD children just might make such therapy helpful to some of them.

Mention should be made of "left brain-right brain" functions and how hemispheric dysfunctions may be responsible for learning disabilities in some children. In normal development, the left hemisphere is predominantly involved in analytic, logical thinking, especially in language, verbal, and mathematical functions. This hemisphere appears to process information sequentially. The right hemisphere seems specialized for holistic rather than analytical cognitive functions. The right hemisphere is primarily responsible for our orientation in space, body image, understanding melodies, artistic endeavors, and other spatial activities. Witelson (1976a) reports that children with developmental reading problems may have spatial functioning usually found only in the right hemisphere represented in both hemispheres (two right-hemisphere syndrome). This phenomenon could be overloading the left hemisphere where language functions occur, thus interfering with the verbal functions of the left hemisphere. She states that deficiency in linguistic, sequential, analytic processing in the left hemisphere could lead to predominant use of the spatial, parallel, holistic mode by dyslexic individuals because they appear to have no difficulty in this area. She notes that LD children readily learn Chinese logographs even though they have trouble with English symbols. The Chinese symbols require visual, holistic processing rather than phonetic, sequential decoding. In another study (1976b), Witelson also noted that boys show a much earlier specialization of the right brain hemisphere for spatial processing than girls.

Implications of Theories and Causes for Remediation

It is difficult to indicate precisely what implications a knowledge of theories and causes would have for the remediation of learning disabilities. The question is partly a philosophical one. On the one hand, there are those who say that unless you know what is causing the problem, your approach to remediation will be based on trial and error and can be very wasteful in terms of teachable moments. On the other hand, there are those who believe that the causes are irrelevant and the theories are inconclusive; therefore, the only acceptable approach to remediation is to determine the strengths and weaknesses of the academic skills required for learning to read (or do arithmetic) and generate a program designed to make the best use of strengths while improving skill weaknesses.

There is a major danger that lurks in theories. That danger is that an illusion might be produced that treats the theory as if it were factual rather than theoretical. An educational program that is prescribed strictly on the basis of a theory may be spurious. Many programs have been developed based on motor development models or sensory process models, such as the Illinois Test of Psycholinguistics Abilities (ITPA) approach, that were unwarranted in terms of the time consumed and the extent to which the total program was unwisely based just on the theory. However, personalities and approaches of teachers do differ. There are some who need to know what is wrong and why; then they feel they can better prepare a program for the child. There are others who say "Don't bother me with the details of the past. Just give me the child and tell me what to do." Others feel that only what can be observed is truly known; therefore, the place to begin is with the child, ascertaining what he can do, and going from there.

We personally like to know what went wrong or what caused the problem because we feel it gives us a better perspective for understanding the nature of the children. We believe this knowledge can help us prepare a better program for the child in terms of his total needs. However, we also recognize that our primary concern is the teaching of skills and academic learning, and if we know nothing else about the child, we should at least build on his strengths and develop his weaknesses. Total understanding can lead to better planning.

Characteristics of Learning Disabled Children

Primary disability readers have certain developmental, behavioral, and physiological characteristics which can be identified and considered in making clinical judgments. These characteristics are not necessarily exclusive to primary disability cases inasmuch as one or two, perhaps several, of these characteristics may be found in normal achievers. However, the primary disability readers will have some characteristics in each of the three areas and will have more of the characteristics mentioned below. The presence of some of these characteristics in a child's developmental pattern does not indicate the existence of primary reading disability, but the more there are present, the greater the need for further study of the possibility of the existence of primary reading disability.

Developmental Characteristics

Perhaps the most meaningful of all the characteristics present in the developmental pattern of a child is the presence of an unusual or abnormal birth situation or prenatal condition. The concept of *abnormal* here is not intended to indicate necessarily some drastically unusual situation but one in which there was some chance of damage being done to the child's neurological system. This damage need not be so extensive that the child be visibly handicapped in any way. The damage could be minute and nondetectable by neurological examinations and instruments presently available. The fact must be recognized that since there is no evidence of damage, we cannot be sure that it does actually exist. Furthermore, a causal relationship is only assumed and not proven.

The abnormal situation might be one of a breech-birth or, perhaps, of an instrument birth. In some primary disability cases there is evidence of long or difficult labor or of a difficult delivery. On the other hand, the birth process may have been too quick, not permitting the neonate to adjust gradually to the outside environment. During the prenatal period the mother may have suffered toxemia of some kind or may have taken some drugs which could affect the fetus. The mother may have had an infectious disease, such as rubella (German measles), during early pregnancy. This is always serious. A premature birth of less than 180 days would also be considered unusual. It would be well to remember that, by medical standards, even a full-term baby is considered premature if it weighs less than five pounds. In working with one child, one of the authors learned from the mother that there was a double placenta when the child was born. This, of course, is by no means normal. Recently, it has been learned that a general anesthesia taken by the mother at the time of birth could also anesthetize the neonate. In summary, the more difficult the birth situation, the greater the possibility of the occurrence of primary reading disability.

A second characteristic is the absence of some major area of maturational development in the sequential process. Delacato (1959) places great emphasis upon the absence of either a crawling stage or a creeping stage in the child's growth pattern. By crawling, he means the pulling of one's self along the floor with the stomach constantly in contact with the floor. By creeping, he means quadruped walking by moving about on hands and knees with no part of the stomach touching the floor. The child may have crawled around a playpen and then begun to pull himself upright prior to walking, thus omitting the creeping stage. Occasionally, there is a child who bypasses both the crawl and the creep and first moves by walking. A large number of play-pen babies, babies who have been rather restricted to the space of the playpen, have become primary disability reading cases. However, a serious question can be raised as to whether there is a causal relationship between the lack of crawling or creeping and reading disability or whether it is a correlative relationship. Our clinical observations imply a correlative relationship. The older child who cannot do adequate creeping usually has a motor problem due to some cause other than skipping the creeping stage. The point here is that it is important to be aware of any observations which may have been made about the developmental patterns.

Another developmental characteristic is the presence of a speech abnormality in the child's history. It may be that the child did not begin to talk until much later than other children or, in a few cases, speech started at a very early age. The child's early, and sometimes later, speech may have contained reversals of words or syllables or spoonerisms. He may have said such things as "bottlemilk" for "milkbottle" or, perhaps, "bilkmottle" for "milkbottle". He may have had difficulty with some sounds beyond the period when other children could articulate them with ease. Unlike normal children, he may never have stammered or stuttered. The average child at about the age of three or four often has trouble getting words out; hence, he stammers or stutters. This is a transitory thing which disappears as rapidly as it appears. Many primary disability readers never have this stammering or stuttering problem.

Behavioral Characteristics

One of the more significant behavioral characteristics is the presence of a history of "headbanging" in early childhood. In such a case, a child between the approximate ages of 8 and 36 months seeks to strike or bang his head on the floor, against the wall, or the side of his playpen. In addition to, or in place of headbanging, the child may be unusually rhythmic. He is constantly moving while doing other things, such as rocking his body to and fro even while eating. Sometimes this child is noted as one who has always been able to follow rhythm without having had any apparent learning period.

A second noteworthy behavioral characteristic which is found in many primary reading disability cases is the presence of either lethargic behavior or hyperactivity. The lethargic child appears to be sluggish and indifferent or apathetic. He seems to move only when he has to, and he seldom makes any voluntary responses or energetic movements. The hyperactive child is just the opposite. This child may be so active that he makes a person tired or nervous just to be around him.

Frequently the primary disability reader is a child whose parents claim he was seemingly normal or even precocious in his preschool life. Generally the child showed a better than average intellectual ability by being able to learn and say things orally far in advance of his peers. Never once were the parents given any hint that trouble was in store for the child when he was to begin school. Many parents of remedial readers have indicated that they were certain they had a gifted child and that they could hardly wait for him to start school to show how well he could do.

Some primary reading disability (PRD) children also have an amplified ability to learn by hearing. "Tell it to him just once and he'll remember" is the kind of comment heard again and again. Many of these children develop this aural learning ability so acutely that they can repeat a conversation almost verbatim a week after it has occurred.

The fifth behavioral characteristic is an extreme fluctuation of the child's retention and learning rate. Some days a child may behave almost as if he had no difficulties and may seem to learn as rapidly as his classmates. Yet, the next day he may not be able to learn a single thing. For a month, he may be able to recognize a word every time he sees it, and then, suddenly, he no longer recognizes the word. Two weeks later, he will just as suddenly begin to recognize the word again.

Physiological Characteristics

As an area, the physiological characteristics are more closely related to primary disability readers than are developmental or behavioral characteristics.

A physiological characteristic of a primary reading disability case is that most of the sensory equipment, including acuity, appears normal in the child. The child's intelligence is usually average or better; the visual apparatus seems to be intact and functioning without anomalies; the hearing seems normal; medical examination fails to show any glandular disturbance. Thus, most of the usual contributory physical restrictions are not present.

The second physiological characteristic is the seemingly accurate functioning of the separate physical and cerebral areas related to the reading process. The reading process involves (a) recognition, (b) language significance, and (c) motor response. The primary disability reader may be able to perform each of these functions individually but not all of them in a series as he should. An examination of the child to determine the degree to which he can recognize objects reveals no object agnosia. He indicates that he possesses language significance since he can respond appropriately to oral commands. Likewise, his motor speech patterns seem to be intact since he can speak and carry on conversations. Yet, even though each factor functions adequately when pursued individually, when they must integrate and work together, as they must in the reading process, something happens and a dysfunction exists.

The physiological consideration of body laterality as reflected in mixed dominance and/or in cross dominance is another characteristic. Body laterality refers to *sidedness*, the preferential use of one side of the body, especially in tasks demanding the use of only one hand, one eye, or one foot. Lateral dominance implies that a child has a preferential use of one side of the body, either all right side or all left side. Crossdominance indicates that at least one hand, eye, or foot is dominant on the side opposite the usual dominant side of the body. A child possessing this might be right-handed and right-footed but left-eyed. Or he could be left-handed but right-eyed and right-footed. Any combination can occur. Mixed or incomplete dominance, however, implies that a child has not developed a preferred hand or perhaps eye or foot. Therefore, a child with a mixed manual dominance will use his right hand sometimes and other times, his left. This mixture is not the same as being ambidextrous which means being equally skillful with both hands or with both sides of the body. The combination of some left-right disorientation and mixed or cross dominance in children nine or older seems especially significant.

It should be noted that there are some normal achievers who also have mixed or cross dominance. Therefore, primary reading disability should not be identified on the basis of a lack of lateral dominance alone. The research literature generally discredits laterality as a symptom or cause of reading disability. In our clinics, we generally check for laterality but seldom use the results in our conclusions because, frankly, we are not sure that it tells us anything significant other than that the child probably had trouble learning to read in first grade.

One other observation: some children with primary reading disability do appear to have developed lateral dominance. In these cases, however, there is often a form of lateral rigidity producing a situation in which one side of the body is strongly dominant but the other side is so significantly underdeveloped that it is completely incapable of performing certain motor acts or else does very poorly as compared to the preferred side.

Richardson's Study of Characteristics

Among the better summations to be found of characteristics of children who have "specific learning problems" is that of Sylvia O. Richardson, M. D., as reported in the conference report of the Third Annual International Conference of the Association for Children with Learning Disabilities (1966). She reviewed the literature and reported what classroom teachers, pediatricians, neurologists, and psychiatrists had to say in their description. The classroom teachers reported such characteristics as the following:

1. Poor visual discrimination and memory for words.
2. Poor auditory memory for words or for individual sounds in words.
3. Persistent reversals of words, syllables, or letters in reading, writing, and speech. Rotation or inversion of letters; reverse sequence of letters and syllables; mirror writing or transposition of numbers.
4. Poor recall for reproduction of simple geometric forms.
5. Poor memory for auditory or visual sequence.
6. Weakly established handedness.
7. Clumsiness and poor hand control.
8. Immature articulation.
9. Hyperactivity and distractibility.

Psychologists generally refer to perceptual-motor problems, inferring the lack of normal functioning of (1) the perceptual intake processes such as visual, auditory, or tactile; (2) the motor processes, such as speaking, writing, manipulating, walking; or (3) a combination of both. The implication is that there are signs present of disorganization in the integrative perceptual-motor mechanisms of the brain.

Richardson presents the following physical signs as given by pediatricians, neurologists, and psychiatrists as characteristics of children who do not learn:

1. Mild tremor, especially on effort; mild choreoform or athetoid movements.
2. Hyper-reflexion.
3. Excessive clumsiness.
4. Monocular vision or minor ocular imbalance.
5. Disturbance of body image.
   a. Right-left confusion and absence of, or weakly established, laterality.
   b. Finger agnosia or impairment of finger-localizing ability.
   c. Impaired spatial concept.
6. Impaired form perception.
7. Immature articulation.
8. Hyperkinetic behavior with distractibility, short attention span, irritability and emotional lability.

The characteristics of children with learning disabilities as agreed upon by the three disciplines and reported by Richardson are:

1. Poor auditory memory.
2. Poor auditory discrimination.
3. Poor sound blending.
4. Poor visual memory.
5. Poor visual discrimination.
6. Inadequate ability in visual and visual-motor sequencing.
7. Lack of, or weakly established, cerebral dominance.
8. Right-left confusion with problems in laterality and directionality.
9. Fine motor uncoordination.
10. Nonspecific awkwardness or clumsiness.
11. Ocular imbalance.
12. Attention defect and disordered or hyperkinetic behavior.

Many of the above characteristics are frequently observed in children with severe reading disabilities who are seen in our clinical setups. Our concept of primary reading disability resembles that of the so-called "learning disability child."

Kaluger/Kaluger Study of Characteristics

Meriem and George Kaluger (1973), both workers in the field of learning disabilities, analyzed 300 of their psychological reports on LD children to determine what characteristics they observed in disabled learners. They concluded that all the characteristics identified could be classified under five headings: (1) difficulties in academic learning, (2) perceptual-motor difficulties, (3) language and speech disorders, (4) difficulties with thought processes, and (5) behavioral and affective characteristics. Of the 52 characteristics listed, LD children were found to have 5 to 7 of them on the average. Occasionally a child would have only one characteristic, but had it to a severe degree. The particular characteristics a child had appeared to depend on the cause of his learning disability. Normal children also have some of these characteristics but disabled learners have more of them and to a greater degree of deficiency.

The characteristics, by categories, are as follows:

I. Difficulties in Academic Learning

1. Achievement in reading is one or more years below mental age level.
2. Poor oral reading fluency.
3. Poor reading comprehension.
4. Poor ability in phonetic analysis of new words.
5. Reverses letters, words, sounds of syllables in reading.
6. Reverses letters and numbers in writing.
7. Words spelled show little relationship to the sound they contain.
8. Achievement in arithmetic is below mental age level.
9. Little or no application of skills learned in reading or arithmetic. (No transfer of learning from isolated skills to application.)

II. Perceptual-Motor Difficulties

1. Poor auditory perception (awareness, discrimination, memory, sequence, etc.)
2. Poor visual perception (discrimination, memory, sequence, etc.)
3. Confusion about lefts and rights and directional orientation.
4. No consistent use of preferred hand or preferred foot. (cerebral dominance)
5. Preferred handedness and footedness not on same side of body. (laterality)
6. Gross motor awkwardness or clumsiness.
7. Cannot coordinate use of hands and/or feet. (ex. skipping)
8. Poor visual-motor coordination. (fine motor)
9. Illegible or distorted handwriting.
10. Mild tremor of hands, fingers or feet on effort.
11. Uses only one hand (or side of body) with no assistance from the other.
12. Cannot pull main visual or auditory stimulus from background stimuli. (figure-ground)
13. Unable to discriminate different phonetic sounds.
14. Impaired form perception, space conception, and/or poor recall of form or space.
15. Ocular imbalance or poor adjustment.

III. Language and Speech Disorders

1. Speech defect beyond immature articulation.
2. Indistinct or distorted speech (omits or adds sounds).
3. Distortion in repeating sounds.
4. Poor ability in blending sounds.

5. Long, rambling conversation or story-telling.
6. Poor word or sentence structure.
7. Halting, stumbling or very slow oral delivery.
8. Miscalls word but gives appropriate substitute. (ex. Dad for man)

IV. Difficulties with Thought Processes

1. Takes a long time to organize his thoughts before he can respond.
2. Capable at concrete thinking but poor at abstractions.
3. Unable to pay attention or respond in an orderly fashion (poor ego control).
4. Unable to shift attention or to change behavior, ideas or words. (perseveration)
5. Pays too little attention to details or to the internal construction of words.
6. Pays too much attention to details: cannot see the total pattern of form, thought or idea.
7. Poor organization of work time and work space.
8. Cannot follow directions. Cannot remember them.
9. Cannot understand or remember gestures or words.
10. Cannot transfer learning from isolated skills to application.

V. Behavior and Affective Characteristics

1. Excessive body or verbal activity (hyperactive or hyperkinetic).
2. Rather lethargic and nonactive (hypoactive).
3. Easily distracted visually.
4. Easily distracted by sound (auditorially).
5. Short attention or concentration span.
6. Works better when someone is standing by him but not when the person moves away.
7. Takes much more time than others to do his work.
8. One day seems capable and remembers but the next day he does not (variability of performance).
9. Unplanned, impulsive or "forced" motor responses which appear meaningless or inappropriate (impulsivity or disinhibition).
10. Overreaction or overflow of an emotional response (emotional liability).

Selected Characteristics: Discussion

Left-Right Disorientation

Left-right disorientation or a poor sense of directionality refers to the inability of a person to readily identify his left or right, the left or right on another person, or the directions as to top, bottom, dorsal, or lateral. Benton (1959) has developed a test of left-right disorientation whereby the child is asked to do such things as show his left hand, point to his right eye, or touch his left ear with his right hand. The child is also asked to look at pictures and to identify whether the part of the body shown is the right or left side.

Many specialists believe that children learn their rights and lefts by the age of 8. Any child after that age who exhibits left-right disorientation or hesitation should be definitely checked for other indications of primary reading disability. By the time a child reaches secondary school, he will have usually devised some scheme for identifying his right and left. Such schemes as "This is my right hand because it's the one I write with," or "I wear my ring or watch on my left hand" can sometimes be detected by watching the person's face and seeing if he is hesitating and trying to figure out his left and right. Older left-right disorientation cases often have difficulty with directional relationships, such as pointing left and saying "right," or having difficulty with directional terms such as anterior and posterior. College students who are compensating for left-right disorientation frequently have trouble learning which part is the dorsal side. Left-right disorientation is also a form of body agnosia in that the person has difficulty with body image and lacks the knowledge or facility to coordinate the halves of his body laterally or cross-laterally.

Distractibility and Short Attention Span

It is difficult to separate distractibility in a child from the characteristic of having a short attention span. Distractibility, having one's attention diverted from one's task by inconsequential or minor stimuli, will result in a short attention span, but not all children with short attention spans are necessarily distractible. Among other things a child may have a short attention span due to a physical problem, such as a thyroid condition; hypoglycemia or hunger pangs; a nonstimulating environment or teaching session; inability to understand what is taking place; poor auditory or visual acuity resulting in not being able to grasp enough of the content being presented; a low frustration level due to inability to perform the task required; or, even bothersome clothing, tight shorts or pants, or an itch.

Distractibility implies an inability to screen out unimportant stimuli. Severe brain-damaged individuals are distracted by the slightest sounds, movements, or attention-getting elements such as colors, jewelry, and even cosmetics. Few of the learning disabled children most teachers encounter are that distractible. Children can be either visually distractible or auditorially distractible; seldom are they both. Possibly about 30 to 35% of LD children are distracted enough to require special attention. The older a child gets, the more he can compensate for his distractibility. However, one thing is certain: distractibility must be controlled first, otherwise little or no learning will take place because the teacher will not have the attention of the child.

Most LD children who have distractibility are *visually* distractible. A bird flies by a window; the child's eye is attracted by the movement. A child in the back of the room bends over to pick up a piece of paper; the visually distractible child notices this. The teacher, sitting behind her desk, reaches for a pencil; the distractible child's attention is diverted. The implication of all of these distractions is that the child finds it very difficult to finish his desk work in a reasonable time. The teacher complains that it takes him forever to complete his assignment. What is worse, the teacher notices that when she stands beside him, he can keep at his work; but when she goes back to her desk, he's looking all over the room. So many times we hear the question "If he can do his work while I'm standing beside him, why can't he do it when I'm at my desk?" There is an answer. The closeness of the teacher helps the child pull his visual field into a small area so he can concentrate on his words or problems and complete a line before he is distracted again. The best help for the visually distractible child is to create a situation or structure in which his field is limited. A cardboard box or carrel on his desk, large enough for him to work inside, can be very helpful. A large cardboard box, such as those in which refrigerators are shipped, in the back of the room can serve as an "office" where he can go to do his work. This child could even work better sitting under his desk or under the teacher's desk. A recent development is the construction of an inflatable plastic bubble that can be set up in a room. Several children can work quite well within such an enclosure.

Occasionally there will be a child who is *auditorially* distractible. He gets overloaded with sound input and cannot handle it (overstimulation), or he is triggered by even the slightest of sounds (low arousal level). Anything that can be done to dampen sound will be helpful. Carpets or rugs on the floor and drapes or acoustical tile on the walls or ceiling can be both attractive and sound absorbent. For the child, Swedish wool (not cotton or lamb's wool) can be used to screen out sounds. Swedish wool is used as ear plugs by some industrial workers on excessive sound-producing jobs. The wool is soft and comfortable to the ear. It diminishes the intensity of the sound to a tolerable level. Some of the polyvinyl soft plastic eardrum protectors used by swimmers are also suitable. Of course, comfortable earphones can be of some help. We have found that the small gadgets designed to emit "white noise" shut out distracting sounds and children (and adults) can tolerate, without any effort, the steady production of "white noise."

Hyperactivity

Hyperactivity has become a fashionable, popular layman's term and is frequently used to imply a child with a learning disability. This inappropriate use of the term has created many misconceptions. In the first place, there are many children in regular LD self-contained classrooms who are not hyperactive. In a center of 240 LD children where we formerly had some responsibilities, not more than 10% in any one semester were overly active or restless to the point that they were a problem to themselves, to the teacher, or to the class. Hyperactivity means excessive motor activity or restlessness to the point that it interferes with normal functions of the classroom or of individual learning.

Hyperkinesis or *hyperkinetic* is a medical term and implies a child who has detectable brain damage that causes excessive physical activity. This is the child who is "born running and never takes his track shoes off." He is a driven child. He drives his parents, his teachers, and himself up a wall. What is important to realize is that not all hyperkinetic children are learning disabled. This would be true if the brain damage were only in the motor areas. These children are usually classroom, and even social, problems because it is difficult for them to control their movements.

An unpublished study by Kaluger and Kaluger from 1971 to 1974, at the Capital Area Intermediate Unit centers for learning disabled children in Cumberland County, Pennsylvania, revealed several types of hyperactive children. It is possible to categorize overactivity into five groups, according to types of behavior. The most common and noticeable type of hyperactivity is motor hyperactivity. This child finds it very difficult to sit still. He has to be on his feet, moving around, in and out of things, and constantly a source of irritation to his teacher and parents. As this child gets older, we find him seeking to control by wrapping his feet around the legs of the chair, or, with his legs and feet coiled on the seat of the chair, sitting on them so they will not move about. A second type of hyperactive child is the one who can control gross motor movements but who is verbally active. This child talks, talks, talks, to anybody and anything. These children are pleasant enough "if only they wouldn't talk so much." A third type of hyperactive child is one we call the *pseudo-hypoactive* child. This youngster never moves in the classroom. You can see that he is trying very hard to control. He appears tense and stiff, but he does not appear to be learning in spite of paying attention. This child is expending so much energy controlling his movements that he has little energy left for learning. The teacher usually learns of his hyperactivity from the parents who ask "How can you put up with him all day? He's never still at home." The teacher is dumbfounded and says "But he's not a problem at school at all!"

The fourth type of hyperactive child is the one who is *developmentally hyperactive*. The specific meaning of the term, as it is used here, is that the child has no neurological or biochemical basis for the hyperactivity but has never been taught to sit still; he may also be "hyper" due to emotional or psychological distress. Unfortunately, there are children who come to school never having been taught how to behave. Frequently these children have a psychological concern and have not learned how to handle their problems except through aggressive, forceful, loud-talking behavior. Often their behavior is actually for emotional and personal survival; they simply have developed maladaptive forms of behaviors by which they are trying to handle their problems. They have not been taught more appropriate forms of behavior.

The fifth type of hyperactive child is the one in whom hyperactivity is artificially induced by food intake, resulting in central nervous system allergies. Artificial coloring, especially red and orange food dye, and artificial flavoring and preservatives added to certain food products can affect neurological functioning and produce hyperactivity in children and in adults. Dr. B. Feingold of the Kaiser-Permanente Hospital Center (1974) learned that many of the children referred to him improved in behavior when placed on a salicylate-free diet for two weeks or so. Salicylate can be found in a natural state in fruits and vegetables such as apples, grapes, oranges, peaches, strawberries, cucumbers, and tomatoes. Foods with added salicylates include ice cream, sugar-coated cereals, bakery goods, candy, mint flavors, luncheon meats, hot dogs, artificially colored fruit drinks, and soda pop. We have had striking success with some such children simply by taking them off "junk" foods. Most of the children we have worked with have had only two to four items of food that were producing the hyperactivity. We also learned that not all kinds of ice cream, fruit drinks, or luncheon meats produced hyperactivity. Each individual had to learn what he could or could not take.

As you can see, not all hyperactivity can be treated in the same manner. The causes vary, so the treatment must vary. Hyperactivity caused by physical factors must be treated accordingly. Physical factors that cause excessive restlessness are as varied as such conditions as inadequate oxygen intake to the brain due to such factors as a vein engorgement, a low level of glucose (hypoglycemia) that affects nerve cells, and an inadequate level of calcium (Walker, 1974). Food sensitivities and allergies have already been mentioned. A study conducted in Sarasota, Florida with four first-grade classes using two different types of fluorescent lights showed that there was more hyperactive behavior in rooms using the standard, cool white fluorescent tubes as opposed to the rooms using the full spectrum tubes with long, ultraviolet wavelengths (Treichel, 1974). We have had some cases who were excessively restless because of tight-fitting clothing, and others who were merely growing rapidly physically, and the bone to muscle ratio was out of proportion. The implication is that just because a child is hyperactive, the solution is not necessarily medication to slow down motor actions. Drugs should not be used prematurely and without careful differential diagnosis.

Suggestions for teachers having hyperactive children in their class are:

1. Make assignments short. Ten short, 5-minute assignments might be better than two half-hour assignments.
2. Structure his activity and space. Teach the child self-control.
3. Give immediate verbal and nonverbal reinforcement for appropriate behavior.
4. Allow him to stand up to do his assignments if he wants to. Standing eliminates physical stress. Use a higher desk where a child can work in a standing position.
5. Have him sit on a stool without a back.
6. Build a short quiet time into the schedule.
7. Do not overload or frustrate the child with difficult work.
8. Try a screen or carrel arrangement within which he can work.
9. Be aware of his diet and note if certain types of breakfast or lunch foods tend to increase activity. Eliminate foods that stimulate and increase restlessness.
10. Work with the parents and share ideas and feelings.

Use of Medication for Modifying Behavior

In January 1975 the Food and Drug Administration estimated that between 150,000 and 200,000 children were being treated with stimulant drugs on a long-term basis (Wolf, 1975). The stimulant drug most widely used to control distractibility is Ritalin, invented in 1950 by the CIBA Pharmaceutical Company. Other drugs such as Dexedrine and Deaner are also used. Methyphenidate, Librium, Cylert, Equanil (Heprobamate), Thorazine, Mellaril and Haloperidol are among the many anti-anxiety drugs employed. The Department of Health, Education, and Welfare earlier reported that the use of these drugs was beneficial in only one-half to two-thirds of the cases in which they were tried. By beneficial, they referred not to solving the problem of hyperactivity with drugs, but to putting the child back into a position to interact with his environment to the extent that his condition permitted (HEW Report, 1971). According to the Drug Panel of the Office of Child Development, no evidence has been reported that children who are treated for hyperactivity by the use of stimulant drugs have become drug users in later life (Office of Child Development, 1971).

How does the use of stimulant drugs affect the learning behaviors of hyperactive children? Generally, it has been theorized that medication has an effect on social variables, in that the child may become more responsive to the environment or to the teacher. Studies, however, do not provide a clear understanding of how medication improves the actual scholastic or learning achievement of the child (Bosco, 1977). Campbell, Douglas, and Morgensten (1970) did a study concerned with cognitive styles in hyperactive children at the Montreal Children's Hospital. One of its goals was to assess the success of Ritalin in alleviating the cognitive and learning problems found in hyperactive children in comparison with normal children. The results of this study indicated that Ritalin did modify the cognitive behavior of the children so that they were able to take more time in responding to problems and therefore made more correct responses. These data suggest that improvement in scholastic achievement after the administration of Ritalin may result from a general increase in attention, response organization, and impulse control.

A research study by Burleigh, Cupta, and Sadderfield (1971) determined that hyperactive children tended to repeat inappropriate behavior in problem-solving tasks. Burleigh then divided the hyperactive children into two groups. One group he treated with Ritalin, the other with a placebo. He then repeated the procedure on the original experiment. His findings point to significant improvement in the children treated with Ritalin as compared to the children on the placebo.

A research study comparing the efficiency, side effects, and safety of Cylert and Dexedrine to a placebo was conducted by Conners (1971) at the Massachusetts General Hospital in Boston. His subjects included 81 children ages 6 to 12 who had been referred because they exhibited major symptoms of hyperactivity and distractibility. All had an I.Q. over 80 and one or more signs of minimal brain dysfunction. Conners then randomly assigned children to one of three groups where they received the designated treatment (Dexedrine, Cylert, or the placebo) for a period of 8 weeks. During that period, the children were evaluated medically and psychologically, and by teacher and parent ratings. The results indicated both drug groups showed significantly reduced hyperactive behavior over the children on the placebo. Dexedrine exhibited a more immediate and outstanding effect, but Cylert produced fewer side effects. Side effects evidenced were insomnia, sadness, and irritability. In another study, Connors found that Ritalin helped improve verbal learning, while Dexedrine helped improve motor performance.

Other positive effects of the stimulant drugs are listed by Renshaw in *The Hyperactive Child* (1974). Included are the following:

1. more controlled activity (quieter)
2. more goal-directed activity
3. fewer disruptive impulses
4. less distractible
5. better coordination (handwriting, drawing, gym, sports)
6. improved personal neatness
7. more friendly, less negativistic
8. sometimes better sleep habits

Some concerns are evident, however. Although side effects are rare in the small doses of stimulant drugs used to treat children, they do exist. Side effects of commonly used amphetamines might include loss of appetite, depression, headaches, stomachaches, bedwetting, irritability, and dizziness. Schrag and Divoky (1975) fear that children who reach adolescence have the additional problem of overcoming a dependence on the drug to maintain self-control. When they are removed from the drug, they haven't had the practice in building self-control or the practice in learning to cope with daily stress. The drug panel for the Office of Child Development further cautions against the use of stimulant drugs in children whose problems stem from such factors as hunger, emotional stress, poor teaching or crowded classrooms.

From the above findings, there seems to be some validity in the use of stimulant drugs for modifying the behavior of hyperactive children. Not all children are improved, however, as they sometimes are affected by the medication in a different manner than is expected. The use of medication with children is quite an emotional issue for some people. Our position is that medication should be used only as a last resort. We define the last resort as being that point in time when the child cannot improve in his academic learning without the use of medication. We are fearful of the child getting too far behind in his educational learning because we know of the distress and emotional problems that can erupt when the child is 12 to 14 years of age and only achieving on a second- or third-grade level.

In the matter of gaining self-control, we recommend the child be taken off the medication on weekends, holidays, and summer vacations so both the child and the parents can see what the behavior pattern is and what self-controls need to be learned. We also recommend that the teacher, not just the parents, talk with the physician to indicate how the child is responding to the medication. We caution the proper dosage usage. A mother of one of our cases gave her boy the entire dosage for the day in the morning before sending him to school "so he would behave." The poor child was so sedated that he did not begin to respond until two o'clock in the afternoon. There is one final point we have noticed. If the parents are dead-set against the use of medication, or if the child is adamant against taking medication, the medicine will be of little or no help.

chapter 5

Severe Language, Reading, and Motor Disorders

It is important to recognize that a reading or learning disorder can be a mild, moderate, or severe deficiency. Most often the degree of severity of a problem is assumed by noting how far below grade level (or mental age level) the child is functioning. This approach is not all bad, but it is limited in providing pertinent information necessary for developing a good educational plan. It is essential to discover the nature and cause of the deficiency, at least in terms of the functional levels of the sense modalities and of the central nervous system processing involved in learning to read. Knowledge of why the child has not been able to learn to read will suggest approaches and media that should be used. Knowing the severity of his problem may suggest the proper placement for him for instructional purposes. We cannot overlook the fact that even among remedial readers, there are some children who deviate so much from the others in terms of their deficiencies and inability to learn that they require a very special kind of help. There is such a thing as a mentally bright adult who is a total nonreader in spite of the fact that he truly tried to learn to read while in school. This person could have been born with, or he could have acquired, a central nervous system condition that resulted in alexia or dyslexia. There are children and adults who are aphasic. About 1% of the school-age population will have a severe learning disorder.

The symptoms of primary reading disability frequently persist with an individual into adulthood. Fortunately, it is possible for a child or an adult to learn to compensate for some of his disabilities. Witness the elaborate schemes some individuals have for identifying left and right or for doing arithmetic by the use of tally marks, dots, counting on fingers, touching the lips with fingers while counting, or just using rote memorization of the procedures or steps involved in computing a problem. The individual whose writing paper has many words crossed out or who exerts much pencil pressure to make the writing look darker may be compensating for a mild case of dysgraphia. It is true that a severely affected individual may still be able to learn to do some reading and some arithmetic, but he will function on a much lower level of learning efficiency than he would otherwise. If measuring instruments could be made sensitive enough, or if the observer were knowledgeable enough in knowing what to look for, symptoms of central nervous system dysfunctions

102

could be detected, even if the individual is compensating to make up for his deficiency. One final point: It should be noted that the severity of dysfunctions varies among individuals and that the severity can be ranked on a continuum that ranges from very mild at one extreme to very severe or profound at the other.

Basic Understandings

From a historical perspective, it is interesting to note that severe learning, reading, and language disorders were discussed in the medical literature many years before they appeared to any extent in educational literature. By contrast, however, it was the strong educational emphasis on the topic of learning disabilities in the 1960s and 1970s that brought such terms as *dyslexia*, *asphasia*, and to a lesser degree, *dysgraphia* to the attention of parents, teachers, and the public in general. Although there is some merging of medical and educational views concerning these learning disorders, there remains a distinct difference in orientation and approach to the study and remediation of the problems. Medical orientation emphasizes neurological implications and organic considerations, while educational orientation stresses behavioral factors and functional usage of learning skills.

The popular media, magazines, and newspapers in particular, in an effort to make a difficult but timely topic more understandable, have distorted and misused the original medical definitions of aphasia and dyslexia. Today, there is much confusion in the minds of educators, medical personnel who work with LD children, and concerned laymen as to what exactly is meant when these terms are used. For example, not all poor readers are dyslexic; yet, all dyslexics are poor readers. How do you tell the difference? Neurologists would answer by saying the dyslexic would have a central nervous system involvement that produces a handicapping condition, which in turn impairs the ability to learn to read. Most educators would state that a dyslexic is one who has a severe reading deficiency. Many laypeople and parents would claim that a dyslexic is a child who is not reading on grade level and, therefore, is a poor reader.

The following explanation may help clarify some of the confusion that surrounds the use of terms like *aphasia*, *alexia*, and *dyslexia*. The use of the letter *a* as a prefix literally means *without*, implying a rather complete lack of ability. The letter combination *dys* used as a prefix infers a serious disturbed condition but not a complete lack of ability. To illustrate the difference, let's apply the prefixes *a* and *dys* to the stem *lexia*, which in Latin means the written or printed word. The definition for alexia would be "without the capacity to read or interpret letters or words." Dyslexia is defined as "a disturbed function in the process of reading or interpreting letters or words." The medical definition for alexia is "inability to read, due to a central lesion; word blindness." For dyslexia, the medical definition is "difficulty in reading as a result of brain lesion." In both definitions, there is a neurological involvement included. The difference between the two terms, alexia and dyslexia, is a matter of degree of incapacity; alexia is more serious than dyslexia.

The true nonreader would have alexia. A very poor reader would have dyslexia, usually due to a neurological dysfunction involving the reading process. Why emphasize the difference between a dyslexic child and a nondyslexic if they are both poor readers? Because the very nature of their inability to learn to read will suggest (a) techniques and materials appropriate for teaching each type of disabled reader since neurologically involved children will need more help than is provided by typical developmental reading approaches; (b) the nondyslexic child has his neural mechanism for learning to read intact and, as a result, should be more amenable to remediation; and (c) the prognosis for succeeding in learning to read is usually better for the nondyslexic individual.

Not all individuals with brain damage are poor readers. Severe learning disorders due to central nervous system dysfunctions may result in deficiencies in areas other than reading. This observation explains why it is possible for a learning disabled child to be very capable in one academic area but very poor in another, such as good in reading but poor in math (or vice versa), good in math but very poor in handwriting, or good in sports (gross motor movements) but poor in reading. The following terms imply various areas of the brain that could be affected and, as a result, produce serious limitations in different kinds of learning:

Alexia (Dyslexia)—Inability to read or interpret letters or words.

Agraphia (Dysgraphia)—Inability to make fine motor movements. specifically in writing and drawing.

Acalculia (Dyscalculia)—Inability to understand and interpret numbers and to do arithmetic or mathematics.

Agnosia (Dysgnosia)—Inability to recognize an object by a specific sense, such as touch, sight, taste, smell, or sound.

Apraxia (Dyspraxia)—Inability to perform certain purposive movements without loss of motor (muscle) power, sensation or coordination, such as in speaking or walking.

There are other terms that are intended to be more specific as to function such as *dysarthria*—difficulty in the articulation of words due to involvement of the CNS; *dyskinesia*—partial impairment of voluntary movement abilities resulting in incomplete movements, poor coordination, and apparently clumsy behavior; and *dysnomia*—a condition in which an individual knows the word he is trying to recall, recognizes it when it is said for him, but cannot recall it at will. We would like to mention one more condition which is found in some disabled readers—*verbal paraphasia*—the misuse of words or word combinations spoken, or the substitution of a word with the same meaning as the stimulus word. This condition is a form of aphasia sometimes encountered in a reader who looks at the word *man* and says *father*. Literal paraphasia is the inability to pronounce a word the subject has heard. Quite often the subject will distort the sound composition of the word or replace it with a word that sounds something like it and that very often has a similar meaning (Bannatyne, 1971).

Aphasia

Aphasia is a temporary or permanent language disorder associated with brain damage. It is characterized by loss or impairment in the use of spoken or written symbols for the formulation, reception, or transmission of ideas. Aphasia is not an absence of speech, but rather a lack of language communication mediated through speech (Agranowitz & McKeown, 1966).

Osgood and Miron (1963) give a more discriminative definition by stating that aphasia is a nonfunctional impairment in the reception, manipulation, and/or expression of symbolic content whose basis is to be found in organic damage to relatively central brain structure.

Characteristics of Aphasia

Aphasia is a condition of not being able to handle the structure of written and/or oral language itself. The aphasic does not comprehend the grammar (syntax) of the language he hears, speaks, or writes. He may be able to learn symbols such as letters, numbers, and punctuation cues, but his disability is that he does not understand how the overall language fits together. Therefore, he is unable to communicate effectively with others because he either cannot express his thoughts in meaningful sentences, or he does not get a clear idea of what the material he hears really means (Jordan, 1977).

A classification of the aphasic disorders is typically divided into four types: (1) predominantly receptive or sensory aphasia, where the person can hear and see but cannot understand spoken or written language; (2) predominantly expressive or motor aphasia, where although the vocal apparatus is not paralyzed, the individual cannot formulate speech properly or write properly; (3) mixed expressive-receptive or global aphasia, where all language forms are affected, and (4) the amnesis or nominal disorder, where the memory for language is the primary defect. A less frequently mentioned category is conceptual or central aphasia, where the individual is unable to formulate language or concepts. In conceptual or global aphasia, the neurological damage is more diffuse than it is in the other categories (Mohr, 1973).

There are many ways in which a language loss may be manifested. For example, one patient may think of the word *dog*, but his tongue, teeth, and lips do not get the message from the brain telling them how to pronounce this word. This example is expressive aphasia. Another patient may not be able to understand the word *dog* when someone else says it. This is an example of receptive aphasia. He does not have a hearing loss but the words sound like a foreign language to him. Still another patient may see a dog and recognize it is a dog, but may not be able to recall the word *dog*, indicating nominal aphasia.

The difficulties are not only with speaking. A patient may not be able to read, to write, to do math, or to comprehend spoken language. Rarely has a patient only one or two of these defects; more commonly he will have a combination of them.

Brain-damaged persons tend to become ego-oriented and show increased difficulty in dealing with the abstract. One of the frequent behavioral modifications of brain-damaged persons is the phenomenon of perseveration. This is a tendency for a specific act or behavior, an attitude, or a set to continue in operation when it is no longer appropriate to the situation at hand. Other changes in this defect might be catastrophic behavior, affective behavior, disturbance of attention and memory, and inconsistency of response.

Developmental Aphasia

Developmental or congenital aphasia is a lack of symbolic language development due to brain damage before, during, or after birth up to the age of normal language development. Congenital aphasia, or primary aphasia, presents a much more difficult problem than the acquired types. In congenital aphasia, one is discussing a child who presents failure in the development of language function, often without a history of neurological signs of brain disease or brain injury. Failure to develop language may also be due to mental deficiency, deafness, or severe emotional disturbances, but children with these problems present special problems of their own and should not be considered aphasic (Rappaport, 1964).

Myklebust (1957) has listed the characteristics of children with developmental aphasia as follows: (1) *predominantly expressive*—a relatively common diagnosis, showing less emotional disturbance, flat affectivity, good comprehension, and better motor functioning than other groups, but offering difficulty in retaining; (2) *predominantly receptive*— characterized by erratic auditory behavior, hearing words on some occasions but not on others, appearing often to ignore auditory stimuli; (3) *mixed receptive and expressive*—the most common type, which is difficult to differentiate from receptive types because of the retardation of expressive language in the latter; (4) *central aphasia*—a type displaying disturbance of "inner speech" which reflects itself in both receptive and expressive difficulties of a symbolic nature.

The etiologies of developmental aphasia include glandular deficiencies, cortical lesions, anoxia, rubella, and agenetic causes (i.e., lack of development of cerebral structures). Predominantly expressive aphasia usually has an agenetic or a forceps delivery etiology; central aphasia usually has anoxia or forceps delivery in the etiology. The site of the injury, not the agent (e.g. forceps), is the determinant.

Functional Aphasia

Aphasia really means loss of the power of speech but there are a number of conditions which are also properly classed as functional aphasic manifestations, such as alexia (inability to read) and agraphia (inability to write). One speaks of two kinds of functional aphasia, sensory and motor. Sensory aphasia indicates an inability to understand words heard or seen. Motor aphasia does not impair the ability to hear and read words but the ability to talk (express) or write is lost.

Lesions centered in the inferior frontal convolution of the left cerebral hemisphere cause the loss of speech. The individual who has forgotten how to make the movements necessary for speech is said to have *Broca's aphasia*, a form of apraxia.

Lesions centered in the superior temporal convolution produce sensory disturbances. This is called *word deafness*, indicating the individual cannot comprehend spoken symbols. With lesions in the angular gyrus, the speech disturbance involves chiefly the visual elements. The individual cannot recognize pictures. This disability is called *alexia* or *word blindness*. Writing may be involved although articulation is intact. Lesions in the posterior part of the second frontal convolution just anterior to the motor area of the arm produce agraphia or inability to write (Myklebust, 1957).

Receptive and Expressive Aphasia

There are two main types of aphasia among children: expressive or motor aphasia, and receptive or sensory aphasia.

Expressive aphasia is characterized by:

1. Very limited speech and language.
2. Adequate understanding of speech and language.
3. Limited one- or two-syllable patterns of vocalization.
4. Partial or complete inability to imitate tongue, lip, and jaw actions, sounds, or words.
5. Absence of muscular paralysis.
6. Adequate intelligence for speech.
7. Gestures frequently used for communication.
8. Presence of echolalia or patterns of vocalization are repetitious in intensity.

The expressive aphasic child can understand what is said to him, but cannot reproduce sound patterns and sequences. Usually a limited pattern of one or two syllables is repeated whenever he attempts verbal communication. Vocal inflections vary appropriately with what he is trying to express, but he relies mainly on pulling, pointing, and gesturing for expressive communication.

Receptive aphasia is characterized by:

1. Lack of understanding of speech.
2. For all practical purposes, child does not speak.
3. Discrepancy between nonverbal intelligence and the understanding of spoken language.
4. Discrepancy between hearing and the understanding of spoken language.
5. Uses few or no gestures.
6. Greater responsiveness to nonverbal stimuli than to verbal.

The parents of a receptive aphasic may think that their child is deaf, or may be confused because he seems to "hear at one moment and not the next." Some aphasic children hear within the normal range, but most respond to sound inconsistently and thus are difficult to test audiometrically. When an aphasic child has a severe hearing loss, the presence of aphasia may not become apparent until he fails to learn when taught as a deaf child.

It should be stressed that each individual aphasic child possesses the characteristics described above in varying degrees and combinations, and these characteristics are frequently complicated or obscured at first by uncooperative behavior. The diagnostic classification of some children, therefore, can be made only after observing their response to teaching.

Assessment of Aphasia

How may a teacher, untrained in clinical procedures, go about assessing a brain-injured child in order to determine his problem and start a remedial program?

Before the teacher attempts an evaluation, he must have a good idea what normal child expectancy is in developmental areas. Before starting the evaluation, the teacher should study all available reports from doctors, clinics, hospitals, or other referring agencies, as well as any psychological or intelligence test results.

THE HISTORY. The first step in the evaluation is the study of the child's history which is primarily a parent's impression of the child. This must include pertinent information on the following (Kostein & Fowler, 1954):

Pregnancy
Delivery   } any deviations
Family

Motor development
    Age when sat up
    Age when walked
    Motor skills

Illnesses
    Surgery
    High temperatures

       Diseases such as meningitis or encephalitis
       Reaction after accidents
       Hospitalization
    Social development
       Toilet training
       Feeding
       Dressing
       Sleeping habits
       Eating habits
       Behavior
    Communication
       Family's impression
       How are wants conveyed?
       Does he use words and sentences meaningfully?
       Does he respond to environmental sounds, to voices?
       Are his responses consistent?
    Education
       Any therapy, group experiences, or schooling?

THE HEARING EVALUATION. It is possible for these children to have a peripheral hearing loss although their problem is usually not in hearing sound but understanding it. Some expressive aphasic children have no auditory problem at all. Formal hearing tests are sometimes unreliable with aphasic children and in some cases it may not be possible to measure their auditory capacity.

It is necessary to test for awareness of sound, of voice, of speech, and then for discrimination of gross sounds, vocalizations, and speech patterns. Tests should also be made for auditory perception and auditory memory (Barry, 1969).

EVALUATION OF LANGUAGE. Language can be divided into three types:

1. Inner, or the language used to communicate with oneself.
2. Receptive, the language used to understand others.
3. Expressive, the language used to make ourselves understood.

Toy objects representing the child's daily experiences are used in language testing. These are preferred to pictures since pictures are in themselves symbols, and also because objects can be moved to show relationships.

EMOTIONAL AND SOCIAL ADJUSTMENT EVALUATION. Observation of the child's emotional and social adjustment behavior during the evaluation and analysis of the history should guide the teacher. Any deviation in behavior should be noted.

MOTOR ABILITIES EVALUATION. Several types of motor skills are tested.

1. Gross Motor Skills. The teacher may check these in a general way by a comparison with the normal child using the New York Development Scale, or by comparing with standards of Gesell (1940) or Myklebust (1954).

2. Fine Motor Skills. These may be checked by observing how the child handles crayon, scissors, buttons and button holes. The character of his grasp should be noted, as well as the time needed to attempt or complete a task.

3. Speech Motor Control. The ability of the child to imitate speech sounds must be checked. Any deviation of speech motor control noted throughout the evaluation should be added to notations made here.

Other Tests of Aphasia

The Language Modalities test for aphasia is the outgrowth of extensive study by Wepman and Jones of the language performance of brain damaged patients (1961). The patient's difficulties in handling free response items are summarized by the examiner. Following the scoring, the examiner arrives at an impression of the classification category best suited for the subject, making use of Wepman's fivefold classifications: syntactic, semantic, pragmatic, jargon, and global aphasia.

The Minnesota Test for Differential Diagnosis of Aphasia developed by Schuell (1965) in a series of research editions provides for exhaustive testing in six major areas of possible disturbance. Using these tests, Schuell has been able to follow the language recovery of large numbers of aphasic patients for substantial periods of time. On the basis of her repeated testing of these patients and her work with them in therapy she has developed a fivefold classification of aphasic disorders which couples observation test results with prognosis for language recovery.

The Porch Index of Communicative Ability (1971) is useful in charting progress in recovery. Table 5–1 (pp. 110–11) presents the test format used by Agronowitz and McKeown (1964, p. 34).

DeRenzi and Vignole (1962) have devised a test for discovering mild receptive aphasia. Preliminary use of this test indicates that it is sensitive enough to reveal auditory-language disturbance which may go unrecognized in patients whose expressive-language skills appear normal.

Other tests that may be used are: Eisenson's Examining for Aphasia (1954), the Halstead-Wepman Screening Test for Aphasia (1949), and the Assessment of Aphasia and Related Disorders by Goodglass and Kaplan (1972).

At the conclusion of the evaluation, the examiner carefully reviews the history, the evaluation results, and her own observations and impressions. From these she plans suitable therapy. It is quite possible that in some cases she may not be able to come to a definite conclusion and so she proceeds with "diagnostic teaching," a combination of continued evaluation and therapy.

A more detailed approach to the examination of aphasic individuals, one that would cover all of the sensory and motor areas related to aphasia, would include the following:

1. A review of available test results and previous educational experience.
2. Ascertaining if the child is right- or left-handed and the occurrence of handedness in the family.
3. Can the child speak spontaneously or reply to questions?
4. Can he repeat letters, words, and sentences?

5. Does the child show that he understands words heard, such as his name, simple or complicated words, or directions?
6. Show an object; can the child pick up a duplicate of the object?
7. Does the child recognize common sounds?
8. Can the child name objects shown?
9. Is the child aware of odors? Can he name them?
10. Can he identify the taste of sugar, lemon, salt, coffee?
11. With his eyes shut, can he recognize and name objects placed in his hand? Can he identify writing on his palm and forehead?
12. Can he read printed letters, short and long words, headings and paragraphs?
13. Can he write spontaneously? Can he copy written or printed words with understanding?
14. What is the quality of his drawings of the Bender-Gestalt figures?
15. Is singing and playing of music understood? Can tone be reproduced correctly?
16. To what extent are gestures used and understood?
17. Can the child perform skilled or semiskilled actions such as lighting a candle, brushing a sleeve, beating time to music, copying a rhythmic pattern or walking with normal gait and coordination?
18. Is his memory of places, location of objects and forms motor (tracing it out with his finger) or visual?

Group the results of the above activities according to (a) receptive disorders, (b) expressive disorders, (c) mixed receptive and expressive disorders, (d) amnesic or anominal disorders, or (e) global disorders that include a disturbance in language function involving all of the above categories.

TABLE 5–1. The Agranowitz-McKeown aphasia test.

	Test Items	Explanatory Notes	Remarks on Performance
VISUAL RECOGNITION AND COMPREHENSION			
1. ALPHABET LETTERS	Does the patient recognize alphabet letters by sight? A M t L v r O (One at a time)	He has indicated recognition if he can read them aloud or point them out as the examiner reads them.	
2. INDIVIDUAL WORDS	Does the patient recognize individual words by sight? CUP SING RED TEACHER MAN APPLE CAT (One at a time)	He has indicated recognition if he can read them, point to them as examiner reads them, match them with objects or pictures, or pantomime their meaning.	
3. SENTENCES	Can the patient read silently and carry out WRITTEN commands? Button your coat. Open your mouth. Give me the pencil.	Caution: Do not give a hint by gesture or demonstration of any kind. He must button his coat. To read the statement is not recognition of its meaning.	
4. NUMBERS	Does the patient recognize numbers? 5 2 7 25	He has demonstrated recognition if he reads them, points to them or holds up appropriate number of fingers.	
AUDITORY RECOGNITION AND COMPREHENSION			
5. COMPREHENSION OF SPOKEN LANGUAGE	Can the patient carry out SPOKEN commands? Hand me the book. Close your eyes.	Do not make any gesture which might give a clue. Patient must not be permitted to read the commands.	

TABLE 5–1. The Agranowitz-McKeown aphasia test. (*Cont.*)

	Test Items	Explanatory Notes	Remarks on Performance
MOTOR FUNCTIONS			
6. PRONUNCIA-TION OF IN-DIVIDUAL WORDS	Can the patient produce words in imitation? AH! MAMA PIPE SEVEN WINDOW MASSACHUSETTS	Let him pronounce each word after the examiner.	
7. PRINTING	Can the patient write or print?	Patient may protest if he has recently become hemiplegic necessitating use of his minor hand; however, with guidance, he probably will comply.	
8. LONGHAND	He is to copy a few words in longhand or in printing.		
LANGUAGE FUNCTIONS			
9. RECALL OF NAMES	Can the patient name items pointed out to him? THUMB PENCIL LAMP PAPERCLIP	Patient must *name* them, not merely point them out as he hears them named.	
10. ORAL LANGUAGE	Appraisal of patient's spontaneous speech. Does he use wrong words, distorted words, block, etc?	Examiner ascertains this from language used in the entire examination or from such a request as: Tell me about your work.	
11. SPELLING	Can the patient spell? CUP HOUSE MONDAY HOME	Patient is to write the words as the examiner pronounces them or shows an object.	
12. WRITTEN SENTENCE FORMATION	Can the patient compose and write a sentence unaided?	Examiner may suggest various *topics* but must not dictate *sentences*.	
ARITHMETIC			
13. BASIC ARITHMETIC	Can the patient do the basic arithmetic processes? 45 25 23 +15 −15 × 7 2) 26	Patient may work these orally or on paper.	

SOURCE: Agranowitz, A., & McKeown, M. R. *Aphasia handbook: For adults and children.* Springfield, Ill.: Charles C Thomas, 1964. pp. 34–35. Originally from Homans, John. *A textbook of surgery* (6th ed.), 1945. Reprinted by permission of the publisher.

Teaching the Aphasic Child

In training children with language disorders, there are three important considerations.

1. The Physical Set-up
2. Corrective Therapy for Psycho-motor Dysfunctions and Disturbed Behavior
3. The Development of Language and Other Skills Involving Language

THE PHYSICAL SET-UP. Because each child is an individual problem in behavior and learning, classes are kept small. The rooms are uncluttered, adequate rather than spacious, and for beginners, free from distractions. The children are seated apart from one another. Easily distracted children should face a wall, backs to all activity. This arrangement eliminates overstimulation and helps the child organize and relate better to his environment. Printing or writing is done in white on a black background.

Provisions must be made for the teacher to work with each child individually at some time during the day. She sits near him so she may frequently establish eye-to-eye contact. Her closeness helps him to pay attention to the training materials which have been placed in his visual field. As the child gradually gains ability and control of himself, the teacher moves further away until he can be left to work independently. She is then free to help another child. In a class where each child's needs are different, where each may be at a different level, this ability to work alone is absolutely essential, and achieving it is one of the teacher's first aims.

CORRECTIVE THERAPY FOR PSYCHO-MOTOR DYSFUNCTIONING AND IMPAIRED PERCEPTIONS. The child may not be able to control his behavior and to integrate his experiences. This problem is often referred to in terms of *distraction, disinhibition,* and *perseveration,* sometimes called the *Strauss Triad* (Strauss & Lehtinen, 1947). This disintegrated behavior must be dealt with before specific language training can be started. Firm, deliberate procedures are helpful in handling these characteristics. Removal from the situation, mild restraint, soothing vocalizations, substituting another activity, knowing the child's tolerance level, and structuring are the most successful approaches.

This therapy includes training impaired body images and training impaired perceptions—visual, tactile, and auditory.

LANGUAGE-TRAINING AND TRAINING IN OTHER SKILLS INVOLVING LANGUAGE. If the child's inner language is impaired, this must be trained first. If the child's inner language is intact but he is impaired receptively, receptive language training must take place. If, however, he has a receptive and expressive impairment, he will need intensive receptive language training followed by expressive language training. The child whose only language disorder is an expressive one is the easiest to handle, as his behavior is usually not so disturbed and as he needs training in expressive language only.

From the child's history and from the evaluation and observations made by the teacher, she can judge at which level of language training to start and how to plan a program for each child. Language training and training in the other areas are usually started at the same time and are coordinated.

Training in the language areas includes: language, reading readiness and reading, writing, and number concepts. Table 5–2 gives a quick reference to the kinds of activities that should be used for various types of disorders.

TECHNIQUES FOR IMPROVING AUDITORY-VERBAL APHASIA. According to Agranowitz and McKeown, (1966, pp. 77–81) the following are good techniques to use in helping an aphasic child with auditory-verbal aphasia.

1. *Using Oral Commands.*   Give the child oral commands to be carried out.
2. *Using Pictures of Single Objects.*   Show a group of pictures of single items. Pronounce aloud the name of each article pictured and ask the child to point to the corresponding picture.
3. *Using a Practical Situation.*   Enter into a make-believe lunch, using questions and commands.
4. *Using Individual Words for Auditory Recognition.*   Write the word list on the board. As the words are pronounced the child points to each (not in order).
5. *Following Silent Reading.*   The child follows silently while the teacher reads orally. The teacher will stop and have the child read the next word.

TABLE 5–2.   Basic reference index for beginning language therapy.

Aphasia Test Item in Table 5–1	Language Function Affected	Typical Behavior from the Defect	Basic Retraining Needed
4, 13	Arithmetic (acalculia)	Patient cannot count or recall numbers; cannot do the four basic processes.	Counting, copying numbers, recognition of numbers; addition, subtraction, multiplication, division.
7, 8	Handwriting (motor agraphia)	Patient has lost the memory patterns for movements of handwriting.	Motor patterns of handwriting.
11, 12	Written Spelling and Sentence Formulation (amnesic agraphia)	Patient cannot spell or formulate sentences in writing.	Written spelling and sentence formulation.
1, 2, 3, 4	Reading (alexia)	Patient cannot recognize letters or words; cannot understand simple or complicated written statements.	Recognition of alphabet letters and words; silent reading for comprehension.
9, 10	Recall of Language (anomia and amnesic aphasia)	Patient cannot recall words and phrases on intent. He is often heard to say, "I know what it is, but I can't tell you."	Associating names with objects, people, and places; formulating language.
5	Auditory Recognition of Spoken Language (auditory-verbal agnosia)	Patient has no hearing loss, but does not recognize or understand spoken language. He often does not detect errors of his own speech; therefore, unknowingly uses the wrong words (paraphasia and jargon).	Auditory training; recognition and comprehension of individual sounds, words and sentences.
6	Ability to Pronounce Sounds and Words (motor aphasia)	Patient cannot recall the placement of the organs of speech (tongue, teeth, lips, etc.) in pronouncing sounds and words. He *knows* the appropriate word but cannot form it.	Practice in making individual sounds and words. Drills before mirror and in imitation of the therapist.

SOURCE: Agranowitz & McKeown, *Aphasia handbook*, p. 36

6. *Using Group Reading.*   Each group member reads aloud. When one stops suddenly, the next one continues.

ACTIVITIES AND MEDIA

What Is It?   The children close their eyes. The teacher makes a familiar sound. The children should not see the object used by the teacher to produce the sound. If they cannot keep their eyes closed, the teacher should go behind a screen.

Possible Sounds

tearing paper
sharpening a pencil
clapping hands
ringing a bell
snapping fingers
snapping the lights on
clicking the tongue
blowing a whistle
jingling money
bouncing a ball
closing a pocketbook

(Van Witsen, 1967, p. 31)

Loud and Soft.   Have objects that are similar in appearance. Example: big bell and little bell; ruler and toothpick; large lid and small lid. Have the child close his eyes. Make a sound with an object. The child will point to the one that made the sound (Van Witsen, 1967, p. 33).

Animal Sounds.   Materials: Tape recording of animal sounds and pictures of the animals. Procedure: Ask the child to listen to the sounds of one of the animals. Show him the matching pictures. Do this several times. Say *dog,* for example, with the sound of his bark, at the same time showing his picture. Introduce other pictures in the same manner. Ask the child to listen to the sound and choose the appropriate picture to match the sound (Agranowitz & McKeown, 1966, p. 271).

Music Sounds.   The same procedure is followed as in *Animal Sounds,* substituting musical instruments for the animals. The best instruments to use are the drum, piano, and xylophone.

The Voice.   (An interpretation of what is said is not important in this exercise; only to recognize that it is a voice.) Someone is to hum a tune, call out "Hello," or speak a phrase. Make a game by asking the child to point to the producer of the sound: the teacher, the child or someone else. When possible, use children's voices and masculine and feminine adult voices with accompanying pictures to aid in distinguishing various voice qualities (Agranowitz & McKeown, 1966, p. 271).

Simple Commands

1. A Game of Simple Directions.
   a. See the ball.
   b. Get the ball.
   c. Bounce the ball.
   d. Throw the ball.
2. Using Body Scheme.
   a. Hold up your hand.
   b. Close your eyes.
   c. Point to your toe.
   d. Open your mouth.
   e. Shake hands.
3. Simple Commands. Show a picture such as a person closing the door. Ask the child to carry out a similar command: "Close the door" (Agranowitz & McKeown, 1966, p. 274).

The following activities are taken from Wallace and Kauffman (1973).

a. Have the child clap for various reasons when he is being read to. For example: "Clap for every person's name." "Clap for every word that rhymes with _____."
b. Have the child match objects that produce particular noises with the actual noise.
c. Read a poem or story to a child with obvious missing words. Have the child supply the missing part.
d. Pass out various objects to each child. Ask the children to stand if they have the object that is described.

Dyslexia

Dyslexia is a medical and educational mystery. Doctors do not know what causes it, few teachers know how to recognize it, and some educators question whether it exists at all. Instead, they put the blame on the way reading is usually taught. It was estimated at a recent conference sponsored by the U.S. Office of Education that there are 3.5 million children who are dyslexic in the United States.

Since many dyslexic children are above average in intelligence, it is not considered a form of retardation. For some reason their brains are simply unable to translate the symbols on paper.

Dyslexia is an impairment of the ability to read or to understand what one reads silently or aloud. The word *dyslexia* has been loosely defined in the literature lately so that it has come to mean "severe reading disability," regardless of cause. The illustrations below are of the reading disability, not necessarily of "technical" dyslexia. Taken to an extreme, these illustrations would imply dyslexia.

Characteristics of Mild Dyslexia

Dyslexia can be manifested in several ways. It can be indicated by the child who uses only one clue from a word to guess what the word is. The child looks at the word *house* and calls it *horse*. It is as if the child were paying attention only to the beginning and the end of the word and ignoring the other letters within the word. The child might have merely looked at the configuration of the word and read *horse* because it has the same shape as *house*. A child with dyslexia may be able to learn words presented one at a time, but he will miss these same words when they are placed in context. It is not unusual to find a child who has been drilled on 14 to 17 words in a first preprimer to the point where he can recognize each word in isolation, failing to recognize these same words when they appear later in the middle of the book.

The child may mispronounce or miscall words because of his improper spatial orientation (left-right in space). He may say *bog* for *dog* or *was* for *saw*. The fact that he cannot tell from the context of what he is reading that the pronunciation is wrong only serves to illustrate the low level of comprehension that the child has. Certainly, no normal reader paying attention to the context of what he is reading and comprehending would substitute *bog* for *dog* in the sentence, "The dog bit the man." It is possible for some children to misread or mispronounce a word and still know what they are reading. We have good evidence that a child's reading input (what he takes into his cerebral area) is adequate and correctly received even if he reads *Bill* for *Bob* in oral reading but shows in a comprehension check that he knows the name as *Bob*. His reading output (what he says) is incorrect but internally he knows the word correctly. We have come to recognize the importance of checking a child both for input and output in the reading process. If a child is handed a list of words and asked "What is this word?" he may miscall many of the words. But if, after the child has read the words, he is asked to pick out from the list certain words which are now presented to him orally, he often shows that he does recognize the words internally even though he miscalls them outwardly when he reads them.

Specific characteristics are as follows:

1. They show no evidence of any significant impairment of vision or hearing, generally no brain damage or primary personality deviations or any history thereof.

2. They show difficulty remembering whole-word patterns and do not learn easily by the sight method.
3. They are poor oral readers and poor spellers.
4. They usually come from families in which there is left-handedness or language disorders or both.
5. In their early attempts at reading and writing, they show marked confusions in remembering the orientation of letters.
6. They show some evidence of delayed development of one-sided motor preference.
7. They often show delays or defects in more than one language area (Money, 1962).

Basic Understanding

Earlier in this chapter mention was made of a medical orientation and an educational orientation to the definitions of severe learning and language disorders. In regard to a study of the causes of dyslexia, the research literature is inconclusive and confusing. It is true that not all brain-injured individuals have dyslexia because it is possible for the brain damage to be in parts of the brain that do not affect the processes involved in reading. There are many persons with cerebral palsy who are very capable readers. It is also true that there are some individuals with no brain dysfunctions at all who are severely disabled readers. There are persons whose reading ability has been adversely affected by factors of an environmental or psychological nature. Then, of course, there are some individuals with cerebral dysfunctions who are also very poor readers. Thus, we have three general groupings of poor readers. There is a growing tendency to group all severely disabled readers as having dyslexia.

Spache (1976) gives an extensive review of the definitions of dyslexia as presented by both educators and medical personnel. A reading of these definitions illustrates how the applications, meanings, and causes of dyslexia have proliferated from the original medical definitions. Interestingly enough the bulk of these definitions was published between 1967 and 1969. For the most part they dealt with descriptions or characteristics of dyslexia. The Geneva Medico-Educational Service (1968) criticized most definitions of dyslexia because they either emphasized heredity alone or merely presented a list of symptoms. This group recognized four types: (a) damage to the central nervous system, (2) disorganization following the disorder of hemispheric function, (c) a constitutional and hereditary disorder, and (d) learning problems due to immaturity. In more recent years several investigators such as Lillywhite, Young and Olmstead (1971), Naidoo (1971), Klasen (1972), and Marshall and Newcombe (1973) have made strong points for considering dyslexia not just as a specific disease entity, but also as a behavioral syndrome, bringing together the medical and educational orientations. Our position is that we still need to have some idea of the cause(s) of a child's dyslexia because it will make a difference in the materials and techniques that should be used to help him. A child with a neurological dysfunction will require considerations that need not be used with a child who has an extrinsic or nonorganic involvement.

An interesting recent research finding concedes it is possible that some dyslexic children may have spatial functioning, which is mostly restricted to the functions of the right hemisphere, present in both hemispheres. According to Witelson of McMaster University (1976), dyslexic children in her study proved to be equally adept at using both the left and the right hemisphere to recognize shapes presented to either hand. Nondyslexics could not do this. She concluded that dyslexic children used both hemispheres to perform spatial tasks and so, in some way, overloaded the left hemisphere and interfered with the linguistic, sequential, analytical processing performed by that hemisphere. As a result, the child took a spatial, holistic, whole word approach to reading and could not do phonetic, sequential decoding required to unlock difficult words. She suggested a reading program balanced between the two approaches if a dyslexic is to learn to read.

Special note should be made of dyslexia that is acquired after a child is born. The reading defect may occur following an injury to the brain caused by an accident or by a postnatal degeneration of brain cells due to an infection or a high fever. This cause of dyslexia is known as *traumatic* or *acquired* dyslexia. Traumatic injuries to an infant's or juvenile's brain do not produce the same functional effect and symptoms as do the same injuries to an older person's brain that has already matured in function. The immature brain has greater plasticity that allows it to compensate for injury, both by using substitutive pathways and by localizing certain minor language functions in the nondominant hemisphere if their normal location in the dominant hemisphere has been damaged. It was once believed that all language functions were contained in the left hemisphere. Now it is recognized that the right hemisphere is also capable of language functions but on a less complex level, somewhat similar to the language capabilities of a typical adolescent, but within the grasp of syntax of a 5-year-old (Zeidel, 1976, 1977). A stroke victim with extensive damage in the left hemisphere may still be able to use some of the simpler language function centered in the right hemisphere.

Types of Dyslexic Readers

According to Jordan (1977), Johnson and Myklebust (1967), and others, dyslexic readers can be classified as having auditory (audile) dyslexia or visual (visile) dyslexia. The most difficult form of dyslexia to correct is auditory dyslexia, which is the inability to perceive the separate (discrete) sounds of spoken language. Auditory dyslexia has little to do with hearing acuity. Most auditory dyslexics have normal hearing, so far as can be determined by audiometer tests. The basic handicap is similar to that of "tone deafness" toward music, or a dormant condition of hearing which is not aware of differences in sounds. Because the dyslexic cannot identify small differences between vowel sounds or consonant sounds, he is unable to associate specific sounds with their printed symbols. Consequently, he is very poor at spelling and composition. Traditional phonics instruction is almost meaningless to most auditory dyslexics. They simply cannot identify the discrete variations of speech sounds or apply the rules and generalizations.

The next most prevalent form of dyslexia is visual dyslexia. This is basically the inability to translate printed language symbols into meaning. Visual dyslexia has little to do with vision itself. It is not a matter of seeing poorly; it is a matter of not interpreting accurately what is seen. Most visual dyslexics see certain letters backward and upside down. To read whole words in the context of a sentence is a jumbled process for such a child. Not only does he perceive individual letters incorrectly, but he also sees parts of words in reverse. When these faults are at work during reading tasks, the child has a disorganized, meaningless, and frustrating experience. Consequently, he does everything in his power to avoid reading.

A study by Mattis, French and Rapin (1975) suggests three groups or types of dyslexics according to their syndromes and their effect on reading disability. One group reflected a language disorder syndrome in which speech-sound sequencing deficits were noted. A second group was labeled as having the articulation and graphomotor dyscoordination syndrome with very poor phonic attack, inability to utter or blend phonemes, and much writing and handwriting difficulty. The third group had a visuo-perceptual disorder, making it difficult to discriminate letters and to store and retrieve visual stimuli. The implication of this study was that it would be difficult to develop a prescriptive teaching program for a given child based primarily on his pattern of reading and spelling errors. The suggestion was to plan for children according to their pattern of deficits in higher cortical functions and to suggest a treatment program specific to the syndrome.

Assessment of Dyslexia

A child is retarded in reading if he is not able to read at the proper level in relation to his age and years of instruction. It is a simple matter to make the differential diagnosis of reading deficits, but no one has yet devised a foolproof way of assessing specific dyslexia.

Reversal and translocation of letters are examples of persistent reading errors not peculiar to dyslexics. These errors are notoriously common among all beginners in reading and writing. Usually, however, they are eliminated after a brief history of only weeks or months. The dyslexic individual is not the only one who makes reversals and translocations, but he is unique in that he makes so many of them for so long a time. His confusion of visual and body images seems to underlie his difficulties of directional orientation. His problem is not a simple one of left-right confusion, nor is it a matter of difficulty with perception of form in two dimensions. It is truly a three dimensional space-movement, perception problem.

Jordan (1977) has devised a very comprehensive informal checklist for identifying symptoms of auditory and visual dyslexia. The complete checklists are in his book *Dyslexia in the Classroom*. The following major headings indicate the nature of his tests. The details under the headings, as given in his book, are most significant.

A. *Auditory Dyslexia Symptoms*

1. Confusion with Phonics
2. Confusion with Words
3. Confusion with Spelling
4. Reinforcement While Writing or Reading (pp. 47–48)

B. *Visual Dyslexia Symptoms*

1. Confusion with Sequence
2. Difficulty Following Directions
3. Faulty Oral Language
4. Faulty Reading Comprehension
5. Slow Work Rate
6. Difficulty with Alphabet
7. Confusion with Symbols
8. Errors in Oral Reading
9. Errors in Spelling
10. Errors in Copying (pp. 29–31)

Our interest is not so much in pegging or labeling a child as it is in identifying the educational and learning needs of the child. That is where remediation should begin.

Remediation of Dyslexia Deficits

Frances K. McGlannan, founder and director of the McGlannan Language Arts School in Coral Gables, Florida, explains "You must first develop the skills that underlie reading"

(1967). However, the child with specific dyslexia cannot trust his visual and auditory senses to record accurately the symbols of the printed page. As a result, in every case, overlearning must take place.

The sense of touch and the muscular involvement of the child help him to "see" and to know the letters and words so necessary to his development. The following activities involving the sense of touch help a child to learn letters and words.

1. The alphabet is simply a series of geometric shapes of varying degrees of complexity. Learning, therefore, starts with simple, easily identified forms. Templates of these geometric figures enable the child to feel, associate, match, and combine the different shapes as he tears, cuts out, colors, and pastes these forms in different combinations. More complex shapes follow.

2. Initial contact with the alphabet comes with cut out letters. The letters themselves can be handled by the child, and the groove in the template is carefully designed to fit the child's finger as he traces. (Maximum impact on the memory is made when the eyes are closed.) At a later date, the letters are used to match symbols on a printed page and are combined to form words.

3. The Alpha-Sound Box contains a drawer for each letter of the alphabet and the four digraphs—*ch*, *sh*, *th*, and *wh*. Each drawer contains familiar, miniature objects whose names contain initial sounds that match the sound of the picture on the front. Identifying the drawer representing a given sound, and associating the sound with the sounds of the objects the drawer contains, hasten recognition and strengthen the memory. The children soon begin to "slide" the sounds together to form words.

4. Letters that are spatially confusing for children with poor up-and-down or left-and-right directional sense—*m*, *w*, *n*, and *u* for instance—are mastered through repeated tracing, coloring, and cutouts. Letters rolled and shaped from clay make visually vivid forms that can be identified easily against other backgrounds.

5. As the child develops, the association of symbol and sound becomes increasingly important and he is less dependent on the sense of touch. Pipe-cleaner letters, pasted on colored cardboard squares, provide a refined approach. They are particularly effective when students trace letters with closed eyes and repeat the sound of the letters at the same time.

6. After the child has begun to read, he is even less dependent upon the supplementary aids to learning, but he continues to form new words with pipe cleaner letters. Daily drills with vowel sounds and word patterns remain necessary and are made more effective through the continued use of the sense of touch.

7. At a later date the child is ready for still further reduction of his dependence on the "feel" of letters, but muscular involvement in learning continues to be important. Cut-out cardboard letters in bright colors form vivid word patterns as they are placed in proper sequence—and prompt corrections can be made when a wrong letter is chosen.

There is obviously no real barrier to teaching a dyslexic child. The basic prerequisite is a teacher with knowledge of the problem and its treatment, patience, and ingenuity in adapting techniques to the individual child. It is important for parents to understand and to be willing to learn with the child. Most important, the problem must be identified early.

The Perceptual Research Center seeks to help dyslexic children learn to read by providing developmental training through various activities. Some specific areas of the Perceptual Educational Research Center (PERC) or Randolph Program are (Small, 1967):

Phonemes are clarified through the use of large lowercase letters cut from wood. A sanded back prevents reversals.

Language is emphasized by coordinating physical action with verbalization wherever possible. The aim is first to improve listening skills, then memory and recall in sequence.

Reading is done in small groups. One group works with sound and symbol relationships while another works at sight words. Others work on comprehension, recall, oral expression, interior letter design, smooth scanning, or oral delivery. Older children help younger, and sometimes vice versa.

Writing involves alphabet drill in lowercase letters. This helps sequence patterning. Cardboard forms and even tracing activities help to untangle shapes.

Brush Drawing is used with music for control and freedom of expression through line and rhythm.

Mathematics involves objects used with corresponding numerals with new math concepts in sensory activities. Writing numerals sequentially is helpful.

Physical Education activities and tests include crawling, right-and-left games, locomotor movements, coordination, obstacle relays, marching and dancing, sequentially developed rhythms, and posture exercises.

Music is a daily activity with singing and games, echo response, and rhythmical patterns.

Social and Emotional Development is phenomenal in activities which involve factors of elasticity, creativity, and self-discipline.

Through this program children who have experienced only failure as a result of previous efforts now have an opportunity to discover the fun of learning and the joy of developing confidence.

Mildred McGinnis (1963), developer of the Association Method for aphasic children, gives some very pertinent suggestions and techniques for working with both aphasic and dyslexic children. McGinnis, as does McGlannan, emphasizes a language development by association approach. The child is asked to write, spell, and trace certain letters and groups of letters until he finally, after much drill, is able to see the small written words correctly. McGinnis associates learning, seeing, sounding, and writing the symbols of the sounds. McGlannan, in addition, provides a concrete object such as a toy tiger to emphasize or associate the letter *t* to the sound made in the word *tiger*. Drill or practice is carried on until there is ease of memory and facilitation of recall. McGinnis suggests the following procedures for teaching:

1. Attention getting exercises.
2. Development of single sounds.
3. Combining sounds into nouns.
4. Associating meaning with nouns.
5. Writing readiness exercises and writing of nouns.
6. Lipreading and acoustic association, first with sound elements and then with nouns.
7. Association of the meaning of commands relating to daily class routine from both oral and written stimulation.

Agraphia and Dysgraphia

Agraphia may result from a loss of memory of the movements used in writing or from a symbolic or formulation loss. Paragraphia results in garbled spelling due to faulty recall. The act of writing is a combination of motor and mental processes so complicated that its loss of it—called *agraphia*—is the most difficult of all the aphasias to analyze.

There are two types of agraphia. The term *apractic* or motor agraphia applies to the person who cannot write because he no longer knows how to form the letters although he may or may not be able to spell orally. Agnostic agraphia is a spelling loss. The child can form letters but does not know what to write. Agraphia individuals who have a primary disturbance in the ability to use tools have an apraxia; one who has a paralysis of the hand and arm previously used for writing has a motor disability. The solution of this may take the form of an immediate change of handedness for writing.

Dysgraphia is the inability to coordinate hand and arm muscles to write legibly. Many bright dyslexic children have been seriously misjudged because their teachers could not read their written responses. The work of extremely dysgraphic children actually resembles "chicken scratches," with few recognizable letter or word forms on the page. Often these disabled students fill page after page with scribbling in order to appear busy. Frequently they can read their own writing, although no one else can. It is difficult for such dyslexics to learn to write legibly, although certain handwriting drills can increase the legibility of their work. Usually such students can learn to type, thus acquiring a substitute script through which they can communicate in printed form.

Symptoms of Dysgraphia

There are three manifestations of writing deficiencies which can be found in the writing of dysgraphics: misphonetic, malphonetic, and nonphonetic.

Misphonetic writing is writing which is phonetically sound but not correct. *Tellafone* is phonetically correct for the word *telephone*, but it is not correct spelling wise. Apparently the child cannot visualize words so he depends upon phonics. As a result his misspellings are usually spelled phonetically. The youngster may write *biznes* when the stimulus word is *business*. Other examples are:

apon	for	upon
awfer	for	offer
littel	for	little

Malphonetic writing is writing which gives indication of some knowledge of phonics but of an inability to apply phonics. *Telabout* might be written for *telephone*. It begins correctly but fails to maintain phonetic synchrony throughout the word. Other examples of malphonetic agraphia are:

stop	for	top
gril	for	girl
accdient	for	accident
big	for	bad
roar	for	road

The writing of the student may be nonphonetic even though the student may possess enough phonic knowledge to prevent such errors. To the stimulus word *book* the child may write *topie*. The child may be able to correctly identify the sounds the symbols *c-a-t* represent, yet write *maux* when asked to write *cat*. The word *telephone* may be spelled *pelmetur* or may be an illegible *denlem* .

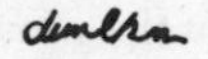

Some authors label the three as *global*, *dyseidetic*, and *combined*. We prefer the terminology *nonphonetic*, *misphonetic*, and *malphonetic* because these terms seem more indicative of the specific disability.

Dysgraphia is an impaired ability to express ideas by means of writing or written symbols, probably due to a neurological defect. It is characterized by the inability to form letters properly, or the inability to combine well-formed letters into meaningful words or symbols. If the impairment is extensive, the handwriting is not much more than an illegible scribble. In less severe cases, several things can occur. The child may have a tendency to telescope or to run letters together in writing a word. It is as though he is paying attention to each letter without paying attention at the same time to what came before or comes after the letter. *Any* may turn out to be *any* with the *a* and *n* formed perfectly but the *n* and *y* telescoped together. Since the second mound of the letter *n* is also the beginning of the letter *y*, the child writes only the part of the *y* which is missing. The word *heavy* may also be written by a primary reader as *hvy*. Telescoping accounts for the fact that many primary disability cases have a discrepancy in favor of oral spelling ability versus written spelling.

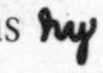

Reversals and rotations are also evident in the writing of primary disability readers. Often *d*'s come out *b*'s and *n*'s come out as *u*'s. It is as if the primary disability case finds the task of letter formation so cumbersome as to preclude any attention to spatial orientation. In other instances, the letters will be deformed or the writing of letters will lack the details which distinguish them from other letters. The *o* may be like an *a* or a *t* which is not crossed. Sometimes the writing appears to be depicting a roller-coaster ride with its up and down curves. In some writing, lowercase letters are larger than uppercase letters. The ascenders, the parts of letters such as *l*, *t*, or *d* which extend above the main body of the word, may be smaller than *a*'s, *c*'s, and other small letters. Illustrations of dysgraphia are given in Figure 5–1.

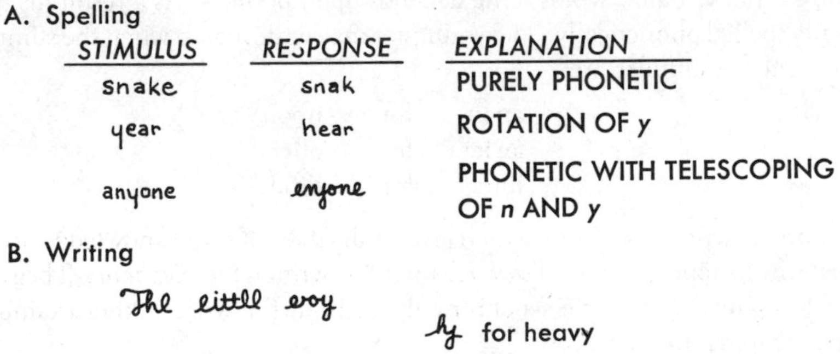

A. Spelling

STIMULUS	RESPONSE	EXPLANATION
snake	snak	PURELY PHONETIC
year	hear	ROTATION OF *y*
anyone	enyone	PHONETIC WITH TELESCOPING OF *n* AND *y*

B. Writing

The little eoy

hy for heavy

FIGURE 5–1. Examples of poor spelling and dysgraphia.

Assessment of Dysgraphia

The Eisensen *Tests for Aphasia* and the Slingerland Tests have sections which claim to test for agraphia and dysgraphia. In both tests objectivity is lacking. If subjectivity is to be used to determine the presence of agraphia, why use subjective measures such as these tests? It is much better to examine the student's writing.

If a spelling test is given during the normal classroom procedure, an analysis of the test can indicate the presence of dysgraphia. Generally, the student spends the largest portion of his spelling-study time on the first word. The next largest amount of time is spent on the second word, and so forth. If a comparison is made between the writing of the first and last word, and if the words look as if they have been written by two different people, the child is probably dysgraphic.

Agraphia is a pathological loss of the ability to write. Whereas the dysgraphic child can write but writes badly, the agraphic child is virtually a nonwriter. Both the dysgraphic and the agraphic child tend to become emotional, or a disciplinary problem when placed in a writing situation. Both laboriously form the letters they are attempting. The dysgraphic student will produce one-half of what his nondysgraphic classmate will write in the same amount of time, and the dysgraphic will use about one-half as many different words. At present, the best indicator of the presence of dysgraphia is if, without any effort, the teacher can recognize that the child's oral production is immeasurably better than his written production.

Remediation of Dysgraphia

We cannot recommend a system, a technique, or a procedure which will eliminate dysgraphia. We can, however, recommend some things which seem to work with some children. Systems which emphasize the tracing technique, such as the Gillingham-Stillman, Fernald, Stanger-Donahue, and others like them, can sometimes help the child develop correct letter formation and the ability to write. Youngsters in first grade and beginning second grade seem to have a 50% success rate in eliminating dysgraphia if they are given the Winter Haven Perceptual Forms program combined with a highly structured phonics program. Beyond second grade we believe the child should be taught to type. Dysgraphics who experience difficulty in letter formation and sentence construction when writing many times have no problem, or have less of a problem, when using a typewriter. One of the authors is dysgraphic and cannot spell or compose with paper and a pencil but has no difficulty when he types. A typing program that has proven effective is: *Typing Keys for Remediation of Reading and Speaking,* by Maelta Davis, published by Academic Therapy, San Rafael, California, 1971.

Filling the Gap

Educators have not always been aware of the child with dysgraphia. Hence, many students in junior and senior high schools are getting low grades and failing tests because, although they know the academic content being tested, they either cannot write or write so slowly as to never finish the test. It is imperative that classroom teachers be made aware of this problem and of their responsibility to test the child in a manner which will give an accurate picture of his knowledge content. Some schools are putting the tests on cassettes and allowing the dysgraphic child to record his answers on a cassette. Some schools have an older student read the test question while another student records the dysgraphic's oral answer.

Acalculia

Acalculia is a disturbance in arithmetic resulting from a loss of the significance of numbers or an inability to perform mathematical functions. Fortunately, much of arithmetic effort is entirely automatic by the time the individual becomes an adult. Because of this, many aphasics can arrive at correct results without being able to name the numbers or tell what they did to arrive at their results.

This disturbance may be present on a twofold basis (1) because of actual difficulty on the part of the individual in dealing with arithmetic processes, or (2) because of related difficulty in oral or written production of the symbols involved in calculation. If the latter is the case, the difficulty is really one of word-finding (anomia) rather than of acalculia.

Frequently we will find that an aphasic person may do well in simple arithmetic computation, especially if he is permitted to write his answers. This apparently well-retained ability can probably be explained by the fact that most of us learn to do simple arithmetic automatically. The tables become so automatic for most adults that most of our computations are carried on without the need for quantitative conceptualization or reasoning. Despite this general finding, it is not too rare to come across an aphasic who cannot perform simple arithmetic operations accurately but who can do fairly well in numerical problem-solving situations.

Dyscalculia is an impaired ability to do calculations or to work with numbers. Dyscalculia manifests itself especially by causing difficulty in working with multi-digit numbers or with more than one column of numbers. It may also cause an inability to comprehend the value of numbers. The child may be able to recognize the number symbols as objects but is unable to shift from the concrete symbol to an abstract level of sophistication which shows greater understanding. He may be able to recognize the figure 7 as a symbol and to call it by name but he may not be able to think of it as the symbolic representation of seven items, or 6 items plus 1, or 5 and 2. He may be able to apply the skills which he has learned by rote memory, but his achievement level in arithmetic will suffer because he has no number concepts.

Since he also has difficulty with directional orientation (left-right), he begins to falter when he is faced with multi-digits and the basic operations of arithmetic. In addition and subtraction we begin to work at the right and move to the left. In division, we begin at the left and move to the right. In long division, this entails an altering of directionality: first left to right, then right to left for the subtraction, and so forth to the completion of the problem. The child with directional disorientation becomes confused as to where to begin (left or right) and in which direction he should work.

Agnosia

Agnosia is an inability to interpret sensory impressions because of imperfect perceiving. Specifically, agnosia is the loss of ability to recognize and identify familiar objects through a particular sense. Nielsen (1965) describes different types of agnosia in the fields of vision, hearing, and tactile appreciation. Visual agnosia refers to the inability of the visual field to recognize some written or printed words, musical symbols, and sometimes figures. In object and picture agnosia (ideational agnosia) there is an inability to identify and recognize intellectually certain objects though the person may be able to visually identify verbal and musical symbols. Auditory agnosia always has symbolic involvement but it is possible to maintain understanding of some sound effects even though the understanding of other sounds is impaired. *Word deafness* for certain words or sounds may be present. Tactile has to do with touch. Tactile agnosia would involve an ability to be able to tell where one is being touched or what one is touching. If there is a loss or defective appreciation of parts of one's own body, this is autotopagnosia and implies a poor body image.

Of course not all of the types of agnosia will be found in all primary disability readers. In fact, agnosia appears to be one of the first symptoms which can be overcome or bypassed by the child. For example, finger agnosia (not knowing which finger is which when the defective recognition finger or fingers have to be identified by name, number, or touch) is common in very young children. However, finger agnosia is usually overcome by the age of 7 in most cases. The agnosia of the impaired sense of body image, however, persists on into later life.

Agnosias are significant, because when they exist, they are primary disturbances which impair symbolic evaluation. If agnosia exists, the person must be trained to overcome this difficulty in order to be able to understand language symbols.

In evaluating visual agnosia, a distinction must be made between optical disturbance and visual agnosia. An optical disturbance concerns eyesight or visual perception without any attempt to interpret what is seen. Often the services of an ophthalmologist are needed for refractions, prescriptions for glasses, or other recommendations.

Since an agnosia is a loss of recognition by one sense organ only, substitute senses must be used for identification purposes. By running the hand around the form of a cup, by tracing with the fingers the outline of a picture of a house, or by handling utensils, tools, and small objects, the patient aids visual recognition by using the tactile sense. To test for visual agnosia, check to see if the child can identify objects by using various senses.

Apraxia

Apraxia indicates the loss of the ability to perform purposeful movements in the absence of paralysis or sensory disturbance; it is caused by lesions in the cerebral cortex.

A patient may have difficulty producing words because of faulty motor control of the articulators or because he has somehow forgotten the patterns of movement necessary to produce words. A differentiation must be made if possible between dysarthria and apraxia. Although some authors include dysarthria as apraxia, a distinction will be made between them here. The term *dysarthria* will refer to impairments of motor control due to faulty innervation of speech musculatures or imperfect coordination of the musculatures in complex acts. The term *apraxia* will refer to difficulties in voluntary control of the musculators in the absence of paresis or incoordination. *Verbal apraxia* would refer to a specific difficulty in performing the oral acts involved in articulating speech sounds and ordering them sequentially into words. This may occur although the patient's understanding of speech is adequate and he responds meaningfully in writing.

chapter 6

Informal Assessment

More and more educators are recognizing it is the teacher's responsibility to assess the learning abilities and achievement levels of the children in her classroom. To some teachers, this statement will come as no surprise because they have known and followed that principle for years. Other teachers may be shocked, or at least startled, to be told that they should and must assess their children. "That's the job of the psychologist (or of the counselor)" will be the protesting response.

At any rate, the belief that specialists should be doing the testing is faulty and inappropriate reasoning on several points. The truth is that in most places there are not enough properly trained individuals to do all of the testing that teachers want done. A second factor is that psychologists or counselors usually approach a referral from a point of view different from that of the teacher. The psychologist or counselor usually tries to find out what is wrong with the child in order to determine why he cannot learn. The teacher does not generally want to know what is wrong; she wants to know what to do to help the child learn. Frequently, a teacher will refer a child who is failing because he can't read and she will get a report back stating, in effect, that the child is not learning because he is a poor reader. The teacher cries out in anguish "I know he can't read. That's why I sent him to you. Tell me what to do about it!" From our perspective, this type of a request is an inappropriate use of the psychologist. The job of the psychologist is to test and diagnose.

Many, if not most, school psychologists are not thoroughly grounded in all school subjects on all grade levels. They are not knowledgeable about specific techniques and materials for specific learning needs. Their training centered on children and how to evaluate and diagnose their learning capacities and styles. They can tell you what is wrong and possibly why it is wrong but not necessarily specifically how to remediate the problem. They can generalize a remediation approach. Frankly, the teacher must learn how to teach all types of children assigned to her. It is her job to know techniques and materials, what to do about a child who cannot learn phonics, and how to find out for herself, in keeping with her limitations as a classroom professional, what is wrong with a child's efforts to learn. She is the one who knows the child best, how he acts under different conditions, and what he can or cannot do. She can make better conclusions about the child's ability and needs if she knows what to look for. Moreover, she can assess the child in reading situations as they are

126

encountered in the classroom, whereas the psychologist may have to do his testing in some closet or boiler room! Our intent is to convey the message that teachers can and must learn to identify most of their children's learning problems; they must have more confidence in their own abilities. They can learn what to do. There are tools, procedures, and techniques that are very helpful to teachers in assessing learning problems. They must also, however, learn to identify the types of problems that do require referrals to specialists—and there are such problems—as well as to identify which problems they should be able to assess and remediate in the classroom.

Basic Understandings

What is meant by informal assessment? First of all, assessment means to appraise, to analyze, or to determine the quality, the value, or the nature of a child's performance in order to determine how effectively he is learning. In this case, we are basically concerned with how well the child is learning to read, what skills he possesses, where his weaknesses are, how well he has achieved in learning relevant skills. The word *assessment* is used to imply the same thing as the word *diagnosis*. But, for various reasons, educators avoid the term *diagnosis* because of its medical connotation. It's no big deal; just a case of "render unto medicine that which is medicine's and unto education that which is education's." The deeper implication is that medical practitioners have been making a good point about parents and teachers recognizing what a physician can or cannot do. For example, look at the case of the parent who takes her child to a pediatrician because the child has a perceptual problem and cannot learn. The medical professional's reply is the same as that given by a pediatric neurologist to one of the authors regarding state regulations that insist that all learning disabled children be examined by a neurologist: "Teaching and learning are pedagogical problems, not medical problems."

Assessment is a term used by educators to imply the determination of the current status and nature of a child's achievement in learning subject matter, cognitive skills, and/or behavioral skills. The term *evaluation* is used in determining how well a child is doing after being subjected to a particular teaching program or plan. In other words, an evaluation comes after the initial assessment of needs and after the child has been exposed to a program of instruction. Finally, the term *informal assessment* means that subjective techniques such as observations, checklists, error analysis of the child's written, oral or behavioral responses, and similar teacher judgment procedures are used as opposed to standardized tests with established norms. The teacher is supposed to know what to look for. She is with the child for long periods of time and has more opportunities to observe his strengths and weaknesses, what skills he knows or does not know, and what helps him learn most efficiently. Informal assessment, in the hands of a sensitive, aware, knowledgeable teacher, is more important and significant than any 10 psychological reports. That statement may be a slight exaggeration, but it does convey a thought that has much truth in it.

Factors Affecting Reading Ability

Generally five categories are given as causes of reading disability: mental factors, physiological factors, psychological factors, environmental factors, and educational factors.*

---

* For an indepth study of the research related to these factors, consult Bond and Tinker, *Reading difficulties: Their diagnosis and corrections*, 3rd ed., Appleton Century Crofts, 1973, chapters 5 and 6.

MENTAL FACTORS

Each child has in reality two ages: a chronological age, which refers to the number of years and months he has lived, and a mental age, which refers to his level of mental development. Although most schools in the United States set a minimum entrance age, which is a chronological age, it is generally conceded that there is little correlation between chronological age and reading success. Educators are more and more emphasizing the use of mental age for school entrance purposes since a number of studies have shown a correlation between mental age and reading potential. Kirk (1940) used mental age to predict the probable maximum reading potential of different I.Q. groups. Kirk even developed a beginning reading age chart for the different I.Q. groups, as noted in Table 6–1.

PHYSIOLOGICAL FACTORS

Sex. Studies made in clinics invariably show a greater percentage of boys than girls classed as remedial readers. Some have postulated the theory that since reading is a passive subject, it has more affinity to girls whose early training is geared toward passive play, i.e., dolls, house, cooking, whereas passive reading is diametrically opposed to the hyperactive type of early training of boys, i.e., wrestling and tree climbing. Sex differences are greater in first grade, in favor of girls, than they are in third grade (Stouffer, 1968).

Visual Factors. Although the results concerning the importance of vision as a cause of reading disability are negligible, it is generally accepted by educators that since the eye is the sensory organ through which printed symbols are relayed to the brain for storage and interpretation, each child's visual mechanism should be functioning as effectively as possible. The child should have the visual acuity necessary for distant vision so that he may be able to take in printed materials presented at far point, such as on the chalkboard. Since book reading is done at near point, the child's near point acuity must also be functioning effectively. Many learning disability cases lack good near point acuity; most of them are farsighted. In addition, the child's vision should be free of defects in the mechanism which coordinates the two eyes in binocular vision so that he can maintain a single clear image with a minimum of nervous tension. Khoudadoust (1967) of Johns Hopkins Hospital examined 1,000 newborn children in the first 24 hours of life after normal deliveries and found that 20% of the infants showed evidence of retinal pathology characterized by hemorrhage.

In addition to the mechanical aspects of vision, certain visual perceptual abilities must be present: the ability to draw generalizations concerning likenesses and differences of forms, the ability to minimize the importance of size, the ability to distinguish figure from background.

Kirschner's (1960) theory of Dynamic Prehensile Vision which likens the eye to a hand reaching out to select specific portions of the environment ties in with the reading situation. The eye must select the line to be read or the word to be learned from the total visual environment.

Hearing. As with vision, auditory skills can be divided into two categories—the mechanics of hearing and auditory discrimination. It is generally accepted that auditory problems can be contributing causes to reading disability. The order of vocabulary development is from understanding vocabulary (hearing) to speaking vocabulary to reading vocabulary. If the understanding vocabulary which depends so much on hearing is hampered, then speaking and ultimately reading vocabulary will be affected.

In addition, a child must develop the skill to make fine discriminations between sounds which are almost similar. The *p* and *b* are sounds of language which must be discriminated

TABLE 6–1. Expected levels in reading according to mental age.

I.Q.	Classification	Age of Beginning Reading	Minimum and Maximum Reading Achievement to Expect at Completion of Schooling
Below 50	Mentally defective	14–16	Will learn only a few words. Reading instruction futile for school purposes.
50–59	Mentally handicapped	10–12	First to third grade
60–69	Mentally handicapped	9–10	Second to fourth grade
70–79	Borderline defective	8–9	Third to seventh grade
80–89	Dull normal	7–8	Fourth to eighth grade (some go through H.S.)
90–109	Normal or average	6–7	
110–119	Bright normal		
120–139	Superior	do not begin reading too early because of vision	
140–and up	Very superior		

Notes:

1. A child's background (home, family, and environment) is very important in determining the extent to which a child will read and how soon he will read.
2. For I.Q.'s of 70–79, many will read up to 7th grade level in textbooks, but on reading tests will score only on a 4th grade level.
3. Most newspapers are on a 5th to 7th grade level. Magazines vary from 5th grade to 9th grade level.

Adapted from Kirk, S.A. *Teaching reading to slow-learning children.* Boston: Houghton Mifflin, 1940.

properly if the child is to respond in a desired manner to the sentence "Pat the little dog." Part of reading is knowing the sounds signaled by language symbols. A child who has not learned this skill cannot attach sounds to printed symbols.

Neural Transmission. A number of researchers have worked in the area of the central nervous system (CNS) and postulated inadequate neural transmission as a possible cause of reading disability. Walton (1957), using the ophthalmograph, measured the speed of synaptic transmission in the visual system. Smith and Carrigan (1960) tried altering synaptic transmission speed through drugs. Kolson, Odom, and Bushong (1964) demonstrated the same through the use of a supplementary diet.

Motor Coordination. Studies have attempted to correlate poor motor coordination with reading disability. Kephart's book *The Slow Learner in the Classroom* (1971) gives many suggestions for developing the necessary motor skills. Kirschner (1960) seems to feel motor coordination should be checked and developed before actual remedial training is started. Brenner and Gillman (1968) found that pupils with good verbal ability but with very poor visuomotor performance were likely to be severely handicapped in reading whether age 10 or age 17.

PSYCHOLOGICAL FACTORS

As pointed out, most children with reading disability manifest signs of psychological problems, although we feel that many psychological problems are contributory causes rather than initiating causes. Much research has been done on the psychological problems of the reading disabled child. High correlations have been found between reading disability and delinquency, sibling position and sibling rivalry, masculine mother versus feminine mother, home pressures and high levels of aspiration. Competent psychological evaluation of disabled readers is a must. A major aspect to be determined is the child's self-concept— how he feels about himself and his ability to read.

EDUCATIONAL FACTORS

The quality and continuity of the educational program may contribute to a child's reading disability. A school which treats all children as if they were visual learners may contribute to a child's disability. Improperly trained teachers can keep the child from reaching his potential. "Panacea Cure" lay pressure groups have in some cases forced schools to use a one method approach which invariably produces reading disabled children. In addition, infrequent attendance or long periods of absence on the part of the child can leave gaps in his grasp of the mechanics of reading thereby seriously disabling him.

ENVIRONMENTAL FACTORS

Labov's classic study of ghetto children leaves no doubt about the contribution of environment to reading disability (Labov & Robins, 1967). If children fail to hear the same sounds as the teacher, rapport and communication can break down with resultant reading disability. A home where books are conspicuously absent is certainly not conducive to the development of interest in reading. Project Head Start has shown that a child who has not been read to or who has not been allowed to express himself has many problems to overcome before he even enters school.

Factors Related to Success

Attempts have been made to classify conditions which artificially disrupt the reading and learning processes. The approach is usually to seek to specify factors or conditions which are responsible for learning problems. In one way or another the list becomes inadequate because it is quite impossible to mention all of the causes or sources of difficulties. The better lists are considered so because they include more of the problems which most children have.

We would like to present a guide for the general evaluation of children who have reading and learning disabilities in any of the skills. The approach taken is one which considers the conditions which must be fulfilled before a person can achieve or attain success in any endeavor. The abbreviated guide presented here takes a psycho-philosophical approach, and must be considered as such. It does, however, give a direction for considering the various elements necessary for success in learning.

MOTIVATION. Motivation and the proper attitude on the part of the learner are necessary for the attainment of success. Teachers are acquainted with pupils who do not care to learn, who see no purpose in learning, or who think they cannot learn and so inhibit their learning capacity. How to motivate pupils has often been cited as one of the major problems of teachers. The teacher provides the climate and material for learning in such a way that the child hopefully will want to learn, but it is just as significant to be aware of other attitudinal conditions which can also affect learning. A lack of proper attitudes and motivation is found to a larger extent among older pupils than among children in the first four grades.

SKILLS. A requirement for success is the possession of the necessary background and/or readiness to accomplish a task or for learning new material and skills. Each task requires that a person possess certain knowledge and skills before success can be attained. The implication is that the teacher must see to it that a child learns or has the necessary background before embarking on a new task. The academic and physical conditions required for learning must be fulfilled.

CAPACITY. Certainly a person must have the physical and mental capacity required for success. Teachers have been conscious of the importance of an adequate mental ability, but there is some question as to whether or not they have used this knowledge intelligently in their teaching. We all recognize the mentally retarded child who is special education material and the child who is intellectually gifted, but we tend to group the rest of the children into one large category without any consideration of the *real* existence of significant individual differences. It is surprising the number of reading teachers who make little or no effort to determine a child's learning expectancy level or mental age and to compare his academic or reading achievement to this level. Particular tasks require a particular level of mental ability or physical potential before success can be attained.

VOLITION. A fourth condition which must be met before success will take place is that the pupil must make an effort to learn and must devote sufficient time to the learning task. Often we are too quick to designate this condition as the area of failure. We are prone to think that "If he really wants to learn, he can—all he has to do is study harder," or "If he would only try." This cliche is the answer many teachers give for learning difficulties. Nevertheless, it is true that a person must devote the time and effort needed to practice or study if he wishes to succeed.

OPPORTUNITY TO LEARN. The last condition which must be fulfilled in order to have success is to have the opportunity to learn. Not all of the children who are in school may have a chance to learn. They may be denied this opportunity by an inept teacher, a weak curriculum or course of study, the use of improper or inadequate teaching techniques, the absence of the right learning materials, a poor climate for learning in the classroom or at home, or some other similar factor.

Regardless of the task, these five requirements must be met before success can be attained: (1) the presence of motivation and good attitudes, (2) the attainment of the necessary knowledge, skills, and readiness, (3) the appropriate mental and/or physical capacity, (4) sufficient time and effort, and (5) the opportunity to learn. Reading and learning disability will have one or more deficiencies in some aspect of these five conditions.

What to Assess?

Children with learning disabilities usually have more than one anomaly present. In H. M. Robinson's (1953) classic studies she indicates that many factors were causing difficulty, and she promulgated the Multiple-Causation Theory. This theory states that a constellation of factors causes a learning disorder.

Because Robinson examined children who were remedial readers of long standing, she saw children who had time to develop many of the side effects associated with remedial readers. Most children with learning disorders have a psychological problem as well. The unsolved question is did the psychological problem cause the reading difficulty or did the reading difficulty cause the psychological problem. One could speculate that a child with a reading problem would develop psychological problems which would intensify his reading problem and in turn magnify the psychological problem and so on and on. Since it is virtually impossible to determine which came first, multiple-causation is suggested as the problem.

We propose to call those causes initiating the disability *initiating causes,* and the side-effects developed therefrom and intensifying the disability we propose to call *contributory causes.*

The five general questions which must be answered in order to provide the data needed to program for proper remediation are:

1. Does this child have the mental ability to be more successful?
2. What are his reading strengths and weaknesses and how strong or weak are they?
3. What is/are the probable cause/causes of his reading disability?
4. If the child is a Primary Learning Disability case, what is his disorder pattern; what learning deficiencies are there?
5. What is his learning pattern and what sensory modalities can he best use to learn?

A general classification of areas to be assessed would include:

1. Mental ability level.
2. General achievement levels in word recognition, vocabulary, and comprehension, and in some cases, grade levels in arithmetic, spelling, and writing ability.
3. Specific assessment of reading skills to determine strengths and weaknesses—avoid generalizations (needs phonics); be specific (doesn't know *k* sound).
4. Analysis of reading/learning deficits or disorders, according to primary or secondary factors involved in the components of the reading/learning process, the determinants of the pattern for learning, and/or the various elements which contribute to success in achievement in reading.

Approach all observations and results in a sensitive, qualitative, analytic manner. The scores resulting from the tests will be meaningful only if interpreted in terms of the total picture and tempered by professional judgment.

Process of Assessment

The process of assessment should proceed from (1) preliminary diagnosis in which mental ability level and achievement in reading and related subject matter areas is evaluated, to (2) a differential diagnosis in which it is determined whether or not the child has a perceptual or learning deficit or just an educational deficiency, to (3) a therapeutic diagnosis when the exact nature of the reading disability, in terms of skills, is evaluated. An etiological diagnosis, one which seeks to determine the "cause" of the disability, is not needed in the case of a secondary reading disability. In case of a primary learning disability, an etiological diagnosis would only be helpful in evaluating extreme reading disability cases.

More specifically, Jennie DeGenaro (1975) suggests that the teacher consider assessing the following areas for younger children:

1. Visual discrimination and memory for letters, digits, and pictures by teacher-made materials or the Detroit Test of Learning Aptitude.
2. Auditory discrimination and memory for words and digits by use of teacher-made materials or the Wepman Auditory Discrimination and Auditory Memory Tests.
3. Letter identification by naming letters from a mimeographed sheet.
4. Writing the alphabet sequence.
5. Assessing phonetic knowledge by asking children to write the beginning sounds of words.
6. Determine tactual ability by having the child use only his sense of touch to identify geometric shapes and objects.
7. Determine if the child makes reversals or rotations of letters or words in reading or writing.
8. Check verbal skills by handing the child an object and having him describe it.
9. Copying short sentences from the board to assess far point vision and motor ability and from a sheet of paper to assess near point vision and motor ability.
10. Use of informal reading inventory or cloze technique to determine reading level.
11. Appraise child's self-concept by having him react to a set of faces rated from the saddest to the happiest face by responding to questions on "This is how I feel about. . . ."
12. Eye-hand coordination and written language can be assessed by having the child draw a picture, followed by writing a story about it.
13. Determine how many directions a child can remember and follow. Directionality insights can be revealed by having the child do such things as "Write your name on the left side of your paper," and "Draw a circle at the bottom of the paper."
14. Gross-motor development can be assessed by having the child hop on one foot, skip across the room, throw and catch a ball.

Naomi Zigmond, University of Pittsburgh, in the Written Language Sample Test she is developing, suggests that in assessing a written sample one should look for error patterns in the following categories: (1) what the child says and how he says it (in written language); (2) auditory analysis of sound and symbol relationships; (3) eye-hand coordination to determine if formulation aphasia is present; (4) visual processes in remembering and copying words; and (5) grammatical correctness. Her approach shows much promise.

Principles of Assessment

A teacher may conduct an assessment of a child's achievement level for several reasons. First, it may be the beginning of a school year (or in the case of a remedial reading teacher, a resource room teacher, or a tutor, a time when the child is first encountered) and the teacher wants to know what skills the child possesses so she will have some idea where to begin teaching. Second, during the year the teacher may observe that nothing is happening; the child is on a learning plateau and no progress is being made. She may want to do an assessment to determine who and what is bogging the child down in his efforts to learn. Third, the teacher may become aware that the child is actually regressing or deteriorating in learning progress. An assessment is needed to determine what is wrong, what areas have weakened and need to be overlearned, and whether something else besides a knowledge of reading skills might be responsible for the lack of progress.

There are several principles that need to be kept in mind when doing an assessment. The following are important to obtaining reliable findings:

1. Establish rapport with the child. For the child to respond best, he must be able to relate and talk to the teacher without fear or concern.
2. The purpose of assessment is a pragmatic one with the ultimate goal of finding out what the child needs to be helped. Work toward the end of developing a teaching plan, not merely for the accumulation of observations and results; certainly, do not assess for the purpose of labeling a child.
3. Recognize that a child may perform differently in a group than he does in a one-to-one situation. Assess in both types of situations and note what differences occur; then determine what makes the difference.
4. Be aware of all areas affecting learning. Check as many aspects as you can of the total developing child. It may be that his reading problems are a result of poor peer relationships on the playground, or of a deficiency in body metabolism or sugar level. The point is that the child's total life situation is involved in his having the freedom to learn to read.
5. Assessment should be combined with evaluation in an ongoing, continuum process of keeping track of how well the child is doing. If there is no progress, either the assessment was wrong or the teaching method is not working effectively.
6. Look for patterns of errors or deficiencies. Detection of a single weakness may be significant but it is more likely that the problem is more complex and interrelated with other learning factors. Do not be mislead by splinter or isolated defects.
7. In your analysis be specific as to the need. Do not say that the child is "weak in phonics." Determine what sounds he does not know, what sounds he cannot hear, or the specific subskill that is lacking.
8. Look for weaknesses, but also look for strengths. In the final analysis, you will be teaching 80% to the child's strengths, while teaching 20% of the time to overcoming weaknesses.
9. Use a variety of assessment measures. Since a child can use a variety of learning modalities in various teaching situations, it is important to expose the child to different types of approaches in order to determine if some work better than others.
10. Remember, it is much better and more important to teach, teach, teach than to be obsessed by the inclination to test, test, test.

Determining Unreadiness for Reading

The kindergarten teacher's responsibility is to determine which children are ready for instruction and which are not. Then she must determine the kinds of experience each child who is not ready will need in order to bring him to that level of developmental maturity which we call reading readiness. The evaluation of each child is accomplished by the use of various screening processes, intelligence tests, readiness tests, and teachers' judgment. Please refer to Chapter 9 for more complete information on assessment of reading readiness.

Vision Screening

It would be ideal if each child could have a thorough visual examination prior to his entry to school. However, unless some glaring condition of vision exists, few parents bother taking their children to an eye specialist for a visual examination. Hence, most schools have to provide some kind of visual screening.

The oldest and probably most widely used visual screening device is the Snellen Chart. The Snellen Chart examination is usually administered by the school nurse. Children failing the examination are referred to a vision specialist for a thorough examination. Dissatisfaction with the Snellen Chart has been expressed because it is designed primarily for far point vision which is vision of objects which are more than fourteen inches from the eyes. This dissatisfaction has led to the inclusion of other informal vision tests in the screening process.

One of these informal vision tests is the Cover Test. This test shows whether the alignment of the two eyes is maintained when one eye is covered and therefore relaxed. A small card is held in front of one of the child's eyes while he focuses with the other eye on a small light. The examiner notes whether or not the child maintains alignment with the covered eye. The test is then repeated for the other eye. The presence of any shift of alignment of the eye when focused for far point vision or an abnormally large shift when the eye is focused at near point vision suggests the child should be referred for a thorough visual examination by a competent eye specialist.

Another informal test is the Push-up Test. The child is asked to fixate on a pencil with a thumbtack attached to the eraser. The pencil is positioned 20 inches from his nose, then moved toward his nose. Within 6 inches from the nose, one eye will "kick off" or swing out (usually the nonleading eye). If the eyes break sooner or hold closer than 4 inches from the nose, the child should have the services of a vision specialist.

The Skeffington String Test is another informal test sometimes used. A piece of string 14 inches long is held on the bridge of the nose and extending out. It is held parallel to the eyes and even with the center line of the nose. The child is asked:

Question	*Correct Answer*
1. How many strings do you see?	2
2. They start out here (indicate far end of string). Where do they go?	To center of each eye

Any other response indicates possibility of visual problems.

Many schools are using the *Keystone Visual Survey Test* as a vision screening procedure. This consists of a stereoscopic type of instrument with controlled lighting. The child is tested by a set of cards which test for near point visual acuity, far point visual acuity, fusion, vertical and horizontal imbalance, stereopsis, and color. Some vision experts have been critical of the use of the telebinocular as a screening device since they claim that the results of telebinocular tests refer too many children for further eye examinations when none are needed.

In an attempt to define the areas of reliability, validity, and adequacy in visual screening and thus eliminate unnecessary referrals, the classic Orinda Study stands as a monument to comprehensiveness and cooperation (Henrick et al., 1959). Eleven hundred practicing optometrists and ophthalmologists were sent a questionnaire pertaining to all of the various aspects of vision. From the responses, a comprehensive set of criteria was formulated on the basis of what practicing vision specialists thought the cut-off points for visual anomalies and for visual functions should be. The criteria specified clinically acceptable cut-off points for visual acuity, myopia, hyperopia, astigmatism, problems of coordination, and organic problems such as medical anomalies, pathological conditions, and structural defects.

Once the criteria was established, in the Orinda study, school children were screened with each of the following vision screening techniques: the Snellen Chart, the California state recommended procedures, the Keystone Visual Survey, Telebinocular, and the Massachusetts Vision Tests. These screenings were followed by another screening given by vision specialists using a process which is now called the Modified Clinical Technique. Each child was further given a thorough visual examination at the University of California School of Optometry or at the Stanford University Department of Ophthalmology.

The findings showed the Modified Clinical Technique to be about 95% efficient. This means that this technique detected 95 out of 100 children who needed eye care. It also missed two or three children who needed care, and it referred two or three who did not need care. No other screening procedure came near the efficiency of the Modified Clinical Technique.

As a result of the findings of the Orinda study, pressure is mounting to have the Modified Clinical Technique incorporated into the school screening program. A major obstacle for the widespread use of this technique is the need for a vision specialist to administer the screening. This could be costly. However, the process takes only about five minutes per child and it only needs to be administered to a child twice during his elementary school years. Proponents point out that it would be no more time consuming nor costly than the use of inadequate screening procedures which are administered yearly.

Hearing Screening

As with vision, the examination of hearing is a health service. The schools are often forced to offer this service since few parents take their children to doctors to have complete physical examinations prior to beginning school. Nevertheless, the school can profit in its work with the child if it has some of this information. The schools usually employ an audiometer as the screening device. This device, called a pure-tone audiometer, makes use of different frequencies of sounds presented at different intensity levels. The child listens to the sounds through earphones. If a group is tested at one time, a record is played as each child listens through earphones to a voice and writes down the numbers which are spoken at different frequency and intensity levels. The audiometrist, or the school nurse, plots an audiogram of the hearing level of each child and interprets it to determine if professional help is needed for the child. Other hearing screening tests occasionally used are the watch "tick" test and the whisper test. More recently "speech threshold" tests have been found to be more meaningful than pure-tone audiometer tests in detecting hearing losses related to reading. We prefer speech threshold tests to all other types because spoken words are used. The loudness of the words is decreased gradually. The words missed first indicate the type of hearing loss, if any, that the individual has.

Readiness for Schooling

A psychologist once said "Teachers will give a battery of tests to determine if a child has six toes and all they really have to do is take off his shoe to see." What he was trying to emphasize was the need for the teacher to rely on her extensive training and experience to help her make judgments. The old concept of the test being more scientific and accurate than the teacher's judgment is slowly being replaced by the attitude that the test should be considered as just one more tool for the teacher to use to supplement her professional judgment. This by no means implies that standardized tests should be discarded. It means, rather, that these tests should be used wisely.

The good remedial teacher seeks to evaluate her child to determine if a sufficient level of development has been reached in routine readiness, conceptual readiness, verbal readiness, perceptual readiness, and motor readiness. Many teachers employ a Readiness Evaluating Scale such as the one in Figure 6–1. After using formal tests, informal teacher-made tests, and observations, the teacher fills in a profile for each child in her group. From this evaluation she determines which children are average and above average and begins formal

Readiness Evaluating Scale

Pupil's name _____   Score _____

Characteristic	low −1	average 0	high +1

Routine Readiness

Takes care of personal needs _____
Adjusts to school routine _____
Follows directions _____

Perceptual Readiness

Adequate sensory input mechanism _____
Can visually discriminate letters _____
Can auditorially discriminate sounds _____
Can distinguish foreground from background _____

Verbal Readiness

Has a speaking vocabulary sufficient to make the printed vocabulary he
will encounter meaningful _____
Has an interest in symbols _____
Likes to listen to stories _____
Can relate several things in sequence _____
Likes to look at picture books _____

Conceptual Readiness

Has had the kind of experiences which will make printed matter meaningful _____
Has acquired generalizations _____

Motor Readiness

Has good hand-eye coordination _____
Can stay within lines when coloring _____
_____
Algebraic total _____

FIGURE 6–1. A minus score indicates an unreadiness for reading. A zero score or plus score indicates the child is ready for reading.

reading instruction with them. Those children who score in the "low" column must be given exercises and experiences to overcome their deficiency.

Learning Expectancy Level (LEL)

In order to determine if a particular student is a disabled reader or not, one must have an idea of that child's mental potential for learning to read. In informal diagnosis, this must be the first step. Cleland (1964) has summarized some of the formulae and statements made concerning a child's potential for learning which could be compared to the pupil's performance in reading.

He quotes Harris, Broom, and Strong as all saying that "reading potential can be assessed from measures of intelligence." The Durrell-Sullivan reading capacity test gives a score which Cleland has concluded tends to be too high. Bond and Tinker use a formula for finding estimated reading level (ERL). They say ERL equals number of years in school $\times \frac{I.Q.}{100} + 1$. Cleland himself believes that a valid and reliable listening test is as good an instrument as can be found for determining readiness for reading.

We like to determine a Learning Expectancy Level (LEL) which indicates the grade level at which a child may be expected to learn to read, all other factors being normal (Kolson & Kaluger, 1963). Our formula is LEL equals mental age minus 5. The 5 represents the number of years the child is not in school or exposed to a developmental reading program. This approach is similar to the reading expectancy concept of Harris.

The Learning Expectancy Level formula is predicated on the assumption that there is a difference of 5 years between grade placement and the age of an average child with no anomalies.

Grade	Difference	Age
1	5	6
2	5	7
3	5	8
4	5	9
12	5	17

Since C.A. is not the important age but rather the M.A., we can determine potential by substituting M.A. for C.A. and subtracting five. McLeod (1968), however, raises an issue by questioning whether an intelligence test giving a mental age is adequate enough to determine the learning expectancy level of a child. He suggests that the elements of decoding, encoding, and the auditory modalities be invoked because a "general" mental age score can cover up some very serious deficiencies.

An important thing to remember is that reading and learning expectancy formulae have one limitation in common. No formula is valid if the child has not been taught reading skills and performance in keeping with his mental age. For example, if a child in beginning second or third grade has a mental age two or three years above his grade level, he cannot be expected to be achieving on his mental age level unless he has been taught the skills consummate with that grade and mental age level. With the learning disabled child, the reading expectancy formulae will be limited because such formulae do not apply to children with learning deficiencies. This is the point that McLeod was seeking to make.

The most important score obtained is the mental age. A normal child entering first grade is usually 6 years of age. The numerical difference between grade one and the chronological age of 6 is 5. A normal second grader is 7 years old. Again we find a difference of 5 between the age and the grade. A normal third grader is 8, and once more a difference of 5 is obtained between age and grade. From this we can hypothesize that a child's grade level potential can be secured by subtracting 5 from the mental age. The mental age can be determined by an individual mental ability test such as the Revised Stanford-Binet or estimated from the Wechsler Intelligence Scale for Children which are tests given by psychologists. Tests such as the Slosson Intelligence Test (1963), the Ammons and Ammons Full Range Picture Vocabulary Test (1962), or the Quick Test (1962) can be given by teachers. These tests give a mental age and correlate somewhat with the Stanford-Binet vocabulary scores. I.Q.s or M.A.s obtained on group intelligence tests which require reading are not satisfactory for this purpose because poor reading ability will artificially lower the score.

When using the LEL formula to find a child's potential level, use his chronological age (C.A.) in years and months (ex., 8 yrs., 3 mos.) as if it were the time that a reading achievement test was given to him. If an I.Q. is known but not the M.A. use the following procedure:

I.Q. × C.A. = M.A. − 5 = Learning Expectancy Level

1. Multiply I.Q. (with a decimal placed before the last *two* numbers) times the chronological age, also given with a decimal value (ex. 8 years 3 months = 8.25). (See Table 6.2.)
2. Then subtract 5 (always 5).
3. Answer is Learning Expecting Level, which is the grade level at which he should be accomplishing, all things being normal.
4. Always list the reading achievement test scores with the LEL so they can be compared.
5. Recognize that the greater the difference between the LEL and the C.A., the more likely that extenuating circumstances could affect the reading level. Example:

I.Q.	×	C.A.(yrs)	=	M.A.(yrs.)	−	5	=	LEL
.93	×	8.25	=	7.7	−	5	=	grade 2.7

Use this table to convert months into percentages of a year:

11 months = .91	5 months = .42
10 months = .83	4 months = .33
9 months = .75	3 months = .25
8 months = .67	2 months = .17
7 months = .58	1 month = .08
6 months = .50	

Table 6-2 can be used to obtain a quick estimate of Learning Expectancy Level by comparing the chronological age with the intelligence quotient. Locate the chronological age in the first vertical column. Trace with the eye or finger along the horizontal line of the C.A. to the vertical column headed by the I.Q. most similar to that found for the child. It is possible to interpolate if necessary. The junction of the C.A. horizontal column and the vertical column of the I.Q. will indicate the grade placement Learning Expectancy Level. A number below 1.00, including minus numbers, indicates a grade placement below first grade.

TABLE 6-2. Learning Expectancy Level (LEL) according to the Chronological Age (C.A.) and the Intelligence Quotient (I.Q.). Example: a chronological age of 8 with an I.Q. of 105 would have an LEL of grade 3.4.

C.A.	Intelligence Quotient (I.Q.)													
	75	80	85	90	95	100	105	110	115	120	125	130	135	140
5–0	−1.25	−1.00	−.75	−.50	−.25	.00	.25	.50	.75	1.00	1.25	1.50	1.75	2.00
5½	−.87	−.60	−.32	−.05	.25	.50	.78	1.05	1.33	1.60	1.88	2.15	2.43	2.70
6	−.50	−.20	−.10	.40	.70	1.00	1.30	1.60	1.90	2.20	2.50	2.80	3.10	3.40
6½	−.12	.20	.53	.85	1.18	1.50	1.83	2.15	2.48	2.80	3.13	2.45	3.78	4.10
7	.25	.60	.95	1.30	1.65	2.00	2.35	2.70	3.05	3.40	3.75	4.10	4.45	4.80
7½	.63	1.00	1.38	1.75	2.13	2.50	2.88	3.25	3.63	4.00	4.38	4.75	5.13	5.50
8	1.00	1.40	1.80	2.20	2.60	3.00	3.40	3.80	4.20	4.60	5.00	5.40	5.80	6.20
8½	1.38	1.80	2.23	2.65	3.08	3.50	3.93	4.35	4.78	5.20	5.63	6.05	6.48	6.90
9	1.75	2.20	2.65	3.10	3.55	4.00	4.45	4.90	5.35	5.80	6.25	6.70	7.15	7.60
9½	2.13	2.60	3.08	3.55	4.03	4.50	4.98	5.45	5.93	6.40	6.88	7.35	7.83	8.30
10	2.50	3.00	3.50	4.00	4.50	5.00	5.50	6.00	6.50	7.00	7.50	8.00	8.50	9.00
10½	2.88	3.40	3.93	4.45	4.98	5.50	6.03	6.55	7.08	7.60	8.13	8.65	9.18	9.70
11	3.25	3.80	4.35	4.90	5.45	6.00	6.55	7.10	7.65	8.20	8.75	9.30	9.85	10.40
11½	3.63	4.20	4.78	5.35	5.93	6.50	7.08	7.65	8.23	8.80	9.38	9.95	10.53	11.10
12	4.00	4.60	5.20	5.80	6.40	7.00	7.60	8.20	8.80	9.40	10.00	10.60	11.20	11.80
12½	4.38	5.00	5.63	6.25	6.88	7.50	8.13	8.75	9.38	10.00	10.63	11.25	11.88	12.50
13	4.75	5.40	6.05	6.70	7.35	8.00	8.65	9.30	9.95	10.60	11.25	11.90	12.55	13.20
13½	5.13	5.80	6.48	7.15	7.83	8.50	9.18	9.85	10.53	11.20	11.88	12.55	13.23	13.90
14	5.50	6.20	6.90	7.60	8.30	9.00	9.70	10.40	11.10	11.80	12.50	13.20	13.90	14.60
14½	5.88	6.60	7.33	8.05	8.78	9.50	10.23	10.95	11.68	12.40	13.13	13.85	14.58	15.30
15	6.25	7.00	7.75	8.50	9.25	10.00	10.75	11.50	12.25	13.00	13.75	14.50	15.25	16.00
15½	6.63	7.40	8.18	8.95	9.73	10.50	11.28	12.05	12.83	13.60	14.38	15.15	15.93	16.70
16	7.00	7.80	8.60	9.40	10.20	11.00	11.80	12.60	13.40	14.20	15.00	15.80	16.60	17.40

Informal Reading Inventory (IRI)

Standardized reading tests generally give the frustration level of performance. Hence to get a more accurate placement of the child's instructional level, remedial reading specialists and reading teachers generally administer an Informal Reading Inventory (IRI). This is the second step in an informal diagnosis. Because the IRI must be administered individually, the teacher can more closely observe the child's test behavior.

The IRI is an informal individual testing device which employs the use of a basal set of readers or graded reading paragraphs which are unfamiliar to the child. After the teacher establishes rapport with the child, she selects a basal reader several reading levels below the level generally used with normal achievers of the child's age. Often a word recognition flash test is given first and the IRI is started one grade level below the level at which the first error was made on the word recognition flash test. The teacher selects a story from the book. The story should not be chosen from selections in the first twenty pages of the book since the first twenty pages are usually just a review of the previous year's work. The selection should have from 100 to 150 words.

The child is asked to read the selection silently and to ask for any words he does not know. The teacher records the words he asks for. As the child is reading the teacher observes and notes specific reading behavior such as pointing, vocalization, symptoms of visual disability, etc. When the child has finished, the teacher asks questions concerning the material read in order to check the child's comprehension. The teacher also has him read some selections orally in order to determine his word attack skills. The testing is continued until four reading levels have been determined for the child: Independent Level, Instruction Level, Frustration Level, and Capacity Level.

Reading Levels

The pupil's basic level must be found and reading instruction must begin there, regardless of his grade placement. The basic level and the levels shown below should be ascertained through informal checks with basic readers.

Independent Reading Level is the level at which the pupil reads independently with approximately 99% pronunciation of words, 95% comprehension of meaning, and 90% interpretation of meaning. This is the level of supplementary reading. The pupil should be able to read the book at home or at school without aid. The material should cause no difficulty and have high interest value. There should be no head movements, no finger pointing, and no vocalization, and the child should phrase well.

Instruction Level is the level at which the pupil begins to experience sufficient difficulty so that learning elements can be pulled out for teaching purposes but the material is still easy enough that the pupil can enjoy reading and will not be discouraged. There should be approximately 85 to 90% interpretation. This is the teaching level and, although the material should be challenging, it should not be too difficult. This is the level at which we use the steps recommended for the teaching of a reading lesson, to be found in Chapter Eight.

Frustration Level is the level at which the content is so difficult that the pupil is frustrated in pronouncing words or getting meanings with any degree of satisfaction: less than 70 to 75% of the words are pronounced correctly; he scores below 70-75% on comprehension, and below 60% on interpretation. This is the level to be avoided. It will frequently be characterized by head movements, finger pointing, tension, withdrawal and short concentration span, vocalization in silent reading, substitutions, repetitions, insertions, and omissions. He is usually unable to produce more than one out of ten running words.

Capacity Level. From this point upward, the teacher reads the selections and then asks comprehension questions. The highest level of comprehension of reading material read to the individual is called his Capacity Level. He should attain a comprehension score of 75%. This is the level at which the pupil should be expected to understand well in terms of his mental capacity. This is the equivalent to what some authors speak of as the Expectancy Level, the hear-level, i.e., the highest level of readability at which a child is able to understand when listening to someone read or talk. The IRI gives us the answer to the question "At what level does he read?"

Constructing an IRI

Usually teachers construct their own IRI based on the basal readers they are using. From the same section (but not the first twenty pages) in each grade level book of a basal series, select a portion for the child to read. The length of the selection should be:

> for first and second graders — 35- 50 words
> for third and fourth graders — 50- 75 words
> for fifth and sixth graders — 75-100 words
> for Junior High   — 100-150 words
> for Senior High   — 150-200 words

In making the selection try to find a passage from which a diversity of comprehension questions can be drawn.

1. A "Who" or "What" question: "Who was the little girl?"
2. A "How" question: "How did she learn to swim?"
3. A "Why" or inferential question: "The little girl opened the package. 'Oh!' she said, 'A doll. Just what I wanted.' " "Do you think the little girl was happy? Why?" Although the story does not say she was happy, the inference can be made.
4. A General Vocabulary question. This asks for the most used meaning of the word.
5. A Specific Vocabulary Question. This asks the meaning of the word as used in this content.

By making certain of a diversity of questions, the examiner can pinpoint some comprehensional and vocabulary needs of the pupil. Kender and Rubenstein (1977) remind us by their study, however, that by simply asking questions, we may be testing memory rather than comprehension. They suggest that the child be allowed to reread or reinspect the passage before answering comprehension questions; otherwise, we may be emphasizing memory factors. This is important to note with learning disabled children who may have memory problems.

Several standardized IRI type assessment tools are on the market. These include:

Smith, Nila B. *Graded selections for reading diagnosis.* New York: New York University Press, 1959, 1963.

McCracken, Robert A. *Standard reading inventory.* Klamath, Oregon: Klamath Printing Co., 1966.

Silvaroli, Nicholas J. *Classroom reading inventory* (2nd ed.). Dubuque, Iowa: William C. Brown, 1973.

Sucher, Floyd, & Allred, Ruel A. *Sucher-Allred reading placement inventory.* Oklahoma City: The Economy Co., 1973.

Miller, Willa H. *Reading diagnostic kit.* New York: Center for Applied Research in Education, Inc., 1974 (includes a separate IRI for various grade levels).

We have personally used the Silvaroli and the Miller materials and have found them very useful. For an indepth look at the construction and use of IRI s, consult Marjorie S. Johnson and Roy A. Kress, Informal Reading Inventories, Reading Aid Series, Newark, Delaware: International Reading Association, 1965.

Informal Assessment of Strengths and Weaknesses

Several general suggestions will be given in this section. For a comprehensive and extensive list of teacher-made items to assess reading strengths and weaknesses, refer to Arthur W. Heilman, *Principles and Practices of Teaching Reading*, Columbus, Ohio: Charles E. Merrill Publishing Company, Chapter 8.

Utilizing Vocabulary Lists

At this point it is advisable to get a rough approximation of the vocabulary level of the child. The 220 abstract words in the Dolch List is a good starting point (Dolch, 1950). These words make up from 50-65% of all words the child will encounter in the elementary school basal readers. According to Dolch, if the child knows one-third of the words, he is reading at the end of first reader level; two-thirds, at the end of the second reader; and all the words, at the third reader level. To find levels beyond third reader level, the teacher can have the child pronounce the words in the glossary of the advanced level books from a basal series.

Not only can the teacher or school psychologist arrive at a vocabulary level by following the above procedure, but she is also able to determine specifically what vocabulary to teach. When the child has gone through the Dolch cards, the teacher marks on a mimeographed sheet whether the child knows (ν), miscalled (X), or omitted (O) the word. The teacher then begins developing the child's recognition and understanding of the miscalled words. By using color combinations to mark the same sheet periodically the teacher can sense changes in the child's vocabulary. If the first marking is done with red ink and the date written in red ink, the second marking in black ink, and the third in blue ink, the teacher has a one-sheet summary of progress.

For a more recent and currently widely used word list, consider the Kucera-Francis Word List (1967). This list is a computational analysis of many other word lists that purport to reflect present-day American English. The Kucera-Francis Word List is more extensive than the Dolch List and covers more grade levels.

Reading and LD teachers can make good use of the Functional Reading Resource Manual for Teachers, developed by the Maryland State Department of Education for older nonreaders and poor readers (1975). Volume I provides directions for assessment and remediation for (a) following directions, (b) locating references, and (c) attaining personal development. Volume II covers (a) gaining information and (b) understanding forms.

Teacher Observation

Teacher observation is most effective if used minute by minute to evaluate a lesson and a child. The skillful teacher always notes the feedback from the pupils in order to determine if the approach being used is reaching them. If the child makes an error she can also use this observation to diagnose the reason for the error and to determine the direction of the next movement.

A good teacher bases her appraisal of the child on her overall experience with the child. She observes how he reads orally. Does he read word by word? Does he read in thought units? Does he read in monotone? During the silent reading, does he have lip movement? Does he rely on finger-pointing? Does a test confuse and frighten him? These questions and others like them cannot be answered by a paper and pencil test; they can only be determined by the observant teacher. There is no substitute for the good judgment of the teacher based on careful observation.

This same observation serves the purpose of ongoing diagnosis. Many good teachers will realize through observation that their present teaching methods fail to reach the children and will alter their methods and materials on the spot. This continual evaluation of the effectiveness of what is being done through the feedback from the children seems to mark one of the basic differences between good teachers and less successful teachers.

The following statements are typical of observational comments made by teachers:

1. Andy has difficulty understanding directions and often needs help in carrying them out.
2. His attention span is short, even for a first grader.
3. He often forgets how to perform a new skill that he seemed to do so well just the day before.
4. He often fails to turn in written assignments.
5. He is always the last one to get a written assignment done. It may take him an hour to do what others do in 15 minutes.
6. He is often distracted by things going on in another part of the room.
7. He has a low frustration level; gives up easily.
8. He frequently misreads numbers or letters.
9. His writing is poor, with letters misformed and poorly spaced; pencil pressure is heavy.
10. He seldom volunteers in class, although it appears that he knows the answer or has the correct information.
11. He tires easily and becomes noticeably irritable as the day wears on.
12. He requires extra readiness development, much repetition, and much time to obtain overlearning.
13. He is inattentive and does not concentrate well.
14. He becomes confused when given directions involving more than one step.
15. He can do arithmetic better than he can read.

As a help to teachers and future teachers of reading who are not quite sure how to do informal classroom assessments of children and write prescriptions or educational plans for each child, Geyer and Matanzo (1977) wrote a comprehensive instructional book to guide teachers in learning how to do both procedures, *Programmed Reading Diagnosis for Teachers with Prescriptive References*. The unique features of this book are (a) it is programmed instruction so that a teacher can work her own way through learning assessment and prescriptive procedures; (b) it covers the diagnosis of word recognition, silent reading comprehension, oral reading, word attack, and prescription writing; (c) it emphasizes error analysis and how teachers can detect, record, and analyze miscues in a structural, objective way; (d) it provides many opportunities for practicing the detection of errors and miscues and, in the appendix, indicates how accurate the diagnosis has been; and (e) it mentions sources that will enhance prescriptive writing for specific errors. A set of four cassette tapes with seventeen activities is available. On each tape a teacher is working with a child in reading assessment. The teacher-student can practice recording errors, and then have a follow up for immediate feedback of accuracy of detecting miscues.

Tests Accompanying Basal Series

Tests accompanying basal series make their greatest contribution by affording insight into the effectiveness of a specific series of lessons and into the amount of assimilation and retention of very specific knowledge and skills by the group as a whole. Most basal series supply the teacher with tests to be given after the preprimers have been read. The tests are designed to measure whether or not a child has learned a particular group of sight words and reading skills purportedly taught by the preprimers, in order to determine if he has the level of attainment necessary for success in the primer. It does not measure any of the things taught by the teacher which are not included in the basal program.

Generally, the tests are relatively easy to give and to score. They give an overview of the effectiveness of the teaching and learning and assist the teacher in planning further activities for learning. Those children who have not made enough progress in the material tested may have to be formed into a subgroup and given additional experiences in order to increase their chance of success in future learning activities. Those children who have made successful progress can now be led into the newer materials by the teacher with some confidence that they come to the new situation adequately equipped for success.

Experience has led us to believe, however, that not too much reliance should be placed on the quantitative or quantitative-like aspects of these tests. Instead, the teacher should make a qualitative subjective judgment of the meaning of the results and should not be swayed completely by a numerical score. In some school districts, it is known that a child can be held back from moving to the next reader just by failing a basal reader test by one point. When the entire test only has 10 points and the cutoff score is 6 points, it is possible to imagine how easily such a test could be unreliable for a child on a day he is not feeling well or is simply restless.

Informal Procedures of Phonics Analysis

A very fine form has been prepared by Kottmeyer (1959) called *Diagnostic Inventory of Reading Skills* through which he enables the user to make a rather extensive diagnosis of the skills that a reader has in phonics. The analysis seeks to informally answer the following questions:

(1) How much sight vocabulary has he? (Dolch words)
(2) Does he try to use context clues?

(3) Does he know the name of letters?
(4) Does he know the consonant sounds?
(5) Can he substitute beginning consonant sounds?
(6) Can he hear the short vowel sounds in words?
(7) Can he tell when vowel sounds are long in words?
(8) Does he know the common vowel digraphs?
(9) Can he blend letter sounds to form words?
(10) Does he make reversals?
(11) Does he see the common prefixes as units?
(12) Does he see the common suffixes as units?
(13) Does he see compound words as units?
(14) Can he divide long words into parts?

The remedial reading teacher or clinician will be able to find other informal techniques which they can use in evaluating a variety of reading skills. The use of previous school records, periodic achievement tests in basal workbooks, the child's own workbook which gives a rough appraisal of progress, day by day diagnosis in observing the child read, and the use of a self-inventory or questionnaire by the child are all helpful. The teacher could prepare informal tests to evaluate initial consonants, final consonants, consonant blends, rhyming words, vowel sounds, compound words, root words, errors in oral reading, level of reading, learning rate, auditory discrimination, hearing sounds in words, visual discrimination in words, and so forth.

Lazar and Lazar 1973–74 have produced a Pupil Profile of Reading Skills (PPRS) which is reproduced in Table 6–3. The PPRS was developed to assist in the assessment of 110 specific factors related to the reading process that should be considered in the educational history of a pupil.

Early Identification of Children with Learning Disabilities

Preliminary Statement

It would be a mistake to be concerned with learning disabilities and not to be concerned with the early identification of youngsters who are potential learning disabled individuals. If a learning disability is not identified and remediated early, many problems can be generated, such as anti-school behavior, maladjustment, emotional problems, and defeatism. The longer the time the student is not given treatment, the more the likelihood of success will diminish.

The child with a learning disability generally is not functioning in one or more of five areas: affective domain, psychomotor domain, perceptual domain, cognitive domain, or volitional domain. The affective domain includes the child's feelings about self and relationships with peers and groups. The psychomotor domain refers to the development of effective use and control of large and small muscles. The perceptual domain refers to the manner in which the student processes sensory information. The cognitive domain includes the mental activities which lead to understanding, reacting, and evaluating. The volitional domain includes all aspects which engender motivation of the student.

TABLE 6–3. Pupil profile of reading skills.*

INSTRUCTIONS: The purpose of this entry behavior rating scale is to allow the special class teacher to develop an initial pupil reading skills profile. This profile sheet will assist the teacher or psychologist in making a specific diagnosis and evaluation of a pupil's strengths and weaknesses in reading. It helps facilitate for the teacher an initial survey that will eventually lead to modifications and reconsiderations after the teacher and pupil have had sufficient time together and is especially helpful in that the teacher can pinpoint with greater precision the specific needs of the student. Finally, the profile allows for developmentally sequenced observation and study of pupil behavior in operational terms that lend themselves to prescriptions to be written in behavioral terms which are measurable.

In coding the behavior of the student the teacher might rely on both formal instrumentation and informal teacher-made devices that will tap the specific skills in question. Regardless of sources, the following symbolic code is suggested: (1) H—which implies that the student has demonstrated this skill to acceptable criterion, (2) D—which implies a deficit and an area for work and remediation, and (3) NA—which means "not assessed for" at this time.

I. PERCEPTUAL READING SKILLS:

A. Auditory Skills:

_____ 1. matching rhyming words
_____ 2. identifying consonant sounds
_____ 3. identifying vowel sounds
_____ 4. hearing word variants
_____ 5. recognizing syllable length
_____ 6. listening for accent

B. Visual Skills:

_____ 7. notices likenesses and differences
_____ 8. notices differences between upper- and lowercase and between letters
_____ 9. discriminates between colors and knows names
_____10. discriminates between shapes and knows names
_____11. discriminates between texture
_____12. discriminates between sizes
_____13. can use picture clues

C. Motor Skills:

_____14. left-right eye movements
_____15. gross eye-hand coordination
_____16. fine hand-eye coordination
_____17. one-foot balance with eyes open
_____18. one-foot balance with eyes closed
_____19. hop forward on favorite foot
_____20. hop backwards on favorite foot
_____21. general motor awareness and coordination
_____22. spacial discrimination (i.e.: up and down, toward and from, near and far, on and under, bottom and top, between, and directionality)

NOTE: These can also be included under visual skills.

II. WORD IDENTIFICATION & ATTACK SKILLS:

A. Sight Vocabulary

_____23. can associate pictures to words
_____24. has oral reading ability
_____25. has silent reading ability

*Permission to reproduce the PPRS is granted by the authors. Lazar, A. L., & Lazar, P. E. Profile development—for educational remediation. *Academic Therapy*, winter 1973–74, 9:3, 175–182.

_____26. estimated number of words _____ from the Dolch List?

_____27. estimated grade level in reading _____?

B. Phonic Analysis Skills:

_____28. recognizes consonant sounds

_____29. recognizes consonant blends

_____30. recognizes consonant digraphs

_____31. recognizes vowel sounds

_____32. recognizes diphthongs

_____33. recognizes vowel digraphs

C. Structural Analysis Skills:

_____34. recognizes affixes

_____35. recognizes compound words

_____36. recognizes roots

_____37. recognizes contractions

D. Context Clue Skills:

_____38. uses definition clues

_____39. uses experience clues

_____40. uses comparison clues

_____41. uses synonym clues

_____42. uses familiar-expression clues

_____43. uses summary clues

_____44. uses reflection-of-mood clues

E. Syllabication Skills:

_____45. can recognize syllables

_____46. makes use of syllabication generalization

_____47. recognizes accent

III. COMPREHENSION

A. Comprehension Skills:

_____48. matching words and pictures

_____49. recognizes meaningful phonograms

_____50. can match definitions and word symbols

_____51. recognizes antonyms

_____52. recognizes synonyms

_____53. recognizes homonyms

_____54. can see literal and interpretive meanings

_____55. uses context clues

_____56. understands unit meaning of sentence—paragraph—chapter—section—article—book

_____57. recognizes main idea and supporting detail

_____58. recognizes sequence

_____59. can make generalizations and conclusions

_____60. can follow oral directions

_____61. can follow written directions

B. Comprehension Rate:

_____62. uses correct left-right eye movements

_____63. lip movements evident

_____64. points with finger

_____65. reads word by word

_____66. good steady flow of words in oral reading

_____67. eye regressions evident

_____68. can adjust rate to purpose for effect

_____69. number _____ of words in sentence, or sentence length to be used in writing stories or paragraphs.

_____70. uses various word-attack techniques meeting his own needs

_____71. can demonstrate at least 80 percent level of comprehension

IV. ORAL READING:

_____72. uses a steady rate

_____73. can adjust rate to purpose

_____74. can use phrasing to read

_____75. can use sufficient eye-voice span to read

_____76. uses pleasant pitch and volume

_____77. enunciates correctly

_____78. pronounces correctly

_____79. uses punctuation correctly

_____80. appears relaxed during oral reading

_____81. enjoys oral reading

V. STUDY SKILLS FOR EFFECTIVE READING:

A. Organizational Skills:

_____82. can arrange things in alphabetical order

_____83. can use a Table of Contents

_____84. can use an index

_____85. can read abbreviations

_____86. can interpret diacritical markings and symbols

_____87. can identify topic sentences

_____88. can outline and summarize major points

_____89. can synthesize materials from several sources

B. Library Skills:

_____90. can use a library card catalogue

_____91. can use vertical files

_____92. can use a glossary in a book

_____93. can use a dictionary

_____94. can use an encyclopedia

_____95. can use an atlas

_____96. can use abstracts

_____97. can use the Reader's Guide

_____98. has a library card for public library near home

_____99. how many _____ times per month does he go to the library?

_____100. how many books _____ are checked out per month on an average?

VI. INTERPRETATION AND APPRECIATION READING SKILLS:

_____101. detects cause-and-effect relationship

_____102. recognizes figurative language

_____103. recognizes difference between fact and opinion

_____104. recognizes the mood of the story

_____105. can detect the author's purpose

_____106. demonstrates ability to infer and conclude

_____107. can read for verification

_____108. enjoys poetry

_____109. enjoys choral reading

_____110. reads the newspaper

SUMMARY OF RESULTS:

Indicate the number of D items per major section.

_____ I. Perceptual Reading Skills
_____ II. Word Identification & Attack Skills
_____ III. Comprehension
_____ IV. Oral Reading
_____ V. Study Skills for Effective Reading
_____ VI. Interpretation and Appreciation Reading Skills

Total H   —   _____
Total D   —   _____
Total NA —   _____
110

List five skills that should be given priority for development:
(Use number and title)

1. _____ _____
2. _____ _____
3. _____ _____
4. _____ _____
5. _____ _____

In the instructions given with the rating scale, one will see that only three simple symbols are employed: H—which implies that all is well and that the student has demonstrated the skill; D—which implies a need for remediation; and NA—which indicates that this item was not assessed. Considering the range of demands on a teacher's time in the classroom, it becomes essential that a simple but meaningful coding system be utilized.

A program for the early identification of a child who might have a learning disability must assess the beginning student in the five areas. How to do this has eluded educators in the past. (See last paragraph on p. 146.)

The Maryland Program for Early Identification

In 1973 the Maryland State Department of Education conducted a multidisciplinary workshop on early identification. Participants were optometrists, ophthalmologists, pediatricians, psychologists, special educationists, reading specialists, psychiatrists, learning disabilities specialists, psychometrists, early childhood educationists, college professors, and parents. The first conclusion arrived at was "There doesn't exist a single test which will identify potential learning disabilities cases." By the end of the one-week workshop, the participants proposed a four phase program for early identification.

Phase I: Screening. The goal of Phase I was to screen 100% of Maryland students using parent information and teacher expertise. Using a 36-item teacher observation instrument, the teacher observed the child for 60 days. On the basis of this observation, parent information, and any tests administered, the teacher modified the program for each student having deficiencies in any of the five areas (cognitive, perceptual, affective, psychomotor, and volition). At the end of 100 days those children still showing deficits (estimated at 15% of the total population) were referred to the Educational Management Team for study and prescription.

Phase II: Educational Assessment. The purpose of Phase II was to provide an indepth diagnosis by appropriate specialist(s) and to write an educational management plan for each of the youngsters identified through Phase I. (It was estimated Phase I would identify approximately 15% of the total screened as children likely to have learning disabilities.)

Phase III: Comprehensive Services. The purpose of Phase III was to provide comprehensive and indepth assessment and/or educational activities unavailable at the local level.

Phase IV: Special Placement. The purpose of Phase IV was to recommend special placement in an outside agency for a child needing a kind of program unavailable at the local level.

A Suggested Plan for Early Identification

Until a test is devised to accurately differentiate children with a reading disability potential from those with no potential disabilities, educators must rely on teacher observation. The problem with teacher observation is its subjective nature. To lower the effect of subjectivity it was necessary for all teachers to use a structured systematic observation guide. We suggest the use of the *Maryland Systematic Teacher Observation Instrument* because we believe it to be the most validated instrument designed for the purpose of observation (Maryland State Department of Education, 1975). This instrument is shown in Table 6–4.

A multidisciplinary committee developed 126 statements of behavior which they believed differentiate between the child with a potential learning disability and the normal child. The statements were separated into three lists, each containing 42 items.

A 5-point scale (*strongly disagree, disagree, undecided, agree, strongly agree*) was used by experts from many disciplines to rate each statement using three standards: clarity, observability, and validity. Approximately one thousand persons rated the behaviors. Those items with the highest rating were selected. Using standard statistical procedures, 96 of the 126 were found to be acceptable.

The 96 items were then divided into the categories listed earlier (cognitive domain, affective domain, etc.). The first 7 items having the highest median in each category were selected. The total number of items after this procedure was reduced to 44. These were field tested, resulting in 36 items which did discriminate the normal child from the child with a potential learning disability.

The total possible points for the 36 items is 180. Kindergarten children who score 139 or lower and first graders who score 153 or lower are considered "high risk" students and must be screened further. If a student rates three or lower on three or more items in a particular area, further screening will be needed in that area. Remember, this teacher observation instrument only alerts the teacher to a potential problem; it does not identify or classify a potential learning disability.

Follow Up of High Risk Children

Once the possible "high risk" student has been identified, further testing of these children should follow. If the school system employs school psychologists, psychometrists, or reading specialists, the screening tests can be administered by these professionals. If,

TABLE 6–4. Maryland systematic teacher observation instrument.

	ALWAYS	OFTEN	SOMETIMES	SELDOM	NEVER
1. Says "huh" or "what" after he has been told something or asked a question.	○	○	○	○	○
2. Finishes task late.	○	○	○	○	○
3. Can tell about a picture while looking at it.	○	○	○	○	○
4. Names and locates at least five parts of his body.	○	○	○	○	○
5. Knocks over things when reaching for them.	○	○	○	○	○
6. Fumbles for words, uses a wrong word, or says he forgot what he was trying to say.	○	○	○	○	○
7. Cringes or pulls away when approached by others.	○	○	○	○	○
8. Can recognize own name in print.	○	○	○	○	○
9. Stays with the activity at hand.	○	○	○	○	○
10. Can tell about a recent school activity (i.e. field trip).	○	○	○	○	○
11. Follows directions.	○	○	○	○	○
12. Can repeat sentences such as "I like to play outside" in correct order.	○	○	○	○	○
13. Drowsy, sleepy, or sleeps.	○	○	○	○	○
14. Names common objects such as chair, desk, table.	○	○	○	○	○
15. Fights, shouts, or shakes his fist as a preferred means of solving problems.	○	○	○	○	○
16. Identifies likenesses and differences in pictures, objects and forms.	○	○	○	○	○
17. Gives own name and age when asked.	○	○	○	○	○
18. Stares into space.	○	○	○	○	○
19. Can identify colors (i.e., red, yellow, blue, green) by name.	○	○	○	○	○
20. Says, "I can't" when presented with school tasks.	○	○	○	○	○
21. If child prints, he prints words, letters and/or numbers backwards.	○	○	○	○	○
22. Hurts children and/or animals for no apparent reason.	○	○	○	○	○
23. Speech is understandable.	○	○	○	○	○
24. Works and solves problems independently.	○	○	○	○	○
25. Destroys or damages things, breaks toys.	○	○	○	○	○
26. Matches objects to pictures (i.e., toy truck to picture of truck).	○	○	○	○	○
27. Gets along with other children in various situations.	○	○	○	○	○
28. Can tell about a story after listening to it.	○	○	○	○	○
29. Stumbles, trips or falls.	○	○	○	○	○
30. Can copy a circle, square, and triangle so that it is recognizable.	○	○	○	○	○
31. Can tell how many objects up to five.	○	○	○	○	○
32. Classifies objects by categories, such as food or clothing.	○	○	○	○	○
33. Speaks in sentences of more than three words.	○	○	○	○	○
34. Discriminates between fine differences in sounds heard (i.e., boy, toy).	○	○	○	○	○
35. Arranges a three-part picture story in correct sequence.	○	○	○	○	○
36. Retells story in correct sequential order.	○	○	○	○	○

however, specialists are not available, then the classroom teacher must do the assessing. To ask the classroom teacher to give individual assessment tests would take away too much of the teaching time; hence, group tests should be used. Table 6–5 lists group tests having reliability and validity which the classroom teacher can use to assess children in the five domains. Table 6-6 which follows lists individual assessment instruments having validity and reliability.

TABLE 6–5. Group assessment instruments.

Test	Administrative Time
I. Affective Domain	
Animal Crackers	30 minutes
Pupil's Assessment in School (PASS)	20–25 minutes
Slingerland Pre-Reading Screening Procedures (K^2-1^1 levels only)	35–40 minutes
II. Psychomotor Domain	
Pintner-Cunningham Primary Test Form A	20–25 minutes
Slingerland Pre-Reading Screening Procedures (K^2-1^1 levels only)	35–40 minutes
Metropolitan Reading Test (K^2)	60 minutes
III. Perceptual Domain	
Pintner-Cunningham Primary Test Form A	20–25 minutes
Slingerland Pre-reading Screening Procedures (K^2-1^1 levels only)	35–40 minutes
Metropolitan Reading Test (K^2)	60 minutes
IV. Cognitive Domain	
Pintner-Cunningham Primary Test Form A	20–25 minutes
Metropolitan Reading Test (K^2)	60 minutes
V. Volitional Domain	
Animal Crackers	30 minutes
Pupil's Assessment in School (PASS)	20–25 minutes

TABLE 6–6. Individual assessment instruments.

Test	Administrative Time
I. Affective Domain	
Carrow Test for Auditory Comprehension of Language (TACL)	20 minutes
Animal Crackers	30 minutes
Self-Control Behavior Inventory (SCBI)	5–8 minutes
II. Psychomotor Domain	
Meeting Street School Screening Test (MSSST)	20 minutes
Cognitive Skills Assessment Battery (CSAB)	20 minutes
III. Perceptual Domain	
Carrow Test for Auditory Comprehension of Language (TACL)	20 minutes
Meeting Street School Screening Test (MSSST)	20 minutes
Cognitive Skills Assessment Battery (CSAB)	20 minutes
IV. Cognitive Domain	
Meeting Street School Screening Test (MSSST)	20 minutes
Cognitive Skills Assessment Battery (CSAB)	20 minutes
V. Volitional Domain	
Classroom Behavior Inventory (CBI)	5–8 minutes
Self-Control Behavior Inventory (SCBI)	5-8 minutes

What to Do about What You Found

If the youngster scores low on a test in the affective domain, the teacher can:

1. Provide tasks based on child's interest.
2. Assist child in setting realistic goals.
3. Recognize success to reinforce positive behavior.
4. Encourage the child so as to develop a positive self-image.
5. Select a compatible partner.
6. Assign only one task at a time.
7. Involve the child in the planning.
8. Encourage the child to bring in items to share with others.
9. Make certain the child understands the directions.
10. Set limits firmly and consistently.
11. Provide a quiet area so the child can focus on the task at hand.
12. Set reasonable time limits for job completion.

If the youngster scores low on psychomotor domain, the teacher can:

1. Introduce games and songs that identify parts of the body.
2. Provide people puzzles so children can learn to identify parts of the body.
3. Supply the child with building blocks.
4. Provide tapes for listening by the student.
5. Pace child by setting time periods for completion of assignments.
6. Read to child.
7. Use rhythmic activities.
8. Have the child play on a jungle gym.
9. Play stepping stones.
10. Play hop scotch.
11. Play kick ball.
12. Do finger painting.
13. Trace letters and words.
14. Let the child work at an easel.
15. Have the child match shapes.

If the child scores low on the perceptual tests, the teacher can:

1. Teach sound discrimination through musical activities.
2. Play "Simon Says."
3. Use telephones or walkie-talkies.
4. Have the child locate words in print.
5. Have the child match colors, sizes, and shapes.
6. Have the child match letters and words.
7. Have the child match pictures.
8. Play "Connecting Dots."
9. Have the child trace geometric forms.
10. Play "Rhyming Words."
11. Sequence pictures of a story the child has heard.

If the child scores low in the cognitive domain, the teacher can:

1. Encourage sharing time.
2. Introduce games which identify parts of the body.
3. Provide people puzzles.
4. Give the child purpose for listening.
5. Set up a listening center.
6. Have a "Child of the Week."
7. Present rhymes.
8. Provide materials for classifying.

If the child scores low in the volitional area, the teacher can:

1. Locate the child's interest and use it to motivate.
2. Set realistic goals.
3. Recognize success.
4. Help the child develop positive self-image.
5. Provide science center, listening center, and play center.
6. Carefully choose another child to assist.
7. Set limits.
8. Show interest in child's efforts.

Early identification of "high risk" students and planning programs tailored to their needs can prevent many problems in the later grades.

Bibliography Related to the Early Identification Program

Montgomery County Public Schools. *Early identification of learning disabilities and suggestions to assist in program design.* Rockville, Md.: MCPS, 1975.

Curriculum & Evaluation Consultants. *The development and validation of screening instruments for the early identification of learning disabilities.* Annapolis, Md.: MSDE, 1975.

Aukerman, Robert. *Approaches to beginning reading.* New York: John Wiley & Sons, 1971.

Hoepfner, Ralph, Stern, Carolyn, & Nummedal, Susan. CSE-EGRC *preschool/kindergarten evaluations.* Los Angeles: UCLA Graduate School of Education, 1971.

Hymes, James. *Before the child reads.* New York: Harper & Row, 1958.

Possien, Wilma M. *They all need to talk—Oral communication in the language arts program.* New York: Appleton-Century Crofts, 1969.

Weber, Evelyn. *Early childhood education.* Worthington, Ohio: Charles A. Jones Publishing Co., 1970.

Kolson, E. J., & Kaluger, G. *Clinical aspects of remedial reading.* Springfield, Ill.: Charles C Thomas, 1963.

chapter 7

Formal Assessment

Although an informal diagnosis of reading skills will be sufficient to analyze the needs of most children with reading disabilities, there will always be a group of problem readers for whom the informal methods will not be enough. These youngsters may have more complex reading problems, have disabilities which are more severe in nature, or be bothered more by a learning disorder than a reading deficit.

Many remedial teachers and psychologists who are not as experienced and sensitive to reading disabilities as they would like to be will welcome the availability of formal, standardized testing techniques. The fact that the literature reports so many studies in reading demands that a reading teacher be knowledgeable concerning the validity and reliability of standardized testing materials and remedial techniques so that he can properly evaluate what he reads. A person doing research in reading must use standardized procedures.

Please note that each of the chapters dealing with specific categories of reading and learning skills tells about a wide assortment of assessment tests and procedures. The reader should refer to those chapters for specifics. The purpose of this chapter, as well as the preceding chapters, is to present background information and a consolidation of materials and ideas related to the total approach to assessment. There are many factors that can affect a child's learning or reading capability. To look at only one element of a multicomponent process is incomprehensible and lacking in understanding of what reading and learning is all about. The moral of the statement is somewhat like that of the story of five blind men trying to describe what an elephant looked like when each of the blind men was touching and feeling only one part of the elephant—a leg, the trunk, the side of its body, an ear, and its tail. Each described what he thought the elephant looked like and could not understand how the others could be so wrong. It took a sixth person, one who could see what was happening, to put all of the descriptions together.

Basic Understandings

In considering formal assessment, one of the first things to be done is to put the whole matter of testing into its proper perspective. There appears to be a kind of mystique about tests that seems to give them some magical quality and give you insights that you never dreamed of. This misconception is evident in the fact that many teachers when confronted with a child who is not learning want the child tested immediately to find out what is wrong. "Give him a test" seems to be synonymous with "Tests will tell me what to do." This is an illusion; tests have many limitations, one of the greatest of which is that they may not be able to measure what the examiner thinks they should, or even that they may not uncover what they (the tests) are said to be able to determine. It is strange that in spite of our intellectual understanding of test limitations, we still consider their results as valid, as if they were carved in stone by some all-knowing, all-seeing, all-encompassing Being.

Tests are only as good as the user's understanding of what they measure and how well they measure. Test titles seldom tell you what or how well they measure. Tests built on the basis of a theory generally measure only in terms of the theory. But is the theory correct to begin with? Mechanical, routine use of tests without insight as to their nature and adequacy will only give superficial results, which may be of little help. In the final analysis, the teacher who knows her subject matter and knows how children learn can probably get more pertinent information concerning a particular child from informal assessment and error analysis that she does in her classroom than she can from a battery of formal tests that she knows very little about.

Statistical Considerations

We will not go into deep statistical analysis or jargon but there are a few basic things test users must know. Tests are constructed by human beings. They are usually intended to measure rather complex cognitive, affective, or motor qualities. It is extremely difficult to put together a test that will do the job that the test maker intended it to do. If a test is not used for the purpose for which the test maker constructed it, if it is not administered in the way the test manual stipulated that it be administered, or if it is not given to the population from which the test maker designed the norms, then the test is improperly used to begin with and the results will be spurious or inappropriate.

In selecting a test, first determine what you want to find out about the child. Do you want to know the reading level of the child (a very intangible general objective), or do you want to know how well he does in word recognition skills, literal comprehension of words, comprehension from paragraph reading, or knowledge of vocabulary? Do you want to know specifically what his weaknesses are in phonetic analysis, structural analysis, or study skills? Perhaps you want to determine how effectively the child can use auditory skills, such as discrimination, sequentialization, or memory of words. The point is, first know exactly what you want to find out; then select a test, or part of a test, to measure exactly what you want. Now we encounter our first statistical consideration: Is the test selected "valid" for your purpose? *Validity* is a statistical term; it means "the degree to which the test actually measures what it purports or says it measures." The title of the test or a subsection may say one thing, but the content items may measure something else. They may be contaminated by other variables so that you really do not know exactly what the results reflect. The best place to check on the validity of the test is to read the test manual and see how the author established the validity of the test. If this information is lacking, then look in the literature and see if any research has been done on validity. If none is found, you're on your own and you had better beware of what use you make of the test results.

A second major statistical factor that must be considered in selecting a test is the *reliability* of the test. Statistically, reliability means "the degree to which you would get the same results if the same test were to be given to the same children a second time." The point here is that a test can be quickly or haphazardly put together, without any consideration or realization as to whether items are constructed in such a way as to elicit the same response from the child each time the items are presented. A number of variables may enter into the picture to change the way a child would respond on a second occasion. If you cannot count on the child responding consistently, then you cannot count on the strength or adequacy of the results. They may be high one time and low the next. Reliability factors are represented by a test-retest correlation. A correlation of .90 or higher is considered to be good reliability for group tests that measure content. A reliability of .75 for subtest scores is considered adequate. To help examiners make better use of the scores, a standard error of measurement is frequently given. The standard error would give the range of scores, such as 35 to 39, within which the testee will score 50% of the time the next time he takes the test. The standard score gives some indication of the adequacy of the reliability correlation.

There are other statistical terms that the serious user of tests should know, even though validity and reliability are the prime considerations in selecting a test. Certainly persons using tests should understand the meaning of the terms used with the results, such as *percentile* (at what percentage level of the group tested originally for the establishment of the norms does this score fall?), *mean* (the average score), *median* (the middle score), and *grade equivalent* (or age equivalent) scores. *Standard deviation* gives the range of scores within which 68% of all scores fall; this would be considered the average group and anything beyond one standard deviation would be either higher or lower than the average group. For the more seriously involved test user, it would be important to know about *factor analysis* (how many different things does this test really measure?) and *analysis of variance* (how many things influence the results of this test?).

It is important to understand the meaning of *correlation*. Correlation is a statistical procedure by which the relationship between two or more factors is determined. A perfect positive relationship (correlation is indicated by the letter r) would be a $+ 1.0$. A perfect negative (opposite) relationship would be a $- 1.0$. A correlation of 0.0 would indicate a scatter or no relationship. A correlation above 0.0, that is, .10 or higher, would be positive. At least a .5 or better would be needed to be considered adequate. A .8 or higher would be very high. The best way to determine the adequacy of a correlation would be to check on the significance difference between two scores. A significance difference at the .5 or 5% level means that the relationship would occur 95 times out of a hundred. A significance difference at the 1% level means it would occur 99 times out of a hundred. A 5% level or higher is extremely significant.

The important concept to remember about correlations is that they only indicate degree of relationships—a correlative relationship—and *do not* imply that one of the factors caused or was responsible for the other factor. There is no cause-effect relationship implied. For example, some researchers show a high correlation, .8 or better, between children possessing good auditory discrimination ability and children achieving well in reading. In other words, a child with good auditory discrimination ability also tends to be a good reader. However, that is not to say that the good auditory discrimination ability is responsible for producing good reading achievement. To illustrate: Whatever ⓧ is, it might be responsible

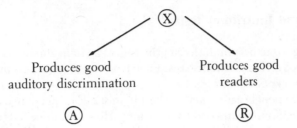

for producing Ⓐ (auditory discrimination) and, separately, producing Ⓡ (reading achievement). But, you cannot assume from this study that by improving the child's Ⓐ you can improve Ⓡ. It might be true that Ⓐ does effect Ⓡ, but *this particular study does not prove that relationship*. Another study, a cause and effect study, must be done. There is a difference between a correlative relationship and a causative relationship.

One last but very important statistical concept that needs to be understood by all teachers who use tests is the makeup and meaning of the *norms*. Norms are the tables or scores to which we compare the child's raw scores in order to get a comparative meaning or result. The child gets 15 items correct. What does that mean? The table of norms tells us that 15 is 75 percentile, or grade equivalent of 4.7, or age equivalent of 10.2. But, is that true? We will not know until we learn what the sample or norm population was to whom we are comparing our child's score. The first thing we need to do is to find out what grades or ages made up the sample population. If the grade norms are based on a first and second grade (or 6 and 7 year age group), should we be comparing the scores made by our average ability 10 year old in fourth grade? No! Suppose our school population is semirural, in one of the Plains states, and the sample population is made up of children from populated urban and suburban schools from the Northeast? Better be careful of the interpretations. Suppose our children are inner city blacks or children from Spanish-speaking neighborhoods; would norms from basically middle class, white population areas be appropriate? Again the answer is "no." Can something be done about these inappropriate norms so that the tests can still be used? Yes; develop your own norms, locally, but be sure they are constructed properly.

Is there ever a time when the inappropriate norms can be used? Yes, but only when it is necessary to determine how well the child could function in a situation dominated by the population on which the norms were based. For example, consider the inner city child who moves into a different cultural and economically based school setting (similar to the norm sample). The test results would not indicate what potential the child possesses; they would only indicate how well he would function within that system if he were taught as these children were taught. The fault is with the teachers and the system for not recognizing the special needs of the child and administering to his needs. Every child deserves the right to be taught in the way by which he can best learn. No school and no teacher has the right to say "he doesn't belong here because he does not fit in with our way of doing things, so let him sink or swim on his own." Teachers and schools must be flexible and adaptive and not try to escape their task by segregating the child into a special class or ignoring him. To determine actual potential, use appropriate assessment tasks.

For a good, readable checklist for test evaluation, see George D. Spache, *Investigating the Issues of Reading Disabilities*, Allyn & Bacon, 1976, Chapter 11.

Group Tests and Individual Tests

Some tests are designed to be administered primarily to a group at one time, and others are developed to be used on a one-to-one basis. Each type of tests have their purposes, their strengths, and their weaknesses.

Group tests are convenient because they can be administered to an entire class (or group) at one time. The savings in time and effort are obvious. However, these tests do have their weaknesses. There are such intangibles as some children not understanding the directions; some children reacting to test fright or test shock, and the teacher not being aware of this fact; some marking their answers in the wrong spaces; and, of course, guessing. If these factors are not detected, the distorted results will not be recognized by the teacher. A more significant point is the need for the teacher to know how to properly administer, score, and interpret the test. The truly capable teacher will also know how to analyze the errors on the test to learn what specific deficiencies the child has.

Individual tests are intended to be administered to one child at a time. The teacher can observe how the child approaches his work, can involve the child in oral communication, and can keep a record of the type of errors made. There is no question but that an individual type test can give the teacher many subjective, qualitative insights she could not get from group test results. A group test can be given individually, but it is not generally designed to reveal the kinds of information that come from individual tests.

Some interesting observations on the use of group tests and individual tests, especially with reading and learning disabled children, were made in studies done by David Malley (1975) and by Silberberg and Silberberg (1977). Silberberg and Silberberg sought to pinpoint the concept of "reading level," typically defined by a test score. They used the results of the HEW Anchor Test Study (1975), which made use of the California Achievement Test, The Comprehensive Tests of Basic Skills, Gates-MacGinitie Reading Test, Iowa Test of Basic Skills, and Metropolitan Achievement Tests. This study found that the tests were quite comparable and that most children could be expected to score within ± 5 percentile points if they took any two of these tests. The Silberbergs then gave individual reading tests—The Gilmore Oral Reading Test, Wide Range Achievement Test, and the Gray Oral Reading Test, plus parts of the Bond-Barlow-Hoyt and the Metropolitan Achievement Test—to 100 children entering remedial reading classes. They found wide discrepancies among the results of these tests. They found they could not use the results interchangeably. Wallen found the same type of results when specific areas of reading were being investigated. The only positive conclusion was that the higher the score a child made on any of the tests administered, the better his overall reading ability. We only wish to demonstrate the care that must be taken in comparing details of test results from one test to another, and especially in comparing results from individual tests to group tests.

For detailed descriptions and frequent research reviews of different tests, consult Oscar K. Buros, *The Seventh Mental Measurements Yearbook* (or a later edition when it is available), Highland Park, New Jersey, the Gryphon Press, 1972. Buros also has Reading Tests and Reviews 2, 1972, with the same publisher, and Tests in Print II, 1974.

Formal Assessment of Reading

Norm-Referenced Tests

The norm-referenced or standardized test gives adequate objectivity as well as supplying standards by which the deviation from the average can be ascertained. There are two types of norm-referenced tests available to the teacher: (a) reading survey tests, which are designed to give an indication of grade placement, and (b) diagnostic tests, which are designed to give an appraisal of the basic reading abilities.

Most reading survey tests have sections on vocabulary and comprehension. Survey tests for the intermediate grades many times have a check on the pupil's rate of reading. Survey tests generally require about 45 minutes to an hour to administer and can be administered to groups of children. The raw scores are then translated into norms for particular grades and expressed in terms of grade levels.

The results of the survey tests are generally reliable for a class but are somewhat less reliable when applied to an individual within a class. Test publishers recognize this. "This means no single test can be equally well suited to the entire range of achievement. It is inevitably too easy or too difficult, frustrating or unchallenging for many pupils. The only solution to the problem is to provide different tests for pupils at different levels of achievement" (Hieronymus & Linquist, 1971). When the teacher must apply the score of the test to an individual, the results should be used as a contribution to the teacher's own judgment of the level of attainment of the student and not as the sole determiner of that level.

When using survey tests with an entire class, it is wise to do step-up and step-down testing. Those youngsters in the class who score off the top of the test should be retested with a higher form of the test. Those students who score below the guess score of the test should be retested with a lower form of the test.

Diagnostic tests are said to measure the various reading abilities comprising the general reading ability. The problem here is that the makers of the tests have little agreement in defining the subtest tasks that they believe comprise these abilities. An analysis of the subtests in diagnostic tests finds a wide variety of abilities mentioned. Yet, an analysis of the kinds of tasks measured in the diagnostic tests reveals little difference among the tasks measured by the test makers. Some of the more common abilities measured are word recognition, sentence and paragraph comprehension, visual discrimination, auditory discrimination and word attack skills.

Criterion-Referenced Tests In Reading

Recent years have witnessed the increasing use of criterion-referenced tests to measure the reading achievement of students. A criterion-referenced test is a test in which the items are keyed to specific skills or objectives. Unlike norm-referenced tests which give either an overall general level of achievement or level of acquisition of broad subcategories, the criterion-referenced test measures the student's mastery or nonmastery of very specific skills or objectives.

The first step in the development of a criterion-referenced test is to identify the skills or objectives to be measured. It is important that the skills or objectives be stated in very specific terms. *Phonics* is not specific enough; the initial blend *gr* is specific. Stated as a generic objective, there can be seven parts.

Input: 1. Modality—How the stimulus is presented.
        2. Quantity—The number to be presented.
        3. Qualities—The special qualities of the stimulus.
        4. Item—What is to be presented.
Output: 5. Action—The observable behavior of the student.
        6. Object—What the student acts upon.
        7. Limitation—What limits the object.

Example of a generic objective:

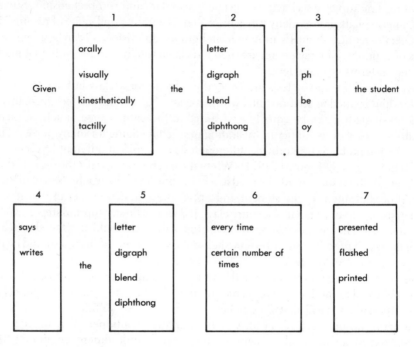

The generic objective then can be translated into any number of instructional objectives.
     1   2 3   4   5

Given visually / the / letter / r / the student will state / the name of the letter /
    6   7
every time / *it is presented.* The underlined portion is the standard of performance. A mnemonic device for remembering the main components is GASP: The Given,
the Action, the Standard of Performance. G is 1, 2, and 3; A is 4 and 5; S is 6; P is 7.

The second step in the development of a criterion-referenced test is to write test items
keyed to the skills list. If the test items are multiple choice, then care must be taken to insure
that the distractors are from a level commensurate with the level of the stimulus. A situation
in which the student is to select a word from five choices is worthless if all five of the choices
are not from the same level of difficulty.

The third step is to have the test items edited for clarity and meaning.

The fourth step is validation by experts. The skills list and test items are submitted to a
group of experts. Generally, 80% agreement by the experts is needed to keep a skill or
objective in the list. Eighty percent of the experts must agree that the test item does measure
the skill or objective it is keyed to in order to give the item authority validity.

The fifth step is to select a sample of the items to comprise a test. Generally there should be a minimum of five test items per skill or objective to be tested.

The sixth step is to field test in about ten classrooms, five classrooms who should have mastered the skill and five who have not. Here the administrative directions are checked for ease and clarity. The results of the field test allow statistical analysis of the results to determine the statistical validity of each item and the levels of mastery for each item on the test. A quadrant of item effectiveness for each item is then constructed.

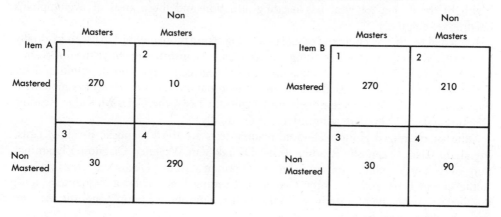

Blocks 1 and 3 are the determiners. The higher the total of 1 and 3, the greater the effectiveness of the item. Item A is more effective than Item B in the blocks because Item A was known (mastered) by 270 of the Masters as compared to only 10% of the Non-Masters. Item B was known by 210 of the Non-Masters, so it was not a new or unknown item. There is little agreement concerning what the cut-off should be. Ideally 80% or more of the Masters should be in #1 and 80% of the Non-Masters should be in #3.

The seventh step is to revise the test on the basis of the field test. It is then ready for administration.

Criterion-referenced tests are more useful for instructional planning than norm-referenced tests.

For further information on criterion-referenced testing consult:

1. Livingston, S. A. Criterion-referenced applications of classical test theory. *Journal of Educational Measurement*, 1972, 9, 13–26.
2. Popham, W. J. Indices of adequacy for criterion-referenced test items. *Criterion-referenced measurements*. Englewood Cliffs, N. J.: Ed. Tech Publ., 1971.
3. Rovinelli, R. J. Methods of validating criterion-referenced test items. Unpublished doctoral dissertation, University of Massachusetts, 1976.

Group Diagnostic Reading Tests

One of the more widely used group diagnostic tests is the Bond-Barlow-Hoyt (Silent Reading Diagnostic) Test (1970). This battery of tests gives a refinement of information which goes far beyond the listing of the subtests. From the subtest Words in Isolation, one can also get a pattern of the type of errors the child makes: initial errors, terminal errors, or reversals. The same is true with Words in Context. Other subtests are Reversible Words in Context, Locating Elements (which although not stated by the test authors also gives an indication of possible figure-ground perception problems), Syllabication, Word Elements, Beginning Sounds, Ending Sounds, and Letter Sounds. The subtest Word Synthesis seeks to test the child's ability to mentally combine elements of a word into a word. A close look at the kinds of comprehension questions on this subtest suggests that the test also assesses the child's ability to answer inference questions.

To get the most utility from the Bond-Barlow-Hoyt tests, a reading survey test must also be given in order to establish what Bond calls *Lines of Importance*. The Lines of Importance highlight those areas of weakness needing attention and those areas of overemphasis needing de-emphasis.

Remedial reading teachers and school psychologists are more inclined to use individually administered group diagnostic reading tests as diagnostic instruments since the one-to-one relationship of this type of test situation can often give insights into the child and his problems which are not afforded by a group testing situation. If it is necessary to supplement the information from the Silent Reading Diagnostic Tests, the Gates-McKillop Reading Diagnostic Tests (1962) are administered individually.

Other standardized group diagnostic reading tests are the Diagnostic Reading Tests, Ingraham-Clark Diagnostic Reading Tests, Dvorak-Van Wagenen Diagnostic Examination of Silent Reading Ability, Monroe-Sherman Group Diagnostic Reading and Achievement Tests, and the Doren Diagnostic Reading Tests. There are other tests, also, but they will not be mentioned here. Table 7-1 lists a number of group diagnostic tests and the subskills covered by each.

Individual Reading Tests

A number of worthwhile individual oral reading survey tests are used by reading experts. Some people tend to use one test repeatedly. This statement is by no means a criticism since continued use of a given test provides the remedial reading specialist or psychologist with a broader base of understanding for analysis of the responses to the test than does the employment of several tests with which the teacher may be only partially familiar.

Because of the one-to-one relationship involved in individual reading tests, the remedial reading teacher can do an informal analysis, in terms of clinical judgment, while obtaining scores which have some degree of standardization. The Gilmore Oral Reading Test (1968) measures accuracy (pronunciation), paragraph comprehension, and rate. The recording of errors on the accuracy part of the test permits the examiner to detect slight to moderate difficulties. As a quick check, this is a very usable test. The Gray Oral Reading Tests (1967) include thirteen passages to provide data for analysis of errors and is also a widely used test.

In our work, we find the Gilmore test very effective when used with a child reading at third reader level or above. A child reading below third reader level finds the Spache Diagnostic Reading Scales (1972) more comfortable. The Spache Diagnostic Reading Scales make use of word recognition lists which are quite good, reading paragraphs for accuracy and comprehension, and a quick phonetic ability check. Examiner judgment is needed to evaluate how well the testee has done. Norms are given but the manual explains that different teaching programs and definition of terms would affect the standards. The norms for the phonics subtest of Spache appear to be too high, although the test is effective.

For a more extensive study, the Durrell Analysis of Reading Difficulty (1955) is one of the more widely used individual diagnostic tests. Subtests include: Oral Reading, Silent Reading, Listening, Comprehension, Word Recognition and Word Analysis, Visual Memory of Word Forms, Auditory Analysis of Word Elements, Spelling, and Handwrit-

	Group	Individual	Vocabulary	Study Reading	Comprehension	Reading Potential	Auditory Discrimination	Visual Discrimination	Phonics	Syllabication	Learning Rate	Grade Level
Diagnostic Reading Tests	✔	✔		✔		✔	✔	✔	✔			K-Coll
Gates-McKillop		✔	✔	✔			✔	✔	✔	✔		2-6
Durrell Analysis		✔	✔		✔	✔	✔	✔	✔	✔	✔	1-6
Gates Read. Diag. Tests		✔	✔	✔					✔	✔		1-HS
Gilmore Oral Reading		✔	✔	✔								1-HS
Gray Oral Rdng. Para.		✔	✔									1-HS
Diag. Reading Scales		✔	✔	✔					✔	✔		1-8
SRA Reading Record	✔		✔	✔	✔							6-HS
Stanford Diag. Tests	✔		✔		✔		✔	✔	✔	✔		2-6
Silent Reading Diag. Tests	✔		✔	✔					✔	✔		3-6
Calif. Phonics Survey			✔							✔		7-Col
Doren Diag. Reading Test of Word Recognition Skills										✔		1-9
Primary Reading Profile			✔	✔						✔		1-2

TABLE 7–1. Diagnostic reading tests.

ing. This test, however, is not for the severely disabled reader. The Monroe Diagnostic Reading Examination (1932) goes into greater depth and can be used with the moderately severe to severe remedial reader. The Iota Word Test on the Monroe Test is especially useful.

For a quick check on the highest reading level, we like the Wide Range Achievement Test (1965). This test measures oral word recognition level as well as grade level in spelling and arithmetic. The reading test can be used for informal analysis of word attack skills and types of reading errors, but the examiner must be alert to detecting the person with a good sound-symbol relationship who is actually a "word caller" but has no comprehension. It is often helpful to analyze the achievement in spelling and arithmetic. The spelling test may indicate how a child "hears" words. The spelling score is usually close to the reading grade level. With learning disabled children 10 years old or older, the arithmetic score is two and usually three grade levels higher than the score made in reading. With a combination of a high arithmetic and low reading score, we assume that the child has ability to learn but for some reason cannot apply it to the field of reading.

Much has been done with Bormuth's "Cloze Technique" (1969). This technique involves:

1. Selecting a passage.
2. Deleting words (not omitting proper names or first word of a sentence).
    a. Every 10th word for fact-laden textual material.
    b. Every 5th, 6th, 7th, or 8th word for narratives.
3. Keeping the first and last sentence intact.
4. Scoring (deleting every 5th word in narrative content).
    44% of the items correct would indicate the Instructional level.
    57% of the items correct would indicate the Independent level.

The New York State Department of Education has been working on standardization of cloze paragraphs.

Other tests used for a quick measure are the McCracken Standard Reading Inventory, Leavell Oral Reading Tests, and the Silvaroli Classroom Reading Inventory.

Three good sources of detailed descriptions of reading tests are:

1. Buros, O. K. *Reading tests and reviews* 2, Highland Park, N.J.: The Gryphan Press, 1972.
2. Spache, G. D. *Diagnosing and correcting reading disabilities.* Boston: Allyn & Bacon, 1976.
3. Bond, G. L., & Tinker, M. A. *Reading difficulties: Their diagnosis and correction* (3rd ed.). New York: Appleton-Century-Crofts, 1973.

Formal Assessment of Learning Disabilities

The definition of primary learning disability implies that the individual has normal mental ability (I.Q. of 85 or higher for our purposes) but that his organic mechanism for learning is not intact or is not functioning properly. This type of person will be a more severe reading disability case and, in the extreme, will be a nonreader. He may have a perceptual handicap, may have a neural dysfunction of a variety of types, or may have a maturational or developmental lag. In general, the areas to be evaluated are learning modalities. Conclusions based on neurological diagnosis and other medical evaluations are to be made only by medical specialists. Although competent and properly trained psychologists may suspect cerebral dysfunctions on the basis of test performances, a diagnosis and conclusion of the presence of a neural impairment should only be made by proper medical sources. The question still remains as to whether or not the relatedness between neural dysfunctions and reading deficiencies is causative or correlative.

Preliminary Study

Having determined a child's learning expectancy level and analyzed what reading deficits he has, a decision must be made as to whether or not a more detailed analysis is needed, especially in terms of identifying a moderate to severe disabled reader. The decision to test for learning modalities, perceptual handicaps, and other characteristics of a primary disability reader is made if (1) the reading disability is severe, the child reads two years or more below expectancy level and has no signs of emotional disorder present; (2) a wide discrepancy exists between the verbal and performance I.Q.s on the WISC-R or an abnormally low score occurs on a significant subtest such as vocabulary, digit span, block design, or digit symbol; or (3) clinical judgment based upon results found in the informal or formal reading analysis seems to indicate a deficiency in either the visual or auditory learning modalities. The areas which are examined, according to the needs of the child, and tests which are used will vary from clinic to clinic, but the tests most frequently used by us will be listed in accordance with our classification of perceptual handicaps. The various areas will be listed separately, but it should be understood that a child may have deficiencies in several areas at the same time.

Suggested Batteries of Tests for Learning Disabilities

Test batteries used in diagnosing learning disabilities cases vary according to the theory or orientation of the researcher or examiner involved. The areas of learning disabilities, minimal or subtle neural dysfunction, and perceptually handicapped are not well-defined in terminology, causes, elements of the problems, remedial needs, or anything else. Yet, it is interesting that in spite of differences in points of view, there are some similarities in approaches. No implications are intended here that there are "standard" batteries of tests. The good clinician chooses each test to fit the needs of the individual child.

Silver and Hagin (1966) have done extensive work in this field. They evaluate five areas in their research: first, reading level, using the Wide Range Achievement Test (WRAT), the Metropolitan Reading Test, the WRAT spelling test, and a writing sample; second, intellectual level, using the WISC, while at the same time gathering qualitative data on speech and language patterns using an articulation inventory, and ascertaining approaches to thinking and reasoning; third, educational opportunity in terms of grade placement and examination of the child's work papers and notebook; fourth, since Silver is an M.D., neurologic status including both the classic areas and the more subtle defects of patterned motor acuity; fifth, in the perceptual areas related to a combination of intellectual and neural functions, they check (1) the visual modality with the Bender-Gestalt and Marble Board, (2) auditory modality, especially discrimination (Monroe), blending (Gates), sound matching (Gates), and word meaning (Durrell), (3) tactile and kinesthetic perception, including the use of finger agnosia, the figure-ground test of Strauss and Werner, the face-hand test of Bender, and stereognosis, (4) body image, orientation in space and in a mirrored image by use of the Goodenough Drawing, and (5) various types of sequencing, such as objects, digits, words, sentences, and the check test of H. Head. The neurological tests include right-left orientation, laterality, postural reflexes, the extension test, fine movements, and the EEG.

Levitt (1967) says that characteristically a diagnosis might include any of the following tests: the Illinois Test of Psycholinguistics Abilities (ITPA), the Parsons Language Sample (PLS), the Detroit Tests of Learning Aptitudes, the Wepman Auditory Discrimination Test, and various reading measures already mentioned.

In the Baltimore County remedial reading program (Schiffman, 1962), the following tests are given in addition to a case study: the WISC or Binet, a personality evaluation including Rorschach or Draw-A-Person, a reading battery including IRI, the Gates Associative Learning Tests, Detroit Tests of Memory Span, Laterality Tests, Bender-Gestalt, Frostig Perceptual Developmental Examination, and Eisenson Examination for Aphasia.

Bannatyne (1967), who developed the Psycholinguistic Color System, suggests the use of the WISC, the ITPA, Frostig's Visual Perceptual Tests, Bender-Gestalt, Memory-for Designs, tests for auditory and visual coding processes, the Lincoln-Oseretsky Test for Motor Functioning, articulation, auditory discrimination, and an EEG.

The EEG, however, is very limited in its use for diagnosing primary learning disability cases. For those who are interested in the use of the EEG or the usual tests given by neurologists, it should be noted that a number of medical people interested in learning disabilities do not believe that the typical or usual neurological tests are adequate for interpreting the types of dysfunctions, which admittedly may not be neural in nature, found in primary cases or those with "minimal brain damage." Gross and Wilson (1964), however, in their work on subconvulsive dysrhythmia found that this disorder was revealed by cerebral dysrhythmias on the EEG. These children had behavior and learning problems. Furthermore, they could be helped by medication.

A promising battery of tests for determining perceptual handicaps was developed by Rosner and Richman (1968) for the Division of Mental Health Services of the Pittsburgh (Pennsylvania) Public Schools. The Rosner Perceptual Survey requires the services of an optometrist or ophthalmologist, but the Rosner-Richman Perceptual Survey does not. The RRPS contains directions for administration and scoring criteria for the following tests: General Adjustment Response, Word Repetition, Auditory Organization, Gesell Copy Forms, Motor Skills (balance, hop, skip, throw, kick), Identification of Body Parts, Rhythmic Hopping and Tapping, Auditory-visual, and the Rutgers Drawing Test. In addition to these tests, the Rosner Perceptual Survey also includes Near Point Acuity, Stereopsis, Cover Test, Near Point Convergence, Pursuits, Retinoscopy, Split-form Board, and Tactual-visual Integration. A Behavior Rating Scale for use by the teacher is included in the publication. This scale is one of the best we have come across for the teacher.

Auditory Modality for Learning

In many ways, we consider the auditory modality to be most significant to the reading and learning process. This is a modality which is frequently underemphasized in diagnostic evaluation by too little testing. We consider auditory perceptual abilities more important than visual above the first grade. Components of the auditory modality which are related to reading are (a) auditory acuity, (b) speech discrimination, and (c) auditory memory and sequencing. We are concerned with auditory-verbal ability (ability to develop sound-symbol relationships), auditory comprehension or recognition of words, and degree of auditory awareness or alertness.

Auditory discrimination of speech-sound can be quickly tested by Wepman's Auditory Discrimination Test (1958) which consists of 40 pairs of words similar except for one sound. These words are read to the child who indicates whether they are the same or different. A problem in using this test with primary children is to determine whether or not they are actually listening for differences or just guessing. The Boston University Speech-Sound Discrimination Picture Test (Pronovost & Dumbleton, 1953) consists of 36 cards on each of which appear three pictures. Two of the three drawings represent words similar in sound or identical such as *cat—cat* or *cat—bat*. The child points to the pair of pictures representing what the examiner says. Informal tests of phonetic analysis and phonics, such as a modified Kottmeyer test, are also used to determine discrimination ability. We always check for ability to do blending, visually, auditorially, and verbally.

Some speech specialists caution users of speech discrimination tests to be aware of a possible general deficiency on the part of an articulation-impaired person in discerning differences between speech sounds. Remediation for poor auditory discrimination usually involves some form of auditory or speech stimulation through intensification of sounds (not hearing aids, necessarily).

Auditory acuity is always a possible source of problems so a hearing test should be given to all severely disabled readers and to those who show a deficiency on the auditory discrimination test. An observation made in our work, but not proven, is that children who have as small a loss as 15 decibels on pure tone audiometers very frequently have discrimination problems involving consonants. Some children have nerve hearing loss which only affects high frequency sounds. Either way, these children could be handicapped in learning phonics. A speech reception test or a test of speech articulation or intelligibility given by a speech therapist is usually recommended in addition to a pure-tone test.

Auditory memory is occasionally found to be the only deficit that a disabled reader may have. This auditory retention ability is measured by the digit-span test on the WISC-R or WAIS, the auditory sequencing subtest of the ITPA, or the Schuell Sentence-repetition Test (1957). Remediation involves developing the auditory retention span through a variety of appropriate memory games involving hearing numbers, letters, names, vowels, or consonant sounds. This approach, with some slight changes, can also be used to promote sound-symbol relationships and recognition.

In analyzing the WISC-R or WAIS subtests, we postulate that a low score on digit span, along with a low score on the digit symbol test, usually supports a conclusion of poor general memory ability. High or average digit span but low digit symbol scores usually reflect poor motor ability, poor visual memory, or a lack of drive and concentration.

Visual Modality for Learning

The visual modality is complicated by the fact that it has many aspects, some of which are perceptual and others mostly cognitive; also, there may be a visual-motor involvement. Some of the visual elements to be tested are (a) acuity, (b) memory and sequencing, (c) with severe cases, figure-ground perception, and (d) with younger children, perceptual discrimination, form, and configuration. Generally visual-motor performance is also observed in connection with the other tests of visual modality.

Visual acuity screening is done in most schools. However, for reading disabilities, cases should have a more thorough examination. Since vision is much more than mere acuity, the Keystone Visual Survey Tests should be administered. Tendencies toward lack of near-point and far-point fusion, nearsightedness, farsightedness, muscular imbalance, astigmatism, lack of stereopsis, and poor binocular efficiency can be detected through the use of these tests. Getman (1960), an optometrist, has developed a manual for the Optometric Extension Program Foundation which presents more advanced techniques and diagnostic criteria for the optometric care of children's vision. Many vision specialists interested in children with reading problems are making use of this method.

Among the more useful tests for estimating perceptual ability in children are the Block Design subtests of the WISC or WAIS, the Bender-Gestalt Visual Motor Test (1962), and the Marble Board Test (Cruickshank et al., 1965). The Block Design subtest requires that a child be able to perceive patterns or forms and to analyze and reproduce them by using blocks.

The Bender-Gestalt consists of nine configurations which the testee must copy. Levels of maturity and possible neural dysfunctions have been said to be revealed by this test. However, further evidence should be sought before jumping to conclusions. A study by Koppitz (1975) states that if a child has reading problems and reveals perceptual immaturity or malfunctioning on his Bender record, then two possibilities present themselves. First, the child may be slow in his visual motor development or be of limited intelligence. Second, there may be perceptual deficiencies present caused by poor visual functioning due to organic problems, to emotional problems (if auditory perception has been ruled out), or to dull, normal children living in an educationally nonstimulating environment. Koppitz has also developed a scoring scale which can be used with children ages 5-11. The designs of the Bender-Gestalt are in Table 7-2.

The Marble Board Test is designed to measure visual perception through motor performances. This test is frequently given to severely retarded readers or those suspected of brain-damage. Caution must be used in interpretation, as low mental ability children respond as many brain-injured children do.

The Minnesota-Percepto-Diagnostic Test (Fuller & Laird, 1936) claims to differentiate between primary disability learners and secondary reading disability cases. Fuller, the author, believes that it is a sensitive test when used with children who are two or more years behind in reading. He surmises that the problem of the primary case is not one of perception per se but one of association. A limitation of this test, as with the Marble Board Test and the Bender-Gestalt, is that a perceptual or cerebral problem may be detected in the visual or visual-motor realm, but it does little to detect the child with an auditory perception problem.

For visual memory, either the Memory for Designs Test (Graham & Kendall, 1960) or the Benton Revised Visual Retention Test (1955) are used. Both tests have been found to be effective for their purposes.

The Frostig Developmental Test of Visual Perception (1964) measures eye-motor coordination, figure-ground, constancy of shape, position in space, and spatial relationships. This series of tests seems to be receiving wide usage and is being subjected to considerable research studies. The fact that a remedial program is provided with this test makes it attractive to many people.

The Street Gestalt Completion Test (1931) is administered to the child in order to get insight into his constructive perceptual abilities. The items on the test consist of incomplete silhouettes of familiar forms. If the child's ability to see the parts and integrate them into a meaningful entity has not developed, he cannot function well on this test. Generally, primary reading disability cases have a tendency to try to identify one small part of the total silhouette, rather than the whole.

TABLE 7–2. Bender-Gestalt test designs.

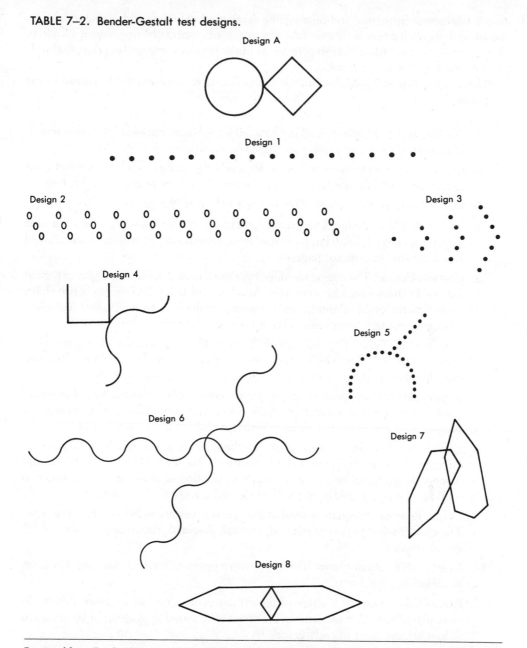

Reprinted from: Bender, Lauretta. "A Visual Motor Gestalt Test and its Clinical Use." Research Monograph No. 3, *American Orthopsychiatric Association*, 1938. Copyright, the American Orthopsychiatric Association, Inc. Reproduced by permission.

Motor Patterns

Perceptual-motor patterns as well as motor patterns by themselves are diagnosed by many psychologists. The significance of muscle patterns to reading and learning ability has not been fully determined, but there is considerable evidence to say that if motor patterns are not causative to reading development, then they certainly are correlated at least. This point is a fundamental distinction and must not be overlooked. Much is said of motor development and its relatedness to intellectual development, especially in younger children. Kephart has done extensive work in perceptual-motor development, so his perceptual scale will be presented in some detail.

The Purdue Perceptual-Motor Survey Tests (Roach & Kephart, 1966) consist of the following:

1. Walking Board. Similar to walking on a rail for balance. Backward direction reveals spatial orientation and projection. Sidewise direction is for laterality.

2. Jumping. Five techniques are given to reveal the child's ability to control gross musculature and to alternate activities across the center of gravity of his body.

3. Identification of Body Parts. This is a test related to the problem of body image.

4. Imitation of Movements. The requirement of moving from one position to the next involves unilateral, bilateral, and crosslateral movements. It requires translation of visual patterns into motor patterns.

5. Obstacle Course. The course includes a yardstick placed across two chairs as high as the child's knees which he steps over. Another yardstick is laid on top of two chairs lower than the child's shoulder and he is asked to duck under it. Another obstacle is squeezing through two chairs. This is for body awareness.

6. Angels-in-the-Snow. The child lies on the floor. He is asked to make ten movements with his arms and legs. The instructor points to his arm and says, "Move this arm, etc." Pointing is the only clue as to which arm or leg is to be moved.

7. Stepping Stones. Stepping stones are 6-inch squares of cardboard. Ten of these are black and ten are red. A pattern is given. Sometimes a right foot lead is demanded. Sometimes a left. This test shows whether a child is too asymmetrical.

8. Chalkboard. One of the most direct methods of testing a child's inadequacy in directionality is observing him at a chalkboard. Ask the child to draw a circle and observe the preferred hand, size of drawing, position of drawing with reference to midline of body, accuracy of production, and direction of movement.

9. Ocular Pursuits. Adequate control of the eyes is necessary to follow a target in view. The child is asked to pursue a lateral, vertical, diagonal, rotary, and a right and left eye movement.

10. Visual Achievement Forms. This deals with a figure-ground relationship. Children are asked to copy forms.

11. Kraus-Weber Tests is a series of performances designed to measure minimum muscular fitness. Certain items in the series were found by Kagerer to be related to school achievement in early grades.

The Perceptual Form Test (Sutphin, 1964), developed by research sponsored by the Winter Haven Lions Research Foundation, has been found useful in determining the perceptual maturity level of kindergarten and first grade children. The test is actually a battery of tasks, including (1) the Goodenough Draw-A-Man Test, (2) the Perceptual Form Test proper in which the child is asked to copy seven figures from complete and incomplete designs, (3) the testing of a variety of motor skills such as throwing a ball, skipping, hopping, walking a beam, angels in the snow, (4) a dominance test of eye, hand, and foot, (5) a test of near-point working distance, (6) visual screening by a device such as the Massachusetts Telebinocular Vision Test, (7) the Whisper Test, (8) the Articulation Test using a speech test such as the Speech Cards from Scott, Foresman, (9) the String Test to determine visual readiness by ascertaining how many strings a child sees, (10) the Block Test in which the child is asked to visualize a block to determine if the child is basically a kinesthetic type of learner (6% are), and (11) the Metropolitan Readiness Test for those who scored 60 or higher on the second Perceptual Form Test.

For the evaluation of finer motor skills, per se, the Lincoln-Oseretsky Motor Development Scale (Sloan, 1955) is very valuable as a diagnostic instrument. The test covers ages 6 to 14 and measures for each age level (1) general static coordination, (2) dynamic coordination of the hands, (3) general dynamic coordination, (4) motor speech, (5) simultaneous voluntary movements, and (6) ability to perform without superfluous movements. As an index of gross motor control and general locomotor coordination, the Health Rail-Walking Test (1953) can be used. The Purdue Pegboard Test is being studied by some researchers as an indicator of motor dysfunction.

Language and Speech Development

In diagnosing speech development, we use no measuring device except subjective judgment as to whether or not the child has a speech defect. We are aware of primary disability cases that have speech problems or who were slow in developing normal speech sounds. We are mindful that many normal children who are 6 and 7 years of age may have not developed certain consonant sounds. However, if a child is deficient in reading and appears to have a speech defect, we ask a speech therapist to check the child. In a minor unpublished experiment with only twenty children, we separated kindergarten children with speech defects into an experimental group and a control group and had a speech therapist work on speech training with the experimental group. This study was done two years in a row. Each time, the children receiving the speech training progressed better in learning and reading skills in first grade than did the other group.

In evaluating older children, we always check to see if they may have had a history of speech problems and speech therapy in the primary grades. By the same token, we also check with the teachers or cumulative folders to see if there was a history of poor motor development or incoordination on the playground or in games.

Language development is evaluated by the score on the vocabulary test of the Binet or the WISC-R. The Binet scale gives a mental age level. We also seek to learn if the child is a nonspontaneous talker who seldom, if ever, initiates conversation and says as few words as possible in answering your questions. The child may be different when among his peers, so this possibility is considered in the diagnosis. A nonspontaneous talker often has auditory modality or verbal problems.

Among language and speech tests that have been used are (a) Detroit Tests of Learning Aptitude (Baker & Leland, 1955), (b) Illinois Test of Psycholinguistic Abilities (Kirk et al., 1968), (c) Picture Story Language Test (Myklebust, 1965), (d) Parsons Language Sample (Spradlin, 1963), (e) Basic Concept Inventory (Engelmann, 1967), and (f) Templin-Darley Screening and Diagnostic Tests of Articulation (1960).

Cognitive Factors

The element of cognition is determined by the subtest scores on the WISC-R, especially in comprehension and similarities (abstract reasoning). The child who is culturally or language disadvantaged generally does worse on general information, arithmetic, and vocabulary on the WISC-R but frequently holds up better on the similarities test. By diagnosing the types of answers given by the child on the WISC-R, some attempt can be made to determine if he is correct in his answers and if he shows some reasoning. Also, his thinking is evaluated to determine if it is rigid and so structured that once he gets on an idea, he cannot change his thinking, or if he is flexible in his thinking and can manipulate ideas.

Neural Patterns of Learning

We use the phrase *Neural Patterns of Learning* to include a variety of physical responses which may give some clue as to the developmental level of neurological maturity in aspects which some researchers believe may be related to learning. We have observed that the higher the I.Q. of the child, the more likely he is to be able to compensate even though he has some inability to perform on age level on some of the following tests.

DIRECTIONALITY OR LEFT-RIGHT ORIENTATION. We determine the degree to which a child knows his rights and lefts. We assume that most normal 6-year-old children can show you their left hand, right eye, left ear, right knee, without hesitation. The average 7-year-old can cross the midline of the body and do such things as point to his left ear with his right hand. The 8-year-old can generally tell lefts and rights, even in crossing the midline, on the examiner. We do not know that these are accurate norms, but our observations are that a child who is nine years old or older and still has trouble telling lefts and rights, or has to hesitate to figure them out, probably also is a primary case and will be less efficient in his learning processes. Again, is the relationship causative or correlative? We do not know. In remediation, simply teaching a child his lefts and rights does not do much, if any, good in helping him become a better reader. We use the test of directionality as a check for immaturity in development in the 6- to 8-year-old and as a sign which says "look further." We do show concern for the child who is nine or older and is still confused about directionality. We frequently use a stereo reader with such a child.

Benton has a Left-Right Discrimination and Finger Localization Test (1959) to determine the level of directionality the child has developed. The first four questions are at the level of body concept. The next four questions are projections into space. Questions 9 through 15 force the child to make 2 choices, some homolateral and others bilateral. The last four questions deal with isolated parts of the body which are identifiable. The task difficulty here is that no other visual clues are permitted.

The examiner must be aware of signals of trouble: reluctance to cross the body center line, hesitating before responding, eyes rolling up in thought, simultaneous movement of both arms, employment of "gimmicks" such as "I write with my right hand," "I wear my watch on my left hand." In the clinic we always ask the child, "Are you sure that's right?" Not being certain, many times a child will change a right response to an incorrect one.

Subjective judgment on left-right disorientation may be noted in such activities as a lack of perspective or dimensional confusion in spontaneous drawings. Many children will have reversals of letters or numbers in writing or reading, such as in reversing columns in adding numbers, in saying *left* for *felt*, or writing *dose* for *does*. Many disoriented persons will say *left* and point right, or say an incorrect but related word such as *Christmas* for *Easter*. Some control is shown if the person makes a spontaneous correction. Children with good intelligence and adults can compensate for these deficiencies in reading or speaking by close attention and concentration on what they are reading or saying. This extra effort explains why many primary cases talk and read more slowly. The primary case *must* develop concentration and attention abilities. An interesting speculation and demonstration has to do with how children tie their shoe-strings. Many primary cases tie them backwards. The Jordan Left-Right Reversal Test (1974) measures letter and number reversals in children ages 5 through 12.

DOMINANCE OR LATERALITY. We believe that *laterality*, which means the development of one-side cerebral dominance so that the hand, foot, and eye are all controlled by the same hemisphere, may not actually be measured by the tests usually given for this purpose. Handedness, footedness, and eyedness are peripheral manifestations and may not accurately indicate cerebral dominance.

Handedness is somewhat superficially evaluated by such activities as the hand with which the child writes, throws a ball, brushes his teeth, combs his hair, points to an object, eats, or erases a chalkboard. Footedness is checked by pretending to kick a ball, stamp out a grass fire with one foot, take several steps to stamp out a cigarette. Eyedness is tested at least three times by looking through a tube, a hole in a piece of paper, a kaleidoscope, or a tunnel (opening) made with both hands.

A more specialized test of laterality is the Harris Test of Lateral Dominance (1958), which does more with writing in determining hand preferences.

From the Harris tests we find that we get some valuable information by a modification of his Simultaneous Writing Test. We ask a child to write *cat* or his name with one hand, then the other, then with both hands at the same time. Then, without seeing the paper, the child is asked to write the numbers 1 to 9 with both hands at the same time: the numbers are not given in consecutive order. Reversals with the dominant hand or an inability to write with both hands simultaneously usually suggests a dominance problem of some type.

The Leavell Eye-Hand Coordinator Tests (1958) are a tool psychologists can use for uncovering visual-motor preference. It is a series of tests in which the examinee draws certain figures and is asked to perform certain one-sided tasks such as winding a watch. Scoring is done on the basis of how the figures are drawn, the facing of the figures, and the starting point of drawing. If the results are divorced from the dominance aspect, the presence of neural confusion can be revealed. When combined with the Spache Test for Suppression and the Binocular Reading Test Record (1961) the dominant eye in the reading situation can be discovered.

The research literature is very confused on the meaning of laterality or dominance for reading disability. Our interpretations, by observation only, are that if a child is nine or older and has not developed one-sidedness, we are not concerned about this problem and feel that it no longer seriously affects his reading ability. We believe that it may have affected him when he was beginning to read or at least was a correlative factor in immaturity, so the child may have not learned the necessary skills at that time because of the immature development. We also relate the immaturity concept to children of 6 to 8 who have not developed laterality. In the child 9 years or older, we are concerned if their handedness and footedness are opposite (as in right handed but left footed). We have found this condition in some of our more serious cases, but frankly, we do not know what to do about it. We are also conscious and suspicious of the development of a child who is too strongly onesided and does practically nothing with the other side.

OTHER TESTS. For our own satisfaction in detecting possibilities of maturational lag or neural problems, but not for the purpose of drawing conclusions of a neurological nature, we are interested in the results of such tests as the Schilder Extension Test, the Romberg

Test, test for finger agnosia, and two-point or double stimulation tests of the face. For very severe cases, tactile identification of familiar objects may also be used.

Two helpful tests relating to neural processing for learning are (a) the Quick Neurological Screening Test (QNST) (Mutti et al., 1974), which is made up of 14 subtests, most of them of short duration, and (b) Jean Ayres, Southern California Kinesthesia and Tactile Perception Tests (1966). Ayres has 8 separate tests related to sensory, perceptual, and motor development, but of the group, the kinesthesia and tactile tests are most meaningful to use.

A final note on neural patterns for learning. There are many neurological tests that are not applicable to learning processes related to academics, even though they give positive signs of neural dysfunctions. It appears that only tests that measure functions being processed in the parietal lobe or in the angular gyrus area have anything to do with reading and language learning.

An unusual, but unverified test for handedness and lateral dominance has been suggested by Friedman (1952) who noted the position of the hair-whorl and reported in Critchley's book (1964). He estimated the percentage of a right whorl in a normal community to be 21% and 70% for a left whorl. Tjosseim, Hansen, and Ripley (1962) applied this sign to a series of retarded readers and found a right whorl in 54% and a left whorl in 21%. These differences were regarded as significant in pointing to a greater than normal tendency to congenital left laterality despite the fact that the majority of the children were right-handed. A more recent approach has been considering not only the location of the whorl but whether it turns clockwise or counter clockwise. No conclusions are reported at this time.

To arrive at an indication of the learning modality of each child the Mills Learning Methods Test (1955) can be employed. The teacher finds 40 words which the child does not know at the same reader level. Each day ten words are taught for 10 minutes by a different method—visual, auditory, kinesthetic, or a combination of all three. Immediate recall and delayed recall (24 hours) are checked. On the basis of the results obtained, the child's most efficient learning modality is ascertained.

A final type of test we wish to mention here is a rhythm test. Children with learning disabilites frequently have problems repeating a rhythm produced by tapping or clapping hands. The Knox Cube Test is used as well as clapping or tapping that sounds like variations of the Morse code. This area concerning rhythm and the disabled learner presents one of the more interesting areas for research.

Learning Modalities (the ITPA)

The Illinois Test of Psycholinguistic Abilities (Kirk et al., 1968), was designed to identify psycholinguistic abilities and disabilities in children between the ages of two and one-half and nine. The series of tests seek to follow the perceptual process of "reception, association, and expression" on the representational and the automatic levels. The battery consists of 10 tests plus 2 supplementary tests. The tests are:

Receptive Process (Decoding)	1. *Auditory Reception*—A vocabulary test or simple sentence test requiring a "yes" or "no" answer.
	2. *Visual Reception*—Matching a given picture with one of a group of four (chair to desk).
Organizing Process (Association)	3. *Auditory Association*—a Verbal analogies test.
	4. *Visual Association*—Choose what goes with the central picture, or point to two related pictures similar to what the examiner shows.

Expressive Process (Encoding)	5. *Verbal Expression*—Use of grammatical form in expressing a concept.
	6. *Manual Expression*—Demonstrate physically in what way the object in the picture is used.
Automatic Level	7. *Grammatical Closure*—Complete a sentence accompanying a picture.
	8. *Visual Closure*—Complete a partially visual object.
	9. *Auditory Closure*—Complete the segments of words that are not spoken by the examiner.
	10. *Sound Blending*—Sounds are given at half-second intervals and child is to put the sounds together.
Sequential Memory	11. *Auditory Sequential Memory*—Repeat two of eight digits.
	12. *Visual Sequential Memory*—reproduce sequence of small chips with chips on them.

The test still requires work on both reliability and validity. Test users should recognize its theoretic basis and its limitations in norms and interpretation but, at the same time, recognize its clinical potential.

There are some serious questions being asked by researchers as to what the ITPA actually measures. McLeod (1966) did a factor analysis of the ITPA and came up with only five loadings: (a) sequencing integrative, (b) encoding factor, (c) visual motor factor, (d) auditory language input capacity, and (e) planning factor. Smith and Marx (1971) found only three factors: (a) rote auditory memory, (b) mediated memory, and (c) representational expression. Researchers also believe that 80% of the variance in test scores is due to general linguistic or verbal ability. Maybe this is why language and speech clinicians find the ITPA so helpful. Newcomer et al. (1975) did a construct validity study of the ITPA and found generally favorable results concerning construct validity—that it measures discrete psycholinguistic abilities. They did not find a general linguistic component as was implied in the Smith and Marx study, but they did find something else. Newcomer et al. found that the tests measuring the auditory channel had some validity but that the visual channel was not substantiated as a valid dimension. In a different kind of study, Grill and Bartel (1977) found that the grammatic closure part of the ITPA was an inappropriate diagnostic instrument to use with children who use nonstandard English, even infrequently.

Kolson's Quick Modalities Test (KQM)

Recent emphasis upon children's learning styles has left the teacher in a quandary. The teacher is asked to teach to the student's strongest modality without being given a reasonable way to determine the modality. The Illinois Test of Psycholinguistic Abilities (ITPA) can tell the teacher whether the strongest modality is visual or auditory. The ITPA must be administered individually by a trained examiner. Since it takes approximately 1½ hours to give the ITPA, a teacher with a class of 30 would use from 8 to 10 days of teaching time if she were to administer it individually. In order to make use of those days, she would have to be supplied with a substitute. And, as teachers, you know that this isn't going to happen!

It is important that the teacher be given a quick, easy method for getting an approximation of the student's modality strengths and weaknesses. To do this, Kolson, in 1976, modified the McGill Intrasensory-Integration Test. Admittedly, it is not as accurate as the longer McGill test. However, there may be only two choices—an accurate test that takes much time to give and is difficult to administer, hence probably will not be used; or a less accurate test, easy to administer, that will be used. We're certain that the latter is the more practical of the two. The Kolson Quick Modalities Test (the "poor man's ITPA," as he calls it) is easy for the teacher to give and easy for the pupils to take. If the children can write, then the visual (step one) and auditory (step two) tests can be given as group tests leaving only the tests involving kinesthetic and tactile modalities to be given individually. If the children can write, it takes about 20 minutes to test a class of 30 pupils. To determine the quality of the four modalities, vision, auditory, kinesthetic, or tactile, only the first four parts of this test need be given.

To administer the KQM test, the teacher must be certain that the child can count to at least 30. Once it is determined that the child can count to 30, place a copy of Figure 7-1 before him; then follow eight steps.

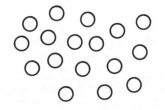

FIGURE 7–1. KQM circles.

Step One: Say, "How many circles are there on this card?" Don't let him point to the circles; it must all be done with the eyes. If the student gives any figure other than the number of circles on the card, his visual mechanism lacks integrity.

Step Two: Say, "I'm going to tap the desk. I want you to tell me *how many times* I tap. Your eyes must be closed." The tester taps an irregular pattern of 13 taps. If the student gives any number other than 13, his auditory mechanism is not intact.

Step Three: The tester takes a wooden pencil. He hands it with the eraser down to the student, saying, "Close your eyes; then tap my hand 15 times with the eraser." If the student taps any number other than 15, his kinesthetic mechanism lacks integrity.

Step Four: Say, "I'm going to tap your back. I want you to tell me how many times I tapped you. You must have your eyes closed while I am tapping." The tester taps 17 times in an irregular pattern. Any answer other than 17 indicates a lack of integrity in the tactile mechanism. Once the individual modalities have been tested, the tester can begin to test how well the student can integrate the modalities. The tester places Figure 7-2 before the student.

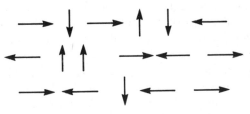

FIGURE 7–2. KQM arrows.

Step Five: Say, "I want you to read these arrows. If the arrow is pointed to the right, say *right*; to the left, say *left*; up, say *up*; down, say *down*." Vision, motor, speech patterns, and directionality are being tested with this test. If the child doesn't know his right and left, tell him to say *side* when the arrow is pointing right or left. If the child can integrate these four factors, go to Step Six. If the child cannot do step five, then skip to step eight.

Step Six: Say, "I want you to read the arrows again, but this time I want you to swing your hands in the direction of the arrow." (Demonstrate) The next step is to integrate the auditory modality with motor.

Step Seven: Say, "I want you to do it again, but this time you must do it to the tapped beat." (Tap desk top, rhythmically, every second.)

Up to this point, Kolson's Quick Modalities test will tell you which of the pupils' modalities lack integrity but will not tell you which is the preferred modality. Do the following to determine the preferred modality between vision and kinesthesis.

Step Eight: Say, "Take this piece of paper (index card) and pencil and when I say 'Go,' put the paper on your forehead and write *cat*. Go!" If he writes *cat* on the paper backwards, he prefers kinesthesis to vision. If he writes *cat* so it would come out forward, he prefers vision. Once the student who prefers kinesthesis knows this, he can be a more efficient learner by taking notes or outlining information. The visual learner, on the other hand, can become a more efficient learner by diagramming or schematicizing materials to be learned. It is senseless to try to teach a child through any modality that is not functioning or lacks integrity. Efficient learning means more time to learn more.

Evaluation of Emotional Factors

Some consideration should be given to evaluating emotional factors which could hinder learning achievement. In particular, it would be interesting to determine the motivational or aspiration level of the child, his self-concept, his degree of satisfactory relationship with his peers, family and school, and his behavior tendencies, such as withdrawal behavior or antisocial behavior. The problem of the reading clinician is that most of the worthwhile tests require special training and interpretation, so the services of a psychologist are required.

Generally, we do not find emotional problems in children in the first three grades unless the children are subjected to undue pressures from the parents. The first signs of emotional concern are noticed during the fourth and fifth grades. By the junior high grades, emotional inhibition is definitely a factor in learning to read. By senior high grades, there may be outright resistance and rejection.

A group test which can be administered to one child at a time and can be used by a reading clinician under the right circumstances is the California Test of Personality (Thorpe et al., 1953). This test is available on the primary, intermediate, elementary, secondary, and adult levels. The testee is required to give a "yes" or "no" answer. The manual claims that young children usually respond truthfully. We found this to be true up to the third grade. The question can be read to the child, and he can mark his own paper. With the first and second graders, we usually mark the papers for them but we pretend not to be looking at the child when he gives an answer.

Test scores on the Personal Adjustment Scale of the California Test of Personality are obtained on self-reliance, feeling of personal worth, personal freedom, feeling of belonging, freedom from withdrawal tendencies, and freedom from nervous symptoms. On the Social

Adjustment Test, scores are obtained on social standards, social skills, freedom from antisocial tendencies, family relationships, school relations, and community relations. Results require clinical judgment, but it is amazing how useful the results can be. Other useful tests are the Personal Adjustment Inventory by Rogers, Minnesota Counseling Inventory, Personality Test for Children by Brown, and the Vineland Social Maturity Scale.

For self-concept, the Adjective Check List (Gough, 1952) and the Q Sort Test (Stephenson, 1953) are frequently used. Anastasi (1976) claims that properly used, self-report inventories can be interpreted as measures of self-concept.

A self-concept booklet that can be used very effectively by teachers of children with a second grade reading level is "All About Me, Myself, and I" (Trzcinski, 1972). The interest level of the content is high enough to appeal even to sixth graders. The topics of this "write on" booklet lend themselves to good group discussions in grades three, four, and five, and have been found to be effective with children with reading and learning disabilities problems.

Among the more specialized but frequently used tests of personal characteristics, emotional and ego functioning are the Draw-A-Person, Bender Gestalt, Sentence Incompletion Tests, Thematic Apperception Test, Children's Apperception Test, and the Minnesota Multiphasic Personality Inventory. These tests should only be administered by psychologists trained to use them. Not all psychologists can give these tests.

Determining Mental Capacity

For many years reading and psychological clinicians have acted as if tests of mental ability were very precise. Today most clinicians realize that tests of mental ability are just one more measure of the student which must be combined with the results of other tests, both norm-referenced and criterion-referenced, and with their observations and judgment in order to make an educational decision concerning a student.

Many tests of mental ability are culturally loaded. "How tall is the average American woman?" This question presupposes that all who take the test have been subjected to many American women and that the brighter ones will be able to generalize that the average woman is between 5' 4" and 5' 6" tall before the mentally slower persons make this generalization. It is obvious that asking an Australian aborigine this question would be unfair, yet it may also be unfair to the ghetto dweller or the child from a rural slum.

The type of questions found on tests of mental capacity many times measure what D. O. Hebb (1949) calls *Intelligence B*, or functional intelligence, developed and influenced by the environment. *Intelligence A* is supposedly innate and so far immeasureable except by measuring the acetycholine-cholinesterase ratio at the synapse, which is most difficult to do. Since we cannot measure Intelligence A, which indicates the potential ability, we must measure Intelligence B, which we assume to be a functional manifestation of Intelligence A.

The work of Kirk has shown that the I.Q. is not static but can be changed. Ferguson (1973) in her book, *The Brain Revolution: The Frontiers of Mind Research*, cites a study which attests to the fluidity of intelligence, as measured by so-called intelligence tests.

At the present time we do not have anything better for measuring mental ability than intelligence tests so they must be used, but never should they be the sole determiner of a student's capacity.

There are many measures available to the clinician trained in the theory and skills of psychological testing. Individual mental ability tests, such as the Wechsler tests for children or the one for adults, and the Revised Stanford-Binet are among the most useful but also the most specialized to give and to interpret. No one should attempt to use these tests without adequate training and preparation. Learning to administer these tests requires a semester course, usually for each type, plus clinical experience. Remedial clinics should have psychological services available, not only to administer these tests, but for other contributions and evaluations that psychologists can make.

Group Tests of Mental Abilities

The scores from group intelligence tests are usually less reliable than the scores from individually administered tests. The child with low reading ability will invariably do poorly on a group intelligence test which is verbal in nature and requires reading. Nonverbal or performance type group intelligence tests do not seem to yield scores of the type of mental abilities related to the reading act. It is wise to remember that intelligence tests measure different kinds, functions, or attributes of intelligence, and we cannot always be sure that what is being measured will relate to the skill we are seeking to teach. For clinical purposes, it is recommended that scores from group intelligence tests not be used, if at all possible.

Individual Tests for the Reading Teacher

An individual verbal mental ability test which a clinician can learn to use effectively is the Peabody Picture Vocabulary Test (Dunn, 1959). In spite of the name of the test, it is designed to reveal mental age; however, we cannot trust the findings as to the I.Q. and the M.A. Theoretically, it can be used at any age level. Our experience is that the test reflects a "verbal" (scholastic or word knowing) type of mental ability and, thus, the results can be affected by any factor which influences verbal ability, such as delayed speech and cultural differences. The test does not reflect any perceptual handicaps, except perhaps indirectly or unintentionally, but the Peabody Test does provide good insight into language development. Tests similar to this one are those developed by Ammons and Ammons, the Full Range Picture Vocabulary Test (1950) and the Quick Test (Ammons & Ammons, 1962). Both of these tests have many uses, also, and are much like the Peabody except that instead of responding with one word to a page of four pictures, as on the Peabody, the Ammons and Ammons tests will ask the child to identify several words on a page containing several pictures. In support of using vocabulary to indicate mental ability level, studies show that there is a strong positive correlation between vocabulary knowledge and verbal-type intelligence.

The psychologists will often ask a child up to the age of 8 to "draw a man." This drawing can be used to obtain a mental age. The test is limited in its effectiveness with perceptual cases, but much can be learned about the motor development and intellectual functioning of the child by analyzing the drawing. This is the Goodenough-Harris Draw-a-Man Test.

Perhaps the best intelligence test for the teacher to learn to use is the Slosson Intelligence Test (SIT) (1963). This test has the same format as the Binet test and will provide a rather adequate I.Q. for verbal learning. It does not do much to reveal learning disabilities, but its score gives a fairly good indication of a child's functional mental capacity for academic, verbal learning. The test must be administered individually but it can usually be given in 15 minutes.

The Wechsler Tests

For interpretative purposes we prefer the use of the Wechsler Intelligence Scale for Children—Revised, (WISC-R) (1974) or the Wechsler Adult Intelligence Scale (WAIS) (1955) to any other individual type test, including the Stanford-Binet. These tests provide a Verbal Scale I.Q., a Performance Scale I.Q., and a Full Scale I.Q.

The Verbal Scale contains six subtests: Information (range of information); Comprehension (common sense judgment); Arithmetic (oral arithmetic reasoning); Similarities (abstract reasoning); Vocabulary (quality of word meaning); and Memory Span for Digits (auditory memory). In general, these subtests measure the type of mental abilities needed to do the type of thinking, reasoning, and remembering which is related to "scholastic" functions or "verbal" areas. Verbal areas pertain to, take the form of, or consist of, words in any form spoken, heard, seen, written, or thought. Achievement on the Verbal Scale is influenced by cultural, emotional, environmental, and/or organic factors involving auditory perception or acuity which can promote or inhibit the acquisition or response of verbal context.

The five subtests making up the Performance Scale are Picture Completion (alertness to essential environmental details); Block Design (spatial perception and visual-motor organization); Picture Arrangement (planning and anticipation of social situations); Object Assembly (practical manipulative ability, work habits, and persistence); and Digit Symbol (concentration and drive in learning new material involving visual-motor coordination, speed, and memory). A test seldom used on the WISC-R because it is not required is the Mazes test, which measures planning and foresight as well as visual-motor ability in speed and accuracy. Some researchers believe this subtest has much diagnostic value. Achievement on the Performance Scale is influenced by factors involving visual perception, visual-motor coordination or just motor response, and knowledge of practical, nonverbal, everyday objects and/or events. The type of mental abilities measured pertain to "practical" or "performance" (visual-manual) activities.

Since the Verbal Scale and the Performance Scale measure different types of mental abilities, it would be interesting to know what, if any, information the I.Q.s, as well as the subtest scores, might provide for the reading clinician. A number of researchers have made observations concerning discrepancies between the I.Q.s on the Verbal and Performance Scales and have implied that the differences, or lack of differences, have meaning when applied to remedial readers. Rabinovitch (1954) states that a big discrepancy between the verbal and performance scores, averaging 22.1 points, suggested primary reading retardation, while lesser discrepancy, averaging 8.8 points, was suggestive of a secondary condition. In discussing the diagnostic use of intelligence tests, Rabin (1965) reports that a V-P discrepancy of 15 points occurs only 13 times out of 100 in a normal population. He does not indicate the reading levels of the people involved in his sample. However, the diagnostic impulse to make much of the discrepancy must be tempered by remembering Rabin's statistics. Clements (1963) says that children with a verbal score of 15-40 points above performance, or a performance score of 10-30 points above verbal, invariably have moderate to severe learning disability.

Our diagnostic interpretations concerning discrepancies between verbal and performance scores, based on clinical observations, are as follows:

1. Any discrepancy of 10 points or more warrants further testing and study; the greater the discrepancy, the greater the need for further analysis to check for perceptual

handicap or cerebral dysfunction. No interpretations are made on the basis of the Wechsler tests alone.

2. If the discrepancy is 15 points or more higher in Performance than the Verbal scale, then we check for (a) a problem in auditory discrimination, perception, or acuity, (b) environmental conditions which may have influenced verbal development adversely, and (c) a "nonspontaneous" talker or one who has had poor speech development.

3. If the discrepancy is 15 points or more higher in Verbal than on the Performance scale, then we check for (a) a visual discrimination, perception, or acuity problem, (b) a motor problem, possibly visual-motor in nature, (c) personality factors such as lack of drive, low frustration level, or lack of interest in this type of testing material.

4. If there is a strong mental disorder (illness) present or the case is an adolescent psychopath or delinquent, then we recognize that these factors may influence the results. Mentally disordered persons generally score higher on verbal scores and delinquents score higher on performance.

Robert Rugel (1974) reviewed 25 studies that reported WISC subtest scores of disabled readers. The subtest scores of the disabled readers are compared with those of normal readers, showing where they scored higher or lower. The results are in Table 7-3. It is

TABLE 7–3. Disabled reader-normal reader subtest comparisons.

	Disabled Readers Significantly Lower Than Average Readers	Disabled Readers Significantly Higher Than Average Readers
DeBruler	Digit Span, Coding, Arithmetic	Picture Completion
McLeod	Digit Span, Coding, Information, Vocabulary	Picture Completion
Belmont et al.	Arithmetic, Information, Vocabulary	Object Assembly
Reid et al. (Average readers)	Arithmetic	Picture Completion
Reid et al. (Above average readers)	Digit Span, Arithmetic, Similarities	Picture Completion
Neville	Digit Span, Arithmetic, Information	Block Design, Picture Arrangement
McLean	Digit Span, Coding, Arithmetic, Information, Vocabulary	Picture Completion
Ackerman et al.	Arithmetic	
Hunter et al.	Digit Span, Coding, Arithmetic, Information, Vocabulary, Similarities	
Lyle et al.	Coding Arithmetic, Information	Block Design, Picture Arrangement, Comprehension
Coleman et al.	Arithmetic, Information	Object Assembly

SOURCE: Rugel, R. P. WISC subtest scores of disabled readers: A review with respect to Bannatyne's recategorization. *Journal of Learning Disabilities*, January 1974, 7:1, 48–61.

interesting to note how often disabled readers score lower than normal readers in the digit span test, yet this is a test not frequently given because it is not required to obtain an IQ score. Normal readers did better than disabled readers mostly in arithmetic, general information, and digit span. Disabled readers generally did better in picture completion, which measures visual alertness to details. This last point surely will have some meaning to those who insist on improving visual perception of poor readers, not realizing that most of them are already very good in visual perception.

The Revised Stanford-Binet

The Stanford-Binet (Terman, 1960) is in a third edition and is still a very popular individual intelligence test. Whereas the Wechsler tests have subtests, the Stanford-Binet has age levels with at least six items requiring different types of mental ability responses on each age level. The test gives a mental age (which the WISC and WAIS do not) as well as an I.Q. The psychologist who is adept at analyzing this test can tell what types of mental abilities are strong or weak by the types of items which were missed on the lower levels and those which are among the last to be missed. The Stanford-Binet, for the most part, measures functional ability of a verbal type on the age levels related to school grades and, as such, is a good predictor of probable scholastic achievement in school. For reading specialists, it does not yield the depth of diagnostic and clinical information usually sought in reading disability diagnosis.

chapter 8

Approaches to
Teaching Disabled Readers

Effective instructional planning depends on three kinds of information:

1. All we know about the child and how he learns.
2. All we know about the subject matter and its component skills.
3. All we know about strategies, techniques and materials that will help the child learn the subject matter.

With such a simple statement of guidelines, it would appear to be a simple task to tie all the parts together into a coordinated, well-structured package. Unfortunately, the task is not that simple. There may be general agreement on the content of the subject and its skills, but there is less agreement and understanding of what it is that we have to know about the child and how he learns. When we consider strategies and techniques of teaching, we are now on even less tenuous ground because specialists and would-be specialists are continually advocating ways to do the job. That endeavor would not be all bad if some of the methods and strategies suggested did not take on the semblance of a panacea and its advocates did not don the robes of a cult, proclaiming that "this approach, and only this approach, is the way to the promised land." Also unfortunate are the strong advertising and public relations programs that accompany newly published materials, trying to sell a technique on the basis of pretty colors, pictures, and words.

The four factors that are frequently missing from many programs are (1) consideration of variability of needs and make-ups of children; (2) the differing philosophies and personalities of teachers, which will indicate approaches and materials they will feel comfortable with; (3) the administrative policies of the schools as they relate to scheduling, curriculum or program structure, and teacher freedom of choice in how she does her job; and (4) the concern, expectations, and demands of the parents in terms of what they want their schools to do, how they assess school programs and achievement gains, and the money they are willing to commit to promote school programs in academic areas.

This chapter presents thumbnail sketches of various approaches used in teaching reading and in teaching learning disabled children. More detailed presentations will be given on principles of teaching LD youngsters and how to plan a lesson.

Models of Instructional Programs

It is difficult to present clear-cut descriptions of approaches to instructional programs because each basic approach has its proponents who generally decide to do something slightly different with it. For example, the developmental or traditional regular classroom approach has some advocates who stress group instruction, while others emphasize the individualization of instruction. Most likely, teachers will tend to use an eclectic approach to instruction, choosing those elements of instructional programs that appeal most to them. Sometimes administrative policies will decree a certain type of instructional approach by nature of their administrative organizational structure, a time schedule they may institute, a policy passed by the school board, a curriculum plan that must be followed, accountability requirements or competencies that must be met by the end of the school year, or by the very nature of the school building or classroom design. Our position is that a teacher should be permitted to teach in the manner by which she feels most comfortable and secure as long as that approach meets the specific needs of most, if not all, of her pupils. If that approach requires the modification of approaches to teaching, then so be it.

The Developmental Approach

The developmental approach to instruction is the traditional, regular classroom approach. It approximates the basal reader approach to teaching reading. There is a curriculum core of content and skills that must be taught in a somewhat sequential manner. The basic material for instruction is a textbook or a basal reading series that serves as a thread or track that will direct what will be taught and when. A well-balanced core program will make provisions for supplementary materials to be used such as workbooks, wall charts, related activities, learning games, filmstrips, films, and experience charts. The teacher's manual or teacher's guide is used to give direction and help to the teacher. If properly used, the manual can insure a reasonably good program for the majority of the children in a regular classroom.

The innovative teacher can operate within a developmental program with flexibility and variability of instruction in order to provide for individual differences. In addition to basal readers, she can make use of trade books, unit plans of instruction, and pacing of instruction (within reason) by grouping her children according to their ability to learn the material. If she is truly an adaptive teacher, she can structure her daily schedule in such a way that she can individualize instruction by the use of learning centers and other techniques that will permit a choice of learning activities by her children at appropriate times. A rigid, nonflexible, well-structured teacher may find it difficult to deviate much from a routine daily program. In the final analysis, both kinds of teachers still need to provide systematic reading instruction, cope with variability among pupils, integrate reading instruction with subject matter, and provide for both the gifted as well as the disabled readers in their rooms. Moderate to severely impaired learning disabled readers generally do not do well in regular classrooms. The regular classroom teacher usually does not know how to identify their problems, nor how to fit work for that child within her regular program.

The Diagnostic-Prescriptive Approach

The *diagnostic-prescriptive teaching approach* is sometimes referred to as *diagnostic teaching, clinical teaching,* or simply *prescriptive teaching*. There are two administrative formats that make use of the diagnostic-prescriptive teacher (DPT). One approach is to designate certain individuals within a school, or school system, as diagnostic-prescriptive teachers. These teachers will be considered specialists in determining what a child's problems in learning are and will write an educational program (prescription) for him that the regular classroom teacher is to follow. Children are referred to the diagnostic-prescriptive teacher by the regular classroom teacher through designated channels. The child in most cases will attend class in the room of the diagnostic teacher for as long as it takes for this teacher to learn what is wrong and what can be done about it. The child may be in this room 2 weeks, 6 weeks, or as long as is needed for the diagnostician to come up with an answer.

The other administrative format for diagnostic-prescriptive teachers is to make this approach a standard designation for all teachers working with special children. Each teacher who has disabled learners is to be a DPT. It is her job to assess each child as to his strengths and weaknesses, his achievement levels, learning expectancy levels, and his skills, or lack of skills, in each of the basic subjects (reading, arithmetic, spelling, and written and/or oral language). Once the DPT has uncovered the child's needs, she is to write an educational program, frequently including long-range goals as well as short-range goals, and is to indicate what the child needs to be taught, how he is to be taught, and what materials are to be used to teach him. Then she proceeds to teach him on an individualized basis with as much one-to-one instruction as possible.

Teachers of special children are being encouraged to move into the direction of being a diagnostic-prescriptive teacher. Teachers should be doing more of the assessment of their own children rather than asking a psychologist or some other specialist to do this work for them. The teacher knows the child better than any other school person. If she knows how to observe and analyze behavior, knows how children learn and what problems they may have, and knows what cognitive and content skills they should be getting, then she should have the competencies necessary to tie all of those ideas together and emerge with a teaching plan for each child.

Diagnostic and clinical teaching seek to do much the same as a diagnostic-prescriptive teacher. The main difference, in the minds of some authors, is an emphasis on diagnosis. The teacher is to find out why the child is not learning by teaching him and analyzing what errors or miscues the child makes. Then the teacher tries to figure out why the child was making those kinds of errors. According to Lerner (1976), the phases of the clinical teaching process are (1) diagnosis, (2) planning of the teaching task, (3) implementation of this teaching task, (4) evaluation of student performance, and (5) modification of the diagnosis.

We strongly recommend the diagnostic-prescriptive approach to all teachers in special education and elementary education and to those working with problem learners on the secondary level.

Task Analysis Approach

The *task analysis approach* to teaching is sometimes referred to as *target teaching*, *teaching for competencies*, or *deficit teaching*. Task analysis emphasizes specifically what is to be taught. It pinpoints exactly what skills a child is missing and then is very precise as to the sequential subskills a child must learn in order to achieve the desired skill level. Note that no mention is made of analyzing how to teach the student. Task analysis has little to do with instructional methodology; it basically seeks to learn how people go about doing certain tasks, thereby identifying the tasks. To illustrate a task analysis, we suggest that you make a list of the steps that you must go through in using a pair of scissors to cut out the design of a diamond drawn on paper. Where do you begin? Is your first task to cut on the line, to be able to manipulate the scissors, or to be able to hold them correctly? For a more technical task analysis, make a list of steps you must go through to read and understand a paragraph written in a medical or scientific journal.

Why is it necessary to analyze the final task? According to Johnson and Morasky (1977), there are four pertinent reasons: First, to establish a sequential behavior pattern or baseline against which a student's performance can be compared; second, to identify the inner complexities of skills, decisions, and discriminations that must be taught; third, to identify what knowledge a student has in order to know where to begin teaching within the task sequence; fourth, to aid in discovering the proper instructional sequence if a particular one is necessary.

There are three major analysis techniques or approaches in performing a task analysis. These approaches are (a) discrimination analysis, (b) flowchart analysis, and (c) generalization analysis. All three techniques require a final task description and a list of assumptions.

A final task description is a clear, brief description of the task to be performed. It must be specific and concrete. It is not enough to say "to learn phonics"; we're certain you know that. But it is not enough either to say "to learn the consonant sounds." To be specific, the final task description should say "to learn the sounds of the letters *b*, *p*, *d*, and *g*."

The assumptions provide a baseline that assumes certain behavior that anyone must have in order to start learning the final task description. This baseline is known as necessary entering behavior. If the final task description is "to blend the sounds of the letters *b* and *l*, *c* and *h*, and *g* and *r*," then the assumption should state that the child can make the sounds of *b*, *l*, *c*, *h*, *g*, and *r*.

Discrimination task analysis is used when the final task requires the student to be able to identify differences. The basic aspects of discrimination analysis are the identification of subtasks and characteristics that permit discrimination. The job of the student is to be able to see, recognize, or discriminate differences between things. For example, "Identify the difference between the letters *b*, *d*, *p*, and *q*," or "How is the word *horse* different from the word *house*?" Once the parts or attributes have been identified, then the discrimination task analysis can be completed into its segments. The parts of the discrimination task analysis are:

1. The generalized topic or heading.
2. The final task description.
3. The assumptions (what it is assumed that the child can do).
4. The subtasks (what the child must learn to do in order to perform the task).

Flowchart task analysis is used to identify the sequence of behaviors or steps within the task that a student must go through in order to complete the task. Most, but not all, learning tasks involve such sequences. The job of the analyst is to identify the parts of the sequential chain and to prepare a flowchart showing the step by step progression and identifying those steps when action is needed and those steps when a decision must be made. Action steps are indicated by a rectangle ☐ and decision steps by a diamond ⬦.

In developing a flowchart, it is often helpful to begin with the finished task and work backwards. Suppose the task is one of constructing a "memory box" for storing index cards that have single sight words just learned. Begin with the box, how it is to look, how big, etc., then work backwards. At certain points some decisions will have to be made such as how high the sides should be, or whether it should have a cover. The action blocks can be easily identified. Two principles must be followed:

1. All decision diamonds must have at least two paths leading away.
2. All paths must lead to a subsequent point. The flowchart is finished when each of the critical actions and decisions have been identified and placed in a logical order, and a final task description and assumption completed.

Sometimes a task analysis necessitates the use of a generalization such as a rule in syllabication or in the use of short vowels. In this case, the generalized task is identified and examples of the generalization are given. Generalization Task Analysis: When there are two consonants together, the syllable division occurs between the consonants. (Example: bet/ter, hap/py, ap/ple.)

Task analysis does not say much about how to teach, but it certainly helps to identify the small, sequential steps of a task. Most learning disabled children learn best when presented with a step-by-step approach.

Other Models

PROCESS APPROACH. The process approach to teaching emphasizes the different aspects of the learning process, according to the various theories. The Illinois Test of Psycholinguistic Abilities (ITPA) has a series of processes that it advocates, such as auditory reception, visual association, verbal expression, grammatic closure, and sound blending. The theory suggests if a child is weak in any area, that area should be strengthened so the child can learn better. Language teachers work with processes such as receptive disorders, associative disorders, and expressive disorders. Certainly one must be cautious in using the process approach if validity of the theory is lacking or restricted.

MANAGEMENT APPROACH. A recent trend in education is the development of management support systems in reading (Peterson, 1975). This trend is an attempt to transform the role of the teacher from one who dispenses knowledge to that of one who manages the learning environment so the student can guide his own learning. A management support system consists of five components:

1. A skill list which is hierarchical.
2. An entry test to determine the point of entry on the skills list.
3. Commercial materials keyed to the skills list.
4. Diagnostic tests for monitoring the student's program and for guiding the students to practice materials.
5. A posttest.

The teacher administers the entry test and then guides each student to his level of attainment. The student usually administers the diagnostic test to himself and from the results is guided into certain materials. Under this system, the role of the teacher changes from a dispenser of knowledge to a manager of the learning environment.

Some examples of commercial management systems are Random House High Intensity Program, the Fountain Valley Teacher Support System, and to some degree, the Engineered Classroom of Frank Hewett.

TUTORIAL APPROACH. One of the approaches that has much success with learning disabled readers is the tutorial approach. This approach is successful only if the tutor knows what she is doing and if she can establish good rapport with the student. The one-to-one relationship, which can also be established in a classroom if the teacher is ingenious enough, seems to bring about an atmosphere of caring and concern to which the student responds with eagerness. The poor reader has been exposed to conventional methods of reading and has not been successful. Perhaps instructions given in a group situation were not adequate enough to reach him. The tutorial approach provides for more direct instruction, quicker feedback on the adequacy of responses, help, corrections, and assurance at the moment of need, and reinforcement on both the academic (cognitive) and the affective (emotional) levels. Self-concept and confidence can be restored. We highly recommend the tutorial approach.

INDIVIDUALIZING INSTRUCTION. There are many ways by which the individualization of instruction can be done. The approach is primarily a matter of teacher initiative, creativeness, and interest. Diagnostic-prescriptive teaching can provide for individualized programs whether the class is treated as a group with separate work tasks or as a class in which each child is met individually. Techniques and materials that can be used for individualization within the classroom are learning centers, modularized instruction, teaching machines, self-pacing materials, and self-selection of supplementary reading. Examples of commercial materials that can be used are:

1. Individually Guided Education (IGE), Wisconsin Research and Development Center.
2. Individually Prescribed Instruction (IPI), Learning Research and Development Center, University of Pittsburgh.
3. Program for Learning in Accordance to Needs (PLAN), American Institute for Research in Behavioral Science.
4. The Power Reading System, Winston Press.
5. SRA Reading Laboratory Series, Science Research Associates.
6. Individualized Reading from Scholastic, Scholastic Book Service.
7. Personalized Reading Center, Xerox Corporation.
8. Springboards: Reading Motivation, Noble & Noble, Publishers.
9. Skills Box (Language), Holt, Rinehart, Winston.
10. Building Reading Power, Charles E. Merrill Publishing Company.
11. Readers Digest Skill Builders, Reader's Digest.

THE BOND APPROACH. One of the most unusual sets of basal readers produced in recent years has been the set of readers authored by Guy Bond. In reality, Bond produced two parallel sets of basal readers. For each grade level there are two matching books containing the same stories, the same pictures, and matched page by page. One set of readers is called the *regular edition* and the other the *classmate edition*.

The difference between the regular and classmate edition is in the difficulty of the material. The classmate edition is written several grade levels lower than the regular edition. An easier vocabulary is used, and the sentence structure is less complex than found in the regular edition.

Because the stories match page by page, the teacher can teach a classroom of children from one lesson plan, except for a few modifications, and she can treat the class as a single group, even though she has, in reality, two separate reading groups.

Approaches to Teaching Reading

It is impossible for anyone to know what is abnormal unless he first becomes acquainted with what is normalcy. For this reason it is advisable for the prospective teacher of learning disabled readers to have classroom experience. The Letson Committee on Standards of the International Reading Association (IRA) suggests a minimum of 2 years successful classroom experience. The successful classroom experience cannot be too strongly emphasized. Remedial reading demands a personality and a knowledgeability far beyond that required of a classroom teacher; hence, a teacher whose enthusiasm is lacking in a classroom will find even greater difficulties in a remedial situation. The following approaches to reading are used by regular classroom teachers.

Basal Reading Approach

The *Basal Program* is a systematic attempt to teach the mechanics of reading through a sequential development of skills. Although this can be done through programmed instruction, individualized reading, or other means, generally, the Basal Program centers around a set of basal readers. Book companies employ a team of experts—reading specialists, learning theorists, grammarians, psychologists, and others—to produce a set of readers with a sequential development of the mechanics of reading. Several years and millions of dollars are spent before the readers are ready for distribution. The time and money are spent to make certain the tool developed will conform to recent research. In order to center concentration on the development of the mechanics of reading, the vocabulary is controlled and the repetition of words introduced conforms to the laws of learning as to time and frequency.

Usually the basal text is accompanied by a teacher's manual, which gives the teacher concrete teaching suggestions. Much of the effectiveness of the teacher can be lost if she does not follow the manual or at least consult it regularly in planning her reading lessons. The manual serves as a source of suggestions for the enrichment of the experiences of the children and a guide for the teacher in using different approaches and senses in learning. The text, the teacher's manual, and the accompanying children's workbook provide the kinds of activities which contribute to the learning of word attack skills (including phonics), the development of comprehension, and a steady increase in the rate of reading.

Without question, the basal reading approach has been the most widely used program in regular classroom teaching of reading. Here are the advantages of the basal approach: (a) The basal readers are comprehension-oriented and somewhat sequential in content from prereadiness levels through the upper elementary grades; (b) The teacher's manual or guide provides suggestions, activities, and a step-by-step outline for teaching; (c) The development of reading skills is presented in a systematic, sequential manner; (d) A core vocabulary is established and repeated frequently enough to provide reinforcement; and (e) Assessment, evaluation, and diagnostic materials are usually provided. A more recent advantage of basal reading programs is the development of a number of techniques and materials which were not provided before but which have been found by teachers of the learning disabled to be helpful in improving reading skills. Directed Reading Activity (DRA), which is the heart of a successful basal series, is presented later in this chapter.

Disadvantages of the basal program center around the fact that they are so well-structured and comprehensive that the teacher and children may have little opportunity to be flexible or to branch out into personalized styles of teaching and away from a traditional approach. The basal approach tends to encourage group instruction, fails to deal in content areas, and is frequently geared to concepts developed by middle-class, white suburban children. In terms of learning disabled children, they are frequently subjected to the same readers, the same stories, and the same method years after year, with no appreciable success but with much increase in resistance to reading and in frustration. We have found, however, that an LD child usually does not believe that he is learning to read unless he has a hardback covered book in his hands, so this idea must be kept in mind.

Language Experience Approach (LEA)

Lee and Allan (1963) point out that the *Language Experience Approach* (LEA) is based on four premises:

1. What a child thinks about he can talk about.
2. What he can talk about can be expressed in writing or some other form.
3. Anything he writes can be read.
4. He can read what he writes and what other people write.

The language experience approach relies heavily upon the pupil's oral language, which is more developed than his reading ability. Reading is conceptualized as essentially a thinking process, rather than a translating or decoding process. Much importance is given to the child's having meaningful experiences with print so as to establish firmly the notion that print is a representation of oral language and that what can be said can be written, as well as what can be written can be read.

Proponents of language experience methodology feel that using the pupil's dictated responses to a vivid experience will foster desired effective responses to reading. Stauffer (1970) describes the effect of this approach on children in special education classes: "These children showed special delight when they found a word in a magazine or book that they learned to recognize through a dictated and recorded account. The 'Look, Mom, I can read' radiance is energizing as well as illuminating."

The language experience approach also assumes that children will get powerful memory cues as they read material which they have recently dictated. As they read, they will in fact be recalling their ideas in the exact language they used to express them orally. When the child fails to recognize in print the words he has dictated, the teacher can stimulate correct responses by specific memory aids such as "Do you remember where you told us your dog slept?" or "For what special occasion did you tell us you got your bike?"

Finally, the language experience approach assumes that poor readers experience fewer failures reading their own ideas, expressed in familiar vocabulary and sentence patterns, than they experience when they must read less familiar ideas expressed in less familiar language. The satisfaction the poor reader receives from responding accurately to his own ideas in print is more rewarding than the satisfaction he might receive from getting new ideas with less facility. The disabled reader needs this kind of success and security.

From the preceding discussion it is apparent that the pupil's dictated stories, descriptions, and other commentary constitute the content of the reading material used in the language experience approach. Since seriously disabled readers usually write with great difficulty, the material they dictate could be typed for them. We have also found that some students perform best with material that is prepared on a kindergarten-type size typewriter. Asking pupils with written language deficits to write, type, or copy their own dictation almost always defeats the purpose of the language experience approach.

When pupils are reading the typed copy of their dictation, the teacher should listen carefully and insist upon complete accuracy. Care must be taken to make sure that bright students do not repeat from memory rather than read their material. As instruction proceeds and pupils acquire a functional sight vocabulary, the teacher should structure the dictating sessions so that high utility words are included in the material to be read. Phonics and other word attack skills are taught incidentally as instruction proceeds and as pupils indicate a readiness to derive generalizations from observing their oral language in print. Specific skill development exercises may be incorporated into the later stages of the language experience approach. Ultimately, pupils transfer words from their own material to library books, textbooks, magazines, newspapers, and the writing of other students. Care must be taken, however, to move children gradually from their own dictated material to reading material written by others. Care must also be taken to avoid giving pupils material written by others that contains too many words that have not been thoroughly learned from reading their own material or that cannot be analyzed effectively with the word attack skills they have learned.

The advantage of the language experience approach (LEA) is that it makes use of the child's own language to teach him what reading is all about. It makes the child more sensitive to his language, to his environment, and to his experiences. He learns to share ideas. The disadvantages for the learning disabled reader, however, center around the same points that are considered strengths of the program. Usually the LD child has some language or speech deficits. A child may come from a culturally different background and has little English that he can bring to the development of an LEA reading chart. The biggest disadvantage for poor readers is the fact that LD children require a structured, systematic approach to learning reading skills. The language experience approach does not provide enough of the stability that a disabled reader needs. We find the LEA helpful as a supplement or as an application of what has been taught, but not as a primary approach.

Individualized Reading Program

A review of the articles on *individualized reading* makes it difficult to define what is meant by the term since there appear to be many personal ideas concerning the definition of individualized reading. Every writer seems to have his own concept of what the term embodies. However, the common elements from these articles have been extracted for presentation here.

The basic principle of the individualized concept is that all children differ as to level of development and rate of learning. To require all children to read from the same book and to subject them to the same exercises violates this difference. Instead of using the basal reader as the primary tool for instruction, the individualized programs use a wide variety of trade books as the primary tool. A trade book is designed for the general public and is written primarily for individual reading. It does not constitute a basal text. Proponents argue that basal readers are dull and deadening whereas trade books are interesting. These books are found in abundance, and any child can find something he is interested in reading.

The second principle of individualized reading is the principle of seeking. All humans are curious. This causes them to continually search their environment. In addition, each human has certain needs and thus searches the environment in an attempt to satisfy these needs. Therefore, the teacher using the individualized reading approach sees to it that the environment is saturated with a wide variety of attractive and interesting books at varying levels of difficulty and covering a wide range of topics. The child, in his seeking activities, will explore this environment which contains books.

This seeking activity leads to the third principle, that of self-selection. In his seeking activities the child will find a book which he feels satisfies a need or arouses his curiosity. He will begin to read this book. Although the teacher may, on request, help guide the child in making a selection, she never interferes with his selection even though she may feel that the book is wrong for this particular child.

The fourth principle is that of pacing. Under what the individualized reading proponents call the *look, say* method of the basal reader, it is the teacher who determines how fast the class and the individuals in the class will go. Under individualized reading the child sets his own rate of reading and, therefore, is never pushed ahead as children under the basal approach often are.

As the children read their individual books, the teacher serves as a guide and helper. Through this guiding and helping activity, she identifies needs of individuals and organizes small group practice for children needing the same skill development. She sets up individual conferences and prepares practice sessions for individual pupils. The teacher is expected to have individual conferences with each child at least once a week to check on his progress, his needs, and his plans for future reading.

The individualized reading program must not be confused with individualization of reading instruction. Individualization merely seeks ways by which the pupil can learn on his own. The main elements of an individualized reading program center around (a) self-selection or freedom for the child to select his own reading materials as they are suited to his interests and his reading ability, (b) diagnosis being the teacher's main role, evaluating progress in terms of goals and skills that were identified before beginning such a program, and (c) a conference period in which the child and the teacher discuss reading choices, share feelings, and decide future directions in reading. For capable readers, these factors are all advantages because they can understand what they are supposed to do and are capable of handling their reading development with a minimal amount of help. For the disabled reader, however, these elements of an individualized reading program may well spell disaster. As we have said, the LD child needs structure and organization; therefore, to be placed into a position of selecting his own reading materials may be very upsetting to him. Even more upsetting is the lack of a structured outline of study that insures the presentation and study of specific developmental skills needed in reading. The conference time could be helpful for the LD reader because it could give teacher and pupil a chance to establish a close personal relationship and provide an opportunity for the teacher to strengthen self-concept, to identify hidden problems in learning or living that the child might have, and to provide guidance and reinforcement of learning.

The Linguistic Approach to Reading

A *linguistic approach* to reading can mean a number of different things, depending on which linguist is being quoted and whose program is being examined. Basically, linguists are concerned with the structure of oral language. The relationship of sounds (phonemes) to symbols (graphemes) usually forms the structure for the linguistic method of teaching reading. Linguists emphasize the relationship between letter patterns and sound patterns as they appear in rules of English grammar and oral communication.

Most linguistic approaches suggest that letters should be learned by name and not by sound. Beginning reading words should consist of three letter words following a consonant-short vowel-consonant (C-V-C) pattern. Minimal variation of words is frequently used by simply changing one letter in the word such as *mat, sat, bat, cat.* These words are then used in sentences. Pictures and illustrations are usually discouraged so the children will not be diverted from emphasizing the printed word forms.

Advantages of the linguistic approach for disabled readers are that the words that are learned initially are phonemically regular; only after some skills are developed do they progress to semiregular and irregular spellings. The frequent repetition of words to insure overlearning is a definite asset. A major disadvantage has been a lack of emphasis on comprehension and reading for meaning in the early stages of learning to read. Linguists believe that reading is a process of decoding; hence, that must be the major emphasis. Other disadvantages are (a) the lack of agreement as to what is the linguistic approach to reading, (b) the development of instructional materials and methodology based on linguistic theories but which have not been field-researched, and (c) the carefully, extremely controlled vocabularies do not take into account the usually spoken vocabulary of the child, but do include words less frequently used, such as *ram* and *dam*.

Phonic Approaches to Reading

The *phonic approach* teaches word recognition as a sounding-blending process. The goal is to enable the child to unlock unfamiliar words. In actual practice, the content of phonic approaches differs from program to program. One group of programs uses the synthetic approach, whereby the child learns letter sounds in isolation which are then blended or synthesized into words. *K-a-t* becomes *cat*. Most phonic programs are of this type. The other group of phonic programs makes sound generalizations or deductions from words that have been learned as sight words. "Yes, that is the word *sat*; what is the sound made by the first letter in the word?" In this approach, phonics instruction is not introduced until the child has learned enough words to provide examples of letter-sound relationships (Matthes, 1972). Most basal readings series will contain some phonics instruction, but their emphasis, synthesis or analytic, will differ.

Reading experts and the research generally agree that phonics instruction is an important part of any reading program. The advantages are that phonics produce efficiency and independence in unlocking new words and that the child learns of the association between printed letters and the sounds they represent. An informal analysis of our psychological reports of learning disabled readers shows that very few of our cases could read beyond a second-grade level without some use of phonetic analysis to unlock words. Therefore, we strongly recommend phonics instruction for learning disabled readers. Some disadvantages of the phonetic approach are (a) the tendency of some teachers to teach phonics as isolated sounds without associating the sounds to unlocking words, (b) the emphasis on the pronunciation of words without stressing comprehension, and (c) a confusion that arises with words that are exceptions to the rules.

Other Reading Approaches

MODIFIED ALPHABET APPROACHES. For various reasons, some authors believe it to be an advantage to reconstruct or change the traditional alphabet so that reading can come easier to an individual. The Initial Teaching Alphabet (ITA) is the best known of these alphabets. It uses a 44 character alphabet with one symbol for each sound made in reading. The capital letters are designed the same as lowercase letters except that they are larger. Words in Color (Gattegno, 1962) is another alphabet system. It uses color to represent differing speech sounds. There are 47 colors for 47 phonemes. Sounds and colors are taught through the use of wall charts. See Chapter 11 for further information. The Psycholinguistic Color System (Bannatyne, 1966) takes a color-coded approach also by giving colors to 17 vowel phonemes. The color-coded approaches of Gattegno and Bannatyne have been found to be helpful with some learning disabled readers, including adults. The Peabody Rebus and the DISTAR programs, which will be discussed later, are also modified alphabet programs.

PROGRAMMED READING. Programmed reading materials usually take the form of workbooks but they can be programmed for machines or computers. The information or tasks are presented in a series of frames that are presented in a small step format so that each step will almost always insure accuracy of response. The small, sequential steps are the "programmed" part of the material. The steps may require different types of responses, such as answering a question, supplying a missing word, or responding to true-false or multiple-choice questions. Feedback of the accuracy of the child's response is immediate. On workbooks, the answers are frequently given in the margins; on teaching machines, a light or a sound give the student immediate feedback, or the answer may be unmasked; on computer-assisted instruction (CAI), a response may be provided on the screen. One of the better programs provided is the Sullivan Programmed Readers. Most younger learning disabled children find this format too difficult to cope with; they need direct instruction of skills. Some older LD children do respond well to the Sullivan Readers, however.

OTHER PROGRAMS. Following is a list of other programs used to teach developmental reading to marginal or mildly severe learning disabled readers:

1. Merrill Linguistic Readers, Charles E. Merrill Publishing Company.
2. SRA Basic Reading Series, Science Research Associates.
3. Linguistic Readers, Harper Row Publishers.
4. Let's Read, Charles L. Barnhart, Inc.
5. Basic Reading, J. B. Lippincott Company.
6. Palo Alto Sequential Steps to Reading, Harcourt, Brace, Jovanovich.
7. Diacritical Marking System (DMS), Edward Fry, Elementary English, May 1964.
8. Individually Prescribed Instruction (IPI), Robert Glaser and John Bolvin, School of Education, University of Pittsburgh.
9. Open Court Correlated Language Programs, Open Court Publishing Company.
10. Stern Structural Reading Series, Singer Publishers, Syracuse.
11. SRA Reading Labs, Science Research Associates.

Approaches to Teaching the Learning Disabled

Several studies and observations in our clinics lead us to conclude that it is important to consider the particular type of learning disability that a child has and to take the finding into consideration when planning a program for the child. A question concerning remediation raised by Silver and Hagin (1965) was whether to seek to stimulate defective perceptual areas and to develop them or to detect the strongest perceptual areas and seek to work through them. Their thinking, although inconclusive, was to stimulate the defective areas and to improve them. More important, they found that the traditional techniques used with remedial readers were not effective.

In a study by Fernald (1932) it was learned that the multisensory approach used with the cases of total disability also seemed to give satisfactory results with cases of partial disability. These cases could not be helped by traditional methods but they were helped by the multisensory technique.

In the extensive remedial reading research program conducted in the Baltimore County Public Schools, Schiffman (1962) found it valuable to use the Fernald VAKT approach in analytical breakdown, the Gillingham approach with VAKT in synthetic methods, and a basal or experience approach using VAKT instead of simply the VA techniques. (VAKT stands for Visual, Auditory, Kinesthetic, Tactile.)

Critchley (1964), after reviewing the literature on dyslexia, concluded that a dyslexic, once diagnosed, should be taken away from a milieu where the analytic method of teaching is practiced, in order to receive special instruction along totally different lines. To him, the analytic method is the "look and say," "flash," "sight-reading," or global system of teaching.

A summary of approaches used in teaching learning disabled children follows.

Multisensory Approach

The *multisensory approach* to teaching a task is one that makes use of more than one sensory input to get the stimuli messages to the brain. The method is generally referred to as VAKT or the *tracing technique*. Most teaching makes use of the V-A modalities (visual and auditory), but few use the K-T (kinesthetic and tactile). Kinesthetic refers to awareness of movement and position through the muscles and joints. Tactile means awareness through touch, usually through the skin of the fingers. Smell and taste are other sensory modalities that could be used for input of stimuli, but they are only occasionally used in developing awareness of stimuli. We know of one case where a boy has such extensive neurological distortions that only his sense of smell was intact. This boy was being taught to be aware of and to identify reading symbols through the use of different smells. As it were, he was learning to read through his nose.

The VAKT approach is sort of a shotgun approach. It uses a variety of sensory modalities to pick up stimuli, hoping that some will make a breakthrough to the brain and, if more than one modalitity permits a transmission to the brain, it will serve to reinforce the others. The K-T modalities are the first to be developed in a child, and therefore, are more basic or fundamental in terms of sophistication of input and identification. Note how often an individual who cannot interpret an idea, visualize a symbol, or mentally work out an arithmetic problem will use his fingers to write, to sketch in the air or on the back of his hand, to better "see" or figure out the problem. When the auditory and visual approaches fail, we always move down to the tactile and kinesthetic levels.

The VAKT is used in a variety of educational approaches, as will be noted later. It is also modified to serve different purposes. For example, Frances McGlannan in her Language Arts School in Coral Gables, Florida, uses the vaAkt approach, with the larger A standing for Association. She uses the VAKT but also uses some device or technique that will enable the child to develop a cognitive or conceptual insight. In teaching the sound of a letter, she has an object, such as a toy tiger, standing for the letter T, that the child can hold in the palm of his hand or finger when he wants to make the T sound. As many teachers do, she uses letters made of pipe-stem cleaners glued to cardboard for the children to trace and to make word families. The toy serves to provide the initial (or final) sound. Another modification is the blocking technique where, instead of VAKT, the teacher may use only AKT, with sight or vision blocked out (Blau & Blau, 1969). This approach is used when it is believed that one of the modalities may actually be interfering with the others. Since Blau and Blau believe that the visual channel is the one that interferes most frequently, they eliminate it. We find some children who are overloaded with stimuli, often auditory stimuli, to the point that they shut out or tune out auditory input. Blocking of the auditory modality may be of some help to these children.

Margaret Rawson (1975) clearly depicts the mutual interaction of the senses as the learner hears while he speaks and looks while he writes and, all in all, integrates the input from the sensory processes. Figure 8–1 sketches her illustration of the association of the sensory

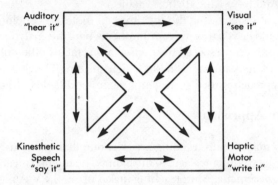

FIGURE 8–1. Sensory association in language learning. In Rawson, M. B., & Duane, D. *Reading, perception, and language*. Towson, Md.: Orton Society, 1976.

modality in language, including reading and learning. Stressing the four sensory avenues, VAKT, presumably results in their reinforcing each other in an integration-type process for more effective learning.

Grace Fernald (1943) was somewhat of a pioneer in developing remedial techniques for working with children. Work in the clinic school at the University of California taught her the importance of having a child gain successful learning experiences. She advocated the application of remedial techniques, as a preventative measure, before a child would be affected by failure in learning. Her work dealt with two major approaches: first, with relieving the cognitive blocking actions of emotional factors and the stress they produced through a technique she called the *analytical method*; second, the introduction of a learning procedure that would result in successful learning through what she called the *reconditioning method*. Today her reconditioning method has been shortened to the VAKT approach, which is but one step of her technique. The VAKT technique is explained in detail in Chapter 10. All four stages of the reconditioning method are used primarily with very severely disabled learners. Stage one is the technique described in Chapter 10. The child selects a word he wants to learn. The word is written large on a piece of rough paper. He traces the word with his finger (K and T), saying each letter aloud as he traces (A), and at the same time, of course, looking at the letter (V). The word is said before the tracing starts and after it stops. When the child thinks he can write the word, the copy is removed and the child writes the word from memory.

Stage two eliminates the tracing. The child looks at the word, vocalizes the word, then writes the word without directly copying it. Stage three eliminates the copying of the word. The child learns the new word by looking at it and saying it to himself. Stage four begins when the child can generalize; he now has the ability to recognize new words by their similarity to words, or parts of words, that he had previously learned.

We find the VAKT approach and its modifications very helpful, not only for school children, but also for college and graduate students as well. We have had students learn shorthand symbols by tracing and had graduate students learn to spell difficult words and to make phonetic applications in unlocking unfamiliar words.

Specialized Phonic Systems

ORTON-GILLINGHAM. The Orton-Gillingham Phonics approach, formerly known as the Gillingham-Stillman (1965) or simply the Gillingham approach, is a very intensive phonic system that makes use of VAKT in conjunction with stress on auditory discrimination ability. The method is highly structured and strongly emphasizes phonics.

The program is based on 8 steps that form the association of auditory, visual, and kinesthetic stimuli. Once the child knows the sounds, he is introduced to phonograms, a letter or a group of letters which represent a phonetic sound. The steps are as follows:

1. Phonogram is presented visually and auditorially; the child repeats the sound which is associated with a letter.
2. Phonogram is demonstrated, traced, copied and written from memory by the child.
3. Phonogram is presented visually; the child names it.
4. Child writes the phonogram from dictation.
5. Phonogram is presented visually; the child produces the sound. Hand is moved to form letter, child gives sound. Basis for reading is established in this step.
6. Name of phonogram is given; the child gives phonogram name.
7. Teacher produces the sound; the child gives phonogram name.
8. Teacher gives the phonogram sound; the child writes the letter symbols and names the phonogram. Basis for spelling is established in this step.

Some teachers are leery of using this approach because it is not a method you can use without some insight and training in what you are doing. We can say that once the teacher obtains the proper training (learning) and materials, she can be very effective in helping children ages 9 or older who have not been able to learn by any other approach. We generally recommend this approach to be used with moderate to some severely disabled readers. Further mention is made of this method in Chapter 11.

SPALDING UNIFIED PHONICS APPROACH. The Spalding approach to teaching reading is found in Spalding and Spalding, *The Writing Road to Reading* (1957). The title of the book suggests the main emphasis of their approach, the use of writing incorporated in a phonic program. Spalding claims that unless children write correctly, they do not see the correct symbols for the sounds. Therefore, the best time to stop bad habits is before they begin. Correct handwriting is taught from the very beginning. Further mention of the Spalding method is made in Chapter 11.

There are nine basic steps in the Spalding teaching procedures:

1. Teach the phonograms.
   a. Pupils are shown phonograms and say the association sound in unison.
   b. After the phonogram is pronounced, the students write the letter symbol.
2. Do not name the letters; just the phonetic sounds are used.
3. Refer to multiple letter phonograms by the sound associated with them; ex. *ea, eigh*. Never spell them letter by letter.

4. At the beginning teach and demand correct writing and pronunciation.
5. Students should say each phonogram of short words or each syllable of longer words. They should write the letter form after pronouncing the sound or syllables.
6. Basic rules for spelling are taught when necessary.
7. Words that cannot be taught phonetically or to which no spelling rules apply must be taught as sight or "learned" words.
8. Spelling must be emphasized as the basic key to the understanding of both written and spoken language.
9. Only when children can read common words easily enough can they read from reading books, and be able to understand the meaning.

PHONOVISUAL APPROACH. Lucille Schoolfield and Josephine Timberlake (1974) devised a phonetic approach based on pictorial charts along with training in auditory and visual discrimination. The 26 initial and final consonants, plus 18 vowels sounds are sounded out in a sequencing manner and taught through the use of games, books, charts, and manuals. The child recognizes the letter he sees (visual) and the sound it makes (auditory), leading to finer discrimination and eventually to better comprehension. There is a key word or "common reference word" for each sound. The instructor introduces the first five sounds (child says the sound, teacher says it while child watches her mouth, child writes the sound of the picture). The same general procedure is followed for all 44 sounds, with minor variations. This approach provides for some sequencing, auditory and visual discrimination practice, a variety of experiences, a secure self-concept, and adequate phonetic instruction. When properly used with a basal reading program and spelling instruction, the Phonovisual approach can be used with low mental ability levels and young mild to moderate disabled readers. It corrects minor speech difficulties, helps eliminate reversals, and improves spelling. In this "sound-symbol" approach, a child learns and understands that a particular sound goes with a particular letter or word.

This method had to be altered because the children ran into difficulty whenever the letter had more than one sound. This method can be used as a supplement to a regular basal program through the use of a vowel and consonant chart, which Phonovisual provides. The child is taught to recognize the letters and to associate sounds with these letters. The following steps can be used to accomplish the procedure:

1. Visualization of the letters.
2. Presentation of the letter's sound.
3. Visualization of the speech apparatus when the sound is produced.
4. Visual presentation of a picture and key words as a reference for remembering the sound.

The lessons are presented in a game fashion. We have found that with proper timing and materials, this approach has been very effective with young, mild to moderate disabled readers, ages 6 to 8. See Chapter 11 for further information.

Language Development Approach
(Johnson & Myklebust)

Doris Johnson and Helmer Myklebust collaborated on the book *Learning Disabilities: Educational Principles and Practices* (1967) to produce one of the most comprehensive texts in the field. The text presents an extensive remediation program based on Myklebust's psychoneurological theory of language (and reading) development. Basically, Myklebust speaks of psychoneurological integrities for learning, suggesting that adequate functioning of the perceptual and central nervous systems, as well as psychological strength, is essential for normal language development and functions. If functional development in any one of the necessary integrities is less than adequate, then a variety of learning and/or language problems will arise, such as perceptual disturbances in sensory discrimination and recognition; disturbance of imagery to recall perceived auditory and visual experiences; inability to acquire facility in dealing with symbolic processes; and/or inability to generalize, conceptualize, or categorize experiences. Reading of the Johnson and Myklebust book is highly recommended, not only for a discussion of the theory of language and cognitive development, but also for an indepth look at the remediation programs they advocate.

According to Myklebust, there are five general groups of learning disorders. First, there are disorders of auditory language such as disorders in auditory receptive language, auditory expressive language, and generalized or mixed deficits in auditory learning. Second, there are disorders of reading which includes two common forms of dyslexia—visual and auditory. Visual dyslexia is characterized by such conditions as confusion of similar words and letters, slow word recognition, frequent letter reversals (*d* for *b*) or inversions (*m* for *w*), difficulty with visual sequence and visual memory, poor drawings, problems with visual analysis, visual synthesis, and visual integration. The auditorially dyslexic child will be able to learn by the whole word approach but will have trouble with phonetic word attack skills.

A third disorder is in written language. Poor written language implies inadequate integration or development of the sensory and motor processes for receptive and expressive purposes. Disorders of arithmetic is a fourth group of learning disorders, involving either arithmetical deficiencies related to language disorder or disturbances in quantitative thinking in the comprehension of the mathematical principles themselves. The fifth area of dysfunction is nonverbal disorders of learning involving aspects of the environment such as space, size, direction, self-perception, and time, resulting in characteristics such as left-right disorientation, distractibility, poor self-image, disinhibition, and perseveration.

According to Johnson and Myklebust, the fundamental principles that should be followed in the remediation of psychoneurological learning disorders are:

1. Individualize the educational plan for each child according to his strengths, deficits, needs, learning style, and background of experiences.
2. Teach to the level of psychoneurological capability—perceptual, imagery, symbolization, or conceptualization.
3. Teach to the type of psychoneurological strength or involvement—verbal, nonverbal, intrasensory, intersensory, or integrative functions.
4. Teach a balanced program according to readiness levels.
5. Remember that input precedes output and that either may be involved in the learning disorder.
6. Do not overload the child with stimuli; consider tolerance levels.
7. Use the multisensory approach if appropriate for the tolerance level.
8. Teaching only to the deficit or weakness is limited and unacceptable.
9. Teaching only to and through the integrities is inappropriate if the capability for interneurosensory learning is not developed.
10. Do not assume the need for perceptual training. It may not be needed.
11. Control important variables related to learning and teaching such as attention of the child, rate of presentation, size of print or objects, and proximity of pupil and teacher.

12. Emphasize both verbal and nonverbal areas of experiences.
13. Keep both behavioral criteria and psychoneurological considerations in mind when implementing educational remediation.

Specific remedial techniques, as well as the approach to what Myklebust calls *clinical teaching,* are to be found in the book.

Other Approaches

ASSOCIATION METHOD: MCGINNIS. Mildred McGinnis (1963) was concerned with developing a language development program for aphasic children. The program, the Association Method, has been used at the Central Institute of the Deaf (CID) in St. Louis since shortly after World War I. The method has been effectively used with severe learning disabled children who had difficulty or delay in developing vocal language skills. Individual speech sounds are taught rather than sentences, phrases or words so that the child's attention can be maintained and some success in achievement is assured. The major principles of the Association Method are (1) words are taught phonetically or by an elemental approach; (2) each sound is overarticulated to develop preciseness of pronunciation; (3) the articulated word is associated with its letter-symbol written in cursive script; (4) expression, rather than meaning or comprehension, is the starting point and foundation of the program; and (5) systematic sensorimotor association is used. The Association Method is also presented in Chapter 11. It is included here because it is an approach that deserves recognition for its effectiveness with school-age children.

MWM PROGRAM: MINSKOFF, WISEMAN, MINSKOFF. The MWM Program for Developing Language Abilities (1972) is psycholinguistic-oriented in approach. Remediation is attempted in 12 psycholinguistic areas, somewhat related to the processes theoretically measured by the Illinois Test of Psycholinguistic Abilities (ITPA). The areas in the MWM program include auditory reception, visual reception, auditory association, visual association, verbal expression, manual expression, auditory sequential memory, visual sequential memory, grammatic closure, visual closure, auditory closure, and sound blending. The subskills for each of the 12 areas are presented, and suggestions are given for development of the skills. This remedial program was designed for children whose functional language level in any of the areas falls between the chronological ages of 3 to 7 years. A teacher's guide with specific directions for implementation of the program is provided, as are an inventory of language abilities, 6 teaching manuals for remedial strategies, and specific activities and supplementary remedial materials consisting of flash cards, a phonograph record, a story book, and a word book.

We have had some exposure to this program and it looks like it has something to offer. It is necessary, however, to accept the theoretical concept of the processes as presented in the ITPA.

PEABODY REBUS READING PROGRAM. The Peabody Rebus Program (Woodcock, 1967) is a form of a modified alphabet approach. The word *rebus* means "picture word." In this approach, picture-words are used as a programmed approach to readiness and beginning reading instruction. The idea is that children should first learn about the nature of reading and develop basic reading skills by the use of an easily learned rebus vocabulary. The pictorial representation of words is supposed to be easily learned and remembered. Much of the teaching load is carried by the instructional material, rather than by the teacher.

For example, a picture of a can stands for the word *can*; a dot inside a square stands for the word *in*; a hand with a finger pointing stands for the word *the*; a face profile with an arrow pointing from the eye means *see*; I stands for *I*. Put these symbols together and you have a sentence. I ⬚ ⬚ ⬚ ⬚ ⬚ ⬚ The Peabody Rebus Program includes three programmed workbooks and two readers. It appears that reading skills such as left-to-right, down-the-page, page-to-page progression, and context clues are effectively taught by rebus reading. The rebus approach can be used by mentally retarded children, bilingual, or non-English speaking children who have never read in any language, certain older LD children, and preschool programs in general.

DISTAR PROGRAM. DISTAR stands for Direct Instructional Systems for Teaching Arithmetic and Reading (Englemann & Bruner, 1969). The program is basically a method whereby a teacher trained in the program can help prepare children to compete and learn. The program is highly structured, fast-paced, and intensive with directive programming, immediate feedback, and apparently logically sequenced. The teacher is definitely in charge. She learns and teaches certain hand signals and phrases that gain the attention of the children, and she structures when they will respond and when they will listen. For example, the teacher points to herself and says "My turn," and says the sound or word. Then she points with her hand to the child (or group) and says "Your turn," and they repeat the sound or word. Then the order might be "Say it fast." A training film is available to teach the techniques. DISTAR is designed to quickly remediate below-average reading skills by providing exercises in sequencing events, rhyming, and blending. There are two levels in the reading program with a teacher manual and four presentation books for each level. The DISTAR program is receiving some recognition and usage with children needing remedial work, but more research is needed to truly indicate the effectiveness of this approach.

Other Approaches and Techniques

We would like to just mention by title a few more of the systems and techniques developed for teaching reading.

1. *Computer Assisted Instruction* (CAI), with student terminals equipped with a teletypewriter and audio headset.
2. *DOVACK*, Differentiated Oral Visual Kinesthetic, a computer approach where a child dictates a story, which is then programmed for the computer. The computer feeds back the story, with the teacher's voice carefully pronouncing the words.
3. *Black English*, a language in its own right, being taught first with a "Ghetto Reader." Then the transition is made to Standard English versions of the stories.
4. *The Marxman*, a series of comic books developed in English by Cliff Edwards to be used with slow readers. Cars can cr-a-a-a-sh! and girls can scr-ea-ea-ea-m.
5. *The Responsive Environment Approach*, involving the use of an automated or a talking typewriter.
6. Edith Norrie's *Letter-Case*, a box with many small compartments in which small cardboard pieces with a letter or blend printed on it are placed. The child selects letters and spells a word. The letters are color-coded.
7. *Alpha One*, a beginning reading program that makes use of puppets and humorous material to introduce readiness and reading skills.

8. *Edmark*, a beginning reading program for severely affected learners, even on the level of the trainable mentally retarded. Through the use of pictures, it teaches sight words.

It will be helpful for you to refer to Chapters 9, 10, and 11, where a number of more widely known approaches to various skills in reading are presented in greater detail.

Principles of Remediation

Remedial teaching is basically good teaching. The teacher takes the child where he is and seeks to bring the child to increased standards of competence. Remediation is based on careful diagnosis and geared to the needs and interests of the child.

Remediation is threefold. First, it attempts to do away with ineffective habits which were incorrectly learned and to teach these skills so that they are performed correctly. Second, it teaches skills which were never learned but which are vitally needed for good reading. Third, after the basic skills for learning to read are developed, remediation should help the child catch up on the material he had not learned because he kept getting further and further behind. In summary, remediation is concerned with doing away with bad habits, establishing good habits, and bringing the child's achievement up to learning expectancy level.

General Principles of Remediation

Almost every classroom contains students with learning disabilities. Classroom teachers can help pupils cope with their learning difficulties by adapting some principles that have been found useful in corrective and remedial teaching. The following list combines accepted learning principles and specific applications for pupils with learning difficulties. This list, adapted from the article by Otto (1965), should be helpful to any teacher working with remedial readers.

1. Secure the learner's cooperation. This is, of course, more easily said than done. The point here is that the active participant is more apt to permit himself to learn than is the passive spectator.

2. Begin instruction on the learner's level. To do this the teacher must first have a clear picture of the pupil's present skill development and his capacity for further achievement. Existing test scores should be utilized and additional diagnostic information should be sought through both formal and informal measures when needed. In addition the teacher must have access to and be familiar with materials and sequences of skills to be learned at various levels of difficulty. Teachers who rely upon a single test for diagnostic information cannot implement this basic principle.

3. Take small steps. Make each step so small that a correct response is virtually assured. The student should be led toward his goal through a series of minimal changes for which interim models are provided. Pupils need help, too, in setting realistic goals on their own. Unless a pupil perceives a small step as one that is significant, he is not likely to be satisfied with the small step. Disabled learners need to see that they must walk before they can run.

4. Reinforce success. In many cases a success experience is its own reinforcement. It is important that the learner know at once whether his response is correct. In individualized corrective or remedial teaching, the teacher can supply this knowledge of results.

5. Keep learning tasks and materials meaningful. Many research studies have made clear the fact that meaningful tasks and materials are mastered more readily than materials that have no

meaning or tasks that are not understood. The teacher's problem is not merely to be sure that tasks and materials have inherent meaning, however; materials must be meaningful for the particular pupil being taught, and tasks must be understood by the pupil.

6. Facilitate remembering. Most psychologists agree that forgetting is due primarily to interference. Teachers can combat this interference by taking care to see that the unique features of each new learning are stressed and understood. With some tasks the best way to insure remembering is to provide for overlearning and to reinforce with frequent review. This overlearning is especially useful in the basic skill areas, *e.g.* production of letter forms in handwriting, service words in reading, multiplication tables, and proper language forms.

7. Encourage pupil discovery of relationships. Transfer to new tasks is most likely to occur if the pupils are able to discover important relationships and generalizations for themselves. The suggestion here is not that the pupils should be abandoned to proceed at random as they seek to make their own discoveries. Instead the learning sequence should be so structured as to lead the pupil to the place where relationships are clear and self-discovery is a logical next step.

8. Guard against motivation that is too intense. Too much of any good thing can be harmful. Too much motivation is likely to be accompanied by distracting emotions that interfere with efficient learning.

9. Build a backlog of success experiences. Pupils' tolerance for failure is derived from their reserve of success experiences. Good achievers have a backlog of success to sustain them when they encounter problems. But poor achievers typically do not have a success reserve, at least not in all academic areas, so their tolerance for failure is extremely limited; a habitual withdrawal response in the face of even minor failure is common. Thus, teachers must take care to insure that all pupils be given opportunities to add to their store of success experiences. They should be particularly aware that pupils with learning problems have a special need to build a reserve of success to sustain them as they work toward a full participation in the regular instructional program.

Bond and Tinker (1973) present a fine set of principles of remediation that the reader may wish to consult.

Principles of Remediation for Moderate to Severe Cases

Reading deficiencies due to secondary factors are usually psychosocial in nature, implying that the inability to learn to read is due to failure in activating the mental processes of learning. The ability to learn is there but for some reason it has not been utilized. This inability to learn to read may be due to a variety of conditions which may be mental, physiological, emotional, environmental, or caused by poor teaching. Remedial work with secondary disability readers would require an approach which would overcome the inhibiting factor or factors and then provide the proper remedial techniques needed to overcome the specific defective reading skills involved.

Primary learning disability implies that there is a central nervous system impairment in the capacity to learn to read. This defect makes it impossible for the learner to learn as efficiently as he normally would. It could make it impossible for him to learn to read at all. There are some adult primary disability readers who can read to some degree, but they are restricted from reading much better than they are doing. These adult PRD cases are usually individuals with high intelligence levels. All remedial reading teachers are also familiar with young people of senior high school or young adulthood ages who are normal in intelligence but who are still reading on a first- , second- , or third-grade level.

Remediation begins with adequate interpretation of assessment results which indicate (a) the type of the educational deficit, (b) the existence or absence of a perceptual or learning disorder, (c) the severity of the deficiency, and, possibly, (d) the cause of the disability.

Most primary disability cases (a) have difficulty simply learning associations between letter symbols and letter sounds, especially in the blending process, (b) use insufficient word recognition clues by attending primarily to initial letters, length, and general shape while ignoring clues of details within words, and (c) experience confusion of left-right reversals in letters of similar shape or tranposition of letters in a word. Based on these findings, Bryant (1965) recommends the following principles:

1. Work on one discrimination or association problem at a time until that problem is overcome. The simplest and easiest should be established first.
2. Each new word should be taught by writing the word or filling in missing letters to direct attention to the details within the word. Associate sounds with letters and word parts.
3. The task must be made repeatedly until automatic or overlearned.
4. Provide discrimination between each new word and words of similar shapes. Do not cause "learning interference" by giving too many new words or associations at one time.
5. Give much success by using the most basic simplest relationship or smallest step. Use "micro-units" so that the chances of failure to learn are lessened.
6. Give frequent reviews of basic perceptual, associational, and blending skills.
7. Left-right confusion requires distributed kinesthetic practice and discrimination training with materials of increasing difficulty.
8. No other discrimination tasks should be taught while working on overcoming left-right reversals.

Cruickshank (1962) considers the following to be the major elements in educational planning: (a) individualized planning, (b) rational structure between the teacher and the pupil, (c) a nonstimulating environmental structure (we found that controlling auditory distractions was much more important than controlling visual distractions), (d) a structural program so that it does not vary greatly and become threatening, (e) structural teaching materials used according to the needs of the child, (f) motor training, and (g) language development through speech therapy and verbalization.

The First Two Steps

The first step toward a successful remedial program is the establishment of rapport with the child. Until rapport is established, nothing else should be done. Too often clinicians and reading teachers immediately begin testing the child. This practice is one of the worst things that can be done. To begin with, this child has had a succession of failures with tests, and what is even worse, each time he has taken a test he has gotten into trouble. Results from tests given before rapport is established are not valid and can be of little use to the teacher.

Some of the techniques used to establish rapport are: explanation, humor, and sincerity. For example, knowing the child is bright enough to wonder why he has difficulty learning something other children learn easily, we try to provide him with an explanation. We explain Primary Disability and identify successful people who have primary disability. The child many times does not fully comprehend the explanation, but at least he knows there is a reason, and he is not "dumb" or "stupid." Also, he knows he is not alone.

Most children coming to a reading center are tense. Anything which can be done to ease the tension by getting the child to laugh or smile should be done. A professional attitude and bearing is great, but it can scare the daylights out of a frightened child.

If you can convey to the child the knowledge that you are sincerely interested in him and his problems, a firm rapport will be established. This is easy to do if you are interested in children and their problems and impossible to do if you are not.

The second step toward a successful remedial program is making certain the child has a great deal of success. A history of failure has preceded your meeting with the child, and he has no reason to believe that this meeting will be different. You, as the remedial teacher, while establishing rapport, must somehow determine a task level at which this child can succeed. Nothing succeeds as well as success. If the child's first experience with you is successful, he will be more willing to continue.

The Draw-a-Man test, the Hand-Face test, Benton Screening, and the Arm Extension Tests make the child feel successful because he has no understanding of what constitutes failure in these areas. Also they involve a completely different kind of activity than he expected. Sometimes we teach something we know he can learn—a sound or a word. If the teacher takes the time to establish rapport and a feeling of success, she will have made a great step toward improvement.

Teaching a Developmental Reading Lesson

How to Teach a Reading Lesson

From the very first day of school the first-grade teacher uses the assessment approach. She is faced with the task of dividing her children into two groups: those ready to read, and those not ready to read. This calls for a determination of each child's level of development. Once this division is accomplished she must continue to assess in order to locate errors in the original grouping. In addition, the groups must be tested in order to determine exactly the kind of experiences each group will need. After setting up the situations which will provide for the needs of each group, she must follow these experiences with some type of evaluation in order to determine the effectiveness of the lessons taught. This in turn leads to the planning of new experiences to meet the new needs uncovered. Continuous evaluation and assessment must permeate the entire school life of each child and each group. The teacher uses readiness tests, intelligence tests, rating scales, and her own judgment based on what she has learned through her training and experience to make a continuous assessment. Other means of evaluating at her disposal are the tests constructed by the authors of the basal text she is using and the response made by the children.

The teacher does not wait for the preliminary assessment to be completed before she initiates an approach to the use of the basal text. She does this through the whole-to-part-to-whole approach. Through the labeling techniques of Watkins, she tries to develop a sight vocabulary. Items in the room environment are labeled and attention is called to these labels. Children's desks and coat hooks are labeled with the child's name. Some kinds of action-direction exercises are employed. More words are added to this sight vocabulary through experience charts and modifications of experience charts. Children's common experiences are discussed. Stories concerning these experiences are composed by the class, dictated to the teacher, and then reread by the pupils. Chalkboard newspapers, such as the one in Figure 8–2, are used to add to the child's sight vocabulary. The teacher hopes that the daily reappearance of the newspaper will entrench these words into the child's basic sight vocabulary.

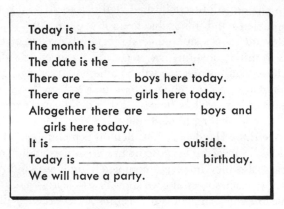

Today is _____.
The month is _____.
The date is the _____.
There are _____ boys here today.
There are _____ girls here today.
Altogether there are _____ boys and
    girls here today.
It is _____ outside.
Today is _____ birthday.
We will have a party.

FIGURE 8–2. An example of a first grade chalkboard newspaper.

When the child has developed a sight vocabulary of from 50 to 75 words, as determined through the assessment approach, the teacher is ready to begin with the first pre-primer. Now, the basal approach takes over.

While the child was accumulating his basic sight vocabulary, the children and teacher were playing games in which the teacher asked them to listen to sounds and to identify sounds which were the same and sounds which were different in initial, medial, and terminal positions in words. These games were not for amusement purposes. In reality, this was laying the foundation for the future program in phonics. Basal text authors and reading specialists use the word-sound games to teach auditory discrimination. This is an attempt to develop the child's ability to discriminate sounds. Later, symbols will be attached to the sounds, and thus, we have phonics.

No sooner does the child begin to read than the teacher begins to develop unit activities in social studies, usually around the theme of community helpers. The study approach begins to operate. The child is guided to picture books on the theme of the unit. Experience charts are made of the activities in connection with the unit. These charts are read. Sometimes the words and charts are incorporated into a big reading book for the class. In connection with the unit, letters will often need to be written—requests, invitations, thank-you letters, and such. These are composed by the class and dictated to the teacher who writes them on the blackboard. Each child then copies the letter. This calls for visual discrimination of letters and letter formations. This suggests that a modified alphabet-spelling method is now being employed.

But first grade is not all work. The teacher has accumulated a wide variety of books on levels from simple picture books to books of third- or fourth-grade level of reading difficulty. Children are given ample opportunity to explore these books and to take them to their desks or home to read. The teacher is using the interest approach to try to inculcate the lifelong habit of leisure time reading for enjoyment.

How to Prepare a Lesson

When it comes to the use of lesson plans, most experienced teachers shudder at the thought of the type of detailed lesson plans which are purportedly written by so many beginning teachers. Beginning teachers, on the other hand, are appalled at the paucity of details that more experienced teachers merely indicate in their plan book, such as the notation that the next lesson in reading covers pages so and so in the basal text and certain pages in the workbook. Surely there can be some middle ground from which both the experienced and inexperienced teacher can begin their planning without going to extremes and still have the benefits which are the results of thoughtful preparation.

Too often, an error committed by many beginning teachers and a fair number of professors teaching methods courses is an insistence on following the mechanical outline of a lesson plan without too much thought being given to its adequacy for use as a tool in actual practice. Frequently, too much space is taken up in a lesson plan with nonessential details and very little space is devoted to the actual teaching part of the period itself. The most important part of any lesson plan, however, is not what is finally written on paper but rather what thinking has preceded the writing of the plan.

Teachers should answer a few questions before they begin to write the teaching procedure. The first question the teacher should ask herself is, "What exactly do I want to teach in this lesson?" A teacher has no direction unless she clearly understands exactly what it is that she is trying to teach to her charges. What specific words are to be introduced and learned? What sound is to be taught? What prefix are we trying to reach? How much more meaningful this approach would be than to merely state "Cover the story on pages 16–20." The content or subject matter of the day's lesson should be specifically identified. The content to be covered can be indicated by that particular unit in the course of study or by the nature of the basal reader itself.

After the teacher has identified what she wants to teach, she must ask the question "Why do I want to teach this particular subject matter?" This question has the impact of forcing the teacher to consciously assess the value, the significance, and the ultimate goal to be gained by the child in learning this material. The teacher may come to recognize the importance of this new content in the sequential development of skills; or, the teacher comes to realize the communicative value and the meaningfulness that the new subject matter may have for the child; perhaps the teacher herself gains a new perspective of this material and its importance. These and other considerations will enable a teacher to provide more adequately for the better teaching of the content. She becomes more alert to the techniques, materials, and activities which will be needed to bring about the desired results. In some ways, this question may reflect the aims and outcomes of the lesson in terms of the skills, knowledge, or attitudes to be gained. Whether the aims and outcomes should be stated first and then the content selected to fit these aims, or whether the content of the day's lesson should be selected first on the basis of broader objectives of the unit and then the aims and outcomes of that lesson's content deduced, is somewhat of a moot question of the "chicken-or-the-egg" variety. If a teacher knows her content, perhaps the aims should be stated first. However, if the teacher is a beginner with little knowledge of content, perhaps the determination from the course outline or basal text of the content to be taught might well be done first. In either case, the teacher must see that the content to be taught is vital to the further development of the reading ability of the child.

Once the teacher knows what she wants to teach and why she wants to teach it, she must now ask the question, "What are the techniques, activities, and materials by which this content can be taught?" There will be a variety of ways by which the subject matter can be taught. The first idea that comes to a teacher's mind is not always the best idea. The techniques used with yesterday's lesson may not be appropriate for today's lesson. New ideas must be constantly pursued so that the teacher will be able to make a meaningful choice. A teacher's creativity often shows at this point. All teachers can make use of the teacher's manual as a source of suggestions. Other sources are professional magazines, source books for teachers, professional textbooks, conversations with other teachers, activity curriculum outlines, and the like.

The next question facing the teacher is "For this subject matter, with these pupils, in this school, what is the most efficient and effective approach for the teaching of this material?" Notice that the teacher takes several factors into account here: First, the nature of the material; second, the nature of the pupils in the class; third, the educational climate of the school and the community. A fourth factor to be considered is the personality of the teacher. A quiet and reserved teacher with little classroom control would not do well to have many active, social participation activities in which the pupils are much on their own. When a teacher has come to a conclusion concerning the most efficient and effective means of teaching the subject matter, she is now ready to concern herself with the procedures for actually teaching the material: "How am I going to teach this lesson?" or, as it is professionally called, *the directed reading activity*.

Directed Reading Activity (DRA)

The *directed reading activity* is the procedure to be followed in the actual teaching of the lesson. The questions asked and answered up to this point have been preparations made with a view of eventually being used to answer the question "How am I going to teach this?" The teaching part of any lesson usually consists of 6 parts: (1) development of motivation, (2) preparation or reading for the new material, (3) presentation of the new story and material, (4) development and strengthening of the newly learned content, (5) follow up and application of the newly learned material, and (6) the evaluation of the lesson. Steps 3, 4, and 5 are the most significant inasmuch as it is in these three steps that the actual learning takes place. Notice that reinforcement of learning is sought through the process of meaningful repetition. The elderly preacher advocated this same approach when asked what his secret was for being so successful in having his congregation always remember his sermons. "Well," he said, "first I tell them what I'm going to tell them, then I tell them, then I tell them what I've told them." Varied, meaningful repetition seldom hurts learning.

The first step in a directed reading activity is to motivate the pupils to want to learn the new material. By motivation we mean creating in the child a lively interest in the fact to be learned or the skill to be developed. Learning implies that the pupil must be an active participant in the learning process. The child must actively seek to involve himself mentally in the learning of something new. The passive spectator, the withdrawn or resistant individual, the disinterested pupil, will not learn as readily as the child who is enthusiastic and eager to seek for the new, the unknown, the exciting. The teacher can establish in the children a desire to learn which can permeate all of the activities of the year, but it will also be important to pinpoint the motivation to want to learn the particular skill, knowledge, or attitude being taught in that day's lesson. This motivation may be encouraged by group discussion, introduction by pictures or stories, questions which direct thinking into desired channels, or sometimes just a statement. Every teacher's manual gives numerous suggestions for motivating each lesson.

The second step in a directed reading activity is the preparation or readiness necessary to undertake the lesson of the day. The new concepts to be presented in the story to be read must be developed in order for the children to get meaning from the story. Good teachers use pictures, objects, slides, motion pictures, and community resource people to develop concepts prior to the reading of the story. In addition to the development of the concepts, the teacher must present the new vocabulary to be found in the story. Before the class reads the story, the teacher takes the new words from the story and introduces them one at a time by writing them on the chalkboard; she then tries to develop the meaning of the word as it is used in the story. By the use of game type drill, directed action exercises, or discussion she tries to entrench the word and its meaning into the child's reading vocabulary.

Once the children have been motivated and readied for reading, the teacher guides the children in reading the story. This is the presentation step. In most cases, the children will silently read short parts of the story in response to a guide question given by the teacher, such as "Read the next paragraph to find out where Bill was heading." In other words, the children have a specific purpose or goal for their reading to make their work more meaningful or purposeful. After most of the children in the reading group have indicated that they have found the answer, many teachers will have one of the children read the section orally.

After the story has been read, the next step is to develop and strengthen the skills which are related to or part of the material just read. These skills could involve the use of the new vocabulary words, a new concept or a new word attack skill. It is at this time that the teacher also checks to see how well the children learned what they were supposed to learn and how accurate their learning was. This development and strengthening can be done through workbook activity, teacher-made drills, or drills suggested by the teacher's manual.

The next step in the directed reading activity is generally referred to as the follow-up activity. During this phase the children apply the skills, knowledge, or attitudes acquired during the lesson. This step can be an assignment for work at their desks or at home and can consist of independent activities, practice exercises, workbook drill, and so forth. In some situations, the children may re-read the story for a different purpose, such as to prepare a dramatization, or for role playing; or, they may read stories in other books which parallel the content of the story read; or, the teacher may merely conduct a discussion. Many teachers in Los Angeles County refer to this portion of the lesson as the "clincher," the nailing down of the newly learned material to make certain the pupil will retain it.

Having taught the lesson, the teacher should perform one more step, the evaluation of the lesson procedure and of how well the children learned what they were supposed to learn. The teacher should have some idea of how effective her lesson planning was in terms of accomplishing what she set out to do. Parts of this evaluation will be subjective in nature as the teacher mentally reviews the conduct of the lesson and notes where the lesson went well and where the children were having difficulty grasping what she was trying to teach. The teacher could use tests or just an informal analysis to identify what the children have learned, what needs to be retaught, what was good about her lesson, and what needs improvement.

A sample lesson plan outline will follow. The teacher should consider each of the major points in the outline in preparing a lesson plan but she should feel free to modify the outline as to the amount of details to be included. How much she should put into a lesson plan depends on the nature of the lesson, the needs of the children, and her own needs based upon her experience and insight.

SUGGESTED FORM FOR A DAILY LESSON PLAN

Name_____   Subject_____

Grade_____   Date_____

I. Preparation

    A. What material do I want to teach in this lesson? (Content)

       Be specific as to the new words, new skills, new sounds, etc., which are to be presented. What skills, knowledge, or attitudes will be developed? List the pages of the basal reader and the workbook to be covered.

    B. Why do I want to teach this particular content? (Values and Outcomes)

       What values does this subject matter have for the child who is learning to read? How does it fit into the total reading program, what sequence of a skill is being developed, or what is the signficance of the new material? How will pupil behavior, in reading or otherwise, be affected?

    C. What are the techniques, activities, and materials by which this content can be taught? (Techniques and Aids)

       This section will serve as a "source of ideas and materials" for the teaching of the content. From the teacher's manual, other reading, and other persons, collect ideas of the materials or activities which might be used. Be imaginative and creative.

    D. For this subject matter, for these particular children in this particular school, what is the most efficient and effective approach for the teaching of this material? (Method)

       Make a decision and choose from the sources listed in the previous section which technique, materials, or activities will be most helpful in terms of the content, the nature of the pupils, the type of school, and the personality of the teacher involved. List them.

II. The Teaching Period (Directed Reading Activity)

    A. Motivation

       What specifically will I do to create an interest in the children to want to learn the new material?

    B. Preparation and Readiness

       How will the new concepts or vocabulary be presented initially to the children to make sure they will have the meaning and readiness needed when they confront them in the new story?

    C. Presentation of the Story

       How will this be done? Will the children read orally or silently? What guide questions will I use?

    D. Development of the New Learning

       How will the new skills, knowledge, or attitudes be practiced? What will be done to strengthen the newly learned material? How will I check to see if the children have learned the new content correctly?

E. Follow up and Application

How will the newly learned content be applied or further used to "clinch" the lesson? What assignment will be made?

III. Evaluation of the Lesson

To be completed after the lesson has been conducted. Did I accomplish the objectives? Why was the lesson successful or why not? What would I do differently if I were to teach it again?

Individualized Educational Program (IEP)

The concept of individualized instructional plans, prescriptive plans, or educational programming has been with us for some time, but it was not until Public Law 94–142 became effective that there was a widespread effort made to put into practice what was being advocated. Public Law 94–142 seeks to guarantee all handicapped children a free, public education geared to their own special needs. It requires that a specialized education program be written for each handicapped child. The educational program, which is to be reviewed yearly, must specify instructional goals and must indicate what special education and related services the child will receive.

Specifically, the IEP or individualized education program must be a written statement developed in a meeting by a qualified representative of the local educational agency, the teacher, the parent or guardian of the child, and, whenever appropriate, the child. We assume that the teacher and her support services will be responsible for making suggestions and writing the initial plan for consideration. The statement must include:

1. The present levels of educational performance of the child.
2. Annual goals set for him in different academic and developmental areas specifying the behavior to be reached through the individualized educational program.
3. A list of short-term objectives that serve as the steps in achieving each annual goal.
4. Specific educational and related services and special instructional media and materials to be provided to the child.
5. An indication of the extent to which the child will be able to participate in regular education programs.
6. The date when special services are to begin and the anticipated duration of such services.
7. The tests or appropriate objective criteria used to evaluate the child's progress to determine if the instructional objectives are being met.

Basically, the writing of the individualized educational program involves three steps:

1. Determining present levels of educational performance of the total child in academic, behavioral, and learning or cognitive areas by (a) surveying available information such as psychological and medical reports; evaluations and reports written by specialists such as in reading or in speech and language; reports from resource people such as previous teachers, parents, counselors, school nurses, and home and school visitors; and (b) collecting additional information by the use of formal and informal assessment instruments and techniques.

2. The writing of annual goals that will identify, in a general way, anticipated growth in skills and knowledge in instructional and developmental areas that can be reasonably expected of the child by the end of the year.
3. Specifying short-term objectives, derived from the annual goals, in smaller, specific, more manageable segments or units of learning tasks, that can be learned in a relatively short time, evaluated for progress, and eventually will result in the achievement of the specified annual goal.

The short-term objectives are the specifics that must be taught. They are derived from a task analysis of the topic under consideration within a specific instructional area. For example: The instructional area is "phonetic analysis of words;" the annual goal is use of consonant blends; the task analysis identifies the specific consonant blends to be taught and stated as short-term objectives; instructional media and evaluative criteria are included. The short-term objectives, then, are the vital part of the educational plan because they indicate precisely the nature and content of the skill to be taught. Short-term objectives, or the task analysis of an instructional area or skill, are not always easy to establish. However, some sources are available for ideas: curriculum-based objectives or published collections of tasks; published sequences of objectives accompanying commercially or locally prepared materials; and teacher-written objectives written at another point in time.

The law requires that appropriate evaluative techniques or materials be used to determine if the child has mastered the short-term objectives. The evaluative criteria can be expressed in terms of frequency, the length of time, the terminal behavior, the allowances or restrictions, the percentage of successful performance, or the consistency of learned behavior. For example, the criterion for successful mastery of an objective may be 4 out of 5 correct responses for three consecutive instructional periods. This type of evaluation lends itself very readily to the criterion-referenced measurement (CRM) approach. This approach is well-structured in terms of specific objectives and specified levels of successful performance. The teacher operates on a test-teach-test cycle for each skill.

The format for a comprehensive individualized instructional plan would be something as the following:

    I. Personal Identification Information on the Pupil.
   II. Background Information (if applicable).
      a. Developmental history.
      b. Pertinent family data.
  III. Present Levels of Educational Performance (consider the whole child).
      a. Formal assessment.
      b. Informal assessment.
      c. Information from available sources.
      d. Summary of strengths, weaknesses, skill deficiencies.
  IV. Long-Term or Annual Goals (for each instructional area).
   V. Short-Term Instructional Goals (in terms of the annual goals).
      a. Task analysis of skills.
      b. Sequential order (if appropriate).
  VI. Teaching Plan.
      a. The tasks or skills to be learned.
      b. The instructional technique, material or media to be used.
      c. Evaluation material or criteria of successful performance.

The previous form will serve as a base from which daily lesson plans or daily instructional procedures can be derived. The individualized educational program says "This is where we're going, how we're going to get there, and how we will know when we've arrived." The daily plan, which is really the individualized teaching aspect of the program, is the nuts and bolts that make the whole project work. It's important to know where we're going, but it's more important to develop a daily format that will get you there. The techniques of individualized teaching such as using folders with daily work materials to be completed, compiling a daily schedule that includes time for individual instruction, record keeping and assignment of daily facts by the teacher; and keeping an individualized sheet for each child listing tasks to be accomplished that day, become the mainstay of teaching and learning activities. The "big plan" is informative and serves as a guideline to instruction; but it's the "little plan," the daily one, where the job of teaching is spelled out.

Media for Teaching Reading

The Basal Text

The *basal text* is one of a series of carefully graded readers designed by a team of specialists to provide a sequence of development consisting of short easy steps which will lead the child from inability to read to independence in reading. The basal reading series will usually have two or three preprimers in addition to a primer and the first reader to be used in first grade. The *preprimers* help to develop the mechanics of reading, such as developing the habit of reading horizontally left to right, moving down one line and reading left to right again. Sounds and symbols are introduced in the pre-primers, also. Most preprimers appear in paperback covers. The *primer* is the first hardback book in most series. It seeks to put to use some of the skills learned in the pre-primers in addition to developing a basic vocabulary of sight words. The first reader, usually known as the 1^2 book, is introduced during the second half of first grade. Each grade beyond the first will have at least two readers designated by grade level and as the first or second one for that particular grade. The designations are indicated as the 2^1 and 2^2 readers in second grade, 3^1 and 3^2 in third grade, and so on. Sometimes readers will have a number of stars, circles, or dots equal to the grade level of the book on the cover to indicate the grade for which the book was written.

All basal readers have controlled vocabularies which have been scientifically determined. Research has been conducted to determine which words are part of a child's understanding vocabulary, which ones are more likely to be encountered and used at this level of reading, and which words have a structure which will permit more effective and efficient learning. Only so many new words will be introduced in any one book. The new words which are presented will be repeated frequently enough to become entrenched. The elements of repetition, supporting key pictures, application of the words in classroom experiences, all tend to strengthen a child's knowledge of the new words. Each basal text is accompanied by a teacher's manual which gives accurate directions and suggestions for teaching.

It should be noted at this point that a number of vocabulary lists for different grade levels have been developed on the basis of research. For years these lists have served as the basis for the selection of words to be used in the texts. Although not all of the basal readers use the same new words, the vocabulary lists have had the effect of controlling which words and how many words would be learned by the children. In recent years, some reading specialists have sought to make more use of the speaking and understanding vocabulary and experiences which a child brings to school with him. Such an approach is the Coordinated Language-Experiences Curriculum being developed at the University of Pittsburgh and being tried out in some Pittsburgh Public Schools. The intent is to teach the child how to unlock words which he understands and uses and to provide him with a wider reading vocabulary at an earlier grade. The implication of this and other similar approaches is not to do away with basal readers, however. What will occur will be the development of a set of readers with a vocabulary content which is somewhat different from the readers of today. This approach warrants close observation by teachers of beginning reading.

Basal readers are used so extensively and have been proven by research studies to be as good as or better than so many other approaches to the teaching of reading that most reading experts classify basal readers as the best tool presently available to classroom teachers.

Associated Teaching Materials

Each basal series has an assortment of associated devices to parallel the work of the basal text. These devices are designed to reach the child through different avenues of learning and to help the child crystallize his new reading skill or vocabulary. In learning a new skill or word in the basal reader, the child is usually taught on his instructional level of reading. The associated materials accompanying the new learning, however, can be understood by the child working on his independent reading level, which is lower than his instructional level of reading. Thus, the associated materials become a definite aid in learning new material, as well as providing practice and relating the lesson to previously learned material.

One of the most significant associated materials is the workbook. The workbook accompanying the basal text parallels the text in order to provide worthwhile practice exercises to help the pupils master the material of the text. In addition, the workbook provides independent activities which the children can pursue on their own at their desks. The experience of working on their own is valuable and, at the same time, it releases the teacher so she can work with another reading group in her room.

Another associated material frequently found in the first grade is the "big reading book." Generally it is an oversized version of the first preprimer. This book can be seen by any child no matter where he is sitting in the classroom. It is used by the teacher in the early stages of beginning reading to develop the proper use and handling of books, the teaching of good reading habits, and the emphasizing of the social nature of reading.

Most companies which produce basal texts also produce cut-out figures of the principle characters in the beginning reading books. These cut-outs help the teacher make the characters more concrete for the children. In addition, many companies produce flashcards, wall charts, achievement tests, and even diagnostic tests.

Supplementary Study Materials

A wide variety of supplementary study materials are available for the teacher. These materials are designed for a number of different purposes. Some give additional practice with the skills and knowledge learned through the basal program. Other materials are intended to enrich the basic offering by providing added reading or meaning. Still other materials are designed to provide for the specific individual needs of each learner.

Some of the better known supplementary study materials in use in the schools today are high interest-low reading level books, the *SRA Reading Laboratory*, *The Reader's Digest Skill Builders*, and commercial games and devices such as word wheels and practice readers.

The Teacher's Manual

The teacher's manual for the basal text is a detailed description of the sequence of the lessons and activities the authors of the basal series thought would develop the desired skills, knowledge, and attitudes. The teacher's manual gives concrete suggestions for teaching a particular lesson. It is also a source of ideas and suggestions. Some teacher's manuals even give the teacher background information she should know about the content being taught. Teacher's manuals vary in organization. Some manuals are planned as detailed lesson plans whereas others are basically sources of many suggestions for the teaching of a lesson. The teacher may choose the activities she wishes to present in the classroom. Beginning teachers usually follow the manual rather closely during their first year of teaching. After they have gained some confidence and "know-how," they begin to modify the suggestions to fit their personality and style of teaching and the climate of the learning situation in their classroom.

Teacher's manuals are generally in agreement with the procedures of teaching reading as recommended by most experts in the field of reading. The manuals pursue accepted objectives and outcomes through the use of approved methods, materials, and devices. To expect a beginning teacher with limited training and experience to produce lesson plans and to develop sequential skills as good as those produced by a staff of experts with years of experience and training would be foolish. Even teachers with many years of experience find worthwhile suggestions and ideas in their manuals. Beginning teachers can do at least this much. The most pointed criticism concerning teacher's manuals seems to be directed at the kind of use the teacher makes of it. Many teacher's manuals provide structured lesson plans for use with the basal reader. If a teacher merely makes use of the plan provided, she is not taking into account the nature of the learners in her class. She is not making any attempt to adjust the textbook to their needs. This is a criticism of the use of the tool and not of the tool itself. The teacher's manual should be considered more or less as a guide or a source book and not as a regimentor of a teacher's activities.

A further argument offered against the use of teacher's manuals is the restriction which it imposes when it seeks to develop skills and lessons in sequential order. Many educators feel that the basal reader should be correlated with other subject matter areas of the curriculum and should not necessarily be read in sequence or have the lessons developed in sequence. Use of the teacher's manual can influence some teachers to follow the lessons in sequence and, thereby, keep them from correlating purposes for reading such as "learning to read" with a "reading to learn" situation.

Criticism of Workbooks

A significantly large number of educators bewail the use of the workbook in the classroom. They state that workbooks are designed for the average child in class and thus prevent the teacher from structuring the practice material to fit the needs of individual children. Fast learners zip through their workbook without too much challenge while slow learners work as well as they can but still find it difficult to complete the necessary work. Furthermore, many educators feel that workbooks provide practice exercises which a child may or may not need. They argue that, in many cases, the exercises provided in workbooks do nothing more than provide busy work for a number of children, teaching them very little at a great expense of time.

Some educators are not as vehement in their denunciation of workbooks as they are in their criticism of the manner in which the workbooks are used. The misuse of workbooks in all subject matter areas has long been denounced. The workbooks are to provide needed practice and direction in the development of a new skill or knowledge. Many educators feel that to require all of the children to do all of the pages in the workbook indicates a lack of understanding on the part of the teacher. These educators would prefer that the child not be given a workbook but that the teacher should tear certain pages out of a workbook and give these pages to specific children to meet their particular need. This approach would be one way of individualizing the practice material.

Most teachers still count heavily on the use of workbooks, in spite of the criticisms. Certainly if a teacher wishes to use the workbook as a teaching tool, she should be aware of its limitations and should seek to use it advantageously.

Instructional Technology

The introduction of technology in the schools is the most revolutionary change in classroom instruction to date. Everything is changing at once. The curricula, the methods of teaching subjects, concepts of how children learn, and most dramatically, the tools of teaching.

Research with the electronic "talking" typewriter developed by O.K. Moore indicates that youngsters from deprived backgrounds communicate with the machines better than they do with people. The talking typewriter has infinite patience and never tries to hurry a child. As the child strikes a typewriter key, the letter appears on a large screen before him, and, through earphones, he hears a soft voice name the letter. The computer now locks all the other letters on the typewriter and will wait indefinitely for the child to strike that letter again. When the child does, the letter appears again, on the screen, and the voice names it. Thus, through touch (the typewriter key), through sight (the screen), and through hearing (the voice) the technique makes use of three senses in teaching the letter. The computer is programmed to eventually work with words and with sentences. Moore claims to have taught 2½- and 3-year-olds to read by this approach.

Other devices having teaching possibilities are educational or "public" television, programmed-instructional textbooks, workbooks, and teaching machines, computer learning as directed from distant centers and related at a pupil "console desk," extensive use of earphones, tapes, and slides, all electronically controlled, automated libraries with direct dial access systems, and other such imaginative devices. Not all devices are massive and prohibitive in cost. One machine which projects a story, sentence by sentence, for a child to read has a key which can be pressed whenever a child wants to know a word and the machine gives the word.

Generally, the traditional mechanical devices used in the teaching of reading can be classified into four categories: flashmeters, pacers, screeners, and perceptual developers.

FLASHMETERS. The flashmeter is a mechanical device for controlling the length of exposure on the screen of items to be seen by pupils. The principle of its construction is the same as used in cameras to control the length of time of exposure of a film. In the case of flashmeters, it is used to control the length of time the light from the slide projector is permitted to pass through a slide and out the lens onto a screen. Most flashmeters have a control range from constant exposure to 1/100 of a second.

Companies producing flashmeters also produce slides to be used during the flashmeter training. Slides can be bought which contain geometric figures, digits of varying lengths, unrelated letters, short words, long words, phrases, and sentences. Generally the companies also produce manuals for the teacher to follow in the development of her lessons.

The procedure is to locate a point where the child or pupil can see with ease, then to concomitantly increase the speed of exposure and the number of spaces to be included in the span of recognition. The lessons are usually conducted with the lights out or lowered. The teacher says "Ready" and the pupils fix their eyes on a portion of the screen previously indicated as the spot where the material will appear. She then says "Now" and flashes the materials. This is followed by the instruction "Write." When a slide has been completed the teacher reads the material in sequence, and the pupils check their accuracy.

Because there is a constant change from dark to light and because of the contrast between the exposed material and its background, the flashmeter has been criticized since all factors are ripe for production of vivid after-images which assist the learner in going faster than he really is capable of going. As a result of this criticism, many of the newer flashmeters expose all of the materials only all out of focus. The teacher can bring into focus the material to be seen. Some of the more frequently used flashmeters are the tachistoscopes of the Mast/ Keystone View Company and the Educational Development Laboratories.

PACERS. Reading pacers are devices for controlling the speed of reading of the learner. They are generally of three types: the place marker, the blinker, and the film.

Place marker type of accelerators or pacers are distinguished by a wire, light, or window blind arrangement, which comes down over the material placed in the machine. The rate of descent of the place marker can be controlled to move from very slow speeds to very high speeds. The student is instructed in how to operate the machine and given stories and material written on his instructional level to place in the machine. He is then told to fix the rate of descent at a point where he can read comfortably, then to set the speed just a little higher in order to speed up his rate of reading.

Manufacturers claim the device pushes the pupil to increase his speed while at the same time training eye movements since the reader finds it impossible to go back and reread the material since it is covered.

Most pacers of the marker type are operated electrically; however, a recent pacer designed by SRA has its mechanism controlled magnetically, thereby eliminating the need for cords.

Two companies producing this kind of pacer are Science Research Associates and Mast/Keystone View Company.

The blinker type of pacer is characterized by having slots in which the cover to each can be raised in succession. In illustration, the old metronoscope was a big box-like affair into which were placed stories printed in rolls. On the face of the metronoscope were three slots in line with a cover. When operating, the first cover went up, then down; this was followed by the same movement of the second cover and then the third. The procedure was then repeated. As each cover went up it exposed some of the story going through the metronoscope on a roll.

The manufacturer contended that this prevented regressions and pushed the reader for speed since the speed of both the covers and the roll could be controlled. In addition the metronoscope was said to have developed a smooth return sweep. Some manufacturers even made small ones for individual use although the most frequently used kind were designed for group use.

The third kind of pacer is the film. Stories are printed on films and are put through film projectors designed to enable the controller to control the speed of the film. Some control the exposure through a tapered mechanism inserted in the projector, others control it through a device which brings selected sequential parts into focus then back out of focus. Usually these films are accompanied by booklets containing materials designed to check on comprehension. Manufacturers claim these pacers, too, improve eye movements and increase rate.

Some of the better known film pacers are the Controlled Reader, Harvard University Reading Films and the State University of Iowa Reading Films. One of the most ingenious of recent products is the Perceptoscope which combines everything but the metronoscope.

SCREENERS. Visual screening has become a big thing in our public schools and, as a result, mechanical devices are available here, too. One of the earlier visual screening devices was the telebinocular which was described in detail in the chapter on readiness. Another one which follows much the same procedures is the Orthorater.

The spiral wheel is a mechanical device used to screen for organic brain injury. This device is a black wheel which has been imprinted with a white spiral. When the wheel is spun and watched, the viewer gets the impression that the white spiral is moving. When the wheel is stopped, ordinary people have the impression that it is continuing and report an after-image. Brain-injured persons on the other hand are reported not to have experienced this illusion. The research results on this finding are not conclusive.

PERCEPTUAL DEVELOPERS. There are mechanical devices available to the teacher which, for want of a better name, the authors have classified as perceptual developers. These machines are designed to improve the pupils' efficiency of perception through a variety of channels. One of the most used is the Leavell Hand-Eye Coordinator which claims to improve the perceptual abilities of the pupil by developing better visual-motor-cerebral coordination. The hand-eye coordinator is an ordinary stereoscope attached to a clip board. Sheets from specially designed pads are placed in the clip board so that the subject can trace them with his dominant hand while viewing them with his dominant eye which sees the image to be traced. The nondominant eye does not see the image but remains open.

This same mechanism is used with different kinds of pads for the Delacato materials which purport to improve perception by establishing neurological unity through procedures reminiscent of the Leavell materials.

A unique instrument is the bar reader which is much like a one-gallon can with the top and bottom removed. Stories are printed on cards and inserted in the bottom. The pupil looks down through the top at the card. The complication is that a series of bars are between the reader and the card to be read. The claim is that this helps to develop Gestalt closure. This device is used frequently by optometrists who have become interested in reading problems.

OTHER DEVICES. Mention should be made of three media devices that provide a multisensory approach to learning to read. The machines are the Hoffman Reader, Systems 80, and DuKane. Each of these systems operates somewhat the same. A filmstrip, usually about 9 slides long and enclosed in a cardboard strip, is inserted in the appropriate place on the machine. A light is turned on and the slides appear individually on a screen in front of the child. The slide strips are designed to teach specific reading skills and/or to present practice material for reading. A record or tape is synchronized to go with the filmstrip. The child usually wears earphones to direct auditory input and to keep from disturbing others. As the child looks and hears, he follows in his text or works in a workbook. Thus, he gets a variety of input and reinforcement. There are reading programs developed for different grade levels. The children find these machines very fascinating and interesting to use.

The major drawback of the machines is cost. Not only is the machine expensive, but so are the programs. DuKane is the least expensive of the machines. However, the cost of the materials and the machine must be weighed in terms of benefits to the child. And many, if not most, teachers who use these machines say that they are worth their price in terms of their aid in teaching learning disabled children to read.

Preventing Reading Disability Through the Improvement of the Developmental Program

The surest means of preventing much reading disability is for a school system to bring their teachers to a point where each one can readily determine the reading capacity and instructional level of each child and, through informal and formal means, determine the three specific subskill weaknesses of each child. Undoubtedly, this improved developmental program is the aim of every school administrator in every school system. The problem lies in the means for upgrading the program. At present, upgrading of programs is done on a trial-error basis. Attempts are made through workshops and through importation of college reading personnel to stimulate the staff. Supervisors are hired in the hopes that somehow or other, in the process of interacting with the teachers, there will be a sudden upsurge in the developmental reading program. In most cases, there are some results. In many more, however, no changes take place.

If the change is attempted through dictatorial decree by an interested superintendent, then teachers will flounder and try to conform to regulations emanating from the office of the chief administrator. In the meantime, they will have no concept of what they are doing and why they are doing it—a vital need, if there is to be real improvement.

Experience has shown us that active participation of all the staff is a must if there is to be real improvement. If a board or chief administrator tries to improve the program through subsidizing teachers' expenses in taking courses in reading, some value can be felt. The problem becomes one, however, of uncoordinated effort. Teachers going to different universities will get different viewpoints and different techniques, each good in its own, but in a school system these splinters will not provide a coordinated program.

A real program for the improvement of the developmental program must be a three stage program. Stage 1 is the dissemination of information so that all teachers are using the same vocabulary, are acquainted with the same techniques, and have the same rationale behind their efforts. This alone will not accomplish the purposes. Stage 2 must be inaugurated. Stage 2 is the active participation of all the teachers. This means work—getting in, digging, making things, applying things. The major part of this participation stage is the confidence teachers acquire in their knowledge of reading, its scope, sequence, and techniques. The third stage then is active implementation in the classroom where specific tasks are given to the teachers to perform such as finding each child's instructional level and determining his weaknesses. During this phase there must be much assistance by the supervisors or the chief school administrator if the program is to be improved.

Stage 1—Organization and Dissemination of Information

For the dissemination of information, we generally require that the school provide 15 four-hour sessions with all teachers. During this time the staff presents the following topics.

> The nature of reading.
> What is a total reading program?
> What is a total coordinated reading program?
> The background for reading.
> Approaches to the teaching of reading.
> Using the basic materials effectively.
> Word attack skills.
> Phonics.
> Other word attack skills.
> Vocabulary lists and vocabulary builders.
> Rate of reading.
> Developing study skills.
> Reading in the content areas.
> Appraising reading growth.
> The remedial reader in the classroom.
> Mechanical devices in reading.
> Teaching reading to the exceptional child.
> New ideas and trends in reading.
> Divergent opinions in the teaching of reading.

Experience has shown a workshop scheduled at the end of the school day finds the teachers tired, bedraggled, and worn-out. Yet to have them come back disrupts their evening. Possibly the best technique would be to pay them two extra weeks and have them come back to school two weeks before school starts and do the workshop then. However, boards are reluctant to pay the teachers for this type of activity. Hence, we try to run the four-hour session at the end of the school day with a built-in dinner, which seems to provide relief. In fact, no one ever gets irritated when he is eating. The dinner also provides an opportunity for informal discussion and eliminates antipathy. We run the class for an hour-and-a-half, have an hour break for a dinner provided by the school board, and then come back for another hour-and-a-half. The class sessions use filmstrips, other audio-visual aids, lecture technique, Socratic method, group discussion and group dynamics, as means of getting across the information. The staff provides a well-equipped library of professional books and other materials as a source of reference for the participants in the workshops.

We have found it highly desirable to give a pretest and a posttest. The pretests and posttests contain the same items so that the teachers can get a comparison of growth. Each test consists of vocabulary and terminology, techniques, diagnosis, remediation, and informal and formal means of appraising progress. The aims of the dissemination part are (1) to make certain teachers are talking the same language, (2) to make certain teachers are familiar with the same techniques, (3) to stimulate a reading drive in the school, (4) to coordinate the entire staff as a team working to improve developmental reading, and (5) to provide interaction between the administration and supervisory personnel and the class-room teacher. If the school has a director of reading or a reading consultant, it is quite possible for her to provide this 15 session workshop. However, we have found that the teachers are familiar with the director of reading or the reading consultant's ideas and, hence, a great amount of antipathy toward the time spent develops. However, bringing in a recognized authority uses the principle that a prophet is without honor in his home and country. Many times the authority may not know as much as the director of reading, but the fact that he is an outsider attached to a university and a somewhat recognized authority lends impetus to the reading drive.

Stage 2—Participation

Experience has shown us that talking to the teachers accomplishes nothing. Involvement is the key to progress. This involvement is accomplished by breaking the teachers up into grade-level groups in which they develop a philosophy of reading for each grade level. Later the individual groups are brought together and a total school philosophy of reading is developed.

The teachers are then redivided into grade-level groups with a charge to develop a reading skills chart for each group's grade level which conforms to the total philosophy of the school. This requires the teachers to look into the basal reader's manual for their grade and to extract reading subskills into chart form. It requires them to investigate other manuals for their grade levels to determine if there are things that should be taught at this grade level which are not in the basic manual used. By the time the skill chart for the grade level is constructed, each teacher has a thorough understanding of what should be taught at his grade level.

With the accomplishment of the grade-level skill charts, the individual groups are once again reassembled as a total faculty where, starting with the kindergarten, the skill charts are presented. During this time, discussion of grade placement of items takes place. By the time all grade-level charts have been presented and discussed, each teacher on the faculty knows the sequence of development of skills. Each teacher has some understanding of what goes before and after his grade.

Once again the total faculty is broken down by grade levels with the charge to take those subskills which the group has developed for their grade level and briefly outline five procedures for teaching each skill. These procedures should contain purpose, materials needed, and procedure. In the give and take of fulfilling the charge placed on them, teachers in the selection of procedures grow in their understanding of various ways of teaching a given item. The teacher who has taught the same subskill, in the same way, time after time, now at least has four additional means of teaching it, if not more.

Once again the total group is reassembled and their procedures presented, affording the excellent teacher the opportunity to devise modifications of many of the procedures presented at other grade levels for his own grade. The final product is turned into a handbook for teachers.

While these group meetings have been going on, each teacher has been given a Reading Services Unit Preference List worksheet. She is asked to fill out all the columns for her grade level. This is done to force her, for the first time in many cases, to look at each child as an individual—what he is capable of doing, and what he is doing. Many times this is the first time the teacher has ever made a distinction between the slow learner and the remedial reader.

After this is done, each teacher is given an informal analysis of subskills sheet and is asked to locate the principle weakness of each child within her class. The consultant's administra-

Reading Services Unit

Preference List Work Sheet

Classroom Teacher_____   School_____

Name of Pupil	Grade Level	I.Q. or M.A.	(MA-5.0) Expect. Level	Reading Achiev. Level	Achiev. Grade Minus	No. of Teacher Requests	Clinic Pref. Order
1.							
2.							
3.							
4.							
5.							
6.							
7.							
8.							
9.							
10.							
11.							
12.							
13.							
14.							
15.							
16.							
17.							
18.							
19.							
20.							
21.							
22.							
23.							
24.							
25.							
26.							
27.							
28.							
29.							
30.							

FIGURE 8–3. Worksheet of reading services unit.

tive staff many times must go into the classroom to help the teacher rearrange schedules, times and classes so that she may find the time to work with the child to determine his principle weakness. This generally takes about four weeks the first time. The teacher is told to inform each child what his principle weakness is and then she is helped to set aside one day every week where there is a 45-minute skill period. At this time each child knows his skill weaknesses and means are provided to give practice at that skill level. The teacher is assisted by the consultants and the supervisory staff in accumulating practice materials. Generally, cardboard boxes labeled with subskill headings are made and materials gathered and labeled for that subskill. For example, a box would be labeled *phonics.* Workbooks would be torn apart, pages of drill practice would be identified (such as 3 for grade three—"phonics blends, *cl.*") The child knows his principle weakness is blends and knows he needs practice on *cl.* During the skill period he would go to the box, pull out the page with practice for *cl* which has been put on oaktag. The child then puts a piece of plastic over the oaktag, does the exercises on the plastic with crayon. After he has completed it, he goes to the answer sheet and checks his answers to see his errors. He can then wipe the crayon off the plastic and get another drill practice if he did not do too well. If he did very well, he can go to his next subskill need.

During the second year of the program, the teachers are asked to identify three skill weaknesses for each child. We do not allow them to say his weakness is phonics; we insist they say "His weakness is phonics—he doesn't know these letter names, he needs to know these letter sounds, he needs to know these blends." They must be specific. Teachers in the system who devise outstanding methods, procedures, or organization, present their techniques to the total group which is a stimulus to the other teachers to perform well.

Stage 3—Implementation

This is the diagnostic part for the school program. The consultants visit classrooms, watch, and identify needs, and then present these needs to the total group with methods for fulfilling the needs. The visits can not be spotty. They must be done regularly in order to maintain a high degree of reading drive.

chapter 9

Developing
Reading Readiness
and Perceptual Skills

The term *reading readiness* has broad significance. Traditionally, reading readiness refers to that point in time in the child's development when he is constitutionally and mentally ready to make his first venture into reading with confidence and with a good chance for success. In addition, it refers to subsequent stages in the child's development when he can profitably and effectively move from one level of reading achievement to a more exacting, challenging, productive level. Reading readiness should not be considered the exclusive domain of the kindergarten and first-grade teacher. Readiness applies to any grade level, achievement level, or skill development level or subject area where a child must attain certain prerequisities of learning (readiness) in order to move on to higher, more sophisticated, levels of learning. An appropriate example, although not in the field of reading, is the case of the college freshman who was excellent in arithmetic but had never taken a course in algebra. This student had to develop algebraic readiness skills before embarking on a study of calculus. In the field of reading, regardless of a reader's age, he will not be able to do effective phonic analysis and syllabication until he has learned the basic elements of phonics and the rules for the syllabication of words. A 14 year old reading on a first- or second-grade level will need readiness development in order to learn the phonics that have eluded him for years.

The learning disabled child can present a very special kind of problem to the teacher attempting to teach him reading. In the first place, the LD child in need of prereadiness or readiness skills may well be considerably older than the chronological age when children are normally taught readiness skills. For any number of reasons, the LD child could have been delayed because of maturational, environmental, neurological, perceptual, or language factors from absorbing and learning the readiness skills when they were initially taught. In the second place, a young, moderate to severely impaired LD child may not have the ability to begin his school program at the point where prereadiness and readiness skills activities begin in most basal reading programs. The readiness materials available to the teacher may be too advanced for some LD children. The level of readiness needed by the LD child may have to be on the developmental level of a 2 or 3 year old, instead of that of a 4, 5, or 6 year old.

This lack of maturational readiness for some children is the reason why many school districts will not admit children into a kindergarten program if they are not 5 years of age by October 1 of the admission year. It is accepted that many children (especially boys) with post-October 1 birthdates benefit from an additional year of maturational development before exposure to conventional reading methods. On the other hand, some children are ready for school even if their chronological age does not fit the criteria for entrance. These children, however, can usually be admitted on the recommendation of a competent psychological examiner who can verify their readiness for kindergarten learning.

Basic Understandings

An Age for Reading Readiness?

The traditional researcher in the field of reading believes that a child needs a mental age of 6 years and 6 months in order to profit from formal reading instruction *as it is generally taught in the schools in the United States.* This was the conclusion reached in the classic study of Gates (1931). The point of emphasis to be noted here is that the mental age of 6–6 is needed to be able to learn to read *by the methods presently used in the schools to teach reading.* There is no question but that a child must have the mental maturity or other maturity required by a task before the learning of that task can take place. The fallacy in our thinking up to this time has been to assume that the difficulty of the subject content of reading required a mental age of 6–6 when, in reality, it was the complex nature of the methods used to teach a child to read that required an older child to understand what was to be done. Johnson (1974) reviewed the research and concluded that there is no best chronological or mental age for learning to read.

Children are regularly being taught to read at the age of 5 in Scotland. However, in these schools they are using a different kind of teaching approach from that used in the United States, and they also have some very different objectives in their reading program. Gates taught some 4 year olds to read, and Moore some 3 year olds. Certainly it is possible to teach a child to read before he has a mental age of 6–6, but the important question is, "Should we teach a child to read before he is 6 years old? Does a child need to know how to read before he enters school?" One of the criteria for determining at which point in the school's curriculum a skill or a knowledge should be placed is the criterion of "need." So far, no research has demonstrated nor has anyone shown that a child needs to know how to read before the age of 6.

The old argument of nurture versus nature also applies to reading readiness. Can a child be taught to progress more quickly to a higher level of development than his maturational readiness level would normally permit? Does environment make a difference? Gesell (1946) supported a maturational, developmental theory with his studies. Reading ability was viewed as part of the total maturational process which included physical and intellectual factors. Therefore, readiness for reading could not be accelerated. Gesell concluded that children, for the most part, performed certain tasks at certain ages and progressed through sequential stages of growth with few exceptions. He considered attempts at speeding up dangerous, or a waste of effort. Parents were often told their children would read when they were ready.

Piaget's theories of child development hypothesize that children can learn only those concepts for which they are developmentally ready. Before the approximate age of 8, a child can be taught to use such words as *tall, short, wide,* and *narrow,* but because he is incapable of mastering the ideas of conservation, he will not understand that a tall, narrow glass contains the same amount of water as a short, wide one, even when the water is poured from the short glass into the tall glass. The child must have demonstrations, illustrations, and personal experiences, but the child must first and foremost be ready for the learning to take place.

Bruner (1960), however, maintains that children are capable of dealing with any kind of information provided the material is presented in a way that is meaningful to them. Smedslund's (1961) research shows that younger children can be taught the Piagetian principle of conservation usually learned at ages 7 to 8, thus moving them from one developmental stage to the next before the normal maturational age. The pupils trained in his study were between 5½ and 6½ years of age. However, when some of the clay and beakers with liquids used in the conservation of material experiment were moved out of sight of the children in the study, they gave poorer explanations for the changes in the experimental materials than did children of a higher chronological age who had matured naturally to the understanding of conservation.

Wallace (1974) shows that a complex rather than a simple environment stimulates development. Rats who have been experimented with in enriched environments show an increase in neural junctions, as compared to those in nonenriched environments. If this is also true for humans, it would indicate that experiences stimulate physical growth of the brain and that these, in turn, increase the capacity for responding to more experiences. Yet, while enriched experience seems necessary for growth, physical maturation must have proceeded to a point where the individual is capable of making a response to a particular stimulus. A middle approach views learning as an interaction between physical and mental factors and between heredity and environment. Learning is not viewed as the result of either maturation or conditioning but as a combination of these two factors.

It would appear that early, formal instruction simply may not benefit the child who has not reached the teachable "moment" for reading. A fundamental principle indicates that insistence upon too early formal instruction may actually harm the child. Self-image is formed during infancy and early childhood. Consequently, placing a child in a situation where demands are made upon him for which he is unready may create a negative self-image, especially if the child makes comparisons with children who are ready. According to Kagan (1965), this would not occur if the child had been permitted to arrive at the moment of readiness at his own pace.

Our opinion as it relates to conflicting theories and results of research is that all data and research designs must be evaluated carefully. Perhaps both schools of thought on the issue of nurture versus nature are partially right. If every child is different, one child may benefit by training while another may not.

Factors of Reading Readiness

Attempts to clarify the relationships, if any, between physical, intellectual, social and emotional, and experiential readiness and success in beginning reading are many and varied. Karlin (1971) contends that most of the research has these five conclusions in common:

1. There appears to be a small but significant relationship between physical development and success in beginning reading. Girls seem to be more mature physically than boys,

and have a lower failure rate in first grade than boys. The relationship may be a correlative one and not a causative one.

2. Hearing and visual impairments might interfere with progress in learning to read. Poor health and general physical condition could be detrimental factors in beginning reading achievement. Good physical health and fitness are helpful.

3. Intelligence is a major factor in learning to read. However, the possession of high intelligence is no guarantee of reading success. Furthermore, the possession of a particular mental age does not assure success in beginning reading. The child should have attained the cognitive level of being able to do concrete reasoning (operations) in Piaget's scheme.

4. Children who are emotionally and socially immature are less likely to respond satisfactorily to difficult learning tasks than those who have self-confidence and feel secure. Good self-concept and self-esteem always help.

5. Children with rich language and experiential backgrounds seem to do much better than children with meager ones. Children who participate in activities that are associated with beginning reading seem better prepared for the learning task than children who have not engaged in them. Of course, cultural differences in language experiences must be taken into consideration as a negative factor.

According to Elkind (1975) children who have an attachment to an adult who enjoys, appreciates, and rewards good reading behavior tend to do better in learning to read. Age is dismissed as a relevant factor.

With regard to vision, studies indicate that many 6-year-old children are not mature enough in visual perceptual development to perform well on beginning reading tasks (Snyder et al., 1967). The eyes of a 6 year old are still immature in size and shape.

It has been determined that poor hearers are poor readers. (Lindgren, 1969). Auditory discrimination of beginning sounds may be a predictor of later reading success. Aural remediation should begin as early as possible. Young children should be tested for hearing difficulties before the beginning of formal reading instruction.

Richard Smith (1974) found a definite link between general verbal ability, including oral expression, and reading ability. Using children's own oral language patterns in written material does increase language comprehension. Although "silent speech" (subvocalization) during silent reading occurs in all persons, good readers do less of it. Norm Chomsky's theories closely connect the development of thought with the development of language. At a certain point it seems that speech becomes internalized as thought. The degree to which this can occur smoothly during reading may depend upon the opportunity that the individual has had to practice developing language skills. An interrelated developmental continuum marked by levels of speech, oral reading, and silent reading has been found to exist (Ketcham, 1951).

While there have been various programs of reading readiness in the schools, many come too late. Language development activities should begin early in life. What may be needed is the training of parents in the art of "parenting" and in ways of developing language and cognitive skills in a child. Parenthood is probably the only major human undertaking for which there is no specific formal training, and many people who become parents are simply ill-equipped for developing their child's learning potential.

An example of a preschool program which seeks to facilitate reading readiness in the early years at home is one which is run by the public library in Glassboro, New Jersey (New-combe, 1974). Meetings are held for parents to teach them how to use toys to encourage the development of specific skills such as sound matching, auditory discrimination, visual-motor coordination, and exploration. Parents are educated through films, speakers, and exposure to children's literature. The importance of reading to children when they are young and of encouraging them to relate experiences is emphasized. Parent-child interaction and individuality are other concepts included in the training which perpetuates itself when the mother-trainees become mother-trainers upon completion of the 8-week program. Well-coordinated children's activities center on relating physical involvement and sensory experiences through films, stories, and songs. Books are available to the child, but formal instruction in reading is not proposed. Special trips are planned to broaden the children's perspectives so that they will have more concepts to relate to their stories when they eventually learn to read. The program operates for children from birth to age 4. In such a learning-centered environment, a major goal is simply to help the child learn to enjoy learning.

Reading Readiness and the LD Child

The factors necessary for the acquisition of reading that have been mentioned up to this point apply to both normally developing children and learning disabled children. The LD child will have a number of other factors that could hinder his learning to read. Most of the characteristics of LD children outlined previously in this text would be appropriate factors to consider in assessing a child's readiness to read. Instead of restating these specific factors, we would like to just refer to a few basic concepts. First, some of the traits that many LD children have that hinder learning to read are an inability to learn symbols, an inability to learn incidentally, an inability to learn from vicarious experiences, and an inability to learn from abstract concepts (Serio, 1973). If a teacher recognizes these limitations in LD children, she can provide experiences and materials that will help eliminate these pitfalls.

A second concept that a teacher of LD children must keep in mind is that most of these children have difficulty processing information. They may have difficulty with basic sensory input of language, sounds, or visual symbols. They may have a problem unraveling all of the sensory stimuli that are coming into their brain and, as a result, may not be able to unscramble and organize them into meaningful, perceptual units. Even if they can organize and structure the incoming information, they may have trouble making sense out of it. Their cognitive or conceptual processes may be handicapped or underdeveloped so that no meaning can be attached to the assembled visual, auditory, or verbal pieces. The puzzle has been put together, but they may still not know what it portrays because of imperfect conceptual or perceptual processing; a faulty or inadequate memory; distortions due to poor neural functioning; inability to formulate responses; or a maturational lag in neurological development of essential learning processes. The message has to get into the brain, be processed, interpreted, programmed for response, and then expressed. An LD child may have any or all of these problems.

A third understanding is that many LD children lack a normal rate of neurological development. Maturational lag is a major problem for 4, 5, 6 and some 7 year olds. As a result, many of these children, some of whom are far above average in intelligence but below average in ability to process information, will not be ready for the level of prereadiness and readiness material that is being used in kindergarten or first grade. It is essential to assess the level of reading readiness of every child in the classroom. Then the teacher must provide each child with the appropriate skill building techniques and materials regardless of the fact that, in some essential areas, the child may be operating on the level of a 2 or 3 year old. The same principle applies to a teacher or tutor of older LD children who may not have learned the basic readiness skills necessary for beginning phonics or structural analysis.

Context of Reading Readiness

In some ways there is a relationship or overlapping of ideas when we consider factors of reading readiness on one hand, as we did in a previous section, and on the other, the prereading or readiness skills that must be taught in order to get to the basics of reading. A summary listing of factors of reading readiness might be stated as follows, without elaboration:

I. Physical and Physiological Readiness

    A. Visual acuity and discrimination ability.
    B. Hearing acuity, auditory awareness, and perception of speech sounds.
    C. Health and physical alertness.
    D. Motor coordination ability and skills. *tracking*
    E. Early development of graphic discrimination and writing, including differentiating print from pictures.

II. Mental Readiness and Background Experiences

    A. Mental maturity and capacity.
    B. Perceptual development for visual, auditory, and haptic functions.
    C. Conceptual adequacy and concept formation.
    D. Thought-processing and problem-solving ability.
    E. Memory and sequentialization facilitation.

III. Social-Emotional Readiness

    A. Cooperation with teacher and others.
    B. Independent self-care.
    C. Sharing with and caring for others.
    D. Ability to listen and understand.
    E. Communication and social skills.

IV. Psychological and Educational Readiness

    A. Self-adjustment and adaptability to changes.
    B. Mental set and interest in learning.
    C. Attention span, alertness, and willingness to respond.
    D. Acceptable responses to frustrations.
    E. Freedom to learn and to respond.
    F. Has a learning style or mode of learning that can be developed.

Teaching Tasks on the Readiness Level

In some ways it is possible to take those factors of readiness for reading and to extend them into teaching tasks on the readiness level. For example, Dechant (1970) lists eight major areas of readiness skills that must be developed.

1. Training in concept formation.
2. Training in auditory discrimination.
3. Training in visual discrimination.
4. Knowledge of the alphabet.
5. Training in left-to-right progression and in reading on a line.
6. Acquisition of a sight vocabulary.
7. Ability to associate meaning with printed symbols.
8. Independence in working out the pronunciation of words.

Other teaching tasks might include story sense and memory for sequence, love of books and reading, and attention to the reading task. A comparison of the two lists above shows that there is an extension of prerequisites for learning readiness skills to the task of developing these skills.

Barbe and Abbott (1975) include a checklist of reading skills in their book. The list, developed by Barbe, extends from the readiness level to sixth-grade level. Not only is the checklist a good assessment list, it is also very specific as to what competencies or skills a child should achieve on each level. Each grade level is different, of course, but a developmental thread runs through all the levels. An outline of the major headings* of skills to be taught on the readiness level includes:

I. Vocabulary

   A. Word recognition (name, letters, numbers).
   B. Word meaning (place words, quantitative words, descriptive words).

II. Perceptual Skills

   A. Auditory (related to hearing and reproducing words).
   B. Visual (related to discrimination and part to whole).

III. Comprehension

   A. Interest (motivation).
   B. Ability (mechanics and awareness).

IV. Oral Expression

   A. Spontaneous expression.
   B. Use of complete thoughts.
   C. Repeats sentences.
   D. Retells stories.

Reading Readiness Tasks and Activities

The following is an attempt to correlate some of the factors of reading readiness to readiness tasks that must be learned. Activities are suggested for each area.

---

* For insight on readiness concepts such as children's understanding of words, sounds, sentences, etc., consult Downing, J., & Oliver, P. Child's conception of a word. *Reading Research Quarterly*, 1973–74, 4; 568–82; and Downing, J. What is decoding? *Reading Teacher*, November 1975, 29, 142–4.

A. *Wholesome attitude toward learning to build a feeling of success.*

    1. Give the child tasks with which he can succeed. It is important that there should be a number of such experiences the first day and the first week.

    2. Make the learner aware of small increments of growth. From time to time go back and point out the words which have been learned, the facts which have been accumulated, and other learnings which may have seemed so slight in significance that their presence is apt to be overlooked.

    3. Show the necessity for education and for what the school has to offer.

    4. By using games and attractive materials, show that learning can be a happy, pleasant experience.

    5. Your attitude toward learning is the most important factor influencing the attitude of the child.

B. *Background of experience to develop concepts.*

    1. Share experiences through a news or story period. There should be a specific time for this *each* day.

    2. Discuss experiences. These should grow out of a situation which has developed, rather than arising from a command by you.

    3. Look at pictures and discuss them; tell related stories.

    4. Look at books and follow the same procedures.

    5. Excursions wherever and whenever possible. If this is not feasible for a group, it is possible for the children to tell about the trips they have taken.

    6. Read stories and informational articles. Allow the children to ask questions and talk about the content. Stimulate questions.

    7. Talks by you, other teachers, or parents.

C. *Understanding of many words to develop a vocabulary.*

    1. Call attention to new words as they appear in the discussions, stories, and the reading activities of section B.

    2. Help the child to find the right word during his own conversations and discussions.

    3. You can insert a few new words in your own speech, call attention to them, and clarify the meanings.

D. *Facility in language expression.*

    1. The activities of sections B and C will tend to develop language facility.

    2. Games both on the playground and in the classroom will help. The child is usually more ready to talk in a play situation.

    3. The children will imitate your language. Insist upon completeness of thought. The sentences may be very short, but they should be complete statements of a thought.

E. *Can carry a sequence of ideas in mind.*

    1. Interpret a picture progressively.

    2. Practice in following directions. These should be simple at first and may gradually become more complex.

    3. Discuss any experience, keeping the details in the order of occurrence.

4. You tell a story, and then ask the children what happened first, then what happened next, and so on.
5. Counting.
6. Following each other in line.
7. Telling what they have done this morning in the proper time order. There are many variations of this.

F. *Can see relationships.*

1. Call attention to relationships between objects, people, spaces.
2. Discuss accidents, emphasizing cause and result.

G. *Articulate speech and desirable speech habits.*

1. In every activity which involves speech, strive for clearness. Locate the sounds with which each child has difficulty and provide practice with those sounds.

H. *Can make visual discriminations.*

1. In similar objects, drawings, and pictures, have the children point out likenesses and differences.

I. *Has a fair memory span.*

1. Child repeats numbers or words or a sentence.
2. Child follows directions which he must remember.
3. Any memory game.

J. *Concept of reading for meaning.*

1. Make child aware of the importance and the use of reading skills.
2. Bulletin board notices which the child must read. Also name cards, clippings, and the like.
3. Comprehension exercises in connection with the stories which have been read or told.

K. *Can organize and classify ideas.*

1. Group objects, animals, words, ideas; that is, put like things together.
2. Find all the ideas in one story about a given subject.

L. *Left-to-right progression.*

1. Tracing from left to right.
2. Coloring from left to right.
3. Drawing lines under objects from left to right.
4. Read comic strips as they follow the pictures.

M. *In dealing with pictures.*

1. Ask many questions which will call for interpretation and the use of imagination.
2. Pick out details.
3. Insist on answers of more than one word.

Assessment of Readiness

Before we can talk intelligently about assessing preschoolers to determine if they have a readiness for learning what is to be taught in kindergarten (or in first grade), we must know what is taught at those grade levels and what ability a child must possess in order to be ready for that learning. This principle is more easily stated than implemented because there are various points of view on what constitutes learning, what constitutes readiness, and even what content a child must be taught in a readiness program. A developmental view would assess the child's mental, social, and physical maturational level for learning. A process point of view would attempt to determine the child's adequacy in perceptual processes and motor development or skill areas as an indication of his readiness for schooling. A task analysis or competency point of view would be interested in the child's acquisition of letter, number, and writing skills; this could be considered a base line for comparison with the level of readiness that a teacher would expect or demand because that is the level on which she expects to begin her teaching. As you can imagine, the assessment of reading levels is no simple matter, although many teachers would hardly surmise that fact if they have been evaluating "readiness tests" or "criteria" for entering schools. All three major points of view have something to offer to a good readiness assessment program.

The Approach of Most School Psychologists

The developmental approach forms the basis for most school psychologists in assessing the readiness of a specific child. The testing is done on a one-to-one basis. The expectation of the referral person (parent or school) is that the psychologist can—and will—determine if the child is ready for school. A good psychological evaluation will assess mental ability level; social development; language development; self-help skills pertaining to eating, dressing, and related items; number, letter, and writing readiness; and a general consideration of motor development, physical maturity of body build, visual maturity, physical stamina, and attentiveness. The individual intelligence test used generally is either the Wechsler Preschool and Primary Scales of Intelligence (WPPSI) (1967) or the Stanford-Binet, Form L-M (Terman & Merrill, 1960). The Wechsler Intelligence Scale for Children, Revised (WISC-R) is frequently used if the child is 5-0 or older. The WPPSI can be used with children between the ages of 4-0 to 6-6. We prefer the WPPSI because it has 12 subtests, measuring a variety of intellectual abilities. The Stanford-Binet is more strongly loaded with verbal items than the WPPSI. Since it is more verbal and language oriented, children with language problems—maturational, cultural, or emotional in nature—will not do as well on the Binet as the WPPSI. The WPPSI and the Binet are good predictors of success in school; but the Binet does not give the indicators of limitations in perceptual and motor areas or the signs of possible learning disabilities to the degree that the WPPSI does.

A test aimed at assessing younger children is the McCarthy Scales of Children's Abilities (MSCA) (1972). The test kit was designed to provide for six scales: Verbal, Perceptual-Performance, Quantitative, General Cognitive, Memory, and Motor. The McCarthy Scales are appropriate for children ages two years, six months through eight years, six months. There are 18 component tests; some subtests are very short and some are not sufficiently reliable when used alone. However, if the score of only one scale is desired, all 18 subtests need not be given. The test is well put together but independent research attesting to its adequacy and uniqueness is lacking at this time. We find the McCarthy

Scales good enough to warrant the consideration of school psychologists working with younger children and with possible learning disabled children.

The Illinois Test of Psycholinguistic Abilities (ITPA) (Kirk et al., 1968) is sometimes used by psychologists to assess children for school readiness. The ITPA is more "process" oriented. It provides scales for composite scores on the representational level in auditory-vocal and in visual-motor areas. The same two categories receive composite scores on the automatic level of cognitive functioning. The scores are derived from eight regular and two supplementary subtest scores. The subtests are titled Auditory Reception, Visual Reception, Visual Memory, Auditory Association, Auditory Memory, Visual Association, Visual Closure, Verbal Expression, Grammatic Closure, Manual Expression, and the two supplementary tests, Auditory Closure and Sound Blending. These tests are outlined and defined in Chapter 7. The ITPA has been more thoroughly researched than the McCarthy Scales because the ITPA, revised edition 1968, has been widely promoted for use with learning disabled children to determine their perceptual disorders. The results of research of factor analysis suggest that the ITPA may only be measuring three factors (some say five), instead of eight (McLeod, 1966). The labeling and grouping of the subtests is somewhat questionable. In our experience, unpublished results of the administration of the ITPA to 50 children with learning problems make us reluctant to use it for either preschool teaching or testing of children with learning disabilities. For our purpose, which is to determine the LD child's learning capacity for reading, we find the time better spent in using other assessment tools that give us more information related to what we want and need.

The other assessment techniques used by school psychologists in determining readiness for schooling are varied and do not usually require specialized training as do the Wechsler tests, the Stanford-Binet, the McCarthy Scales, and the ITPA. These other tests are generally chosen from those mentioned in the following sections.

Teacher Assessment of Readiness

In many districts preschool readiness tests are given before a child enters school. Therefore, many kindergarten and first-grade teachers are not involved in readiness testing unless they are assigned that task as part of the school registration procedure. Teachers involved in readiness testing will probably use a standardized test or a combination of criteria factors established by the district. If a child is admitted to school on the basis of age alone, the teacher will then need to assess a child's readiness for learning while he is in her class. She may use two basic techniques in order to make a judgment: A standardized readiness test, or informal reading readiness techniques and observations.

FORMAL ASSESSMENT. Standardized reading readiness tests must be evaluated carefully to determine if they measure for what you need to know about a child. You must also know if what you want is what you need. For example, a task analysis must be conducted to determine exactly what it is that a test measures. You simply cannot go by test titles. Frequently, a readiness test will not measure anything substantial besides visual-motor skills or visual-perceptual skills. In the past teachers have noted that frequently a child does quite well on a readiness test but very poorly in school. Why? Well, likely the traits measured by the test were not the traits required for learning the tasks presented by the teacher. This point is central to our second caution, which asks whether what you are measuring is what you need to determine if the child is ready for schooling or reading.

A review study by Rude (1973) suggests that there are four basic categories of readiness skills: (a) grapheme perception—how well the child can identify and use the characteristics of letters and words; (b) left-to-right visual scan—the ability to be consistent in processing eye movements in a left-to-right directionality orientation; (c) understanding of grapheme-phoneme relationship—not only knowing that letters stand for sounds, but also that sounds can be used to unlock unknown words; and (d) phoneme blending ability—being able to put two or more letters together in a sound-making or sounding relationship. In addition, the child must have some skills such as attentiveness, appropriate learning style or mode, and an experiential verbal background that can contribute to learning to read.

Following are some widely used standardized tests. You must use good judgment in the selection of a test to insure that the test meets your needs.

1. Gates-MacGinitie Reading Tests: Readiness Skills. Grades Kindergarten–1, 1968, Teachers College Press, Columbia University. This test consists of eight subtests; listening comprehension; auditory discrimination; visual discrimination; following directions; letter recognition; visual-motor coordination; auditory blending; word recognition. Subtests scores are weighed on the basis of their predictive value in assessing readiness. Individual test time varies.
2. Harrison-Stroud Reading Readiness Profiles. Grades Kindergarten–1, 1956, Houghton Mifflin. The six subtests are: using symbols; making visual discrimination; using the context; making auditory discriminations; using context and auditory clues; letter naming. Time: 79 minutes.
3. Lee-Clark Readiness Test, 1962 Revision. Grades Kindergarten–1, California Test Bureau. The subtests are: letter symbols; concepts; word symbols. Time: approximately 15 minutes.
4. Metropolitan Readiness Tests. Grade 1, 1966, Harcourt Brace Jovanovich. The seven subtests are: word meaning; listening; matching; alphabet; numbers; copying; draw a man (optional); reading readiness; number readiness. Time: approximately 60 minutes.
5. Murphy-Durrell Diagnostic Readiness Test. Grade 1, 1965, Harcourt Brace Jovanovich. The subtests are: sound recognition; letter naming; learning words. Auditory, visual and learning rate scores. Time: Part 1–2, approximately 60 minutes; Part 3, approximately 35–50 minutes.

Other readiness and screening tests frequently used by professionals interested in locating children with high risk for learning disabilities involvement include:

1. Anton Brenner Gestalt Test of School Readiness. Grades Pre-school, Kindergarten, 1964, Western Psychological Services. Group test that assesses readiness for school.
2. Detroit Test of Learning Abilities. Bobbs-Merrill, Battery of 19 tests with separate subtests and mental age norms for ages 4–0 to adult.
3. Evanston Early Identification Scale. Grades Kindergarten–early first grade, Follett. A quick objective screening for human figure drawing. Yields classification as high, middle, or low risk.
4. First Grade Screening Test. 1966, American Guidance Service. Identifies beginning first graders who need special help to make sufficient progress to be ready for second grade. The test can be given to children finishing kindergarten.
5. Kindergarten Evaluation of Learning Potential (KELP). 1967, McGraw-Hill. Helps teacher measure learning potential on the basis of classroom learning.
6. Mann and Suiter Handbook of Diagnostic Screening. Grades Kindergarten–1, 1974, Allyn & Bacon. Series of 20 short developmental screening tests or checklists. Teachers' Handbook provides ditto masters.

7. Meeting Street School Screening Tests. Grades Kindergarten–1, 1969, Crippled Children & Adults of Rhode Island, Providence, R.I. Assesses language, visual-perceptual-motor skills, and gross-motor control to process symbolic information. High risk cut-off score.

8. Maturity Level for School Entrance and Reading Readiness. Grades Kindergarten–1, 1959, American Guidance Service (Banham). A checklist of 25 items in five categories: bodily coordination, eye-hand coordination, speech and language comprehension, personal independence, social independence. Norms are based on a point count.

9. The Predictive Index. Kindergarten, 1966, Harper, Row (de Hirsch, Jansky, Langford). A diagnostic test of potential reading disabilities comprised of 10 subtests.

10. Preschool Inventory. Ages 3 to 6, 1967, Educational Testing Service, Princeton. A 64-item checklist assessing basic information and vocabulary; number concepts and ordination; concepts of size, shape, motion and color; concepts of time, object class, and social functions; visual-motor performance; following instructions; independence and self-help. Gives a percentile score for chronological age.

11. The Pupil Rating Scale. Norms based on 3rd and 4th Graders, 1971, Grune & Stratton (Myklebust). A screening for learning disabilities in school children. Scores are obtained in five areas: auditory comprehension, spoken language, orientation, motor coordination, personal-social behavior. Teacher can use this scale as an observational checklist for any age level.

12. Screening Tests for Identifying Children with Specific Language Disabilities. Grades-Primary, 1962, Educators Publishing Service, (Slingerland). Three sets of screening tests to detect symptoms of possible language disabilities.

13. Valett Psychoeducational Inventory of Basic Learning Abilities. Grades Kindergarten–1, 1968, Fearon. Contains 229 developmental test items arranged in six categories: gross motor development, sensory-motor integration, perceptual-motor skills, language development, conceptual skills, social skills.

14. Vineland Social Maturity Scale. Ages 6 months to adult, 1953, Psychological Corporation. Binet-type age scale designed to measure the successive stages of social competence or self-help skills in eating, dressing, locomotion, communication. Not very effective above age 7.

15. A Parent's Guide to School Readiness. 1972, Academic Therapy Publications (Anthony J. Cedoline). Not a test but a booklet presenting informative guidelines for parents and teachers in five individual development areas: physiological (includes perception), social, emotional, intellectual, and language.

In administering these or any tests it is essential to observe for distractibility or inability to pay attention to the task. It is also necessary to take into account that the child may not understand the language of the examiner or may be unable to interpret illustrations that are unclear or ambiguous. This must be considered since every child brings different experiences to the testing situation. Review the items with the child to see why the wrong response is made.

INFORMAL ASSESSMENT. Studies indicate that experienced teachers through teacher observation and error analysis may be just about as accurate as any test (Rude, 1973). Variables that are not found in a readiness test but that are pertinent include: (a) teachers should know what they will be teaching; (b) teachers must determine the methods they will be using; (c) teacher's attitude toward a student's success may affect the learning outcome; (d) teachers use different goals which would influence their predictions. A checklist adapted from the New York Reading Readiness Test, Form A, that would be valid for most classrooms is as follows:

Guide to Judgment of Readiness

Physical Functioning. Child:

1. Has adequate vision.
2. Has adequate hearing.
3. Has adequate vitality and energy.
4. Has good general health.
5. Has adequate motor coordination.
6. Shows consistent use of one hand and has not changed from left- to right-handedness.

Mental Functioning. Child:

1. Shows ability to learn.
2. Shows ability to follow directions.
3. Shows ability to observe.
4. Shows ability to remember.
5. Shows ability to reason.
6. Shows adequate attention span.
7. Shows curiosity and interest.
8. Shows interest in books and learning to read.

Social Functioning. Child:

1. Gets along with other children.
2. Can adapt to group activities.
3. Responds well to group controls.
4. Participates actively in group projects.
5. Is satisfied with a reasonable amount of attention.
6. Can perform usual classroom routines.

Emotional Functioning. Child:

1. Is emotionally well-controlled for age.
2. Is relatively free of nervous habits.
3. Shows sufficient personal independence.
4. Usually seems happy.
5. Usually works with confidence.
6. Shows relative freedom from hyperactivity.

Language and Speech. Child:

1. Speaks clearly.
2. Has English-speaking background.
3. Has adequate vocabulary.
4. Expresses his ideas adequately.

Experience Background. Child:

1. Has had many opportunities to go places, see things, discuss his experiences with others.
2. Has had many experiences with pictures, books, stories.
3. Has had many experiences in expressive activities—painting, clay, dramatics.
4. Has had kindergarten experience.

Not all of this checklist pertains directly to reading, but it is important to consider the whole child in classroom functions. If we accept the checklist as applicable to reading or any form of academics, we can see just how detrimental the "symptoms" of a learning disability can be. The children in most LD classrooms cover a wide range of the checklist's skills in a negative way. Some of the problems a learning disabled child is likely to exhibit are lack of motor coordination; handedness difficulties; inability to follow directions due to auditory or visual memory and/or sequencing problems; inability to remember; inadequate attention span; inability to observe through lack of attention or due to distractibility; inability to function in a group activity or with group controls; need for much individual attention; lack of emotional control due to organic problems or frustration; lack of confidence due to past failure; and hyperactivity. These are the obvious problems you may expect to find in some form in the learning disabled student when going through the reading readiness checklist. Assuming the validity of the checklist, is it any wonder these children have trouble reading? Even on the secondary level, the learning disabled student has problems in "reading readiness."

Teaching Readiness Skills

A reasonable question concerning the teaching of readiness skills is "Who needs what, when, why, and how?" To manufacture a readiness program that is applicable to all pre-first graders is unthinkable. There are many individual differences in children aged 4, 5, and 6 years. To expose all children to the same program is to violate all that is known about growth, development, and the way different children learn. A hint of learning disabilities in a child's make-up is all the more reason to deny the use of a standard readiness program. When you consider children with unreadiness for reading because of language, cultural, environmental, or psychological factors, then you must be even more cautious and careful of the type of readiness program being structured for a class of kindergarten children.

Philosophical and Professional Considerations

A number of philosophical and professional concerns have resulted in the issuance of a joint statement by seven national organizations relating to present practices in pre-first grade reading instruction.* Some of the concerns expressed in the statement, as reported in the *Right to Read '77* bulletin (1977), are (a) a growing number of children are enrolled in pre-kindergarten and kindergarten classes in which highly structured prereading and reading programs are being used; (b) decisions related to the teaching of reading are increasingly being made on economic and political bases, instead of on our knowledge of young children and how they learn best; (c) in pushing for high scores on widely used measures of achievement, teachers of young children sometimes feel compelled to use materials, methods, and activities designed for older children, thereby producing negative attitudes towards reading; and (d) recognition of a need for alternative ways to teach and to evaluate progress in prereading and reading skills.

---

* The seven organizations are (1) American Association of Elementary/Kindergarten/Nursery Educators; (2) Association for Childhood Education International; (3) Association for Supervision and Curriculum Development; (4) International Reading Association; (5) National Association for the Education of Young Children; (6) National Association of Elementary School Principals; (7) National Council of Teachers of English.

Among the recommendations made in the joint statement are (a) provide reading experiences in a broader communication process that includes listening, speaking, and writing (the language experience approach was endorsed); (b) continually appraise how aspects of each child's total development affect his reading development; (c) use evaluative procedures that are developmentally and professionally appropriate; (d) insure feelings of success for all children; (e) plan flexibly in order to accommodate a variety of learning styles and ways of thinking; (f) respect the language the child brings to school and use it as a base for language activities; and (g) provide opportunities for children to experiment with language and simply have fun with it. In a way, the recommendations imply a need for preschool programs that will provide cognitive and affective learning in keeping with principles of child growth and development.

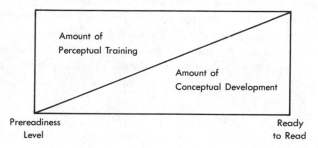

How much perceptual training and how much conceptual training is necessary for the pre-first grader? An adaptation of the paradigm designed by Neville Kephart has merit if grade levels in his chart are ignored. The research is not clear on how much perceptual training should be given at ages 4, 5, and 6. It does imply that little or no perceptual training is helpful after age 7. The statement is often made that "the sooner or younger we can get the child, the easier and better he can be helped." We appreciate the logic of the statement, but we have yet to see any research to justify that idea. Certainly a child should be seen before he develops emotional hang-ups because of frustration in reading. But we do know of LD cases in young adulthood who were helped—some very dramatically—because they wanted and sought help. On the first point, the study by Belmont, Flegenheimer, and Birch (1973) found that beginning first grade children who were poor reading risks and who, in addition to regular developmental reading instruction, received supplementary instruction for 7 months in perceptual training while others received remedial reading, made *equivalent* advances in reading level in first grade. Both groups gained the same amount. The only difference in performance was that children who received the perceptual training made fewer attempts to pronounce difficult words than those who just received remedial training.

Our position is simple. Know your children and their learning needs and styles; know your subject matter and the skills required; try to put the two together by whatever means is comfortable to you, the teacher, and appropriate and acceptable for the children. It is not a technique, a method, or a certain material that is of utmost importance. In the final analysis, it is the quality of the teacher and her style that makes the difference in learning receptiveness. No child fails alone; no teacher succeeds alone.

Frostig Visual Perception Program

Frostig's most significant contributions are in the area of evaluation and education of children with visual perceptual difficulties. However, before discussing Frostig's program based on perception, her concept of perception should be understood. Perception is the ability to recognize stimuli and is one of the prime psychological functions. The sensory perception of stimuli occurs in the eye, but recognition—the process of relating them to previous experiences—occurs in the brain. Maximum development of visual perception normally takes place when the child is in kindergarten and the lower primary grades.

When a child is slow to develop visual perception—and many are—he has difficulty recognizing the relationship of visual symbols. Many times children have trouble recognizing shapes and colors and following directions. Most of this is caused by a lack of visual perceptual development. A program to help these children should be started in kindergarten or in nursery school.

Frostig maintains that in deciding upon a child's educational program, it is first of all necessary to take into account his ability in each of the six major psychological functions which develop during infancy and later childhood: sensorimotor functions, language, perception, thought process, emotional development, and social adjustment. The child's performance in sensorimotor development, perception, language, and higher cognitive functions largely determines the teaching strategy; his emotional development and social adjustment have important implications for classroom management (Frostig, 1966).

Frostig's sensorimotor training program is concerned with four different areas:

1. Physical education (training in movement skills).
2. Development of body awareness (suggestions to help a child develop body concept, scheme and image).
3. Training in manipulatory skills.
4. Training in eye movement (tracking).

In the basic Frostig Program for the Development of Visual Perception (1964) there are sections of worksheets which are divided into five areas of visual perception so that the teacher can become aware of a pupil's difficulties in a particular area and will be able to put the necessary emphasis on that area. The five areas of perception are visual-motor coordination, figure-ground perception, perceptual constancy, spatial relationships, and position in space. Frostig recommends the use of worksheets, physical exercises, and three-dimensional activities.

Frostig's own analysis of the *visual perception problem*, or *lag*, as she terms it, is that children are simply not able to see with their mind's eye the same picture as viewed by the eye itself. A child may have excellent vision, but still see a distorted picture because he is unable to put into proper perspective what the eye views. Frostig's studies have repeatedly shown that there is a definite correlation between children in the lowest quartile in the primary grades and those with perception lags.

Basic Visual Achievement Forms

The Basic Visual Achievement Forms and Perceptual Training Procedure are the result of rather extensive research pertaining to perceptual training and hand-eye coordination (Lowder, 1963). The initial studies were directed to working with beginning readers. Although the achievement forms are not highly accurate predictors of achievement in specific school subjects such as reading and writing, they can identify children who are perceptually disturbed or who are lacking in that degree of hand-eye coordination which is necessary for beginning school tasks.

The Perceptual Achievement Forms consist of seven forms: a circle, a cross, a square, a triangle, a divided rectangle (it looks like a Union Jack flag), a horizontal diamond, and a vertical diamond. This test is given to determine how well the children can copy these forms. The templates have only five forms, omitting the vertical diamond and the cross.

The training procedure makes use of templates. For group training, there is a master template which contains all five of the forms which a child may use at his desk as he traces around the inside part of the cut-out form on to an 8½" × 11" sheet of paper. The class is instructed to "bump" each corner, except in the circle, of course, so that no corners are "rounded-off." Each session with the master template consists of four parts:

1. Starting with the circle, the class will trace around the edge of the form at least ten times without stopping and in unison to the count.
2. After removing the master templates, the children are instructed to trace over each of their work samples the same number of times as done originally. They are urged to stay "right on the line."
3. The children turn the sheet of paper over and are asked to draw the forms they have just completed in the same size and position as they did before.
4. The children now place the template on the side they have just completed and trace around each form one more time to see how closely they were able to copy their previous activity.

The child who scores low on the Perceptual Achievement Forms test is given individual training. He receives a large single form template which he uses at the chalkboard. Placing the template on the chalkboard at eye level, the child presses the palm of his hand on the long end of the template and uses chalk to trace the cut-out figures. He must be conscious of "feeling" the edge of the form as he moves his chalk around the outline 20 times. When the template is removed, he retraces the figures. The form is then erased and the child is asked to draw the form identical in size to the one erased. The template is then placed on the drawing and one more line is traced, preferably using a different color of chalk. Three forms are used at one session.

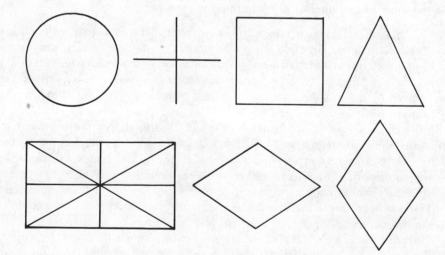

FIGURE 9–1. The Basic Visual Achievement Forms.

The training involved in the tracing process is carried over into classroom activities as much as possible. The training development consists of (1) copying, (2) matching, (3) size constancy, (4) organization into meaningful wholes, (5) visual memory, and (6) eye-hand-motor performance.

Kephart's Perceptual-Motor Training

Kephart sought to increase each child's self-awareness and to give each child an adequate body-image through the use of games and motor skill exercises. Kephart made use of the *Basic Visual Achievement Forms* in his procedure, but he adds a number of other activities. He made use of trampolines, walking rails, balance boards, Marsden Ball technique, and angels-in-the-snow. Kephart apparently believed that the basis of all learning was motor development. Motor development follows an orderly sequence. Motor skills, including self-awareness and body image, must be properly and adequately developed on each level in order to build a good foundation for learning. Kephart would diagnose a case to determine which skills were under-developed. He would then prescribe exercises which are supposed to strengthen the skills which are weak or nonexistent. All of his procedures are designed to bring about the full motor development of the child. Most of the suggestions he makes have been used successfully by others. However, his system (Kephart, 1971) is the first to incorporate all of these ideas into a total program. As yet, no research that we know of has been published to show the relatedness of motor development to learning achievement or of the effectiveness of his total program.

Kephart's remedial program is one which focuses simultaneously on visual receptive, assimilative, and motor expressive behaviors at the lower levels. There is a gradual ascendance to more symbolic behavior. His work stresses the importance of "readying a child for more complex educational tasks by special emphasis on the basic perceptual motor components of learning; these are undertaken at the exploratory level." His perceptual program stresses the need to develop laterality, including an awareness of the difference between the left and right side of the body. This program is based on the development of motor coordination and eye movements. It includes training in four main areas: blackboard training, sensorimotor training, ocular control, and form perception.

CHALKBOARD TRAINING. This is one of the most direct methods of testing the child's adequacy in directionality. The child is asked to produce a movement which will leave a trace in the form of a line on the chalkboard which will possess certain characteristics of size and shape. He is required to develop a visual image of a given shape in response to the directions given by the monitor, translate this into a motor pattern, and produce the required movements.

While the child is making his figures on the chalkboard, the examiner should be observing such things as the preferred hand, the size of the drawing, the accuracy of the production, visual direction and attention during tasks done by both hands, the use of the body during the drawings, whether he can cross his body midline without difficulty, and whether he can visually monitor his motor performance. One of the most important observations is of his ability to match motor performance with visual control, for often he will draw a production on a purely motor basis and completely suspend visual control.

One of the first things a child is asked to draw is a circle, using either hand he wishes. Observation here includes seeing if the child will draw the figure markedly toward the side of his body represented by his preferred hand. If he does, he is trying to avoid crossing the midline because he has not mastered the translation of movement patterns which occurs here.

Another drawing which the child is asked to make on the chalkboard is that of double circles. He is told to take a piece of chalk in each hand and to draw two circles at the same time. Children are also required to draw lines, both vertically and horizontally, which connect *x*'s which the examiner has placed on the board.

SENSORIMOTOR TRAINING. This area of training includes everything from the *walking board* to *stepping stones*. It deals with such activities as walking, balancing, bouncing, and rhythm. The walking board is similar to the childhood game of walking fences or rails or a railroad track. The primary function to be observed in this activity is balance, though postural flexibility should also be observed. Laterality is involved, too, since it affects balancing. The child is directed to walk not only forward, but also backward and sidewise.

Another activity the child must do is jumping, which also has to do with balance and posture. He jumps first with both feet, next with the right foot, and then with the left. In addition, he must skip and hop in different patterns of using the left and right foot. These activities are related to his ability to control his gross muscles and to alternate activities across the center of gravity of his body.

Kephart includes techniques which are designed to reveal how much the child knows about his body and how to control its parts. In the first part, he is asked to point to various parts of his body; but in the second, he must imitate the movements made by the examiner. These movements are designed so that unilateral, bilateral, and cross-lateral movements are required.

The child is asked to do an obstacle course in which he must step over an obstacle, duck under an obstacle, and squeeze through a narrow opening without touching it. These tasks are related to his awareness of the space occupied by the parts of his body in various positions.

Finally, in stepping stones, the child is required to take steps of different lengths and in different directions. The examiner watches to see if he is able to change control of the legs and trunk under conditions which demand irregular performances.

Another activity, *angels-in-the-snow*, is done with the child on the floor, lying on his back. His arms are at his side and his feet are together. He is asked to move his arms up over his head and to move his feet apart. If he has trouble in this area, it shows that he is experiencing problems in controlling the parts of his body individually or in prescribed combinations.

OCULAR CONTROL. This part of the survey attempts to investigate the child's ability to control ocular movements. The child is given a target to follow and must keep this target in sight. Adequate control of the eye is necessary if the child is to do this operation.

Using a penlight as the target, the examiner is able to observe such important behaviors as whether the child perfers to move his head rather than his eye, whether the eye wanders off the target, whether the child can find the target quickly if he does lose it, and if there is any jerk or hesitation as the eyes cross the midline.

During the pursuit, four performances are to be rated: Both eyes together, right eye alone, left eye alone, and convergence. Basically, this part of the survey merely entails having the examiner shine a penlight about 20″ in front of the child and having the child follow this light.

FORM PERCEPTION. In this area of the survey called *visual achievement forms*, the child is asked to copy seven simple geometric designs: circle, cross, square, triangle, horizontal diamond, vertical diamond, and divided rectangle. His performance is rated by his form perception as well as his method of organizing his drawings on the page.

If the child's performance indicates that he is dealing with the forms as wholes, he demonstrates adequate form perception. If he draws one line at a time and pauses between each stroke, his form perception is poor. In the latter case, the corners will frequently not be closed and the relationship between the elements will be poor.

Leavell Hand-Eye Coordination and Language Training Series

The Language Training Series (Leavell, 1961) centers around a drawing board to which a stereoscope has been attached and the use of any one of a series of three pads. Pad #1 consists of drawings placed within a frame. The first drawings are simple in design but the drawings become more complex as the child progresses through the pad. Pad #2 consists of pages on which the drawings alternate somewhat with words. One page has a drawing and the next page usually a word. Pad #3 is composed entirely of words. The child does all of his work looking through the stereoscope onto the drawing board where the picture to be traced

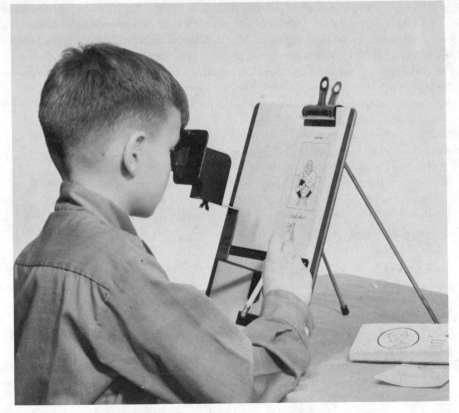

FIGURE 9–2. Keystone Stereo-Reader.

Photo courtesy of Keystone View, Mast/Keystone, Davenport, Iowa 52803.

is placed before the eye which is on the same side as the preferred hand. The opposite eye has nothing before it but the same color background found on the drawing. The child is instructed to trace the drawing using his preferred hand.

Work done by Murroughs, Leavell, Berners, and others seems to indicate good results when this series is used with primary learning disability cases who score confused or mixed dominance on the Leavell Tests for Neural Confusion or the Harris Tests of Laterality.

Kolson-Kaluger Method

The Kolson-Kaluger Method utilizes the stereo-reader and a series of pads to combine good features from a number of the preceding methods. It borrows the tracing of figures from the Leavell method, the sound-symbol relationship developed by tracing from the Gillingham-Stillman method, the key picture technique from the Association Method, and the VAKT technique used to develop whole words from the Fernald method. In addition, it contributes a controlled field and a controlled vocabulary (Kolson & Kaluger, 1965).

Four sets of pads are designed to be used with the stereo-reader. Pad #1 contains pages with controlled fields. Each page has a symbol presented with a key word and a picture which embodies the sound signaled by the symbol. The child traces and pronounces as he traces the symbol thereby insuring visual-auditory-kinesthetic-tactile impressions and coordination. Pad #2 teaches the child to look to the internal construction of words while at the same time being aware of the entity. Words in Pad #2 are introduced by configurational groups. Syllabication through the use of the VAKT techniques is developed by the use of Pad #3. Pad #4 begins a breaking away from the tracing practice by introducing short stories which are to be read while using the stereo-reader. A blending series has also been developed.

The Doman-Delacato Method

The Doman-Delacato Method places great emphasis on preremedial training which, according to Delacato, is designed to bring about an organized neural system (1963). It consists of teaching the child how to crawl, creep, and walk properly. While the child is learning these motility stages to establish neurological unity, concomitant work is done to develop the visual system through exercises akin to orthoptics. Alternating vision exercises and visual pursuit exercises which are guided by both hand-eye coordination and cerebral functioning are used to develop the visual system. Later the child may be given trampoline work to further strengthen the neural organization. When the child begins the reading task, he is first taught by the use of a stereoscopic reader. The material with which he is working is placed in the stereoscopic reader before the eye which is ipsilateral (on the same side) to his preferred hand.

Delacato also uses the placing of the nonpreferred hand in a sling, the regulation of fluid intake, whispering in oral reading, and the elimination of any musical activity as part of his therapy. In the final stages, he pursues a whole word approach utilizing a visual-auditory-kinesthetic-tactile approach.

The Doman-Delacato Method has not yet been proven effective. There has been some adverse criticism and research of the technique (see Robbins, 1966). Another of Delacato's methods, the Doman-Delacato Patterning Method, is used with severe brain-injured cases but was rejected by the American Medical Association (1967).

The Body Alphabet

The Body Alphabet is a system of teaching letters and letter sounds and reading to children with severe learning problems. A. J. Kirshner of Montreal believes that the Body Alphabet makes use of motor pathways which resist deterioration to reinforce the shape and the sound of the letters (1960). The child uses a total body response to reproduce a letter with his body. In so doing, he develops an "anti-gravity motor experience area of the sub-systems to vision." Children with learning difficulties lack a body image which would indicate an awareness of their body in space. Once awareness of body in space is achieved, visualization capacity or form perception based on movement can be developed by making the child aware of the image his body is making in the eyes of the observer who must "read" him. Coupled with the saying of the letter sound, the child makes a total response to the letter. He, and others with him, can "play games" by spelling out words made by their bodies. For example, a child may bend over to make the *E* posture. With this posture, he is asked to read all the words with the short *E* sound. Whenever he reads the words, he is asked to bend over in the *E* posture to help him recall the sound. Then the child is taught the short *I* sound, and once more he reads the words with the short *I* sound and makes the *I* posture at the same time. Usually 30 minutes is enough to teach a sound.

Kirshner claims that children at the age of 3½ years can imitate with the appropriate body posture all the letters of the alphabet, whereas writing letters requires a visual motor skill of age 5 or 6. Hyperactive children and others with motor problems can respond to the body alphabet approach to letter learning sooner than by the visual motor approach because the level of readiness (motor) needed for learning letters is much lower than required by the visual-motor approach. Many games are used.

An example of a Body Alphabet game is to provide each child with a three-foot dowel and a six-foot dowel, which are used by a "monitor." Another child forms a body letter and the first child acts as monitor, correcting the second if his letter is in error. Another game involves projecting the body letter made onto a screen and asking the child to "copy cat" the letter and, after successful imitation, go to the chalkboard and draw the letter. Phonetic sounds are incorporated only after the child has achieved facility with the body shape and the written letter. Usually six lessons are needed to learn the letters; then the sounds are taught.

The Montessori Method

Montessori's research indicates that children have a very natural desire to learn between the ages of 2 and 6 years, the period she terms *the sensitive period* (1967). Young children respond favorably to order and logic in the arrangement of things around them and will work diligently within a carefully prepared structured environment in which the child is given only as much freedom as he can handle. The approach is to use concrete tools to lead the child to abstract concepts. Montessori advocates writing—using movable letters, not a pencil—before reading sounds before words, and reading from slips of paper before any reading, per se, is taught (Guyer, 1974–75). She was thoroughly convinced that much verbal instruction and conversation should precede writing, sounding, or reading.

The Montessori Method is divided into three parts: motor education, sensory education, and language (1965). This method is based on the idea that the care and management of the environment itself afford the principle means of motor education, while sensory education and the education of language are provided by didactic materials. The environment is stimulated by having available materials such as solid inserts, sets of solids in graduated sizes, various geometric solids, rectangular tablets with rough and smooth surfaces, collections of various stuffs, different weights, colored tablets, closed boxes with different sounds, musical bells, sandpaper letters, small sticks for counting, and frames for lacing and buttoning, as well as other objects. Considerable literature and material are now available on this method.

Avoiding the "Panacea"

The problem of working with the primary disability case is complex since each one presents an entirely different problem, and a technique which works with one may prove ineffective with another. To a classroom teacher who has a successful record of teaching children to read —85% do learn—the clinic loaded with severe problems, need for specialized techniques, and a need for one-to-one relationships many times is completely disrupting. To achieve tranquility out of all this chaos, too often the novice remedial reading teacher will take his first successful method and apply it indiscriminately and rigidly to all cases.

To begin with, if there existed one method usable with all cases there would be no need for a diagnosis. Secondly, there would be no need for extensive training of remedial reading specialists. All that would be necessary is to take a person and indoctrinate him in the application of the one technique.

This "panacea method" approach must be guarded against. Experienced teachers know that a structuralized technique used successfully with one case must be somewhat altered when used with a similar case. The specialist must not only assess his case but also evaluate *constantly* his approach to remediation in order to alter it to provide efficient teaching for maximum growth.

Good teachers many times take techniques from several structuralized methods and combine them into a new entity tailored to a given child. Modifications of structuralized techniques many times can be made to provide more effective and efficient remediation. Listening centers where the child may hear the story as he visually reads it provide a kind of modified "neurological impress" which frees the teacher to work with another child. Also, through a VAKT technique, one child who has just learned a word can teach it to a child totally unfamiliar with it and each profits. The one who instructs overlearns, which is so necessary, while the second child learns the word.

It is probable that the worth and skill of the remedial reading teacher is related to the number of modifications and combinations of methods he can devise and how well he can adapt them to specific children.

Media for Teaching Reading Readiness and Perceptual Skills

Developing Readiness Skills in Attention and Letters

Some children will have high learning rates, good knowledge of letter names, and fair ability in hearing sounds in speech. These children will need little practice in readiness skills and should start a formal program in reading. They may work with some of the other children as group leaders, getting additional security in the skills they have acquired. Emphasis should be placed on sounds in varied positions in words, beginning, middle, and final. A second group will have average learning rates, some knowledge of letter names, and be able to recognize "like" sounds in speech. These children will benefit from some of the material for readiness provided in the manuals of the basal readers. A third group will have low learning rates, little knowledge of letter names and sounds, and poor attention and low persistence. Drills to improve attention should be provided for this last group before the exercises in matching letters and letter names are introduced.

The following exercises are samples of some of the kinds of things which may be provided in order to develop the necessary readiness skills. These are only suggestions; you will be able to devise many varied ones to fit the special needs of your children.

ATTENTION DRILLS

1. Visual exercises

   Use things in the immediate environment, asking questions about how things look alike or different. Children's clothing will offer many opportunities for practice. For example: "John's new sweater is red, how is it just like Tom's?" (They are both red.) "How is it different?" (John has buttons; Tom has a zipper.) "Mary and Betty have new shoes. Do you see anything that is just the same about their shoes?" (Each has two, both brown.) "How are they different?" (One buckles, one laces.)

   A flower catalogue offers opportunity for comparisons of colors, size, and numbers in groups. If you have two catalogues which are alike, the pictures in one may be cut out, mounted, and put into packages for the children to match with ones you hold up. Many pictures in magazines may be used in the same way. Also, you may ask a question and have the children respond by showing pictures.

   In all of this work have short periods, give directions clearly and quickly, and keep the children working steadily. Exercises of this type may be given as the children are putting on their hats and coats, or for a few minutes between work periods. As soon as the children are attentive to directions and are responding well, move into exercises using letters and words.

2. Auditory exercises

   The purpose in these exercises is to develop the habit of listening. In the beginning use any noise that happens. Direct the child by naming the object and the noise. For example: "Is the airplane coming toward school?" or "Which direction is the truck going?" Work on differences in pitch and intensity, starting with wide differences and working toward very small differences. Ask two boys to repeat the same sentence, and have the other children listen for the loudest or softest. When the children begin mentioning the noises they hear and the objects making the noises, start ear-training exercises using letters and words.

TEACHING LETTER NAMES

"We all have names. People know who we are because they know our names. We eat many different kinds of food. Each food has a name; meat, candy, ice cream, and bread are names of some of the foods we eat. The things we wear have names; shoes, socks, hats, dresses, and pants are names of some of the clothing we wear. Letters have names, too. We want to learn the names of the letters and how each one looks so that it will be easier for us to learn to read. There are two kinds of letters, large ones which we call *capital letters,* and small ones." Hold up a card with capital A on it and say, "This is a capital A." Show lowercase and say, "This is a small a." Introduce capital M and P in the same way. Hold up the different cards several times, having the children say with you capital a, small m, etc. Then have children name different letters as you hold up cards, giving no help. Have two cards printed, one with A.M. and one with P.M. Hold up the card with A.M. and say "What are the names of these letters? Yes, A.M. This is a short way of saying morning. Let's say together the letters that are a short way of saying morning." Hold up card with P.M. on it. Say "What are the names of these letters? This is a short way of saying afternoon. Let's say together the names of the letters that are a short way of saying afternoon. I'll put up this card (A.M.) because it is morning." Change the card in the afternoon, having the children name the letters. Use the signs for a few days, having them name the letters as the

earning the names of
KZJYWGQUV.
ahvbdlgq. Divide
tice for capital letters,
e letter.

e someone to be the
at your desk, tell him
ands for Post Office."

that have been taught
he end of a street. We
I will choose someone
officer rings the bell
l be the police officer.
ne will be the police

the back of each chair.
en act as ushers. "We are
e of you a ticket. You give
a your ticket. If you tell him

etters?" Discuss local radio and
d, KDKA, WBEI, WGAL, etc.
he station you would like to be
gn that tells the station. We will take
e made, and make original talks like,
his is H.M., your weather reporter."

auditory discrimination of word elements is
in the following order.

th wh ch sh dr tr gr br fr cl fl pl.

Words that rhyme with—*fall, men, play, will, run, pig, bell, in, out, look, fill.*

Final Sounds—*f g b l m d p r k n s t y.*

SUGGESTED ACTIVITIES FOR EAR TRAINING

1. *Fishing.* Have a box with pictures of things which begin with the letters which have been taught. An example of the pictures which might be used for *f, b,* and *l* are:

face	football	farmer	fish	fire fighter
baby	balloon	banana	barn	bear
lamp	leaf	ladder	lettuce	lion

The child selects a picture, names it, and says another word which starts with the same letter. If he fails to name another word, he must put back the picture.

2. *Listening.* Each child folds a paper so that it has 16 blocks. The teacher says a series of words beginning with a given letter. The child writes the letter if the word begins with the letter named; otherwise, the block is left blank. For example:

Listening for *H*, the teacher says:

heart, had, hit, house
mill, mud, he, her
fence, hop, big, have
no, half, hall, how

h	h	h	h
		h	h
	h		h
	h	h	h

3. *Scrap Book.* Each child cuts out pictures of objects that begin with the different sounds. The pages can be used for practice by having the children name the various pictures.

Specific Listening Skills to be Taught

Listening skills may be broadly classified as those concerned with accurate reception and those requiring a reflective response. Both of these types of skills are modified by the listener's personal purpose. Listening skills can be identified as:

a. Determining and evaluating personal listening habits.
b. Listening for details in order to interpret the spoken word and respond creatively or accurately.
c. Following oral directions adequately.
d. Determining and reflecting the mood of listening materials and the sound effects that words symbolize.
e. Determining oral story sequence.
f. Associating descriptive ideas or sounds heard with more concrete objects and true-to-life situations.
g. Discriminating and locating phonetic and structural elements of the spoken word.
h. Retaining ideas from spoken words for future recall.
i. Discovering and identifying sounds, words, or ideas new to the listener.
j. Using oral context clues to build meaningful associations.
k. Interpreting story plot or the feelings and behavior of characters in oral stories.
l. Listening to increasingly longer units of material with accuracy and comprehension.

The level of competency a child acquires in listening skills will be affected by his ability level, but listening ability will be improved primarily by the amount of direct instruction and practice he receives in these skills.

The following are a number of activities and suggestions to improve listening. The letter in parentheses following each activity refers to the corresponding skill listed above:

1. Plan a bulletin board display with the children early in the year. Have them discuss and list the standards of good listening to be used as a checklist in evaluating class conversations from time to time.   (a)
2. Introduce the concept of chain stories to the group. Ask a child to begin telling a story orally while the other children in the group listen attentively so that they may creatively continue the story orally when asked to do so.   (b)

3. Read a poem to the children, asking them to listen for words that suggest the need for sound effects. Ask members of the class to supply the sound effects, using rhythm band instruments.   (d)

4. Read the first half of an unfamiliar story. Ask the children to write a creative ending.   (b)

5. Read a story to the group and have them draw a favorite scene, the most exciting scene, or the funniest scene from the story.   (b)

6. Give the children brief directions for a science experiment, a craft, or some type of construction only once. After they have finished following the directions, have them evaluate their own results.   (d)

7. Read a story to the children. Then give them a number of puppets representing characters in the story. Ask them to activate the puppets and develop story facts sequentially.   (i)

8. Sketch the faces of two clowns, suggesting happy and sad feelings. As you pronounce a number of words, ask the children to associate the word with the clown who represents the feeling of happiness or the feeling of sadness.   (a)

9. Construct the game "Soundo." Ask the children to make cards similar to bingo cards with the word *Soundo* in the top squares. Instead of placing numbers in the other squares as on bingo cards, the children will work with pictures of specified animals or objects. Give the children a list of 20 animals that produce sounds, asking them to sketch or paste pictures of any 17 of them in random locations on their cards. Play specified sounds on a tape recorder or record. As a sound is played, the child places a marker on the corresponding square. A child wins when he covers four corners or six squares either horizontally or vertically.   (f)

10. To develop oral discrimination of beginning and ending sounds, cover two boxes with construction paper and draw a face on each box. Each box character should have a noticeably large set of ears. Place slips of paper with beginning sounds of words in one box and ending sounds of words in another box. Then ask the children to listen to words that you pronounce. The children will respond by selecting the beginning or ending sounds from the appropriate box.   (g)

11. Read a story to the children. Ask them to draw a specific number of sequential steps in the story on a long strip of paper.   (e)

12. Have oral messages carried from class to class, giving children an opportunity to practice retention of ideas.   (h)

13. When a child returns to school after an absence, ask other children to give him the assignments he has missed. Listen in on these assignments to be sure the absentee is receiving correct instructions.   (h)

14. Develop a sensitizing period in listening with the children. Ask them to close their eyes and listen for sounds they know, sounds they have never heard before or paid attention to, and sounds which are man-made as opposed to those which result from natural phenomena.   (i)

15. To extend and deepen meanings, ask the children to listen for certain words that have been listed on the board prior to hearing a selection read. Suggest that the pupils determine the meanings of the listed words by noting the context in which these words were used.   (j)

16. Read descriptions of people with whom the children are familiar—perhaps the special subject teachers or community helpers. Have the pupils guess their identities. (f)

17. Play the game "Who am I?" Have the children listen to a story recording which emphasizes contrast in characterization. Then have a child imitate a particular character from the story and call upon a classmate to guess the character's identity. (k)

18. Construct a group-checking device which incorporates a technique of programmed learning. Draw a large figure of a clown and cut openings 6" in length and 2" in width in the clown's mouth and ruffled collar. Place a strip of paper which can be moved vertically behind the figure. Chart specific rhyming words on the paper. Read to the children a poem which possesses the charted rhyming words. Ask them to look at the word appearing in the clown's mouth and attempt to remember its rhyming word in the poem. After the answer has been given, slide the charted words upward so that the correct answer appears on the clown's collar. (i)

19. Play the game "My Pets." Ask a child to begin by telling the name of one kind of pet. The child then calls on a classmate who will repeat what the first child said and add the name of another pet. The game progresses until a child fails to recall all the pets previously suggested. (i)

Auditory Perceptual Readiness Activities

Activities used in developing auditory discrimination usually pertain to learning to pay attention in listening and developing auditory awareness, remembering, and repeating sounds, words, and letters, learning to recognize sounds, listening for likenesses and differences, becoming aware of rhyming patterns in spoken words, and awareness of sounds, similarities, and differences in spoken words. Table 9–1 presents activities for auditory training. Examples of auditory discrimination activities are as follows:

A. *Recognize sounds*

1. Imitate the sound made by various animals and have the children tell what animal it makes them think of. (dog, cat, cow, chicks, sheep, turkey)

   Records could be used for this activity, for example, the album *Sounds Around Us.*

2. Make a particular sound and have a pupil tell what happened.
   Ex. tap: a desk, blackboard, book, window pane
       drop: a coin, eraser, pencil, stone, plastic dish
       strike: a piano key, two rhythm sticks, triangle with striker

B. *Listening for likenesses and differences*

1. Tell pupils that rhyming words have the same ending sound. Listen to and say rhymes and jingles and tell which words rhyme. You may have to tell which words rhyme at first.

Jack and Jill	Little Jack Horner
Went up the hill	Sat in a corner
To fetch a pail of water	Eating his Christmas pie
Jack fell down	Old Mother Hubbard
And broke his crown	Went to the cupboard
And Jill came tumbling after.	To get her poor dog a bone

2. Say a rhyme and omit the second rhyming word. Pupils supply it. Use nursery rhymes or make up some:

> I saw a mouseo
> Run under the *houseo*.

Rhyming library books can be used this way also after the children have heard the story once.

3. Say three words that rhyme. Pupils repeat words. Call attention to how words are alike. Ex. now, cow, how; book, look, hook; boy, toy, joy; man, ran, tan.

C. *Awareness of similarities and differences in spoken words.* Hold a paper in front of your mouth so that children cannot read your lips. Pronounce words that are alike or different. The children mark "yes" or "no" or "same" or "different" on prepared forms. You can extend the activity to ask for similarities in phonetic initial, medial, or final sounds.

Auditory memory and sequentialization along with auditory discrimination are the auditory perceptual skills most vital to learning to read phonetically. The following are sample activities to be used in training auditory memory and sequentialization skills:

1. Play games that get many children following instructions: "Go and get Tommy. Bring him to the front of the room. Put him beside the desk. Now go get Judy. Bring her up and stand her beside Tommy," etc.

2. Blindfold a child. Do a series of three sounds such as tapping on the desk, ringing a bell, and writing on the blackboard. Then have the child tell you what all you did, trying to get them in the right order.

3. Tell the children to listen to a list of five words. Then give the list again and omit one word. See if they can tell which one you left out. This can be increased in difficulty.

4. Repeat a list of words giving one of the words twice. Then ask the children if they can tell which word has been said two times.

5. Give a series of patterns with a rhythm instrument and have the child repeat the pattern.

6. Give the children a series of symbols vocally. Then ask them to make them on the board. Use symbols that they know such as dot-dash-dot; or square-triangle-circle.

7. Play a game with the child to find locations of the words. For instance, give "tree-cat-dog." Then ask if the word *cat* was in the middle, last, or at the beginning.

8. For older children or more advanced children you might give a sequence of numbers and ask them to repeat them to you backwards.

9. Play the "before and after" game. You might say "What comes before Tuesday?" or "What comes after 7?", etc.

10. Play the "sequence story." The first child starts it with "I saw a horse." The next child adds a sentence and passes it on until the sequence completes a story or can no longer be recalled.

11. Prepare a list of digit sequences. Begin with two digits and increase to eight. Increase difficulty of the task.

6–6	1–2–3–4	2–4–6	1–7
6–6–6	1–2–3–4–5	2–4–6–8	1–6–4
6–6–6–6	1–2–3–4–5–6	2–4–6–8–10	3–8–2–5

Then do the same with letter sequences.

A–A–A	P–T
A–B–C–D	A–C–F
T–T–F–S–S	M–Q–T

Table 9–1. Activities for auditory training.

Area	Observations	Examples of Informal Tasks
1. Auditory Awareness. The ability to be conscious of listening for sounds.	Does the child respond in any fashion to sound? Is the child aware of sounds which are important for self-protection: the sounds of cars, trains, airplanes, firetrucks, telephone, doorbell, or a knock on the door?	Environmental sounds are introduced in a structured manner using a tape recorder or record. "Let's all sit as quietly as we can. What different sounds can we hear?" Identify sounds with eyes closed.
2. Auditory Decoding. The ability to understand sounds or spoken words.	Can the child follow simple verbal instructions? Can he indicate by gesture or words the meaning or purpose of auditory stimuli, such as animal sounds, nouns or verbs?	Play "Simon Says" by always saying the words Simon says. Gradually speed up directions. Use questions requiring "yes" or "no" answers: "Do dogs fly?" "Do cats meow?" Identify nonsense of verbal absurdities: "John has green hair." "I drink water out of a table."
3. Auditory Discrimination. The ability to differentiate and compare sounds.	Can the child distinguish gross and fine differences? Can he discriminate speech sounds as opposed to environmental sounds? Can he discriminate between sounds of varying pitch loudness, direction, and distance? Can he discriminate between similarities and differences in the sounds of words?	Have the child listen to two sounds (a bell and a drum). Are they the same or different? Do the same with words. Find rhyming words. Ask the child to identify an unseen child by hearing his voice. Ask the child to identify loud versus soft by listening to a wooden block and an eraser drop on a desk. Ask the child to tell if the sounds he hears are near or far away.

TABLE 9–1. Activities for auditory training. (Cont.)

Area	Observations	Examples of Informal Tasks
4. Auditory Memory. The ability to retain and recall general auditory information and sounds.	Can the child learn the words of jingles, poems, and songs?	Give the child sentences to repeat, beginning with two or three words and gradually adding more.
	Can he act out charades or simple plots of common nursery rhymes?	Ask the child to repeat a nursery rhyme, retell a familiar story sequence, or remember a story which is unfamiliar.
	Can he follow a series of directions?	Read sentences and ask questions about each.
	Does he know his birthday and address?	Present a series of directions which increase in length and complexity.
	Can he verbally relate yesterday's experiences, meals, television and story plots?	Ask the child to count to himself the number of times he hears your hands clap under the desk.
	How adequate is his short-term memory for auditory sequencing? (see below)	Play memory games such as "I went to the store and bought _____." Each child repeats the list and adds one item.
	How accurately can he respond with increasing delay?	
5. Auditory Sequentialization. The ability to recognize and re-call prior auditory information in correct sequence and detail.	Can the child imitate specific sound patterns of loudness and/or rhythm?	Have the child imitate the sound pattern produced by the teacher using:
	Can the child repeat accurately what has been said?	clapping
	series of digits	drum beats
	series of letters	rhythm sticks
	words	Have the child repeat a series of digits, letters, or words.
	phrases	Start with three and increase until the child cannot repeat the series.
	sentences	Teach the days of the week, months of the year by oral repetition.
	Can he repeat the contents of a story in sequence?	
	Does he know the days of the week and the months of the year?	

TABLE 9–1. Activities for auditory training. (Cont.)

Area	Observations	Examples of Informal Tasks
6. Auditory Figure-Ground. The ability to identify sound when it is surrounded by noise.	Can the child select the source of a sound that has been presented? Can he differentiate speech sounds in the presence of competing background noise?	Tell the child that a particular sound (animal noise) will be "hidden" in a background of noise, and that he is to listen very carefully and indicate as soon as he hears that sound. The background noise could be the taped sound of a vacuum cleaner. The teacher can say a word against the background noise and have the children identify the word. Vary the background to music, competing conversations, etc.
7. Localization of Sound. The ability to be able to tell direction and position from which sounds come.	The child must be able to localize sounds in order to react appropriately; knowing whether a car is approaching from the right or left in order to determine whether to move and, if so, in which direction.	Use games of "Finding the Sound." The child covers his eyes and listens. He points to the place he thinks the sound originates. Use a metronome, timer, or loud clock.
8. Focus. The ability to attend in listening.	Is the child listening and attending before and while a task is presented to him?	The teacher may use such words as Wait, Listen, or Ready before giving an assignment. Wait a few seconds after saying the attention getting word, since a brief moment of quiet aids in listening and recall.
9. Auditory-Vocal Association. The ability to respond verbally in a meaningful way to auditory stimuli.	Can a child associate with verbal opposites, sentence completion, or analogous verbal responses? Does he have the ability to know and understand that a particular sound goes with a particular letter or word, and is he able to apply the sound to those letters?	Have the child supply the analogy: "Soup is hot. Ice cream is _____." Have the child tell which words go together: ball, cow, bat Have him tell how the following items are alike: hammer, saw, axe, stove Have the child match pictures with the same beginning sounds.

Note: There is a certain amount of overlapping in these areas.

258

Then do the same with word sequences.

shoe–dress	cat–dog
shoe–dress–jacket	mouse–cat–hawk
shoe–dress–jacket–shirt	cow–hen–squirrel
shoe–dress–jacket–shirt–hat	

Then do it with nonsense words such as:

wak–lop
ump–lum–wak

12. Present sentences vocally to child. Have him repeat sentences.

See the cat.	Get up.	Pick up a piece of chalk.
See the dog.	Stretch.	Pick up an eraser.
See the bird.	Go to the	Make a circle on the board.
	window.	Put the eraser down.

13. Play the game "Gossip." Whisper a sentence in a child's ear and have him pass it on to the next child. The object is to see whether the sentence has been changed as it is repeated.

14. Play the game "I Went to the Store." The first child says "I went to the store and bought a sled." The next child repeats that and then adds an item to the list. "I went to the store and bought a sled and a doll," etc.

Visual Perceptual Readiness
Skills and Activities

From the following list of visual perceptual readiness skills the teacher should be able to devise or discover activities that would help develop a particular skill.

1. Puzzles (degrees of difficulty).
2. Peg board designs.
3. Reproducing patterns from given copy.
4. Reproducing patterns from memory.
5. Discrimination in likenesses and differences.
6. Recognizing missing parts.
7. Working with parquetry blocks, cutouts of shapes, objects with colors.
8. Identification of wholes through parts.
9. Discrimination in size.
10. Foreground/background stabilization (figure-ground).
11. Stabilization of any form despite any variation of size, color, position.
12. Visual closure of words, letters, numbers.
13. Sequencing of pictures in a story.
14. Differentiating letters and numbers written in different styles.
15. Matching letters, words, designs.
16. Recall of items seen visually (visual memory).
17. Visual tracking ability.

Samples of specific activities to improve visual discrimination are as follows:

1. On the chalkboard are two pairs of words: *happy-happy* and *lazy-sleepy*. Put a circle around the pair that is the same. Now here are some more pairs. Circle the ones which are the same. (Use words that have gross differences, e.g., *hope-run* and *elephant-turtle*.)

2. Same as #1 but for the pairs that are different, use words which differ only in the initial grapheme or blend (e.g., *hope-rope, deer-beer, there-where*).

3. Same as #1 but for the unlike pairs, use words which differ only in the final grapheme (e.g., *hop-hot, bang-bank, mold-mole*).

4. Same as #1 but for the unlike pairs, use words which differ only in a medial grapheme or blend (e.g., *hat-hot, rubber-rudder, master-masher*).

5. Same as #1 but use pairs of letters instead of words, starting first with unlike pairs that are grossly different, such as *m-p* and moving to unlike pairs that require finer discrimination, such as *m-n* or *d-b*.

6. Same as #5 but use cutouts of letters so that children having trouble making discriminations can try fitting one letter on top of another.

7. Same as #6 but use dotted letters and have the children trace over each pair before deciding whether to circle it.

8. "On the chalkboard are a list of words. I'd like you to circle those which begin (or end) in the same way as the first word."

9. Same as #8 but emphasize medial graphemes, instead of initial or final ones.

10. Same as #8 but use letters instead of words. "Circle those letters which are the same as the first one."

11. Same as #8, #9, #10, but have them find the word or letter that is different from all the rest.

Illustrative visual memory activities are as follows:

1. Have children draw shapes with templates on paper, turn the paper over, and try to draw shapes without the template.

2. With geometric cards, show the child three shapes. Cover them, and have the child tell you the shapes in order. Increase the number of shapes as the child progresses.

3. Place four objects in front of the child. After he has studied them, have him close his eyes. Remove one item, and have the child tell what is missing. Repeat, removing two items.

4. Place several familiar objects on a table behind the child. Tell him to look at the objects, turn away, and name as many as he can remember.

5. Cut colorful pictures from magazines, expose and then remove. Check how many things the child can recall at a verbal level. If this is difficult in the initial try, allow the child to verbalize as he studies the picture, then remove it and test his recall.

6. Show a tray of various common items. Allow child to look at the tray for 15 to 20 seconds, then remove the tray from sight. Have the child draw a picture of the tray as he recalls it. You may also let the child tell what was on the tray verbally.

7. A spelling aid to stress and reinforce the visual aspects of the word is to trace and say as the word is exposed. Then remove the word and have the child write it.

8. Draw a design on the board; erase; have the child draw as much of the design as is possible.

Sensorimotor Readiness Skills and Activities

Sensorimotor skills are more complex than they sound because there are various levels and combinations of development to consider. Gross-motor movements involve such things as walking or running forward and backward, marching, balancing, standing on one foot, hopping, kicking, galloping, skipping, leaping, dancing, and jumping rope. Fine-motor movements generally involve the use of hands and fingers, feet and toes, eyelids and other small muscle actions. Sensorimotor skills make use of a sense, usually vision, combining it with the use of gross or fine muscle movements. Readiness sensorimotor skills are as follows:

1. Awareness of self in space.
2. Awareness of self in relation to other objects in the environment.
3. Tracing lines, designs, or shapes.
4. Making one line between parallel lines and other variations.
5. Going through mazes.
6. Following dot and line patterns.
7. Reproducing patterns.
8. Cutting with scissors.
9. Coloring with heavy outlines.
10. Coloring with faint outlines.
11. Dot to dot pictures.
12. Walking, running, skipping, jumping.
13. Building block towers (gaining stability).
14. Manipulation of objects.
15. Use of vertical chalkboard.
16. Rhythms, either in repeating a rhythm or following rhythms made by the group.
17. Able to cope with a large playground area without being given a structured activity.

Sample sensorimotor activities are illustrated by the following:

1. Controlled movements made on the chalkboard. Make circles on the board using the large muscles in the elbow and shoulder, rather than the fingers and wrist.

2. Draw straight lines between goals from left to right on the chalkboard. After doing them with the dominant hand, try doing it with the other one.

3. Let the children copy from the board. Start with simple shapes like ☐ ○ ▽. Then try letters—large ones, M, G, Q, Z, etc. Next put words and finally sentences on the board to copy. If the child is having trouble doing this, *do not* give him too much to copy and don't frustrate him.

4. Label objects around the room. Let the children go around from object to object, copying the label on their papers.

5. Attach a ball by a string to a doorway. Let the child hit the ball gently with a cardboard tube. Try to set up a rhythm for the child.

6. Ball-bouncing is very good for visual-motor perception. Bounce one-to-one and then try to do it in a circle, bouncing to different rows. A variation of this could be to bounce the ball against the building and catch it. Throwing, catching and kicking should be worked on also.

7. Hand objects to the child from various angles, so that he must look and reach for them. Do not let the child move his head, only his eyes.

8. Hold a ring-shaped gelatin mold with a ping-pong ball rolling around in it. Have the child follow the movement of the ball with his eyes only, no movement of his head. Reverse the movement of the ball.

9. Flashlight Game. The teacher shines a flashlight on the chalkboard; the child attempts to follow it and catch it with his light. Move the light in a circle, horizontal, vertical, and oblique fashion. Aim for rapid movement for the child. Two children may play the game when they become familiar with the movement patterns. A more complicated task would be for the teacher to move the light in a pattern and for the follower to guess the pattern and draw it upon completion.

10. Finger Jump. Have the child clasp hands together with thumbs up, hands held directly in front of the face. The child is asked to look from his thumbs to the teacher, moving his eyes only. Directions: "Look at thumbs, look at me, thumbs, teacher, thumbs, teacher." Increase the speed.

11. Ask the child to point out various categories of objects (round, red, wooden) in the room or play yard. Then require that he pick out specific objects such as a book, toy, or picture.

12. Ask the child to find a square button among round ones, a small block among larger blocks, a green marble among blue ones, etc.

13. Sorting. Put objects of two or more types together and ask the child to sort them. The more variables in the group of objects to be sorted, the more difficult the exercise.

14. Ask the child to pick out particular objects you name from boxes containing many different objects. At first the boxes should differ greatly, but later the differences should be minimal.

15. While out on walks, ask the child if he notices things that you see. "Do you see the white house?" "Do you see the little bird in the grass?"

Commercial Materials

(For auditory, verbal and listening development):

1. *The Big Book of Sounds* by Ann Flowers; Interstate Printers and Publishers. Offers ideas on how to construct exercises.

2. *First Steps in Speech Training* by Rodney Bennet. Contains rhymes and jingles for the development of discrimination.

3. *Junior Listen-Hear Book* by Jan Slepian and Ann Seidler; Follett. Features gross listening, discrimination listening, listening to vocal play, listening to rhymes, listening to paired words.

4. *Listen-Hear Books* by Jan Slepian and Ann Seidler; Follett. The sounds of *r, th, k, l, s,* and *f* are taught.

5. *Listening Aids through the Grades* by David and Elizabeth Russell. Auditory activities including auditory discrimination.

6. *Auditory Discrimination Set #1*; Speech and Language Materials, Rhyming Word Games.

7. *Carnival of Beginning Sounds*; Instructo Products. Five games based on 15 common consonants.

8. *Listening Games* by Guy Wagner, Max Hosier, and Mildred Blackman; Teacher's Publications Corp. Games for auditory discrimination—games for upper elementary children as well as nonreaders.

9. *Old Itch:* Lyons and Carnahan; *Phonics We Use Learning Games Kit.* A game like Old Maid using beginning consonant sounds.

10. *Auditory Discrimination in Depth;* The New York Times Teaching Resources. An indepth program for developing auditory discrimination, a complete guide dealing with the gross level, oral-aural level (vowels, consonants, auditory patterns, color encoding), sound-symbol level, coding level, the reading task, and the integration of all of the previous.

11. *Auditory Perception Training: Auditory Discrimination;* Developmental Learning Materials. A series of three levels of tapes and exercises that develop auditory discrimination skills.

The following is a list of materials which may be used to improve a youngster's eye-hand coordination and visual perception:

1. Climbing equipment; Community.

2. *People and Animal Puzzles; Shapes Puzzles; Colored Inch Cubes; Parquetry*—large and small; *Designs in Perspective;* Developmental Learning Materials.

3. *The Slingerland Kit*—Preschool, Intermediate; Educators Publishing.

4. *Ideal Perception Cards; Alphabet Inlay Puzzles; Alpha-Letters* (rubber); *Large Lace Beads and Lace;* Hammett.

5. *Motor-Ocular Training Packet;* O'Connor.

6. *Coordination Board;* Sifo.

7. *The Spatial Organization Series—Primary;* Allied.

8. *Ben-G Reading Readiness Puzzles; Peg Boards and Pegs; Interlocking Train Blocks; Milliken Transparency Duplicating Book* (Motor and Hand-Eye Coordination); *Wipable Perception Ideal Cards;* Creative Playthings.

9. *Fruit and Animal Puzzles; Geometric Shapes in Color; Association Cards; Configuration Cards; Flip and Build; Show you know—Then GO Phonics Game;* Teaching Resources.

10. *Workbench; Chunky Nuts; Figure Craft; Snap and Play Blocks; Lego; Octon; Bolt-It; Space Wheels; Geo-D-Stix;* Childcraft.

11. *Kinesthetic Alphabet Cards;* Instructo.

12. *Visual Discrimination Skills: Pre-School and Kindergarten;* Dr. F. Venditti and E. Murray.

13. *Progressive Visual Perceptual Training Filmstrips Level I—Primary Grades;* Educational Activities.

14. *Perceptual Development Cards, Set I;* Ideal School Supply.

15. *Perceptual Development Cards, Set II;* Ideal School Supply.

16. *String Across—Color Shape Series;* Kurtz Bros.

17. *Multi-Sensory Alphabet—Lower Case Manuscript;* Ideal School Supply.

18. *Space Relationship Cards;* Milton Bradley.

19. *Dubnoff School Program II; Directional-Spatial Pattern Board Exercises;* Bell Dubnoff.

20. *New York Times Perceptual Development Kit.*

21. *Peabody Language Development Kit for Perceptual Training,* all levels.

22. *Reading Readiness Kit 112;* Educational Teaching Aids.

23. *Frosting Program for the Development of Visual Perception.*

chapter 10

Word Analysis:
Visual Skills

In the past both reading and learning disabilities specialists accepted the concept that vision and visual perception occupied a central role in the process of reading. Today, emphasis on their part is somewhat minimized by comparison to the almost unquestioned beliefs of the past. In every way, it seemed logical that the eyes had to be involved in reading; that the brain had to interpret visual stimuli and give them meaning; and that if a child had difficulty remembering words, it almost surely had to be a visual memory problem. Much of the advocacy for visual training and visual perceptual involvement was based on logic and on "peripheral" research; psychological research on perception (visual) was considerable. Although little research was done to indicate the nature and significance of visual perception to reading, it was a foregone conclusion that the two were undeniably related in important and major ways. The fact that the blind could learn to read through their fingers was not pertinent to the question; the fact that many children with very poor eye sight became good readers was not relevant to the central issue. Vision and visual perceptual skills are important to learning to read. But the questions still remain—how important are they, and in what ways?

Basic Understandings

Distinguishing Letters

When a child first becomes conscious of letter symbols, the letters all look similar. An adult can grasp the meaning of that statement simply by thinking of Japanese alphabetic symbols or of Arabic script. An adult's initial impression is "They all look alike or, at best, have only subtle differences." The general reaction is that Japanese or Arabic symbols are very difficult to learn. Yet, Japanese children learn their alphabets; they must learn two alphabets plus Chinese characters. Children speaking the Arabic language learn their letter system, and children of India can learn the Sanskrit, if they so desire. Children in Western societies learn the intricacies of Roman alphabet letters, but it requires the same type of involvement that is required of children of any culture who are learning its language system of translating sounds into graphemes and symbols into sounds.

Each child must learn to focus attentively on the distinctive features of the letters. Features that letters have in common with other letters must be ignored or screened out if identification of the letter is to be attained with a minimum of effort (Ross, 1976). Gibson (1970), in a discussion of the learning of letters, points out that instructional programs should seek to promote efficient strategies of perceptual search and detection of word form, features that will provide a consistent approach to letter and word identification. A haphazard, inconsistent, noncognitive approach will be very ineffective.

Children will seek to identify distinctive features of letters if they are made aware of such differences. Not all children have or can use the kind of cognitive insight needed to be alert to distinguishing features. Learning disabled children may have a compounded problem in that they may be unable to be selective in picking out the features they need to see. They may be lacking in retention and discrimination abilities. Some letters have a number of similar features so that identification is difficult under any circumstances. A study by Gibson, Osser, Schiff and Smith (1963) shows the following letter sets to have significantly high confusion features: M and W, N and M, Q and O, E and F, P and R, K and X. Thorson (1976) made use of a mathematical model based on the work of Gibson (1971) and found that the following letter sets also had a high level of confusability: A, V, and W; K and H; M, N, and K; Y and M; H, T, and E; Y and K. Note that in neither study were b, d, p, and q, the letters most frequently reversed, mentioned.

Visual perceptual skills can be used in identifying letter features such as /, \, -, (,), ᗡ, =, I, <, ∨, ^. Also descenders (parts of a letter that go below the line, such as p, j or g) and ascenders (parts of a letter that go above the midpoint, such as t, b, l, and d) can be used as identifying features. Some remedial educators report an increase in word recognition skills when letter discrimination training was undertaken (King, 1964; Pick, 1965). Generally, studies reporting on visual perceptual training of gross and fine form discrimination show favorable results in improving visual perception skills *but not reading ability*, unless the reading level was first or second grade. Sabatino and Streissguth (1972) show that word form configuration training, directed through the visual modality, is helpful to young visual learners but not to auditory learners. It has been empirically noted that young LD children must be made conscious of the distinguishing features of letter forms in order to learn to identify the letters by name.

Reading as a Visual Process

Reading is a sensory process, and a major sensory system used in reading is vision. Children are born farsighted. Although they still tend to be somewhat farsighted by the ages of 5 and 6, they must read from a book held in their hands. The implication is that they must have adequate near-point acuity and focus ability. Most first- and second-grade basal readers have larger print so the children can focus on the print at distances of 14″ to 20″.

Eye movements in reading were studied extensively in the 1950s and 1960s. Eye movement photography was in vogue. Some interesting observations were made. In reading, the eyes do not make a continuous sweep across the page. They move in quick, short, staccatic movements with pauses between eye shifts. Each time the eye movement stops so the eyes can react to the printed symbols is a *fixation*. *Visual span* is the amount of print seen in a single fixation. Taylor, Frackenpohl, and Pettee (1960) learned by the use of an eye movement camera that up to the fifth grade, the number of eye fixations per line approximates the number of words on that line. Secondary and college students generally read less than three words per fixation. Eye regression, a backward movement of the eye in reading, occurs about once in every two words for first graders; once in three for fourth graders; once in five for ninth graders; and almost one in ten for college students. The immature or poor reader makes extra fixations and many more regressions.

Although fixations imply that thought-unit reading (fixation span) consists of a series of eye movements, this observation is not to imply that the brain only records what the eye sees at that moment. There is an eye-memory span in silent reading that indicates the distance the eyes have traveled ahead of the point at which interpretation occurs. The eye-voice span is the distance the eyes have moved ahead of the point at which the pronunciation occurs. If you were asked to stop reading in the middle of a sentence, you could probably tell what other words or ideas were in that sentence. Mature readers have wide eye-memory and eye-voice spans. Learning disabled readers frequently lack adequate eye-memory and eye-voice spans because they fixate in such small units (word-for-word) and must dwell on each word to unlock it or get its meaning. We frequently encounter bright LD readers who become "key-word" readers, omitting unnecessary or filler words so they can get to the main comprehensive point of the sentence or paragraph.

Concerning other visual skills, note that there is an extremely low correlation between refractive error (optical distortions of the eye, such as nearsightedness, farsightedness, and astigmatism) and beginning reading (Hullsman, 1958; Rychener & Robinson, 1958; Shearer, 1966). Other "end organ" visual functions play a small role at the very outset of beginning reading. These functions include accommodation (focusing), convergence (turning both eyes inward to see at near point), and fusion (two-eyed binocular seeing) (Flax, 1970). In beginning reading where the child has to "break the code" for the first time, he is required to make a visual-verbal match; that is, he has to match the appearance of the word in print to its sound and give the vocal equivalent of the symbol. For the child's first 5 years of life, all of his language experiences were strictly oral and auditory. When he begins to read, he has to be able to make an intersensory shift from audition to vision.

According to Wold (1972), the visual skills involved in kindergarten to second grade are visual directional awareness, visual form perception, intersensory integration, and eye-hand coordination. Letters and numbers in Western culture are oriented on a left-to-right basis. Internal visual coordinates of directionality are needed to see u and n, N and Z, M and W, 6 and 9, 3 and E, in their proper orientation. Since letters consist of shapes, skill in visual form perception is involved. A child's sensory modalities progress through various stages of development until about the age of 5 or 6. Then they are all integrated, and efficient use of the sensory modalities will permit any one of them to take the lead or to substitute, as is needed, in perceptual investigation. Vision ultimately substitutes for the other modalities in beginning reading. According to Birch and Belmont (1964), retarded readers are significantly less able to make judgments of auditory-visual equivalence than are normal readers. Birch (1962) also states that the short attention span and the hyperkinesis of the learning disabled child are frequently due to persistence of a less mature level of visual control. The last vision skill, eye-hand coordination, is needed so that the eyes can lead the hand, such as in the use of the finger as a guide to steer the eyes while reading.

Visual Perceptual Skills and Reading

To what extent are visual skills and visual training necessary for good beginning reading? The question still remains to be answered. The American Academy of Pediatrics, with the

American Academy of Ophthalmology and Otolaryngology and the American Association of Ophthalmology, make the following statements in a paper on the topic (1972):

1. Learning disability and dyslexia require a multi-disciplinary approach.
2. Studies have shown that there is no peripheral eye defect which produces dyslexia, reversal of letters, words, or numbers, and associated learning difficulties.
3. No known scientific evidence has been recorded to show that visual training, neurological organizational training (motor) or perceptual training alone improve learning or academic abilities.
4. Glasses have no value in the specific treatment of dyslexia, except for correctable ocular defects.
5. The teaching of learning disabled and dyslexic children is a problem of educational science.

Nathan Flax, O.D. (1972) takes exception to the paper and its statements. He believes that the research studies cited by the joint academies contain "gross distortions and inaccuracies." Anyone contemplating vision training or visual perceptual treatment should consult the above sources and others before embarking on such an optometric program.

Visual perception is not the same as *vision*. Vision is the ability to actually see the object and bring it into focus. Visual perception is a combination of skills that permit an individual to recognize, discriminate, and interpret visual stimuli by associating them with previous remembered experiences. An LD child may have excellent vision but be unable to discriminate between similar objects, pictures, words, or letters presented in visual form. The visual stimulus is interpreted in the brain, and it is there that a dysfunction may hinder some part of the perceptual-conceptual process.

Many abilities are included in visual perception. Frostig (1964) considers five categories: visual-motor coordination, figure-ground perception, constancy of shape, position in space, and spatial relationships. Others will consider form perception, eye-hand coordination, visual copying, visual rhythm, visual discrimination, visual memory, visual reception, visual sequential memory, visual closure, and visual-motor association. As you see, the visual perceptual process has yet to be properly defined. In the middle and late sixties, a number of tests and media were produced for use with visual perceptual assessment and training. A basic assumption was that when you said visual perception, you said it all. Only gradually did teachers and other educators begin to realize that visual perception was composed of a number of separate abilities. What is needed is a good factor analysis examination of the materials on visual perception—and other processes as well—to determine what is *really* being measured.

Several visual perceptual areas have been selected for presentation here. Activities are listed with these abilities to illustrate what kind of skills the tasks represent and, in many cases, what an LD child would have difficulty doing. The first area under consideration is *visual discrimination*. Visual discrimination is the ability to see likenesses and differences in order to interpret the information. In the following activity you can have the pupil draw a circle around each word which is the same as the first word in the row:

boy	boy	brother	boy	boy

Start by first using words such as *boy* and *brother*, which are decidedly different in appearance and easy to differentiate. Later, use words which are almost alike in appearance, such as *boy* and *bay*. Another approach is to have a row of objects on a table and ask the child to identify the one which is different. A row of spoons with one fork or a row of pencils with a pen can be used.

A second aspect of visual perception is *figure-ground perception*, which is the ability to perceive objects in the foreground and in the background and to separate them meaningfully. Frostig and Maslow (1970) state that training in figure-ground perception should result in improved ability to shift attention appropriately; to concentrate upon relevant stimuli and ignore irrelevant stimuli; to scan adequately; and in general, to show more organized behavior. In our experience we have observed very few school-age children with this particular reading problem. After all, there is very little relevance of figure-ground problems to reading since the "ground" is most always white with no distractions coming from anything other than more graphemes. It is also true that a mental age of 12 is needed before figure-ground problems are completely overcome, but even first graders can find the faces hidden in the trees (or picture) if they are not too obscure. The child reading does not appear to have as much difficulty with the topography of reading print as he does with distractibility or attention factors.

Another area of visual perception frequently mentioned is *position in space*. This ability helps children recognize the position of their body in relation to objects. They may jump *over* a box, crawl *under* a desk, walk *through* a door, run *around* a chair, or step *out* of a box. These activities may be done as a game, using an obstacle course, or by commands. It is often beneficial for an LD child to vocalize what he is doing as it is being done, thus associating the word, action, and position. Some LD children, especially younger ones, experience some difficulty with position in space.

Directionality is an important aspect of position in space. A child needs to know the left and right sides of his body, and also the left and right position of objects in relation to himself. An activity that could involve lefts and rights would be "Simon Says." For example, "Simon says touch your nose with your right hand." The directions can become more complex as competency develops. Children can be asked whether various objects in the room are on their right or left. Verbal commands may also be given; for instance—walk forward, turn right, walk backward, walk sideways to the left, or turn left.

A fourth visual perception ability is *visual memory*. This task involves the capacity to accurately recall previous visual experiences. A child may be shown a single picture, then asked what he remembers seeing on that picture once it is removed from sight. This activity can be used on more sophisticated levels as the abilities of the children become more developed. A memory game can be made by placing various items on a tray such as scissors, pen, eraser, button, thread, and a dime. Ask the children to recall as many items as they can. A number of LD children appear to have visual memory problems. Strangely, for some, the problem may involve only one item or one word; others may forget an entire thought, a series of directions, or an experience.

Constancy of shape or form is another part of visual perception. Can the child identify the form if it is rotated? Marianne Frostig says that perception of three-dimensional objects does not necessarily carry over to perception of two-dimensional objects. Some young LD children have difficulty sorting objects such as circles, squares, stars, and diamonds according to their shape. Sorting objects while verbalizing their names is good practice. Also, presenting the shapes while holding them at various angles is beneficial; thus the child can learn to recognize the shape no matter its position.

How much does visual perceptual training help to improve reading ability or reading skills? Not very much, according to most of the research. A study by Buckland (1973) reveals that visual perceptual training does not signficantly improve reading ability. Other studies confirm these results. After reviewing pertinent visual perceptual studies covering a 15-year period, Hammill, Goodman, and Wiederholt (1974) conclude that the value of perceptual training, especially those programs often used in the schools, has not been clearly established. Silverton and Deichmann (1975) summarize the research done on reading models and make the following observations: (a) Auditory discriminations appear to precede visual discriminations in the initial stages of reading and the acquisition of language arts skills; (b) Auditory and auditory-visual presentations appear to yield significantly greater reading achievements than do visual, tactile, or visual-tactile presentations; and (c) There must be a dominant auditory modality evident for reading behavior to occur. Spache (1976) summarizes 30 perceptual training experiments (excluding the Frostig program) and makes this observation: Most of the preceptual training programs *improve aspects of visual perception but none improve reading performance.* Results of 20 studies done directly with the Frostig program show no significant gain in reading tests in all but two of the studies. The two that show significant gains were both done with kindergarten children and used other programs as well.

Is it worthwhile to do visual perceptual training? It all depends on your purpose. If visual perceptual training is done for the purpose of improving reading skills, then it is probable that the time will be wasted. It could better be used teaching the reading skills directly. If visual perceptual training is used for the purpose of improving visual perceptual skills—as an end in themselves—they will probably work in the majority of cases. There may be some need for certain visual perceptual skills beyond their use for improving reading. The same could be said for motor development training or visual-motor training. Do not use these programs for the improvement of reading ability. But if a child lacks the motor or visual-motor skills needed to play the games of his peers, then by all means, use motor *development* activities (not splinter motor *skills* activities) to improve that child's ability to perform well on the playground.

Context of Visual Word Analysis

When a child is learning to read, he has to respond to the letters and symbols which appear before him. It would be foolish to ask a very young infant to differentiate between various word forms. The very young child has not matured enough to be able to distinguish minute likenesses and differences. This child needs to be shown elements from his environment with which he has become familiar and which he can identify. The young child is shown a picture book and is asked to "Show me the pony" or "Show me the kitty." As he matures, he begins to recognize a difference between letters, and he learns to identify simple numbers. The letters and numbers begin to say something. Soon he gets meaning from letter combinations, such as he would when he learns to print his name. Little by little, and in different ways, the symbols make more sense to him. He is learning to recognize words, and he begins to attach meanings to the words. He is learning to read. Letters or symbols serve as "cues" forming a visual stimulus pattern which recalls to an individual's mind some meaning. The "cue" is actually a hint or an intimation designed to communicate a meaning. Not all cues are visual, however. Some are seen, but others are heard or felt. As a person learns, he needs fewer cues to discover a meaning. This is known as *cue reduction.*

The Concept of Cue Reduction

Credit for the theory of cue reduction goes to Hollingworth. Applied to reading, cue reduction means that when we are faced with an unfamiliar word, we use many cues to identify or unlock the word. However, the more often we are exposed to the word, the fewer the number of cues necessary to help us make a positive identification. When we are faced with a new word in context, we first attempt to identify it by finishing the sentence to see if the meaning and word can be identified through context. We do this because the configuration of the word gave us no clue as to the meaning or the pronunciation. If the context fails, we look at the construction of the word, phonetically, structurally, or both. However, after successive exposures to the word, we would be able to eliminate the cues of phonetic analysis, structural analysis, and even contextual analysis. Eventually, all we would need to recognize the word would be the configuration. In a way, we have reached the point of sight recognition.

The Cues of Configuration

When we speak of configuration, we refer to the general shape of the word. Experimentation has shown, however, that the general shape of the word by itself is not a very good means of identification. The general shape of the word *book*, ⊏⊐, for instance, could be the shape for a large number of words: *took*, *tool*, *beak*, *leak*, *heal*, and *keel* to name a few. There is some evidence, however, that a person can make some use of some types of configuration cues to unlock some words.

The "gridiron effect" is a configuration cue. The person looking at the word *little* may look at the general, outward shape of the word but he may also recognize the gridiron pattern of the up and down lines of the letters. Or, he may use the configuration cue of the "lively effect," which refers to the seemingly flowing structure of the word, such as in *same*.

Sometimes the shapes of letters become cues, and they assist the reader in recognizing a word through configuration. The "ascenders," those letters which rise above the general body of the word, such as the letters *t*, *k*, and *l*, are sometimes the cue used with the general configuration to identify a word. Or the "descenders," those letter structures which are below the main body of a word, such as the letters *g*, *q*, and *p*, may be used. Or, the beginning, the medial, or the terminal letters in a word may be used to identify the word. Configuration is the way by which most beginning reading is developed. The child is taught sight words, which he is expected to recognize by their configuration.

The Cues of Context

Probably the cue most used by adults for unlocking unknown words is the context of the material. When an adult comes to a new word, he generally pauses a moment; then he reads on to the end of the sentence or paragraph hoping the context will identify the word. In order for the context to identify the word, the reader must be familiar with most of the other words in the context. Contextual analysis cannot be applied when there are too many unknown words in the context since each word is a cue for the contextual recognition of an unknown word. Research has shown that if there are more than one out of ten unknown running words in the context, the child gets very little meaning from reading the material. In fact, reading specialists suggest that for instructional purposes there be no more than one out of twenty unknown consecutive words in the context.

One of the more commonly used methods of developing the use of contextual analysis is through skillful questioning by the teacher. Suppose a first grader is reading a page in a basal reader which has a picture of Mother and Father in a kitchen with Mary and Tim. They are all busy cleaning strawberries. Suppose the child is uncertain of the word *home* in the following sentences:

> Mother and Father work at home.
> Mary and Tim work at home.

The skillful teacher, rather than telling the child the word *home* when he asks her what the word is, may say "Look at the picture. Where are Mother and Father working?" After he answers that question correctly, she may ask, "Well, then, where would Mary and Tim be working?" This kind of guidance will usually help the child to get to know the word. This also helps him develop the habit of looking at context to gain meaning.

The child who makes an error in a sentence which leaves the sentence meaningless must be taught to use the context to check the accuracy of his reading. No child paying attention to meaning would ever say "The bog bit the boy," when the sentence really read, "The dog bit the boy." When a child makes this kind of mistake, questioning should be used which would force him to check to see if "that makes sense." This approach will help the child develop his use of contextual analysis, both as a sense of word attack and as a check on the accuracy of his reading.

All workbooks contain exercises which supposedly are directed to the development of the use of contextual analysis. These exercises may be sentences with words blocked out. The child is to supply or think of the right word.

> The boy hit the xxxx with his bat.

Or the exercises may be sentences in which only a part of a word is supplied and the child is asked to supply the missing letter or letters to make a meaningful word:

> When he asked for candy, he always said ____ease.

Some of the more widely used contextual cues are definitions, experience, comparison and contrast, familiarity, and summarization. *Definition* is an indicator of classification. "Peas and carrots are vegetables." *Experience cues* refer to those kinds of things which are common knowledge. In the sentence "When he hit his finger with a hammer, he screamed," the unknown word could be easily identified since everyone screams when he hits his finger with a hammer. *Comparison* and *contrast* refer to relating a known word to an unknown word having commonality or opposition. Consider the phrase "Higher than a mountain." Knowing *high* the child is directed to determine the unknown word by checking it against known high things for one beginning with *m*. "Unlike the tall giraffe, the gazelle was too short to reach it." In this latter sentence the content indicates *tall* is the key word requiring an opposite. The cue *familiarity* would probably be synonymous with "clichelike" and would clarify phrases like "roared like a lion" and "fought like a tiger." *Summarization* is a series of events leading to a conclusion. "We will go to Grandma's. She will fix turkey and cranberries. There will be many good things to eat. We will be stuffed. It always happens on Thanksgiving Day."

The Cues of Structural Analysis

When we refer to structural analysis, we mean the way in which the word is put together. This includes roots, prefixes, suffixes, compounds, contractions, inflectional endings, and syllabication. These cues of structural analysis must be taught to children if they are to reach their maximum capacity in reading.

Root words are called to the attention of children early in the first grade. When a child comes across the word *looked* after having learned the word *look*, the teacher will ask him if he sees a word in *looked* that he knows. When he identifies *look*, she explains *ed* and what it means. Thereafter, it is hoped that he will mentally separate the inflectional ending *ed* and get the root when he is confronted with a word to which this new ending has been added. Later, he is taught the meaning and applications of inflectional changes because some words change in spelling when inflectional endings are added. When *ed* is added to *pin*, the final consonant must be doubled. When *er* is added to *heavy*, the *y* must be changed to *i*. These changes may obscure the root unless definite attention is given to the teaching of these understandings to the pupils.

Although prefixes and suffixes begin to appear in the words taught in second grade, the teaching of prefixes and suffixes is usually delayed until the upper grades. Before prefixes and suffixes are taught as such, the pupils learn to attack the words containing them phonetically. By the time a child leaves the elementary school, he should be able to recognize the most common prefixes and suffixes. Table 10–1 lists some of the more

TABLE 10–1. Common prefixes.

A prefix is a syllable at the beginning of a word. Prefixes usually alter the aspect of the idea.

Prefix	Meaning	Prefix	Meaning
ab	away from	mis	wrong
ad	to	multi	many
ambi, amphi	both	non	not
ante	before	op	against
anti	against	out	over, surpass
auto	self	para	beside
be	by	per	through
bi	two	poly	many
circum	around	post	after
com, con, co	together	pre	before
contra, counter	against	pro	in front of, before
de	from, down	re	back
dis	not, away	semi	half
en	in	sub	under
ex	out	super	above
hemi	half	syn, sym	together
hyper	above	trans	across
hypo	under	ultra	above
in, im	into, not	un	not
inter	between	with	against
il, ir	not		

TABLE 10–2. Common suffixes.

A suffix is a syllable at the end of a word and usually changes the original word to a different class or kind. Some of the most used suffixes are listed below:

able	capable of being
age	act or state of
al	relation to
ate (noun)	one who
ate (verb)	to make
ble, ible	capable of being
cy	state of
den, dom	state or condition
er	little, maker of
est	comparison
ful	capable of being
ian	relating to
ise, ize	to make
ish	state of being
ism	act of
ist, ite	one who
ity, ty	state of being
ly	like, in manner
less	without
ment	state or quality
ness	state of being
ship	relationship
some	state of being
ster	one who
tion	state or condition
tude	state or condition
ure	act or process
ward	direction of

common prefixes and their meaning; Table 10–2 lists some of the more common suffixes and their meaning.

Another structural cue is the recognition of compound words. A compound word is a word made up of two or more words, each having a distinct meaning and each contributing something toward the meaning of the new word. *Streetcar* is a compound word made up of *street* and *car*, which in their combined form means a car running on the street. *Caravan*, on the other hand, is not a compound word even though we can see *car*, *a*, and *van*. Each syllable is a word, but none of these words contribute their individual meanings to the final meaning of the word *caravan*.

Many teachers do not teach compound words in the early academic life of the child. Often this is due to the kind of difficulty encountered by teachers when they use the technique of asking children to "look for a little word in a big word." Children become skillful at doing this but it serves no purpose for them. In many words, pronouncing the little word as it is used in the big word is not like pronouncing the little word when used by itself. Finding *tea* in *steak* contributes nothing to the meaning or pronunciation of either word.

Like prefixes and suffixes, children must be taught the common contractions and the generalizations behind them. This is not as easy as it appears on the surface since many contractions substantially change the form of the root word so that a new spelling occurs. *Won't*, *can't*, and *shan't* are just a few of the contractions which change the root word dramatically.

By the end of the primary grades, children begin to have more and more polysyllabic words in their reading matter. It is at this point that formal teaching of syllabication is begun. Syllabication is the breaking up of polysyllabic words into individual sound units to aid the reader in the pronunciation and recognition of words. Syllabication is tied up closely with phonics, compound words, and other cues of structural analysis. The sequence of the syllabication attack upon an unknown word finds all of these other elements being used. The sequence follows:

1. Every syllable has one sound. Each syllable must have a vowel in it.
2. Usually, a single consonant goes with the vowel which follows it.   v/cv   a/go
3. When there are two consonants together, the syllable division occurs between the consonants. vc/cv: ten/nis pub/lish
4. A closed syllable is one that ends with a consonant.
5. An open syllable is one that ends with a vowel.
6. In a closed syllable the vowel is short.
7. In an open syllable the vowel is long.
8. Prefixes and suffixes are usually syllables.

Basically, the teacher aims at developing a sequence of word attack which will become habitual for each pupil.

Minor Cues: Pictures

Primary grade teachers make extensive use of picture cues. By looking at a picture, the child gets some idea concerning the content of the story. He uses these ideas to help him identify unknown words. For example, the child who has looked at a picture of boys riding bicycles would not think the word *bicycle* meant *wagon* when reading the text. This kind of thing can apparently be overdone, however. One basal series has been sharply criticized by primary teachers who in essence said, "Once the children got through with the pictures there was no need to read the stories."

Assessment of Visual Word Analysis

Informal Assessment

Hafner and Jolly (1972) believe one of the best ways by which a teacher can determine whether a student is having difficulty with visual word attack is to have the child read orally. As the child is reading aloud, the teacher can note the types of errors that he makes. The teacher can then ask questions to determine whether the child knows word attack skills such as root words, beginning and ending sounds, word families, parts of compound words, and contractions of words. As the teacher assesses the usage of structural analysis, the child will reveal his level of understanding of prefixes, suffixes, and syllabication skills. Often a child will indicate his ability to identify words through the use of contextual cues. Error analysis by the teacher is highly recommended; it can form a basis for doing diagnostic teaching.

Teacher-made tests can also be helpful in assessing reading difficulties. Potter and Rae (1973) suggest that a test for knowledge of syllabication should contain four parts. First, you can test the child's understanding of the concept that words contain recognizable parts that can be tested by having the child circle the number that corresponds to the number of parts he hears in a given word. Second, the child can be asked to mark or select a particular syllable. For example, ask him to draw a line under the first syllable in the word *matter*, or before the last syllable in *determine*. A third part of a syllabication test involves dividing both long and short words into syllables without oral cues from the text. In the fourth test, the child can divide nonsense words into syllables. We have found that the use of nonsense words in both assessment and remediation provides a more valid achievement level of unlocking words and a better understanding of the child's ability to abstract the rules for dividing words into syllables.

Kottmeyer (1959) advocates the use of nonsense words to diagnose a student's ability to recognize common prefixes, suffixes, and components of compound words. Common sight words are combined with the most frequently occurring affixes to form compounds. This technique is probably a more objective way of discerning which prefixes or suffixes the student is having trouble with since they are combined with very elementary sight words. Examples of test words that Kottmeyer recommends are as follows:

Prefixes

repan	conjump	inwell	delike	display	combent
ungate	excry	proread	prehead	enstand	

Suffixes

halling	booker	floorest	daytion	skinance
meatness	chairly	waterful	burnant	truckous

Compounds

nightbank	dinnerplayer	basketmeet	broomfeather
paperjumper	eatmobile	spaderoom	carthouse

In assessing structural analysis of words, tests can be devised to determine the child's knowledge of affixes and root words as an aid to pronunciation and meaning. A *root word* is a word from which another word is formed. Often the root word is called the *stem word* or *base word*. Simple endings such as *s, es, ing, ed, er,* and *en* may be added to root words. Prefixes and suffixes are both affixes. They can be added to root words. A teacher-made assessment device could simply ask a child to identify the prefixes, suffixes, or root words. The first level is to identify roots within words. Show a set of five words, four of which contain the same root, and one that has a root that has some similar features but is not the same. For example: *form*ula, in*form*, de*form*, *form*ing, *form*ulate. Word lists can be constructed to check for inflectional endings such as plurals, possessive inflections, and tense inflections. A higher level would deal with the simple identification of prefixes and suffixes, and the highest level would identify these affixes when added to words.

Formal Assessment

Formal tests are somewhat limited in number unless you look for subtests that assess the particular word attack skills you desire. Some of the reading tests that include appropriate subtests are:

1. Indiana Test of Basic Reading Skills. Several subtests can be used, specifically recognition of common endings, auditory discrimination of syllables, visual discrimination of syllables, and pronouncing and blending syllables.
2. McCullough Word-Analysis Tests, experimental edition. Ginn & Co., 1963. Specific subtests for syllabication, root words, and affixes.
3. Silent Reading Diagnostic Test. Lyons & Carnahan, 1955. Some apparent validity is found in the subtests of words in context, syllabication, and root words.
4. Stanford Diagnostic Reading Test. Harcourt Brace Jovanovich, 1968. One subtest measures syllabication.

Vision Problems

Teacher observation can be used to determine if a child has difficulty with visual acuity or visual functions. A child with inadequate ocular performance may be observed exhibiting any of the following characteristics:

1. Note fatigue, strain, discomfort, avoidance behavior, red or weeping eyes.
2. Note squinting, excessive blinking, rubbing of the eyes, tilting of the head, covering and/or closing of one eye.
3. Eye movements tend to be inappropriate and excessive.
4. Saccadic movements also tend to be inappropriate, so that the child cannot look accurately from one object to another.
5. Eyes may tend to cross inward or outward. Eyes may "shake."
6. Eyes or pupils of eyes may be of unequal size.
7. One or both eyelids may droop.
8. May be unable to follow a moving object smoothly.
9. May have trouble with math due to an inability to align digits or the omission of digits.
10. Frequently loses place while reading, continues to use finger to read.
11. Often has trouble copying from the blackboard.
12. May cover one eye or tilt head while doing close work.

Visual perception problems can also be detected by teacher observation. Table 10-3 indicates aspects of visual perception, by definition, and illustrates how a teacher may learn of a deficit in that area by observing classroom behavior or behavior while reading.

Teaching Visual Analysis Skills

How the Word Attack Skills Are Taught

Many of the comments made in the chapter concerning the understanding and teaching of phonics can apply to the teaching of other word attack skills. The three basic steps in the

TABLE 10–3. Visual perception and reading.

Definition	Behavior	Related to Reading
1. *Visual Acuity*—Refers to sharpness of vision, including near and far. The child's vision should be free of defects in the mechanism which coordinates the two eyes in binocular vision, so that he can maintain a single clear image with a minimum of nervous tension.	Poor acuity results in such behavior as moving head excessively, squinting, squirming, poor posture, acting out of feelings of frustration in many ways.	To read, letter shapes must stand out clearly (o,c,a are similar and capital/small letters are different, for example). To read smoothly and with speed requires that eye muscles function together properly without strain.
2. *Visual Focus or Attending*—The ability to keep one's visual attention on the word/lesson/object, at hand without losing attention or being distracted.	Highly distractible movement or change calls attention away from learning; may need the closeness of one-to-one relationship with the teacher in order to focus and concentrate on visual task.	Reading requires: focusing on visual symbols (example: focusing on vowel sounds or parts of words—*oke, tion,* or syllabication); focusing on letters/words without attention shifting to other words and not concentrating on one word too long. Technique: eliminate child's observation of movement by the use of an "office" or "carrel".
3. *Visual Figure-Ground*—to sort out the central visual stimulus in one's environment; in a test, to pick out (visually) objects superimposed on each other on the page, to distinguish the figure from the background against which it is drawn.	Child is confused if he sees only lines, etc., on a page rather than objects, separate letters, etc. This causes frustration, lack of interest in reading or other visual tasks.	To read, one must quickly pick out letters singly and recognize their difference from all other letters Technique: relate pictures/figures/shapes, then letters/words to others which are similar, different, and the same.
4. *Visual Memory*—A decoding process in the brain whereby what has been seen (figures, objects, words) is identified and recalled.	Child may appear to be "scatterbrained;" can't remember words so doesn't have sight vocabulary; fluctuates in recall; has directionality problems and reversals; difficulty with math and spelling; unable to revisualize letters and words.	In reading, child doesn't hold visual image of a whole word in his mind. Technique: help child consciously think where he is to go, what he is to do, etc.; verbalize to impress him. Teach short visual units which he can blend into words (if he has good auditory ability); reinforce later in the day what he read in the morning.

277

TABLE 10-3. Visual perception and reading. (Cont.)

Definition	Behavior	Related to Reading
5. *Visual Sequentialization*—Ability to visualize and remember what has been seen in the order in which it was seen.	Since words are seen as a jumble of letters, he lacks interest in learning to read—too much confusion, makes no sense; may write *house-houes*; can't remember order of letters, blocks, etc., to re-place in given pattern; frustrated; may lead to anger.	In reading, the ability to remember and visualize how letters, words, etc., follow each other in order; failure to remember sequence of letters and sounds results in misreading/mis-spelling. Technique: use tangible items in sequence until child gets the idea; then transfer into letter symbols. Make the child conscious of order and that word letters remain the same in a particular order.
6. *Visual Discrimination*—The ability to distinguish what is seen (shapes, forms, letters) one from the other; alertness to visual detail.	Child confuses letters which appear similar and is frustrated in reading (*bit, bet or came, come*); may invert letters (*m, w,* etc.).	Reading is a process of differentiation of letters and words. These children can't distinguish them at a glance. Technique: find child's best learning mo-dality (auditory, kinesthetic, visual, or combina-tion), and use it to teach similarities and dif-ferences in letters and words.
7. *Visual Spatial Relationship*—Involves ability to visualize letters (figures, forms, etc.) so that, as they are changed in position or place, they re-main constant.	Child gets confused with visual symbols and images; he may reverse words (*on* for *no, saw* for *was*); has difficulty learning sounds and alphabet sym-bols because he confuses them; may become withdrawn or distractible; his self-image may be affected.	To read, a child must know when an *n* is an *n*, or a *u*; he must be aware of spatial relationship of letters to each other and words to each other and know that in a word, when letters change position, the sound and the meaning changes. Technique: manipulating letters to rotate, superimpose, change within words. With this problem, use of tactile perception reinforces learning.

TABLE 10-3. Visual perception and reading. (Cont.)

Definition	Behavior	Related to Reading
8. *Visual Closure*—The ability to make a whole out of part of a letter word.	A child lacks meaning for words and ideas when he lacks closure or synthesis of sounds/words/ sentences that he sees; he lacks interest in reading and visual tasks and will be a nonreader unless helped.	Visual closure leads to meaning and interpretation of what is read; one must synthesize sounds into words and divide them into syllables and parts. Word attack skills require closure. Technique: give experiences involving tangible objects, verbal and printed words. Use a multisensory approach to teach words within words; then integrate them into wholes and break them into parts.
9. *Visual Comprehension*—The ability to associate what one sees with what it means. The ability to relate what one sees with what one reads with what one hears. Example: to learn *cat*, one experiences it, hears the spoken word and sees the printed word. He is able to bring it all together to understand the concept *cat*.	Child is a "word-caller"; may read words fluently but finds no meaning in what he sees, therefore, cannot really read; he may know the auditory symbol for a word, but can't convert the visual symbol he sees into the auditory symbol. He would *understand* if he could transduce.	Reading involves readily associating words, sentences, etc., with meaning; following directions, understanding what is read, both orally and silently. The purpose of reading is comprehension, which leads to interpretation, questioning, comparing.

279

teaching sequence are (1) the identification by the pupil of a need for the new skill, (2) the teaching of the new skill, and (3) presenting meaningful practice so that the new skill can be entrenched.

The teacher begins by having activities or experiences in a meaningful reading situation which suggest the need for new word attack skills. The child must see how the word attack skills can help him become a better reader. Even more significantly, the child must want to learn the new skills. He can be motivated in a number of ways, but he will learn more efficiently and effectively if he can see meaning and purpose for him in the task. Of course the teacher determines, at the same time, which of the word attack skills need more development by the child and by the class. These are the skills which should be pursued. The attempt is made to develop the child's ability to apply all the word cues in his actual reading, however.

After the identification phase, the teacher proceeds to teaching new materials. The teacher plans meaningful activities which will teach the children the skill or knowledge which is the lesson for the period. The teaching of new materials is immediately followed by meaningful experiences in which the pupils are given the opportunity to apply their new learning. Good responses on the part of the pupils can be reinforced by proper comments and actions by the teacher. Thus, the learning is strengthened.

The teacher and the school psychologist may wonder "What are some of the meaningful activities, experiences, and situations which I can use in the teaching of word attack skills?" The answer may be found in the teacher's manual accompanying the basal reading series. For each lesson, the teacher's manual, among other things, suggests introductory comments or motivational approaches, a list of new words to be taught, a series of questions to ask to check for comprehension, a series of planned activities to be used at various steps in the lesson, and a theory for utilizing phonics or other word attack skills more effectively. It is important for the teacher and the school psychologist to be familiar with the teacher's manual. In teaching, the teacher should not stop with the new words, their presentation, and evaluation for comprehension, but rather should go on in the teacher's manual and make use of the suggestions on teaching word attack skills.

Teaching Sequence of Subskills

The learning disabled child will have particular problems in identifying roots and prefixes and in changing roots by using root change rules before adding a suffix or inflectional ending (Cawley et al., 1972). A skill that the learning disabled child is least likely to have a problem with is the identification of the components of compounds. Kochevar (1975) recommends that this be the starting place for the teaching of structural analysis.

Breaking a compound word into its component parts is a relatively easy task. It involves recognizing two complete words within one word. The components are often learned as sight words, but even if a pupil knows parts of compounds as sight words, he will often not be able to recognize the compound itself. Nevertheless, this task is probably the simplest of structural analysis and appeals to remedial students because they can see the logic in it.

The concept of *root word* or *base word* should be firmly established in the mind of the remedial reader as he learns further subskills of structural analysis. After he has had practice breaking apart compound words and has become familiar with the idea that specific skills do exist and that he can successfully acquire them, the learning disabled reader should be taught to recognize the most common inflectional endings: *s, ed, ing, er, est, y,* and *ly.* This task involves separating root words that the reader should already know from common endings. This awareness of root words and endings builds readiness for understanding the concept of dividing words into syllables, a skill to be introduced later in the remedial reading program. A large factor in the reader's success with root words and inflectional endings will be his ability to see both the root and the ending as separate meaning units.

After the reader has experienced success with the above skill, the transition into the subskill of structural analysis that should be taught next—recognition and use of suffixes— will be relatively easy. Here again, the reader must be able to separate the root word from the ending or suffix. A significant part of this task will be for the student to recognize the suffix as a meaning unit and to be aware of how the suffix changes the meaning of the root word. For example, the student should know that attaching the suffix *-able* to a word means adding the meaning "given to" or "tending toward" to the root word; fashion*able* = given to fashion.

Teaching the reader to recognize and know the meaning of prefixes should be the next skill taught to the learning disabled child. Practice with separating root words from inflectional endings and suffixes should be sufficient to provide readiness for the reader to separate affixes that occur at the beginning of the word from the rest of the word. A learning disabled child is more likely to be able to separate root words from affixes found at the end of the word than those found at the beginning. By this time, however, he will have had sufficient practice separating roots from suffixes to be able to transfer this ability to separating them from prefixes. As in the case of suffixes, prefixes must be seen as separate meaning units that change the meaning of the root word. For example, *im-* added to a word negates the word; impossible means not possible.

It is questionable at what point in the teaching of structural analysis the learning disabled child should be taught syllabication. It could be argued that syllabication should be taught before prefixes and suffixes as separate syllables. On the other hand, if a child had mastered the recognition and use of prefixes and suffixes before being taught syllabication, he would already be aware of the fact that they are separate parts of words, both in meaning and in pronunciation. Consequently, the task of syllabication would already be well under way. In other words, if the child knows prefixes and suffixes, he knows them as separate syllables and already has a basis on which to build further principles of syllabication.

Hearing the speech units of which words are composed is the first step in learning to use syllabication as a word attack skill. Auditory recognition of syllables is prerequisite to visual recognition of syllables. Syllabication includes the ability to hear and see places within words where the structural breaks occur between root words, affixes, and syllables. Phonetic analysis plays a big part in syllabication for the major task of syllabication is assigning one syllable per vowel sound. To determine what constitutes one separate vowel sound, a student must be familiar with skills of phonetic analysis.

Reversals in Reading

Why a child reverses letters or words in reading and numbers in math remains somewhat of a mystery. There are a number of theories seeking to explain why a child makes reversals, but none of them can be substantiated by enough research to justify their acceptance. Perhaps one of the problems involved is that there is more than one reason why children make reversals, and no theory covers enough of the causes.

Some definitions and illustrations are in order. According to Harris (1975), there are four types of reversals: (a) whole word reversals—*was* for *saw, on* for *no*; (b) single letter reversal—*bet* for *pet, big* for *dig*; (c) letter order reversals—*left* for *felt, clam* for *calm*; and (d) word order reversals—*I was* for *Was I*. Bannatyne (1972) differentiates between mirror-

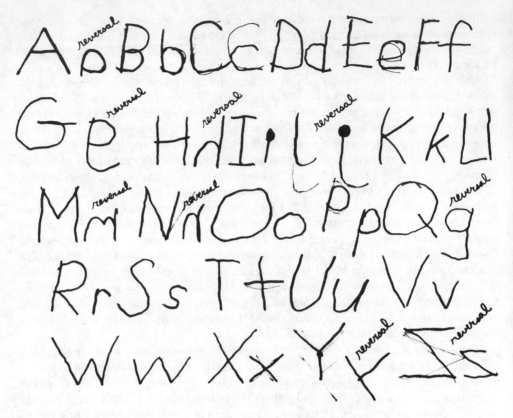

FIGURE 10–1. Reversals by a 7-year-old girl, I.Q. 107.

image and a reversal. He says the term *mirror-image* applies only to the shape of a particular letter as if it were seen in a mirror. Therefore, the child who writes *b* for *d*, or *p* for *q*, has a true mirror-image. If the child writes a letter upside down but not rotated, *p* for *b*, then it is an *inversion*; if the letter is written upside-down and rotated, *p* for *d*, or *on* its side ⊊ for u, then it is a *rotation*. Bannatyne reserves the word *reversal* for a word read or written in reverse—*was* for *saw*, *on* for *no*. It is doubtful that many researchers make the fine differentiations Bannatyne does, but perhaps they should in order to make their research more exacting. Other writers refer to a full reversal—*tar* for *rat*, *pat* for *tap*; a partial or static reversal—*big* for *dig*, *bog* for *dog*; or a kinetic or transposition reversal—*felt* for *left*. In spite of the different interpretations, most people appear to use the word *reversal* in a way that generally includes the four types mentioned by Harris.

RESEARCH ON REVERSALS. A quick review of the research on reversals shows a wide diversity of opinions and theories on the causes of reversals. We will mention only a few theories because it would serve no real purpose in this section to go into details on causes. Among the more prominent points of view are the following:

Writing Equations

Write an equation for each picture.

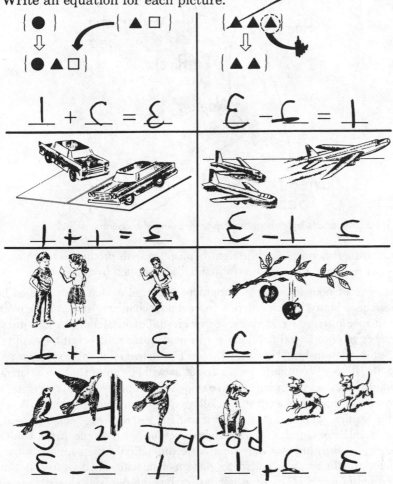

FIGURE 10–2. Reversals by a 7-year-old boy, I.Q. 115.

a. An early pioneer in the field of reading, Dearborn (1933) states that it is easier for a left-eyed person to look and work from right to left. A person with mixed dominance, or lack of dominance, therefore, would have confusion in direction of eye movements, resulting in reversals. (Theory not substantially supported by research.)

b. Another pioneer, Orton (1937) believes that a lack of consistent cerebral dominance produces a deficient visual memory that leads to confusion and conflict in perceiving words. Learned words are recorded in both hemispheres of the brain, although the left hemisphere has the major function of language. Words are recorded in the right hemisphere in reverse patterns, according to Orton, and in the absence of a strong

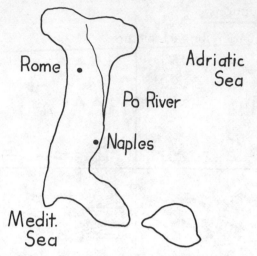

FIGURE 10–3. Reversals by college freshman drawing the country of Italy.

dominant left hemisphere, the right hemisphere will produce a mirror-image or a reversal response. (Theory not substantially supported by research.)

c. The issue of poor laterality development and reading has been studied by many researchers. Harris believes there is more than a chance relationship between lateral dominance and reading disability. However, studies on laterality usually just show the presence of poor lateral development in inadequate readers but they fail to show a causative relationship. They only show a correlative relationship. Major reviews by Spache (1976), Weintraub (1968), and Zangwill (1960) of studies on laterality and reading show overwhelming negative evidence. Monroe (1932b) speculates that premature introduction of word attack skills may be detrimental to a child's development of the reading process if he has not learned to discriminate temporal sequences of speech and letter sounds in a left-to-right direction. For example, in the words *spot* and *stop*, the child must not only be able to differentiate the sounds, but must also differentiate the temporal and spatial pattern of the letters. In a somewhat related way, Bond and Tinker (1973) believe that too much vocabulary introduced at one time may cause inappropriate directional habits because the child attempts to learn and use too many initial and final sounds at one time. Thus, he loses his sense of directionality.

d. Carter and McGinnis (1970) state the teacher may be at fault by placing an emphasis on word endings and looking for a familiar word in a larger unfamiliar word, thus causing some children to work from right to left, as well as from left to right.

Inadequate or distorted visual perception has often been cited as a cause of reversals in reading. Cohn and Strickler (1976), in a study involving 409 children, found that perceptual distortion was not a major source of difficulty in reversing letters. They observed that in young children, at least, the problem may be that they are asked to name letters before they are maturationally ready to do so. The child must first change his original concept of spatial orientation to the idea that an object is still the same object no matter what direction it is printed. *For example: book* is still a *book* even if it is turned over. As one child said when looking at a *u*, "That's an *n*, but it's upside down." When asked why she said *d, b, p, q,* and *g* were all the same, another child answered, "They all have a stick and a ball in them." Cohn and Strickler make a point for cognitive involvement and maturational development in discerning reversals. Many authorities point out that young children learning to read make as many reversals as do disabled learners. What distinguishes the disabled reader is the frequency and persistence of these errors well beyond the point in time when they are no longer common in the normal child. Normal readers seldom reverse beyond the age of 8. Keep in mind also that not all disabled readers reverse letters or words.

We have observed that disabled readers who make reversals in reading and writing never really seem to get over their directionality problem. They merely learn to compensate for their reversal difficulty by finding a way to handle it. At different stages of development, they change what they reverse. For example, a 6 or 7 year old may reverse letters. By 8 or 9, he does not reverse letters as often, but now reverses words such as *was* for *saw*. Later, he makes transpositions—*spot* for *stop*. By the time he is 12, 13, or 14, he can control reading reversals fairly well but has reversal problems in writing and in spelling. He may still confuse *E* and 3 in his writing. He will spell *does* as *dose*. As he compensates further, he learns that *dose* is *dose* like in a "dose of medicine," so he recognizes that dose is the incorrect spelling of the word *does*. However, he may continue to have difficulty with the word *their*, spelling it *thier*. There is nothing to indicate which is the correct spelling for the word *their*. The only way he will learn to spell the word correctly is to become cognitively conscious of the word and to realize that the way he wants to spell it has been consistently wrong; therefore, it must be spelled "the other way" to be correct.

We have also observed that reversals occur in three major areas. First, they occur in reading, as we have been illustrating. Second, they occur in speech, where a person says the opposite word, such as *Easter vacation* for *Christmas*, or the *ventral side* when they mean the *dorsal side*. When in a car, this person is frequently the one who says "Turn left, turn left" while he is pointing to the right. The third area in which reversals occur is in motor response when a child reverses letters or numbers in writing— ∂ for 6, ⌐ for L, И for N. A variation of this third type may be noted on the playground; a child, when confronted with the need to run from the rear to the front of the line, doesn't know whether to go to the left or to the right.

ASSESSMENT OF REVERSALS. Most children exhibit some reversal tendencies while they are learning to read. Reversal tendencies become a problem when the child is 8 years old or when he is moving out of second grade. When a teacher recognizes reversal symptoms in the older child, an interpretation of the nature of the reversal problems should be made and remediation begun immediately. The following tests can be used for detecting and evaluating reversals:

1. Durrell Analysis of Reading Difficulty. Word Recognition and Word Analysis. Test detects reversals of *b* and *d*, *p* and *q*, and the sequence of letters within words.

2. Monroe Diagnostic Reading Test. Oral Reading Test, Iota Word Test, and Word Discrimination Test detect reversals of *b* and *d*, *p* and *q*, *u* and *n*, and the sequence of letters within words, as well as reversal of the order of words.

3. Gates Reading Diagnostic Tests. Oral Reading Test, Reversible Word Test, and Word Perception and Analysis Test detect reversal of the sequence of letters in words.

4. Bond-Barlow-Hoyt Silent Reading Diagnostic Tests. Recognition of Reversible Words in Context Text and Error Classification in the Word Recognition Tests detect reversal of the sequence of letters in words.

An informal test that can be used with older pupils in determining reversal tendencies is a series of sentences that are dictated with the instruction that manuscript writing is to be used (Kolson & Kaluger, 1963). The sentences are as follows:

1. The dog was here.
2. A big ball did roll past me.
3. The man will be down.

Repeated reversals may indicate the child has a directional difficulty so the diagnostician should pursue this lead. It may also indicate a difficulty with comprehension since no child who is comprehending would read, "The pig lay in the mud," as "The dig lay in the mud." A clue as to whether or not the reversals are directionally or comprehensively caused can be gleaned from whether or not the child self-corrects his errors. If after reading a sentence with a reversal, the child goes back and reads it correctly, there is a good chance the difficulty is perceptually or directionally caused. If, however, he fails to correct his errors, the difficulty is probably a comprehension difficulty.

REMEDIATION OF REVERSALS. Basic reversal problems appear to be either directionality (left-right orientation), or cognitive (conceptual) in nature. Therefore, appropriate remedial activities would be those that reinforce or structure a left-to-right movement, and/or make the child consciously think of moving in a left-to-right direction. It may be desirable to first explain to the child the need for a consistent left-to-right sequence in reading; show him how the meanings of words and sentences are changed if the proper sequence is not followed. Hopefully, this explanation, given many times, will make the training meaningful and effective. Launta (1971) says that a child with severe reversal problems may reach a state of *learned helplessness* (our term) and be so frustrated that he will not even try to overcome his reversal tendency. In that case, there is a need to guide the child actively by immediately correcting a reversal response, structuring exercises to have minimal opportunities for eliciting reversal responses, and supplying the correct form of previously reversed sounds, letters, word parts, or words prior to their commission by the child. The following are activities that can be used to overcome reversals:

1. Use an effective tracing technique such as the Fernald or VAKT method.
2. Allow the child to point to the words with his finger as he reads.
3. Teach the sight word *bed* and make a visual bed out of the word by drawing lines bed making the mattress. The *b* is the first letter and it goes into the bed; the letter *d* is the last letter and it goes into the bed. The connecting line is the mattress.
4. Teach the capital *B* and capital *D*, which are not usually reversed. A small *b* can be made by erasing the top curve of the capital *B*. No letter results from erasing the top curve of the *D*.
5. Expose only one line of type at a time by using a line marker or card.
6. Draw a red line at the left of the paper and say "Always begin at the red line to write or to read."
7. Draw an arrow, pointing to the right, under words that are frequently reversed.
8. Color code the first letter of the words to indicate where the child is to start.
9. Cover a word with a card and slowly move the card to the right exposing the letters in the proper sequence.
10. Allow the child to use a typewriter.

11. Have the child trace two different letters printed on rough paper. Afterwards have the child compare the two and tell you the difference between them.
12. Using alphabet cereal, have the child match identical letters. He gets to eat those that he matched correctly.
13. A new idea is to have a right-handed child who writes reversals write his words to the left of the midline of his body. Left-handers write to the right of their midline.
14. Another *b* and *d* mnemonic device is to say that the curve of the *b* is out in front "like your stomach." The *d* goes out in back.

The Fernald Method (VAKT)

The Fernald Method or the so-called *tracing technique* is a whole word approach which utilizes a multisensory technique for developing reading skills (1939). It is a four-stage process whereby the child moves from mere word recognition and word comprehension to the more subtle and sophisticated formulation of reading generalizations. The first stage of the program is of particular interest to us at this time. This stage is a word recognition building activity, and it consists of a highly structured procedure. First the child's interest is secured by having him identify a word he wishes to learn. Once the word has been indicated, the teacher makes certain the child has a clear understanding of the meaning of the word. He is then taught to recognize the word through a tracing procedure. While he traces the word with his finger, he says the word. The tracing utilizes both the tactile and the kinesthetic senses. The oral pronunciation utilizes the auditory senses and the speech motor patterns. Guiding the hand with the eye and brain as he traces a word utilizes vision and the cerebral cortex. The first stage as structured by Kolson and Kaluger (1963) follows:

Clinician	Pupil
1. Finds a word the pupil wants to learn.	
	2. Selects word to be learned.
3. Asks pupil to use word in a sentence or to give the meaning.	
	4. Responds appropriately
5. Asks "How many parts to you hear?"	
	6. Responds. With teacher rendering needed help, the pupil verifies his answer by dictionary.
7. In script with crayon on 4" x 12" paper, writes the word.	
	Pupil observes clinician.
7.1 Says word	
7.2 Says each syllable without distortion, as each part is written. (Pronunciation of each syllable begins with and ends with the initial stroke of the syllable.)	
7.3 Going from left to right crosses *t*'s and dots *i*'s.	
7.4 Underlines each syllable while pronouncing the syllable.	
7.5 Says the word.	Pupil observes clinician.

8. Demonstrates tracing technique.
    8.1 Index and second finger held still while tracing over word.
    8.2 Says word.
    8.3 Says syllable on initial stroke of each syllable. (Without distortion)
    8.4 Cross*est's* and dots*i's* from left to right.
    8.5 Says word.
    8.6 Repeats word until pupil is ready to trace.

9. Traces the word following the procedure demonstrated until he thinks he can write the word without the copy.

10. Checks child's tracing technique.
    10.1 When child hesitates or makes an error, stops him.
    10.2 Records number of tracings.
    10.3 Praises success.

11. Removes copy. Writes word. Pronounces. Says each syllable as he begins to make it. Says again as he underlines each syllable.

12. Checks writing of word.
    12.1 No erasures.
    12.2 Does not stress errors.
    12.3 When child has had two successive writings correct, record word on achievement chart.

13. Compares his writing to original copy.
    13.1 If successful, dates paper and files the word.

    13.2 If unsuccessful, either retraces, or makes a second attempt.

14. Checks retention the next day.

Because of its tremendous possibilities and wide usage, the Fernald approach should be studied in greater detail so that all four stages are understood by the teacher. Stage I which was presented above, seeks to motivate the child and get him to want to learn. New words are taught through the use of the tracing technique, along with visual and auditory emphasis. Once the child has developed facility in the use of the tracing methods and has accumulated a group of sight words which he can use, he moves into Stage II. In this stage the teacher-pupil "step-by-step" procedure in writing the word is still followed except that the child no longer traces the word. The child makes use of oral and auditory modalities. He looks at the word, pronounces the word after the teacher, and studies it until he thinks he knows it. In Stage III, the child learns from the printed word form which is already on the card. Stage IV is started when the child has the ability to recognize new words by their similarity to words or parts of words he has already learned. The child asks the teacher to give the meaning or pronunciation of words he does not recognize in his reading. At all stages, it may be necessary for the child to return to VAKT (Stage I) or VAK (Stage II) to learn certain words.

The Cooper Method

The Cooper Method (1947) is a modification of the Fernald Method. It consists of having the pupil write the words with the tip of the fingers in a shallow tray of sand. We recommend using salt instead of sand. The salt seems to "tingle" the finger more, causing greater awareness. We also paint the bottom of the boxes black to make the tracings stand out. The Cooper Method consists of eight steps:

1. Words are first selected by the child from a controlled list.
2. As the pupil watches, each word is printed on a small card by the clinician.
3. As the word is pronounced, the child examines the word.
4. The pupil tries to write the word in the sand using the tips of his index and second fingers. In the beginning, it may be necessary for the teacher to guide the child's hand.
5. Subject is shown card with the word, and he matches it with his sand model.
6. Pupil shakes and "erases" the sand model and writes the word again in the sand.
7. If an error is made, the process is repeated from step five until the word is reproduced without the benefit of copy.
8. The word is used in a sentence, either orally or in writing.

No book reading is introduced until the pupil has acquired the vocabulary of three preprimers. This method can be used with children who are not too seriously afflicted with primary disability. It should not be used with children who have a problem with visual imagery because the sand tracing does not leave a sharp image.

Action-Direction

More than 60 years ago Emma Watkins advocated what she called the *action-direction exercises approach* to the teaching of reading. Under this approach the teacher labeled objects throughout the room: the window, the door, the desk, the chair. The individual desks and coat hooks were labeled with the names of the children. Each child was supplied with a little basket. Each day Miss Watkins would give the child a toy figure, and she would print the name of the item given. Through labeling everything and by providing items for each child's basket, Miss Watkins developed a sight vocabulary of names of things. Then through demonstration, she would teach verbs, or action words, to the children. When they had learned the action words, she would print directions on cards, such as "Tommy run," or "Mary stand," and have the children perform the action called for. This, too, has contributed something to our modern approach.

The McGinnis-CID or Association Method

The McGinnis-CID Method is used for both receptive and expressive aphasia (1963). The child is taught first to articulate a number of speech sounds, then to produce several sounds in a set sequence and to read and write these sounds in sequence before the sequence is identified as a word and associated with the appropriate picture illustrating the word. By means of a highly disciplined and structured system of drills, the child learns first to say, for example, the sound of the letters *b*, *oa*, and *t*. He learns to say them in sequence but separated into three distinct sounds—"b-oa-t." He learns to read these three sounds in sequence, then to write them, and finally to associate the sequence with a picture of a boat.

In order to effect the memory required to recall the sound of each letter, a multisensory approach is used involving the kinestheology of precise articulatory position and the kinesthetic and visual experiences of writing the sound and seeing it in writing. Different colors are used in writing consonants and vowels in the word in order to further emphasize separation and sequence. Thus the weak auditory memory is reinforced by kinesthetic and visual stimuli. The next steps in the process involve learning to read and write the words from memory and to differentiate by auditory stimulation alone among the sounds and letters learned. As soon as an adequate number of words are learned, the building of sentences begins: first the child memorizes the sentences by rote; then he learns to use them in situations other than drill.

The major principles of this method involve (1) a phonetic approach, (2) precision in articulation of sounds, (3) association of articulatory position and sound and the appropriate cursive script symbol, and (4) systematic sensorimotor association.

In the elementary stages, the Association Method employs seven steps in teaching nouns. The child:

1. Produces, in sequence, the sounds composing a written word.
2. Matches picture of object with written word.
3. Copies the word, articulating each letter as he forms it.
4. Observes teacher articulating the word, then repeats the word aloud.
5. Says the word from memory.
6. Writes the word from memory, articulating the sound as he writes it.
7. Matches picture with word spoken in his ear.

Programmed Instruction

In the field of word attack skills, several types of cues lend themselves nicely to programming: phonics, syllabication, structural analysis, and even contextual analysis. Programming is the preparation of a program or procedure, which, in this case, seeks to alter behavior through the reinforcement of operant behavior. The teaching machine and scrambled books are examples of attempts to program for learning. The approach makes use of an application of the stimulus-response theory. The S-R theory takes into account learning by conditioning and the influence on learning response by a system of rewards and punishment.

The subject matter to be learned by programmed instruction is subdivided into simple, easily accomplished steps. The learner is to make a response on each step. Each response is immediately reinforced, either positively or negatively. This reward tends to elicit this response with greater speed and frequency in the future. If, however, he has made an incorrect response, he immediately receives a negative reinforcement which serves to weaken the frequency and strength of the undesired response.

The advocates of programmed instruction proclaim several advantages for this approach to teaching. They feel that learning will take place under this method because the student is an active participant in the learning process. As the student works his way through the material, giving answers and having his correct answers reinforced, his reflective thinking and immediate recall are strengthened. He actively seeks the knowledge, and he captures it. A second advantage is that the student controls this part of the learning situation. He is responsible to himself, so to speak. He manipulates the material, and he utilizes it as he sees fit. This leads to the third advantage. The student works at his own pace. Relieved of external pressure, he is less apt to have tensions and anxieties which can hinder his learning progress.

The term *programmed learning* has been associated with a teaching machine. The teaching machine, however, is merely a vehicle. The important part of programmed learning is the programmed material which can be used with a machine. Programmed material can also be designed to be used without the machine. A number of programmed courses or subjects are now available in book form and can be used with nothing more than a strip of cardboard.

Although the number of commercially produced programmed instructions in reading is limited at this time, there is a growing number of such programs being made available to reading programs. Public school teachers are taking courses in programmed instruction and are producing specific programs to fit particular classes. This approach to program building under the supervision of an expert is a learning experience. Once a program is constructed, teachers use it.

Much research has been done recently concerning programmed instruction. Indications are that multiple choice items are superior when the aim is recognition. When the aim is total recall, write-in responses seem superior. At present, little research has been done to give conclusive evidence concerning the transfer of learning.

The Center for Programmed Learning has produced several materials for the development of word attack skills: *Phonetic Analysis I, Phonetic Analysis II, Contextual Clues I,* and *Word Analysis Book I.* Reaction to these materials has been mixed.

Misuse of Configuration Cues: Diack

Hunter Diack, a university professor from England and co-author of an English basal reading series (1960), has placed himself in direct opposition to the emphasis placed on visual discrimination readiness exercises used in schools in the United States.

According to Diack, the hours spent on visual discrimination development are a waste of time. He believes that a child 2 years old has enough visual discrimination to be able to distinguish one letter from another. The reason children seemingly cannot distinguish one letter from another when asked to do so at a later age (5 or 6) is not due to poor visual discrimination ability, but rather to a linguistic deficit which makes it impossible for them to understand what the teacher wants them to do. Diack claims that if the questions are worded in such a way as to be in the child's understanding vocabulary, the visual choice of a letter would be immediate and would need little or no practice.

To prove his point, Diack taught a number of young children to discriminate letters and words. In every case, according to Diack, the child learned to make immediate choices or almost so. As a result, Diack feels that it would be better to eliminate our readiness programs and to substitute the learning of word perceptual skills, taught according to his suggestions.

He would begin teaching the letters and their meanings, at the same time teaching that letter placement is a time and sequence indicator. He would eliminate the teaching of configuration cues since he feels that the use of configuration cues helps to develop poor perceptual habits.

Diack's mistake is thinking that visual-discrimination experience comprises the total readiness program. Although his belief that no visual discrimination readiness drill is necessary in kindergarten and first grade may merit research, it should be pointed out that visual discrimination is but one small part of the total readiness program. Too much research and pragmatic knowledge supports the total readiness program to discard the program because Diack has shown that a child of 2 years can visually discriminate a *p* from an *n*.

Diack considers the teaching of configuration cues as a word attack skill useless and even dangerous since it teaches the child poor perceptual skills. Diack alleges that when the child is asked to look at a word, he does not look at the total word but generally fastens his attention on one or several letters and relates them to the larger entity. This is the approach generally taken by a more sophisticated reader in identifying a word. Before this advanced approach in reading can be used, the use of many cues is necessary to grasp the meaning of the word. As the learner has continued exposure to the word, fewer cues are needed to recognize the word. Diack contends that the child being taught by configuration cues is being denied the learning that takes place through the cue reduction process and that the child is being forced to learn to read with the cues already reduced. This method of teaching reading is like asking a child to play Chopin as part of his first lesson in learning to play the piano. The end result of this approach, according to Diack, is that the child does not perceive a word in its letter simplified time sequence, and he develops the habit of guessing. The child does not learn to read to his maximum potential.

Further, Diack feels the educators who insist that letters have no meaning are displaying total ignorance concerning the function and place of letters. Letters do signal a specific sound; hence, they have sound meaning. In addition, the sequence of the letters in a word signifies a time sequence of sounding the word. In the word *cat*, the arrangement of the letters signifies slightly later time presentation of each letter in going from left to right.

To eliminate the bad effects of the use of configuration, Diack and Daniels have constructed a set of basic readers which attempts to eliminate the possibility of using configuration cues in learning to read. Words are presented which have the same configuration. This forces the child to look at the internal construction of the word and to ignore the general pattern. Children are also taught individual letter sounds and are instructed in the time sequence of letters in words. Thus, proper reading perceptual skills are developed, according to Diack.

The readers constructed by Daniels and Diack, *The Royal Road Readers*, have phonic control in a sense that they employ words phonetically structured, but they have no vocabulary control (1957). Most basal series attempt to limit the number of new words with which the young reader must cope. Most first grade reading programs limit the total number of new words introduced in the reading series to about 400 words. This limitation is due to the primary emphasis of teaching by configuration and right recognition even though other word attack skills are taught. Diack feels that this is unnecessary control of vocabulary. He calls the proponents of this approach *configurationists*, and he says "They (the configurationists) start out by keeping letters away from the child and they end up keeping words away from him."

Media for Remediation of
Visual Analysis Skills

Sample Activities for Word Attack Skills

Level One

  I. Configuration cues

    A. Have child match shapes.

                          dog
                          cat
                          book

    B. Match

book	book
book	ball
ball	beam

  II. Context cues

    A. Print sentence on board with unknown word underlined.

       A <u>Buick</u> is a big car.

      Begin with known word *car*. "What are some cars?" "What is the beginning letter in the unknown word?" "What car begins with that letter?"

    B. Put sentence on board, "Mary ate a lot because she was hungry." Direct questions toward why we eat.

    C. Have children fill in the blanks.

       ____ people have more energy than old people.

    D. Have children fill in the blanks.

       He was as ____ as a sheet.

    E. Have children fill in the blanks.

       Three days without food, soaked by the rain, tired from walking, John sat down and just felt ____.

  III. Structural analysis

    A. Put a list of words on the board. Have children pronounce each, then add *ing*.

       see   sew
       call   play
       talk

    B. Compound Words

Level Two

I. Configuration

   A. Match

      b__k   boat
      b_ke   book
      __at   bake

II. Context cues

   A. Classification of words. Put under proper column.

      medicine   chalk
      shovel   eraser
      pill   pointer
      pick   wheelbarrow

      <u>doctor</u>   <u>teacher</u>   <u>ditchdigger</u>

   B. Have child see how many different ways he can use a word. (multiple meanings)

      Run
      I had a home run.
      I run fast.
      She had a run in her stocking.

   C. Play games using antonyms, synonyms, and homonyms.

III. Structural cues

   A. Build word lists using Greek or Latin roots, such as:

      ____phone
      cosma____
      ped____

   B. Build a class book of word origins and history.

   C. List compound words and have children separate them.

      onto ____ ____
      into   ____ ____

   D. Pronounce with pupils. Have pupils decide what two words it represents.

      would've
      can't
      I'm
      he'll

   E. Choose the correct one.

      The ____ nose was cold.   dog dog's
      The ____ chased the cat.   dog dog's

    F. Find the prefix.

refold	untie	behind
redo	dislike	prefix

    G. On a worksheet, write the root and suffix separately.

	root	suffix
tireless	____	____
wonderful	____	____
meanness	____	____

Contextual Cues

Probably the word recognition skill most used by adults is deriving meaning from content. Children should be encouraged to read on to get the meaning of the unknown word in a sentence or paragraph. In order to do this, however, the child must be reading material at his instructional level. Otherwise, other unknown words in the content will prevent his utilization of contextual cues. It is important to note that guessing is the mainstay of contextual analysis. However, guessing, which does not contribute to the meaning of the material, is a symptom of comprehension difficulties.

Remediation in this area calls for the construction of practice exercises in which the child is first asked to read the entire sentence and then to select the right word from several sources. This is the level of recognition. Later, he is asked to read sentences and then to recall and reproduce the correct response-level of recall and reproduction. Caution should be used in constructing these practices to make certain the word to be selected or reproduced is the child's vocabulary and in his conceptual background. Otherwise, you are presenting the child with a dual task.

Syllabication

A student's ability to break a known or unknown word into syllables will depend, to a large extent, on success with recognizing components of compounds, separating root words from inflectional endings, prefixes, and suffixes. If the child has had success in these areas, he is well on his way to experiencing success in breaking words into syllables.

A student's ability in this area will also depend upon his knowledge of phonetic analysis. Since the main task of syllabication is assigning one syllable per vowel sound, a student must know what constitutes one vowel sound before being able to break a word into syllables.

Before any work is done with dividing the written word into syllables, the learning disabled student should master competence in being able to hear the number of syllables in a given word. This is very important for, if the child cannot hear distinct syllables, it is unlikely that he will be able to see them.

The instructional goal of syllabication is simple: that the child begin to hear and see places within words where the structural breaks occur between root words, affixes, and syllables. On one hand, a learning disabled child should not be made to memorize long lists of rules concerning syllabication, but on the other, he should not be left without some basic principles to follow to figure out where syllable breaks occur. Memorization of rules emphasizing memory and parrot-like repetition is not desirable, as it may develop splinter skills, but no application of skills.

SYLLABICATION RULES.   The aim of all remedial teachers should be to develop a pattern of syllabication attack in each child. Through structural learning the child should be taught:

1. Remove affixes

    In order to do this he must be taught the common prefixes and suffixes as sight words and have a grasp of their meaning.

con	together with
de	from, down from
dis	apart, not
ex	out of, from
in, en	in, into, among
inter	between
pre	before
re	back, again
sub	under
super	over, above
un	not

2. The remainder of the word must be divided into syllables.

    To do this, the child needs to know two rules:

    VC/CV—When the pattern is a vowel-consonant-consonant-vowel, we divide between the two consonants.

    V/CV—When the pattern is a vowel-consonant-vowel, we divide before the consonant.

3. He must now be given a method to help him determine vowel sounds.

    To do this he must be taught two definitions and two rules.

    Definitions—Open syllable ends in a vowel

    Closed syllable ends in a consonant

    Rules—Open syllable–long sound

    Closed syllable–short sound

By applying the above listed steps the child will have a procedure for unlocking new words.

SYLLABICATION EXERCISES

1. Hearing syllables

    In Col. I write the number of vowels you see.
    In Col. II the number of vowels you hear.
    In Col. III the number of syllables you hear.

	Column I	Column II	Column III
soft			
butter			
awake			

    Notice that column II and column III are alike.

2. When a single consonant appears between two vowels, the word is usually divided before the consonant.

    a. We have had a vowel followed by two consonants. What sound would a vowel have if it were not followed by a consonant or if it were followed by only one consonant as in:

    me   spi / der

    The *e* in *me* is long. The *i* in *spider* is long.

Write the first syllable in the following, marking the vowel.

baby   paper

pilot   bacon

music

bā pī mū pā bā

Do the syllables look like closed syllables? We call a syllable with a vowel at the end an open syllable. The vowel is usually long. There are exceptions, as in *robin, never, seven*.

3. Write the first syllable of the following words. Tell if it is a closed or open syllable.

	First Syllable	Closed	Open
petty	pet	X	
ribbon			
lady			
scissors			
tiger			

4. Select from the known sight vocabulary several two-syllable words which illustrate the application of a generalization. List the words on chart paper or chalkboard. Explain to the pupil that breaking a word into syllables can often be a help in figuring out new words and that each syllable must contain a vowel.

5. Split a word into syllables using colored chalk to identify the breaking place. Verbalize your line of reasoning as you break the word apart. Example: "Here are two consonants together. That's my cue for dividing this word." Help the pupil divide and verbalize his thinking for the rest of the listed words.

Structural Analysis

COMPOUND WORDS. Teaching the learning disabled child to recognize component parts of compounds is probably the easiest place to start in teaching structural analysis skills. Practice should be given to students both in taking compounds apart and putting them together. However, these compound words should be part of a child's speaking, meaning and sight word vocabulary. The child should be taught that the meaning of compound words is derived from combining the meaning of the component words and that the pronunciation of the compound word remains the same as the two combining forms.

1. Connect the parts of compound words in opposite columns by drawing a line from one part to the part that goes with it, as:

after   berry
can   doors
out   not
straw   boy
cow   noon

2. Dividing compound words with marks.
   Have children:

   Draw a box around each of the words as in | sail | boat |
   Draw a circle around each word as in (pop) (corn)
   Underline each word separately as in *sidewalk*

Draw a line between the two words as in *bee/hive*.

3. To teach component parts in compound words list on the board or print on flash cards compound words composed of two known words:

something	cowboy	sailboat	into
someone	henhouse	cannot	outdoors

Lead the pupils to see the two known words in each word by framing the two words with hands or by underlining the two components with colored chalk.

INFLECTIONAL ENDINGS. In teaching inflectional endings, the remedial teacher will encounter his first opportunity to introduce the concept of *root word*. This should be done in conjunction with activities aimed at separating root words from their endings. The concept of root word should be firmly imbedded in the child's mind as this concept will be transferred to the learning of suffixes and prefixes. Reference should also be made to the language role that the endings play (*s* means more than one, etc.)

1. Write on the board and/or worksheets. Have the children add *s*, *ed*, *ing*.

walk   walks   walked   walking
ask
call
look
jump
show

These should be done only with known words

2. To some words we add *es*.

Write a list of words on the board. Have the children add the ending *es* to them.

fox	foxes	inch
box		dress
dish		lunch
brush		mix
potato		match
class		fish

3. In the space provided add *er*, *est*, *ly* to the first word; then pronounce each word.

	er	est	ly
warm			
great			
high			
soft			
kind			

4. Present an exercise like the following. Ask children to select the word that completes each sentence and then to read the sentence aloud.

a. The boys were _____.

plays, played, playing

b. The man was _____ the car.

        pushes, pushing, pushed

c. Father _____ the car yesterday.

        washes, washed, washing

CONTRACTIONS

Omitting one or more letters.

Sometimes two words are joined to make a smaller word, and one or more letters are left out. We use an apostrophe to show where the letter or letters are left out.

Look at the words in the *Word Box*. Point to the words as I say them—*I am, I'm, I will, I'll, did not, didn't,* etc.

Using the word box, read the sentences below writing the contraction for the words underlined.

Word Box

| I am | we are | she is | did not |
| I'm | we're | she's | didn't |

1. *She is* coming home.
2. He *did not* go today.
3. *We are* invited.

Find the contractions in the story and tell what the contraction means. Read the sentence using the meaning in place of the contraction.

I'll send for the toy.

It's beautiful.

We *can't* see through it.

PREFIXES AND SUFFIXES. For difficulty with prefixes, suffixes and roots (lack of recognition of the common ones and lack of knowledge of their meanings) the student needs to see several familiar words containing the same part (prefix or suffix) to identify the common part, and to determine from the known meanings of the words the contribution of the prefix or suffix to the meanings of the new words. The practice of providing several words with the same affix to help the child come to a generalization about the use of meaning of the affix is supported by many authors on the subject. Here again, students should be brought to the realization that root words retain their meaning and that the prefixes and suffixes are meaningful parts of words.

The prefixes that should be included in the remedial reading program are: *re, un, dis, de, ex, en, in, im, com, con, pre, pro.* The student should also be familiar with the following suffixes (in addition to inflectional endings): *ness, ance, ent, ence, ment, sion, tion, less, able.* The learning disabled student should only be given practice with a selected few of these prefixes and suffixes (*re, un, dis, ment, able, ness*) until it becomes evident to the teacher that he understands the meaning and proper usage of the affixes to the point that he can transfer this knowledge to other affixes.

Many learning disabled youngsters will have trouble identifying affixes as both separate visual units and separate meaning units. The lack of visual perception and discrimination skills necessary to see affixes as separate units should be supplemented with experience with and information into other sensory modalities. The learning disabled child should see, hear, and repeat lists of words with similar affixes. It would also be advisable to provide the opportunity for the learning disabled child to manipulate common prefixes and suffixes written on cards by pairing them up with appropriate root words also written on cards. An exhaustive list of prefixes and suffixes and numerous examples of words for each affix are found in Kottmeyer (1959). He also advocates the use of the Webster Word Analysis Chart, which lists common prefixes, their meanings, and examples of words in which the prefixes are used. He also explains the Webster Word Wheels, which give practice with 11 common prefixes on 20 wheels, and 18 common suffixes on 18 wheels.

Activities related to prefixes and suffixes are:

1. Have children underline the prefix:

   unhappy   enjoy   asleep   dislike
   return   repaint   below   enfold

2. Have children circle or underline the prefix used in the word.

away	be a un	beside	be en un	below	en un be	awake	be a un
undress	en un be	alive	a un en	enlarge	en be un	belong	be un a

3. Make a worksheet. Have the children write the root word and suffix separately.

   kindness   _____   _____
   peaceful   _____   _____
   toothless   _____   _____
   wireless   _____   _____

4. Add a prefix or a suffix to a word to make it convey the meaning in a given definition, as:

   Prefixes: *in*—into, not
              circum—around
              ex—out of, from

   _____*port*:   to send out of the port
   _____*ability*:   not having ability
   _____*navigate*:   to sail around

   Suffixes: *al*—pertaining to
              ward—turning to, direction of
              able—given to, tending toward

   *fraction*_____: pertaining to fractions
   *west*_____: toward the west
   *change*_____: given to change

Nonreading Games for Beginning Reading

1. On a table place several familiar objects, covered by a cloth or paper. Uncover the objects for a few seconds. Replace the cover and ask the child to name as many objects as he can remember. Gradually increase the number of objects.
2. Place several objects under a cover on the table, as above. After exposing the objects for a few seconds, remove one of them while the child closes his eyes. Rearrange the remaining objects. Then uncover them and have the child recall which object was removed. Gradually increase the number of objects on the table and the number removed.

3. Expose a simple pattern for a few seconds. Remove and have the child draw from memory.
4. Expose a picture containing several objects. Remove and have the child name as many things as he can remember having seen.
5. Have the child match objects, colors, numbers, words, phrases, short sentences.
6. Have the child count or name rows of objects from left to right pointing with his finger at first, then with the eyes alone.
7. Describe some object such as "I am thinking of something little and white with long ears and a short tail and pink eyes." Have the child try to visualize the object and guess what is being described. Describe the clothes and appearance of some person in the room or in a picture until the child guesses who is being described.
8. Have the child learn to recognize and copy his own name.
9. Have him learn to recognize and copy the names of familiar objects in the room such as *door, window, desk, clock*.

General principles to follow with the beginning reader are:

a. Select a book with large type.
b. Use liners to help him keep his place and to direct eye movements in the proper direction.
c. Stress the left-to-right direction in all reading games. Don't write the words in vertical columns.
d. An arrow pointing to the right place under a word helps to stress correct direction and to overcome reversals.
e. Tracing over a word several times provides another cue to learning it.
f. Have the child write the word three or four times.
g. Have child compare words that he confuses so he can recognize their differences: *where—there*; *when—then*; *big—pig*; *her—here*.

Remediation of Visual Defects

If the diagnosis reveals a defect in the sight of the child, he should be referred to a professional so that he can receive proper treatment. In 95% of cases eye defects can be taken care of with properly fitted glasses and eye training exercises.

There are some children who have visual deficiencies which cannot be corrected by glasses. A sight-saving program should be set up to take care of these children. The child should be permitted to progress as quickly as possible without harm to the eyes. Typography and illumination are two important factors to be considered in this program. The type in the reading material should be at least as large as that of 24 point print. It should never be smaller than 18 point type.

In this special type of class as much learning as possible should be done through listening. There can be much emphasis on story telling, sharing experiences, and other activities that will not be putting excess emphasis on the eyes. These children will not be at a disadvantage for learning words through phonetic skills, but care should be taken that this approach is not overemphasized. These children still need to know the other word attack skills.

Some sample visual training exercises are as follows:

1. Have child visually track another child who is walking, skipping, or running. Notice if child's eyes stray from the traget and remind him to track.
2. While the child holds his head steady, name simple objects that are placed around the room and have him visually locate them.

3. Put a simple line drawing on an overhead transparency. Have the child draw the object as projected. The child must follow his hand with his eyes as he traces.
4. Have the child trace simple to complex line drawings and geometric forms on the blackboard. Start with large designs, then make them smaller.
5. Suspend a rubber ball from a stick by a length of string. Have the child visually track the ball as it swings. Notify him each time he fails to follow the ball visually. Allow head movements early in the training but gradually work toward having the child track with his eyes only. It may be necessary at the beginning to have the child track with one eye only.
6. Play "Pilot and Spotter." Attach a small airplane to a small pencil or small stick. One child "flies" the plane while the "spotter" attempts to track the plane. The "pilot" attempts to catch the "spotter" each time the "spotter" loses visual contact.
7. Have the child look back and forth from a pencil held approximately one foot from his eyes to a distant object. Work for increased speed and accuracy as well as the ability to endure this type of activity for increasingly longer periods of time each day.
8. For peripheral vision practice, have the child walk forward and try to stop exactly in line with some object while fixating his eyes on an X on the wall.
9. Have the child fixate his eyes on a mark and attempt to identify objects or pictures as you slowly move them toward his center of vision.
10. If a child is unable to track or fixate from a standing or seated position, it may be necessary to begin the training with the child lying on his back as this is an earlier developmental level.

Visual Discrimination
Related to Reading

Activities in visual discrimination include recognizing symbols, recognizing likenesses and differences in objects and symbols, recalling symbols in sequence to develop visual memory, recognizing sight words, letter and number series, and developing word recognition cues. Examples of activities of recognizing likenesses and differences follow:

1. Color the boxes that have the letters that are alike

i r	g g	c c	b d	f t
t f	r r	k h	m m	p q
w w	j i	o o	r z	z z
x k	b p	e e	g i	k k
y y	a e	h h	m n	t t

2. Join the letters in each box that look alike

v	w	c	i	d	x	f	k	p	z
u	u	o	i	x	b	v	v	s	p
b	q	p	z	a	a	v	v	g	k
d	d	s	p	b	d	u	w	k	i
h	h	j	o	t	y	d	x	d	u
a	e	o	i	y	f	x	b	u	p
t	m	l	t	w	r	v	w	c	v
n	p	l	j	w	z	u	u	o	c
p	r	p	r	s	s	p	r	h	q
r	s	q	r	q	p	q	r	q	r

3. Tell me all you can about the word you see here:

                  Home

answers: 1. long *o*
             2. silent *e*
             3. consonants *H* and *m*
             4. means a place to live

4. Visual perception of one and two syllable words. (Put the following words on the blackboard and have the pupils copy them. Then tell them to write beside each word the number of syllables they would hear when the word was pronounced.)

Levels 3—4

     1. acorn
     2. bleach
     3. carton
     4. cough
     5. design
     6. eighth
     7. faucet
     8. gear
     9. motley
   10. pasture

chapter 11

Word Analysis:
Auditory-Verbal Skills

Since most learning disabled readers have difficulty processing auditory-verbal material, we believe it is appropriate to have a chapter emphasizing their most common problem in reading: word analysis. *Word analysis* is an inclusive term that covers all methods of attacking words. Phonics is just one form of word analysis. We have no exact count of how many LD youngsters have auditory-verbal deficits, but of the LD children with whom we have worked, either directly or indirectly, we recognize that by far, the greatest majority of the moderate to severely disabled readers have auditory, perceptual, and verbal problems, as these skills relate to learning to read. Our guess is that at least 80% and possibly 85% of these children have difficulty using auditory-verbal skills.

Basic Understandings

The child in first grade usually learns his first words through the visual method. The words are exposed to him over and over until they are readily identified by their general configuration or by some other visual cue. Children who do not have a visual perception problem and/or who do not have difficulty with directionality can learn the sight words without too much trouble. However, there comes a time, usually about the middle of the second-grade level, when the child has been exposed to too many words which look alike. The child then experiences difficulty in visually separating the words which are similar in shape. It is at this point that the child must learn to apply techniques other than the visual approach to unlocking words. Ability in phonetic analysis is now needed in order for the child to continue making progress in reading. Basic phonics started in first grade begin to pay dividends in learning progress when the child becomes overwhelmed with sight words. It is at this point, however, that the child with an auditory perceptual problem begins to have trouble with his reading because he cannot distinguish the differences in sounds or cannot grasp the idea of how to apply phonics to unlocking words.

There are some subtle differences in the definitions of four reading skill words that are often used interchangeably. The terms are *word identification, word recognition, word perception,* and *word analysis.* According to Zeman (1964), word identification, the first level of development in seeing whole words, refers to the initial time that a child is introduced to a word visually; he pronounces that word orally or silently to himself. In a way, word identification may be thought of as *word encounter,* or *word awareness,* where there has been an exposure to the word, and some degree of internalization or learning has taken place. Word recognition, the second level of development in discerning whole words, involves the use of memory or recall in remembering the word. The child is able to say "Oh, yes, I've seen or heard that word before." At this point, the new word may have no semantic or intrinsic meaning other than the child knows the word is familiar to him. The third level of grasping words is word perception. Now the child or adult associates a meaning to the printed symbol or spoken word and can use the word in a meaningful way for communication. Word identification, word recognition, and word perception are skills which can be aided by other reading skills, such as configuration cues, verbal context cues, picture cues, or language rhythm cues. Three important deductions can be made from the above definitions: (a) Word-calling without word meaning does not contribute to concept development; (b) If too many word identification kinds of words appear in a paragraph, the reading level may be too difficult for the reader; and (c) Word attack skills make use of both visual and auditory aids to unlock words.

Word analysis skills include all skills used to break words into parts. Again, according to Zeman, these include single consonants, consonant blends, consonant digraphs, single vowels, vowel digraphs, diphthongs, consonant vowel combinations, vowel consonant combinations, syllables, roots, prefixes, and suffixes. The last four skills are structure analysis skills, and the rest are phonetic skills. Zeman believes all of these skills are part of spelling or writing, and that these activities can be used to develop word analysis skills. To some degree, Zeman advocates using spelling and writing initially to teach reading skills.

The Place of Phonics in the Reading Program

After reading the articles and books about reading written for public consumption, one is led to believe that a great controversy is raging among educators as to whether or not phonics should be taught as part of a reading program. Indeed, some articles seem to imply that all but a few enlightened teachers and educators are *against* the teaching of reading by phonics or are at least ignoring this area of teaching. It is a shame that critical but uninformed writers outside the field of reading and learning should have such influence on the thinking of the public, especially since their criticism is misleading and unwarranted.

Actually, there is some controversy concerning phonics in the reading program but it does not involve the question of whether or not phonics should be taught. It is generally agreed that phonics *should* be taught. The discussion centers around the question of how to teach phonics and how much is needed. One group of teachers and educators, and this is by far the larger group at present, feels that the better way to teach phonics is in conjunction with the need a child feels to want to learn a word which he sees in context, but which he does not know. He must attack this word in order to be able to say it and to get meaning from it. This procedure is the *whole-to-part approach,* sometimes called the *combination approach,* or *synthetic phonics approach,* to learning words. The other group believes that no words should be taught until the child has been drilled on the letters and the sounds which they signal. After he knows the letters and their sounds, he can apply this newly learned skill to the reading of words. This procedure is the *part-to-whole approach*, sometimes called the *isolated approach*, or *analytic phonics approach*, to the teaching of reading.

Almost all of the basal series of readers pay attention to phonics and consider phonics a vital part of the reading program. Some basal series take the whole to part approach and others the part to whole approach. The teacher's manual accompanying the basal readers presents well-developed suggestions for teaching phonics according to the intended approach. The sequence chart presented with most basal reading series indicates a progression in the development of phonic ability which is the same as or similar to the level of attainment in phonics as suggested by most reading experts. Any teacher who uses a basal reading series in her classroom will have at her disposal specific procedures for teaching the phonics her children need, if she will but follow her teacher's manual.

However, teachers and professional educators consider phonics as only one of many different kinds of word attack skills which a child should be able to use. Teachers believe that a child who is taught only phonetic analysis and no other word attack skills such as configuration, cue reduction, context, structural analysis, will be handicapped in reading ability. Hence, phonics is not the only word attack skill taught by teachers in reading. The teaching of phonics in schools, as a result, is not always as apparent to outsiders as it might be.

The modern school also places great importance upon reading as a communication skill and, as such, it seeks to present reading in a context which is meaningful to the child. In an attempt to make certain that the child grasps the significance of the communicative aspects of reading, the teacher of today begins formal reading instruction in such a way as to make certain that the content has personal meaning for the child. More and more formal reading instruction begins with words which are already part of the child's vocabulary and which have environmental meaning for him. The language experience approach embodies this idea.

Coupled with this emphasis upon meaningfulness is the belief that reading skills should be taught when the child has a need for them and in an applicational or pragmatic manner. In this way, the teacher takes advantage of certain desirable psychological factors involved in learning and also emphasizes the utility of the skill. When the child has added to his reading vocabulary several sight words which contain the same phonic element, the teacher guides the child into realizing that there is a consistency of the sound being signaled by this element. In this manner, the teacher makes use of meaningful aspects while indicating the possibility of using that phonic element in unlocking other words containing that combination of letters.

The place of phonics in the reading program as considered by reading authorities and authors of basal reading series can be summarized as follows:

1. Phonics is an essential and important part of the reading program.
2. A child must have skill in using phonics to unlock words.
3. The child must be able to use other word attack skills in addition to phonetic analysis.
4. Phonics must be taught in a sequential manner.
5. Phonics must be taught in a meaningful situation.
6. Phonics must be taught so as to emphasize its usability.
7. Phonics must be taught in a manner which prevents distortion and confusion.

Chall (1967) purports to have examined all published research on phonics. She attempts to summarize the findings to determine if a "code emphasis" (phonics) or a "meaning emphasis" (visual or whole word) approach is better. Her conclusion is that the bulk of evidence indicates the "code emphasis" approach is the better beginning reading technique.

Understanding Phonics

This is not a book on phonics; therefore, it is impossible to devote the space needed to present a complete survey of the subject. Instead it will present in a concise manner the minimal phonetic knowledge a teacher must have if she is to successfully teach this word attack skill to children and a psychologist must have to understand the remedial sequence involved.

PHONICS, PHONOGRAMS, AND PHONEMES

Phonetics is the science of the sounds of language. It is the study and systematic classification of the sounds made in spoken utterance (Webster). *Phonics* is a method of teaching reading by the application of phonetic sound values to letters and letter groups. Through the use of phonics the reader is able to translate printed symbols into spoken language. To be able to do this, the reader must be able to relate a specific sound to a particular phonogram. A *phonogram* is a single letter or a combination of letters which represent a unit of sound in speech. This unit of sound in speech is called a *phoneme*. The phonemes (units of sounds) in the English language are indicated by the 26 letters of the alphabet used either singly or in combinations. These 26 letters are divided into 19 consonants, 5 vowels, and 2 semivowels. According to linguists, these 26 letters produce about 44 different sounds.

For practical purposes we define a *vowel* as a sound which is easily spoken alone, whereas a *consonant* is a sound which is not easily sounded alone. Speech specialists offer a more technical definition and explanation of a consonant and a vowel. They relate the class of sounds of the phonemes to the position of the so-called speech organs when the sounds and the sound frequencies are made. A *vowel*, according to a speech specialist, is a class of speech sounds in the articulation of which the oral part of the breath channel is not blocked and is not constricted enough to cause audible friction. On the other hand, a *consonant* is a class of speech sounds which is characterized by constriction or closure at one or more points in the breath channel. Consonants in many cases are merely a position of the speech organs. The consonant *b*, for example, must have a vowel sound added to it if a person is to say it loud enough for anyone to hear it. The true sound of a consonant is not in reality an actual sound but a position of the speech organs. The five vowels are *a, e, i, o, u*. The two semivowels are *y* and *w*. All the other letters are considered consonants.

Almost all the letters can represent more than one sound or no sound at all. The sound of *d* is different in *down* than it is in *soldier*. In addition, almost all sounds can be represented by a variety of phonograms. The sound *aw* as found in *straw* would be written as *au* in *Paul*. The same sound *aw* would be written as *a* in *all* and *o* in *olive*. The *o* in *olive* may be stretching the pronunciation somewhat, but most people would be unable to distinguish a difference. In spite of all these seeming inconsistencies and irregularities, most phonograms have a phoneme which is more regularly signaled. The study of phonics is not as confusing and complicated as it might appear.

DIGRAPHS, BLENDS, AND DIPHTHONGS.

Sometimes two letters are used together to represent a single sound, such as the *ph* in *photoelectric*. Two successive letters representing a single sound are called a *digraph*. The sound *ea* in *bread* and *ch* in *chin* are examples of digraphs. When two successive letters form a sound yet the sound of each letter is maintained, such as *sl* in *slang*, we refer to this as a *blend*. If the blend occurs at the beginning of a word such as *bl* in *blue*, it is indicated as an *initial blend*. A *terminal blend* would be a blend at the end of a word, such as *sk* in *desk*. When a blend is composed of two vowels or semivowel combinations such as *oy* in *toy*, we refer to it as a *diphthong*.

Some of the more common digraphs representing a single sound are:

ch (ch)	*th* (breathed or surd)
ch (sh)	*th* (voiced or sonant)
ch (k)	*ck* (k)
ea (ea)	*ph* (f)

Some of the more common initial blends where both letters maintain their sounds are:

bl	*dr*	*pl*	*sm*	*scr*
br	*fl*	*pr*	*sn*	*spl*
cl	*fr*	*sc*	*sp*	*spr*
cr	*gl*	*sk*	*st*	*str*
dw	*gr*	*sl*	*sw*	*tr*

Terminal blend examples are as follows:

ct	*mp*	*rk*
ft	*nd*	*rp*
lb	*nk*	*rt*
lu	*nt*	*sk*
lf	*nb*	*sp*
lt	*nf*	*st*

There are only two diphthongs—blends made up of two vowels or semivowels—which are recognized as such by reading specialists. A few writers in reading will list more than two. The two diphthongs commonly accepted are *oi* and *ou*. Other sounds accepted as diphthongs by some reading experts are:

ai as in *rail*	*eu* as in *feud*
au as in *saucer*	*ew* as in *crew*
aw as in *crawl*	*ow* as in *bowl*

CONSONANT SOUNDS

The sounds usually associated with the consonants are:

b—bed	*k*—kite	*t*—time
c—car	*l*—lid	*v*—very
d—dad	*m*—mother	*w*—wig
f—fun	*n*—no	*x*—x-ray
g—gun	*p*—pan	*y*—yes
h—hat	*r*—run	*z*—zebra
j—jump	*s*—sad	

Secondary sounds of the consonants are:

> c—(s) as in *sent* (before *e, i,* or *y*)
> d—(j) as in *soldier*
> f—(v) as in *of*
> g—(j) as in *gem* (before *e, i,* or *y*)
>
> s—(z) as in *nose*
> s—(sh) as in *sugar*
> t—(sh) as in *education*
> x—(gs) as in *exit*
> x—(z) as in *xylophone*

VOWEL SOUNDS

All the vowels have more than one pronunciation. Generally, vowels are considered to have two main pronunciations which are distinguishable from one another, the long vowel and the short vowel. In reality, there are other vowel sounds but all of these other sounds are too difficult for the average person to distinguish from the usual short vowel sound. Therefore, for practical purpose, we merely consider the long vowel sound and the short vowel sound. The long vowel sound is the same as the alphabetic name of the letter.

> a—*ape*
> e—*event*
> i—*iodine*
> o—*over*
> u—*unique*

The short vowel sounds are:

> a—*apple*
> e—*elephant*
> i—*Indian*
> o—*olive*
> u—*umbrella*

In dictionaries, the correct vowel sound is indicated through diacritical markings. Some of these marks are:

(‐) Macron—an indicator of long vowels, as in *fāmous.*
(◡) Breve—an indicator of short vowels, as in *măntle.*
(⊥) Modified macron—an indicator of half long vowels, as in *ĕlect.*
(~) Tilde—an indicator of nasality, as in *seniõr.*
(^) Circumflex—an indicator of intonation, as in *ûrge.*

The sound of a particular vowel depends upon (1) the number of vowels in the word, (2) the position of the vowel in the word, and (3) the context of the material of which the vowel and word are a part. There are certain rules concerning vowels which teachers and children should know. These rules will help a person phonetically unlock many words. There is no similar list of rules concerning consonants because consonants are rather definite in nature and a memorization of the consonants is all that is needed to apply them in attacking a word. The basic principles concerning the sounds of vowels are as follows:

1. The first vowel in a monosyllabic word containing more than one vowel is a long vowel sound while all other vowels are silent. If the vowels in the monosyllabic word are separated by more than one consonant, then the first vowel has a short sound.
2. The vowel in a monosyllabic word containing one vowel has a short sound, unless the vowel is at the end of the word.
3. The vowel *e* at the end of a word is usually silent.
4. The vowel sound is long if it is at the end of a word or the end of a syllable.
5. When a vowel is followed by the consonant *r* in a monosyllabic word or a monosyllable, the pronunciation of the vowel is altered.

Auditory Perception and Reading

The English language is a phonetic language in which the visual symbols (graphemes) represent sounds (phonemes), and it is the sounds which in various sequential combinations form words. Bannatyne (1971) has developed a very comprehensive model, which he based on logic, definitions, and some research, to demonstrate the importance of an "auditory-vocal psycholinguistic approach" to the teaching of reading, writing, and language. He points out that the visual symbols never directly represent concepts or meanings except in ideographic or logographic language symbols, such as Chinese. In English, the printed word is only *associated* with the spoken word; *meaning* is the property of a spoken word, not the printed word. In a phonetic language, the following associative memory link occurs (Bannatyne, 1973):

Meaning   (concept or object)
↕
Spoken or Heard Word   (auditory-vocal phonemes)
↕
Printed or Written Word   (graphemes)

It is not possible to pass from meaning to graphemes except through auditory-vocal language because the visual symbols only represent *sounds*, not meaning. Meaning is given by translating the graphemes into phonemes. (See also Goodman, 1970 in Chapter 2 for a definition of reading from a psycholinguistic point of view).

Research on the use of visual perception training to improve reading ability has been largely negative or unproductive; the literature on auditory perception and reading has been much more recent than the research on visual perception, and it has aroused much interest. A point of view that has gained considerable acceptance is that visual disabilities may characterize the preschool and kindergarten level learning disabled child, but by the time the child is in second grade, other skills such as auditory perception and auditory-visual integration become more important. There is an element of truth to this statement, but the research results are not complete yet, and the concept itself requires further refinement. One of the problems has been that we have not been able to clearly and precisely delineate and identify, as pure traits, the various visual and auditory processes involved in reading. For example, Price (1973) points out that "poor auditory discrimination" may be an inadequate term to use in assessment and remediation because, although we have a definition for the term (the inability to differentiate between individual speech sounds), it also involves the ability to retain (memory) and to understand the meaning of the sounds (conceptual). In other words, the term *auditory discrimination* is much more complex than it appears at first glance. The research of Witkin (1969) supports this conclusion by pointing to a considerable interrelationship among auditory discrimination, synthesis, and span.

An interesting research study by Wallach, Wallach, Dozier, and Kaplan (1977) concludes that the troubles disadvantaged (poor) children in kindergarten frequently have in learning to read stem not from deficiencies in auditory discrimination, but from inadequate skills in phonemic analysis. Almost all of the 70 disadvantaged and 70 middle-class children in the study could readily hear single phonemic differences in words (*sat* and *cat*). However, almost all of the disadvantaged children (but none of the middle-class children) did very poorly on tasks involving the phonemic or sound analysis of spoken words, in test items such as "Can you hear *mm* when I say *shh?*" "Can you hear *mm* when I say *me?*" Wallach and Wallach (1976) have found that a tutorial program emphasizing training in phonemic analysis was highly successful in teaching poor children to read.

What does the research say concerning auditory perception? In terms of auditory discrimination ability and prediction of reading success, most studies show a high correlation between the two. These findings have been reported by such researchers as Harrington and Durrell (1955), Wepman (1964), Zigmond (1969), and Fox and Routh (1976). These studies were either used to predict success in learning to read, or to identify auditory perceptual skills in good readers. However, they failed to establish a cause-and-effect relationship between the two factors; they only demonstrated a correlative relationship indicating that the two exist side by side.

What is more interesting is that a number of studies suggest that auditory perceptual training in and of itself does not necessarily improve reading ability (Robinson, 1972; Feldman, Schmidt, & Deutsch, 1968b). However, Feldman (1968a) and Rosner (1973) did find an improvement in reading ability when auditory perceptual training was given *in conjunction with the material in reading.* In other words, auditory perceptual training given in an isolated fashion, separate from reading instruction, had some but not much influence on improving reading ability. It did, however, improve auditory perception. When auditory perceptual training and reading instruction were combined, there was a definite improvement in reading ability. Of additional interest are the findings of Morency (1968), who found that only three perceptual processes—auditory discrimination, memory span, and sequential recall—have a positive correlation to reading, writing, and spelling achievement. When inadequate development was found in more than one of these three areas, the likelihood of poor reading ability increased significantly. Morency found in her longitudinal study that significant relationships exist in the same children from first to sixth grade.

Wiig and Semel (1976) survey the literature concerning auditory language processing deficits observed in association with learning disabilities. They cite research indicating that learning disabled youngsters exhibit:

1. Auditory memory deficits.
2. Temporal sequencing deficits.
3. Auditory figure-ground problems.
4. Reauditorization deficits.
5. Auditory-visual integration deficits.
6. Limitations in symbolization, abstractions, and conceptualization.
7. Deficits in linguistic processing and in conceptual synthesis.
8. Deficits in cognitive and logical processing.

What shall we conclude from the research as to how and what we should teach concerning perceptual development? This is what we are telling our teachers:

a. We really don't have all the answers yet. We must continue to be observant of what works with our children, and we must be alert to *good* research, not shabbily-done research.

b. In the meanwhile with LD youngsters, integrate and interlace the teaching of reading skills with training in auditory-verbal skills. Do not teach auditory skills in isolation except, perhaps, at beginning readiness levels. Use appropriate cassette tape programs and earphones when available. Make your own programs.

c. There are very few children who are 7 or older who would benefit from visual perceptual or visual-motor training insofar as improving reading skills is concerned. Visual perceptual and visual-motor training might be helpful for 4, 5, and some 6 year olds who need to develop readiness skills. If your main purpose is to improve visual perceptual or visual-motor skills for their sake alone, or perhaps as an adjunct to developing writing skills, then use them for that purpose, but not for improvement in reading.

d. Do not waste time developing gross motor or fine motor skills for the purpose of improving reading ability. The time can be better spent in other ways. If your purpose is to improve motor skills so the children can play the active physical games of their peers, then motor development programs are appropriate for that goal. Beware of teaching isolated or splinter motor skills.

e. In the final analysis, the best approach to the improvement of reading skills is to *teach* reading skills. If you want to use a supplementary program and do not care to get involved in auditory-verbal perceptual programs, then use a good language program to improve communication skills.

Oakland and Williams (1971) list specific auditory areas that can aid in developing reading skills. They are (1) gross auditory comprehension; (2) gross discrimination of words; (3) fine discrimination of words; (4) discrimination of words in a sentence; (5) discrimination of accented words in a sentence; (6) auditory memory for related and unrelated syllables; (7) auditory closure of words partly heard; (8) discriminating the number of syllables heard within words; (9) discrimination of accented syllables within words; (10) recognition of specific letter sounds; (11) auditory blending or identification of sound blends; (12) recognition and discrimination of word endings; and (13) discrimination of the temporal order of sounds within words.

Auditory Perception Problems of Learning Disabled Readers

The auditory-perceptual process involves much more than just hearing. It also entails the cognitive abilities of listening, interpreting, comprehending, and responding to those stimuli which enter the perceptual field. To insure the occurrence of these cognitive functions, the sound-nerve impulses must be relayed to appropriate neural areas via the cranial nerve where decoding occurs. At this stage, perceptual skills of attention, discrimination, recall, scanning, sequencing, integration, and interpretation are employed to deal with the auditory input. Following adequate perceptual decoding, the conceptual processes of (a) association, (b) concept formation, and (c) planning and programming are used to encode and offer further insight into the meaning of the stimuli. According to Kaluger and Kaluger (1974), the auditory input, once successfully decoded and encoded, can be appropriately responded to by means of neural activation of cerebral expressive centers. This results in motor output in the form of muscle enactment, glandular secretions, speech, writing, or specific behavior.

Auditory Input

↓

Unscrambled and Organized

↓

Interpreted and Meaning Derived

↓

Response Programmed

↓

Motor or Verbal Output

The total auditory-perceptual process, therefore, involves the intricate interaction of the ears, the auditory nerves, the brain, and the motor nerves to make responses to auditory experiences meaningful. Auditory-perceptual problems arise when these components fail to operate as a complete, integrated system. Organic, environmental, or psychogenic factors can create dysfunctions.

A child with an auditory perceptual disorder does not necessarily have an impairment in hearing acuity. In terms of sensation, he is able to hear auditory stimuli. His hearing mechanism is intact; however, his ability to organize, interpret, and deal meaningfully with auditory stimuli may not be. As a result, auditory learning cannot take place as it should or may not occur at all. The child is unable to sort out and associate sounds with particular objects or experiences. He does not recognize or identify sounds. He may ignore or shut out disturbing sounds, or he may react somewhat impulsively to each sound, with a strong determination to seek it out and determine what it is. He will appear very distractible or hyperactive (Zigmond & Cicci, 1968). For example, this child may hear voices in the hallway outside his classroom door. He will run to the door immediately to investigate the sounds and their source before he can continue his work. He will probably do this with every sound he hears because he has not been able to store its meaning in his brain.

A less severe disorder in auditory processing is the inability to discriminate between sounds. The child may be able to distinguish the difference between a knock on the door and the ring of the telephone, but not between the ringing of a telephone and a door bell. He may also have trouble differentiating between similar sounding words like *but-bat-bit*, or between certain printed symbols such as *d* and *b*.

The inability to group the sequence of auditory events may result in poor auditory learning. Words are articulated as sequences of sounds, and difficulties in sequentializing auditory impressions are sometimes reflected in the misarrangement of words (*aminal, emeny*), of compound words (*sitterbaby, belldoor*), or of phrases (*What there are?*). Problems in auditory sequencing may be seen in an inability to learn the days of the week or the months of the year.

Probably one of the most fundamental aspects of auditory perception is *auditory memory*, the ability to remember or recall the sequence of auditory information. Auditory memory is usually checked by having a child recall a sequence of random digits which have been given on a regular interval. A comparison of the number of digits the child can recall with the number of digits other children his age can recall gives the evaluator, a measure of whether or not the child has a deficit in auditory memory. These children will have difficulty comprehending a list of commands or verbal directions. They are usually able to remember only one command at a time. As a result, they have difficulty completing tasks that require remembering a series of commands. For example, if you were to ask such a child to take out his arithmetic book, open to page 150, and do the first two rows of problems, he could remember to take out the right book but forget what he is supposed to do with it, or he could remember that he is to do two rows of problems but forget which book to take out.

Auditory comprehension is another aspect of auditory perception. It is the ability to associate meanings with particular sounds and spoken words. For example, a child may clearly recognize the sound of a siren (acuity). He may be able to hear the difference between a siren and a loud whistle (discrimination). But given both of these conditions, the child may still not be able to recognize that the siren means he should watch out for a speeding ambulance or police car. It is this latter case that points to a deficit in auditory association.

A child with a problem in *auditory closure* will find it difficult to reproduce a whole word correctly when certain sounds have been left out. Auditory closure is closely related to sound blending, phonics, and word attack skills in general. This type of child has difficulty blending sounds together to form whole words (Kroth, 1971).

All of the auditory-perceptual skills mentioned previously are necessary in the development of the reading process. Johnson and Myklebust (1967) maintain that the study of children with dyslexia provides strong evidence of the relationship of auditory processes to reading.

Context of Phonics

General Aims and Outcomes

The desired outcome of the phonics instruction in the elementary school is to develop the habit of using phonics as a means of unlocking new words. The outcome is not to have the child memorize rules and sounds but rather to have a working knowledge of rules and sounds so that he may be able to apply them in a meaningful manner. The implication is that the child must have practice in working with phonics and direction in unlocking new words. New words must be attacked with a conscious awareness of the part rules and sounds play in reading them. Therefore, many reading specialists advise teachers not to teach rules as such to children, but rather to have the children draw their own generalizations and develop their own rules as they gain insights from their experiences in using phonics to unlock words. There is no question but that better learning takes place through this type of an approach.

Every child graduating from elementary school should know the common phonograms and their phonemes. In addition, the child should be able to identify not only the common sounds of the phonograms, but also should be able to indicate their secondary or unusual pronunciations. He should be familiar with the common blends and, what is more important, he should be able to do blending. The difficulties that some radio and television announcers experience when they try to say unfamiliar names or the names of foreign leaders such as Tshombe would not arise if they had learned how to properly blend letters. The child should have the habit of using the following steps when confronted with a new word:

1. He should first try the usual pronunciation of the graphic symbols. If the word is still unknown, he should then—
2. Look at the context of the material for a clue as to the correct pronunciation of the word. If the word is still unknown, he should finally—
3. Try all the secondary pronunciations of the graphic symbols.

Sequence of Phonic Development

The first area of development in phonics is to teach the child to hear, identify, and discriminate the different sounds of language. A child needs to become aware of the fact that there are different sounds and sound patterns. Every child should be able to distinguish the sound of a *b* from the sound of a *p*. Unfortunately, this is one area of readiness preparation for reading which does not receive the attention it deserves. *Auditory discrimination* is essential to good beginning reading. Many reading deficiencies can be eliminated by making certain that the child hears the sounds appropriately. The emphasis at this point is on discriminating language sounds, not on associating the sounds with printed symbols.

Once auditory discrimination of language sounds has been developed, the next step is to present a higher level of *auditory training* which develops auditory discrimination capable of detecting *rhyming sounds* and, later, *beginning sounds*. The child should learn to rhyme *rose* with *nose*, *hat* with *sat*, *tree* and *three* and other rhyming sounds. Once this is accomplished, the child needs to be taught how to detect beginning sounds in words. He should eventually be able to pick out words that have the same sound as a given word. For example, once a child has had auditory training in beginning sounds, he should be able to pick out the word *king* from the words *sing*, *ding*, and *king*, as being the word that begins with the same sound as the word *kind*. Once the auditory training has arrived at this level of auditority discrimination, the child is ready to learn how to associate the sounds with letter symbols.

The next step in phonic development is the use of *consonant substitution* in learning to attack new words. It involves the substitution of a consonant in a familiar word to get a new word. In the word family of *king*, *ring*, and *sing*, note how the first letter, a consonant, is changed to get a new word. The phonograms *th* and *br* could also have been used in this word family to get the words *thing* and *bring*. A child can make effective use of consonant substitution in attacking new words if he can recognize any part of the new word and add the appropriate consonant sound to the part which he knows.

Vowel substitution is a logical next step in the sequence of phonic development. It is the changing of a word through the substitution of another vowel in a word. It comes after consonant substitution because it is a little more complex. There are vowel principles which must be recognized, whereas consonant sounds and phonograms are rather cut and dried. The word *cat* is changed to *cut* by substituting a *u* for an *a*. A sequence for the development of phonetic principles should be followed. First, the child is taught that the vowels have more than one sound. This principle involves a knowledge of long vowels, short vowels, their identification, and markings. The second step is to teach the concept that some letters are silent in some words. Mastery of this principle is followed by a recognition that the number of vowels and the position of a vowel in the word helps to determine the pronunciation. The last step in this sequence is to teach how accents can affect vowel sounds. The four steps in the sequence for the development of phonetic principles need not all be taught as part of vowel substitution; in fact, they should not be thought of as being exclusive to vowel substitution. However, they do have a related connection which must be recognized by the teacher.

Further development in phonics includes the teaching of digraphs, blending, and diphthongs, in that order. To accomplish this, the teacher makes use of lists of these phonograms, teaching so many at a time, accompanied by the appropriate procedure and teaching aids.

The sequence of phonic development may be summarized as follows:

1. Auditory training: Discrimination of language sounds.
2. Auditory training: Rhyming sounds.
3. Auditory training: Beginning sounds.
4. Associating sounds with letter symbols.
5. Consonant substitution.
6. Vowel substitution.
7. Digraphs.
8. Blending.
9. Diphthongs.

Consonants and vowels together are an integral part of the learning process where information about these phonemes are received, organized, stored, and retrieved. The Shoreline School District #412 of Washington has published a *Phonics Handbook* (1970) that is very much involved with auditory and visual discrimination in the learning process. Their process, in a nutshell, is as follows:

1. Auditory Training—Learning to hear.
    a. Identification—Recognition of a sound.
    b. Stimulation—Repetition of a sound.
    c. Discrimination—Selection of a sound.
2. Visual Training—Learning to see.
    a. Identification—Recognition of a printed symbol.
    b. Stimulation—Repetition of a printed symbol.
    c. Discrimination—Selection of a printed symbol.
3. Visual-Auditory Training—Learning to associate.
    a. Identification—Recognize that each sound is represented by a printed symbol.
    b. Stimulation—Repetition of a sound and its corresponding printed symbol.
    c. Discrimination—Selection of a sound and its printed symbol.
4. Functional Analysis—Learning to think.
    a. Analysis—Analyzing unknown words to find familiar phonetic elements.
    b. Synthesis—Combining known phonetic elements to read unfamiliar words.
    c. Substitution—Substituting a known phonetic element for another element.
    d. Context Cues—Using phonetic elements and sentence meaning to read an unknown word.
5. Combination of Word Recognition Skills—Using phonetic cues with any or all other acquired word recognition skills to read an unknown word.

How Phonics Is Taught

Phonics is integrated into the material of most basal reader programs in such a way that a gradual introduction to phonics can be attained by following the sequence of phonic development just presented in the previous section. The teacher's manual will suggest techniques, approaches, and aids for teaching phonics, but the teacher should have at least the minimal knowledge of phonics presented earlier in this chapter. Armed with the teacher's manual and a basic knowledge of phonics, the beginning teacher is ready to introduce her children to the use of phonics in unlocking new words in reading.

The teacher generally waits until the sound to be learned has appeared in several sight words. A *sight word* is a word that the child has learned to read and can recognize at sight. She then follows four steps in teaching the phonic sound: (1) review, (2) generalize, (3) visualize, and (4) entrench. The *review* step is a re-examination of all of the sight words which the child has learned which contain the sound element the teacher wishes to present. The children work with these words seeking to identify the common sounds (phonemes) and letters (graphemes) contained in them. In this way, they *generalize* and draw out on their own the common sounds and words. The teacher is now ready to strengthen this generalization by having the children *visualize* the grapheme—the letter or combination of letters— and the key sound which it represents. *Entrenchment* of the sound and letter is obtained by the use of exercises and practice given the child which force him to use the phonetic generalization just formed.

By way of illustration, let us assume that a class of first graders has come across the words *Daddy, down,* and *day* in their basal reader and the teacher wants to teach the sound of *d.* She could apply the four steps in the teaching of new phonics by following the ensuing procedure.

Review: The teacher prints the words containing the sound element on the chalkboard and has the children identify the words. She could then ask them to mention other words which they know which begin with the same sound. She writes the contributed words on the chalkboard as they are given.

Generalize: The teacher then asks the children to identify how all of these words are alike. When the children have pointed out that the words all start with the letter *d,* she asks if anyone can tell her what sound the letter *d* stands for. After a child has indicated what the sound is, she points to the letter *d* in each word, makes the sound, and says the word. The teacher immediately moves to the next step.

Visualize: The teacher now presents a cue card on which a *d* is printed along with a key word beginning with the letter *d* and a picture of an object whose name begins with that letter. In this case, the word and picture could be *dog.* Some basal readers have accompanying cue cards. In addition, many commerical companies have sets of cue cards available. When the cue card is presented, the teacher identifies the letter, the key word, and the sound. She tells them that if they ever forget the sound of *d,* they should remember the card with the picture of the dog and begin to say the word *dog.* If they will stop as soon as they start to say the word, they will have the sound of *d.* This approach gives the children a point of reference. She then explains how to make the sound, and she has the children watch her make the sound. Then the entire class softly says the sound.

Entrench: The teacher now provides some follow-up drill to entrench the sound, the symbol and the key word, and the picture.

Table 11–1 presents the frequency rank order of letters and consonant clusters in initial and final positions in words. This ranking may not necessarily indicate the sequence in which the letters should be taught, but it does give an indication of the importance of each letter or letter combination.

TABLE 11–1. Rank orders (frequency) of letters and consonant clusters in word-initial and word-final positions.

Rank	Letters	Initial	Final
1	E	TH	N
2	T	H	S
3	A	W	R
4	O	T	D
5	I	B	T
6	N	M	F
7	S	S	ND
8	R	C	NG
9	H	F	L
10	L	D	M
11	D	R	NT
12	C	L	LL
13	U	P	ST
14	M	N	TH
15	F	WH	RS
16	P	PR	W
17	G	G	LD
18	W	St	NS
19	Y	SH	CH
20	B	FR	SS
21	V	V	P
22	K	CH	C
23	X	J	TS
24	J	TR	GHT
25	Q	GR	RD
26	Z	PL	CK
27		BR	RT
28		CL	NTS
29		SK	CT
30		K	WN

Source: Zettersten, A. A statistical study of the graphic system of present-day American English. Lund, Sweden: Studentlitteratur, 1969. In Levin, E. J. and Gibson, H. *The psychology of reading,* Cambridge, Mass.: The MIT Press, 1975. Reprinted by permission of the publisher.

FAMILY SOUND APPROACH VERSUS LETTER SOUND APPROACH. Kottmeyer (1960) points out that there are only two major approaches to the teaching of phonics: The family sound method and the letter sound method. The *family sound approach* makes use of a word family. A *word family* is a group of words containing the same phonic element, such as *king, thing, ring, sing, bring.* The most commonly used variation of the word family approach to teaching phonics is the consonant substitution approach. Under the latter procedure, the child learns to substitute a consonant sound in a word which he already knows in order to make a new word. The child has the word *take* in his sight vocabulary. The teacher guides him into substituting the *m* sound for the *t*, and the child recognizes the word *make* which is already part of his understanding vocabulary. Without too much difficulty, the child can come to transfer the word *make* to his sight vocabulary. Under this approach, it is felt by teachers that both meaning and application contribute to the learning process.

The *letter sound approach* seeks to teach the sound of the letters before the sounds are applied to attack any word. This is the approach that many lay people feel is logical in teaching a child to read. "It makes sense that a child has to know his alphabet and the sounds of the letters before he can begin to use them to figure out how to say a word," they reason. A number of these same people feel that learning the alphabet letter sounds is the same as learning phonics. This belief is based on a lack of knowledge concerning the true nature of phonics. The learning of isolated letter sounds is not too widely accepted by present-day educators, except for use with some special types of remedial readers. Educators tend to set aside the letter sound approach because they feel it is somewhat devoid of meaning to a child, especially as the child quickly comes to realize that one does not always pronounce the letter the same way in different words. It is also believed by many reading experts that letter phonics leads to distortion and confusion. In a classroom, the teacher may be distorting a sound when she has to say it loudly enough for all of the children to hear it. For example, if you will try to say the sound of the letter *b* loudly enough so that a person the length of a classroom away from you can hear it, you will find that you have to add the sound *uh* to the *b* to make it heard. Children will pick up the distorted sound, and when they try to unlock the word *bat*, the erroneous sound impression which they have will make them orally read the word as *buhat*.

It has been previously pointed out that the sound of a vowel is determined by the number of vowels in the word, the position of the vowel, and the context of the reading material. Letter phonics alone cannot cope with these situations. Try to pronounce the word *lead*, for instance. Is it *lead* as "lead us not into temptation" or is it *lead* as in lead sinkers used on fishing lines? You may have begun to say the word according to the rule which states that when two vowels are together, the second vowel is silent while the first vowel says its name. You would then have the word *lead* as in "lead us not into temptation." The *a* is not heard and the first vowel, the *e*, sounds as its alphabet name. Even when you use this rule, you are actually using something more than letter phonics as the determiner of the sound. Letter phonics alone would not be helpful. You are considering both the number of vowels involved, in this case two vowels, and their position within the word, *e* before *a*. Yet, even considering the letter sound, the number of vowels involved, and the position of the vowels, you are still not certain how to pronounce the word *lead* unless you have a context to assist you.

Kottmeyer (1960) maintains that the consonant substitution technique of teaching phonics appears to be a logical approach; however, he feels that it is a highly impractical procedure to use with most children. Consonant substitution teaches a child to unlock new words by thinking of a word family to which the new word belongs and substituting the appropriate consonant sound. In the first place, he states, a child must have very good visual imagery in order to conjure or "think up" a sight word which he knows is similar to the word he is trying to unlock. At the same time, the child must also visualize the new beginning sound, the consonant sound. Then, he must blend this new beginning sound with the "word family" part of the new word he is trying to figure out. Kottmeyer feels that this word attack approach is next to impossible for most children because they do not have the visual imagery to perform this task. In addition to this difficulty, a poor reader has a limited number of sight words in the first place. Consonant substitution is highly dependent upon the child's having a large sight vocabulary, and the poor reader is doubly handicapped.

On the other hand, Kottmeyer believes that single letter phonics has many virtues. He claims that the criticism directed against the use of single letter phonics is not an indictment against the approach but rather against malpractices in the use of the method. He points out that single letter sounds can be accurately taught without the distortions usually found if the proper key words are used. Furthermore, single letter phonics can avoid the problems which arise if word families are learned and the student then finds a word which appears to be part of a word family but is cut differently by syllabic division. For example, *at* is a word family of which *mat* is a member. Although *at* appears in *mater*, *mater* is not a member of the *at* family because *mater* has a syllabic division which makes it *ma-ter*.

It must be pointed out that Kottmeyer basically stresses the use of single letter phonics with remedial readers although his criticism of the use of consonant substitution and word families seems general in application. If one were to consider only remedial readers and their problems, it is not difficult to recognize the fact that some remedial readers, especially those with constitutional cerebral problems, have poor visual imagery and so rely rather heavily on phonics which is more auditory in nature. For these and similar children, the teaching of single letter phonics early in their reading programs could serve as a preventative measure.

LINGUISTICS. The analysis of the speech-sounds of a language so as to develop a systematic, scientific description of that language is known as *linguistics*. The science of linguistics is in its infancy in that the identification and structuring process is still in a developmental stage. As a result, linguists are not yet in common agreement on definitions, interpretations, and principles. You, therefore, should keep in mind that the information presented here about linguistics is what some—perhaps a majority, but not all—linguists believe. Also, this presentation tends to be over-generalized.

The linguists believe that your language is made up of phonemes. A *phoneme* is a unit of sound in spoken language. These phonemes are expressed in writing by graphemes. A *grapheme* is one or more letters of the alphabet. Combinations of graphemes or phonemes which transmit meaning are called *morphemes*. The morpheme may or may not be a word. The key to a morpheme is that it gives meaning, such as the *s* in *cats*. Although there is some disagreement among linguists as to the number of phonemes in the English language, they generally place the number somewhere in the forties, with 44 being close to the central tendency. Significantly, a phoneme may be represented by one or more graphemes. Likewise, each grapheme may signify one or more phonemes. The symbol sound relationship in English is not always predictable. The phoneme *o* can be represented by the grapheme *o* and the grapheme *ough*, as in *dough*. In turn, the grapheme *ough* can stand for the phoneme *uff* as in *tough* or *ow* as in *trough*.

The linguists have divided word symbols into predictable sounds and unpredictable sounds, according to their spelling and the sound symbol relationship. The sound of *d* in *dent* is a predictable sound and can be taught. The sound of *d* in *soldier* is unpredictable and must be recognized as such. The predictable sounds are taught as patterns, whereas the unpredictable sounds are taught as being exceptions to the rule. The linguists claim that if phoneme-grapheme relationships are taught, these patterns can be applied to a large number of predictable words. As a result, this approach would eliminate the necessity of memorizing a large number of word forms in learning to read.

Some linguists raise a question as to the advisability of teaching children to read by the use of present-day basal reading textbooks. These linguists feel that many of these textbooks reveal little understanding of the mechanics of reading and the mechanics of language. The objection seems to be directed at teaching "reading for meaning" without the child first recognizing the spoken linguistic forms which the word shapes symbolize. They allege that the child of six comes to school knowing a great number of words and using most of the kinds of sentences adults use. If the reading material presented to the child were to consist of words which were orally familiar to the child, he would have no difficulty with the meaning of these words since the meaning of concepts and ideas from words is basically a state of mentation. Therefore, the main task in teaching reading is not the derivation of meaning, but rather, the translation of graphemes to phonemes. This is proceeded by first teaching the sounds and the letters these sounds represent.

A review of the literature on linguistics seems to have the following implications for the reading program: (1) Children should first be taught the phonemes and their corresponding grapheme. (2) The vocabularies of beginning readers should be controlled so as to present only two to three letter monosyllabic predictable words; (3) Configuration cues should be minimized, and according to some linguists, configuration cues should be eliminated; and (4) Picture clues should be eliminated since they tend to distract from the main objective of learning to translate graphemes into phonemes.

Assessment of Auditory-Verbal Deficits

Informal Assessment

Diagnosis of auditory-perceptual deficits that are related to reading should be done both informally and formally. Informal behavioral observations of a child in different situations may give clues to his auditory-verbal abilities. The way the child interacts with his playmates can be a very valuable diagnostic tool. Does he seem to understand communication from his peers? You may find he is not able to get along with others as the result of misunderstandings.

Observation of the child preparing for a task in class can also be an indicator of auditory difficulty. Watch for the child who seems to be straining to listen, or the one who asks for, or waits for, a repetition of a verbal request before responding. This child may react tentatively, then wait for the examiner's reaction to his response, as if trying to judge whether he understood correctly.

By listening to the child read orally, consonant and/or vowel errors can be discovered. His level of word attack can be determined by the words he fails to try to pronounce or those he can only say in part. In paragraph reading, note these possible problems: mispronunciation: *bet* for *bit*; refusal: will not attempt the word; or substitution: *cat* for *kitten*. Listen for the omission of initial, medial, or final sounds. Analyze his speech. Does he say *bof* for *both*, *Shears Roebuck* for *Sears Roebuck*, or *Rice Kripsies* for *Rice Krispies*? What kind of auditory problems does he reveal in spelling? Does he have difficulty learning to associate sounds with the appropriate letter symbol? Table 11–2 presents a variety of auditory-perceptual skills, lists deficits that can be observed in the classroom, and shows how those skills are related to reading.

TABLE 11-2. Auditory perception and reading.

Definition	Behavior	Related to reading
1. *Auditory Acuity*—relates to the sense organ, the ear; the sharpness of one's hearing as tested by audiometer or speech threshold test.	If acuity is very low, no response when spoken to: may appear disinterested and quiet; may ask to repeat; may strain to hear; may be a monotone; sounds may be over-amplified instead of too low.	Vocabulary develops from speaking to hearing to reading, so reading is affected if the child does not hear properly; child needs visual approach to reading, placement in a hearing-oriented class if the handicap is severe.
2. *Auditory Awareness*—the recognition that certain sounds are being made in one's environment.	May not respond appropriately to sounds such as bell, commands; does not enjoy sound toys; may be quiet rather than talkative.	To read one must consciously listen for and be aware of sounds in words; may substitute words in oral reading; reads better silently than orally; for words to have meaning, must be aware of auditory environment.
3. *Auditory Focus or Attending*—refers to one's ability to attend (concentrate) on a sound.	Never gets "ready" and "set" to follow a task; appears not to listen; may be distractible; can't focus in on a sound or word long enough to pick it up.	In reading, to comprehend one must have a mind-set and focus on it; for example, vocabulary, memory, word attack skills, forming judgments; technique: eliminate child's awareness of noise through earphones, Swedish wool.
4. *Auditory Figure-Ground*—giving attention to the central sound stimulus in one's environment.	Is distractible because can't blot out sounds in environment that aren't related to the task at hand; may concentrate well on visual tasks; may overreact to extraneous sounds.	In reading effectively, one must be able to block out noises and concentrate on the way a visual symbol would sound when spoken; technique: eliminate auditory distractions when working on reading skills.
5. *Auditory Memory*—a decoding process in the brain whereby all sound information heard is scanned and retrieved (both long and short term memory); refers to how much auditory stimuli one can retain and retrieve for use.	Frustrated; can understand what he hears, but can't remember it; can follow only single command or simple instructions; may not complete assignments; can't remember directions, story sequence, lists of words, numbers, letter sounds.	In reading, doesn't have memory for handling skills necessary for phonetic analysis so best to use whole word approach (develop sight vocabulary first, but teach skills going from whole words to parts); must remember sound sequence in words and word sequence in sentences to comprehend and use words effectively; must recall to relate what is read for organizing, comparing, forming judgments.

322

TABLE 11-2. Auditory perception and reading. (cont.)

Definition	Behavior	Related to reading
6. *Auditory Sequentialization*—the process of putting what has been heard in the proper sequence or order.	Can't structure, so is confused; can't repeat letters, etc., in order heard, so may mispronounce words of more than one syllable; shows difficulty listening; because he can't retain sequence of sounds, may transpose letters in writing or omit/distort syllables in reading, talking, and spelling.	To read, one must hold a pattern of sounds within a word, a series of words within a sentence or series of ideas within a story . . . one must be aware of the number and order of sounds in a word. This is necessary for word attack skills (blending, long words.)
7. *Auditory Discrimination*—differentiating between sounds that are heard so that each sound can be identified.	If a child can't differentiate, he may become discouraged and frustrated. He can't tell differences in letter sounds (*b*, *d*), environmental sounds (may respond inappropriately), is confused and not completely in touch with reality at times; understands words like *sit* and *sat* in context, but can't perceive differences between them in isolation; can't rhyme; may react to gross but not be able to distinguish between fine differences in sounds; misspells and misreads (may hear *watch* for *wash*).	Tests have shown a positive correlation between auditory discrimination ability and success in learning to read; for example, to read one must distinguish letter sounds, especially short vowel sounds; techniques: child has difficulty learning with phonetic approach; determine *his* specific area of difficulty and teach that (ex.: inability to hear similarities and differences in words, to distinguish similar parts of words, to dissect word wholes into syllables, to blend).
8. *Auditory Sound-Symbol Relationship*— the ability to relate a sound heard to its source and the symbol it represents, thus giving it meaning.	Child may appear hard of hearing or deaf; may become lethargic and ignore sounds; responds inconsistently or inappropriately to sounds because he doesn't associate sounds to experience (ex.: doesn't relate fire alarm to danger, so doesn't respond); in reading shows difficulty relating sounds of vowels to vowel letters; doesn't hear rhyming parts of words until first sees them in printed symbols; in spelling and writing may add, omit, or substitute words and letters.	Reading is a process of relating what has been spoken (sounds heard) to visual symbols; therefore, he can't read if he has trouble here; technique: provide meaningful situations in which child consciously relates an auditory symbol to a visual symbol to the thing, experience or object it represents; this gives meaning to words.

323

TABLE 11–2. Auditory perception and reading. (cont.)

Definition	Behavior	Related to reading
9. *Auditory Integration or Closure*—a complex brain function in which total words are perceived as word parts combined—involves synthesizing sounds into parts (syllables) as well as pulling parts together to form complete words. Involves synthesizing words into sentences and sentences into larger units.	Child is confused and frustrated because he only hears sounds, not words—or words, not sentences; his spoken language may be good, but he can't break words into syllables or make words from individual sounds (although he knows letter names and sounds); can't blend.	Interferes with development of syllabication skills; use whole word approach to build sight vocabulary, then proceed with systematic word attack skills, but go from whole words to parts; manipulating letters shows how letters go together to form words.
10. *Auditory Comprehension*—the ability to make sense of what one hears.	Child hears, but doesn't understand; gestures and pantomimes; may be creative in visual tasks; is a follower because doesn't understand enough to challenge or react to ideas; hesitates, lacks self-confidence, may appear dazed; may withdraw or may become a "troublemaker" if not helped.	Reading suffers because he doesn't have spoken language background against which to understand visual symbols necessary for reading. Comprehension can be related to any of the areas in this paper. Determine point of breakdown and remediate it; comprehension will improve.
11. *Other Aspects*	I. Behavior that might be expected with any of these problems: (1) discouragement, frustration (2) poor self-esteem (3) indifference (4) hyperactivity or sluggishness (5) unaware of errors made (6) difficulty listening (7) needs periods of quiet (8) fluctuation in memory and learning rate	

324

TABLE 11–2. Auditory perception and reading. *(cont.)*

Definition	Behavior	Related to reading
11. *Other Aspects (Cont.)*	II. Auditory Expression	
	(1) can't describe adequately	
	(2) poor choice and use of words	
	(3) frustration in speaking before groups, in conversation, and in discussion	
	(4) excellence/rapidity in silent reading and comprehension but can't use correct auditory symbols	
	(5) can't recall exact words read	
	III. The use of a technique depends on the nature of the deficit. The principle is to remediate weakness while stressing strengths.	

325

Formal Assessment

A number of formal tests are available for assessing auditory-verbal deficits. Which one you should use depends on what skills you want to assess, based on the reading skills required for the task you are working on, and on how much information the test gives you beyond the norm- or criterion-reference scores. You should do a task analysis and/or error analysis of the test items. What did the child miss? Is there a pattern of similarity in the errors? What do the errors mean in terms of *reading?*

Some formal tests that might be used follow:

1. Botel Phonics Test. Tests seven areas: Knowledge of beginning consonant sounds; knowledge of five consonant digraphs; rhyming words; knowledge of long and short vowel sounds; vowel digraphs and vowel diphthongs; and knowledge of number of syllables and accents.

2. Botel Word Recognition Test (or similar word recognition test). Can be used to analyze the types of errors a student makes in saying words.

3. San Diego Assessment Test. A graded word list formed by taking words from basal readers and the Thorndike Word List. Can determine a reading level and help detect error in word analysis.

4. Roswell-Chall Reading Test. A practical tool for determining a child's phonic needs. Isolates the sounds or blends needing help, provides a checklist to make certain each element is taught, and guides the instructor in making a diagnosis and prescribing remediation.

5. Gates-McKillop Reading Diagnostic Test. Covers the testing of oral reading, words and their parts, recognizing visual forms of letters, auditory blending, and some supplementary tests.

6. The Nonsense Word Phonics Test. From the Shoreline, Washington School District. Provides nonsense words where true phonetic pronunciations are given because of learned concepts and because of regular words that were learned.

7. Oliphant Auditory Discrimination Memory Test. Screens for auditory discrimination ability by having the teacher say two similar words and having the pupil match a third word to one of the others.

8. Oliphant Auditory Synthesizing Test. Determines ability to listen to the separate phonemes of a spoken word, remember and blend these phonemes in correct sequence. The teacher may pronounce separate sounds and the child chooses the word to make, or she pronounces the separate phonemes and gives the child a choice of three words from which he is to choose the correctly synthesized word.

9. Goldman-Fristoe-Woodcock Auditory Skills Test Battery. Made up of five tests: (a) selective attention, (b) discrimination of speech sound, (c) discrimination of speech-sound problems, (d) a three-part memory test, and (e) a graph of sound-symbol tests.

10. Diagnostic Reading Scales by Spache. Supplementary tests of phonic knowledge, blending, initial consonant substitution and auditory discrimination. Good tests if error analysis is used.

11. Durrell Analysis of Reading Difficulty. Battery of tests contains subtests on word recognition and word analysis plus a number of brief supplementary tests on letters, letter sounds, visual memory, spelling, and handwriting.

Informal error analysis of reading patterns or subjective tests can serve as good assessment techniques if the teacher is alert to what she should be looking for. Messing (1969) indicates that you should look for auditory-verbal weaknesses when the child has (a) no recall; (b) incomplete recall; (c) reversal, omissions or transpositions of sound or syllables in words; (d) irrelevant responses; (e) an answer before instructions are completed; (e) difficulty hearing central thoughts when there is noise present (figure-ground problems); (f) evasive speech; or (g) retrieval difficulties.

TABLE 11–3. Sound-symbol analysis.

NAME _____ DATE _____

SCHOOL _____ GRADE _____ CA _____

I. Say the name of these letters:

   B, A, I, S, C, D, E, F, P, T, M, L, R, Z, J, U, H, G, W, X, Q, K, V, Y, N, O

   r, o, n, l, m, y, t, v, k, p, z, e, a, j, u, s, h, b, c, g, w, d, f, x, q, e

II. Say the sounds made by these letters:

   1. r   m   l   n   v   z   s   f
   2. y   t   k   p   j   h   b   c   g   w   d
   3. sh   ch   th   wh   ng
   4. Say the short vowel sounds for e   i   o   u   a
   5. Say the long vowel sounds for e   i   o   a   u

III. Here are some nonsense words. They really are not words at all, but I'd like to see if you can read them.

   fis   wab   tam   jav
   lote   hin   nobe   nibs
   vin   sut   muts   sult

IV. Say these words: (consonant blends)

   clib   drom   brem   whon   ston
   shup   thun   fris   plup   twir
   grut   smum   flur   swuk   chun

V. Say these prefixes:
   re   in   con   de   dis   com   un   ex   pro   pre   en

VI. Say these suffixes:

   s   ed   ing   y   ly   ty   er   est   tion   ance   al
   ant   ful   ous   able   ent   ness   ment   ive   less

VII. Say these words (compound words/syllabication)

   manletter   afternoonly   betterflynet
   fullenter   probunly   worletterly
   unmanish   bansinglet   aplingstock
   permensub   discandy   contransfor
   repanly   singoptive   basketmeet
   runletter   subentor   truckous

We frequently use the following list of auditory-perceptual skills related to reading as a checklist against tasks that children can or cannot perform.

1. Has learned how to listen attentively.
2. Can repeat sounds, words, sentences.

3. Can identify initial, medial, and final sounds.
4. Can identify the source of sounds.
5. Can identify characteristic sounds.
6. Can tell the initial sounds.
7. Can identify sound and its symbol.
8. Can repeat sounds without visual clues.
9. Can follow directions without visual clues.
10. Can identify sounds, words, directions from recordings.
11. Can identify specific things from music.
12. Can form and identify words that rhyme.
13. Can identify pictures of objects that rhyme (no auditory clues).
14. Has ear sensitivity in auditory closure of words.
15. Has foreground/background stabilization (specific sounds among others; figure-ground ability).
16. Can write initial and final sounds of words that begin and end in consonants.
17. Can understand and use a simple, secure phonics system.

Table 11–3 provides a sound-symbol analysis test that we have used successfully as a screening device. It is aimed at detecting the skills that a child does not know. Teaching must make provisions for teaching those skills. The sections are somewhat hierarchial in nature. If a child knows only half of a section, then it is considered that he is at a transitional stage and with a little more help, preferably individualized help, he will make a break-through in using that level of phonetic skills. At times you will find a child who can say the single blends even though they have not learned (or overlearned) the short vowel sounds. We place more emphasis on being able to pronounce the nonsense word and are not too concerned about the short vowel rules. The child may have functional usage of the rules even though he is not aware of them. The short vowels should now be taught in conjunction with the nonsense words so the child can derive meaning from his proper application of the rules.

If a child is having difficulty with certain sounds, check to see if these may be high frequency sounds that require better hearing acuity from the child. A child with 10 to 15 decibel loss in hearing may not be able to hear the delicate soft sounds of some letters. Some sounds are simply mastered later by some children who are having a maturational lag in development of auditory awareness. Figure 11–1 presents the frequency (high or low intensity sounds in terms of softness or loudness of the different phonetic sounds). Table 11–4 presents the age of mastery of consonant sounds.

TABLE 11–4. Age of mastery of consonant sounds.

Ages 3–4	b, p, m, w, h
4–5	d, t, n, g, k, ng, y
5–6	f, v, z, s
6–7	sh, zh, l, th
7–8	z, s, r, wh, ch, j

Adapted from various sources. Found in Lambert, P. A comparison of pupil achievement in term and self-contained organizations. *Journal of Experimental Education*, 1965, 33, 217–224.

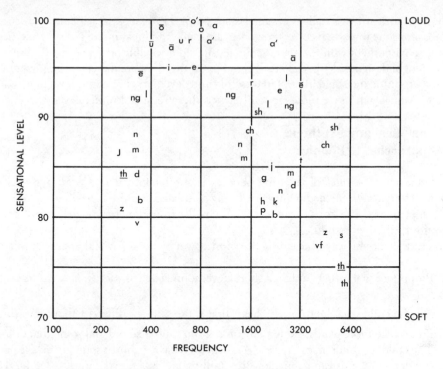

FIGURE 11–1. Position of consonants on frequency bands.

Source: Berry, M. F., & Eisenson, J. *Speech disorders: Principles and practices of therapy,* © 1956, p. 449. Reprinted by permission of Prentice-Hall, Inc.

Characteristics of Children Having Auditory Difficulties

1. The child looks strained and frowns in trying to hear.
2. Things are poorly retained, so directions must be repeated.
3. He confuses words which sound alike—

big—pig	farm—form
bad—bed	bed—bit
wash—watch	barn—born
ship—ship	

4. Phonetics are difficult and confusing.
5. He enunciates poorly or may have speech defects because he doesn't hear the sounds distinctly.

Strategies for Teaching Phonics

Learning disabled children can benefit from program organization and structure, practice, and consistency without distractibility. They need to know what is expected of them skill-wise, what and where the materials are, and what the lesson should be accomplishing.

They need to learn in small, sequential steps (with 95% success), with motivators and rewards along the way when correct responses are made and meaningful skills are acquired. A stable environment with few major changes should be established; a permanent seating assignment or designated "special area" could be arranged. More than anything, you need to show a genuine, personal interest in the child and develop a confidence level in which to operate. Things will move more smoothly when these remedial principles are practiced.

Analytical and Synthetic Approaches to Phonics

The *analytical method* of teaching phonics is similar to a whole word approach to reading. The *synthetic method* requires blending of isolated sounds. You will need to decide which approach is better for a particular child. It is also important for you to be comfortable using the method you choose.

An example of one way of teaching the short vowel by the analytical approach follows:

1. Pronounce words that contain a short vowel sound such as short *a*: *hat, cat, fat, rap, fan*.
2. Ask the child what he thinks he hears that is the same or different about the words.
3. Pronounce more words, some that contain the short *a* sound and some that do not. The child (or children) can raise a "Yes" card if it has the short *a* sound, or a "No" card if it doesn't. Cards can be made with a smiling face ☺ for *yes*, and ☹ for *no*. This provides an easy method of detecting which students know the sound and which do not.
4. Have the child pronounce words with the short *a* sound, adding to the list.
5. Print the words on the board and have the child discover what is the same about the words. The short *a* can be underlined or written in a different color to emphasize the sound. Pictures of objects that contain the short *a* sound can be found.
6. Write words under each picture, underlining the short *a* sound.
7. Have the child learn the letter *a*, both the upper and lower case forms.
8. Have the child use some of the words in sentences so that meaning is brought to the word.

An added step is to have the child draw objects out of a bag with his eyes closed (objects that contain the short *a* sound, for example) and let him guess what the objects are.

A synthetic phonics system is the Gillingham Method (1960). Visual, auditory, and kinesthetic processes are used. Eight steps are included in this method, the steps being called *linkages*. Children are only introduced to linguistic regular words at first. The linkages are:

1. The name of the letter is associated with the printed symbol; then the sound of the letter is associated with the symbol.
2. The teacher makes the letter and explains its form. The pupil traces it, copies it, and writes it from memory.
3. The phonogram is shown to the pupil and he names it.
4. The teacher says the phoneme, and the child writes it.

5. The child is shown the letter and asked to sound it. The teacher moves the child's hand to form the letter, and the child sounds it.
6. The teacher gives the name of the phonogram, and the pupil gives the sound.
7. The teacher makes the sound, and the pupil gives the name of the letter.
8. The teacher makes the sound, and the pupil writes the phonogram.

Phonetic Blending Techniques

According to Whaley (1975) there are two basic principles underlying the blending techniques. The first principle is that the child should develop gross discriminatory abilities and then work toward more complex, specific discriminatory tasks. Second, because the inability to blend is often due to an auditory dysfunction, it is helpful to use the remaining sensory modes to the greatest extent possible while building up the deficient skill.

When a child begins to learn to read, it is beneficial to avoid word attack skills that involve isolation of individual sounds. Do not begin phonetic sounding until the child displays immediate recall of letter-sound relationships. Teach the child that he should hang onto each sound as he sees it and slide it into the next sound.

Some reading experts believe the length of a word in syllables is of consequence in the initial teaching of reading. Groff (1975) states that the most suitable words with which the beginner learns to read are monosyllabic, as opposed to polysyllabic. One syllable words should be used to simplify reading as much as possible *(blue, shut, when, etc.)* While blending the sounds of polysyllabic words many children forget the initial sounds they have pronounced before they come to the end of the word.

The sounds of letters should be taught rather than their names, and students should learn the proper enunciation. The sound *b* should be introduced as the sound that comes at the end of *tub, tab,* and *cab.* Then the transfer to *bu-t, ba-t, bi-t* can be taught. This not only avoids the improper teaching of the sound, but also offers practice in blending sounds (Brooks, 1975).

Teaching should not be limited to each child's dominant modality because first, it may take too long to make an accurate determination, and second, because the average teacher untrained in this area may not be able to determine modality strength. Children with specific learning disabilities should be exposed to all approaches. By being exposed, children often inadvertently reveal the modality with which they feel most comfortable. The following materials can be used to strengthen all modalities: Sight reading cards, anagrams, games that make words, cornmeal letters, beaded letters, sandpaper letters, felt letters, and auditory discrimination games.

The DISTAR reading program uses a technique which has been found to be very helpful when beginning the teaching of blending. The teacher says "When I touch the letter, you say the sound and keep saying it right into the next letter I touch. This is a game, and one of the rules is that you can't take a breath until you run out of letters." As soon as the child has mastered this game, the next step is to eliminate the finger pointing and to ask the child to read through a word as if your finger were pointing. Additionally, the child must be taught that he should use this procedure to attack a word only when the word is unfamiliar to him. However when he does use it, he should use it consistently and in the method you have shown him—by "sliding" through the sound.

Analogies may be used to present a picture to the child of what he should do mentally and orally. It is helpful to draw an analogy between skating and blending and have the child pretend to skate around the room. Make some large letters and place them near each other on the floor. Demonstrate how to "skate" from one letter to the next while saying the letter-sound out loud. When the child practices this, tell him to be sure to make his voice glide in the same way that his feet glide. A similar technique is to have the child stretch a rubberband and sound through a word simultaneously.

Additional kinesthetic reinforcement is sometimes helpful. The following technique is an extension of a demonstration in a film produced by the California Association of Neurologically Handicapped Children, entitled "Why Billy Couldn't Learn" (Vista, Calif., 1968). Tap the child's arm beginning near his shoulder and moving towards his hand, once for each sound in a word, as you demonstrate how to stretch each letter sound orally. Then say the whole word, and simultaneously slide your hand all the way from the child's shoulder to his hand. Have him practice the technique on new words while you tap and slide your hand on his arm. Have him practice the entire exercise using his right hand to tap on his left arm, or vice versa.

Johnson and Myklebust (1967) offer two suggestions for helping children become aware of the parts of words. In one method the teacher says *ta-ble*; the child puts it together. A tape recorder may be implemented for supplementary work. A second technique aids the child in auditorially discriminating the number of sounds in a word, while simultaneously teaching underlying concepts of blending. The teacher says a word very slowly, making a mark on a paper for each sound. After the child can tell the number of sounds, the teacher repeats the word slowly, sound by sound *(s-t-o-p)* and has the child blend them.

The technique from the Hegge-Kirk-Kirk grapho-vocal method (1955) for blending is useful. When using this method, tell the child to form his mouth in preparation for saying the initial consonant of a syllable, but then to say the following vowel instead. Such a technique forces the child to think ahead and be prepared for the second sound, rather than concentrating solely on the first sound. This helps eliminate an undesirable, stuttering, letter-by-letter word attack.

Present a simple three-letter word to the child using scrabble squares or any movable letters. Above each letter, place felt squares or blocks of different colors. Say "This is the word *pat*. Let's pretend these squares (or blocks) also say *pat*." Slowly sound each letter while simultaneously moving the letters and the squares (or blocks) apart. Say *p-a-t*. Slowly move them together again while sounding *p-a-t*. Then say *pat*. "Now you do it." You may wish to begin with squares only and work up to inclusion of letters.

The Phonovisual Method

The Phonovisual Method was designed by Schoolfield and Timberlake (1960) for use as a supplement to the basal reading program. The originators of this method apparently felt that this material was needed to support the phonic program presented in basal readers and so designed it for parallel instruction. The main materials of instruction are a large Phonovisual Consonant Chart (Figure 11–2) and a large Phonovisual Vowel Chart (Figure 11–3). The consonant chart depicts 26 sounds, and the vowel chart illustrates 17 sounds, for a total of 43 sounds. In addition to the charts, there are game books, individual charts for children, a teacher's manual, and various other associated devices. Through these materials the child is taught to recognize the letter, the sound it signals, the position of the speech apparatus when the sound is produced, and is given a key word as a reference for remembering the sound.

The teaching of the sounds begins with the use of the consonant chart, which is approached by the teacher and the pupils as a game. Through the procedures outlined in the

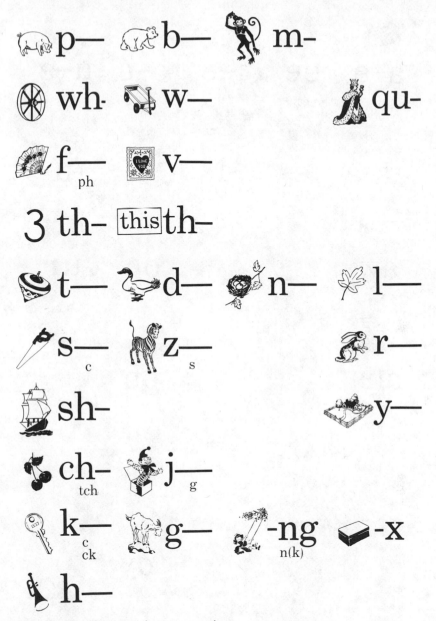

FIGURE 11–2. The Phonovisual consonant chart.

Courtesy of Phonovisual Products, Inc.

manual, the teacher teaches the child the first five sounds. The child says the sound, hears the sound said by the teacher, watches the teacher mouth the sound silently, and then writes the sound of the key picture.

The sequence begins by learning the initial consonant sounds, then proceeds to the medial and final consonants, and finally the vowels and blends.

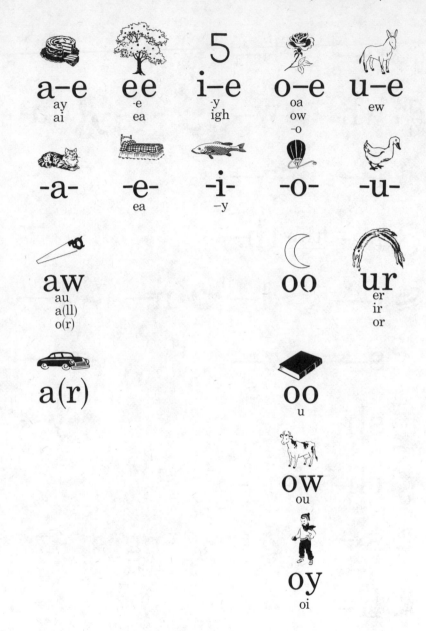

FIGURE 11–3. The Phonovisual vowel chart.

Courtesy of Phonovisual Products, Inc.

  The method employed makes use of several senses in the learning of the sounds. It entails auditory discrimination, writing tactile and kinesthetic senses, and visual discrimination. After the first five sounds have been taught, the rest of the sounds in the first column of the consonant chart are taught. Later the vowels are taught through the use of the vowel chart beginning with the double *e* sound.

The claim is made by the authors of the Phonovisual Method that the method (1) insures an adequate group of phonetics, (2) corrects minor speech difficulties, (3) aids in the elimination of reversals in reading, (4) improves spelling, and (5) gives the child confidence. In addition to being used as a supplement to basal reading programs, some educators, other than the authors of the Phonovisual Method, are suggesting that the approach is an ideal way of starting reading in kindergarten instead of waiting for a child to enter first grade. They claim that the Phonovisual Method is an adjusted program which can be used with children with a mental ability below that needed for the first-grade level of teaching. See Chapter 8 for further information.

Words in Color

Words in Color is a linguistic-phonetic system developed by Calef Gattegno, a British educator, in 1957 (1962). In this method each of the 20 vowels and 27 consonant sounds in English is represented by a color. For example, the *a* in *cat* and the *au* in *laugh* are printed in white on a black surface, while the *a* in *phrase* is a shade of blue. Brown indicates *p* sounds, violet denotes *t* sounds, and gray represents all the *f* sounds, such as *f* in *fun*, *ph* in *phone*, and *gh* in *tough*. Thus, words can be spelled phonetically in colors and written with the proper letters at the same time. The word *fat*, for instance, is color-coded with a gray *f*, a white *a*, and a violet *t*.

Initially, the children learn the short vowel sounds, such as the white *a*, the *e* in *end* (yellow) and the *i* in *ill* (red). Then they are introduced to consonant sounds, so that they can begin to spell words. Through a series of game-like exercises they soon discover for themselves how to read and write in a simple, natural way, much as they learned to talk. As their skill increases, they gradually learn to identify words in black and white and the use of color is discontinued.

After 14 weeks of instruction in the color system, most first-grade children are able to read at the second-grade level.

Success of the program seems to be based upon the principle that English, which is basically a nonphonetic language, can be made phonetic through the use of color to represent the various individual sounds of speech.

Phonetic Keys to Reading

The *Phonetic Keys to Reading* (Harris et al., 1967) attempts to eliminate the objectional portions of older teaching methods of phonics. The older methods stress many meaningless drills and rules. This newer method seeks to develop reading for meaning and phonetic analysis simultaneously. Although the emphasis throughout the series is upon sounds and phonics, the sounds are introduced in whole words, audio-readiness precedes the introduction of the symbol, and some attention is paid to other methods of word attack.

The sounds of the long vowels are taught first so that children will be able to apply these in the early stages of their reading. Later, the short vowel sounds are taught followed by the sounds of the consonants. Concomitant with the learning of the sounds, the children acquire what are called the *phonetic keys*. These phonetic keys are phonetic principles which the child learns through meaningful application. The phonetic rules are called *keys*, and they are very specific. There are 82 such keys covering pronunciation of individual letters, syllables, and spelling. The keys are learned when the children first learn the sounds. There is an insistence that the children memorize the rules and the diacritical marks and verbalize them when attacking a new word. Some educators feel that there is too much stress placed on learning rules. Many studies show that there is no correlation between a knowledge of rules and ability to apply phonics to unlocking words. It must be stated, however, that other word attack skills besides phonetic analysis are presented and liberal use is made of different basal readers. Children taught by the phonetic keys approach do seem to have an advantage in reading, especially in the first and second grades. According to some research, this superiority seems to diminish rapidly after the third grade.

Initial Teaching Alphabet

For some years, experimenters in England have been making use of a new alphabet in teaching retarded readers to read. In recent years, a major center was established at Lehigh University to pursue research on the use of the *Augmented Roman Alphabet,* or as it has come to be known in the United States, the *Intital Teaching Alphabet* (i.t.a.) in the teaching of beginning reading A number of elementary schools are experimentally making use of the i.t.a. The University of London has been doing research in the use of this alphabet to teach 4½- to 5-year-olds, as well as retarded readers, to read (Downing, 1963). The results are still inconclusive and incomplete.

The Augmented Roman Alphabet (A.R.) consists of the *traditional orthography* (T.O.) plus the addition of symbols. The T.O. is the regular alphabet with its 26 symbols. The i.t.a. makes use of a total of 44 symbols. An example of a paragraph printed in i.t.a. is shown in Figure 11–4.

The i.t.a. is designed to simplify the use of the whole-word approach and the phonic approach in the teaching of reading. The whole-word approach is simplified by providing word patterns which are made to appear consistent in the shape of the letters by using only lower case letters plus the 19 augmentations. The teaching of phonics is simplified by removing the inconsistencies which exist between the printed letters and the sounds they signal. There are about 2,000 ways of spelling the sounds of English as represented by the traditional orthography. The i.t.a. uses only 44 ways of spelling the sounds—one symbol only for each sound.

FIGURE 11–4. i.t.a reading paragraph.

The i.t.a. is used when the children are first introduced to reading. They learn the symbols and the sounds that they represent. The children learn to read from books which are printed in i.t.a. Over 200 books have been rewritten into i.t.a. When the children reach an independent reading level of about the end of the second grade, the children are introduced to traditional orthography. The transition from A.R. to T.O. is readily accomplished according to proponents of the new system. All that is needed is a simple adjustment to recognizing the use of capital letters and to new word forms.

The Gillingham-Stillman Method

Like the Fernald Method, the Gillingham-Stillman Method employs a visual auditory-kinesthetic-tactile, or multisensory approach to the development of reading skills (1960). Unlike the Fernald system, the Gillingham-Stillman system begins with parts, i.e., individual letter phonics. The child is first taught the sounds of the phonograms and how to write the phonogram which symbolizes the sound. He sees the phonogram, says the phonogram, traces the phonogram, and then writes the phonogram in the air. Drill cards with key word and picture are given to the child so that he may have a source of reference in order to determine the sound in case he should forget.

Once the child has learned several sounds which can be combined into phonetically correct words, he is given stories to read which have a minimum number of sight words in the context. These words are made up primarily of those sounds he has already learned to say, recognize, and write. He continues to learn other phonograms through Gillingham's "eight linkages" while spelling, dictionary skills, syllabication, and rules are gradually introduced.

A weakness of this method is that it does not place any emphasis on comprehension in the early stages of remediation. It is also very time consuming. However, the system does work. This method is very good for use with severely disabled cases.

Stanger-Donahue Method

The Stanger-Donahue Method (1958) is the British counterpart of the Gillingham-Stillman Method. Although developed independently, it bears many similarities to the latter. It employs a VAKT technique centered on phonics. The child is taught letter names and sounds by tracing over models until he can reproduce them. Script is used. Words are pronounced letter by letter from left to right. Letters are taught in a strict sequence in order to provide a basis for a word list. Unlike the Gillingham-Stillman Method, the Stanger-Donahue Method has developed an elaborate testing system for determining dominance.

This system is successful with the seriously disabled for all the same reasons mentioned for the Gillingham-Stillman Method. Like the Gillingham-Stillman Method, its one chief disadvantage is that it is time consuming.

Spalding and Spalding: The Writing Approach

The Spaldings (1957) have proposed a completely different approach to the teaching of the word attack skills. They propose that reading instruction should begin by correlating writing the letters with learning the sounds of the letters. Basically their approach is a phonic system designed to entrench phonic knowledge through the employment of as many senses as possible. Before any reading is done, the children are taught the letters of the alphabet, and the sounds they signal. As many senses as possible are used in teaching the letters. The children visually see the letter, kinesthetically (through writing) feel the configuration of the letter, tactually (through finger contact) feel the letter, and auditorially hear the letter by saying the sound.

When the sounds are learned, words are blended phonetically. The children learn rules for doing so. If a word gives difficulty, an approach similar to the one used in teaching the sounds originally is employed to overcome the obstacle. The Spalding Method seems to be an attempt to apply the "one to one" techniques of the Gillingham-Stillman Method to larger groups.

The Michigan Reading Program

The Michigan Successive Discrimination Reading Program is a language arts curriculum for beginning reading instruction (Smith, 1966). It consists of a set of self-instruction booklets and tapes and provisions for their use in a controlled classroom environment. The program begins with basic visual and auditory skills and progresses to words, sentences, and paragraphs. Systematic training is provided in the perceptual skills necessary for primer reading. The authors begin on the assumption that all learning tasks must be intrinsically rewarding in order to be learned and maintained. The "intrinsically rewarding" tasks are provided by a programming strategy based upon perceptual learning. A model is provided, then two or more choices, one of which is "the same as" or "equivalent to" the model. The child learns by imitation. The foils or incorrect choices are arranged such that, given a certain level of attention, the child is virtually always able to discover the correct choice and knows what is correct without confirmation. About 97% of his responses are correct. The child works independently, developing good work habits and decision-making ability, and overcomes dependency and other self-defeating behaviors. Tests are available to evaluate achievement.

The Hegge-Kirk-Kirk Method

The Hegge-Kirk-Kirk Method (1955) attempts to develop Gestalt closure, left-to-right progression, and sound-symbol relationship through a series of drills. A VAKT technique called the *grapho-vocal method* is used to teach letter sounds. At this stage associational devices are employed to aid in recall and retrieval—"What sound does the baby make? "Aah, aah" (short *a*). A picture of teeth for the *t* sound. When the child has learned (been introduced to) the sounds, he begins Remedial Reading Drills in which each sound must be made individually in order to develop left-right progression and Gestalt closure. The repetitiousness of the drills provides for overlearning.

The Hegge-Kirk-Kirk Method consists of repeated practice in blending specific sounds. Overlearning is the rule. The child begins with the short *a* sound and proceeds to blend orally long lists of three-letter words containing no other vowel sounds. As the child runs through the drills, fatigue is avoided through a visual-auditory-kinesthetic-tactile approach which is done at the chalkboard. Key clues are given to the child to help him remember the sounds such as: the mother says "shhhh" to the baby for the *sh* sound; the radiator says "ssssss" for the *s* sound, and so on. This method could be called an *integrated phonics method* since, although the child begins with sounds, he practices the sounds in whole words.

This method is well suited to the primary reading disability case who is the least seriously handicapped. Any time the etiological diagnosis indicates limited primary reading disability, the Hegge-Kirk-Kirk Method should be employed.

The Neurological Impress Method

The Neurological Impress Method of reading instruction was developed as a remedial technique for teaching reading to children who were two or three years retarded in reading but who had at least borderline average intelligence on the performance scale of the Wechsler Intelligence Scale for Children. The technique seeks to expose the child to accurate, correct reading patterns and to impress these correct patterns deeply on the neurological system concerned with learning to read. The experimental work was done on children from seventh to tenth grade. The Neurological Impress Method has been developed by R. C. Heckelman and the schools of Merced County, California (1969). The method seems to relate to the research studies reported by Smith (1962) in his book, *Delayed Sensory Feedback and Behavior*.

This is a system of a unison reading process whereby the student and teacher read aloud, simultaneously, at a rapid rate. The disabled reader is placed slightly to the front of the teacher with the student and the teacher holding the book jointly. As the student and teacher read the same material in unison, the voice of the teacher is directed into the ear of the student at close range. In most instances, the student has his right hand free, and he is able to use his finger as a locater. He slides his finger along the line following the words that are being spoken. *The finger must be at the location of the spoken word.* At times the instructor may read louder and faster than the student and at other times he may articulate more softly and lag slightly behind. No preliminary preparation of the reading material is made before the student sees it. The approach to the reading is spontaneous, and as few pauses as possible are made in this reading process. The goal is to cover as many pages of reading material as possible in the time available without causing the student physical discomfort. Dryness of mouth and fatigue of voice are two types of discomfort experienced. At no time does the teacher attempt to teach sounds of the words or word recognition. No attention is called to accompanying pictures or content of the story. After the reading session the teacher refrains from asking a student any questions about what the child was reading but permits the child to volunteer any information that he wishes to give at that time. The teacher always comments positively as to the success of the child and calls attention to the new fluidness with which he is now reading and suggests to him that he is now able to read. Any positive motivation and stimulation that can be given to the child is permitted.

As the sessions progress and as the opportunities present themselves, the instructor lowers his voice or reduces his speed so there is an infinitesimal lag behind the student's reading. *When the student falters, he is reinforced by increased loudness and speed.* The student and instructor alternate between leading and following. After working for several sessions with students, the teacher is generally able to adapt himself to the system and finds very little trouble gearing to the correct speed and approach for the student.

Sessions may last from 15 minutes to 60 minutes in length. Fifteen minutes a session each day, five days a week for six weeks is considered good. An hour session once a week for 12 weeks can be adequate for some students. A minimum of 12 hours over a period of three months is generally recommended.

Although we do not get the same results as the developer of this technique, we have found that in cases displaying some expressive difficulty, when this technique is used improvement occurs in about 50% of the cases. A child with a larger discrepancy between comprehension and accuracy on the Gilmore Oral Reading Test in favor of comprehension may be helped by this technique.

Other Phonic Systems

The controversy and the questions raised by the public and others concerning the use of phonics in the teaching of reading have resulted in the introduction of a separate phonics program. Usually a separate phonics program will have been added to the reading program because of the belief of the teachers and administrators that a special, distinct emphasis on the teaching of phonics would produce better results in learning how to read. Some teachers feel that the amount of work on phonics as suggested by the teacher's manual accompanying the basal readers they were using in their classrooms is not sufficient to answer their purposes. The use of supplementary systems has proven their worth in many places. As a result of these and other reasons, a number of supplementary phonic systems have been produced commercially. Some of the systems are merely workbooks, whereas others are detailed and involved programs. Among the phonic systems available for classroom use are the following:

Breaking the Sound Barrier, Sister Mary Caroline; The Macmillan Company, New York

Building Reading Skills, Leila Armstrong and Rowena Hargrave; McCormack-Mathers Publishing Company, Wichita

Eye and Ear Fun, Clarence R. Stone; Webster Publishing Company, St. Louis

Phonics, Selma Herr; Smith and Holst, Inc., Los Angeles (221 S. Olive Street)

Royal Road Reading, Daniels & Diack; Educators Publishing Service, 301 Vassar St., Cambridge, Mass.

Merrill Linguistic Reading, Fier, Witson, Rudolph; Charles E. Merrill Publishing Co., 1300 Alum Creek Drive, Columbus, Ohio

The Iroquois Phonics Program, Eaton & James; Iroquois Publishing Company, Iroquois Building, Syracuse, N.Y.

Speech to Print Phonics, Durrell & Murphy; Harcourt, Brace and World, New York, N.Y.

Phonics We Use, Mary Meigham, Marjorie Pratt, and Mabel Halvorsen; Lyons and Carnahan, Chicago

Reading with Phonics, Julie Hay and Charles E. Wings; J. P. Lippincott and Company, Chicago

Other programs we would like to mention include (a) Phonics We Use. A series of phonic workbooks which have been around for quite a long time. This series is a conventional set of phonic practice exercises that are widely used by reading teachers; and (b) Speech to Print Phonics. Provided for auditory discrimination, teaching of letter names, sounds of letters and letter combinations and the application of these skills. Context and meaning are also stressed. Fifty-five lessons are presented.

These programs and many more are described in detail in the book *Approaches to Beginning Reading* by Robert C. Aukeman, John Wiley and Sons, New York, 1971. Selection of an appropriate phonics program depends on many factors. Of course, a most significant factor would be whether or not the teacher would receive adequate training in using the program. As far as we can tell, this one factor is more responsible for program failures than any other.

Remediation of Auditory Acuity Defects

Hearing acuity levels vary greatly in the classroom. There may be mildly hard of hearing children or children who are partly deaf. The child with a hearing problem should be given a favorable seat close to where the teacher does most of her speaking. The child should sit with his back to the window so that the light falls on the teacher's face. The teacher must be certain to always enunciate clearly, especially when talking directly to the child with the hearing defect. If it is possible, training in lip reading would be valuable for the child with a mild hearing deficiency. In teaching reading the visual approach to word recognition would be emphasized. The child will have some degree of difficulty in auditory discrimination, but this does not mean that the phonetic approach should be completely neglected. The degree of emphasis in this area will depend on the degree of difficulty the child encounters.

In the case of a partly deaf child, there should be a greater emphasis on silent reading. There is a definite need for special training in lip reading. When the child has developed skill in lip reading, he will be able to get along with little difficulty in the normal classroom. Care should be taken to make the child feel as if he belongs to the group to counteract any emotional problems that may develop.

Media for Remediation in Phonics

Although phonics is only one of the word attack skills, it is one of the more important ones. We are not suggesting an undue emphasis on phonics but merely pointing out that a child who lacks phonics, or who uses phonics inadequately, is seriously handicapped.

In phonics, too, the teacher must determine the level in the phonic sequence at which the child is functioning. If the child is having difficulty with auditory discrimination of letter sounds, exercises to help him develop this discriminating ability must be instituted. With young children, the Phonovisual Method which employs charts and emphasizes the oral reproduction of sounds can be valuable. Speech-to-Print-Phonics with its accompanying games can develop the auditory discrimination and also make the transition to visual recognition and oral reproduction. It must be noted that word position must be checked. Because a child can auditorially discriminate a sound at the beginning of a word is no indication of his ability to discriminate the same sound in a terminal or medial position.

If the phonic weakness is at the level of letter names, these must be taught. In addition to conventional means of teaching letter names, the clinician can employ VAKT techniques such as sandpaper letters, sand tray tracing, etc.

The Language Master can be used at this level or at the level of sound-symbol relationship. The Webster Word Wheels, Phonics We Use, Economy System, Open Court, first grade Basal Readers and workbooks, the McQueen Materials and SRA Phonic Games are some other materials for application at the sound-symbol level. The Peabody Language Development Kit takes the child a step further and seeks to develop verbal skills as well.

The child with a blending problem many times can be helped to develop Gestalt closure through use of the Hegge-Kirk-Kirk Remedial Reading Drills.

More structuralized and specialized materials such as Gillingham-Stillman, Stanger-Donahue, Spalding-Spalding can be used effectively with children with extreme disability.

Remember, the best material is that material tailored by the teacher to most effectively meet this child's immediate skill needs.

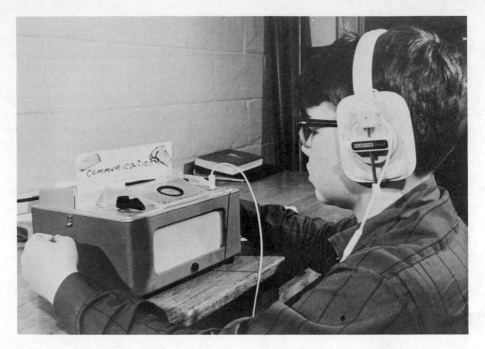

FIGURE 11–5. Language master.

Photo courtesy of Bell and Howell.

Activities for Sequential Development

Level One

   I. Auditory Perception and Discrimination

     A. Recognizing Sounds
        1. Imitate sounds of animals and have children identify each.
        2. Tap rhythms and have children repeat.
        3. Have children put heads down and identify the voice of the child tapped by teacher.
     B. Likenesses and Differences
        1. Say a rhyme leaving out a word and have pupils supply missing word.
        2. Say three words which rhyme. Pupils repeat and indicate similarity.
        3. Say three words, one of which doesn't begin like the others. Have pupils tell which is different.

  II. Visual Perception and Discrimination
     A. Recognition of Language Symbols
        1. On board or mimeographed sheets teacher places confusable letters:

d   d   d   b   d

n   n   m   n   n

u   n   u   u   u

Children put an X on the one which is different.

   2. The same can be done with confusable words.

   dog   dog   god   dog

   on   on   on   no

  B. Likenesses and Differences
   1. Geometric designs can be used as words and letters were used in recognition above.

III. Letter Names

  A. Naming
   1. Teach alphabet song
   2. Distribute alphabet and have children come up in sequence and place letters in order.

IV. Sounds

  A. Consonants
   1. Make a picture chart of words beginning with a consonant and have child say name of picture and point to its beginning letter.
   2. Ask child questions to which he must reply with a word beginning with a given letter.
  B. Consonant Blends
   1. Have child name words beginning with the same blend.
   2. Show child picture cards of items beginning with blends and have the child identify the blend.
  C. Digraphs
   1. Same as with consonant blends
  D. Vowels
   1. Use vowel picture cards

Level Two

 I. Consonants

  A. Call out words having children identify sound at beginning and end.
  B. Have children identify medial consonants in words such as *kitten, penny.*

 II. Blends

  A. Dictate blend words and have child write the blend.
  B. Put a list of blend words on the chalkboard and have child identify the blend.

III. Vowels

  A. Have child raise hand when he hears a short $\bar{a}$ in a list of words pronounced by teacher.
  B. Have children find long vowel words in the glossary of the basal reader. Write these words and say them.

IV. Digraphs

  A. Have child build a picture book of digraphs.
  B. Stepping stones with double *oo* words child must pronounce to get "home."

 V. Diphthongs

  A. Same as in Digraphs

Level Three

 I. Reinforce Consonants

  A. Ask children to fill in the blank with a word like the underlined word only changing the first or last letter.
  B. Make a circular tachistoscope using words that all begin or end with the same consonant.

II. Reinforce Blends

    A. Have children think and say words that begin with certain blends. Teacher writes words on the board and underlines the blend.

    B. To reinforce the endings, repetition may be used. Make new words by changing or adding a consonant or blend to the beginning or end of words.

III. Review Digraphs

    A. Listen for the 'oo' sound: *zoo, room.* Now raise your hand when you hear the sound in these words I am going to say.

IV. Review Diphthongs

V. Review hard *c*, soft *c*, hard *g*, soft *g*, *ir, er, ur, or, ar.*

VI. Review Short and Long Vowels

    A. Find the word under the sentence that has the long (or short) *a* sound and makes sense. Then write it in the blank.

    B. Read each riddle. Draw a line under the word that answers the riddle. You must hear the long *a* sound in the word you choose. "It is something children like to eat."

apple   table   cake

Mispronunciation

Mispronunciations by a child without any speech problems generally follow a pattern. Either the child notes the beginning letters of the word and guesses the rest, or he sees terminal letters or medial letters and guesses the remainder. Lastly, there is the pattern of inconsistent position—i.e., once initial letters, then terminal, then initial again.

The inconsistent pattern generally suggests the child has not developed the pattern of left-to-right progression. Hence, the teacher must concentrate on the development of this pattern. This can be done through a VAKT technique or individual letter phonics drill. In our clinics we have found The Remedial Reading Drills by Hegge-Kirk-Kirk helpful in developing this left-to-right progression.

With the other three patterns, drill designed to force the child to look at that part of the word he is neglecting many times will alleviate the problem.

Example: Initial letter then guess. Circle the word which is like the word in column #1.
Column #1

book	bank	bunk	bang	boss	book
cat	can	cat	cap	car	cot

This type of drill renders the single clue used by the child useless and forces him to look at that part of the word formerly neglected. Similar drills for children using only terminal or medial clues can be designed.

Phonetic Skills

There is so much good material available today on the teaching of phonics that a teacher will have no difficulty finding the teaching techniques. Sample activities are:

A. Consonant Sounds—Initial - Medial - Final

    1. Where do you hear *s* in these words? *sail, shoe, boys, seesaw.*

    2. What sound do you hear at the end of these words? *miss, glass,* etc.

3. Where do you hear the given letter in the word?
   G—*God, glad, bag, sugar*
   L—*tell, love, ladder, lollipop*

B. Consonant Blends

1. Name words that begin with the same blend. *tree, truck, trip, train.* Ask the children for the
   two letters that can be heard at the beginning of the word.
       Print the word on the blackboard. Then ask the children what two letters they see at the
   beginning of the words.
   Let them draw a line under the *tr* in each word. Explain to the children that these are blends.

   Definition: A blend is *two* or *three* consonants sounded together. Each consonant says its
           own name.

2. Print these words on the blackboard.

trade	trap	treat	tramp
track	trick	trot	tray
try	trim	trail	true

Have the children circle the blend. Let them say the word, and use it in a sentence to check
meaning.

Reinforcement of Consonant Blends and Endings.

1. A word wheel is good for reinforcing consonant blends

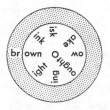

2. To reinforce endings, write words on oak tag without the endings. Hold words in front of
   endings. Class discovers the correct ending.

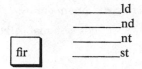

Remedial Exercises: Nonreading Games

Nonreading games help develop general auditory abilities for a child who is just learning
to read.

1. Make a chart containing pictures of objects beginning with the same sound. Child points to each
   picture, naming it and listening for the initial sound.
2. Tell a simple story of two or three sentences. Have the child repeat it as accurately as possible.

3. Tap on the desk several times while the child listens, counts mentally, and then tells the number of taps. Vary this procedure by tapping slowly at times, quickly, or in irregular rhythm.

4. Have the child listen while words beginning or ending with the same sound are repeated. Then include a "different" sound, such as *man, milk, money, sled,* and *gate, late, state, come.* See if the child can hear the "different" word.

5. Have the child suggest other words beginning or ending with the same sounds.

6. Have the child listen to nursery rhymes and jingles, especially those like Bye Baby Bunting which emphasizes a particular sound.

7. Have the children say rhymes and poems in chorus.

8. Give oral directions involving two actions, then three or more. "Put a pencil on the desk, shut the door, then stand beside my desk." Vary this by having the child repeat the directions before acting them out.

Remedial Exercises to Develop Auditory Abilities in Reading

1. Child should sit close to the teacher during the reading period.

2. Speak clearly and distinctly, repeating as often as necessary and not giving too many or too complex directions at one time.

3. Have child repeat aloud the directions given to make sure he has heard correctly.

4. Work on sight method more than phonetic method.

5. Reinforce sight method with tracing.

6. Give a more sympathetic type of phonetic training than usual.

    a. Review or teach initial sounds.

        (1) Make a sound dictionary.
        (2) Make a sound chart.
        (3) Make the sounds as vivid as possible by using motor exercises such as:
        —Show how paper flutters before the lips for the sound of *p* but not for *b*.
        —Blow on child's hand to show the difference between *wh* and *w*.
        —Show how the tongue protrudes for the sound of *th*.

    b. Review or teach the blends and phonograms.

    c. Review or teach the vowel sounds systematically.

        (1) Short vowels.
        (2) Long vowels with final *e*.
        (3) Vowel combinations, such as—*ai, ea, ei, ea*.
        (4) Discrimination of vowels in sentences, such as:

                He wore a (hat, hate).
                I have a (dim, dime).

    d. Teach him to make words grow longer.

walk	walking	walked
hop	hopping	hopped
go	going	
shine	shining	

    e. Have him make longer words of two short ones.

in	to	into
sun	set	sunset
up	on	upon
black	board	blackboard

  f. Have him find little words in big words.

seat	sea	eat	
nice	ice		
something	some	thing	
butterfly	but	butter	fly

Avoid choosing words that change the pronunciation of the larger word, such as, *flower—flow; table—tab.*

  g. Have him make new words by taking off the final *e.*

           hate—hat   cape—cap   cane—can

  h. Make up short phonetic sentences with short vowels, as in *Tom can run.*

Tape Recorder Activities

The tape recorder is a very useful piece of equipment to be used for improving language skills and phonetic analysis skills. It is important for the child to hear the way he speaks and reads and to compare it to the way others speak and read. The following list contains some examples of activities that can be used with a reading group or as an individualized learning center:

1. Tape record the child's reading of a passage. Listen to the tape with the child, picking out problem areas. Allow the child to try the same passage at a later date to see improvement.

2. Have the child repeat words spoken by you as you tape it. Listen to the tape afterward to pick out problem areas.

3. For drilling with rhyming words, record incomplete verses. Allow the child to listen to the verses and add a word to complete the rhyme. The word completions may be tape recorded or given orally.

4. Record words containing a specific consonant sound in the initial, medial, or final position. Using an answer sheet marked *B M E*, the child circles the correct letter indicating in which position he hears that consonant sound.

    Adaptation: Record words to which the child listens for the initial, medial, or final sound. He then writes the letter symbol for the sound that is in that particular position.

More tape recorder activities can be found in the book *Reading Activities with the Tape Recorder* by Frank J. Sciara and Richard B. Walter, Danville, New York, 1973.

Games and Media

1. *Consonant Lotto* (Dolch). Lotto game using consonant sounds.
2. *Vowel Lotto* (Dolch). Lotto game using vowel sounds.

3. *Phonics We Use Learning Games Kit* (Lyons E. Carnahan). Has many different games dealing with different phonic elements. Includes a vowel domino game and a blends race.

4. *Language Master* Phonics Program. The child looks at a card and attempts to identify the word, then places it in the machine and listens as a recorded voice pronounces the word. The child's response can also be recorded and played back.

5. *Cat In the Hat*. Includes storybooks with the stories on each sound, teacher's manual explaining lessons, magnetic board for use with letters, cards with letters and pictures, bigger picture-character cards, large posters, card chart, tapes of songs, puppets, and High Hat Stamp. Workbooks can be bought to accompany kit. Sounds are introduced one at a time, such as *m* with the story "Marty Mouse."

6. *Sea of Vowels Game*. Students choose cards with long or short vowel sounds in words and move so many spaces on a board.

7. *Vowel Sounds Learning Module* (Society for Visual Education). Contains filmstrips, tapes, floor mat with letters, storybooks, game boards.

8. *Learning With Laughter* (Scott Educational Division). Includes filmstrips, activities, and tapes in each kit. The child can watch cartoons dealing with beginning, medial, and final consonants; initial and medial vowel sounds; vowel digraphs and diphthongs; *Y* as a vowel; consonant blends and digraphs; and the alphabet.

9. *Quizmo*. Children mark the letter (or blends) that a given word begins with as the word is pronounced. Played like Bingo.

10. *Magic Cards*. Cards which wipe clean after being written on, contain pictures and letters to match, or capital and lower case letters to match. Practice can be gained in identification of the correct consonant sounds, blends, vowel sounds.

11. *Ear and Eye Fun*. Series of five workbooks with emphasis on exercises that combine meaning, picture, phonic, and structural cues.

12. *Word Builders* (Kenworthy). Capital and lower case letters on little squares to use in making words.

13. *Take* (Dolch). Involves matching the sounds of beginnings, middles, or endings of words.

14. *Go Fish* (Kingsbury). Used to reinforce phonic learnings (initial consonants, blends).

15. *Phonetic Drill Cards*. Flip cards.

16. *Funforms* (Ginn). For practicing phonic skills. The top page is torn off and underneath might be a completed picture of balloons on strings. If the student has circled an incorrect answer, he can tell because the balloon would not have a string. There are many different forms of these activities using this carbon paper method. The child is asked to trace the circle around the words containing the short vowel sounds but not those containing the long vowel sounds.

17. *Phonic Rummy* (Kenworthy).

18. *Picture Phonic Cards*.

19. *Consonant and Vowel Wheels* (Milton Bradley).

20. *Sound Hunt Phonics Game* (American Teaching Aids).

21. *First Talking Alphabet* (Scott Foresman).—Uses records and dittoes to help the children learn the sounds of the letters—includes consonants, consonant digraphs, vowels (long, short, and *r* controlled). Usually the child listens to the record, following along on a colored card, hearing each word pronounced that matches the picture. Then the child must look at the pictures in the next row as their names are pronounced. The child must then tell which picture has the same sound as the first picture in the row. They are also told to trace the "fuzzy" letter at the bottom of the card, and then try to trace it with their eyes closed (A a). The ditto sheets test and reinforce what they have learned about the particular sound they worked with.

A number of commercial companies produce devices which allegedly help the teacher teach phonics to a child. These devices may be drill cards, phonic wheels, word family cards, games, and other such visual aids. Catalogs are available from all such companies. Good ideas for classroom aids to meet special needs can be obtained by the alert teacher from viewing the catalogs. Some of the companies producing phonic devices are:

Bell & Howell Co., Chicago, Illinois
Charles E. Merrill Publishing Co., Columbus, Ohio
Garrard Press, Champaign, Illinois
Ideal School Supply Company, Chicago, Illinois
Kenworthy Educational Service, Buffalo, New York
Milton-Bradley, Springfield, Massachusetts
Steck Company, Austin, Texas
Webster Publishing Company, Austin, Texas
Educational Publishing Service, Cambridge, Massachusetts

chapter 12

Developing Comprehension in Disabled Readers

How can you understand what you are reading if you cannot comprehend it? Comprehend means *to grasp mentally, to understand or know*. Therefore, the term *comprehension* implies the act of, or capacity for, comprehending or understanding. The mental logic thus far sounds reasonable, yet it is circular reasoning and does not even begin to reflect the complex nature of "comprehension" as it is used in the field of reading. Add to this the complexity of the thought processes of the learning disabled reader and we have, indeed, a perplexing problem. A conclusion to this bewildering situation may be to do what Thoreau suggested as an answer for meeting the complexities of life itself: "Simplify, simplify." The LD reader has enough problems, so we must try to simplify the concept of *comprehension* to its most elemental form and build from there.

The term *interpretation* is used interchangeably with the word *comprehension*. Comprehension and interpretation are so interrelated in usage that it is difficult if not impossible to separate the two. It is true that in comprehension we are trying to "understand the ideas of the writer," whereas in interpretation we are emphasizing the mental mediating processes, especially recall. Yet, the two processes both involve understanding and mental manipulation. We use the word *comprehension* to mean the understanding and interpretation of the printed matter.

Basic Understandings

We comprehend the meaning of a word, the meaning of a sentence, or the meaning of a passage or paragraph when we grasp the intention of the writer and succeed in relating his message to the context of our own system of knowledge. Some researchers insist that comprehension requires that the reader "construct" a message from information found in printed or spoken material and then match it to some schematic component already present in his cognitive structure (Gibson & Levin, 1975). Others say we must use our known language and *perceive the concepts* that the words represent, not just providing word

350

meaning as in the sense of a vocabulary definition (Kolers, 1970). In other words, the context of a passage must be used in addition to considering individual words in terms of their meaning. We support this view.

Overview of the Dimensions of Reading Comprehension

A study by Davis (1968) identifies five skills which make a unique contribution to reading comprehension. These are listed in order of the extent of variance (deviation from the mean in a frequency distribution) which they predicted: (a) memory for word meanings; (b) drawing inferences from the content; (c) following the structure of a passage; (d) recognizing a writer's purpose, attitude, tone, and mood; and (e) finding answers to questions asked explicitly or in paraphrase. The first two skills account for a much higher percentage of the variance than the other three. This study points up not only the importance of knowledge of word meaning but also what Davis calls "reasoning in reading." In addition, it becomes obvious that comprehension is not a "unitary (single) mental skill or operation."

Effective comprehension in reading obviously cannot take place if the reader cannot decode the words on the page. However, comprehension can be taught from the beginning of reading instruction by providing constant association between printed words and their meanings. Word recognition is one prerequisite to deriving meaning from words, sentences, and paragraphs.

Adequate language development is another prerequisite to effective comprehension. When the child confronts a series of words in a sentence, relationships between words must be conceptualized as well as individual words. As Wardhaugh (1969) says, "One does not understand sentences by adding together the meanings of words in the same way that beads are added together on a string to make a necklace." The child must have an adequate knowledge of language in terms of underlying sentence structure as well as vocabulary in order to properly encode the meaning of the sentence. Simons (1972) found a high correlation between reading comprehension and the child's ability to understand syntax and grammar of sentences. Items on the test he devised for the study required the student to choose the one sentence out of three that was not a paraphrase of the other two. For example:

  a. The boy gave the book to the girl.
  b. The book was given to the girl by the boy.
 *c. The book was given to the boy by the girl.

McCullough (1976) agrees that there is a need for oral language experience. Children must be able to group words that belong together, derive clues of syntactic structure, and relate the meaning of a word from a previous sentence to a cloze omission in the sentence following. Language development should be taught at the readiness level and in conjunction with later reading instruction.

Reading authorities have long agreed that understanding spoken vocabulary precedes the understanding of printed vocabulary, so perhaps it is rational to assume that aural comprehension should precede printed comprehension. This suggests another prerequisite— the need for teaching listening skills in conjunction with early reading instruction.

Levels of Comprehension

Several writers have set up levels of comprehension which they hope will give more meaning to the nature of reading comprehension and its instruction. A workable classification of levels of comprehension was developed by Nila B. Smith (1969). To Smith there are four levels of comprehension: .

1. *Literal Comprehension*
   Identifying direct and obvious meaning
2. *Interpretation*
   Using the content as a base for deductive reasoning
3. *Critical Reading*
   Analyzing and evaluating the material
4. *Specific Word Meanings*
   Recognizing the implications of multi-meaning of words

Kolson (1977) developed levels of comprehension which he considers to be hierarchical in nature.

1. *Literal Comprehension*
   Identify what the author says
2. *Resolving Conflicting Comprehension*
   Identify the meaning intended when it is in conflict with literal meaning
3. *Inferred Meaning*
   Identify what the author intended
4. *Metaphorical Meaning*
   Identify a less obvious meaning by going beyond the literal presentation to a more implicit observation or analogy

Wilson and Hall (1972) have a comprehension model that is as follows:

1. *Literal Understanding*
   The ability to obtain a message accurately
2. *Interpretation*
   The ability to relate the message to one's own experience
3. *Problem Solving*
   Using Literal Understanding and Interpretation, either critically or creatively, in an application situation

Levels of comprehension for sentence and paragraph meaning are referred to by various terminology; however, most authors agree that the skills range from simple recall to evaluation. Miller (1971) refers to the levels as literal, higher-type, critical, and creative. *Literal comprehension* refers to factual recall, either in reproduction or in translation of the author's words. Miller's *higher-type level of comprehension* includes interpretive and inferential thinking. It reflects the child's ability to think abstractly in answering questions, asking "why," making generalizations, predicting outcomes, and sensing the author's mood. The third level is *critical reading*, which involves evaluation and judgment drawing on past experience. Most disabled readers at the intermediate level will not be reading well enough to be able to profit from instruction in this skill. However, critical thinking can be developed through activities other than reading. *Creative reading* is the highest level of comprehension identified by Miller. At this level, the reader applies knowledge learned from reading to real-life experiences. Although it is a sophisticated skill, it can be developed at early reading stages if material is at the appropriate level.

All of these models should give some insight into the sequence of comprehension skills and what must be considered when teaching objectives are established for a child. Table 12–1 presents the results of a study by Lanier and Davis (1972) in which teachers were asked to come up with a model for writing comprehension questions. The table can also be converted into an individual analysis sheet for comprehension skills.

TABLE 12–1. Information that elicits specific comprehension skills.

Level 1 Literal	Level 2 Interpretive	Level 3 Critical	Level 4 Creative

Recall of
  facts (details)
  sequence
  main idea
  directions
  organization
  cause-and-effect
  comparison
  contrast
  character traits
Recognition of
  facts
  sequence
  main idea
  directions
  organization
  cause-and-effect
  comparison
  contrast
  character traits
	Inferring:
	  sequence
	  main idea
	  cause-and-effect
	  comparison
	  contrast
	  purpose
	  details
	  character traits
	Drawing conclusions
	Generalizing
	Deriving meaning from
	  figurative language
	Speculating
	Predicting
	Anticipating
	Summarizing
		Judging
		Detecting propaganda
		Analyzing
		Checking validity
		Checking author's
		  reputation, biases,
		  purposes
			Applying information
			  to new situation
			Responding
			  emotionally

Source: Lanier, R. J., & Davis, A. P. Developing comprehension through teacher-made questions. *Reading Teacher*, November 1972, 26(2), 153–157.

Sequence of Comprehension Skills

As with all reading skills comprehension skills run from the simple to the complex. Materials specifically designed for one skill should be used for maximum efficiency at mastery in that skill.

Reading specialists generally accept eight skills.

1. *Ability to locate answers.*
   To become proficient at this task the reader must be able to distinguish relevant information from irrelevant information, and to skim to find pertinent paragraphs.

2. *Ability to follow a sequence.*
   Cause-effect relationships must be understood if the reader is to reproduce the story or events in order.

3. *Ability to grasp the main idea.*
   Basic to many other comprehension skills is the ability to skim the material in order to glean a total impression. Grasping the main idea gives the reader the scope and tone of the material to be read.

4. *Ability to note details.*
   Indepth studies require the use of this skill. Until the reader has mastered this skill, he is unable to see the relationship of details to the main idea.

5. *Ability to determine organization.*
   To fully comprehend factual material the reader must recognize elements such as introduction, body, conclusion, headings, subheadings, paragraph organization, and topic sentences.

6. *Ability to follow directions.*
   This skill is the amalgamation of the three skills noting details, determining organization, and grasping sequence.

7. *Ability to read critically.*
   Here the reader must engage the material in a dialogue in which he compares this printed material with other material, or with the total conceptual background he possesses. He must be able to recognize and resist subtle persuasions and propaganda. It is an investigation calling for reason.

8. *Ability to organize and summarize.*
   This highest skill involves all other skills.

Guszak (1969) presents a shorter list of specific skills to be located within written material. The subskills he lists are locating specific: (a) phrases, (b) sentences, (c) paragraphs, and (d) parts of a story. The development of these skill areas through the use of specific purpose questioning should be given much attention in beginning reading instruction. This questioning is done by the teacher when she wants the child to locate and elicit a specific answer that can be found in the material that is being read. In this manner, not only is the child taught how to get the main idea of the story, but he also learns how to get the facts of the story.

The Montgomery County Public Schools of Maryland ("Teaching Reading," 1974) have developed a practical model of the meaning of reading comprehension. It guides their teachers in formulating instructional objectives, performance objectives, and assessment measures. They conceive comprehension to be a continuum, going from (a) literal comprehension, involving location, recall, and translation; to (b) critical comprehension where interpretation, prediction, application, and analysis takes place; to (c) creative comprehension, relating to synthesis and evaluation. Extending throughout all three levels is the area of word meaning. Comprehension is recognized as having both knowing (cognitive) and feeling (affective) components.

Factors Affecting Comprehension

The degree of comprehension achieved by a reader depends on several factors. First, the physical condition of the reader will affect comprehension level. It is obvious that a person with a migraine headache or a severe toothache will be unable to concentrate on the material sufficiently enough to attain a high level of comprehension, but it is just as certain, though less obvious, that minor physical anomalies can affect the degree of the reader's comprehension. Those people in a captive audience at a testimonial banquet who have fastened their belt too tightly and must sit passively through a speech generally hear little of what the speaker says and comprehend nothing. The child with a sensitive nervous system or a defective perceptual process will find it hard to concentrate on what he is to be studying and comprehending.

A second factor affecting the degree of comprehension is the interest of the reader in what the reading matter is about. Interest affects attention, which in turn affects comprehension. Most every college student in his academic life has had to take a course in which he was not only not interested but also antagonistic toward that particular subject. Think back about how difficult the reading was. Page after page had to be reread, then reread again, in order to get even a smattering of understanding of what it was about. Almost anything distracted you and gave you an excuse to stop reading.

A third factor affecting comprehension is the difficulty of the material. Every writer, regardless of the audience level on which he writes, makes certain assumptions concerning the background of the readers who seek to read his book. The authors of this text have assumed that you, the reader, have reached a degree of reading efficiency equal to college level; that you have acquired a better than average vocabulary; that you are interested in children and in working with children; and, that you realize the importance of reading. If we should be wrong in any of these assumptions, the material would then seem difficult for you to read because you lack interest in the subject. Try reading an engineering journal and see how much you "comprehend."

A fourth factor affecting comprehension is the purpose of the reader. The good reader has the ability to regulate the degree and depth of comprehension which he feels is suited to the purpose for which he is reading. Perhaps this idea can be illustrated by a look at the ways different students take notes. Good note takers will take the kind of notes which best fit their needs. If the student has an instructor who has a tendency to give subjective examinations in which he gives more credit to those who can show relationships rather than merely state facts, he will take a different kind of notes than he would if the instructor were the type who gives objective tests and is concerned only with the regurgitation of facts. The poor note taker, on the other hand, takes the same type of notes from both instructors. Likewise in reading. If the purpose is to be entertained, then the level of comprehension may be merely to identify oneself with a specific character and escape from reality by vicariously experiencing his activities. If, however, one is reading to pass a comprehensive examination, he will read carefully and try to assimilate the main ideas and their supportive data.

Relationship of Comprehension to the Perceptual-Conceptual Process

Comprehension in reading has a vital role in the perceptual-conceptual model as it is the desired goal of the reading process. Indeed, it would be senseless to decode printed symbols that have no meaning. At the same time a reader cannot conceptualize words which have not been perceived and decoded.

In reading the first step in the perceptual-conceptual process involves sensory input through the eyes. The reader then attempts to unlock the words using auditory-verbal-visual skills. He may have to scan his memory banks for sound-symbol relationship of the letters in the word in order to sound it out phonetically, or he may scan for memory of the whole word or structural parts of it. In this part of the process he may also be integrating previous experiences with new stimuli in order to recognize the word. The process does not stop here, as the child must again scan memory banks for the meaning of the concept which the word represents in language. Once the meaning of a sentence is understood, the child must decide what to do with the information gained. It may be stored in a memory bank or the child may have to program his response immediately. He must be able to transmit his understanding through expressive means if others are to know that he understands what he is reading.

Bornuth (1969) postulates that there are actually two mental processes needed in reading comprehension. First, the reader must be able to acquire information encoded in language; then he must be able to exhibit the information in some manner. This follows the perceptual-conceptual model. A theoretical question can be posed as to whether learning has taken place if it cannot be exhibited. We cannot observe thinking, nor can we look into the brain to find stored knowledge. Therefore, at least operationally, some form of output has to be taking place.

Response to feedback is the final important part of the perceptual-conceptual process. Can the child go back and restructure the meaning of a sentence if given negative feedback? If the teacher provides an additional clue, can the child reprocess the information using it? Flexible patterns of thinking are a necessary part of the reading process.

An interesting observation in our experiences with LD children is that quite frequently a child who has very good intelligence may score two to five grades higher in comprehension than in oral word reading accuracy. The implication is that the child may have great difficulty in processing the oral sounds of the words, but he is actually getting much meaning from what he is reading. Occasionally, such a child may just read key words, dropping connector words such as *the, and, an, for,* yet he has good comprehension. This child may be developing his own reading approach or technique to getting meaning from paragraphs. We have had several students reach the college level, and even the graduate level, before their approach to reading began to fail them.

Implications for Teaching the LD Child

In teaching LD children, you must recognize that the majority are not able to decode printed words very easily. It is difficult to assess comprehension ability when the child does not have an adequate reading vocabulary. He may be skipping words he doesn't know, or he may be misreading words. You must be particularly careful in assigning reading that is on the child's vocabulary level. In this case a lack of accuracy on comprehension questions would be an indication of lack of comprehension, rather than a result of poor word recognition skills. Johnson and Myklebust (1967) believe LD children have major problems with *processing* information, rather than *understanding* it. We have found this to be true to a large extent with the LD children in classes we observe. In fact, we have been amazed at the amount of information they gain from halting oral reading when errors are corrected.

In a study by Hansen and Lovitt (1976), intervention techniques were used to correct oral reading errors. In the second phase of their study, comprehension errors were corrected. It was found that comprehension of oral reading increased significantly with the second technique. The improvement had a positive effect on silent reading comprehension. Subjects for the study were disabled learners. There is definitely a place for oral reading instruction in an LD class. When a child has had intervention in correcting errors, we at least know that he has achieved the first prerequisite of comprehension. Training can then take place at higher levels of comprehension in oral reading situations. If care is taken that speed is at an appropriate pace, listening tapes could be used in conjunction with reading a selection. These could aid in providing feedback as well as oral expression.

McCroskey and Thompson (1973) conducted a study to determine if comprehension of a spoken message by children with specific learning disabilities was affected by altering the rate with which the message was presented. It was determined that the rate of presentation (2.9 syllables per second versus 5.0 syllables) definitely made a difference in the comprehension levels in children ages 10 or less. It is possible that young children with auditory-verbal learning disabilities need to have incoming speech stimuli presented at rates slower than normal for them to be able to acquire verbal skills.

Wallen (1972) prefers the term *word meaning* to *vocabulary* and limits it to relating of a new name to a concept already possessed. The implication is that teaching word meanings is not a substitute for teaching concepts. However, both skills are necessary for comprehension, and instruction in word meanings plus experience with concepts should be provided in developing vocabulary. In learning word meanings the child must first learn to *identify* an experience he has already had in terms of a new name. For instance, he learns that another name for a *car* is *automobile*. Next he must *generalize* the new term to other examples of car. Generalization is the more sophisticated skill and requires more instruction time.

LD children need to be provided with many success experiences so all comprehension tasks must consider each child's strengths and weaknesses. Not all LD children are the same; knowing each child and his capabilities, as well as the prerequisites for comprehension, are the beginning steps to good teaching.

Assessment of Comprehension

A number of means are available to the teacher for determining difficulties in comprehension. These include observation, teacher-made tests, standardized survey reading tests, standardized diagnostic reading tests, standardized listening comprehension tests, oral reading tests, and individual reading inventories. Each of these can be a useful tool for the teacher who knows what kind of information she wishes to obtain. In other words, obtaining a grade-level score alone is not going to aid the teacher in pinpointing a comprehension problem. Also, although the teacher may be looking specifically for difficulties in comprehension, she cannot afford to overlook other skills being tested. Again, a basic sight vocabulary and adequate word attack skills are prerequisite to understanding the printed word.

There are four basic informal techniques that could be used to assess the child's level of comprehension: (a) general observation, (b) reading group observation, (c) questioning, and (d) the use of an Informal Reading Inventory (IRI). General observation can take place at any time of the day using any type of material. By observing his errors, you can readily see the kinds of difficulties he is having with the reading material, while determining whether he is becoming tense or frustrated. The second technique usually occurs when the child is asked to read aloud in his reading group situation or in any subject area. If the child has problems comprehending, you will sense his frustration in his movements, the tenseness of his face, and in his slow or whispered reading. Oral reading should be stopped at this point and a more successful task given to the child.

Purposeful questioning, the third technique, involves both the teacher and the student. The teacher may ask the child to point to a given phrase, to answer a specific question, or to locate a specific answer in the selection that he has just read. Questioning must have a purpose or it is of little value to either the teacher or the student. Comprehension questions usually are a combination of fact, inference, and vocabulary.

The last technique is the use of an Informal Reading Inventory or IRI. The IRI is composed of two main parts—graded paragraphs to read, and comprehension questions related to the paragraphs. There are three types of inventories: (a) teacher-made, (b) those that go with a basal series and are made by the publisher, and (c) general IRIs such as the Silvaroli (1972). Type A is made by the teacher when one isn't available or if what she has doesn't meet her requirements. The type B is part of the basal reading series that is being used in the classroom. The type C is for general usage. It does not fit any particular series, but it does give a reading level.

In teacher-made or basal series IRIs, time is saved by typing the questions on 5" x 8" cards or a piece of oak tag to check comprehension in each reading situation. Each test card is then inserted at the appropriate page in the test book.

EXAMPLES OF INFORMAL INVENTORIES OF COMPREHENSION

A. *Oral and written responses.*
    1. Either oral or written responses may be required, depending upon the purpose and the type of situation. If the pupil has less than primer or first-reader level reading ability, he is not likely to have much spelling ability, and hence cannot write.
    2. Written responses can be used to check (a) the number of ideas the pupil can recall, (b) the accuracy of sequence of ideas, and (c) the ability to organize. Also, the examiner may observe tremors in handwriting, motor control, spelling errors. In higher grades, special attention should be given to the student's organizational ability. Written responses are especially suitable for group testing.

B. *Techniques to appraise accuracy of comprehension.*
    1. Have a series of questions which may be answered in:
        a. a word
        b. a phrase
        c. a sentence
    2. Have a single question which requires the pupil to reproduce what he has read. Inexperienced teachers sometimes have the habit of unnecessarily repeating questions and the pupil's answers. This practice discourages pupils from listening and encourages "sloppy" answers. While repeating questions and answers is sometimes necessary, it should not be done in a test given to appraise oral language facility.

C. *Example of a teacher-made test.*

    Mary and John go to camp as soon as school closes in the summer. They go on the train and stay until it is time for school to open again in the fall. They have a happy time at camp because there are many other boys and girls there, too. They ride, swim, and play games together every day.

(For interpreting ideas)

1. When do Mary and John go to camp?
   a. Before school
   b. When school is over
   c. In the fall
   d. When school starts

(For understanding words)

2. Which word tells what kind of time the children have at camp?
   a. Lonesome
   b. Sad
   c. Joyous
   d. Funny

(For understanding ideas)

3. How do the children travel to camp?
   a. On a train
   b. On a bus
   c. In an automobile
   d. In a car

(For organizing ideas)

4. The best name for this story would be:
   a. Close of School
   b. Playing Games
   c. A Trip on a Train
   d. A Summer at Camp

(For understanding ideas)

5. Mary and John enjoy camp life because they
   a. are glad to be away for the summer.
   b. like the ride on the train.
   c. have fun playing games with the other children.
   d. are glad to be out of school.

Miller's *Reading Diagnosis Kit* (1974) offers invaluable information on diagnostic procedures. Following is a list of standardized tests that have some relevance to comprehension.

1. Gilmore Oral Reading Test, Harcourt Brace Jovanovich. Assesses oral word accuracy through paragraph reading. Literal comprehension questions are included and norms established.
2. Gray Oral Reading Test, Bobbs Merrill. Assesses oral reading errors and their frequency. Teacher-made comprehension questions are asked. No norms are given for comprehension scores.
3. Durrell Analysis of Reading Difficulty (new ed.), Harcourt Brace Jovanovich. Oral reading and silent reading subtests evaluate literal comprehension.
4. Stanford Diagnostic Test (Level I & II), Harcourt Brace Jovanovich. Includes vocabulary and comprehension subtests. The latter evaluates literal and interpretive comprehension.
5. Woodcock Reading Mastery Tests, American Guidance Service. Includes word comprehension (analogies) and passage comprehension.
6. Peabody Individual Achievement Test (PIAT), American Guidance Service. Includes a reading comprehension subtest which measures comprehension of sentences of increasing difficulty and complexity.

7. Durrell Listening-Reading Series, Harcourt Brace Jovanovich. Teacher can compare a child's listening comprehension to his reading achievement.

8. American School Achievement Tests, Bobbs Merrill. Offers four batteries measuring word recognition, word meaning, sentence meaning, and paragraph meaning.

9. Gates-MacGinitie Reading Tests, Teachers College Press, Columbia University. A battery of subtests measuring discrimination, listening, recognition, and blending skills.

10. Diagnostic Reading Tests, Committee on Diagnostic Reading Tests. The various forms include measurement of vocabulary, silent comprehension, and auditory comprehension.

One more assessment technique for measuring comprehension should be mentioned; it is the cloze test or procedure. The cloze test measures the student's comprehension of a particular piece of material. The technique forces a student who has been concentrating on word-calling to focus on the meaning of the word within the sentence. Usually, when the material is not too difficult to understand, about every fourth or fifth word is deleted. In more technical material, about every tenth word is omitted. The student is to supply the correct missing words. Some times the cloze test will be adapted to serve a particular instructional purpose, such as the testing of pronouns or, by omitting nouns, the testing of comprehending certain facts in content subjects. Gilliland (1974) suggests that completion tests, serving a similar function to the cloze test, may be more easily constructed by the teacher. Both can be used for instructional purposes as well as assessment. In particular, this approach works better with older pupils. The SRA Reading for Understanding Kit and the Using the Context workbooks, for example, use completion tests to teach comprehension skills. Bormuth (1969) reviews the research in the cloze technique and concludes that the scores on cloze tests correlate highly with the traditional, standardized comprehension tests.

Developing Comprehension

Teaching Techniques

The most important technique the teacher can employ to develop the comprehension abilities of her pupils is the skillful use of questioning. Questions guide the reader in looking for significant statements, supportive details, climate of the material, and critical analyzation. The kind of question asked by the teacher determines the kind of reading the child will do. "We have 5 minutes before the bus comes so read to pass the time" leads the child into ambulatory reading. "Read to discover what Kottmeyer considers the elements of phonics necessary for a beginning teacher" leads the reader to assimilative reading. "Read to compare the ideas of Kaluger and Kolson with the ideas of Kottmeyer concerning phonics" leads to critical reading. "Read to produce your estimate of phonic needs for a beginning teacher" leads to creative reading.

In each of the four kinds of reading mentioned in the preceding paragraph, ambulatory, assimilative, critical, and creative, different skills and techniques are called into play. Children do not as of and by themselves learn to do all four kinds of reading. They must be taught.

Ambulatory reading is the kind of reading you do when you cannot sleep at night and read merely to pass the time. Unknown words or phrases are skipped, there is no attempt to remember any or all of the details. Even the plot is given only that attention which will take the minimum of mental activity.

Assimilative reading is the kind of reading a student does in order to pass a course or an examination. Careful attention is given to what is significant, to supporting details, and to the entrenching of all this in the memory in order to be able to recall these at the appropriate time. Mental processes involve mainly memorization and sorting, with little attention to a critical analysis of the real worth of the material being read.

In critical reading the reading is punctuated by periods of pauses during which time the reader conjures up from his memory other related readings with which to evaluate the material being encountered presently. Critical comparisons are made and passages reread for clarification.

In creative reading the reader takes many ideas gleaned from a wide variety of sources and relates them in a new and different way, thereby producing something unique and distinctive. This calls for memory and critical analysis, true, but it also demands original thinking: seeing unusual relationships, looking for an uncommon response warranted by the material, and using the ability to restructure mentally.

To develop the four kinds of reading ability in a pupil the teacher must make certain her questions are the kind which give equal treatment to all four kinds of reading. Only a very low level of assimilative reading is developed when the teacher relies too heavily upon "yes or no" questions or regurgitative questioning.

Another technique for developing comprehension in older youngsters is the teaching of the seven propaganda techniques and having the children apply the techniques to materials read. These seven techniques are:

1. Glittering generalities.
2. Band-wagon technique.
3. Transfer.
4. Testimonial.
5. Plain folks.
6. Mud slinging.
7. Manipulation of figures or facts.

Each of these techniques should be taught and discussed, then materials found which employ them. The reading of speeches and editorials to identify the use of these techniques will go a long way toward developing children's critical reading and comprehension.

The technique of making certain the child has a "child's" reason for reading the material should never be neglected by the teacher. Purposeless reading never does insure depth of understanding, whereas even material too difficult can sometimes be read by a remedial reader who is motivated properly.

The last technique for developing comprehension is one of procedure rather than teaching. This is to make certain the book the teacher is asking the child to read and comprehend is not too difficult for his reading ability. Books with more than one out of twenty running words unknown are too difficult for the child. Hence, his energies must be devoted to word attack skills to the neglect of comprehension. It is in this area where the wealth of high interest-low level reading books can be invaluable.

Tovey (1976) offers ten practical suggestions for improving children's comprehension abilities.

1. Help children select books they can read.
2. Help beginning readers, and especially LD readers, to have successful reading experiences through the use of children's dictated stories.

3. Help children develop an understanding of the nature and purpose of reading—why they read for meaning instead of just sounding out words.
4. Encourage children to read high interest materials.
5. Encourage children to read books with content that is familiar to them.
6. Help children avoid meaningless oral reading.
7. Emphasize reading as communication—in other words, read to learn; de-emphasize the mechanical aspects of reading.
8. Provide children who have comprehension problems with many short selections of high interest.
9. Extend children's interest and thinking related to books they have read by the question approach or the retelling of the story.
10. Motivate children to read, read, read!

Children will find meaning in what they read only if they are looking for it. Many children are looking for nothing—and they generally find just that. You should always give the assignment in such a way as to help the pupil get the meaning from what he reads; the type of assignment made is important; and the child must have guidance. The more meaning he is asked to get, the greater his comprehension. Primary teachers may stress the meaning as much as the appearance of words. Teachers in the later grades should never give an assignment without giving clues as to what the child is to find.

Interesting and attractive reading material should be placed in the child's environment. Just as a merchant fills his shop windows with appropriate merchandise, so may the schools make use of this same means to stimulate a desire to learn how to read. The use of bulletin boards, excursions, caring for pets and flowers, pictures with a short story attached, slides, dramatization of stories, magazine articles, and pictures, games, and samples of good work will help to create this atmosphere. For example:

a. Take easy stories, cut them up into paragraphs, paste the material on the tagboard, and give them to the children for oral reading.
b. Have library sets of easy reading books and supplementary books for the slower readers.
c. Rewrite stories in simplified form, putting them on library tables for children to read.
d. Write short stories on the chalkboard or charts for teaching slow children.
e. If you are faced with the problem of using one book which is too difficult for your pupils, then organize your class into small groups, getting pupils of like ability together as much as possible. With your LD groups, do not be concerned with how much ground you cover, but rather with how well they are comprehending what they read. The first thing you need to do is to see that your pupils have meanings or concepts with which to read it.

The teacher should be so familiar with the material that she can sense the difficulties that the child will meet. Encourage the pupil to relate what is read to past experience. Give any related facts that will make him want to find out more about the material to be read. Make the new concepts in the story meaningful to the pupil before any reading is attempted. As these concepts are taken up and explained, put the words and phrases on the chalkboard so that he will connect the word and the concept. Never give an isolated vocabulary drill before a reading lesson. Connect vocabulary directly with the story that is to be read.

As a child reads a passage, he needs to know some ways of finding the meanings of new words by himself. As a teacher, you should impress him with the fact that he does not have to know absolutely every word in order to be able to read a paragraph silently. Encourage him to read on to the end of the sentence which contains a word he doesn't know. Quite often if he goes back, he can see that he really understands the meaning of the word from its use in the sentence. He may guess the word from the general meaning and the beginning sound. He may look for little familiar words in a big word and then try to pronounce the word and get its meaning. Divide the word into syllables for pronunciation. Teach the child the use of punctuation so that he does not become confused in reading connected material.

Listening Comprehension

More and more educators are coming to the conclusion that pupils need help in listening comprehension as well as in reading comprehension. They argue that the basis for good reading comprehension is laid in the ability of the pupil to comprehend that which he hears. To these educators there is a correlation between proficiency in oral comprehension and proficiency in written comprehension.

Many of the skills involved in the comprehension of printed matter are also involved in the comprehension of the spoken word. Sifting out the insignificant from the significant, noting details, anticipating what follows, drawing conclusions, seeing relationships, and determining author's purpose all are involved in both kinds of comprehension. Hence, the attention paid to one will naturally affect the degree of proficiency with the other.

A forerunner of listening comprehension development has been the SRA Reading Laboratory which includes a series of exercises for the development of listening ability as well as a technique for applying meaning to material being heard. Many basal readers now have listening comprehension lessons included in the teacher's manual, and almost all language arts books pay some kind of attention to this skill. The phenomenon of a listening corner in the primary grades and in some intermediate grades is an outgrowth of this belief in the development of listening skills. Tape recorders are set up in a corner of the room with a variety of materials taped and changed frequently. Children having time available proceed to the listening corner, read the guide sheet, put on headphones tuned to the lesson to which they would like to listen, and use the guide sheet as an indicator of what to listen for.

The developments being made in listening comprehension offer great possibilities. Reading authorities have long agreed that understanding spoken vocabulary precedes the understanding of printed vocabulary, so perhaps it is rational to assume that aural comprehension should precede printed comprehension. Some very carefully designed and controlled experiments are necessary to determine if the rationale holds true.

Comprehension and Recall

The primary purpose of any reading is communication; hence, it is necessary to make a diagnosis of the child's level of comprehension. Is he functioning at a "Who" or "What" level of comprehension, or is he at the next higher level, the "How" level? Or, is he at the "Why" level, the inference level? The teacher can determine the child's level of comprehension through the administration of a properly prepared Informal Reading Inventory. Instruction and practice should begin at the level higher than the level at which the child functions adequately.

The SRA Reading Laboratory is a good source of "Who" and "What" level drills. Although it was not designed for this purpose, we have found in our work that a child's comprehension at the lower levels improves greatly after having been through the SRA

Organizing and Reporting Kit. Commercially produced practice exercises, such as the Charles E. Merrill Diagnostic Reading Workbooks, are also valuable tools to use at this level.

At present we know of no commercially produced material for use at the "How" or "Why" levels of questioning. In our clinics, we teach the child needing remediation at the "How" and "Why" levels to recognize the five most useful paragraph patterns.

1. Question—Answer

   Example—"Do you know how to read a book? You don't begin with the first word and read. Instead you survey the book to get a general idea of its content."

2. Time

   Example—"The sophisticated reading specialist goes through stages. Early he becomes a technician—knowing what to do but not why. Later he becomes research conscious and tries to quote research to back all his actions. When he finds research poor and the results conflicting, he becomes cynical and pragmatic."

3. Comparison—Contrast

   Example—"Both the poor school and the good school have reading problems. Usually it is only the good school that admits it, and tries to provide help for the children with reading problems."

4. Enumeration

   Example—"The experience approach, first, uses the child's egocentricism, second, has a built-in vocabulary controlled, and third, assures that the material is in the child's conceptual background."

5. Conclusion—Proof

   Example—"In dealing with some emotional problems, one must behave opposite to what the child expects; otherwise, he is in control and not you. Further, you would be positively reinforcing the very behavior which you wish to alter if you behaved as he expected."

A word of caution: A child with a comprehension problem will find it easier to begin by finding details than by getting the main idea or summarizing. Too often remedial reading teachers work in reverse and accomplish little.

To improve recall and retrieval we teach children to outline, to use the SQ3R technique, to study aloud, and to employ mnemonic devices. Outlining forces them to employ a kinesthetic modality to reinforce the visual modality employed in silent reading. The SQ3R technique increases the child's proficiency in locating what to study. Oral recitation adds the auditory modality as a reinforcer. Mnemonic devices aid in recall. For example, mnemonically, HOMES can always be used to trigger the names of the great lakes—Huron, Ontario, Michigan, Erie, and Superior.

Comprehension and recall involve location of information, memorization of short selections, remembering several directions, silent reading, and oral reading. Activities included in silent reading are:

1. *Find the main idea.*

   Selecting the best title—Write a paragraph. Write three possible titles for the paragraph. Have the children choose the best possible title for the paragraph.

Tom and John went to the circus. Tom liked to see the elephant show, John liked the monkey act.

_____The Circus
_____Favorite Shows
_____Elephants

Naming a selection—Write a paragraph. Have the children read it and write an appropriate title for it.

Predicting what the author is going to say—Have the children read just the title to a selection. Have them tell what they think the selection will be about.

2. *Locate specific details.*

Noting details—Write a paragraph. Write several questions, some which can be answered from details given in the paragraph and some which cannot be answered from the details. Have the children decide on those which can be answered from the paragraph.

Spot ran to meet the car. He knew that Joe was coming home. Joe had been away on vacation. When the car door opened, Spot jumped quickly into the front seat.

Where did Spot run?
Where had Joe been?
What color was the car?
Was Joe in the car?

Picking out a detail which does not belong—Write a paragraph and have the children read it and pick out one word that does not belong in the story.

It was a very hot day. The children went in for a swim. That was a good way for them to get warm.

3. *Understanding sequence.*

Arranging sentences in proper sequence—Write a sentence in its phrase components. Have the children arrange the phrases in their proper sequence.

_____John asked
_____candy
_____for some

4. *Anticipating outcomes.*

Have the children look at the pictures of the story and try to predict what the outcome will be.

Have the children read part of a story and then make up a possible ending for the story.

Have the children draw pictures in sequence of a story that they have not heard in its entirety.

5. *Evaluating what is read.*

Separating fact from fiction—Have children decide whether the sentences could be true.

6. *Evaluating fact and fiction.*

Bring in articles from several newspapers on the same current topic. Compare the factual content. Note the different points of emphasis and the different interpretations of the same event.

Study magazine advertisements. Prepare sheets with two columns. On one side students list factual statements about the products advertised. On the other side list persuasive or suggestive statements from the ads.

7. *Inferences.*

Give the student several descriptive words. Ask him to identify an animal that the words might fit, then write a short story using the words.

8. *Grasp sequence of events.*

Scramble statements that express the main points of several paragraphs or parts of a story. Have students number statements in order of occurrence:

_____Once they went to a picnic.

_____Joe won first prize in the contest.

_____Mary and Joe were good friends.

_____There was a running contest that day.

9. *Arrange ideas in sequence*

Using story cut-ups. Cut up a story on the children's reading level into different parts and paste on a cardboard. Mix up the cut pieces and pass them to the group. The child who thinks he has the first part of the story reads it. The others follow suit until all parts of the story have been read.

Three Basic Approaches

Remediation procedures for comprehension skills vary from teacher to teacher. Three developmental approaches in the remediation of this skill area are frequently used by classroom teachers. The three approaches are (a) the guided reading or the basal series approach; (b) the language experience approach; and (c) the step-by-step approach, which is a combination of the other two types. There are two approaches that appear to work very well in remediation of comprehension skills in LD children—the guided reading approach and the step-by-step or combination approach.

GUIDED READING OR BASAL APPROACH. The guided reading or basal reading approach has five components in which both the teacher and the student are participants. According to Harris and Smith (1972) the five components are (a) building background, (b) setting purpose, (c) independent reading, (d) follow-up discussion, and (e) development of related skills. These components can all be used in one reading lesson or in a series. Components (a) and (b) are taught by the teacher with as much student input as possible. These components are very important in stimulating the interest of the child and helping to give him a purpose for reading. If this is properly done, the student will be able to complete the independent reading component with little or no help from the teacher. This is important because it helps to build a feeling of success in the child. Usually the teacher has the student read the story orally again or retell it orally in his own words. This permits the follow-up discussion to become a questioning period for both the child and the teacher. Through the use of this follow-up discussion, the teacher can locate any weaknesses in related skill areas and work on those. Activities found helpful with the guided reading approach are the 5W's and Question Drawing.

This approach uses the procedures and materials that are available with the classroom basal reading series. The basal series approach is structured on a sequential development of skills, starting at a dependent level and working up to an independent level. This approach offers many different sources of reading material within its manual. Teachers must try to keep the material interesting for the child yet not too difficult for him (Wallace & Kauffman, 1973).

This approach can be used with an LD child to reinforce what is being read in the classroom. Usually the stories in the basal readers are full of details and allow for practice in locating specific words, phrases, sentences, and paragraphs. The stories are often easily divided into smaller parts to make location exercises more exact and precise. This also helps the child in finding the main idea or main character of the story. The child can reinforce the skills learned through the use of this reading workbook, which is one of the accompanying materials. There are many activities and materials that can be used with this approach. Two that would be recommended are Story Division and Magic Fun.

LANGUAGE EXPERIENCE APPROACH (LEA). The language experience approach deals directly with the child. It is language expressed by the child in the form of experiences or actions that are created for, or have actually happened to, the child. Reading instruction that uses the language of the child automatically builds on what is known by the child. The child's background experiences and self-image should be used in teaching him to read.

The primary advantage of LEA is its emphasis on reasoning and the utilization of skills. At first, the teacher writes the stories as the child dictates to her. In this way, the child sees reading as a method of communication. The child often becomes involved with what he is saying and the story goes on and on. This approach allows a child to interrelate visual, oral, and auditory stimuli into his experiences. He begins to feel that what he has to say is meaningful and important. Having the child locate his own ideas or phrases makes what he has said more meaningful and he can comprehend it much better (Wilson, 1972). The use of the LEA permits a start with relatively easy, interesting material in whatever quantity is desired. But the LEA is a debatable method to use with LD children who need structure. It is also particularly hazardous in the hands of an inexperienced teacher. See Anderson and Dearborn (1952) for a critique of LEA. Some activities that could be tied in with this approach are As I See It and News Reporter.

STEP-BY-STEP APPROACH. This approach is a combination of the other two and works best as an individualized approach. It combines the setting up of a purpose, independent reading, and follow-up questioning which are components of the guided reading approach; the workbook and skill development components of the basal approach; and the experiences of the child in the LEA approach.

Many commercially made materials such as workbooks, skill builders, practice readers, and SRA kits are used in this approach. The experiences of the child are used in the beginning to help locate specific phrases, sentences, and paragraphs. This approach often finds the child creating a long story which can be used extensively in remediation. Gradually the teacher moves to other materials that are on the child's interest level so that he is still motivated to read. The workbook approach allows the teacher to observe the child while he is using his new skills. By doing this, she will be able to locate any difficulties which still exist and try to remediate them in another way.

This approach should work well with a learning disabled child. It allows for remediation to be done in many forms, keeping the child motivated while providing him with success experience at the same time.

Activities for Use with the Three Approaches

Several activities are listed below which can be used with any of the above approaches.

ACTIVITY 1. THE 5 W'S

Have the children write WHO, WHAT, WHEN, WHERE, and WHY to head columns at the top of their papers. They look through their story to find the answers. This activity may be done in small groups or individually (Harris & Smith, 1972).

ACTIVITY 2. QUESTION DRAWING

For this activity either a basal reader or the Specific Skill Series—Book A can be used. Prepare cards that have questions on them. Place the cards in a box and have the child draw one card at a time. Have him locate the answer in the story. When he finds it, have him read it aloud. If the child is to work independently, the cards can be made self-checking (Bloomer, 1964).

ACTIVITY 3. STORY DIVISION

For this activity you will need one copy of the basal reader for each student. Divide a story into parts. Give each child one part of the story to study. After the entire story has been read silently, each child reads his part aloud. Then give the students an oral comprehension check. This activity would be closely associated with finding the main idea (Ekwall, 1970).

ACTIVITY 4. MAGIC FUN

This activity provides practice in locating specific words or phrases. Either the basal reading series or the specific Skill Series can be used. Write a word or phrase on the board; ask the students to locate it in the story. After they have completed this task, they can check with you and then erase it from the board. This activity can be done when working with a small group or with an individual (Criscuolo, 1975).

ACTIVITY 5. AS I SEE IT

This activity fits well with the LEA approach. The story can be either one that is the child's own or one from a book. Drawing paper, paints, crayons, or markers are needed. After the children have either read or written the story, have them illustrate various scenes as they perceived them. Mix up the scenes and have a child reconstruct the story through purposeful questioning (Ekwall, 1970).

ACTIVITY 6. NEWS REPORTER

This activity uses everyday materials such as newspapers, TV guides, want ads, yellow pages, catalogs. The purpose is to have the child locate specific information, facts, or details. The newspaper and TV guide are favorites in most classrooms.

ACTIVITY 7. THE HUNTER AND THE HUNTED

You will need a reading book for each student. This activity is for locating sentences, dialogue, or paragraphs. One child who is designated as the hunter asks the questions. The hunted answers the questions by locating the correct response in the story and reading it orally. If he gets it right, he trades places with the hunter and the game continues. (Ekwall, 1970).

ACTIVITY 8. FIND THE PART

Have the child or children read the story. After they have finished, write an incomplete idea on the board (ex., Why Jimmy felt unhappy.) Direct students to read orally the parts of the story which supply the facts to answer the question. Another approach is to give the pupils sentences from the story and ask them to read the paragraph aloud in which the sentence appears (Criscuolo, 1975).

ACTIVITY 9. WORD CLUES

Refer students to the story being read. Ask them to locate specific words or phrases that are used in place of a word (ex., *said*). Then have the students read what they have found orally (Criscuolo, 1975).

Self-Selection

There are growing numbers of educators who consider the problem of comprehension to be tied closely to the manner in which schools teach children to read. To these educators the assignment of dull uninteresting books to a class in order to develop the mechanics of reading has lead to an overemphasis upon mechanics and a degree of disregard for the real purpose in reading, i.e., comprehending. The educators point out that all children have a natural curiosity about their environment and that this curiosity leads them to exploration. As they explore they self-select items from the environment which are interesting to them at their stage of development and with which they are equipped to cope.

Since in an educational environment there can be placed large numbers of books on varying levels of difficulty and on many topics, the child will be given the opportunity to explore and to select a book which interests him and which is at a level of difficulty commensurate with his ability. Since the problem of difficulty of material and interest will be negated, the child will be able to comprehend the material and hence there is no need for elaborate drills and materials to develop comprehension ability. The basic difference seems to be that under the present plan teachers guess the level and interest of a child's book whereas under self-selection the child knows what book interests him and if he is capable of assimilating it.

The use of self-selection for helping children learn to comprehend is a pioneer idea if it is used as a supplement to a full-range reading program which includes basal, diagnostic, study reading, and interest reading. It borders on cultism, however, to suggest it as the only means to the development of the child's reading ability.

Sample Activities for
Developing Comprehension

Developing comprehension at the literal level.

A. In directed reading activities have "who, what, when and where questions" with comprehension checks. These checks can encompass true-false questions, multiple-choice statements, or completion statements.
B. Show a picture and have children determine what is happening through discussion.
C. Exercises involving short paragraphs on various subjects can be presented for the children to determine the subject of each.
D. Present flash cards with items on them. Then have children recall items when the flashcard is removed.
E. Have children find key words in short paragraphs.
F. Present cards with directions, then have children do in order the things listed: i.e. "Stand up—turn around—raise your hand—whistle—sit down."
G. Cut up story and pass out parts. Have children read each selection in proper sequence.

Developing comprehension at the interpretive level.

A. Tape the auditory portion of a television show and have the children interpret what is happening.
B. Have children supply endings to stories.
C. Use many "why" questions.

    D. Have children write about senses applied unusually, i.e.—Write about:
        1. The sounds of breakfast
        2. The smell of home
        3. The feel of a motor trip
    E. Have children write descriptive phrases about children in the room. Have them read aloud and have the other children guess who it is.
    F. Have children do exercises on similes, metaphors, and figurative speech

Developing comprehension at the critical and evaluative levels.

    A. Teach propaganda techniques and have children identify T.V. commercials.
    B. Present a problem with several solutions. Have children decide which is the best solution and why.
    C. Study and discuss magazine ads.

Specific exercises suitable for the lower grades.

    1. Riddle type—"What am I?"
    2. Telling response. Tell what is wrong.
       Example: Mary went to the store. She bought a bottle of milk. She poured it into a basket.
    3. Give children pictures with precise directions underneath. They are to do what the sentence tells them to do.
    4. Write sentences on the board. Children find answers to the questions in each sentence. Who? When? What?
    5. Jumbled sentences. Children reassemble each sentence.
    6. Play telegram. Simple directions are written on yellow paper. You may use this for individual orders. Children may at times be permitted to send telegrams to one another or to the teacher.
    7. Cut up into sentences a story from an old reader. Paste these sentences on cards. The children reassemble the story.
    8. Write a paragraph on the chalkboard about a person or thing. Below it write a list of adjectives. The child reads the paragraph and chooses adjectives that could be used with the various words in the paragraph.
    9. Give the child a card on which a paragraph is printed. Three or four words appear under the paragraph, one of which tells how someone in the paragraph felt. The child underlines the word.
   10. Give a selection with two paragraphs and ask the child to tell what the first one is about. If he cannot, ask leading questions. Follow the same procedure for the second paragraph.

Exercises suitable for the middle grades.

    1. Guessing pantomimes. Act out parts of a story. Others guess the scene.
    2. Play a game from written or printed directions.
    3. Story-telling from question slips. Prepare a series of questions to be answered by individual pupils.
    4. Question exchange. Teacher or pupils make out questions which are exchanged for answering.
    5. Marking game. Pupils mark certain parts which tell things as you call for them.
    6. Oral reproduction of stories.
    7. Reading to find entertaining material to reproduce to the class later.
    8. Answer fact questions.
    9. Answer thought questions
   10. Match headings and paragraphs.

11. Pair differently worded sentences having the same meaning.
12. Find the main ideas in several paragraphs and construct a summary paragraph from them.
13. Select the most interesting sentence. Discuss choices.
14. Describe an imaginary trip from a railroad, steamship, or tourist folder.
15. Check differently treated topics. Pupils look through the tables of contents or indices of several books, for instance, to find several versions of the same story.

Media for Developing Comprehension

The basal reading series with its accompanying workbook, spelling workbooks, and materials for the development of proficiency in grammar all contribute to a child's ability to comprehend. There are, however, many supplementary materials available to the teacher which can be used profitably to develop the comprehension abilities of the pupils. The listing at the end of this section gives a representative list of such materials and the name of the publisher. Many more are available for the classroom teacher's use.

The SRA Reading Laboratory is basically a comprehension developer. This box of multilevel stories with accompanying comprehension questions can be used very profitably as a supplement to any grade-level program.

Another kit of the Science Research Associates, the SRA Organizing and Reporting Kit, can contribute much to the development of the comprehension abilities of school children by developing an understanding of the organization of materials. The analysis of good reports and why they are good gives the child insight into the organization design of good writers while the sequential lessons leading to the composition of a good report by the student make him aware of the elements of printed matter organization, i.e., the topic sentence, supportive details, etc.

The Reading for Understanding Materials can be used at the junior and senior high school levels to develop comprehension abilities. Also, the various books published by the Reader's Digest Association are found very interesting for children of all levels and contribute heavily toward the development of comprehension.

A listing of materials found useful in developing comprehension follows:

1. Reading Booster Cards
   McGraw-Hill

2. Context Puzzles
   Scott Foresman Reading Systems

3. Scholastic Record & Book
   Companion Sets
   Scholastic Records

4. Reading Thinking Skills
   Continental Press

5. Sprint Libraries
   Scholastic Reading Center

6. Action Reading Kits
   Educational Activities

7. Sentence Formulation & Syntax Development Kit
   Educational Activities

8. Specific Skill Series
   Barnell Loft

9. Structural Reading
   Random House

10. Crossword Puzzles for Reading-Thinking Skills
    Continental Press

11. SRA Reading Laboratories
    Science Research Associates

12. Reading Skilltext Series
    Charles E. Merrill

13. Reading Incentive Program
    Bowmar

14. Highway Holidays Series
    Bowmar

15. Concepts for Communication
    Developmental Learning Materials

16. Read-Study-Think
    Xerox

17. Reader's Digest Reading Skill Builders
    Reader's Digest Educational Services

18. System for Success
    Follett

19. New Modern Reading Skill Text Series
    Charles E. Merrill

20. Individualized Reading from Scholastic
    Magazines

21. Reading for Meaning
    Lippincott

22. Comprehension Audio Lessons
    Reader's Digest Educational Services

23. My Weekly Reader
    American Educational Publications

24. Learn to Listen, Speak and Write
    Scott Foresman

25. Listening Aids through the Grades
    Columbia University Bureau of Publications

26. Help Yourself to Improve Your Reading
    Reader's Digest Educational Services

27. Listen and Read
    Educational Development Laboratories

A very good list of activities for development of comprehension skills can be found in *The Teaching of Reading* (4th ed.) (Dallman, Rouch, Chang, & DeBoer, 1974).

chapter 13

Improving Vocabulary
Growth and Content Reading

> 'Twas brillig and the slithy toves
> Did gyre and gimble in the wabe;
> All mimsy were the borogoves,
> And the mome raths outgrabe. (from *Jabberwocky*, by Lewis Carroll)

Many people have tried to get literal meaning from this poem but to no avail. The reason they could not make any sense out of it is because of the 23 words in the stanza, 11 are nonsense words. Yet these words are so cleverly written that they can be easily pronounced, and a person gets the impression that they must mean something. In terms of vocabulary reading the implication is clear: vocabulary building involves more than mere word recognition and pronunciation; it also involves word meaning, which implies concept development.

When we speak of vocabulary we refer to the total number of oral sounds or printed symbols to which a child can attach a meaning which is similar to the meaning others in his culture would attach to the same symbol or sound. The 2-year-old daughter of an acquaintance, when confronted with something for which there is no name known to her, calls the unknown object a *dwa-dwa*. This *dwa-dwa* might have meaning for the child, but to anyone else in her culture, no meaning is attached. On the other hand when the young child says *mother,* she has the concept which is somewhat similar to the concept anyone else would attach to the word.

Basic Understandings

Kinds of Vocabulary

Generally, people have five kinds of vocabularies: an understanding vocabulary, a speaking vocabulary, a reading vocabulary, a writing vocabulary, and an emerging vocabulary. The understanding vocabulary is the first to develop with young children. Long before the baby can talk or read or write he can recognize and respond to words spoken to him by members of his family. In fact, the baby does try to communicate with others, especially mother, as early as 3 weeks after being born by using different kinds of cries to convey different needs. In return, baby soon begins to respond to key words such as *bottle*, indicating that he has certain expectations concerning the meaning of that word.

The second vocabulary to develop is the child's speaking vocabulary. From his understanding vocabulary words and concepts will come into his speaking vocabulary. Once he begins to speak the speaking vocabulary grows so rapidly that it is difficult to determine the extent and rate of growth. We are certain, however, that by the time he comes to school he has a minimal speaking vocabulary of 3,728 words.

The third vocabulary the child acquires, the reading vocabulary, begins for most children prior to school entrance; however, in the majority of cases, the acquisition has been so very small that it is safe to generalize and say the reading vocabulary begins to grow in the first grade. Here he learns to apply a new type of symbol, a printed word, to the oral symbol and the concept he has previously acquired.

It is the first grade, too, where most children begin to acquire the fourth vocabulary, the writing vocabulary. Learning how to reproduce the printed symbols of the reading vocabulary proceeds very slowly and in most cases continues to lag behind the other three vocabularies throughout the life of a person. The Craig study of best sellers shows that authors who have written several best sellers, perhaps as much as forty years apart, wrote on the same level, using the same level of vocabulary in all of their works. The only exception is Shakespeare. The fact that his level of writing changed leads some people to disbelieve that he wrote all of the books credited to his authorship.

The fifth kind of vocabulary is one that is found in each of the first four vocabularies. We refer to it as an *emerging vocabulary*. We hear a word, or see a word, for the first time. We do not bother to look it up in a dictionary or to ask the user what it means but instead get a very vague delineation from the context. On the second confrontation of the word, we may recall the first context and, combining it with the second context, we further delimit the meaning. We still cannot say it is in our understanding vocabulary because the meaning is as yet too vague. Eventually, however, after a number of exposures in different contexts, the word will become incorporated into our vocabulary. Up until the time it does, however, it is in our emerging vocabulary. As an example let us trace a word through the emerging vocabulary into the understanding and reading vocabulary.

First exposure: The child died of marasmus.

What is marasmus? You now know that marasmus is something that can be fatal. But what is it?

Second exposure: Many orphans of victims of the flu epidemic after World War I died of marasmus even though they had the best of diets and medical care.

Now you are beginning to taste the impact of the thing called *marasmus*. It isn't a nutritional affliction, apparently. And, seemingly, medical care cannot help.

Third exposure: Death when seemingly nothing physically was wrong with the child, when he was given the best care, and lived in a clean and orderly environment made marasmus puzzling. Because of the large number of children, the harassed nurses could not fondle the babies but they did give them the best of care.

Want to guess?

Fourth exposure: Since lack of bodily contact with other humans appeared to be the only variable, the deaths were attributed to that and the term *marasmus* was born.

By now the word *marasmus* has passed from your emerging vocabulary into your understanding vocabulary and reading vocabulary.

Fifth exposure: Knowing now that the word *marasmus* means a physiological wasting away of organic tissue and organs due to psychological distress, a person becomes intrigued to learn later that even a Burmese cat will also suffer from marasmus when separated from those who gave him love, attention, and care.

Now the concept of the word *marasmus* in the understanding vocabulary takes on expanded meaning as its implications and applications have been broadened. A person's understanding vocabulary throughout life is the largest of the five. By fourth grade the reading vocabulary generally surpasses the speaking vocabulary. The writing vocabulary seems to stay the smallest throughout life. Reading specialists believe the progression of vocabulary development is from understanding to speaking to reading to writing in the elementary grades.

Size of Vocabulary

The size of the vocabulary of children has been researched thoroughly. In 1907 the vocabulary of preschool children at specified ages was reported. Reading vocabularies of beginning reading books have been studied. The writing vocabularies have been studied. The size of children's vocabularies when entering school has been investigated. Surprisingly enough there seems to be wide disagreement concerning the size of vocabularies.

Possibly the differences in conclusions concerning size can be attributed to the manner in which the various studies have been conducted. Two techniques are generally employed when conducting a vocabulary study: frequency count and sampling. Under the frequency count method the research tabulates every word the child uses on the assumption that if the child uses the word, it is in his vocabulary or at least it is in the particular kind of vocabulary being researched. Generally a person using the frequency count method will employ stimulus objects in order to get the child to talk about a certain area and to give the child a wide range of experiences in which to use his vocabulary. The areas frequently used are farm, store, travel, church, city, holidays, seasons, stories, radio, television, movies, space, mechanical equipment, and uniformed personnel. One such study used pictures of cross sections of the culture. Under the sampling technique, words are usually chosen from an unabridged dictionary through a statistical procedure and then the children are subjected to a test of recognition of the words. By using a statistical procedure the results can be extrapolated into what would have happened if the child had been subjected to the entire dictionary. It can be easily seen that the two techniques offer many possibilities for discrepancies in results. Possibly the safest thing we can say is that a child has a minimal vocabulary of 3,728 words, but his maximal vocabulary may be as high as 26,000 words.

A study directed by J. Wepman (1966) under a National Institute of Mental Health grant found that whether a person were a Ph.D., a cab driver, a laborer, or a clerk, their basic everyday speaking vocabulary was about the same. Just 403 words are used by people regardless of their educational background in more than 80% of their everyday conversation. Only 33 words comprise half of a person's vocabulary. These 33 words are generally the less specific words which hold our language together. *Is, the, and, a, I* make up one-sixth of our vocabulary.

Wepman had a 54-person sample divided equally between men and women ranging in age up to 90-years-old. They were shown 20 pictures about which they told stories. All words were recorded and a frequency count compiled. Although the list was designed to aid in the retraining of aphasia victims, it offers possibilities to education.

Of the estimated 600,000 words in the English language, the average eighth grader knows about 10,000, the average high school student about 15,000, and the college graduate, approximately 20,000 of those words. However, of those 600,000 words, only about 4,000 are in constant daily use. Cramer (1961) lists these words and suggests that the first 2,000 constitute approximately 95% of an individual's reading and writing vocabularies. All 4,000 words make up 98% of the words most commonly used by people in reading and writing.

Vocabulary Tasks Facing the Teacher

The vocabulary tasks facing the classroom teacher can be classified into (1) attaching a new symbol to an old concept (a meaning of a word symbol); (2) attaching an old symbol which is known to the child to a new concept; and (3) attaching a new symbol to a new concept.

Attaching a new symbol to an old concept is the kind of activity engaged in by the first-grade teacher. We have seen in the preceding section that first graders come to school with at least 3,728 words and concepts in their understanding vocabulary. Reading authorities and psychologists agree that the concepts and words in a child's understanding vocabulary are more than enough to get him through the first two grades, inasmuch as most first-grade reading programs have only about 400 words. However, in first grade and much of second grade, the child is faced with the task of attaching to his old concept of the meaning of a word a new symbol, a printed word.

Attaching a new symbol to an old concept can best be illustrated through the reading specialist's old friend, the word *cat*. To a very young child, the word *cat* may mean a particular cat with whom the child has numerous contacts. Eventually, however, the child will see other cats and be forced to change his basic concept of the word *cat* from that of a specific cat to the generalization for cat. When he begins to study animals, he will be told that a tiger is a cat and a lion is a cat. Once again, a more inclusive cat concept must be attached to an old symbol. When he joins the teen-agers he will be told that a *cool cat* is a T-shirted young teen-ager who knows his way around. Once more, a new concept must be attached to the word *cat*.

Attaching a new symbol to a new concept is the kind of activity most high school classes engage in. In science the child must simultaneously acquire a new concept that an atom is a miniature universe held together by force fields and invisible to the eye while he learns the verbal symbol *atom* to go along with the concept.

It is evident that these three kinds of tasks present different levels of difficulty. If teachers were more aware of these three levels of tasks we would not find so many teachers devoting 15 to 20 minutes and myriads of art work and activities to developing the concepts "up" and "down" when so much research has shown that these concepts are already a part of the child's understanding vocabulary. Therefore, the task is at the level of attaching a new symbol to an old concept—in other words, not developing the concept, but teaching the word.

Bond and Tinker (1973), Lamb and Arnold (1976) and Samuels (1976) have additional information on the definitions of sight words and sight vocabulary that the reader may find interesting. Samuels, in particular, also stresses the importance of automaticity, the development of automatic habits in reading. What is remarkable about automatic responses is that they enable a person to understand what is being read without the need to focus undue attention on the reading matter.

The LD Child and Vocabulary Development

A learning disabled child could have learning dysfunction problems in any one of three language areas: (a) receptive language, (b) inner or associative language, and (c) expressive language. Vocabulary disorders can be caused or further disrupted by sociocultural factors influencing language, a language or speech problem, or by central nervous system dysfunctions that interfere with language processing. Only the latter case can be considered a learning disability, but certainly many LD children have further language complications brought on by having learned nonstandard English, restricted language and verbal development in general, or a second language which is the primary language spoken in the home.

A facet of language acquired early is auditory reception and the ability to comprehend the spoken word. It must be noted that receptive language can be either auditory or visual, and either or both may be deficient in a child. It is here that we begin to note how interrelated the three language areas are in affecting the overall performance of the child. The receptive process introduces experience (stimuli) to the inner language process. Inner language is dependent on the quality of the receptive process for its development; the expressive process, then, is dependent on the quality of performance of the inner language process.

Many children who have disabilities in auditory receptive learning commonly show deviant behavior characterized by excessive restlessness, perseveration, distractibility, and poor sustained attention. Johnson and Myklebust (1967) state that one of the most common symptoms is "misunderstanding." The LD child has difficulty in vocabulary development because he is misperceiving what he hears. In the perceptual-conceptual process, this limitation would restrict the effectiveness of the conceptual or language formulation process, in turn making it difficult for language to be formulated for use in the expressive or output phase.

An essential aspect of language development is that word meaning must be acquired before words can be used to communicate and understand. For a word to have meaning, it must relate to a unit of previous experience or learning. This phase is called *inner language*. It is here that the transformation of experience into symbols takes place. In relation to the perceptual-conceptual process of learning, this would be noted as *language formulation* and takes place during the conceptual process. The child with a disorder in inner language may have difficulty in acquiring meaning from the experience, or he may have a deficiency in his ability to transform the experience into verbal symbols. The inner language disorders have been found to be the most difficult to remediate. Johnson and Myklebust have done much research in this area of processing learning experiences and the changing of these experiences into abstract, meaningful symbols such as are found in reading or writing.

Where the spoken word is concerned, comprehension must precede expression. Understanding must be attained before the word can be used meaningfully in communication. Output difficulties are more easily observed than input problems. For example, it would be very evident if a child had expressive difficulties since speaking would be a problem. Children who have expressive language disabilities appear to have (a) difficulty in recalling, (b) trouble holding words and directions in mind, and (c) difficulty activating the motor system for the appropriate *expressive* response.

Spache (1976) maintains there are three major categories of how language development occurs. One group of theories relates to operant conditioning and the imitation of the adult. The second group emphasizes the cognitive development of language based on concept acquisition and spontaneous experiences. The third theory stresses Piaget's organismic development on a biological basis, plus a state of readiness promoted by experiences.

All of these have one common thread—the need for the child to be fulfilled and to have much exposure to an experiential background. Without the appropriate experiences plus sensory-verbal stimulations, the child remains undeveloped in his knowledge and usage of vocabulary. Spache says there are many characteristic areas to consider as indications of a socioculturally disadvantaged background: low socioeconomic status; poor relationships with peers and teachers; racial and ethnic discrimination; poor familial relationships and child-rearing patterns; and the lack of good home conditions. The learning disabled child will have poor vocabulary development because of a lack of adequate verbal stimulation needed to overcome whatever central nervous system malfunction he may have in processing information. The difference between the LD child and the socioculturally disadvantaged child is in the processing mechanism. The LD child has an organic defect, while the other child has a social or emotional limitation. The culturally disadvantaged child can be taught by developmental methods. The LD child, however, will require techniques which emphasize a multisensory approach and which adhere to principles and procedures that can be used effectively by the child within his operating capacity and his neural structure.

Johnson and Myklebust point out that it is necessary to recognize that the visual, auditory, tactile, and kinesthetic sensory signals can be intact but still be specifically deficient in relation to language. They also emphasize that the child should first be assessed as to his problem and then have the appropriate remedial education planned for him.

How Concepts Are Developed

Basically, children acquire concepts in two ways: through experience or vicariously. Of the two, experience is probably the best; however, much learning in life is abstract, and hence, impossible for acquisition through experience alone.

For practical purposes, concepts are generalizations which can be categorized. To form any generalization one must be subjected to many experiences with the elements of the category to be able to distinguish the common attributes which delimit the category. Hence, the importance of the experiential background to the beginning reader. Without concepts and words to categorize them, he is at a loss to acquire meaning. Studies have shown that a correlation exists between the breadth of experience of the reader and the degree of his achievement. Culturally deprived children illustrate this point.

It is necessary to point out that exposure is not necessarily experience. For the child to experience a particular thing sometimes it is necessary that his attention be focused on the particular stimulus in the total environment. What we mean is that taking a child to a zoo may not necessarily mean that the child is having the experience of seeing many and varied kinds of animals. If his attention has been attracted to the concession stands selling gas filled balloons at the entrance to the zoo, and if he is captivated by the balloons, he may spend all his time looking at the balloons held by other children and give the animals only a cursory inspection. Teachers and parents trying to engage children in planned experiences must take the time to focus the child's attention on the desired experience through discussion and questioning. This concentration enables the child to employ the oral symbols associated with the concepts they are trying to develop.

If children and adults developed concepts through experience only, their knowledge would be rather limited. Many concepts are developed through vicarious means. Television has contributed much to the development of concepts in children, sometimes to the dismay of teachers and parents. Movies, books, and discussions are other informal means of developing experiences vicariously. Just telling a child is probably the most inefficient means of trying to give him a vicarious experience. For a vicarious experience to have any worth the child must become mentally involved. Telling gives the child the mental responsibility of assimilation and nothing else. All teachers know that it is impossible to be sure that a child is assimilating when you want him to. If, however, he is put in a position where he is given what Dewey called "an obstacle to surmount," or a vital need for mental participation, the teacher can be reasonably sure that he will assimilate. Dewey says reflective thinking only takes place when a person is confronted with a situation or problem he must solve.

Vocabulary Control

BASAL READERS. Until recently the basal texts have seen a constant shrinkage of the number of new words introduced in the basal readers. This situation has been misconstrued by some critics as indicative of the inefficiency of the present methods of teaching reading. In reality, the criticism is a testimonial to how little the critic knows about the total reading program. As pointed out in an earlier chapter the total reading program has four approaches: basal (containing a controlled vocabulary), diagnostic, reading to learn, and interest approach. The controlled vocabulary of the basal readers is limited because the main purpose of the basal reader is to develop the mechanics of reading; hence, by maintaining a controlled vocabulary of a limited number of words, introduced slowly and with many repetitions, the teacher becomes free to concentrate on the mechanics and the child is not bogged down with the dual task of acquisition of vocabulary and acquisition of skills simultaneously. Yet, the vocabulary to which the child is subjected in the other three approaches is not quite so limited and adds a substantial amount to the total number of words a child is exposed to under our present systems of teaching reading. The other three approaches confront the child with more words to learn than he is confronted with in the basal approach, so he really learns more words than are found in the basal reader. Yet, critics seem to talk as if the basal reader was the sole program. It is to be remembered that the basal reader has a limited vocabulary because the basic purpose is to teach the mechanics of reading.

Controlling the vocabulary in the basal text assures that the child will be faced with only those words which are in his understanding and speaking vocabulary. It also provides for overlearning those words which make up a large percentage of the running words the child will encounter in his elementary reading activities. Vocabulary control offers the best assurance that the child will have a solid foundation for the refinement of his reading.

Authors of basal texts take much time and effort to make certain that classic studies of the vocabulary of children at the level for which their book is being written are consulted. Some of these basic vocabulary lists which are considered useful are as follows:

1. Daniel W. Fullmen and Clifford J. Kolson. A beginning reading vocabulary. *Journal of Educational Research*, 1961, 54.

   A list of 184 words appearing in most of the beginning reading books. The list is divided into subsections based on frequency of occurrence.

2. Edward W. Dolch. *Teaching primary reading.* Champaign, Illinois: Garrard Press, 1960.

   Lists of 220 abstract words and 95 nouns which make up from 50% to 65% of all running words encountered in the elementary school.

3. Ernest Horn. *A basic writing vocabulary.* Iowa City: Bureau of Publications, University of Iowa, 1926.

   A classic study which gives some indication of what words children use in writing.

4. Edward L. Thorndike and Irving Lorge. *The teacher's word book of thirty thousand words.* New York: Bureau of Publications, Teachers College, Columbia University, 1944.

   A graded list of words indicating a difficulty index. It is the most comprehensive study of words and their difficulty available.

5. Clifford J. Kolson. *The vocabulary of kindergarten children.* Unpublished doctoral thesis, University of Pittsburgh, 1960.

   Gives the minimal oral vocabulary of kindergarten children.

THE SOCIOECONOMIC BASIS OF VOCABULARY. One of the most fascinating studies of vocabularies was done by J. Allen Figural (1964). Figural set out to find the vocabulary of underprivileged children. He felt that previous studies had made contributions to education but that they were designed for the average socioeconomic class. If a significant difference existed between the vocabularies of underprivileged children and those of children of another socioeconomic group, then the vocabulary list designed for the average was at best questionable when used with a specific socioeconomic group.

The results of Figural's study showed many differences between the underprivileged and his more privileged counterpart. First, the underprivileged came to school with a much smaller vocabulary than his counterpart. Second, the underprivileged and his counterpart had only a school vocabulary in common at the end of the elementary school. There were also other differences.

The Figural study never has been given as much attention as it deserves. Perhaps he was a pioneer in making researchers and authors in reading conscious of the various needs of children from different socioeconomic groups.

BASIC ENGLISH. C. K. Ogden, a semanticist, believes much confusion results because of the vagueness of many English words. Words do not always signify the same meaning to two different people. Ogden seems to feel that if the language could be simplified much confusion would be eliminated. With this in mind Ogden reduced English to a basic vocabulary of 850 words (1934). The list is divided into (a) operations such as *come, get, with;* (b) things such as *chalk, business;* (c) qualities such as *able, round, sweet, strange.* There are a few simple rules to follow. With the vocabulary and the rules, most books can be translated into Basic English. A large number of books have already been transferred into Basic English.

Although Ogden designed his vocabulary for a purpose other than reading, its application to the teaching of English to non-English speaking peoples and its use with some remedial readers seems to indicate a move for an even more controlled vocabulary than is found in our basal series. The fact is that all basal series contain more words in the elementary books than are found in Basic English.

THE ULTIMATE IN INCIDENTAL CONTROL. Laura Zirbes (1928, 1964) advocates allowing the control of vocabulary to rest with the children. Under her proposal, therefore, the words they use must be in their spoken vocabulary, and hence, in their understanding vocabulary. According to Zirbes, if the reading materials the children develop come out of their own experiences and vocalizations, the vocabulary is automatically controlled. For years Zirbes advocated the use of the experience approach to teaching reading, not as an adjunct to the basal reader, but rather as the way. Recently she seems to have accepted the individualized reading approach along with the experience approach. In the individualized reading approach, theoretically, the child uses self-selection in his choice of reading matter and probably would not choose a book he could not understand. So, he automatically controls the vocabulary.

Context of Vocabulary Building

The Development of Vocabulary

The first approach to the development of vocabulary could be labeled the *incidental approach*. Under this approach children are subjected to a wide variety of experiences such as trips, pictures, television, and reading matter through which it is hoped they will steadily increase the size of their vocabulary. There can be no doubt that this kind of approach will add to the child's vocabulary. Most preschoolers come to school with an extensive vocabulary because of their experience, even though prior to their schooling no conscious effort was made to increase their vocabulary.

The second approach to the development of vocabulary could be labeled the *correlated approach*. Here the teacher attempts to identify beforehand the new concepts and new words to be found in all of the children's reading matter. When a new word is encountered in reading, the teacher knows it is a new word and can give time to the development and entrenchment of the word in the child's vocabulary. This approach is the kind used under the basal reader system. The authors have identified new words and give, in the teacher's manual, suggestions for insuring the acquisition of the word by the children.

The third approach could be labeled the *directed practice approach*. Under this approach the teacher has a separate program where she consciously tries to develop the understanding and recognition of new words without reference, necessarily, to the books the children are reading. *Word Wealth Junior* by Ward Miller is this kind of a plan. The book contains a large number of words which have been subdivided so that there are weekly lists and sequential lessons for the study of the lists.

The fourth could be labeled the *author approach*. More and more authors of books written for children are trying to develop vocabulary in the text where the word appears. This can be done by inserting a clause or phrase in the sentence which explains the meaning of the word. Some authors use a *synonym approach* by inserting a synonym in the sentence such as "The divan or couch. . . ." Some authors even give a brief explanation of the word in a footnote or in parentheses in the sentence in which it appears.

The modern school uses all these avenues to develop the child's vocabulary. The correlated approach is found in the basal reader. This reader has been chosen many times because of the author's approach. The incidental approach is used in interest and study reading and activities for the children. In a sense, the directed practice approach can be found in the spelling program, and in many cases, in the employment of books designed to do the job. As a result of the use of the different approaches, of a more sophisticated childhood, and of more experience, the vocabulary of our children is steadily increasing. The International Kindergarten Union (IKU) study in 1928 found kindergarten children to have a minimal vocabulary of 2,596 words. When this study was replicated by Kolson in 1959 he found the minimal vocabulary had grown to 3,728 words. In addition he found today's children had eliminated baby talk and animal noises and had replaced them with a more sophisticated vocabulary.

Assessment of Vocabulary

In the area of vocabulary we must not only determine what words the child is ready to learn but also his level of mastery. Is he at the lowest level of mastery, *recognition,* or is he at the *reproduction* or the *application* stage?

The basic sight words on the Dolch cards can be used to determine the level of recognition and oral reproduction. Since these are basic sight words, we have an indication of vocabulary level through the number of words known. We also have an indication of the level of oral reproduction through the words miscalled which will be the ones to be learned. If the child knows all the Dolch words, the new vocabulary lists in the back of the basal readers can be used to build a vocabulary list to be learned.

The vocabulary area in which remediation is sought should be based on an assessment of competency in meaning vocabulary knowledge. One of the more convenient ways for a teacher to do an assessment is to do an error analysis of the student's use of vocabulary in his oral language and to examine the nature of the errors made in his creative or free expression writing. Does the student have a limited meaning vocabulary restricting how much and how well he can express his ideas and elaborate on them? Does he use the vocabulary impressively and inaccurately? Does he overuse some words, such as "you know" and "OK" to convey an implied but not an expressed meaning?

It is also possible to determine competency in vocabulary by use of the vocabulary subtest, usually called the *word meaning* subtest, on a standardized survey reading test. There are some limitations to these tests, as reflected by cultural bias, the use of words with multiple meanings, and the need for word-recognition ability. However, they can give a relative ranking and some indication of the functional level of vocabulary reading ability. Some commonly used standardized tests with word meaning or vocabulary subtests are:

1. California Reading Tests. Psychological Corporation, 757 Third Ave., New York 10017.
2. Gates-MacGinitie Reading Tests. Teachers College Press, Columbia University, 525 West 120th Street, New York 10007
3. Durrell Listening-Reading Series. Harcourt Brace Jovanovich, 757 Third Ave., New York 10017.
4. Metropolitan Achievement Tests (revised). Harcourt Brace Jovanovich, 757 Third Ave., New York 10017.
5. Stanford Achievement Tests (revised). Harcourt Brace Jovanovich, 757 Third Ave., New York 10017.

An informal analysis of vocabulary and language usage can also be made by the teacher observing the difficulty that a child may have in forming words into sentences and into correct syntax. Use a series of questions that cannot be answered with a *yes* or *no.* The Peabody Kit has some excellent activities and questions that could be used in a diagnosing teaching situation. Stories could be read and the child asked to tell what he heard. Another technique to use is to make up a series of cards and place them in context with objects around the room. Some words could be nouns (object names) and others, verbs (*filing,* placed on a file) or adjectives (*alive,* placed by a plant). The Peabody Picture Vocabulary Test can give ideas for cards. The concept of *learning rate* is significant in assessment because it indicates how many words a child can learn in one day.

How to determine learning rate

Purpose—to establish a rate at which new vocabulary can be presented.

Procedure—Select 10 words two years above the present reading level. Present these words to the class in the morning using all the modalities of learning. Spend 10 minutes on this activity. Individually check the class one hour later, at the end of the day, and the next day for word recognition. The average number of words recalled will give an approximate number of new words which can be presented and learned in one presentation.

Sample list of words

appetite
elastic
engineer
feather
introduce
lemon
narrow
scold
obey
tease

Teaching Vocabulary Building

LANGUAGE EXPERIENCE APPROACH. Since nothing is really learned until it can be used, the child should be taught to write the word and to use the word. This will insure the highest level of mastery—application. Experience charts function well in insuring mastery at this level. The language experience method can be used to build vocabulary, to build correct grammatical and syntactical form, and to form words into sentences. The language experience approach is developed around three major ideas:

(a) An emphasis on experiencing communication (vocabulary) in natural ways.
(b) An emphasis on the study of communication (vocabulary) that helps a person to be literate in our society.
(c) An emphasis on ideas and on language as other people use it to communicate their ideas. In other words, the child experiences vocabulary, studies vocabulary, and relates the vocabulary of others to self.

Children can learn new vocabulary words and learn to build sentences which, in turn, are grammatically and syntactically correct through the multiple media provided in this approach. In this technique one could experience new learnings through talking, painting, singing, dancing, acting, or writing. One could study vocabulary through the acquisition of name words, place words, and through learning natural speech patterns which help in formulating sentences. The child can also relate communication of others to self through reading or being read to, seeing films, listening to records and tapes, listening to music, enjoying fine art prints, and handling sculpture.

This approach lends itself greatly to the needs of the learning disabled child. It allows for success in a variety of areas, can be adapted to the presentation of short bits of information at a time, and, above all, treats all the senses through a wide variety of media.

Following is a sample of specific activities suggested by Van Allan (1976) for vocabulary growth using the language experience approach.

1. *Concepts for names.*
   a. Use the names of students to extend vocabulary: Allan—*boy, friend, brother, son, grandchild, student, baseball player*
   b. Collect words that change when we talk about a group

   tree⟶ grove   ship⟶ fleet
   cow⟶ herd   person⟶ crowd

   c. Make a list of homonyms and leave it open for students to add sound-alike words

   I—eye   sun—son
   mail—male   dear—deer

2. *Concepts for verbs.*
   a. Say words of movement and ask children to pantomime them as you change the meaning of the word

   Pull—a heavy load
   —weeds from the ground
   —a tooth

   b. Use stories, poems, and songs and invite children to move like animals

   Hop like a bird
   Jump like a rabbit
   Walk like an elephant

   c. Observe weather movements from day to day. On a chart collect words with inflections that indicate tense

   to drip   drips   dripping   dripped
   to shake   shakes   shaking   shook

3. *Concepts for words of description.*
   a. Choose a category of description such as the shape of things and look for examples—*square, round.*
   b. Listen for sounds. Identify their source and try to write the sounds with alphabet letters so others can duplicate the sounds.
   c. Cook something. Examine the ingredients and describe them before and after cooking.

MULTISENSORY APPROACH. The idea of building a sight word vocabulary for labeling and reading purposes and overall increase of vocabulary can best be learned by the VAKT or tracing approach. This approach uses the visual, auditory, kinesthetic, and tactile senses to learn sight words.

In all stages of VAKT, words are learned as the child needs them to express his ideas. At first, all the words come from the oral language of the learner as he attempts to write, record, or label pictures he has made. At no point does the child copy words. Rather, he studies the word, fashioned appropriately to his development, until eventually he can write it from memory. The child always writes at least two successive correct copies before he uses the word in his story or report. Repeated contact with the word must then be provided through the directed rereading of a typed copy of his own written materials and a variety of reading experiences with teacher-prepared materials. These words must be checked regularly for retention.

Activities which supplement this approach must be done in step form. Money (1966) suggests the following sequence:

1. A word to be learned is identified.
2. The teacher directs attention to its structure by asking about parts and syllables.

3. The child listens and watches as the teacher writes the words on a large sheet of paper, saying the word before it is written, saying each syllable on the first stroke of that syllable, and again saying the word as a whole after the writing has been completed.
4. The child then traces over the word following the same pronunciation routine.
5. If correct, he writes it twice; if successful, he is ready to put it into use.

WORD BANKS. The use of word banks can be a highly motivating medium for developing vocabulary as well as other reading skills. A *word bank* is a collection of a child's voluntary sight word vocabulary. It is a collection of cards on which a single word—the one just learned—is written by the child or his teacher and stored in one place, usually a box or an envelope. Quant (1973) suggests follow-up activities for use in classrooms where word banks are used. He indicates that word banks can be used for (a) the development of classifying skills by asking children for words that are things they can see, hear, or feel, or words that make them feel happy, sad, etc.; (b) sight word recognition, using words collected from word bingo or word concentration games, or matching words to wall charts; (c) practice in phonics—finding the words in the bank that begin with a certain consonant or that have a given vowel sound, sorting the cards according to sounds, or arranging them in alphabetical order; (d) structural analysis—finding words that can be combined into compound words, sorting the word cards according to the number of syllables. The word bank can also be used for an individualized spelling program, the development of a picture dictionary, or the construction of sentences.

WORD LISTS. The use of word lists chosen from those mentioned in the previous section would certainly provide a good basis for beginning work in vocabulary development. We have often said to teachers of LD children "If you don't know where to start, begin by assessing knowledge of the words in the Dolch list and then teach the unknown Dolch words." The Dolch List is outdated and has been under some criticism. Several studies recently, however, suggest that the Dolch List has withstood time (Mangieri & Kahn, 1977). Lowe and Follman (1974) compare the Dolch List to several recent lists and find that the first 150 words can be used without reservation or limitation. They suggest an expanded use of the list, however, by teaching the words with another word, such as *the dog* or *a dog*.

An interesting note on the use of word lists was sounded by Pope (1975) when she pointed out that most sight word lists were lists of frequently used words and often did not contribute much to usage with the decoding aproach. She has developed a list she feels will help with phonetic emphasis in reading. Jerry Johns (1972) developed a list of 63 words for older disabled readers based on the Dolch List. Kucera and Francis (1967) also put together a list of words that are most frequently used by adolescent and adult readers.

The Dolch List and the Kucera/Francis lists are in Appendix B. The use of sight words is not out of style. A core vocabulary is needed before going on to higher level books. The sight vocabulary, however, should never substitute for context and stories which provide meaningful reading experience (Hood, 1977).

Specialized word lists available in addition to those mentioned earlier are:

1. Ogden, C. K. Basic English for adults, 850 words. *The system of basic English.* New York: Harcourt Brace, 1934.

2. Figural, J. A. Vocabulary for underprivileged children. From Limitations in the vocabulary of disadvantaged children: A cause of poor reading. *Improvement of reading through classroom practice.* Newark, Del.: International Reading Association, 1964, 164–165.

3. Jones, L. V., & Wepman, J. M. A spoken word count. Chicago, Illinois: Language Research Associates, 1966.

4. Wilson, C. T. An essential vocabulary. *Reading Teacher*, November 1963, 17, 94–96.

5. Durrell, D. D. Graded word lists. In *Improving reading instruction*. New York: Harcourt, Brace & World, 1956.

6. Kucera, H., & Francis, W. N. *Computational analysis of present day American English.* Providence, R.I.: Brown University Press, 1967.

   Analysis of 500 samples of adult printed material. Shows the 220 most frequently used words.

7. Harris, A. J. & Jacobson, M. D. Basic vocabulary for beginning reading. *Reading Teacher*, 1973, 26:4, 392–395.

   Word list based on computerized study of 14 series of elementary textbooks grades one through six.

8. Otto, W., & Chester, R. Sight words for beginning readers. *The Journal of Educational Research*, July-August 1972, 65, 435–443.

   Compiled a list for beginning readers from the Carroll (see #12) list: The "Great Atlantic and Pacific Word List" of 500 words for instant sight recognition.

9. Fry, E. Teaching a basic reading vocabulary. *Elementary English*, January 1960, 37, 38–42.

   List of "Instant Words" derived from three primary basal readers.

10. Johns, J. A list of basic sight words for older disabled readers. *English Journal*, October 1972, *61*, 1057–1059.

    A revision of the Dolch list and a comparison with other checklists to get a list of words reflecting adult language.

11. Hillerich, R. L. Word lists—getting it all together. *Reading Teacher*, January 1974, 27: 4, 353–360.

    A list of 240 starter words in a basic language arts vocabulary for children.

12. Carroll, J. B., Davies, P., & Richmond, B. *The American heritage word frequency book.* Boston: Houghton Mifflin, 1971.

    Based on samples from 1,045 printed school texts grades 3–9; shows the most frequently used words.

13. Johnson, D. D. A basic vocabulary for beginning reading. *Elementary School Journal*, October 1971a, 72, 29–54.

    A list of 306 words based on printed and spoken words of the kindergarten and first grade levels.

14. Pope, L. Sight words for the seventies. *Academic Therapy*, Spring 1975, 10:3, 285–289.

    A list of 200 words for beginning readers given in three sections; these words are considered suitable for use with a phonetic approach rather than sight recognition as found in most other lists.

If a reader is severely disabled and approaching adolescence or adulthood, then it is advisable to use a "survival word list" for developing a reading vocabulary. These are words frequently encountered in society and are important to one's safety and well-being. The list includes words such as *danger, exit, fire alarm, men, women, go slow, hospital, push, pull,* and *live wires.* A list of these words is included in Appendix B.

OTHER SAMPLE ACTIVITIES FOR INCREASING A CHILD'S VOCABULARY

A. Building a conceptual background

    1. Provide opportunity to touch, to taste, to hear, to use, to manipulate the thing for which the symbol to be learned stands.

2. Have dramatic play, games, excursions.
3. Use pictures, models, drawings, slides, overhead projectors, and films. Follow with a discussion.

B. Developing oral expression and listening
1. Provide opportunity for story telling, reporting, explaining.
2. Read to children and have them read to each other.
3. Provide listening centers in each room.

C. Building sight vocabulary
1. Have child develop "My Book of Words."
2. Develop interest reading.
3. Teach dictionary skills.

D. Developing multi-meanings
1. Collect sentences using word in different way, i.e.—*run*
   a. I had a *run* in my stocking.
   b. The bobsled *run* was fast.
   c. Let's *run* home.

E. Context clues
Circle the right word
1. We_____our pet.
      look   like
2. Help_____find our dog.
         up   us
3. Come_____, Mother.
        here   he
4. We_____you to come.
     what   want
5. Spot is a funny_____.
              get   pet
6. We_____find Spot.
      can   car
7. Father_____for us
      want   works
8. Mother_____us.
       helps   here
9. I cannot find my hat. _____is it?
            Where   What

Media for Vocabulary Building

1. *Word walls.* A portion of wall space devoted to lists of words that children can use when writing or can point out words for spelling. The teacher can incorporate these sight words into games.

2. *Large pictures on a variety of topics.* The pictures can be used to stimulate verbal growth and to motivate the children toward correct structure. Have a child tell the story about one of the pictures followed by discussion.

3. *Books on a variety of topics.* Benefit is gained because the child can hear more words and hear them in appropriate context and syntactical form. The child listens to a story, then tells the story back, using the words heard.

4. *Walks and field trips.* Encourage the child to discuss appropriately the things in his environment. Have the child draw pictures of things seen on a walk; talk about the picture and label each one. The class could play "What Did I See?"

5. *Filmstrips and movies.* The opportunity is provided for children to see and hear words in correct context. Discussions, dramatizations, book making, or picture collections can be activities developed from filmstrips.

6. *Lotto games, dittoes, and a variety of commercially produced games to stimulate vocabulary growth, sentence form, and labeling.* These can be used as small group or individual activities. Instructo, School Craft, Creative Playthings, and Gel-Sten Co. are only a few of the companies offering such materials.

7. *The MacMillan Reading Spectrum, Vocabulary Development Booklets.* These booklets can be used with older primary children to develop word knowledge and skills.

An excellent book filled with vocabulary activities for the learning disabled youngster is *Everyday Problems and the Child with Learning Disabilities* (Bernstein, 1967). Other materials are:

Title	Address
1. Vocabulary Building Series	Educators Publishing Service, 75 Moulten St., Cambridge, Mass. 02138
2. Wordly Wise	Educators Publishing Service
3. Spectrum of Skills	Macmillan Co., 866 Third Ave., New York 10022
4. Words—A Programmed Course in Vocabulary	Science Research Associates, 259 East Erie St., Chicago, Ill. 60611
5. Making Friends With Words	Globe Book Co., 175 Fifth Ave., New York 10010
6. Ginn Language Kit	Ginn Publishing Co., Waltham, Mass. 02154
7. Peabody Language Development Kit	American Guidance Service, Circle Pines, Minn. 55014
8. SRA Reading Laboratories	Science Research Associates, 259 East Erie St., Chicago, Ill. 60611
9. Growth in Word Power	Reader's Digest Services, Educational Division, Pleasantville, N.Y. 10570
New Advanced Reading Skill Builders	Reader's Digest Services
10. Merrill Reading Skill Text Series	Charles E. Merrill, 1300 Alum Creek Dr., Columbus, Oh. 43216
11. Word Power	In each monthly issue of Reader's Digest
12. 30 Days to a More Powerful Vocabulary	Pocket Books, New York 10010
13. New Ways to Greater Word Power	Dell, New York 10010
14. Word Power Made Easy	Perma Books, New York 10010
15. Word Power: Short Guide to Vocabulary and Spelling	Everett-Edwards, DeLand, Fla. 32720
16. Words Are Important (series)	Hammond Press, Maplewood, N.J. 07040

There are many other materials available. Attend a state, regional, or national conference of the International Reading Association or the Council of Exceptional Children and visit the book exhibit or exhibitor's booths. A vast amount of material is available. In the final analysis, however, some of the very best material, in terms of being suitable and appropriate for the child, is the material prepared by the teacher for the specific need of the child.

Reading and Content Fields

Reading for study purposes is one of the four avenues a good teacher uses in order to develop the child's fullest reading potential. It is in the content area where this study type of reading is developed. Here the child learns to apply the general reading skills he has learned in the basal approach and it is here where he is given instruction in the specific reading skills peculiar to a given content field.

The first task of the teacher when working in the content areas is to determine the degree of efficiency of application of general reading skills by the student in the content area. A child may function very well during basal reading, yet not transfer the skills learned in basal reading to the content area. The teacher must ask herself:

1. Does this child transfer the reading assignment study technique to the content reading?
2. Does this child adjust his speed for the more meticulous kind of reading characterizing study reading?
3. Has this child the general vocabulary level to succeed at this reading task?

The teacher's reaction to the evaluation based on the three preceding questions may be to give the child a book covering the same material but on a lower level of difficulty in order to make certain the child is reading at his instructional level. She may organize individual instruction, or small group instruction, or total class instruction for lessons applying the general study techniques to the content material if her evaluation shows the transfer is not being made. Sometimes she may just have a conference with a child to point out the fact that he is reading too fast for the best assimilation of the content material.

Once the teacher has made certain that the child is equipped to the fullest of his capacity with the general reading skills she must turn her attention to the development of reading skills specific to a particular discipline. Each discipline has reading skills peculiar to itself. Map reading is peculiar to geography and history, diagram reading is essential to arithmetic, and cut-away pictures are frequently used in health. These specific skills must be taught. In addition every discipline has its own terminology which must be developed through the meticulous vocabulary development procedures.

Principles for Developing Reading
Skills in Content Areas

The first principle for developing specific reading skills is to attend to vocabulary. It is amazing to watch a capable elementary teacher work for 15 minutes to develop the concepts of up and down, which the children probably knew in the first place, then to watch the same teacher teach a social studies lesson and fly right over a difficult concept such as logic making absolutely no effort to employ concept or vocabulary development procedures. Most of the technical vocabulary of the content areas is difficult and needs the best vocabulary development techniques in order to insure maximum comprehension.

The second principle is to control the learning steps. All learning is sequential and requires step-by-step development. Specific reading skills in the content area require these same short steps in sequential order if the learner is to develop to his maximum potential. Confronting a child with a weather map before the preliminary instruction in map symbols can only lead to catastrophic responses. Map reading is a skill which must be developed through stages of academic growth just as much as long division must have been preceded by the learning of the division facts.

The third principle is to provide adequate practice. As each concept is developed, each word learned, or each reading skill introduced, the teacher must make certain there is follow-up application of these factors and that these activities conform to what is generally spoken of as the laws of learning. Introduction is just the first phase in any teaching. It must be followed by entrenchment activities.

The fourth principle is to provide continuous evaluation of the learning and to use this evaluation to replan the learning activities. One of the greatest shocks a beginning teacher faces is the fact that her charges have not learned all those things she so skillfully taught. Constant formal and informal evaluation techniques must be applied in order to insure progress.

The easiest way for a teacher to make certain she applies these four principles in the content area is to assume that the discipline lesson is also a reading lesson and to apply the directed reading activity (DRA) format to the learning situation.

Specific Reading Skills in Subject Areas

The specific skills in the arithmetic field can be classified into vocabulary, comprehension of symbols, and comprehension of relationships. Arithmetic is replete with terms such as *augend, addend, subtrahend*. These are many times new terms and new concepts, and care must be taken to see that the learners understand them. Arithmetic also involves the use of a system of digits. Digits are just as much symbols as are words and letters. Each digit must signal certain concepts and the relationship of one digit to another may alter the concept of a digit as much as the relationship of one letter to another alters the sound signaled by a letter. The letter *e* has a common sound, but when it is combined with other letters into the word *here*, its sound is changed. Likewise the figure 2 signals a concept, but when the digit 2 is combined with other digits into the number *123*, the concept signaled by 2 has been altered. This reading skill, though mainly arithmetic, is also a reading skill and must be taught as such.

Operational symbols are another specific reading skill the learner must master in arithmetic. *Add* means one thing, whereas *subtract* means another. Attention must be given to this kind of symbol reading if we wish to avoid the impression that "An arithmetic book is a series of problems interspersed with directions which children inevitably fail to follow."

The teacher must take pains to make certain the child learns the skill of comprehending the peculiar relationships inherent in mathematics. Equations are an expression of relationships and the teacher must see that the child understands the generalization principle involved in a relationship expression such as an equation, graph, or chart.

Some specific suggestions for improving the specific reading abilities in arithmetic are:

1. Include irrelevant facts within problems.
2. Develop the habit of estimating before working the problem.
3. Practice the restating of problems in the child's own terms.
4. Give the pupils practice in formulating arithmetic problems.
5. Practice with verbal problems not containing numbers and have the students indicate the process.

If the teacher would follow these suggestions and what has been said in the preceding paragraphs, she will be attending to specific arithmetic skills.

In the field of science the special reading abilities are those of vocabulary, direction following, drawing generalizations, location of information, and application of information. Modifications of those things suggested for the development of specific reading abilities in math are also applicable here. In addition, however, it must be pointed out that the concepts in math are sometimes condensed into symbols which have a great deal of information and fact behind them. This means that the person who is to interpret these condensed symbols must have a broad background of experience from which to draw. Hence, it is imperative in the area of science that a child have a wide experiential background since this is the only way in which he can gain deeper understanding and insight into the relationships and principles which function in his environment.

In addition to map reading, picture reading, cartoon reading, and document interpretation, the major problem in the area of the social studies is one of vocabulary. Nowhere is the vocabulary burden more difficult. It is often repeated that one picture is worth a thousand words but in the area of social studies one sometimes finds the reverse and discovers that one word is worth a thousand pictures. How many pictures would you have to draw in order to get across the concept embedded in the word *equality*? Social studies is loaded with terms so abstract that relating them to a child's known vocabulary is a Herculean task. How can you make *justice* concrete?

The area of aesthetics combines the task of new symbol learning with what Spencer calls the *broad view* of reading. Music has its symbols—the clef, the key; art has its symbols in the two dimensional drawings which represent three dimensional objects in the environment. These symbols must be taught and the concepts behind them developed. At the same time the pupils must be given practice in recognizing parts of music and parts of pictures and relating them to the total work. This is the kind of broad reading which calls for interpretation and patterned eye movements. Is the difference between the skilled musician and the unskilled measurable through eye movements? Does the skilled musician take in more than one note at a time as compared to a poor musician who reads note by note? We think we view a picture without eye movements, yet studies show the eyes in viewing a picture move from point to point on the picture. Artists must determine the correct eye patterning for efficient reading in art.

Because one of the major reading problems in all the content fields is the problem of technical vocabulary, teachers have tried to use many kinds of media to help develop concepts and vocabulary. A multitude of audio-visual aids have been devised to do the job. Slide films are available in every area as are films, mock ups, and records. Although all of these have more or less contributed toward conceptual and vocabulary development the problem remains with us. These materials are designed to reach the middle of the academic spectrum and therefore, may or may not be appropriate for a given area; or what is more often the case, they do not quite coincide with what the classroom teacher is doing. The recent use of closed circuit television programs designed to complement the classes or class of a particular area seem to have overcome these obstacles.

One such program was a supplementary science program beamed to the Washington D.C. area. Because a large number of classrooms were participating, they were able to show the kinds of persons and materials which are somewhat beyond the realm of the classroom teacher. Study guides were issued which gave the teacher specific methods and directions for preparatory activities which introduced terminology and motivated interest. The television lessons which followed then proceeded to give vicarious visual experiences which deepened the understandings and entrenched the learning.

Televised sessions of the city council can do more to develop understanding of the function of local government than textbooks and discussions. Days in court can develop the idea of civic responsibility and protection far beyond the scope of the classroom situation.

A number of sources offer further suggestions on how to study in various content areas. Gilliland (1974) offers specific suggestions for causes of inadequate reading in subject fields. Bond and Tinker (1973) have a good chapter on improving reading in the content areas of social studies, science, mathematics, and literature. Shepherd (1960a, 1960b) and Strang et al. (1967) also provide excellent descriptions of reading in content areas, and the latter reference has a good set of exercises for remedial training.

Content Reading and the Secondary Teacher

Recent studies have shown that using the secondary reading teacher in a tutorial role is not only costly but also ineffective. Most youngsters having difficulty in reading when they reach junior high school have had anywhere from one to six years of one-to-one or small group remediation outside the classroom setting. If the remediation has not prepared them to function in secondary content materials, then more of the same remediation is of questionable value.

To begin with, a youngster whose reading skills are so poor that he cannot read the five or six content area texts is not helped by entering a remedial class where more reading materials are loaded upon the student. Secondly, this type of youngster usually has an antagonistic attitude toward remedial reading.

These things have led to a change in the role of the secondary reading teacher. The trend is to use the reading teacher as a resource teacher to the content teachers. Her role is to:

1. Inform the content area teachers of the kinds of disabilities students in the class exhibit.
2. Suggest alternative methods, media, and techniques for teaching the students with learning problems.
3. Provide short-term therapy for small groups of students exhibiting similar needs.
4. Assess students' reading and study skills.
5. Provide liaison with the elementary feeder schools and the high school into which the junior high school feeds.

6. Conduct inservice workshops to train content area teachers in methods of teaching reading through use of the content materials, thus improving the teaching of the content while helping the student gain reading skills.
7. Serve as a resource to the content teachers.
8. Organize volunteers.
9. Serve as a substantive advisor to the principal.

chapter 14

Improving Reading-Study Skills,
Interest in Reading,
and Rate of Reading

The first three grades in elementary school are the years when the basic skills of reading—word recognition, phonetics and structural analysis, comprehension—are taught. The content matter during these years is basically narrative in nature and related to the experiences of the children. The upper elementary grades are the years when these basic skills are used to give meaning to the content of specific academic fields, such as social studies, science, health, geography, literature, and written problems in mathematics. The content is factual and developmental and contains a vocabulary that is endemic to the subject. Special reading-study skills for locating information and using it effectively become a necessity for the older child and adult because he must be able to locate and isolate meaningful facts, ideas, and generalizations from the vast content to which he is exposed.

Some skills relating to location and organization of information can be taught as early as the first grade. Even a first grader can be introduced to a table of contents as presented in some readers. Other skills learned in the primary grades include noting the title of stories as they appear, finding page numbers, knowing where books of interest can be found, and using a dictionary for children. It is the older child, however, who is confronted with a need to know basic reading-study skills if he is to be an efficient functional reader. He is one who must use a discovery, inquiry approach to "unlocking" the structure and meaning of new subject matter. It is also the older reader who must expand his reading interest horizons if he is to develop a taste and a thirst for information gained through reading. Hopefully, the child will develop good reading habits, attitudes, and interests.

Consider the disabled reader who, at the age of 12 or so, may only be reading on a second- or third-grade level. He is still trying to learn the basic skills of unlocking new words and gaining meaning from what he is reading. However, as an adolescent or an adult, he will still need reading-study skills; he should also have broad interest in reading materials. But after years of frustration in just learning basic reading skills, the chances of his developing a good feeling about independent reading are practically zero! His frustration with reading is usually so great that he would prefer to be doing something else other than reading— anything else! He will not be motivated easily to pursue reading for learning because he has failed so often in learning how to do simple reading.

Basic Understandings

The terms *learning to read* and *reading to learn* are indicative of the difference between basic reading skills (learning to read) and reading-study skills (reading to learn). Whereas the former term includes areas such as sight words, phonetic analysis, structural analysis, comprehension, and vocabulary development, the latter term (reading-study skills) relates to topics such as locating information, reading for specific information, organizing, evaluating, and retaining material, and using that information as a stepping-stone to a more sophisticated level of knowledge.

Basic Reading-Study Skills

The core components of reading-study skills are outlined as follows:

BASIC LOCATIONAL SKILLS

1. Using a table of contents.
2. Using an index.
3. Using a glossary.
4. Using an appendix.

Skills required are (a) locating words when arranged in alphabetical order; (b) finding the specific page pertaining to needed information; (c) deciding on a key word; (d) identifying an entry word; and (e) knowing the content to be found in various reference books.

ABILITY TO USE VARIOUS TYPES OF BOOKS

1. Using a dictionary.
2. Using an encyclopedia.
3. Using other reference books such as the *World Almanac*, a telephone directory, an atlas, bus and railway timetables, and a TV guide.
4. Using nonreference books such as textbooks and nonfiction works.

Skills required are the locational skills listed above, plus the ability to interpret information, to know how to use it, and to judge the appropriateness of the information for its intended use.

ABILITY TO USE THE LIBRARY TO LOCATE MATERIAL

1. Using the card catalog.
2. Knowledge of coding and filing systems.
3. Locating books on the shelves.
4. Using indexes such as the *Reader's Guide to Periodical Literature* for information sources in magazines and journals.
5. Locating other materials in the library.
6. Knowledge of the services of a library.

Skills required are (a) the specific skills and rules of library usage; (b) knowledge of basic information related to library organization of books, journals, and other media; and, (c) learning how to operate the various machines, such as the micro-reader, Xerox copier, microfiche, microfilms, and video dial access systems being used in more and more libraries.

DEVELOPING STUDY SKILLS

1. Interpreting graphic aids such as a picture, diagram, chart, graph, or map.
2. Identifying, evaluating, and organizing significant information.
3. Outlining a paragraph, subsection, or chapter.
4. Note taking from reading material or lecture.
5. Summarizing what was read.
6. Frequent use of the glossary.
7. Retention of material.
8. How to study for a test.
9. Critical reading.
10. How to interpret and follow directions.

Skills required are the development of basic study habits and study attitudes conducive to good study reading, note taking, and the learning of new material.

The Learning Disabled
Reader and Study Skills

The learning disabled reader has difficulties developing reading-study skills as well as with enhancing reading interests and increasing his speed or rate of reading. A simplistic explanation for these limitations cannot suffice. The causes and types of learning disabilities are too broad to channel an explanation into a few sentences. Whether it is limited auditory or visual memory capacity, inability to function because of a short attention span brought on by distractibility or excessive restlessness, or failure to respond correctly even though they have the proper information (expressive difficulty), certainly all learning disabled readers have one thing in common: they are behind grade or mental age level in reading achievement. To expect these readers to function on the same learning level in developing reading-study skills as regular classroom readers is inappropriate and incomprehensible.

Yet, the older child must learn some basic reading-study skills for his own survival. The individual's learning style must be determined and used to its best advantage in learning as many basic study skills as possible. Forget about improving the rate of reading; concentrate on the rate of comprehension. "Reading" without comprehension of meaning is *not* reading. Be concerned about improving interest in reading, however, because existence as an independent, competent adult requires that the individual be interested in at least reading those materials that are essential for his well-being. One last point: remember that a learning disabled child with a high I.Q. could be making passing grades in high school; however, he should be making top grades. This youngster needs to learn as many reading-study skills as he can absorb because he needs all the help he can get to learn enough to keep up with his class.

Developing Reading-Study Skills

Locating Information

The first problem faced by any student when he wants to pursue an area for study is to locate materials. In order to locate materials the student must have acquired four kinds of knowledge: knowledge of library procedures, knowledge of numbers, knowledge of letters, and knowledge of sources.

Although libraries differ somewhat there are certain constancies associated with libraries. Every library has a librarian, a card catalog, a reference materials center, a system for classification of materials, and rules governing use of materials. The primary job of the elementary school in developing knowledge of library procedures is to first guide the child to mastery of the elementary school library to which he has access, and then to help him develop generalizations which will enable him to function efficiently in any library. This task is best accomplished through classes in library science along with application of what is learned during the classes to real problems correlated with the direction of academic growth of the child.

Since the two most used systems of classification, the Library of Congress system and the Dewey decimal system, both employ numbers in the classification, a child must enter the library with number knowledge if he is to be expected to function independently.

Even though the child may be acquainted with library procedures he is still faced with an impossible task if he does not have an adequate grasp of the alphabet. Classification may be by number, but the card catalog is organized according to the alphabet. The child who has no idea of alphabetizing goes to the library handicapped, and hence must spend an undue length of time locating materials in the card catalog. Probably it is safe to say that alphabetizing is the basic locational skill. Many reading authorities deplore the teaching of the alphabet as an aid to reading, but even they must accept the proposition that if the child has not learned the alphabet incidentally by the time he is first confronted with the use of the library, effort must be made to entrench the sequence of the alphabet in the learner.

The last locational skill is knowledge of sources. Knowing where to go for specific information is a time saver to any researcher or beginning researcher. By the time the average student leaves the elementary school, he should be familiar with the following sources through teaching and use:

1. *Encyclopedias* for an overview of a subject and as a source of other materials on the subject. Also as a source of biographical data.
2. *Who's Who* as a source of biographical data on contemporary persons.
3. *Dictionaries* as a source of meaning, spelling, pronunciation, and derivation.
4. *Reader's Guide to Periodic Literature* as a source of articles appearing in magazines.

This is merely a list of minimum essentials and not indicative of what more advanced students can be taught. The knowledge of sources is most effectively taught through a combination of direct teaching and guided practice.

How to Use Materials Efficiently

The first skill to master is the use of the textbook. Children should be taught to use the table of contents as an indicator of the major topical headings. Likewise they should realize the table of contents helps locate major topics. The use of the index as a more detailed listing of topics and as an indicator of where specific material is covered in the book must also be taught. The skill of skimming in order to locate specific items and to get a general idea of the kinds of material covered by the book or pages can be taught through application in the textbook.

Some textbooks can be used to introduce the glossary as a source of pronunciation and meaning. It is here that the teacher can develop the habit of referring to key words in order to unlock the pronunciation of a word in a dictionary. If the glossary contains guide words, the teacher can use the textbook to entrench usage of guide words and knowledge of the alphabet.

The skills covered in the last two paragraphs are skills which are applicable to any kind of book a child may read; hence the teacher must guide the child into making a transference of these skills learned through application in the basic text into other subject textbooks, reference books, and other reading materials.

There are a number of good sources of information on reading-study skills (Dallman et al., 1974; Miller, 1975; Potter & Rae, 1975; Gilliland, 1974).

Teaching Dictionary Skills

The first experiences a child has with a dictionary make him aware that it is a source for learning the meaning of unknown words (Gray, 1960). Learning dictionary procedures should begin in the early grades to encourage independence in a child. Readiness for locating words must develop sequentially. The tasks involved include:

1. Establishing left-to-right directionality in reading movement.
2. Knowing the alphabet and using alphabetical sequence.
3. Alphabetizing by use of more than the first letter of the word.
4. Recognizing the general position of letters within the alphabet.
5. Identifying root words, as in structural analysis.

Once the individual has achieved readiness in locating words, he can begin to examine the book itself for its arrangement. According to Anderson (1972), children should be able to find the guide words on any given page. They should know that the guide word at the top of the left page is the first word defined on that page, and the word at the top of the right page is the last word defined on that page. Then by guided practice, they can decide if the word they want to find is before, after, or between the guide words. They must also learn the idea that the word is to be found in the front, middle, or back of the dictionary.

In working with a dictionary, a child must understand the following terminology: *alphabetical order, guide word, root word, entry word, definition, pronunciation key, syllable, accent,* and *schwa.* Readiness procedures must be continued to extend and reinforce the knowledge already established. Along with locating words, two more areas are involved in establishing readiness—pronunciation and definitions. Phonetic skills and relationships developed in the early reading stages can supply readiness for learning how to interpret dictionary pronunciations and for using a pronunciation key. Training should develop the ability to hear consonants and vowels, syllables, and accents. If the child cannot hear these sounds, they will not mean much when seen in the dictionary.

In developing readiness for using dictionary definitions, a child needs to have early context cue skills. In early school development, he must be aware that words may have multiple meanings and that context is important in determining the exact meaning. He should also be shown that some dictionaries have pictures that can aid the formulation of a definition in his mind. In early exposure, picture dictionaries can be helpful, as can a child-made picture dictionary. The subskills and sequence of development involved in this level of readiness are (a) associating words that mean the same thing (synonyms); (b) selecting the meaning that fits the context by recognizing that some words have more than one meaning and that there are some words that sound the same but are spelled differently (homonyms); and (c) forming simple definitions for a word from context cues.

Usage of the dictionary should progress simultaneously in the areas of word location, meaning, and pronunciation, from simple to complex skills. The introduction of certain skills will depend on the development of prerequisite skills. In using a dictionary for definitions, a child could be trying to clarify a vague meaning he has received through context, checking spelling, choosing an exact or more appropriate meaning, or finding a substitute for an overworked word.

A child needs to understand why we must have pronunciation symbols in order to develop this skill of deriving pronunciations. He should be encouraged to use the dictionary when he does not know how to say a word.

Various ideas will need to be reviewed before children use a pronunciation key. Word lists can be grouped according to a letter the words have in common. By saying these simple words, they can hear that the common letter of each list does not sound the same in all of the words.

Next, children can examine words such as *eat, treat, threat* to see that spelling is not always a clue to pronunciation. They should also compare words that contain the same sound, but are represented by a different letter or letters, such as *no—know, though—toe.*

Children must understand the idea of silent letters because the spelling of a word won't always match the pronunciation. This can be done by writing words containing silent letters, saying them, and determining which letter(s) is silent.

In developing dictionary skills in any child, whether learning disabled or a normal achiever, that child is being supplied the means for independence. The major difference in teaching these skills in a regular class as opposed to an LD class will come about in the amount of time spent on a skill and the method by which it is taught. It is especially important in the case of an LD child that the means for supplying necessary skills match the needs at a successful level. Only through sequential skill development will a child be confident and capable enough to progress alone. Through observation of a child's progress, you can evaluate how he is doing. You can devise exercises that serve as checks, so you know when a child is ready for the next level in the sequence. Table 14–1 presents a representative sampling of the types of materials available for teaching reading-study skills, including dictionary skills.

How to Develop Reading-Study Skills

Certain study skills assist the pupil to either make a rapid review of material covered or to aid in recall. The techniques of outlining, summarizing, and note taking fall into this category. These skills call for skill in mentally organizing oneself in order to make evaluations of the importance of what is being read.

Children in the beginning should be given guide questions prior to reading a selection in order to have a standard upon which to judge the importance of the material. As the child progresses through the elementary school he should be guided into acquiring the habit of performing certain preliminary activities before reading material. If the material is a book, he should skim through the table of contents to get some idea of the major topics. He should leaf through the book paying attention to major headings and subheadings in order to organize a point of departure for reading the book. Sometimes children may even skim through the index. After having done this skimming the pupil should formulate several questions so he has some objective as he reads. The SQ3R technique discussed in a later section of this chapter is an excellent technique for this purpose. If the material is an article

TABLE 14-1. Representative materials available for developing study skills.

Name	Company	Description
Charlie Brown Dictionary	Scholastic Book Service	Beginning dictionary for 2nd and 3rd graders. Charlie Brown-type illustrations. Designed for high motivation.
Individualized Reading Skills programs (IRS)	Houghton Mifflin	Box of study skills booklets for intermediate levels; includes skills booklets on using the dictionary for pronunciation, meaning, and locating words.
Talking Picture Dictionary	Educational Reading Services (ERS)	Tapes for grades 1–4 go with 16 different volumes of picture dictionaries to teach letter sounds, word meanings, and relationships between words.
The Library Skill Box	Educational Reading Services (ERS)	For grades 3–6, 10 cassettes and 50 duplicating masters give detailed information on things such as dictionaries, atlas, magazine, newpaper, research and report writing, study techniques, and the library in general.
Look It Up: How to Get Information	Educational Reading Services (ERS)	For grades 4–6, filmstrips and cassettes on using and working with dictionaries, atlases, almanacs, encyclopedias, and card catalogs.
Library Skills Transparencies (separate or set)	United Transparency	The whole set includes different facets of library content and organization: 7 individual transparencies work with dictionary usage.
Basic Dictionary Skills	Milliken	For grades 3–6, this booklet of transparencies and duplicating masters focuses on all facets of dictionary usage.
Reference Tools and Study Skills	Milliken	For grades 4–8, this booklet of transparencies and duplicating masters concentrates on study skills, including dictionary usage.
Dictionary Skill Charts and Transparencies	Ideal	Charts develop readiness and beginning skills in how to use a dictionary for spelling, usage, pronunciation, meanings, and locating information.
Cyclo-Teacher Learning Aid	Field Enterprises Educational Corp. (World Book)	This package has programmed material in seven areas. Within the Reference Skills area are units on dictionary usage, encyclopedia, and library research.
Basal Reading Series	Various publishers	Included in this type of series is work with study skills, such as outlining, maps, index usage, glossary and dictionary usage, card catalogs, and encyclopedias in readers, workbooks, and usually, worksheets. Some series stress this more than others, as the Ginn 360 Series does.

or short selection, prereading skimming of the piece to formulate questions will improve retention and the ability to measure the value of the contents.

These kinds of activities will contribute to outlining, note taking, and summarizing but they alone are not enough. Teachers should make certain a schoolwide consistency is maintained in the form of outlines used from grade to grade. In this way children will not become confused as to whether (1) means a minute point or a subheading. The progression of development of outlining skills is from topic sentence to supportive data to minute details. With guided help, teachers can get children to transfer these techniques to note taking, and summarizing.

Two methods are employed by able teachers for making certain their charges develop mastery of the study skills. The first is by direct teaching and the second is by practical application of the skills learned. Neither comes before the other but rather both are developed concommitantly. A need for a skill arises and the children become aware that this skill is vitally needed. The teacher then gives them direct lessons and guided practice to help them satisfy the need which uncovered the problem in the first place

Both individual and group projects are used during the periods when the children are applying the skills needed and learned. Both of these have value. Some educators feel the first exposures should be through group projects in order to take advantage of the individual learnings of the group which when combined probably are greater than the knowledge of any one individual in the group. They argue that this gives the individual members of the group security in that as a group they can usually work out the skill and also each individual knows he is not the only one who needs help. When the members of the group are more secure they can then undertake individual projects. The major objective of all teaching of study skills is the development of an independent learner.

Durrell (1956) maintains that small group study assignments are far superior to individual study. To Durrell all human creatures are gregarious and prefer working with others to working alone. The first advantage then in group work is the feeling of camaraderie engendered by the association with others in an effort to reach a common objective.

A second advantage seems to be one of increased practice and retention. The person studying alone reads and subvocally recites, whereas the person studying with a group reads and subvocally recites but also has the advantage of hearing himself or other members of the group recite. This can lead to greater retention.

Durrell suggests that small groups of around three students be given study guides. One of the students functions as a pupil-teacher reading the questions and then checking on the accuracy of the answers uncovered by the other members of the study group in their reading. Thus instead of a student reading and occasionally reciting, the student now reads and recites on everything.

Another advantage of the small study group is that it relieves the teacher from the task of gathering different materials in order to cater to the capacities of the individual students. With the use of study guides the teacher is able to differentiate the assignment so that the very slow children may be given questions of fact while the bright children may be given questions demanding more penetration.

THE CHINESE TECHNIQUE. A translation of the first degree granted in China many years ago literally meant "flower of pencils." Occidentals have speculated that perhaps this title was conferred because of the manner in which one learned in China in those days. Probably because of ancestral veneration, the Chinese felt that the best forms and styles in writing had already been uncovered; hence, the job of the student was to learn how to replicate these acceptable materials. In order to learn the forms and styles, the student spent countless hours copying the great works and then trying to write in as near a form and style as possible to the writings they had spent so much time copying. You can see this would take a great deal of pencils; hence, the title of the first degree.

Although many American school teachers do not have the same kind of ancestral worship the Chinese had, there are still a significant number who believe that the best forms and styles have already been revealed and the student's job is merely to try to replicate these. As for study skills, the process of copying and imitating the great writings will leave a residue within the student which will automatically enable him to spot major points and to identify minor supportive details.

Great works are read, then analyzed according to the teacher's preconceived notions. All children then engage in outlining the great work with each ending up with a carbon copy of their classmates' outlines. Summaries are written which too are carbon copies of every other one written. In this manner organization skills are thought to develop. A modification of this writing approach has been found helpful for some types of learning disabled readers.

THE SRA ORGANIZING AND REPORTING KIT. One of the newer ideas concerning study skills development is the new SRA Organizing and Reporting Kit. Apparently the authors of the kit have developed it on the assumption that children need direct guidance in developing study skills. This guidance is provided through materials on cards in a box thereby allowing each member of the class to work at his own rate and independently of each other member of the class.

In developing the writing of a report the kit begins with an example of a good report. Through questions, the learner is guided into an analysis of why this particular report is a good report. A series of lessons follow which develop his ability to use the skills associated with the writing of a report and end with the student writing a report.

SQ3R. Francis P. Robinson of Ohio State University has developed a method of study which he calls the SQ3R Method (1962). SQ3R stands for:

1. *Survey.* The reader scans the entire reading assignment. He carefully reads the summaries and introductory statements, main headings and subheadings. If the assignment is a book he will read the preface and table of contents. The purpose is to get an overview of the book or selection.

2. *Question.* While engaging in the survey the reader will automatically form questions in his mind concerning the contents. He should also develop the habit of formulating questions by rephrasing chapter headings and subheadings. The purpose of the question formulation is to give a purpose to the reader's serious reading of the book. That purpose would be to answer the questions.

3. *Read.* The reader now reads the book with the intent of answering the questions he has formulated.

4. *Recite.* After completing the reading of the book or passage either close the book or set it aside and try to recite the answers to the questions you formulated prior to the reading of the book or selection. This recitation checks on what the reader has learned and also helps to reinforce the learning.

5. *Review.* If some of the questions can't be answered the reader reviews the material to find the answers. Even if the recitation uncovers no learning holes the reader should review to overlearn the material.

This method of study has proven to be very effective as it is incorporated in the SRA Reading Laboratory. Many classroom teachers use this technique or a modification in helping children study more effectively.

Study Techniques for Older Students

Have you ever been taught "how to study?" Probably not. Most students are never really given formal instructions on how to study their textbook, how to take notes, how to prepare for tests, or even how to listen in class in order to get the main ideas the teacher is presenting. It is important for a student not only to develop good study skills, but also good work habits and attitudes concerning studying. These attributes are doubly important for the brighter LD student who has the mental capacity but must struggle to keep up with his classmates because he is an inefficient learner. This kind of student is frequently found on the college—even the graduate—level. In high school they could keep up with the crowd, which was made up of a wide range of abilities and desires to succeed. In college the competition is keener and a higher level of performance is necessary. The following materials provide suggestions for improving study habits and techniques of all students:

A. *Basic study habits.*

1. Provide for proper study conditions—quiet place, good light, proper supplies.
2. Prepare a study schedule and stick to it. Do assignments as soon as possible.
3. Start to work immediately; do not "dilly-dally;" avoid interruptions.
4. Force yourself to concentrate; power of concentration can be developed.
5. Pay special attention to the vocabulary of the subject.
6. Know your assignment; have an "assignment page" in your notebook.
7. Keep a progress record—at least know for sure how well you are doing.
8. Review frequently by looking over your old notes or skimming pages already read.
9. Get help from your teacher when it is needed—not when the semester is over.
10. Guard your health—get your sleep, eat proper food, and exercise.

B. *How to keep notebooks.*

1. Use a loose-leaf, three-ring, hardback, 8½" x 11" notebook.
2. Keep notes for each class in order, day by day, and keep them separate from other class notes. Use colored dividers or index tabs to divide the classes.
3. First page of each section should be an ASSIGNMENT PAGE with headings of: DATE DUE ASSIGNMENT COMMENTS
4. At the top of the first page list the name of the course, the teacher, and his office or room number.
5. Use ink or ball-point pen.
6. Have a good supply of paper. Narrow lines are good if you don't crowd notes.
7. Number the pages.
8. Start a new unit or major topic on a fresh sheet, not in the middle or back of a sheet of paper that already has notes on it.
9. Do not crowd your notebook; skip lines and leave lots of white space.
10. Include odd-size sheets given you by folding, pasting, or punching holes.

C. *How to make notes from a lecture.*

1. Study the topic before class to be familiar with it.
2. Be ready to write BEFORE the lecture or teacher begins.

3. If you miss a point, leave a blank space and get the point later.
4. Make the notes in your own words. Copy illustrations off the chalkboard.
5. Condense thoughts into a few words. Good notes are not long, but they are complete. Add explanations given with chalkboard illustrations. Support all major ideas with details or definitions.
6. DO NOT CROWD THE NOTES—leave generous space for additional explanations or illustrations. Uncrowded notes are the easiest to study for a test.
7. Try to grasp the teacher's outline, and then write your notes following this format:

  I. This is the main topic being discussed.
   A. This is the first major idea about this topic.
      1. These are the facts or points being made or discussed about this major idea.
      2.
      3.
   B. This is the next major idea brought up about the major topic.
      1.
      2.

8. Indicate the date of the class period at the beginning of each day's notes.
9. If you must doodle, use a separate sheet for it, not your notes.
10. Be a good listener. Take down enough, yet not everything said.

D. *How to listen in class for important points.*

1. Prepare for what you expect to hear—be familiar with the material by studying.
2. Listen for the main trend or topic in the opening remarks.
3. Note the apparent outline of the teacher's notes or the important divisions of his lecture or class discussion.
4. Listen for "units" of thought such as would be found in a paragraph.
5. Copy down illustrations or figures of speech used in making a point.
6. Pick out the teacher's key word, phrases, or sentences.
7. Listen for a definite statement of a main point.
8. Listen for repetitions which usually indicate important points.
9. Listen for an important thought after "transitional" words, such as *besides, furthermore, accordingly, but, however,* and *yet.*
10. Listen very carefully after a dramatic pause.
11. Keep an outline in mind—as well as in your notes—of the main points and of some of the supporting details.
12. Stop listening long enough to review occasionally.
13. Associate what you hear with what you already know.
14. To yourself, question and challenge the meanings and reasons given by the teacher.
15. Discuss, read, or use what you have heard after the lecture.

E. *Supplies students should have.*

Study desk or own place to study.   Tape; paper clips; rubber bands.
Good study light   Small stapler; large-hole punch.

Proper size notebook.

Lined paper and plain paper.

Fountain pen or ball-point pen.

Red and blue colored pencils.

Ink: blue-black and India black.

Typewriter (if you can afford one).

Ruler with metal edge so ink will not smear.

Reinforcing gum cloth rings for paper holes.

Book shelf or book ends.

Scissors; paste or rubber cement.

Dictionary.

Stamps; envelopes; letter paper.

F. *If you are going to college.*

Adjustment to college life and work involves:

1. Personal adjustment—socially and emotionally.
2. Learning and using proper study techniques.

How to study involves five things:

1. Taking good notes.
2. Knowing how to read properly.
3. Ability to use the library and other resources.
4. Proper mental outlook and attitudes.
5. General pattern of good study habits, such as:

   a. Knowing the assignment;
   b. Using a time budget schedule;
   c. Having the things needed for study;
   d. Making use of all available time;
   e. Getting help when it is needed;
   f. Doing your work instead of just thinking about it; and
   g. Daily review.

G. *Reading textbook assignments.*

1. Determine the type of reading needed for each subject. Textbooks are not read like novels or fictional reading.
2. Do you know what you are to do?
   a. What is the complete assignment?
   b. What should you do in addition to reading? Summarize? Take notes? Outline? Only outline those sections or pages you have trouble understanding.
3. Reading procedures or skills to be followed—the 5-point program.
   a. *Rapid skimming*—To get a preview of the author's outline of the material. (1) Read the section headings and the topic sentences; (2) Make questions out of all topic headings.
   b. *Careful reading*—To fill in the outline. (1) Read straight through from beginning to end; (2) Mark the book if it belongs to you—mark the edges mostly; underline only the most important items such as names, dates, important statements, headings.
   c. *Recall the main ideas*—give supporting details with the book closed.

    d. *Study-type reading*—Reread hazy parts; make sure you can define the important words; make notes or an outline if you cannot get the important ideas in any other way.

    e. *Test yourself*—With the book closed, ask yourself questions and try to answer them. This is a good practice in getting ready for a test.

4. Begin reading your assignments the *first* day and keep up to date with your reading.
5. Budget your time for study purposes.

H. *How to prepare for exams.*

1. Best way to prepare for exams is to prepare your daily assignments effectively. Keep up to date.
2. Take decent class notes. Organize the teacher's lecture.
3. Review frequently to refresh your memory and to organize your thoughts.
4. What to do when a test is announced:

    a. Pay close attention to the announcement—take down the date and comments.
    b. Find out the type of test to be given.
    c. Know the material to be covered.
    d. Set up a special review schedule that allows the time needed for study.
    e. If you need to, study once or twice with well-prepared students.
    f. Go over your notes; go over the main points in the text; ask yourself questions.
    g. The night before the exam, have a review; do not stay up late.
    h. Have confidence in yourself that you will do as well as you can.

5. Know the different types of test items there are and how to answer them.

Sample Activities for Teaching Reading-Study Skills

A. Dictionary Skills

1. Alphabetizing and alphabet order
Knowledge of sequence of letters in the alphabet
Examples: Write in the missing letters of the alphabet.
a b __ __ e f __ h __ j __ l m __ o p __ __ s __ u __ w x __ __

2. Ability to arrange words in alphabetical order when the first letter of each word is different.

Directions: Here are some words that are not in the right ABC order. Write them on the lines at the right in the correct ABC order.

1. coat   1._____
2. eggs   2._____
3. apple   3._____
4. hat   4._____
5. deer   5._____
6. fish   6._____
7. goat   7._____
8. if   8._____
9. baby   9._____
10. jump   10._____

Directions for the next list will be the same as above. The word list this time is more difficult because there are some beginning letters that are omitted.

1. dog	1._____
2. monkey	2._____
3. could	3._____
4. around	4._____
5. funny	5._____
6. pumpkin	6._____
7. happy	7._____
8. kitten	8._____
9. light	9._____
10. monkey	10._____

B. Classification

Make different word classifications. Have the pupils put the words into the proper classification.

Directions: Below are three lists of words. There are also three headings. You are to write the word under the heading to which it belongs:

Animals   People   Food

bread	woodchuck	beans
grandfather	mayor	fisherman
rat	cake	father
shoemaker	milk	wolf
eggs	uncle	reindeer

C. Word Location

1. Look at page 42 of your dictionary. What are the two words printed at the top of the page?

barrow   page 42   bat

They are called the guide words because they "guide" you in finding words. They are clues to the entries. The right guide word is usually the same as the last word on the page. All the entries on the page are in alphabetical order between the guide words. What are the guide words on page 2? Is the word *able* an entry on this page? Why? Is the word *abbey* on page 2? Why not? Is the word *absent* on page 2? See how quickly you can find the guide words for the pages on which you find these words.

kneel   own   trial

Which of these words are listed on the page having these two guide words? Drill-Drown

drive   droop   doctor   drizzle   duck   drape   dust   drive-way

D. Encyclopedias

1. Have a question corner, box or "man"—Mr. Information.

Question for the day—new one daily. Children go to library in free time and try to find answers in encyclopedias.

e.g., What were the original 13 colonies? Who was Betsy Ross?

Use last 5 to 10 minutes of the day to learn answers.

Change questions daily.

At end of day—record answers to question.

2. Take class to library and show them where encyclopedias are found and the different sets.

3. Explain that the letters and numbers on spines of volumes refer to the beginning letter of words and subjects contained within.

4. Show them where on the page to look for guide words.

5. Have individual children look up these words: *space, Viet Nam, Madam Curie, zebra, bat, hyena.*

6. Have children always use more than one particular encyclopedia to gain additional information or a different viewpoint.

E. Library Skills

1. Give children slips of paper with the following information on them

   subject—   _____baseball_____
   title—   _____
   author—   _____
   publisher _____
   date—   _____

   Have different subjects filled in on each—e.g. baseball, scouts, rocks, insects, holidays, people. Using the card catalog, each child has to find one book (minimum) about the subjects he's been given. (Give randomly). He must then fill in correct information using the card catalog.

F. Develop ability to recognize and interpret graphs, charts, time lines, globes, and maps.

Have each child keep an individual record of *how many* and *what types* of books read in one month. Children make bar or picture graphs to show progress, week by week.

G. Miscellaneous Activities

1. *Syllables.*

   If you were writing a very important letter and some of the words you were using were too long to fit the whole word on the same line, it would be necessary to know where to divide the word into syllables. Your dictionary shows you how to divide words into syllables. Use your dictionary to find out how to divide the following list of words into syllables.

Word	Word Divided Into Syllables
Sample: dictionary	dic tion ar y

Word	Word divided into syllables
1. situated	1. _____
2. mechanically	2. _____
3. electricity	3. _____
4. decoration	4. _____
5. attitude	5. _____

2. *Pronunciation—Sharing: Using the Dictionary.*

   a. Copy from your school dictionary the respelling which tells how to pronounce each word correctly. Copy accent marks, too.
   b. Now practice with your partner, each taking a turn pronouncing the words.
   c. Check with the key words at the bottom of the page in your dictionary. Be sure that your partner is pronouncing the word correctly.

Word	Respelling With Accents
1. anchorage	_____
2. communication	_____
3. efficiency	_____
4. pamphlet	_____
5. asparagus	_____

3. *Finding the Right Meaning for Words.*

Read the sentence, then find the underlined word in your dictionary. From the meanings given for the word, select the meaning that best fits the way the word is used in the sentence. Write the number of the meaning on the line beside the word number. Write the meaning you have selected on the line beside the word meaning.

a. The man took the negative to the camera shop to have some pictures made from it.
Number ___ Meaning_____

b. The flowers that were planted in Ipswich Square are now in bloom.
Number ___ Meaning_____

c. His direct answer led the teacher to believe him.
Number ___ Meaning_____

Rate of Reading

Background of the Problem

The credit for the discovery that the eyes do not move in smooth even movements but rather in a series of jerky movements with pauses between has been given to Javal and to Delabarre. Delabarre affixed a plaster of paris cup to the eyes of some students. In the plaster cup was embedded a thin wire which Delabarre wet with ink. As the students read, a written record of how their eyes performed was left upon the printed matter. Javal got the same results by just observing the eyes of a person who was reading.

The work of Javal and Delabarre was followed by much research concerning eye movements in reading. A summary of the accepted results follows:

1. Eye movements are short jerks with long pauses in between.
2. The characteristic eye movements in reading are called *saccadic movements*.
3. The pause the eye makes is called a *fixation*, while the movement between fixations is called an *interfixation*.
4. When the eyes reach the end of a line of print they sweep back in one continuous movement and drop to the next line of print. This sweep is called a *return sweep*.
5. Occasionally while reading the eyes will go back and reread a portion of the line being read. This rereading is called a *regression*.
6. During a fixation the eye sees within its field of vision more than it can recognize. The total of what the eye sees is called the *span of perception*, whereas the amount the brain can interpret and recognize is called the *span of recognition*.
7. The span of perception is wider than the span of recognition.

Much more was discovered, but for our present purposes, we will stop here.

With the above information reading people began to reason that if the span of perception is larger than the span of recognition then the average reader is reading inefficiently since he is recognizing only a a portion of what he sees. If one could widen the span of recognition until it coincided with the span of perception, the reader then would have to make fewer fixations, thereby speeding up his reading. This reasoning was so powerful that for quite a period it influenced much reading activity. Machines were designed to accomplish the purposes stated in the rationale. Exercises and books were made and sold for the same purpose, and speed reading became an American household word. Hardly a reading center or clinic existed which did not offer a course in speed reading.

The courses usually consisted of sessions divided into periods for increasing vocabulary, timed reading, and work with a mechanical device for quick recognition. One of the most popular of these mechanical devices was the flashmeter or tachistoscope. Words, numbers, and phrases were put on slides and placed in a slide projector device. The lens of the slide projector was either built to control the time the aperature was open or an attachment was placed over the lens which did the same thing. By this method the timing of the exposure on the screen could be controlled from around one second to one-one-hundredth of a second. The subjects were first exposed to short words or numbers at slow speed. Then gradually the number of letters, words, or numbers was increased along with the speed of exposure.

The Real Problem of Speed Reading

The major difference between a good reader and a poor reader as far as speed of reading is concerned is in the ability to adjust the speed to the material being read. The good reader if doing ambulatory reading moves along rapidly employing skimming techniques. If, however, he is doing critical reading his reading slows down considerably in order to give him time to make certain of his interpretations and to allow time for him to argue with the material as well as to recall pertinent information. If the good reader who is not a physician reads the *American Medical Journal* his speed slows to a snail's pace. The poor reader, by contrast, will have a tendency to read everything with the same speed making no adjustment for the unfamiliarity or difficulty of the material. What we are trying to emphasize here is that the good reader has many rates of reading. The problem is not one of improving the reader's rate but rather teaching him to adjust his rate to the material and purpose of his reading.

How Fast Can a Person Read?

It is not uncommon to pick up the Sunday supplement to your newspaper and find out such and such a person reads at a rate of 30,000 words per minute or some other phenomenal speed. Advertisements periodically appear which promise to increase your speed of reading into the thousands. One well-known reading institute even promises speeds running into the hundred thousands. It would not surprise the authors one bit if someone now claimed speeds in the millions of words per minute. Yet, physiologically, what are the limits to the speed of reading in man?

The classic study, which has not been given its much deserved acclaim, is the one made by Howard Walton, a professor of optometry at the Los Angeles School of Optometry. Walton (1957) knew from previous research that the average fixation with comprehension took 252 milliseconds. He also knew that interfixation time was somewhere in the neighborhood of one-sixth of a second. From the research done by a colleague, he knew that as one moves out from the *fovea centralis*, the area of greatest acuity on the retina, acuity drops until at five degrees on either side of the retina, the acuity has dropped to twenty-seventy (20/70). Walton combined this information and added to it some research, deriving the average maximum speed which is physiologically possible for humans.

Walton had students learn to fixate points on a card. Since the fixations involved no comprehension, the difference between the time Walton got and the time registered in earlier studies should be the time necessary for mediating processes whereas Walton's time should indicate the neural transmission time. Earlier studies involving comprehension got an average time of 252 milliseconds, while Walton got 219 milliseconds. Since it is impossible to speed up neural transmission in an individual without the use of drugs, we can take the 219 milliseconds as an indication of the shortest fixation time possible.

Walton combined this figure with the knowledge that five degrees on either side of the *fovea centralis* was the peripheral limit of letter discrimination, that this translated into printed page size equals 2.2 inches of print, and that the interfixation time is one-sixth of a second. He showed mathematically that the upper limit of speed reading is 1,451 words per minute for the average person. Any figure beyond this figure is physiologically impossible for the average person. When one reads faster than 1,451 words per minute, he is skimming, which is a good locational study skill but is not reading. Those who claim tremendous speed of reading will have to disprove Walton's high quality proof of its impossibility.

Other limits to reading speed become apparent when one realizes exactly what is done during flashmeter or tachistoscopic training. People are forced to make quick discriminations when words are flashed at high rates of speed. The neurosis created by this demand in turn creates tension and tension limits the visual field so the very training designed to expand the span of recognition in actuality narrows the span of perception, thereby achieving the opposite affect.

A. J. Kirschner in his brilliant papers found the very same results. He noticed that whereas many patients treated at his clinic referred other people for treatment of reading problems, the rate of referral to his speed reading courses was almost negligible. In fact he rarely got a client for the speed reading course who had been referred by a former patient. This bothered Kirschner so he made a survey of former clients of his speed reading courses. Each and every one claimed it was wonderful but when asked why they never referred others tried to evade the question. When they began to realize Kirschner was searching for evidence they loosened up and revealed how they felt. Most said they felt nervous and irritable after the sessions of the class and disliked reading for six to eight months after the course was completed. Kirschner's findings were in line with the findings of Marmo and others who have investigated the problem of what happens after the training period. Patients checked after a time lapse have been found to have regressed to the position they were at the beginning of the speed reading course.

Another factor is that people have many eye movement patterns. There is a direct correlation between the number of regressions and the difficulty of the material being read. Very easy material produces few fixations and few regressions. Very difficult material produces many fixations and many regressions.

The position today is that eye movements are not the cause of poor reading but symptoms of the difficulty of the material. Of the total of 498 milliseconds involved in a fixation and an interfixation, 166 milliseconds of interfixation time and 219 milliseconds of neural transmission time cannot be changed. Hence that leaves only 33 seconds, the time which represents mediating processes, which can be changed. How much can reading be speeded up when only approximately one-fifteenth (1/15) of the total time involved can be changed at all?

Studies by Taylor, Frackenpohl, and Pettee (1960) indicate the approximate rate of reading with comprehension as shown in Table 14–2. Up to grade 8, girls have a definite edge over boys in speed of reading.

TABLE 14–2. Comparison of average rate of reading with comprehension in words per minute by grades and sex.

Grade	Males	Females	Combined
1	75	85	80
2	108	122	115
3	132	146	138
4	152	164	158
5	168	178	173
6	180	190	185
7	190	200	195
8	200	208	204
9	210	218	214
10	220	228	224
11	234	240	237
12	248	252	250
College	280	280	280

Adapted from Taylor, Stanford E.; Frackenpohl, Helen; Pettee, James L. Grade level norms for the components of the fundamental reading skill. Huntington, New York: Educational Developmental Laboratories, Inc. 1960, Bulletin No. 3, p. 12.

Causes of Slower Reading Rates

The intermediate grades are probably the first level at which a concern for rate of reading is justified for developmental readers because at this point emphasis is being placed on the various content areas. The learning disabled reader may not be even close to being ready, as far as reading development is concerned, to even think about improving his rate of reading. Nevertheless, teachers who do not understand the limiting or handicapping characteristics of an LD child may become impatient when he cannot finish his reading assignment and workbook pages in the same amount of time as the others.

It should be recognized that LD children (a) may still be working on developing an efficient method for unlocking words; (b) may have attention and distractibility problems, frequently produced by the large amount of material printed on one page, so that they have to struggle to stay with individual words and to stay on the right line; (c) may have poor mental, ego or conscious control of the learning and thought processes necessary to enable the reading process to progress efficiently; (d) may have trouble vocalizing words and getting meaning from them; and (e) may be lacking in adequate visual, auditory, and/or verbal memory development in order to have a ready storage of information from which they can draw ideas to associate meaning to the words and paragraphs they are reading.

Heilman (1972) points out a number of variables that he believes influence the rate at which different materials are assimilated:

1. The reader's knowledge of the general subject.
2. The vocabulary load, difficulty level of words and concepts.
3. The reader's degree of motivation.
4. The reader's purpose for reading the material.
5. The physiological state of the reader.
6. The length of the reading period.
7. Mechanical factors such as size of print and length of line.
8. The ease of readability of the material.
9. The reader's mastery of the mechanical skills of reading.
10. The number of figures, illustrations, and footnotes the material contains.

In general, the causes of slow reading rate are (a) low mental ability, (b) poor health and fatigue, (c) emotional distress, (d) lack of skill in word recognition, (e) excessive subvocalization or vocalization, (f) pointing to the words (needs to be done by many LD readers), (g) overemphasis on oral reading by the reading program or teacher, (h) inability to be flexible in changing rate of reading for different types of materials, and (i) lack of interest and purpose.

How to Develop Speed and Its Proper Use

It is generally accepted that the best way to develop speed is to pay attention to the difficulty of the material the student is reading. In other words, take care of comprehension and speed will take care of itself. If the reader encounters no strange words or concepts he can speed along. If the reader is familiar with the organization of written matter he can comprehend without rereading. In fact, all of the kinds of things suggested for developing comprehension will contribute to an increased speed. The items mentioned concerning the kinds of questions the teacher asks in the chapter on comprehension should also contribute toward the development of the ability to adjust speed to the materials being read.

There are some things teachers can do which may help students read more efficiently. Explaining to the students the reading process and the function and functioning of the eyes during the reading process can give them an understanding which may help them to read more efficiently. Explaining the idea of reading by thought units and giving the students exercises in this can contribute toward greater reading efficiency. Some examples are:

The art of reading   is an act   needing sequential development for maximum efficiency.

Many readers / read inefficiently / They read / word by word / Good readers / try to read / by thought units /

The teacher in the lower grades should never break up thought units when constructing experience charts since this encourages word-by-word reading.

Teachers can call attention to speed by periodically timing the child's easy reading and having him keep a record of his results. The material to be timed should be very easy so as not to slow the child down in word analysis, and the selections should be about the same length so that he can visually see his increased speed. General comprehension questions should be asked about the material read in order to make certain he is giving some thought to what the printed symbols say. Detailed questions would have a tendency to slow the reader down with retention efforts whereas general questions will not interfere with speed. If no questions are asked after the reading, research has shown there is little accomplished. One must pay attention to comprehension as well as speed.

SPEED GIMMICKS. The increased demand upon students for wide reading and the rapidly increasing body of knowledge and publications are making more and more people feel they must increase their speed of reading. As a result there are growing numbers of so-called reading experts who have devised methods for increasing the speed of reading. Some do it with mechanical gadgets and others do it by using pleasant-sounding words or motor manipulations.

The number of those who advise finger manipulation seems to be on the ascendency. These people have devised a way of manipulating the finger over the page which guides the speed of reading. Some start at the top of the page and run right down through the center. Others begin and make a swirl effect on the page. Still others merely point to the center of the page. Other than developing some hand-eye coordination there is little quality evidence to show that this method has achieved any degree of success.

Another new gimmick is the use of magic words. The student is signaled that he should have completed a line when the teacher says "woshback." The children read and the teacher counts cadence by yelling "woshback" periodically thereby forcing the child to push himself. Little evidence exists to support the use of these magic words.

Another gimmick evident today is censoring. Instructors take stories and mutilate them so that only a small percentage of the original words of the story are included in the final draft:

Example:

> Once upon a time there lived a very sweet young girl who loved to read. Because she read all the time she became very proficient. She also liked to be the center of attention. She attended a speed reading course where she did so well she became a demonstrator and satisfied both her cravings.

Once	there lived	girl
who loved to read.		she be-
came very proficient.	liked to be	center of
attention.	attended speed reading course	
	became a demonstrator	satisfied
her cravings.		

One of the most famous gimmicks employs finger manipulation and good study techniques but is dishonestly called speed reading. Recently advocates of this method opened a clinic in a large city and conducted a demonstration. The demonstration began by having a pupil select a book from a table covered with books. A demonstrator looked at the title, skimmed through the table of contents and the index, and then turned the book page by page while her finger performed a swirling motion. After about 5 minutes she put the book down and talked in generalities about the book for 5 minutes. Scanning of the index and the table of contents and then leafing through the book to get a general idea of the contents is a good study procedure but it is not reading. The skimming, as already pointed out, is a worthwhile locational procedure but it is not reading. As to the 5-minute talk about the book in generalities, anyone can do the same with a book on a general subject. In fact, when asked if she would read a book on optometry an observer had placed on the table before the demonstration began, the demonstrator replied she would not.

THE USE OF DRUGS. A group of specialists have experimented with the use of drugs to slow down or speed up synaptic transmission or neural transmission in order to get a child's speed of reading to a point where he can comprehend and retain those ideas embodied in the material read. The most celebrated of these pioneers are Smith and Carrigan (1960) who, with the advice and counsel of specialists in other disciplines, divided children along the lines of slow transmitters and rapid transmitters. They then prescribed to either slow down neural transmission or to speed it up. The results of their experiment showed surprising results in success of improving reading through this technique.

The experiment assumed that the slow speed or fast speed of reading was correlated with the acetylcholine (ACH) cholinesterase (CHE) ratio of the synapses.

DIET TO IMPROVE RATE. Kolson, Odom, and Bushong postulated that perhaps the ACH-CHE ratio in imbalance was due to inadequate diet which in turn disrupted the endocrine gland balance. To them the drugs merely put in balance the glands which in turn equalized the ACH-CHE ratio. In an attempt to determine if the same thing could be accomplished through diet they conducted a controlled experiment with remedial readers measuring only their improvement in speed over a 6-weeks period during which time they were given supplementary carrot and celery juice to supply an adequate diet. Here, too, the results were in favor of the experimental group which had received the supplementary diet. Because these researchers did not account for the Hawthorne Affect the results are not conclusive but need further replication with allowance made for this factor.

Leon Oettenger (1958), a physician, has reported remarkable results through the use of Deanol 100 with remedial readers. This drug, reported by the *Physicians Desk Reference* as an aid to reading and emotional problems, seems to bring about the same kind of results as reported by Smith and Carrigan and Kolson, Odom, and Bushong. The research of Keith Conners with LD children shows that Ritalin can be used to improve verbal performance in children.

Developing Reading Interests

The Concept of Interest

The concept of *interest* seems to have gotten its impetus in 1913 when John Dewey published his book *Interest and Effort in Education*. In his book Dewey said:

> The genuine principle of interest is the principle of the recognized identity of the fact to be learned or the action proposed with the growing self; that it lies in the direction of the agent's own growth, and is therefore imperiously demanded if the agent is to be himself.

A contemporary of Dewey, Charles Degarmo, in his book *Interest and Education* said:

> It is a feeling of the worth to the self, of an end to be attained.

From these early beginnings interests have expanded to the point where exclusion of the topic from a college textbook in pedagogy would be tantamount to embracing the hickory stick. Dolch (1945) in his book *Manual for Remedial Reading* lists 11 pages dealing with the topic. Yoakam (1955) in his book *Basal Reading Instruction* has an impressive list in his index dealing with interests. Dallman et al. (1974) have an entire chapter dealing with reading interests.

In the school and classroom the word *interest* is bandied about with regularity and frequency. Teachers are condemned because they have not made the subject interesting. All kinds of gimmicks are devised to determine what interests children. Interests lists by ages are published and doctors degrees are granted on the work done to uncover this knowledge.

Interest is the tendency to choose one objective over all others and to direct total effort toward the accomplishment of the objective. The implication in this definition is that the individual makes the choice. If the teacher or other educator makes the choice interest is not totally there. If the teacher uses the child's interest in basketball to "sneak in" the division facts the genuine principle of interest has been violated since the agent, or learner, has not placed the acquisition of division facts above the interest in basketball. Dewey stated it very aptly in *Interest and Effort in Education:*

> When things have to be made interesting it is because interest itself is lacking. Moreover the phrase is a misnomer. The thing, the object is no more interesting than it was before. The appeal is simply made to the child's love of something else. He is excited in a given direction, with the hope that somehow or other during this situation he will assimilate something otherwise repulsive.

A second implication in the definition given for interest is that there is absolutely no assurance the choice made by the pupil is the wisest. Now a contradiction seems to have developed—the agent must choose but no assurance exists that his choice is desirable. It appears from this that the teacher's job is not so much one of discovering what a child's interest is but rather how she can make "the fact to be learned or the action proposed . . ." of paramount importance to the learner. Once this is accomplished the learner will direct his total efforts to the objective desired.

Lamb and Arnold (1976) have a good discussion on interests and tastes that would be worth reviewing.

Discovering Children's Interests

In the area of reading much effort has been expended to determine what kinds of topics interest children of varying levels of development. These lists generally are divided on the basis of sex since the interests of boys and the interests of girls do not completely coincide. Summaries of these lists can be found in the reports of research published by Traxler et al., W. S. Gray, Helen Robinson, and in the *Encyclopedia of Educational Research.*

Generally these studies use four techniques for determining children's interests: the questionnaire, the interview, observation, and planned activities.

The questionnaire can be in the form of a checklist, a completion form, or a combination of both. Children are asked to check or to list those games they like to play, the toys they like, the kind of movies or television they like to view, the kind of work they like to do, the hobby they engage in, and other similar types of questions. From the children's responses the teacher tries to gain insight into the kinds of interests a particular child has or the kinds of interests common to a group.

Interviewing is a technique whereby there is communication for a specific purpose. To get the most from an interview with a child the interviewer must first establish rapport with the child so that the child may feel free to give responses which are truly his and not the responses he believes the examiner wants to hear. The ideal interviewer would be what Peter Spencer would call a master of the broad view of reading, which states that one can "read" moods, weather, and so forth. He must be able to read facial expressions, body movements, symptoms of anxiety, and reaction to the total situation. In addition he must be able to skillfully probe through words to prod the child to reveal himself. The good interviewer must also be able to keep his own bias from being felt by the interviewee and thereby influencing his responses. The results of any interview study of children's interests can be no better than the skillfullness of the interviewer.

Observation in order to determine children's or a child's interests is probably the most used technique as far as the classroom teacher is concerned. The skillful classroom teacher makes mental notes concerning what games a child engages in, what books he favors, what kinds of discussions arouse him, and other details which shed light on his interests.

Many educators employ planned activities as a means to uncover a child's or children's interests. Hobby clubs are formed and the degree of attendance, although dependent on other factors, gives a rough approximation of the interests of the children in the school. Out-of-school trips aid the educator in determining the degree of interest for a particular topic.

How to Broaden and Stimulate Interests

Unless a child has psychological problems, he comes to school with interests. These interests should be the starting point for you the teacher. Once you discover his present interests, your job becomes one of relating these interests to his leisure reading, while at the same time, attempting to broaden those interests.

Many teachers become concerned because a child will pursue a subject to the exclusion of other subjects. You should not be concerned since the child is bound to run out of books on the topic eventually, at which time the teacher can suggest books in a related area thereby broadening his interests. Besides, many times children who pursue a particular subject will find a term or topic recurring in book after book until their curiosity gets the better of them and they explore the recurring topic. The major objective is to get the child reading and then attempt to carefully guide his selections.

Whether we teachers like it or not, many times a child will take the word of another child in preference to the word of an adult or teacher. Knowing this, many skillful teachers permit a child to recommend a book he has read to his classmates either orally or in writing. The forms used range from informal to highly structured. Some teachers have the children tell an interesting episode from the book and then give reasons why specific children in the room might enjoy the book. Other teachers merely have the child say what he wants to concerning the book. Some teachers have a recommendation board where a child may pin up his book recommendation for others to read. These techniques will by no means stir every child to read but they may stimulate several children.

The use of visual means of recording the number and kinds of books read by individual children has been credited with developing interest and stimulating reading. Some of these techniques are boards with houses labeled with children's names on them. When a child finishes a book, he writes his report and places the card in his house. Teachers have made chains out of book reports with each link a book report. The object is to encourage the child to lengthen his chain as well as to give him a quick inventory of his free reading as compared to others in the class.

There is no doubt that an environment heavily loaded with appropriate books can provide some of the best means for developing interests and tastes.

Table 14–3 is the result of a study conducted by Roeder and Lee (1973) to determine which techniques teachers found to be most effective in encouraging children to read for their own enjoyment.

TABLE 14-3. Twenty-five teacher-tested ways to encourage voluntary reading.

	Pri.	Inter.	Sec.	Suggested levels
1.	X	X		*Auction.* "Auction" paperbacks brought in by students. Let children bid with play money. Use student auctioneers who encourage bidding.
2.		X	X	*Teacher interest.* Frequently ask students, "What have you been reading lately?" "Read anything interesting over the weekend?" Keep up with what they are reading.
3.	X	X		*Read to the kindergarten.* Have primary and elementary level students take turns reading books to small groups of kindergarten children.
4.	X	X	X	*Awards.* Students who have read a specific number of books receive an award, for example, "The 5 Book Award."
5.	X	X		*Read-in.* Have each child select a partner and set aside specific times for partners to read to each other.
6.		X	X	*Promotional campaign.* Stage a sales campaign for promoting books. Students can act like advertising executives and "sell" books.
7.	X	X		*Topic of the month.* Colorful posters can be made to advertise a specific topic for each month, such as "nature stories."
8.		X	X	*Critical reading.* Do a unit on the criteria for evaluating a book. Encourage students to find examples in their own reading.
9.	X	X		*Tapes of books.* Have children tape record sections of a book or situations from a book. Develop a game, such as "Which book did this passage come from?" or "I'm thinking of a book in which a character said _____."
10.		X	X	*Quotations.* Use direct quotations from famous figures in history on the value of books. Mount them in conspicuous places around your classroom. Change frequently.
11.	X	X		*Series.* Encourage students to read a book from a series, or to read a book by an author who has written several similar books.
12.	X	X	X	*Home Library.* Encourage students to start libraries of their own. Help get them started with a list of "musts."
13.	X	X	X	*Write books.* Have children write, illustrate, and bind their own books. Encourage "pen" names. Circulate the books around the classroom and, if possible, the school.
14.	X	X	X	*Bookclubs.* Form a classroom book club with specific book reading quotas and activities for members.
15.	X	X		*Bulletin boards.* For example, "Books for Athletes," "Good Books for Girls," "Animal Books."
16.	X	X	X	*Library corner.* Partition off part of the classroom with a screen and load it with a variety of books, magazines and newspapers. Provide students with time to use the library corner.
17.	X	X	X	*Read to children.* Read students brief but complete stories as often as possible. Provide variety—high interest, humor, special interest, timely.
18.	X	X		*Stop at exciting point.* Read orally from a book and stop at the most exciting point. (Have several copies available.)
19.	X	X		*Thought-provoking objects.* Bring in thought-provoking objects which will lead students to read books on specific topics.
20.		X	X	*Community members.* Invite members of the community to speak to the class on their special interests. Be certain to provide a link between the presentation and the reading activity.
21.	X	X	X	*Books from home.* Bring in your own books from home and "talk them up."
22.	X	X		*Paraphrase books.* Using their own works, have students retell stories which they have read. Encourage interested children to read the book.
23.	X	X		*Puppet show.* Have children make up puppet shows based on books which they have read.
24.	X	X	X	*Role playing.* Create enthusiasm through plays and acting out the dialogue in books.
25.	X	X	X	*Exude enthusiasm.* Above all, display a positive, enthusiastic attitude toward reading.

Roeder, H. H., & Lee, N. Twenty-five teacher-tested ways to encourage voluntary reading. *Reading Teacher*, October 1973, 27(1) 48–50. Reprinted with permission of the authors and the International Reading Association.

High Interest, Low-Level Reading Books

In the fifties, if a teacher had a child who was reading on a level which was two, three, or more years lower than other children of his age, the teacher was faced with an unpleasant predicament. How could she provide reading material for this child which would be on his reading level yet have a story content which would be interesting to children of his age? The teacher could write new material for this child so that the child could have reading material which was on his readability and interest level. However, the writing of stories is time consuming and requires a great deal of "know-how" in terms of appropriate vocabulary and content. Although some teachers tried, there was very little writing actually done. The other choice open to the teacher was to provide the child with a book on his reading level. Of course, the book was primarily written to appeal to children of a lower grade level. As a result, the child had a book he could read but the content was far below his interest level. Imagine how a 12- or 14-year-old would feel reading a second-grade book about *The Fairy Princess*.

The past decade has seen a phenomenal rise in the number of publishers of children's books who have begun to produce books written on a level two or three years lower than the interest maturity level of the context. These high interest, low-level reading level books have been a boon to the teacher and especially to the pupil who was experiencing difficulty with reading. What eighth grade boy reading on a fourth-grade level would object to reading or being seen with a book entitled *Stories of Pro Football?* Today, most publishers of children's books will be able to supply you with titles of these kinds of books.

TABLE 14-4. A selected list of high-interest, low-level reading books.

Title	Publisher	Reading Grade According to Publisher	Age Level Interests
1. Action Series Incredible Series Scope Series	Scholastic Book Service 904 Sylvan Ave. Englewood Cliffs, N.J. 07632	4–5	15–Adult
2. Adapted Classics	Globe Book Co. 175 Fifth Ave. New York, N.Y. 10010	5–7	9–12
3. Adult Education Readers	Reader's Digest Educational Dept. Pleasantville, N.Y. 10570	3	9–Adult
4. American Adventure	Harper & Row 10 E. 53rd St. New York, N.Y. 10022	2–6	9–12
5. American Landmark and World Landmark Books	E. M. Hale & Co. 1201 S. Hastings Way Eau Claire, Wis. 54701	5–7	9–12
6. Basic Science Education Series (primary and intermediate)	Harper & Row 10 E. 53rd St. New York, N.Y. 10022	3–5	9

Title	Publisher	Reading Grade According to Publisher	Age Level Interests
7. Basic Vocabulary Series	Garrard Publishing Co. 2 Overhill Rd. Scarsdale, N.Y. 10583	High First	7
8. Beginner Books Easy-to-Read Books	Random House 47 Hahn Rd. Westminster, Md. 21157	1–3	5
9. Beginning to Read Series	Follett Publishing Co. 1010 W. Washington Blvd. Chicago, Ill. 60607	1–3	5
10. Beginning Science Books	Follett Publishing Co. (see above)	2–4	7–9
11. Bowmar Racecar Series	Bowmar Publishing Corp. 622 Rodier Dr. Glendale, Calif. 91201	3–6	5–10
12. Childhood of Famous Americans Series	The Bobbs-Merrill Co. 4300 W. 62nd St. Indianapolis, Ind. 46268	4–5	9
13. Classics for Enjoyment	Laidlaw Brothers Thatcher & Madison Sts. River Forest, Ill. 60305	5–6	9–12
14. Classmate Editions of the Developmental Reading Series	Lyons & Carnahan 407 E. 25th St. Chicago, Ill. 60616	2–4	8
15. Cowboy Sam Series Dan Frontier Series Sailor Jack Series	Benefic Press 10300 W. Roosevelt Blvd. Westchester, Ill. 60153	1–3	7
16. Deep Sea Adventure Series Jim Forest Series	Harr Wagner Publishing Co. 609 Mission St. San Francisco 5, Calif.	F–3	7–9
17. Discovery Series	Garrard Press (see no. 7)	3	9–12
18. Everyreader Series	McGraw-Hill 1221 Ave. of the Americas New York, N.Y. 10020	4	9–12
19. First Book Series	D. C. Heath & Co. 12 S. Spring Street Lexington, Mass. 02173	4–5	9–12
20. First Reading Books	Garrard Press (see no. 7)	1	1–4
21. Folklore Stories	Garrard Press (see no. 7)	2–3	7

Title	Publisher	Reading Grade According to Publisher	Age Level Interests
22. Golden Science Books	Simon & Schuster Educational Division 630 Fifth Ave. New York, N.Y. 10020	4–6	9–12
23. I-Can-Read Series	Harper & Row Publisher (see no. 4)	1–3	5
24. Interesting Reading Series	Follett Publishing Co. (see no. 9)	2–3	9–12
25. Junior Everyreader Series	Webster Publishing Co. (see no. 18)	1–3	7–9
26. Junior Science Books	Garrard Press (see no. 7)	3	9
27. Life in America Geographies	The Fideler Co. 31 Ottawa Ave., N.W. Grand Rapids, Mich. 49502	4–5	9–12
28. My Weekly Reader	American Education Publications 245 Long Hill Rd. Middletown, Conn. 06457	1–6	4–12
29. Pleasure Reading Series	Garrard Press (see no. 7)	3	9–12
30. Reader's Digest Skill	Reader's Digest (see no. 3)	2–6	4–9
31. Read-to-Know Books	Follett Publishing Co. (see no. 9)	8–10	2–4
32. Scholastic Magazines Weekly	Scholastic Magazines 33 W. 42nd St. New York, N.Y. 10036	1–6	4–12
33. Simplified Classics	Scott Foresman & Co. 1900 East Lake Ave. Glenview, Ill. 60025	4–5	9–12
34. What Is It Series	Benefic Press (see no. 15)	1–4	4–8
35. Teen Age Tales	D. C. Heath & Co. 125 Spring St. Lexington, Mass. 02173	3–6	12

Write to each publisher for literature regarding these materials.

The Central Library—Room Library Controversy

There has been a great deal of controversy over the merits of the central library in the elementary school and the merits of the room library. Proponents of the central library claim the advantage of a qualified librarian who knows books and understands children's reading needs. Being a specialist the school librarian can teach use of library, order the most appropriate materials, and transfer some of the natural enthusiasm for books all librarians have to children. They point out that the division of books to rooms narrows the choice for the child, hence limits the possibility of arousing his interests.

Room library proponents on the other hand claim the classroom teacher gets to know and understand her children much better than any librarian could since she spends more time with them and has a smaller number with which to become acquainted. It is true that the librarian is a specialist but she is a specialist in generalizations concerning children and not a specialist in a particular child, whereas the classroom teacher in her undergraduate preparation has been exposed to the generalizations but she is also a specialist concerning the interests of the specific children under her charge.

The true position combines the best features of both. The trend is toward a central library where children can go and learn through browsing and class sessions to use the library and to be stimulated by the librarian's enthusiasm. The classroom teacher is permitted however to withdraw numbers of books from the library to place in a room reading corner. This allows her to include in a child's immediate environment books which may interest him and books which correlate with what is being learned in the content areas.

Television, Comic Books, and Reading

Everything from grandfather's falling arches to murder have been blamed on television and comic books. Periodically some militant soul addresses a PTA or writes a letter to an editor decrying the content and widespread use of comic books and television. Yet, the actual facts are that so far no evidence has been produced which gives substantiation to the claims that television and comics have injurious effects. True there are isolated cases where a specific child has been adversely affected, but for the majority of our pupils no proof of ill effects exists. In fact, the comic book and the television program many times have good effects. Children viewing television may be stimulated along a line in which little interest previously existed. As a result they may go to books to explore the area further. As for comic books, it is better for a child to be reading comic books than nothing at all. Diverting the reading of a child into a new channel is much easier than getting a nonreader to read.

As to the blood and gore in the two media, Hebb among others postulates the theory that the meaning gleaned by a child who watches TV shows with violence is not the same meaning gleaned by the adult viewer. A colleague of the authors points out that in all gory comic books and television programs good always triumphs and the criminal is punished, whereas not the same can be said about some of our so-called children's classics. Look at the tremendous rewards given to a lazy ne'er do well who was stupid enough to trade his mother's only cow for a handful of beans. Here good did not triumph. Jack not only stole from the giant which violates moral and legal precepts, but actually murdered the giant in the end and escaped any punishment!

Most educators today accept television as an integral part of a child's life and are noting that opportunities are present that may help a child in language development and reading readiness. Programs such as Sesame Street, Captain Kangaroo, Mister Rodgers, and the Electric Company have made an impact; of that there is no doubt. The only question for the researchers is to determine how much of an impact. Regardless, prominent reading specialists such as Smith (1974) and Gattegno (1969) are urging teachers to seek ways to use television as a reading resource.

Adams and Harrison (1975) reveal that in their study of 228 students in fourth, fifth, and sixth grade reading classes in parts of North Carolina, the following conclusions were reached: (a) Students watched TV approximately five hours per school day, approximately eight hours on Saturday, and four hours on Sunday; (b) Approximately one-third of the children could watch TV anytime they wanted to, and one-third could watch any program they selected; and, (c) Half of these pupils could read most of the words they saw on TV, while only 10 to 15% ignored or didn't read the words.

These findings were replicated in unpublished studies which we did in our areas and in other research as well. One such study (*Scholastic Newstime*, 1974) points out that between the ages of 2 and 14, the average child spends 6.6 years sleeping, 1.5 years watching TV, 1.4 years in school, and 2.5 years doing everything else, including chores, playing, eating, going places. The article by Adams and Harrison (1975) makes some very good suggestions on how TV can be used to improve competency in such reading areas as consonant clusters, phrase meaning, word meaning, recalling information, outlining, note taking, dictionary definitions, classifying conclusions and summary, and interpreting charts.

It is interesting to compare the British and American approaches to teaching reading with TV. Feeley (1976) provided some insight into the techniques used by BBC program broadcasts as compared to the American broadcasts of "Sesame Street" and "Electric Company" as produced by the Children's Television Workshop. The initial and major difference noted was due to the nature of programming in the two countries.

The American TV broadcasting is strongly oriented to the use of commercials while British broadcasting is strongly controlled with few or no commercials. The difference in approach results in the kind of TV that the children become accustomed to. American children are used to a fast-paced approach with a number of interruptions of the main programs; British children are used to more continuity, a story form program. As a result, the programming for Sesame Street and Electric Company seeks to teach a variety of decoding skills through brief, unconnected, humorous, but finely focused sequences built on basic learning principles. The British approach, in their programs Look and Read for ages 7 to 9 and older remedial readers, and Words and Pictures for ages 4 to 6, follows a serialized format, generally built around a high-interest adventure story. Chovil (1975) believes the British approach is more likely to motivate children into reading a book in addition to teaching basic skills. The TV programs are supplemented by a "book of the film" containing not only the story and still pictures, but also comprehension activities that can be used by teachers. According to Liebert (1975), 35% of the elementary schools in the United States tune in Electric Company; Chovil finds that 39% of the British schools are using Look and Read. Over 20% of the infant schools make use of Words and Pictures, according to the Morris study (1974).

Although there are many remediation materials available commercially for LD children, none are as universally available or as economical as comic strips. Hallenbeck (1976), in an interesting article on remediating with comic strips, points out that comic strips can be used to develop left-to-right sequencing; provide material that can improve cognitive development by interpreting picture absurdities; increase attention span; remediate perceptual deficits such as alertness to details; provide practice in reading material that the children find enjoyable; and help to develop self-concepts and a sense of mastery of the environment by teaching the child to distinguish between fact and fantasy in an objective way. By training LD children to appreciate comic strip humor, they can develop their own sense of humor at the same time they are improving their reading and conceptualizing skills. Certainly, comic strips, properly chosen, can be used for enrichment and incidental education. The use of comics and humor for teaching are supported by researchers such as McGhee (1971) and Paine (1974).

Craig's Theory of Adult Standards for Children's Books

James C. Craig made a study of the readability of best sellers in the United States. From the readability level of the so-called children's books appearing among the best sellers compared to books recommended by educators and librarians Craig made certain observations which can be summed up in the following quote;

> Children's books, like electric trains, are bought for the gratification and edification of the parents.

Craig found many books beyond the grade level for which they were recommended. Coupling this with the Rankin study which indicated a discrepancy between adults' and children's enthusiasm for the Newberry books and the Kolson, Zimmerman, Robinson study which indicated a discrepancy between the publisher most purchased and the publisher preferred by children in self-selection activities, one can only come to the conclusion that with all the research into children's interest there is much that still needs to be done. Perhaps children's book awards should be given and controlled by children but just how this could be done is speculative.

Many educators are discussing the possibility that the emphasis in interest has been misplaced. We have tended to think in terms of what interests children and then use these interests to slip in learning. In reality our efforts should be directed toward trying to determine the inherent interest of the material to be learned so that we may be able to create interest in the learning rather than "sneak it in."

What are the inherencies of interest in academic matters? First, there is the matter of difficulty. Easy tasks soon lose their interest value whereas tasks which present a little difficulty seem to have an attraction. Dewey, in his *Interest and Effort in Education*, said:

> It is not too much to say that a normal person demands a certain amount of difficulty to surmount in order that he may have a full and vivid sense of what he is about, and hence have a lively interest in what he is doing.

The second inherency is one of curiosity. All children are by nature curious about unknowns in their environment. Anything new which is slightly related to something known will arouse this natural curiosity. Hence, if the teacher makes certain the material to be learned is related to what has been learned, that the material is new, that it presents an obstacle to surmount, yet is capable of being surmounted, there is no need to rely upon sneaky techniques.

The Literature Sampler and the Trade Book

Constance McCullough (no date) and others have designed a box of selected selections from 44 good books. The selections are printed on individual cards with accompanying cards containing guides to discussion and enrichment. This sampler was designed for the junior high school. The stories are organized within the box along lines of interest such as adventure, humor, etc. After the student has read a selection, he is given a list of stories along similar lines to which he can go for additional reading.

We hope that McCullough will someday give her talents to the development of a similar kind of sampler for the elementary school. The kit could save the teacher much effort in helping children become acquainted with worthwhile materials and in locating similar kinds of materials of which they have indicated an interest.

One of the greatest allies of the public school teacher is the trade book. The number of companies producing children's books has increased and, what is more important, the new merchandizing techniques are increasing the consumption of trade books. Hardly a super-market exists which does not have a stand where trade books of all kinds are exhibited. Bored children of tired shoppers spend time consuming these materials whereas prior to this phenomenon the children would have been getting into mischief. Admittedly many of these materials are inferior but at least they offer competition for the so-called gory comics. Further, out of want of something better to do, children are reading and this is good.

These cheap trade books offer the teacher an inexpensive source of materials to use during the interest portion of her total reading program, and also a wide variety of topics.

The Use of the Newspaper

Of all the resource materials, the newspaper offers the widest variety of high interest contemporary reading materials. *Diversity* is the key word. The newspaper as a resource for teaching reading skills, including study skills, is not a new idea but it still is only being used on a limited basis. The teacher's task is to adapt the articles, columns, and ads into reading materials for her own unique teaching situation. The materials or content can be adjusted to meet the needs of individual pupils according to their reading level, rate of learning, high-interest areas, special difficulties, and needs for enrichment. Newspapers that have special contributions to make can be reused many times once the teacher has developed the activities to go with a particular issue. Newspaper lessons can be used on a group or individual basis as a follow up to a teacher-directed lesson. Of course, they can also be used as an independent activity for freely selective reading. Reading the daily paper and discussing the news, sports, and weather can also develop an interest in pursuing the daily reading of the paper outside the classroom.

Whisler (1972) points out the wide variety of uses to which a newspaper can be put in teaching reading skills. She mentions skill in finding the main idea, skimming, summarizing, outlining, analytic reading for special purposes, reading graphs, critical reading. She does suggest a slow, careful organization of a guided program to promote these skills, beginning on a low level of difficulty and gradually increasing in complexity by using a wide variety of activities.

appendix a

Aids and Tools for Children
with Learning Disabilities

The following list of tools are used as aids in teaching reading and arithmetic to children with learning disabilities in the preschool, primary, and intermediate grade levels.

Aids in Reading

PRESCHOOL LEVEL

1. *Picture matching boards.*

   The picture matching boards put into manual form one area of reading readiness, that of matching identical pictures. It encourages closer observation and keener perception, and gives practice in eye-hand coordination. The perception of similarities is a difficult concept for many cerebral palsied children but it is basic in beginning reading.

2. *Picture interpretation board.*

   The picture interpretation board puts into manual form the "picture reading" area of reading readiness. It allows the child without speech to demonstrate that he understands the contents of a picture. For children who find matching difficult, it gives further practice in seeing relationships.

Although a strictly academic program for mentally handicapped children is generally discouraged, reading is one of the skills most emphasized in special classes.

Intelligence tests have shown that on the whole, mentally handicapped children learn to read up to their mental age reading grade expectancy, as do children of normal or superior intelligence.

The following general guides will aid teachers in knowing what reading ability to expect of mentally handicapped children:

1. Children with chronological ages 7 to 9 and with mental ages of 4 to 6:
   a. have not begun to read.
   b. should be showing interest in reading, in books, and in pictures, in the interpretation of pictures, labels, their own names.
   c. should be engaging in an intensive reading readiness program.

2. Children of chronological ages of 9 to 11 with mental ages of 5½ years to 7:
    a. should be having an intensive reading readiness program with incidental reading of charts, signs, labels, if readiness is not adequate.
    b. should be interested in drawing pictures, interpreting pictures, and reading and writing stories about these pictures.
    c. should begin to read preprimers, primers, and simple books.
3. Children of chronological ages 11 to 13 and with mental ages of 7 to 8½ years:
    a. should be reading first- to third-grade material with adequate understanding.
    b. should be grouping words and phrases into thought units, but are slow in reading.
4. Children of chronological ages of 13 to 16 with mental ages of 8½ to 11 years:
    a. should be utilizing reading for many activities and using books from third through fifth grade level.
    b. should be using dictionary, telephone directory, and library, and reading newspapers and maps.
    c. should be spontaneously reading for information and pleasure.

PRIMARY LEVEL

1. *Word charts.*
   These charts are used to help child develop a recognition of rhyming words, different words, alike words, action and naming words. Help child begin reading and begin spelling.
2. *Show-Me card pocket.*
   Used as a class procedure. Gives teacher a chance to see if children are progressing and at what pace.
3. *Who gets it?*
   Child uses word and picture combinations to develop concepts that words portray.
4. *Basic sight word test.*
   Test 25 or more children. Teacher can tell which children need remedial work. Helps child recognize words and word combinations.
5. *Alphabet picture.*
   Used to teach child to recognize objects, to learn letters in alphabetical order, and to learn to spell simple words.
6. *Flash words.*
   Used to teach child words that cannot be pictured.
7. *Dial-n-spell.*
   Helps child learn to spell and develop a concept of word meanings.

INTERMEDIATE

1. *Sentence builder.*
   Word cards which help child develop an ability to recognize words and place them properly in sentences. These cards also further develop left to right eye movement.
2. *Phonetic quizmo.*
   Helps child increase his phonetic sounding ability, and his capability in using phonics to pronounce words.
3. *Happy bears reading set.*
   Develops child's ability to read words and sentences. It develops child's comprehension. Develops left-to-right movement of eyes. Prepares child for more varied primary reading.

Aids in Arithmetic

1. *Number puzzle.*
   By handling these numbers, the child becomes acquainted with the first five numbers or higher, develops color recognition, and develops motor skills by placing the numbers in correct cut out area.

2. *Number peg board.*
   This board is used for teaching beginning number concepts. Counting and grouping are the main purposes.

3. *Numeral peg board.*
   The purpose of the Numeral Peg Board is to develop an association between the number and the quantity it represents. The sense of touch is brought into play to cause recognition of number sequence by placing in correct order. The teacher or child may use this tool.

4. *Domino and number board.*
   This is used to develop relationship of numerals and their quantities. Domino Dots are raised to give child an opportunity to learn the tactile sense.

5. *Number picture board.*
   Child begins to match the picture of a number of objects with the number itself. Emphasis is on counting pictures.

6. *Addition board.*
   Used to perform simple addition. Develops meaning of the equal and plus signs. Child can actually add 2 pegs and 2 pegs and see that it equals 4 pegs.

It is a commonly accepted fact that most handicapped children will achieve between the third and fifth grade in their arithmetic ability. Consequently, arithmetic materials are presented to learning disabled children in the same order, in the same manner, and with the same emphasis as they are presented to average or normal children. The only adjustment made for the mentally handicapped is that the materials designed for 8-year-old normal children will be used for mentally handicapped children with a mental age of 8.

The learning disabled should be taught a solid foundation for the arithmetical needs they will have in adult life. These include:

1. The development, understanding, and use of an arithmetical vocabulary.
2. The development of number concepts and skills.
3. The development of the ability to apply number concepts.
4. The development of an understanding of various units of measurement.
5. The development of an understanding of fractional parts.

1. *Stick-o-mat flannel board.*
   The flannel board may be used by the teacher to develop almost all arithmetic concepts. It may be used by the child to instill those concepts. Cut-outs of all kinds may be used.

2. *Relative sizes set.*
   These cut-out circles are used to develop the concept of size in terms of smallest, smaller, small, large, larger, largest.

3. *Cubical counting blocks.*

Used to develop counting sense, color recognition, and motor skills through construction.

4. *Counting frame.*

This can be used to develop counting sense, concept of 10, and could be used by the child to solve simple addition and subtraction problems.

5. *First counting board.*

This can be used to motivate a child's interest in counting, especially at the primary level. It develops skill in manipulation by putting things in correct cut out position. It develops recognition of sounds and the quantities represented when counting to five.

6. *Clock puzzle.*

Used to develop concept of time and how it affects a child's daily life. Can be used to develop number sequence, seconds, minutes, hours, and days. In intermediate level, it could be used to develop concept of Roman numerals and possibly clockwise and counterclockwise.

7. *Counting discs.*

Used to develop skill in counting, adding, and subtracting. Helps child understand the plus and minus signs.

8. *Number scale.*

Develops concept of balancing. Also used to prove basic addition facts.

9. *Teach and fun telephone.*

Used in primary level to develop number recognition and number sequence. Could be used also to develop skill in addition.

10. *Peg board.*

A concrete tool used to develop coordination and motor skills. Also used to develop counting sense and color recognition.

11. *Place value pegs or sticks.*

Used to develop ten-ness of numbers, place or position value and recognition of the function of zero.

INTERMEDIATE LEVEL

1. *Calendar.*

This calendar can develop a concept of time in terms of days, weeks, months, and years. It can be used to develop the child's ability in addition and subtraction and the sequence of numbers.

2. *Educational thermometer.*

This thermometer could develop the concept of counting by tens and also the concept of munus. It may be used to help the child understand temperature. This could be used to further addition and subtraction abilities.

3. *Flash cards.*

Can be used at all levels to develop recognition of numbers and their different combinations in addition and subtraction. Used in a learning process because opposite side has answers.

4. *Place value indicator.*

Used to develop concept of 10 as the base of our number system. Develops recognition of place value of numbers and the importance of zero. This also helps child understand two and three place numbers.

5. *Toy money.*

Used in special education to develop concept of our money value, making change, and counting sequence by ones, fives, tens, etc.

6. *Toy scale.*

Used to develop concept of weight. It can develop ability in recognizing number sequence. Helps further child's ability in addition and subtraction.

7. *Fraction kit.*

Can be used by the teacher and the child. Used to develop concept of whole and part or fractions of a whole.

8. *Number games.*

There is a great variety of arithmetic games that may be used for the child's enjoyment but at the same time will further his arithmetical ability.

appendix b

Three Word Lists

KUCERA-FRANCIS CORPUS*

1. the	35. her	69. two
2. of	36. all	70. may
3. and	37. she	71. then
4. to	38. there	72. do
5. a	39. would	73. first
6. in	40. their	74. any
7. that	41. we	75. my
8. is	42. him	76. now
9. was	43. been	77. such
10. he	44. has	78. like
11. for	45. when	79. our
12. it	46. who	80. over
13. with	47. will	81. man
14. as	48. more	82. me
15. his	49. no	83. even
16. on	50. if	84. most
17. be	51. out	85. made
18. at	52. so	86. after
19. by	53. said	87. also
20. I	54. what	88. did
21. this	55. up	89. many
22. had	56. its	90. before
23. not	57. about	91. must
24. are	58. into	92. through
25. but	59. than	93. back
26. from	60. them	94. years
27. or	61. can	95. where
28. have	62. only	96. much
29. an	63. other	97. your
30. they	64. new	98. may
31. which	65. some	99. well
32. one	66. could	100. down
33. you	67. time	101. should
34. were	68. these	102. because

*From Kucera, Henry, & Francis, W. Nelson. *Computational analysis of present-day American English.* Providence, R.I.: Brown University Press, 1967. Reproduced by permission of the publisher.

103. each	142. come	181. left
104. just	143. since	182. number
105. those	144. against	183. course
106. people	145. go	184. war
107. Mr.	146. came	185. until
108. how	147. right	186. always
109. too	148. used	187. away
110. little	149. take	188. something
111. state	150. three	189. fact
112. good	151. states	190. though
113. very	152. himself	191. water
114. make	153. few	192. less
115. would	154. house	193. public
116. still	155. use	194. put
117. own	156. during	195. thing
118. see	157. without	196. almost
119. men	158. again	197. hand
120. work	159. place	198. enough
121. long	160. American	199. far
122. get	161. around	200. took
123. here	162. however	201. head
124. between	163. home	202. yet
125. both	164. small	203. government
126. life	165. found	204. system
127. being	166. Mrs.	205. better
128. under	167. thought	206. set
129. never	168. went	207. told
130. day	169. say	208. nothing
131. same	170. part	209. night
132. another	171. once	210. end
133. know	172. general	211. why
134. while	173. high	212. called
135. last	174. upon	213. didn't
136. might	175. school	214. eyes
137. us	176. every	215. find
138. great	177. don't	216. going
139. old	178. does	217. look
140. year	179. got	218. asked
141. off	180. united	219. later
		220. knew

A Basic Sight Vocabulary of 220 Words

E. W. Dolch

Since these 220 words make up from 50 to 75% of all ordinary reading material in the first three grades, they should be recognized instantly by sight by all school children.

a	always	are	ate	before	blue
about	am	around	away	best	both
after	an	as	be	better	bring
again	and	ask	because	big	brown
all	any	at	been	black	but

buy	four	is	old	show	two
by	from	it	on	sing	under
call	full	its	once	sit	up
came	funny	jump	one	six	upon
can	gave	just	only	sleep	us
carry	get	keep	open	small	use
clean	give	kind	or	so	very
cold	go	know	our	some	walk
come	goes	laugh	out	soon	want
could	going	let	over	start	warm
cut	good	light	own	stop	was
did	got	like	pick	take	well
do	green	little	play	tell	went
does	grow	live	please	ten	were
done	had	long	pretty	thank	what
don't	has	look	pull	that	when
down	have	made	put	the	where
draw	he	make		their	which
drink	help	many	ran	them	white
eat	her	may	read	then	who
eight	here	me	red	there	why
every	him	much	ride	these	will
fall	his	must	right	they	wish
far	hold	my	round	think	with
fast	hot	myself	run	this	work
find	how		said	those	would
first	hurt	never	saw	three	write
five	I	new	say	to	yellow
fly	if	no	see	today	yes
for	in	not	seven	together	you
found	into	now	shall	too	your
		of	she	try	

Source: Dolch, E. W. *Basic sight words cards*. Champaign, Illinois: Garrard Press, 1960.

Survival Words*

1. Stop
2. Go
3. Danger
4. Keep Off
5. Keep Out
6. Poison
7. Hands Off
8. Fragile
9. Private
10. Watch Step
11. Police Station
12. Hospital
13. Emergency Ward
14. Quiet Zone
15. Fire Station
16. Fire Alarm
17. Fire Escape
18. Fire Extinguisher
19. Entrance
20. Exit
21. No Entrance
22. Bus Station
23. Bus Stop
24. Subway
25. Ticket Station
26. Cashier

27. Pay Here
28. Pay As You Enter
29. Cafeteria
30. Restaurant
31. Not Responsible
32. Hotel
33. Elevator
34. Stairs
35. Downstairs
36. Upstairs
37. Escalator
38. Bank
39. Post Office
40. Drug Store
41. Prescriptions
42. Office
43. Toilet
44. Rest Rooms
45. Powder Rooms
46. Men
47. Women
48. Ladies
49. Gentlemen
50. Out of Order
51. Telephone
52. Live Wires
53. Stay Out
54. Stay Off
55. Keep to the Left
56. Keep to the Right
57. Straight Ahead
58. Slow Down
59. Slippery When Wet
60. Speed Limit
61. Reserved
62. Dead End
63. Street Closed
64. One Way Street
65. No Turns
66. No Left Turn
67. No Right Turn

68. No U Turn
69. No Parking
70. Turn Right
71. Turn Left
72. Detour
73. Temporary Detour
74. Low Bridge
75. Railroad Crossing
76. School Zone
77. Parking One Hour
78. No Smoking
79. No Trespassing
80. Do Not Enter
81. Do Not Pass
82. Do Not Handle
83. Do Not Touch
84. Do Not Deposit Rubbish
85. Do Not Deposit Mail
86. Do Not Talk to the Driver
87. Do Not Litter
88. Push
89. Pull
90. This Side Up
91. This Way Out
92. Handle At Own Risk
93. Handle With Care
94. For Sale
95. For Rent
96. Help Wanted
97. Hot Water
98. Cold Water
99. Deep Water
100. High Tension
101. Explosives
102. Waste Can
103. Trash Can
104. Disposal
105. Step Down
106. Watch Your Step
107. Watch Your Coat
108. Watch Your Head

*When a symbol accompanies the word, this symbol should also be taught.

appendix c

Names and Addresses of Companies That Publish Materials for Use in Reading and Learning Disabilities

Academic Therapy Publications
1539 Fourth St.
San Rafael, Calif. 94901

ACI Films
35 W. 45th St.
New York, N.Y. 10036

Acoustifone Corp.
8954 Comanche Ave.
Chatsworth, Calif. 91311

Adapt Press
104 E. 20th St.
Sioux Falls, S.D. 57105

Addison-Wesley Publishing Co.
Reading, Md. 01867

American Book Co.
450 W. 33rd St.
New York, N.Y. 10001

American Education Publications
Education Center
Columbus, Oh. 43216

American Guidance Service
Publisher's Bldg.
Circle Pines, Minn. 55014

Ann Arbor Publishers, Inc.
2057 Charlton Ave.
Ann Arbor, Mich. 48104

Association for Childhood Education
 International
3615 Wisconsin Ave., N.W.
Washington, D.C. 20016

Association for Supervision and Curriculum
 Development
Room 428, 1201 Sixteenth St., N.W.
Washington, D.C. 20036

Association Instructional Materials
600 Madison Ave.
New York, N.Y. 10022

Atheneum Publishers
122 E. 42nd St.
New York, N.Y. 10017

Bell & Howell Co.
Audio Visual Products Division
7100 McCormick Rd.
Chicago, Ill. 60645

Benefic Press
10300 W. Roosevelt Rd.
Westchester, Ill. 60153

Bobbs-Merrill Co.
4300 W. 62nd St.
Indianapolis, Ind. 46268

Borg-Warner Educational Systems
7450 N. Natchez Ave.
Niles, Ill. 60648

Bowmar Publishing Corp.
622 Rodier Dr.
Glendale, Calif. 91201

Burgess Publishing Co.
426 S. Sixth St.
Minneapolis, Minn. 55415

Calif. Assoc. for Neurologically Handicapped
  Children
Literature Distribution Center
P.O. Box 790
Lomita, Calif. 90717

California Test Bureau/McGraw-Hill
Del Monte Research Park
Monterey, Calif. 93940

Cambridge Book Co.
488 Madison Ave.
New York, N.Y. 10022

Cassetts Unlimited
Roanoke, Tx. 76262

Center for Applied Research in Education
521 5th Ave.
New York, N.Y. 10017

Child Study
Association of America
9 E. 89th St.
New York, N.Y. 10028

Childcraft Equipment Corp.
150 East 58th St.
New York, N.Y. 10022

Continental Press
520 E. Bainbridge St.
Elizabethtown, Pa. 17022

Cooperative Tests and Service
Educational Testing Service
Box 999
Princeton, N.J. 08540

Creative Playthings
Box 330
Princeton, New Jersey 08504

Croft Educational Services, Inc.
100 Garfield Ave.
New London, Ct. 06320

Thomas Y. Crowell Co.
666 Fifth Ave.
New York, N.Y. 10019

CTB/McGraw Hill
Del Monte Research Park
Monterey, Calif. 93940

Cuisenaire Company of America
9 Elm Ave.
Mount Vernon, N.Y. 10550

Curriculum Associates
P.O. Box 56
Wellesley Hills, Mass. 02181

John Day Co.
257 Park Ave. S.
New York, N.Y. 10010

Dell Publishing Co.
750 Third Ave.
New York, N.Y. 10017

Denoyer Geppert Co.
5235 Ravenswood Ave.
Chicago, Ill. 60640

Dept. of Health Education and Welfare
U.S. Gov't Printing Office
Washington, D.C. 20402

Developmental Learning Materials
3505 North Ashland Avenue
Chicago, Ill. 60657

A. B. Dick Co.
5700 W. Touchy Ave.
Chicago, Ill. 60645

Docent Corp.
24 Broadway
Pleasantville, N.Y. 10570

Dodd, Mead & Co.
79 Madison Ave.
New York, N.Y. 10016

Doubleday & Co.
501 Franklin Ave.
Garden City, N.Y. 10017

Dutton, E. P. and Co.
201 Park Ave. So.
New York, N.Y. 10002

Early Years Magazine
P.O. Box 1223
Darien, Ct. 06820

The Economy Company
P.O. Box 25308
Oklahoma City, Ok. 73125

Edmark Associates
655 I. Orcas St.
Seattle, Wash. 98108

Educational Activities
P.O. Box 392
Freeport, N.Y. 11510

Educational Aids
845 Wisteria Dr.
Fremont, Calif. 94538

Educational Book Division
Prentice-Hall
Englewood Cliffs, N.J. 07632

Educational Developmental Laboratories
A Divison of McGraw-Hill
Huntington, N.Y. 11743

Educational Games
P.O. Box 3653
Grand Central Station
New York, N.Y. 10017

Educators Publishing Service
75 Moulton St.
Cambridge, Mass. 02138

Educational Records Bureau
21 Audubon Ave.
New York, N.Y. 10032

Eric/Crier Clearinghouse
NCTE
1111 Kenyon Rd.
Urbana, Ill. 61801

Eye Gate House
146-01 Archer Ave.
Jamaica, N.Y. 11435

Exceptional Products Corp.
Box 6406
Richfield Branch
Minneapolis, Minn. 55423

Fawcett Publishers
1515 Broadway
New York, N.Y. 10036

Fearon Publishers
6 Davis Dr.
Belmont, Calif. 94002

Follett Educational Corp.
1010 W. Washington Blvd.
Chicago, Ill. 60607

Garrard Publishing
2 Overhill Rd.
Scarsdale. N.Y. 10583

General Learning Corp.
3 E. 54th St.
New York, N.Y. 10022

Gillingham-Slingerland
Reading Workshops
75 Moulton St.
Cambridge, Mass. 02138

Ginn and Co.
9888 Monroe Dr.
Dallas, Tx. 75229

Goodyear Publishing
15115 Sunset Blvd., Pacific
Palisades, Calif.

The Grade Teacher
Riverside, N.J. 08075

Grolier Educational Corp.
845 Third Ave.
New York, N.Y. 10022

Harcourt Brace Jovanovich
757 Third Ave.
New York, N.Y. 10017

Harper & Row
Library Dept.
10 E. 53rd St.
New York, N.Y. 10022

D.C. Heath & Co.
125 Spring St.
Lexington, Mass. 02173

Highlights for Children
2300 Fifth Ave.
Columbus, Oh. 43216

Hoffman Information Systems
5623 Peck Rd.
Arcadia, Calif. 91006

or

4423 Arden Dr.
El Monte, Calif. 91734

Holt, Rinehart & Winston
383 Madison Ave.
New York, N.Y. 10017

Houghton Mifflin
110 Tremont St.
Boston, Mass. 02107

Ideal School Supply Co.
11000 S. Lavergne Ave.
Oak Lawn, Ill. 60453

Individualized Instruction Inc.
P.O. Box 25308
Oklahoma City, Okla. 73125

Initial Teaching Alphabet Foundation
52 Vanderbilt Ave.
New York, N.Y. 10017

Innovations for Individualizing Instruction
Box 4361
Washington, D.C.

Instructo Corp.
Cedar Hollow and Mathews Rds.
Paoli, Pa. 19301

Instructor Publications
Seven Bank St.
Dansville, N.Y. 14437

International Film Bureau
332 S. Michigan Ave.
Chicago, Ill. 60604

International Reading Association
800 Barksdale Rd.
Newark, Del. 19711

Learning Corp. of America
711 Fifth Ave.
New York, N.Y. 10022

Let's Read
Box 250
Bronxville, N.Y. 10708

J. B. Lippincott Co.
E. Washington Square
Philadelphia, Pa. 19105

Love Publishing Co.
6635 E. Villanova Pl.
Denver, Colo. 80222

Lyons and Carnahan
407 E. 25th St.
Chicago. Ill. 60616

Mafex Associates
Box 519
Johnstown, Pa. 15907

M.K.M. Inc.
809 Kansas City Street
Rapid City, S.D. 57701

McCormick-Mathers Publishing
    Co.
300 Pike St.
Cincinnati, Oh. 45202

McGraw Hill Book Co.
1226 Avenue of the Americas
New York, N.Y. 10036

David McKay Co.
750 Third Ave.
New York, N.Y. 10017

Macmillan
866 Third Ave.
New York, N.Y. 10022

Mast/Keystone
2212 E. 12th St.
Davenport, Iowa 52803

Charles E. Merrill Publishing Co.
1300 Alum Creek Dr.
Columbus, Oh. 43216

Milliken Publishing Co.
Sound Photo Equipment
Box 2953
Lubbock, Tx. 79408

Milton Bradley
Springfield, Mass. 01101

C. V. Mosby
11830 Westline Industrial Dr.
St. Louis, Mo. 63141

Open Court Publishing Co.
Box 599
LaSalle, Ill. 61301

F. A. Owen Publishing Co.
Instructor Park
Dansville, N.Y. 14437

Pacifica Foundation
Pacifica Tape Library
Department E
5316 Venice Blvd.
Los Angeles, Calif. 90019

Parker Publishing Co.
West Nyack, N.Y. 10994

Phonovisual Products
12216 Parklawn Dr.
Rockville, Md. 20852

Playskool
Division of Milton Bradley
Springfield, Mass. 01101

Prentice-Hall
Educational Book Division
Englewood Cliffs, N.J. 07632

The Psychological Corp.
757 Third Ave.
New York, N.Y. 10017

Rand, McNally
P.O. Box 7600
Chicago, Ill. 60680

Random House
457 Hahn Rd.
Westminster, Md. 21157

Reader's Choice
Division of Scholastic Magazines
904 Sylvan Ave.
Englewood Cliffs, N.J. 07632

Reader's Digest Services
Educational Division
Pleasantville, N.J. 10570

Reading Laboratory
55 Day St.
S. Norwalk, Conn. 06854

Reading Newsreport
11 W. 42nd St.
New York, N.Y. 10026

Right To Read
400 Maryland Ave. S.W.
Washington, D.C. 20202

W. B. Saunders Co.
West Washington Square
Philadelphia, Pa. 19105

Scholastic Book Services
50 West 44th St.
New York, N.Y. 10036

Science Research Associates
259 East Erie St.
Chicago, Ill. 60611

Scott Foresman
1900 East Lake Ave.
Glenview, Ill. 60025

Silver Burdett Co.
Morristown, N.J. 07960

Singer Co./Graflex Division
3750 Monroe Ave.
Rochester, N.Y. 14603

Singer Education & Training Products
SVE-Society For Visual Education
1345 Diversey Parkway
Chicago, Ill. 60614

Skill Development Equip. Co.
Division of Port-a-Pit
1340 N. Jefferson
Anaheim Calif. 92806

Slosson Educational Publications
140 Pine St.
East Aurora, N.Y. 14052

Society for Visual Education
1345 Diversey Parkway
Chicago, Ill. 60614

Stanwix House
3020 Chartiers Ave.
Pittsburgh, Pa. 15204

Superintendent of Documents
Gov't Printing Office
Washington, D.C. 20402

Teacher
866 Third Ave.
New York, N.Y. 10022

Teachers College Press
1234 Amsterdam Ave.
New York, N.Y. 10027

Teaching Resources
Educational Service
100 Boylston St.
Boston, Mass. 02116

Charles C Thomas
Publisher
301-327 E. Lawrence Ave.
Springfield, Ill. 62704

University of Chicago Press
5801 & South Ellis Ave.
Chicago, Ill. 60637

University of Michigan Press
615 E. University
Ann Arbor, Mich. 48101

University of Minnesota Press
2037 University Ave.
Minneapolis, Minn. 55455

George Wahr Publishing Co.
316 S. State St.
Ann Arbor, Mich.

Walker Educational Book Corp.
720 Fifth Ave.
New York, N.Y. 10019

Webster Publishing Co.
1154 Reco Ave.
St. Louis, Miss.

Weekly Reader
American Education Publications
Education Center
Columbus, Oh. 43216

Joseph M. Wepman
950 E. 59th St.
Chicago, Ill.

Western Psychological Services
12031 Wilshire Blvd.
Los Angeles, Calif. 90025

Westinghouse Learning Corp.
2680 Hanover St.
P.O. Box 10680
Palo Alto, Calif. 94304

John Wiley & Sons
605 Third Ave.
New York, N.Y. 10016

Wisconsin Design For Reading Skill
c/o Interpretive Scoring Systems
4401 W. 76th St.
Minneapolis, Minn. 55435

Wisconsin Research and Development Center
   for Cognitive Learning
Madison, Wis. 53706

Word Games
P.O. Box 305
Healdsburg, Calif. 95448

Xerox Education Publications
Education Center
Columbus, Oh. 43216

Zaner-Bloser Co.
612 N. Park St.
Columbus, Oh. 43215

appendix d

Recommended Professional Journals

Name and Publisher	Content	Issue
Academic Therapy 1539 Fourth St. San Rafael, Calif. 94901	Interdisciplinary journal directed to an international audience of teachers, special teachers, parents, and specialists working in the field of reading, learning, and communication disabilities. All ages. Methods of identification, diagnosis, and remediation emphasized.	Issued six times per year, September, October, December, February, March, and June.
Bulletin of the Orton Society 8415 Bellona Ln. Towson, Md. 21204	Official bulletin by the Orton Society, a nonprofit scientific and educational organization for the study and treatment of children with specific language disability (dyslexia). All ages, international in scope. Many useful reprints available.	One issue annually.
Exceptional Children	Covers all of the areas of exceptionalities in children. It presents a variety of articles, including many on reading and language, for different types of children.	Alternates every other month with Teaching Exceptional Children.
The Journal of Learning Disabilities 101 East Ontario St. Chicago, Ill. 60611	Multidisciplinary, primarily concerned with learning disabilities (diagnosis and treatment). All ages, international in scope. Theoretical and practical contributions.	Issued monthly. June/July and August/September combined.

441

Name and Publisher	*Content*	*Issue*
Journal of Reading International Reading Association 800 Barksdale Road Newark, Del. 19711	Primarily directed to secondary teachers, the journal also concerns itself with older poor readers and motivational techniques. Its purpose is to exchange information and opinions regarding reading skills.	Eight times annually, October through May.
The Journal of Special Education Buttonwood Farms 3515 Woodhaven Rd. Philadelphia, Pa. 19154	Primarily devoted to all types of handicapped children in a special setting, the journal contains relevant material for remedial reading approaches.	Quarterly.
Language Arts (formerly *Elementary English*) National Council of Teachers of English 1111 Kenyon Rd. Urbana, Ill. 61801	Encompasses the teaching of all the language arts in the elementary school, but has many articles and features dealing with reading.	Eight times a year.
Reading Clinic The Center for Applied Research in Education 521 Fifth Ave. New York, N.Y. 10017	Directed to grade 1-8 classroom teachers and reading specialists, this practical publication provides tested activities and materials for both developmental and remedial reading programs. Includes ready-to-use activity worksheets for diagnosing specific weaknesses and reinforcing specific skills.	Monthly issues, September through June.
Reading Newsreport Multimedia Education 11 West 42nd St. New York, N.Y. 10036	Covers broad spectrum of reading problems and includes articles of interest to the remedial reading teacher, e.g., tutoring relationship, use of comic books in class, etc.	Monthly issues, October through May.
Reading Teacher International Reading Association 800 Barksdale Road Newark, Del. 19711	Primarily directed to elementary school teachers, the journal also brings articles on remedial reading. Occasionally it deals with problems such as minimal brain dysfunctions, paraprofessionals, and motivational techniques.	Eight times annually, October through May.

Name and Publisher	Content	Issue
Slow Learner Workshop Parker Publishing Co. West Nyack, N.Y. 10994	Primarily directed to elementary educators, this publication provides practical, tested techniques and activities for teaching children with all types of learning difficulties. Includes successful new ideas and programs from across the country.	Monthly issues, September through June.

GLOSSARY

abasement: humiliation; feeling of degradation.

aberration: an unexpected or severe departure from the normal.

abstract ability: the ability to comprehend relationships and to react to concepts and abstract symbols.

acalculia: a disturbance of the ability to manipulate arithmetic symbols or to do simple mathematical calculations. *Dyscalculia:* partial yet serious impairment in the above.

accommodation: movements that prepare a sense organ (the eye) for receiving impressions or stimuli.

acetylcholine (ACH): believed to be the chemical agent of transmission at the synapse.

acquired behavior: behavior which is ascribable primarily to experience.

acuity: level of functioning capability of a sensory mode, e.g., visual acuity.

adjustment: the process whereby an individual finds and adapts modes of behavior that bring about a more satisfactory relationship with his environment.

affix: a bound morpheme that is attached to the beginning of a base (as a prefix) or to the end of the base (as a suffix).

agitographia: a writing disability characterized by very rapid movements and the omission or distortion of letters, words, or parts of words.

agnosia: inability to interpret sensory impression; loss of ability to recognize and identify familiar objects through a particular sense organ. There is auditory agnosia, auditory-verbal agnosia, color agnosia, geometric-form agnosia, picture agnosia, tactile agnosia, tactile-verbal agnosia, and visual or optic agnosia.

agraphia: inability to recall the kinesthetic patterns that go into writing. It is the inability to write words or to express oneself in writing. *Dysgraphia:* partial yet serious impairment in the above.

alexia: a disturbance of the ability to evaluate or interpret written symbols. A severe reading disability usually considered the byproduct of brain dysfunction. *Dyslexia:* partial yet serious impairment in the above.

alpha waves: an electroencephalographic record of neuronal firing in the cerebral cortex. It is characterized by a 8–13 frequency. The alpha wave is found in most adults.

ambulatory reading: the kind of reading one does when he is just passing time.

amusia: loss of ability to produce or to comprehend musical sounds.

anarthria: loss of ability to form words accurately due to brain lesion or damage to peripheral nerves which carry impulses to the articulatory muscles. *Dysarthria:* partial yet serious impairment in the above.

angular gyrus: area of the brain (left hemisphere) which governs some speech functions.

444

anomia: an inability to name objects or recall and recognize names. *Dysnomia:* impaired ability.

anoxia: the lack of oxygen to the brain. May occur in the newborn. The brain cells are particularly vulnerable to continued anoxia.

aphasia: loss or impairment of the ability to use language due to injury or disease of the brain centers. It may be inability to comprehend, manipulate, or express words in speech, writing, or signs. There is auditory aphasia, expressive aphasia, formulation aphasia, nominal aphasia (recalling names of objects), and paraphasia (substitution of parts of words or of inappropriate words).

apraxia: loss of ability to perform purposeful movements, in the absence of paralysis or sensory disturbance; caused by lesions in the cerebral cortex. An inability to perform a motor act.

articulation: the production of speech sounds.

ascenders: those letters which project above the base configuration of the word. In *lady* the *l* and the *d* are ascenders.

association: cognitive development of relationships by integrating experiences.

assimilative reading: reading directed to the exact understanding of what the author says. It implies retention.

astereognosis: a form of agnosia. Cannot recognize objects or conceive of their forms by touching or feeling them.

asymbolia: loss of ability to use or understand symbols, such as those used in mathematics, chemistry, music.

ataxia: marked incoordination in movements of the voluntary musculature and disturbed equilibrium.

athetosis: uncontrolled muscular movements marked by slow, recurring, weaving movements of arms and legs, and by facial grimaces (a form of cerebral palsy).

auding: listening, recognizing, and interpreting spoken language. Not merely hearing and responding to sounds.

audiometer: a hearing screening device. It may be a pure-tone audiometer or a speech threshold audiometer.

auditory association: the ability to relate spoken words in a meaningful way.

auditory blending: the ability to put separate sounds together to form a meaningful whole; e.g., the *b* sound and *l* sound to form *bl* as in BLUE.

auditory closure: ability to recognize the whole from the presentation of a partial auditory stimulus.

auditory discrimination: ability to distinguish auditorially between slight differences in sounds.

auditory dyslexia: difficulty encoding (translating) speech into printed or written symbols; difficulty identifying ("hearing") discrete phonic elements of speech accurately; difficulty making sound-symbol associations.

auditory memory: ability to recall words, digits, etc., in a meaningful manner; includes memory of meaning.

auditory perception: ability to receive sounds accurately and to understand what they mean.

auditory reception: ability to derive meaning from orally presented material.

auditory sequential memory: ability to reproduce a sequence of auditory stimuli.

autism: a condition of being dominated by subjective self-centered trends of thought or behavior, showing a paucity of social or communicative relations.

basal reading: a systematic attempt to teach children to read by giving them daily systematic instruction in reading.

basal text: the major tool used for basal reading instruction.

base: a morpheme which carries the principal meaning of a word and to which affixes may be added. Examples: *type—retype, typ*ist. Two bases may be combined to form compound words. Example: *type*writer.

basic sight words: the child's stock of words which he recognizes without having to analyze them.

Basic English: a list of 850 words compiled by C. K. Ogden with which it is possible to express almost anything in English.

basic sight vocabulary: a list of 220 words compiled by Dolch. They are said to make up 50 to 75% of all running words an elementary child will encounter in his reading.

basic skills: those areas of study that can be used to describe reading behavior.

basic visual achievement forms: seven geometric forms developed during the Winter Haven Project. They can be used to determine the child's degree of coordination, and as a prognosticator of probable success in reading.

behavior modification: a technique for systematically changing or developing targeted (designated) behaviors.

binocular vision: vision that involves joint focusing of both eyes.

blend: the combining of two letters into a sound in which each retains its distinctive sound.

body image: awareness of one's own body (conscious mental picture or subconscious knowledge of one's position in space and time). Includes the impressions one receives from internal signals as well as feedback resulting from contact with others. How one thinks he looks is referred to as body concept or body image. Body schema is the pattern.

bradyslexia: extremely slow rate of reading, writing, or spelling.

brain damage: any structural injury or insult to the brain, whether by surgery, accident, or disease.

breve: a diacritical mark used to indicate a short sound of a vowel.

broad view of reading: refers to the Claremont concept, also known as Spencer's concept, that all activities involved with seeing relationships and interpreting them are reading activities.

catastrophic reaction: response to a shock or a threatening situation with which the individual is unprepared to cope. Behavior is inadequate, vacillating, inconsistent, and generally retarded.

central nervous system (CNS): that part of the nervous system to which the sensory impulses are transmitted and from which motor impulses pass out; in vertebrates, the brain and spinal cord.

cerebral dominance: assumption that one cerebral hemisphere generally leads the other in control of bodily movements. In most individuals, the left side of the brain controls language and is considered the dominant hemisphere.

channels of communication: the sensorimotor pathways through which language is transmitted; e.g., auditory-vocal, visual-motor, among other possible combinations.

chiroscopic drawing: the tracing of an image guided by the eye which does not see the image. The image is seen by the other eye.

cholinesterase (CHE): an enzyme believed to remove the acetycholine from cell walls at synapse. It seems to perform a circuit breaker action.

choreiform movements: spasmodic or jerky movements which occur quite irregularly and arhythmically in different muscles. Characteristically these movements are sudden and of short duration distinguishing them clearly from slow tonic athetoid movements.

chronological age: refers to the number of years a person has lived.

circumflex: a diacritical mark.

clinical teaching: an approach to instruction that emphasizes recognition of and response to the individualized needs of a pupil.

closed syllable: ends in a consonant.

closure: the process of achieving completion in behavior or mental act. The tendency to stabilize, close, or complete a situation or a figure.

cloze: a technique for the purpose of measuring comprehension and readability of reading materials. Cloze tests are constructed by deleting words in a regular manner from a passage and substituting blank spaces. Exercise is to fill in the spaces with appropriate words.

cluttering: bursting, nervous speech marked by frequent omissions and substitutions of sound.

CNS: central nervous system.

cognitive: the faculty of knowing; of becoming aware of objects of thought or perception, including understanding and reasoning.

cognitive style: an individual's characteristic approach to problem solving and cognitive tasks (e.g., some persons tend to be analytical, seeing parts, while others tend to holistic, seeing things in their entirety with little awareness of components).

compound word: a word consisting of components that are words. Compounds are distinguished in speech from similar grammatical constructions by intonational contrast (*bluebird* as contrasted with *blue bird*).

comprehension: undertaking the meaning of printed or spoken language.

compulsiveness: insistence on performing or doing things in habitual ways.

concept: a classification or systematic organization of the total meaning an individual has for any idea, person, place, thing, or word.

conceptual background: refers to the generalizations the student has before he begins a particular book or level of reading.

conceptualization: ability to infer from what is observable.

concretism: an approach to thinking and behavior in which a person tends to approach each situation as a unique one and is situation bound. Such a person does not see essential similarities between situations which normal persons would accept as similar or even identical.

configuration: the general shape of a word.

congenital: present at birth; usually a defect of either familial or exogenous origin which exists at the time of birth.

conservation: in Piaget's theory, the ability to retain a concept of area, mass, length, etc., when superficial changes are made in the appearance of an object or scene.

consonant: a sound which cannot easily be sounded alone.

consonant cluster: (1) adjacent consonants in a spoken word, articulated as separate sounds but somewhat blended together in normal speech; (2) two or more adjacent consonant letters in a written word, each of which represents an articulated sound in the spoken word. Also called *consonant blend*. Examples: *cl, pr, st*.

context: the parts of a spoken or written expression that surround a word or passage and can throw light upon the meaning.

contextual analysis: using the rest of the sentence to get the meaning of an unknown word.

control group: the group in an experiment to which the variable in the study is not applied.

convergence: the ocular pointing mechanism by which the eyes are "aimed" at a target. It enables one to see a single object at varying distances.

corrective reading: reading designed for children experiencing minor difficulties in reading.

cover test: an informal vision screening device.

creative reading: reading designed to produce something original either in content or in an unusual relating of already known facts.

crossing the midline: the movement of the eyes, a hand and forearm, or a foot and leg across the midsection of the body without involving any other part of the body; i.e., without turning the head, twisting or swaying the trunk, or innervating the opposite limb.

cross-modal: involving more than one sensory channel.

cue reduction: the process by which a smaller part of the total stimulus situation becomes adequate to render a response to the meaning of the total situation; e.g., the meaning of the letter E when it appears on the gasoline gauge of an automobile.

decode: to go from written or oral language (code) to *meaning*; to recreate in the mind of the listener or reader the *meaning* expressed by the speaker or writer.

delta wave: an electroencephalographic record of neural firing in the cerebral cortex. It is characterized by a frequency between .5–3.5. It is the normal record of sleep activity. When it occurs in the wake adult, it is thought to indicate possible pathology.

descenders: those letters which extend below the base configuration of the word. In *lady* the *y* is a descender.

developmental reading: reading designed for those children who learn to read to their capacity regardless of what their capacity may be.

diagnostic test: a test designed to identify strengths and weaknesses.

digraph: two letters representing a single sound.

diphthong: a blend of two vowels which seem to flow together without losing the identity of each vowel. Example: *oy* in *boy*, and *oi* in *oil*.

directionality: the outward projection of laterality so that the organism can organize the external environment.

directional orientation: the awareness of left-right direction in reading.

discrimination: the process of detecting differences.

  Auditory discrimination: sometimes referred to as ear training, involves identifying sounds with respect to their likenesses and differences.
  Visual discrimination: discriminating between different objects, forms, and/or letter symbols.

disinhibition: lack of ability to restrain oneself from responding to distracting stimuli. In other words, a child would not inhibit these responses from within. Example: child asks a visitor, "How come you have white hair?"

dissociation: the inability to see things as a whole, as a unity, or as a gestalt. The tendency to respond to a stimulus in terms of parts or segments.

distractibility: the tendency for one's attention to be easily drawn to extraneous stimuli or to focus on minor details with a lack of attention to major aspects. Often used synonymously with short attention span although the latter suggests an inability to concentrate on one thing for very long even without distractors.

DRA: abbreviation for Directed Reading Activity.

DRTA: abbreviation for Directed Reading Thinking Activity.

Dynamic Prehensile Theory of Vision: a theory which states that the eyes are not passive receptors but are more akin to the hands, which reach out into the environment and abstract a specific sensory event present at the time.

dysacusis: hearing impairment which involves distortion of loudness or pitch, or both, rather than loss in sensitivity.

dysarthria: an articulatory disorder or disorder in motor speech due to a CNS dysfunction.

dysbulia: difficulty in thinking and in giving attention.

dyscalculia: partial inability to do arithmetic or to work with numbers. See acalculia.

dysdiadochokinesis: inability to perform repetitive movements such as tapping with the finger.

dysgraphia: partial inability to express ideas by means of writing or written symbols. Usually associated with brain dysfunction.

dyskinesia: partial impairment of voluntary movement abilities, resulting in incomplete movements, poor coordination, and apparently clumsy behavior.

dyslalia: refers to speech impairment due to defects in the organs of speech. Not the same as slovenly speech.

dyslexia: partial inability to read, or to understand what one reads silently or aloud. Condition is usually, but not always, associated with brain impairment. (Some authors refer to genetic dyslexia, affective dyslexia, experiential dyslexia, congenital dyslexia, developmental dyslexia, etc.)

dysnomia: the condition when an individual knows the word he is trying to recall, recognizes it when said for him, but cannot recall it at will.

dysphasia: difficulty in speaking or writing due to mental impairment.

dyspraxia: impairment of coordination or movement. See apraxia.

dysrythmia: abnormal speech fluency, characterized by defective stress, breath control, and intonation.

echolalia or echophrasia: apparently uncontrollable response characterized by repeating a word or sentence just spoken by another person. In young infants about the age of ten months or so, echolalia refers to persistent repetition of sounds.

EMR: educably mentally retarded child; has an I.Q. from 50–75.

electroencephalograph: an instrument for graphically recording electrical currents developed in the cerebral cortex during brain functioning; often abbreviated EEG.

emotional blocking: inability to think or make satisfactory responses due to excessive emotion, usually related to fear.

emotional lability: the tendency toward cyclic emotional behavior characterized by sudden unexplainable shifts from one emotion to another.

encode: to go from *meaning* to *code*: either written or oral. (1) written: to *produce* written language; to transform meaning in the mind of a writer into a graphic sequence, following the written language code. (2) oral: to *produce* oral language; to transform meaning in the mind of a speaker into a sound sequence following the rules of the language code. The expression of meaning in language through speech or motion.

endogenous: due to hereditary or genetic factors.

etiology: the cause of a condition.

etiological diagnosis: a diagnosis designed to uncover the causes or origins of the disorder.

exogenous: due to something other than hereditary or genetic factors.

experience chart: a teaching device which employs the pupil dictated story of an experience for the teaching of reading.

expressive language skills: skills required to produce language for communication with other individuals. Speaking and writing are expressive language skills.

eye-hand coordination: this skill consists of the mind's-eye steering the hand(s) accurately and skillfully through the three coordinates of space—right and left, up and down, for and aft—, which are matched with the coordinates of the body and vision, for the purpose of manipulating tools or forming the symbols of language. The ability to organize perceptual inputs and to reproduce manually.

face validity: refers to the fact that a thing appears to do what is claimed it will do.

feedback: the sensory or perceptual report of the result of a somatic, social or cognitive behavior.

figure-ground: refers to the relationship between a specific pattern (figure) and its ground (background); clinically, the figure is that part of the field of perception that is the center of the observer's attention, the remainder of this field is the ground.

fine motor development: the maturation and refinement of the small muscles in the extremities of the body such as finger and wrist movements and eye-hand coordination.

finger agnosia: inability to recognize the name or identify the individual fingers of one's own hand.

fixation: the pause of the eye in reading.

flashmeter: a device for timed and rapid exposure of items.

fovia centralis: the area on the retina which has the greatest acuity.

frustration level: the maximum performance level of a child.

Gerstman syndrome: a constellation of symptoms indicating lack of laterality and a disturbance of body image. The symptoms are: agraphia, acalculia, right-left disorientation, and finger agnosia.

gestalt: a term used to express any unified whole whose properties can not be derived by adding the parts and their relationships. The something which is more than the sum of its parts.

global: perceived or perceptually taken as a whole without attempt to distinguish separate parts or functions.

gnosia: the faculty of perceiving and knowing.

grammatic closure: ability to make use of the redundancies of oral language in acquiring automatic habits for handling syntax and grammatic inflections.

grapheme: a letter or symbol of written language. The graphemes of printed English are the 21 consonant letters, the 5 vowel letters, 11 punctuation marks, and such nonphonemic features as lower case and capital letters, italics, and small caps. Space between words is also considered a graphemic feature of printed English.

gridiron effect: an arrangement of letters in a word whereby they all have the same slant. The word "little" is an example of the gridiron effect.

gross motor activity: an activity or output in which groups of large muscles are used and the factors of rhythm and balance are primary.

handedness: refers to hand preference of an individual.

hand-eye coordination: ability of the hand and eye to perform easily together.

haptic: touch or tactual and kinesthetic awareness.

hard neurological signs: physical symptoms of brain injury which can be identified medically.

hemiopia: the condition where one has only one half of the field of vision in one or both eyes.

hemispherical dominance: refers to the fact that one cerebral hemisphere generally leads the other in control of body movement, resulting in the preferred use of left or right (laterality).

heterogeneous grouping: the placing of children without regard to achieving homogeneity.

homogeneous grouping: the placing of children with the same characteristics together.

homolateral: occurring on the same side of the body.

hyperactivity: excessive activity—the individual seems to have a surplus of energy.

hyperkinesis: excessive mobility or motor restlessness sometimes referred to as drive.

hypoactivity: pronounced absence of physical activity.

hypokinesis: diminished motor function or activity often appearing as listlessness.

ideation: reflective thought.

ideational agnosia: inability to visualize or recall constructions of words; inability to remember which letters are needed for correct spellings; difficulty in recalling correct order (sequence) of letters within words; handwriting may be clearly legible, but content does not make sense.

idioglossia: phenomenon of "invented language" caused by the omission, substitution, distortion, and transposition of speech sounds. Same as idiolalia.

idiopathic: self-originated; of unknown origin.

imagery: representation of images.

imperception: lack of ability to interpret sensory information correctly. A cognitive impairment rather than a sensory impairment.

impulsiveness: the tendency to act on impulse. Inability to control an impulse.

individualization: that process by which the teacher, through diagnostic and evaluative procedures, pinpoints the combination of skills and methods of presentation that are uniquely motivating and specific for a particular child.

individualized reading: an organizational device for teaching children to read through materials chosen through self-selection activities.

inner language: language of inner thought, probably developed prior to any other language (expressive, etc.).

instructional level: the level at which a child can be taught.

integration: the pulling together and organizing of all stimuli impinging on an organism at a given moment. Also involved is the tying together of the present stimulation with experience variables retained from past activities. The organizing of many individual movements into a complex response.

interfixation: the movement of the eyes from one fixation to another in reading.

interneurosensory: a learning process that involves more than one system in the brain.

intraneurosensory: a learning process that involves only one system in the brain.

inversion: turning letters upside down within words while reading or writing (way for may—yelp for help).

ipsilateral: homolateral; occurring on the same side.

IRI: the abbreviation for informal reading inventory.

itinerant teacher: a teacher who travels among several schools usually providing individual help for children with special problems.

Joplin plan: an organizational arrangement whereby wide ranges of achievement are somewhat cut down by having children go to reading classes geared to their own levels regardless of grade placement.

kinesthetic: pertaining to the sense by which muscular motion, position, or weight are perceived. Thought of as being in muscle and joints.

kinesthetic method: a method of treating reading disability by having pupils trace the outline of words using muscle movement to supplement visual and auditory stimuli.

kinetic reversal: transposing letters within words, or numerals within number groups (*aet* for *ate*; 749 for 794).

laterality: the internal organization of the organism so that there is an awareness of sideness, left or right; also used to imply the tendency to use one side of the body for most tasks, such as using the right hand, right eye, and right foot.

learning: acquiring new behavior patterns; changes in performance as a result of experience that engenders insight.

learning disability: a retardation disorder or delayed development in one or more of the processes of speech, language, reading, writing, arithmetic or other school subjects resulting from a psychological handicap caused by possible cerebral dysfunction and/or emotional or behavioral disturbance. It is not a result of mental retardation, sensory deprivation or cultural or instructional factors. (Kirk & Bateman).

learning disabilities specialist: is involved in the diagnosis and classification of severely handicapped children. This includes an estimate of the child's sensory abilities as well as an estimate of his strengths and weaknesses in academic learning. The learning disabilities specialist is aware of the individuality of each child, and individual differences are considered when the educational prescription is made. The learning disabilities specialist is a "child-oriented" master teacher.

LEL: stands for learning expectancy level which is derived by subtracting 5 from the mental age.

legasthenia: inability to relate ideas (concepts) to symbols (percepts); a bridge is out between ideas (experience) and the symbols representing the ideas.

linguistics: the scientific study of human speech or language, and relevant relationships between speech and writing.

lively effect: an arrangement of letters in a word whereby the word seems to flow.

locomotion: movement from one location to another (walking, crawling, rolling, etc.).

long vowel: in phonics the vowel sounds heard in *ape, eat, mine, doe,* and *use,* which coincide with the names of the letters *a, e, i, o, u.*

macron: a diacritical mark indicating a long vowel sound.

maturational lag: the concept of delayed development of areas of the brain; of the perceptual process which matures according to recognized patterns longitudinally. A lag signifies irregularity in these patterns without a structural defect, deficiency, or loss.

memory span: the number of related or unrelated items that can be recalled immediately after presentation.

mental age: the level of mental ability development.

minimal cerebral dysfunction: a child's history and symptomatology resembles that found in the "neurologically impaired" child but for whom there is no evidence of specific and definable central nervous system disorder. Also there is no indication of a lowering of general intellectual capacity.

mirror writing: a term applied to writing which is completely reversed in letters and form. Example: *emoc* for *come.* May be upside down and/or backwards.

mixed cerebral dominance: the theory that language disorders may be due wholly or partly to the fact that one cerebral hemisphere does not consistently lead the other in the control of bodily movement (i.e., hemispheric dominance has not been adequately established). Ex: The individual may use either hand (or foot, or eye) instead of having a preferred hand, foot, or eye.

mixed laterality: a condition where laterality has not been established and the individual uses either hand (or feet or eyes) to perform tasks.

modality: the pathways through which an individual receives information and thereby learns. The "modality concept" postulates that some individuals learn better through one modality than through another. For example, a child may receive data better through the visual modality than through his auditory modality.

modified clinical technique: a visual screening procedure which requires the services of a vision specialist.

modified macron: a diacritical mark.

monosyllable: means one syllable.

morpheme: the smallest unit of *meaning*. An indivisible meaning-bearing language element patterned out of phonemes. Examples: *girl, -s, un-, tie, -ed.* Thus *girls* consists of two morphemes (*girl* + *-s*) the *-s* has the meaning of plurality; *untied* consists of three morphemes (*un-* + *tie* + *ed*) each of the morphemes having a different meaning. Morphemes may be free (whole words such as *girl*) or bound (prefixes, suffixes, and bases which cannot stand alone, such as *-ceive*), (*-ceive* is a Latin root and means *take*). See *affix, base, bound base, free base.*

multiple-causation theory: a theory advanced by Helen M. Robinson which states that the cause of poor reading is a constellation of symptoms not necessarily the same in all cases.

multisensory: making use of more than one sensory modality to bring stimuli to the brain for interpretation.

negativism: extreme opposition and resistance to suggestions or advice. Normally observed in late infancy.

neurological examination: an examination of sensory or motor responses, especially of the reflexes, to determine whether there are localized impairments of the nervous system. Generally considered the "classic" examination.

neurologically impaired: a child who manifests hard neurological signs; that is, there is evidence of specific and definable central nervous system disorder.

nonreader: the child who is unable to profit from the best instruction in any of the skill areas; therefore, is unable to learn to read from conventional methods. The nonreader is generally identified as one who has made scant progress in learning after two or more years of instruction in reading. The number of words he recognizes at sight is negligible, perhaps twenty-five or less. He confuses words and has difficulty in spelling.

nosographic definition: gives a description of the disorder without reference to the causes.

nosological definition: gives a description of the disorder as to its cause or causes.

nystagmus: an involuntary rapid movement of the eyeball; lateral, vertical, rotary or mixed.

ocular pursuit: the process of the visual tracking of movement.

ontogeny: how an individual organism develops—its developmental history.

open syllable: a syllable which ends in a vowel.

ophthalmologist: a vision specialist with an M.D. degree. He is licensed to prescribe refractions and to treat eye diseases.

optometrist: a vision specialist with an O.D. degree. He is licensed to prescribe refractions and to treat the functional aspects of vision but cannot use drugs or treat eye diseases.

organicity: impairment of the central nervous system.

percept: a mental impression derived both from immediate sensory experience and the mental reaction thereto.

perception: the interpretation of sensory information. The mechanism by which the intellect recognizes and makes sense out of sensory stimulation. The accurate mental association of present stimuli with memories of past experiences.

Perception of position in space: the accurate interpretation of an object as being behind, before, above, below, or to the side.

Perception of spatial relationships: comprehending the position of two or more objects in relation to oneself and in relation to each other.

Figure-ground perception: the accurate selection from the mass of incoming stimuli, which should be the center of attention. These selected stimuli form the figure in the person's perceptual field, while the majority of stimuli form a dimly perceived ground. The figure is that part of the field of perception that is the center of the observer's attention. A disturbance in figure-ground may result because the individual confuses figure and background, reverses them, or is unable to see any difference between figure and ground.

perceptual constancy: the accurate interpretation of stimuli (objects, symbols, etc.) as being the same in spite of their being perceived in various ways (e.g., being turned upside down, partially concealed, inverted and rotated).

perceptual-motor: refers to deriving meaning from sensory stimuli and integrating the sensory with the motor processes so that there is a purposeful response, or the understanding thereof in the presence of a handicap impeding the response.

perceptual-motor match: the process of comparing and collating the input data received through the motor system and the input data received through perception.

perceptually handicapped: a perceptual handicap, in the auditory, visual, or tactile modalities of learning, or in motor response. The perceptual handicap may be receptive (taking in), expressive (giving out or responding), or associative (giving meaning).

perinatal: connected with or occurring during the birth process.

perseveration: continuing to behave or respond in a certain way when it is no longer appropriate (e.g., repetition of a word several times before going on, continuing a movement such as letter writing even at the end of a line, bringing up an idea over and over, or writing the same number(s) over and over).

phonemes: the smallest unit of sound in spoken language, such as /s/ in son.

phonetics: the science of the sounds of language.

phonetic analysis: the science concerned with identifying, describing, classifying, and recording individual speech sounds. Phonetics deals with speech sounds in general, whereas phonemics is concerned with the significant sounds of a particular language.

phonic analysis: a method of teaching beginning reading which starts with whole words in sentences and stories and then uses these words to call attention to letter-sound relationships in order to arrive at generalizations about these relationships.

phonic synthesis: a method of teaching beginning reading which starts with generalizations about the letters of the alphabet and the sounds they represent and proceeds to their combination into words and syllables.

phonics: the application of phonetics to reading.

phonogram: a letter or combination of letters signaling one sound.

phylogeny: evolutionary development of an entire species. (Contrast with *ontogeny*.)

polysyllable: more than one syllable.

position in space: refers to perception of the relationship of an object to that of the observer.

postnatal: occurring during the period following the birth.

prefix: an affix which precedes the base. In English, prefixes are always derivational; that is, they do not make inflected forms such as plurals or past tense. See affix.

prenatal: connected with or occurring during the period preceding the birth.

primary learning and reading disability: the organic mechanism for perceptual learning is not intact or ready for learning due to any of a variety of factors, all of them organic in nature. The child is considered to have normal mental ability for learning.

projection technique: a method of teaching reading through the use of the projector.

psycholinguistics: the study of the language process from the shared viewpoint of the disciplines of psychology and linguistics.

psychomotor: interaction of motor or movement behaviors with psychological processes.

psychoneurology: a term suggested to designate the area of study that concerns itself with the behavioral disorders associated with brain dysfunctions in human beings.

readability: the sum total of all the factors which make a selection comprehensible.

readiness: the developmental level necessary for reading instruction.

reading: a cerebral process whereby printed symbols stimulate a reorganization of past experiences into a new and meaningful entity.

reading clinic: a centrally located area drawing children from more than one school and offering diagnosis and remediation of serious reading problems.

reading pacers: mechanical devices for pushing a reader to read faster.

reauditorization: the ability to recall the name or sounds of visual symbols (letters). Some individuals remember what letters look like but not which sound they make.

recall: a demonstration of retention through repeating what previously was learned; for example, an individual's speaking vocabulary is dependent upon his ability to recall.

receptive language: the process of understanding language produced by others; e.g., reading, listening.

recode: (1) word calling or sounding out—to go from the written code to its oral counterpart: or (2) to go from the oral code to its written counterpart (as in taking dictation); both *without meaning necessarily being involved.*

remedial reading: reading designed for children experiencing serious difficulty in learning to read.

remediation: that function which redirects or circumvents an impaired procedure in learning. It implies compensatory methods that facilitate learning rather than cure learning disorders.

resource teacher: a specialist who works with children with learning disabilities and acts as a consultant to other teachers, providing materials and methods to help children who are having difficulty within the regular classroom. The resource teacher may work from a centralized resource room within a school where appropriate materials are housed.

reversal: a transposition of letters.

reversal, kinetic: a transposition of letters in a word. Example: *was* for *saw.*

reversal, static: an interchange or reversal of form. Example: *iorn* for *iron, bog* for *dog.*

revisualization: ability to retrieve a visual image of a letter or word that is heard from one's memory so that it can be written.

right-left disorientation: the inability to distinguish right from left; having no awareness of directionality.

rigidity: maintaining an attitude or behavioral set when such a set is no longer appropriate.

ritalin: medication given for control of hyperkinesis; a form of the amphetamine class of drugs which is not habit forming in hyperkinetics; side effects are sometimes seen (insomnia, constipation, decreased appetite, drop in white cell count in blood test); cancels out the violent impulses of hyperkinetic behavior, allowing the child to concentrate and change his attitudes toward school.

rotations: the turning around of letters in a word. Example: *p* for *d.*

saccadic movements: the jerky movements of the eyes while reading.

secondary reading disability: an acquired reading disability having no specific syndrome but one in which the organic mechanism is intact for perceptual learning.

semantic aphasia: pronouncing or repeating words correctly without comprehending their meanings; often seen when children can decode fluently but have no idea of what they have just read.

semantics: the study of meaning. *Detailed definition:* Philosophical semantics deals with notional meaning—ideas, notions, concepts, images, feelings. General semantics deals with referential meaning—objects, relationships, or classes of objects or relationships in the outside world that are referred to by a word. Linguistic semantics deals with distributional meaning—the positions a word fills in the system of the language, that is, in what contexts it can be used and what it contributes to those contexts. Examples: in dictionaries, defining a word by synonyms or longer expressions which suggest a concept associated with a word gives its notional meaning; defining it by means of a picture or diagram gives its referential meaning; using it in illustrative quotations gives it distributional meaning.

sensorimotor skill: a skill in which muscular movement is prominent but under sensory control. For example, riding a bicycle is not simply a pattern of skilled movements. The bicycle rider has to watch the traffic and the bumps in the road and be guided by them. These considerations in calling attention to the sensory control of skill explain the somewhat awkward term *sensorimotor skill.*

sequential development: a step by step plan of development wherein one skill is built upon another.

short vowel: one of the five simple vowels heard in *bat, bet, bit, box,* and *but.*

sight vocabulary: those words whose retrieval is immediate because extended language analysis skills are no longer required.

slow learner: a child with an I.Q. of from 75 or 80 to 90.

Snellen chart: a vision screening device.

soft neurological signs: behavioral symptoms that suggest possible minimal brain injury in the absence of gross or obvious neurological abnormalities.

sound blending: ability to synthesize the separate parts of a word and produce an integrated whole.

space perception: the direct awareness of the spatial properties of an object, especially in relation to the observer. The perception of position, direction, size, form, and/or distance by any of the senses.

span of perception: what the eye can encompass during a fixation.

span of recognition: what the eye sees and the brain recognizes during one fixation.

spatial orientation: awareness of space around the person in terms of distance, form, direction, and position.

spatial relationships: an ability of the observer to perceive the position of two or more objects or subjects in relation to himself and in relation to each other.

specific language disability: often the term is applied to those who have found it very difficult to learn to read and spell, but who are otherwise intelligent, and usually learn arithmetic more readily. More recently any language deficit, oral, visual or auditory, is referred to with this term.

splinter skills: highly specific skills having limited relationship to the activities of the total organism, a motor pattern or skill, usually achieved by rote drill, which exists in isolation from the remainder of the individual's motor activity or ability.

standardized tests: tests which have been given to a large and representative sampling of the population to which the test will be applied, and it is characterized by the norms which enable comparisons.

stem: the part of a word that remains morphemically constant as various prefixes and suffixes are added. A stem always contains a base; it may also contain affixes. Example: in the set *dog-dogs, dog* is the stem; in the set *reader-readers, reader* (consisting of base *read* and suffix *-er*) is the stem.

stereognosis: an ability to somatically perceive objects, forms, materials, according to shape, size, quality of materials.

strabismus: an eye condition in which there is a lack of coordination of the eye muscles, characterized by a squint or cross-eyes.

Strauss syndrome: the cluster of symptoms characterizing the "brain-injured" child; includes hyperactivity, distractability, and impulsivity.

strephosymbolia: etymologically means "twisted symbols." The term first used by Orton to denote difficulty in learning to read without evidence of other gross mental defects. It also denotes a condition in which objects seem reversed, as in a mirror.

structural analysis: using visual modality to reveal the component parts of a word, such as affixes, configuration.

structuring: the act of arranging an activity in a way that is understandable to children and conducive to performance, or in other words, arranging the task so that children are aware of what is expected of them. Once the task is structured, the children should be left to perform without additional cueing.

substitution: mentally or physically replacing one letter or word with another while reading or writing (*bottle* for *battle*, *run* for *ran*); also refers to failure to observe minimal cues, such as minor details that distinguish similar letter forms, punctuation cues, printer's cues, and so forth.

suffix: an affix which follows a base.

suppression: a visual anomaly in which, although the eye continues to function, the brain apparently ignores the image from the crossing eye.

survey test: test designed to give comprehensive coverage of an area.

syllabication: a word attack skill consisting of breaking the word down into its appropriate syllables.

syntax: the order of words in sentences, the structure of the language. Syntax is the division of grammar dealing with patterning of morphemes and words into larger structural units (noun and verb groups, phrases, clauses, and sentences).

tachistoscope: an apparatus in psychology and in reading, used for exposing colors, figures, or other visual stimuli for fractions of a second.

tactile: pertaining to touch or touch-pressure (tactual).

tactile perception: an ability to perceive tactile stimuli as to localize, discriminate, quality as in identification of form, shape, size, texture of touch-pressure. (In many situations tactile and kinesthetic stimuli would be combined, as in manipulating an object).

task analysis: the examination of a certain task for the purpose of noting its component parts or subtasks.

team learning: when two children study together for the growth of each.

team teaching: an arrangement whereby two or more teachers with special skills which complement each other assume joint responsibility for guiding educational growth of a group of learners.

telebinocular: a mechanical device used for visual screening.

telescoping: the result of the writer's inability to see a word as an entity. Hence he combines aspects of individual letters. Example: *hy* for *heavy*. The *h*, *v*, and *y* are telescoped into the substitute symbols.

temporal: pertaining to time or time relationships. The ability to recognize the limits of time with understanding. In early childhood time is not "an ever-rolling stream" but simply concrete events embedded in activity. Time and space are not differentiated from each other. Movement must occur in time, and the child must project awareness of time into object relationships.

therapeutic diagnosis: a diagnosis to determine what can be done to remedy the disability. Little attention is given to the cause or causes.

tilde: a diacritical mark.

toxemia (of pregnancy): a kind of blood poisoning associated with abnormal changes in body chemistry during pregnancy and producing a variety of symptoms including nausea, vomiting, shortness of breath, albumin in the urine and convulsions.

trainable child: a child with an I.Q. from 30–50.

ungraded primary: an organizational device for breaking the primary grades into more and shorter steps.

vision screening: a sampling of visual skills for the purpose of locating visual problems.

visual acuity: refers to the sharpness of vision.

visual agnosia: inability to perceive overall configurations; the reader sees only isolated symbols instead of clusters, syllables, whole word units, or whole number units.

visual aphasia: inability to recognize printed words as representing the person's listening-speaking vocabulary; inability to comprehend the fact that print is talk written down; sometimes a synonym for *legasthenia*.

visual association: the organizing process by which one is able to relate concepts presented visually.

visual closure: ability to identify a visual stimulus from an incomplete visual presentation.

visual discrimination: ability to discern visually similarities and differences.

visual dyslexia: difficulty interpreting ("seeing") printed or written symbols accurately; tendency to perceive symbols upside down or in reverse.

visual fusion: coordination of the separate images in the two eyes into one image.

visual-motor: ability to relate visual stimuli to motor responses in an appropriate way.

visual-motor coordination: an ability to coordinate vision with movements of the body or with movement of a part or parts of the body.

visual-motor skills: skills normally accomplished through visual perception and an integrated motor response or responses; often involve spatial relations and tactile perception; a kinesthetic perception is included, although not stated.

visual perception: the identification, organization, and interpretation of sensory data received by the individual through the eyes.

visual reception: ability to gain meaning from visual symbols.

visual sequential memory: ability to reproduce sequences of visual items from memory.

vocabulary control: an attempt to limit the vocabulary to words already in the child's understanding vocabulary.

vowel: a speech sound which can easily be sounded alone.

word-attack skills: the ability to analyze unfamiliar words by syllables and phonic elements and so arrive at their pronunciation and possibly recognize their meaning.

word recognition: recoding pronunciation and decoding meaning of a printed word.

REFERENCES

Adams, A. H., & Harrison, C. B. Using television to teach specific skills. *Reading Teacher*, October 1975, 29 (1), 45–51.

Agranowitz A., & McKeown, M. R. *Aphasia handbook*. Springfield, Illinois, Charles C. Thomas, 1964.

Ammons, R. B., & Ammons, H. S. *Full-range picture vocabulary test*. Missoula, Montana: Psychological Test Specialists, 1950.

———. *Quick test*. Missoula, Montana: Psychological Test Specialists, 1962a.

———. *Full-range picture vocabulary test*. Missoula, Montana: Psychological Test Specialists, 1962b.

Anastasi, A. *Psychological testing*. New York: Macmillan, 1976.

Anderson, I. H., & Dearborn, W. F. *The psychology of teaching reading*. New York: Roland Press, 1952.

Anderson, P. S. *Language skills in elementary education*. New York: Macmillan, 1972, 225–226.

Artley, A. S., & Hardin, V. B. A Current dilemma: Reading disability or learning disability. *Reading Teacher*, January, 1976, 29 (4), 361–366.

Ayres, A. J. *Southern California kinesthesia and tactile perception tests*. Los Angeles: Western Psychological Services, 1966.

Ayres, J. *Sensory integration and learning disorders*. Los Angeles: Western Psychological Services, 1972.

Baker, H. J., & Leland, B. *Detroit tests of learning aptitudes*. Indianapolis: Bobbs-Merrill, 1955.

Bannatyne, A. D. Matching remedial methods with specific deficits. In International Convocation on Children and Young Adults with Learning Disabilities, Pittsburgh, Pa., 1967.

———. *Language, reading and learning disabilities*. Springfield, Illinois: Charles C. Thomas, 1971.

———. Mirror-images and reversals. *Academic Therapy*. Fall 1972, 8 (1), 87–92.

———. Reading: An auditory-vocal process. *Academic Therapy*, Summer 1973, 8 (4), 429–431.

Barbe, W. B., & Abbott, J. L. *Personalized reading instructions: New techniques that increase reading skill and comprehension*. West Nyack, N.Y.: Parker, 1975.

Barnes, B. Specific dyslexia and legislation. *Journal of Learning Disabilities*, January, 1968, 1 (1), 60.

Barry, H. *The young aphasic child*. Washington, D.C.: Alexander Graham Bell Association for the Deaf, 1969.

Bateman, B. Learning disabilities—yesterday, today and tomorrow. *Exceptional Children*, December 1964, 31 (4), 167–177.

————. Learning disorders. *Review of Educational Research*. 1966, *36*, 93–119.

Belmont, I.; Flegenheimer, H.; & Birch, H. G. Comparison of perceptual training and remedial instruction for poor beginning readers. *Journal of Learning Disabilities*, April 1973, *6* (4), 230–235.

Bender, L. *Bender visual-motor gestalt test for children*. New York: Psychological Corp., 1962.

————. Neuropsychiatric disturbances. In A. H. Keeney and V. T. Keeney (Eds.), *Dyslexia*. St. Louis: C. V. Mosby, 1968.

Benton, A. L., *The revised visual retention test: Clinical and experimental application*. New York: Psychological Corporation, 1955.

————. *Right-left discrimination and finger orientation*. New York: Harper & Row, 1959a.

————. *Right-left discrimination and finger localization*. New York: Hoeber, 1959b.

Bernstein, B. *Everyday problems and the child with learning disabilities*. New York: John Day, 1967.

Best, R., & Bernard J. *Winners and losers, sex, the group and learning in the primary grade*. In press.

Betts, E. A. *Foundations of reading instruction*. New York: American Book, 1957.

Birch, H. G. Dyslexia and the maturation of the visual functions. In J. Money, *Reading disability*. Baltimore: John Hopkins Press, 1962.

Birch, H. G., & Belmont, L. Auditory visual integration in normal and retarded readers. *American Journal of Orthopsychiatry*, October 1964, *34* (5).

Birch, L. B. The improvement of reading ability. *British Journal of Educational Psychology*, June 1950, *20*, part 2, 73–76.

Black, W. F. Self-concept as related to achievement and age in learning disabled children. *Child Development*, 1974, *45*, 1137–40.

Blau, H., & Blau, H. A theory of learning to read by "modality blocking." In J. I. Arena (Ed.), *Successful programming: Many points of view*. Pittsburgh: Association of Children with Learning Disabilities, 1969.

Blommer, R. H. Skill games to teach reading. New York: Instructor, 1964, *46*.

Bond, G. L., & Tinker, M. A. *Reading difficulties: Their diagnosis and correction* (2nd ed.). New York: Appleton-Century-Crofts, 1967.

————. *Reading difficulties: Their diagnosis and correction* (3rd ed.). New York: Appleton-Century-Crofts, 1973.

Bond, G. L., & Dykstra, R. Coordinating Center for first grade reading instruction programs. (Final Report of Project No. X–001, Contract No. OE 5–10–264). Minneapolis: University of Minnesota, 1967, also in *Reading Quarterly*, Summer 1967, *4*, 115–126.

Bond, G. L.; Barlow, I. H.; & Hoyt, C. *Silent reading diagnostic tests*. Chicago: Lyons & Carnahan, Meredith Corp. 1970.

Bormuth, J. R. Factory validity of cloze tests as measures of reading comprehension ability. *Reading Research Quarterly*, 1969a, *4* (3), 358–365.

————. An operational definition of comprehension instruction. In K. S. Goodman and J. T. Flemming, *Psycholinguistics and the teaching of reading*. Newark, Del.: International Reading Association, 1969b, 48–60.

Bosco, J. Behavior modification in drugs and the schools: The case of Ritalin. *Phi Delta Kappa*, March 1977, *56*, 489.

Brenner, M. W., & Gillman, S. Verbal intelligence, visuomotor ability, and school achievement. *The British Journal of Psychology*, February 1968, *38* (1), 75–78.

Brooks, C. H. A combined phonics and multisensory approach promotes reading improvement. *Reading Improvement*, Summer 1975, *12* (2), 87–93.

Brueckner, L. J., & Lewis, W. D. *Diagnostic test and remedial exercises in reading*. New York: Holt, Rinehart & Winston, 1947.

Bruner, J. S. *The process of education*. Cambridge: Harvard University Press, 1960.

————. *Toward a theory of instruction*. Cambridge, Mass.: Harvard University Press, 1966.

Bryant, N. D. Some principles of remedial instruction for dyslexia. *Reading Teacher*, April 1965, *18* (7), 567–572.

————. Subject variable: Definition, incidence, characteristics and correlates. In N. D. Bryant and C. Kass, (Eds.), *Final Report: LTI in Learning disabilities* (Vol. 1). (U.S.O.E. Grant No. OEG–0–71–4425–604, Project No. 127145). Tucson, Arizona: University of Arizona, 1972.

————. Role conflict in providing services to learning disabled children. Speech given at South Central Regional Conference of Council of Exceptional Children and reported in *Division for Children with Learning Disabilities Newsletter*, December 1976, 2 (2), 32–33.

Buckland, P., & Barlow, B. Effects of visual perceptual training in reading achievement. *Exceptional Children*, January 1973, 36, 302.

Burleigh, A. C.; Cupta, W.; & Sadderfield, J. C. Development of a Score that Separates Hyperactive and Normal Children and Demonstrates Drug Effect, ED 048 374, New York, 1971.

Campbell, S. B.; Douglas, V. I.; & Morgenstern, G. Cognitive styles in hyperactive children and the effect of methylphenidate. *Journal of Child Psychology and Psychiatry*, January 1970, 12, 55.

Carter, H. L. J., & McGinnis, D. J. *Diagnosis and treatment of the disabled reader*. New York: Macmillan, 1970.

Cawley, J. F.; Goodstein, H. A.; & Burrow, W. H. *The slow learner and the reading problem*. Springfield, Illinois: Charles C. Thomas, 1972.

Chalfant, J. D., & King, F. S. An approach to operationalizing the definition of learning disabilities. *Journal of Learning Disabilities*, April 1976, 9 (4), 228–243.

Chall, J. S. *Learning to read: The great debate*, New York: McGraw-Hill, 1967.

Chomsky, C. Stages in language development and reading exposure. *Harvard Educational Review*, February 1972, 42 (1), 1–33.

Chomsky, N. *Language and mind*. New York: Harcourt, Brace, World, 1968.

Chovil, C. Reading programmes on BBC school television. Paper presented at the International Reading Association Convention, New York City, 1975.

Cleland, D. C. Clinical materials for appraising disabilities in reading. *Reading Teacher*, March 1964, 17, 428–429.

Clement, S. O., & Peters J. E. Minimal brain dysfunctions in the school age child. *Archives of General Psychiatry*, 1963, 6, 185–197.

Cohn, M., & Strickler, G. Inadequate perception vs. reversals. *Reading Teacher*, November 1976, 30 (2), 162–167.

Conners, K. Comparative effects of stimulant drugs in hyperkinetic children (ED059, 556). Vienna, Austria: International Congress of Pediatrics, 1971, 1–8.

Cooper, J. L. A procedures for teaching non-readers. *Education*, April 1947, 67, 494–499.

Cott, A. Megavitamins: The orthomolecular approach to behavior disorders and learning disabilities. *Academic Therapy*, Spring 1972, 7 (3), 245–257.

Cramer, W. *Keys to your reading improvement*. Portland, Maine: J. Weston Walch, 1961, 124.

Cravioto, J. Nutritional deprivation and psychobiological development in children. In Sapir and Nitzburg, *Children with learning problems*, 1972, 218–240.

Criscuolo, N. P. 137 activities for reading enrichment. New York: Instructor, 1975, 35–36.

Critchley, M. *Developmental dyslexia.* Springfield, Illinois: Charles C. Thomas, 1964.

————. Correlated disturbances: Etiologic, associated and secondary. *Dyslexia: Diagnosis and treatment of reading disorders.* Keeney & Keeney (eds.), St. Louis: C. V. Mosby, 1968, 38.

Crosby, R. M. N., & Liston, R. A. *Reading and the dyslexic child.* London: Souvenir Press, 1968.

Cruickshank W. C. *A teaching method for brain injured and hyperactive children.* New York: Syracuse Press, 1962.

Cruickshank, W. C. et al. *Perception and cerebral palsy.* Syracuse: Syracuse University Press, 1965.

Curriculum and Evaluation Consultants. The development and validation of screening instruments for the early identification of learning disabilities. Maryland State Department of Education: Baltimore, Md., 1975.

Dallman, M.; Rouch, R. L.; Chang, L. Y. C.; & DeBoer, J. J. *The teaching of reading* (4th ed.). New York: Holt, Rinehart & Winston, 1974, 182.

Daniels, J. D., & Diack, H. *The phonic word method of teaching reading.* London: Chatto & Windus, 1957.

Davis, F. B. Research in comprehension in reading. *Reading Research Quarterly,* Summer 1968, 3, 499–545.

Dearborn, W. R. Structural factors which condition special disability in reading. Proceedings of the American Association of Mental Deficiency, 1933, 38, 266–285.

Dechant, E. V. *Improving the teaching of reading* (2nd ed.). Englewood Cliffs, N.J.: Prentice-Hall, 1970, 165.

DeGenaro, J. J. Informal diagnostic procedures or what I do before the psychometrist arrives. *Journal of Learning Disabilities,* November, 1975, 8 (9), 557–563.

DeHirsch, K.; Jansky, J.; & Lanford, Q. *Predicting reading failure.* New York: Harper, Row, 1966.

Delacato, C. H. *The treatment and prevention of reading problems: The neuropsychological approach.* Springfield, Illinois: Charles C. Thomas, 1959.

————. *The diagnosis and treatment of speech and reading problems.* Springfield, Illinois: Charles C. Thomas, 1963.

Dennis, W. Causes of retardation among institution children. *Journal of Genetic Psychology,* 1960, 96, 47–60.

Department of Health, Education and Welfare, Report on the Conference on the Use of Stimulant Drugs in the Treatment of Behaviorally Disturbed Young School Children, ED 051–612, Washington, D.C. (1971).

DeRenzi, E., & Vignolo, E. The token test: A sensitive test to detect receptive disturbances in aphasics. *Brain,* 85, December 1962, 665.

Diack, H. *Reading and the psychology of perception.* New York: Philosophical Library, 1960.

Dolch, E. W. *A manual for remedial reading* (2nd ed.). Champaign, Illinois: Garrard Press, 1945.

————. *Dolch sight word test.* Champaign, Illinois: Garrard Press, 1960.

Downing, J. A. *Experiments with Pitman's initial teaching alphabet in British Schools.* New York: Initial Teaching Alphabet Publications, Inc., 1963.

Drug Panel, Office of Child Development, The use of stimulant drugs treating hyperactive children. *Children,* May 1971, 18, 11.

Dunn, L. M. *Peabody picture vocabulary test,* Circle Pines, Minnesota: American Guidance Service, 1959.

Durrell, D. D. *Improvement of basic reading abilities.* New York: Harcourt, Brace & World, 1940.

———. *Durrell analysis of reading difficulty.* New York: Harcourt, Brace Jovanovich, 1955.

———. *Improving reading instruction.* New York: Harcourt, Brace & World, 1956.

Ebersole, H.; Kephart, N. C.; & Ebersole, J. B. *Steps to achievement for the slow learner.* Columbus: Charles E. Merrill, 1968, 65–66.

Eisenson, J. *Examining for aphasia.* New York: Psychological Corporation, 1954.

———. *Aphasia in children.* New York: Harper, Row, 1972.

Ekwall, E. E. *Locating and correcting reading difficulties.* Columbus: Charles E. Merrill, 1970, 72, 77, 81.

Elkind, D. We can teach better reading. *Today's Education,* November-December 1975, *64,* 34–38.

Englemann, S. *Basic concept inventory.* Chicago: Follett Publishing Co., 1967.

Englemann, S., & Brunner, E. C. *DISTAR: An instruction system for reading instruction.* Chicago: Science Research Associates, 1969.

Eustis, R. S. The primary etiology of specific language disabilities. *Journal of Pediatrics,* 1947, *31,* 255–448.

Federal Legislation, Department of Health, Education and Welfare, Office of Education, 1968.

Feeley, J. Reading with TV: British and American approaches. *Reading Teacher,* December 1976, *30* (3), 271–275.

Feingold, B. F. *Why your child is hyperactive.* New York: Random House, 1974.

Feldman, S. A study of the effectiveness of training for retarded readers in the auditory perceptual skills underlying reading. ERIC ED 013 749, March 1968a.

Feldman, S.; Schmidt, D.; & Deutsch, C. A study of the effects of auditory training on remedial reading. ERIC ED 016 579, July 1968b.

Ferguson, M. *The brain revolution: The frontier of mind research.* New York: Taplinger, 1973.

Fernald, G. *Remedial techniques in basic school subjects.* New York: McGraw-Hill, 1939.

———. *Remedial technique in basic school subjects* (Rev. ed.). New York: McGraw-Hill, 1943, 32ff.

Figural, J. A. Limitations in the vocabulary of disadvantaged children: A cause for poor reading. *Improvement in reading through classroom practice.* Newark, Del.: International Reading Association, 1964, 9.

Flax, N. Problems in relating visual function to reading disorder. *American Journal of Optometry and Archives of the American Academy of Optometry,* May 1970, 47, 366–372.

———. Comment: The eye and learning disabilities. *Journal of the American Optometric Association,* June 1972, *43* (6), 612–617.

Focus on TV. *Scholastic Newstime,* October 3, 1974, 4.

Fox, B., & Routh, D. K. Phonemic analysis and synthesis as word attack skills. *Journal of Educational Psychology,* February 1976, *68,* 70–74.

Frostig, M. The relationship of diagnosis to remediation in learning problems. *International Approach to Learning Disabilities of Children and Youth,* March 1966, 46.

Frostig, M., & Horne, D. *The Frostig program for the development of visual Perception.* Chicago: Follett Publishing Co. 1964.

Frostig, M., & Maslow, P. *Learning problems in the classroom.* New York: Grune & Stratton, 1970, 176.

Fuller, G. B. Perceptual considerations in children with a reading disability. *Psychology in the Schools*, July 1964, 3 (3), 229–232.

Fuller, G. B., & Laird, J. T. The Minnesota percepto-diagnostic test. *Journal of Clinical Psychology Monograph Supplement*, 1963, No. 16.

Gates, A. I. *McKillop reading diagnostic tests, reading diagnostic test.* New York: Teachers College Press, 1962.

Gates, A. J. The necessary age for beginning reading. *Elementary School Journal*, March 1937, 37. Also reported by M. Morphett and C. Washburne. When should children begin to read. *Elementary School Journal*, March 1931, 31, 496–503.

Gattegno, C. *Words in color.* Chicago: Learning Materials, 1962.

———. *Towards a visual culture: Education through television.* New York: Outerbridge & Dienstfrey, 1969.

General Brown Central School, Summary of Developmental and Prescriptive Reading Program. Mimeograph Report, New York, Title I, ESEA, No. 22–04–01–66–001, 1967.

Geneva Medico-Educational Service, Problems posed by dyslexia. *Journal of Learning Disabilities*, 1968, 1 (3), 158–171.

Gesell, A., & Amatruda, C. S. *Developmental diagnosis: Normal and abnormal child development, clinical methods and practical applications.* New York: Harper, Row, 1941.

Gesell, A. & Ilg, F. L. *Child development: An introduction to the study of human development.* New York: Harper, Row, 1949.

Gesell, A. et al. *The first five years of life*, New York: Harper, Row, 1940. Also in A. Gesell and F. L. Ilg. *The child from five to ten.* Harper, Row, 1946.

Getman, G. N. *Techniques and diagnostic criteria for the optometric care of children's vision*, Duncan, Oklahoma: Optometric Extension Program Foundation, 1960.

Geyer, J. R., & Matanzo, J. B. *Programmed reading diagnosis for teachers, with prescriptive references.* Columbus, Ohio: Charles E. Merrill, 1977.

Gibson, E. J. *Principles of perceptual learning and development.* Englewood Cliffs, N.J.: Prentice-Hall, 1969.

———. The ontology of reading, 1970, 25, 136–143.

———.Perceptual learning and the theory of word perception. *Cognitive Psychology*, 1971, 2 351–368.

Gibson, E. J., & Levin, H. *The psychology of reading.* Cambridge, Mass: The MIT Press, 1975.

Gibson, E. J.; Osser, H.; Schiff, W.; & Smith, J. An analysis of critical features of letters, tested by a confusion matrix. In Final Report on a Basic Research Program on Reading, Cooperative Research Project No. 639, Cornell University & U.S. Office of Education, 1963.

Gibson, J. M. *Damn reading: A case against literacy.* New York: Vantage Press, 1969.

Gilliland, H. *A practical guide to remedial reading.* Columbus: Charles E. Merrill, 1974.

Gillingham, A. B., & Stillman, B. L. *Remedial training.* Cambridge, Mass.: Educators Publishing Service, 1960.

Gillingham, A. B., & Stillman, B. L. *Remedial training for children with specific disability in reading, spelling, and penmanship* (7th ed.). Cambridge, Mass.: Educators Publishing Service, 1965.

Gilmore, J. V. *Gilmore oral reading test.* New York: Harcourt Brace Jovanovich, 1968.

Goldberg, H. K. The ophthalmologist looks at the reading problem. *American Journal of Ophthalmology*, January 1959, 67, 56–59.

Goodglass, H., & Kaplan, E. *The assessment of aphasia and related disorders*. Philadelphia: Lea & Tebiger, 1972.

Goodman, K. S., & Niles, O. S. *Reading process and program*. Champaign, Illinois: National Council of Teachers of English, 1970.

Gough, H. G. *The adjective check list*. Berkeley: University of California Press, 1952.

Graham, F. K., & Kendall, B. S. Memory for designs test. *General manual, perceptual motor skills*, 2, Monthly Supplement, 2 (7), 1960, 147–158.

Gray, W. S. *On their own in reading*. Glenview, Illinois: Scott, Foresman, 1960, 205.

Gray, W. S., & Robinson, H. M. (eds.), *Gray oral reading tests*. Indianapolis: Bobbs-Merrill, 1967.

Gregory, R. L. *Eye and brain*. New York: McGraw-Hill, 1966, 160–163.

Grill, J. J., & Bartel, N. R. Language bias in tests: ITPA grammatic closure. *Journal of Learning Disabilities*, April 1977, 10 (4), 229–235.

Groff, P. Long versus short words in beginning reading. *Reading World*, May 1975, 14 (4), 277–286.

Gross, M. D., & Wilson, W. C. Behavior disorders of children with cerebral dysrhythmios. *Archives of General Psychiatry*, December 1964, 11, 610–619.

Gross, S.; Carr, M. L.; Dornseif, A.; & Rouse, S. M. Behavior objectives in a reading skills program, grades 4–8. *Reading Teacher*, May 1974, 27 (8), 782–789.

Guilford, J. P. *The nature of human intelligence*. New York: McGraw-Hill, 1967.

Guyer, B. P. The Montessori approach for the elementary-age LD child. *Academic Therapy*, Winter 1974–75, 10 (2), 187–192.

Guzak, F. J. Questioning strategies of elementary teachers in relation to comprehension. In *Reading and realism*, J. Allan Figural (Ed.). Newark: Del.: International Reading Association, 1969, 110–116.

Hafner, L. E., & Jolly, H. B. *Patterns of teaching reading in the elementary school*. New York: Macmillan Co., 1972.

Hallahan, D., & Cruickshank, W. *Psychoeducational foundations of learning disabilities*. Englewood Cliffs, N.J.: Prentice-Hall, 1973.

Hallenbeck, P. H. Remediating with comic strips. *Journal of Learning Disabilities*, January 1976, 9 (1), 22–26.

Hallgren, B. *Acta Psychiatricia and Neurologica*. Copenhagen, Supplement, No. 65 (1950).

Hammill, D.; Goodman, L.; & Wiederholt, J. D. Visual-motor processes: Can we train them? *Reading Teacher*, February 1974, 27 (5), 469–478.

Halstead, W. C., & Wepman, J. M. *Manual for the Halstead-Wepman screening test for aphasia*, Chicago: University of Chicago Clinic, 1949.

Hansen, C. L., & Lovitt, T. C. The relationship between question type and mode of reading on the ability to comprehend. *Journal of Special Education*, Spring 1976, 10, 53–60.

Harrington, M. J., & Durrell, D. Mental maturity versus perceptual abilities in primary reading. *Journal of Educational Psychology*, 1955, 46, 375–380.

Harris, A. J. *Harris tests of lateral dominance*. New York: Psychological Corp., 1958.

Harris, A. J., & Sepay, E. R. *How to increase reading ability* (6th ed.). New York: David McKay, 1976.

Harris, J. D. *Emotional blocks to learning*. New York: Free Press, 1961.

Harris, L. A., & Smith, C. B. *Reading instruction through diagnostic teaching*. New York: Holt, Rinehart & Winston, 1972.

Harris, T.; Creekmore, M.; & Greenman, M. *Phonetic keys to reading.* Oklahoma City: The Economy Co., 1967.

Harrower, M. Reading failure: A warning signal. *Woman's Home Companion,* July 1955, p. 43.

Heath, S. R. Relation of rail-walking and other motor performances of mental defectives to mental age and etiologic type. *Training School Bulletin,* October 1953, 50, 119–127.

Hebb, D. O. *The organization of behavior: A neuropsychological theory.* New York: John Wiley & Sons, 1949.

Heckelman, R. G. A neurological impress method of remedial reading instruction. *Academic Therapy,* Summer 1969, 277–282.

Hegge, T.; Kirk, S.; & Kirk, A. *Remedial reading skills.* Ann Arbor, Michigan: George Wehr, 1955.

Heilman, A. W. *Principles and practices of teaching reading* (3rd ed.). Columbus: Charles E. Merrill, 1972, 502.

Heiser, K. F., & Wolman, B. B. Mental deficiencies. In B. B. Wolman (Ed.). *Handbook of clinical psychology.* New York: McGraw-Hill, 1965.

Henrick, L. et al., Visual screening for elementary schools. *The Orinda study.* Berkeley: University of California Press, 1959.

Herman, K. *Reading disability.* Springfield, Illinois: Charles C. Thomas, 1959.

Hieronymus, A. H. & Lindquist, E. F. *Teacher's guide for the administration and interpretation and use of Iowa test of basic skills, forms 5 and 6.* Boston: Houghton Mifflin, 1971, p. 3.

Hinshelwood, J. *Congenital word blindness.* London: Lewis, 1917.

Hollander, S. K. Reading: Process and product. *Reading Teacher,* March 1975, 28 (6), 550–554.

Holmes, J. A., & Singer, H. *The substrata factor theory: Substrata factor differences underlying reading ability in known groups.* Cooperative Research Project, Washington, D.C.: U.S. Office of Education, 1961.

Hood, J. Sight words are not going out of style. *Reading Teacher,* January 1977, 30 (4), 379–382.

Hullsman, C. Some recent research on visual problems in reading. *American Journal of Optometry and Archives of the American Academy of Optometry,* November 1958, 36, 146–148.

Hunt, J. McV. *Intelligence and experience.* New York: The Ronald Press, 1961.

Huus, H. Developing reading readiness. *The Instructor,* March 1965, 74, 59.

Ilg, F. L., & Ames, L. B. *School readiness: Behavior tests used at the Gesell Institute.* New York: Harper, Row, 1965.

Jastak, J. F.; Byou, J. W.; & Jastak, S. R. *Wide range achievement test* (Rev. ed.). Wilmington, Del.: Guidance Associates, 1965.

Johns, J. A list of basic sight words for older disabled readers. *English Journal,* October 1972, 61, 1057–1059.

Johnson, D. J. The teaching of reading. *The Journal of Educational Research,* May-June 1974, 67 (9), 412.

Johnson, D. J., & Myklebust, H. R. *Learning disabilities: Educational principles and practices.* New York: Grune & Stratton, 1967.

Johnson, S. W., & Morasky, R. L. *Learning disabilities.* Boston: Allyn & Bacon, 1977.

Joint statement of the American Academy of Pediatrics and the American Academy of Ophthalmology and Otolaryngology, and the American Association of Ophthalmology. The eye and learning disabilities. *Pediatric News,* February 1972, 1, 63–66.

Jones, L. V., & Wepman, J. M. *A spoken word count.* Chicago: Language Research Associates, 1966, 607.

Jordan, B. T. *Jordan left-right reversal test.* San Rafael, California: Academic Therapy Publications, 1974.

Jordan, D. R. *Dyslexia in the classroom*, Columbus: Charles E. Merrill, 1977

Kagan, J. Reflection—impulsivity and reading ability in primary grade children. *Child Development*, 1965, 36, 688.

Kagan, J. Guatemalan Children and effects of early childhood deprivation: Longitudinal study, Address to American Association for the Advancement of Science. In *APA MONITOR*, February 1973, 4 (2), 1, 7.

Kaluger, G., & Heil, C. Basic symmetry and balance. *Progress in Physical Therapy*, 1970, 1 (2), 133–136.

Kaluger, G., & Kaluger, M. *Human development: The span of life*. St. Louis: C. V. Mosby, 1974.

Karlin, R. *Teaching elementary reading*. New York: Harcourt Brace Jovanovich, 1971.

Katz, P., & Deutch, M. Visual and auditory efficiency and its relationship to reading in children. Cooperative Research Project, No. 1099, Washington, D.C.: Office of Education, HEW, 1963.

Kawi, A. A., & Pasamanick, B. The association of factors of pregnancy with the development of reading disorders. *Journal of American Medical Association*, 1958, 166, 1420–1423.

Keeney, A. H., & Keeney, V. T. (Eds.), *Dyslexia: Diagnosis and treatment of reading disorders*. St. Louis: C. V. Mosby, 1968.

Kender, J. P., & Rubenstein, H. Recall versus reinspection in IRI comprehension tests. *Reading Teacher*, April 1977, 30 (7), 776–778.

Kephart, N. C. *The slow learner in the classroom* (2nd ed.). Columbus: Charles E. Merrill, 1971.

Kerr, J. School hygiene in its mental, moral and physical aspects. Howard Medal Prize Essay. *Royal Statistical Society Journal*, 1897, 60, 613–680.

Ketcham, W. A. Experimental tests of principles of developmental anatomy and neuroanatomy as applied to the pedagogy of reading. *Child Development*, September 1951, 22, 192.

Khoudadoust, A. Examination of 1,000 newborn. Speech presented at Wilmer Institute Annual Meeting, April 1967.

King, E. M. Effects of different kinds of visual discrimination training in learning to read words. *Journal of Educational Psychology*, 1964, 55, 325–333.

Kirk, S. A. *Teaching reading to slow-learning children*. Boston: Houghton Mifflin, 1940.

Kirk, S. A.; McCarthey, J. J.; & Kirk, W. *Illinois test of psycholinguistic abilities*. Urbana, Illinois: University of Illinois Press, 1968.

Kirschner, A. J. Reading training, 1945–1958. *Optometric Weekly*, April 1960, 51, 855–859.

Kirschner, A. J. *Body alphabet: Visual motor game*. Montreal, Canada: The Author, 4950 Queen Mary Road, 1960.

Klasen, E. *The syndrome of specific dyslexia*. Baltimore: University Park Press, 1972.

Kochevar, W. J. *Individualized remedial reading techniques for the classroom teacher*. West Nyack, N.Y.: Parker, 1975.

Kolers, P. A. Three stages of reading. In H. Levin and J. P. Williams (Eds.), *Basic studies on reading*. New York: Basic Books, 1970, 90–118.

Kolson, C. J. Private correspondence, German Farms, Maryland, April 1977.

Kolson, C. J., & Kaluger, G. *Clinical aspects of remedial reading*. Springfield, Illinois: Charles C. Thomas, 1963, 16–23.

Kolson, C. J., & Kaluger, G. *Primary learning disabilities series*. Shippensburg, Pa.: The Authors, 1965.

Kolson, C. J.; Odom, R.; & Bushong, J. The effect of supplementary diet on remedial readers. Unpublished report, Oregon State University, 1964.

Koppitz, E. M. *The Bender Gestalt Test for Young Children*. New York: Grune & Stratton, 1964, 63–64.

————. *The Bender Gestalt test for children* (2nd ed.). New York: Grune & Stratton, 1975.

Kostein, Sr., & Fowler, E. P. Differential diagnosis of communicative disorders in children referred by hearing tests. *American Medical Association Archives of Otolaryngology*, October 1954, 60.

Kottmeyer, W. *Teacher's Guide for remedial reading*. St. Louis: Webster, 1959.

————. *Teacher's manual for remedial reading*. New York: McGraw-Hill, 1960.

Kroth, J. A. A *programmed primer in learning disabilities*. Springfield, Illinois: Charles C. Thomas, 1971.

Kucera, H., & Francis, W. N. *Computational analysis of present-day American English*. Providence, R.I.: Brown University Press, 1967.

Labov, W., & Robins, C. A note on the relations of reading failure to peer-group status in urban ghettos. Monograph, New York: Columbia University Press, 1967.

Lamb, P. M., & Arnold, R. D. Reading: Foundations and instructional strategies. Belmont, Calif.: Wadsworth Publishing Co., 1976.

Lanier, R. J., & Davis, A. P. Developing comprehension through teacher-made questions. *Reading Teacher*, November 1972, 26 (2), 153–157.

Launta, R. E. Reversals: A response to frustrations? *Reading Teacher*, October 1971, 25 (1), 45–51.

Lawson, C. A. *Brain mechanisms and human learning*. Boston: Houghton Mifflin, 1967.

Lazar, A. L., & Lazar, P. E. Profile development for educational remediation. *Academic Therapy*, Winter 1973–74, 9 (3), 175–181.

Leary, B. Information please. A monograph on Reading, No. 28. New York: Harper, Row, 1965.

Leavell, V. W. *Leavell hand-eye coordination tests*. Davenport, Iowa: Mast/Keystone View Co. 1958.

————. *Manual for instruction for language development*. Davenport, Iowa: Mast/Keystone View Co., 1961.

Lee, D. M., & Allen, R. V. *Learning to read through experience* (2nd ed.). New York: Appleton-Century-Crofts, 1963.

Lerner, J. W. *Children with learning disabilities* (2nd ed.). Boston: Houghton Mifflin, 1976.

Levine, M., & Fuller, G. Psychological, neuropsychological and educational correlates of reading deficit. *Journal of Learning Disabilities*, November 1972, 5 (9), 563–571.

Levitt, T. C. Assessment of children with learning disabilities. *Exceptional Children*, December 1967, 34 (4), 233–241.

Liebert, R. J. The Electric Company. *In-school utilization study, vol. 2: 1972–73 school and teacher surveys and trends since fall, 1971*. Florida State University, Tallahassee, 1973.

Lillywhite, H. S.; Young, N. B.; & Olmsted, R. W. *Pediatrician's handbook of communicative disorders*. Philadelphia: Lea & Tebiger, 1971.

Lindgren, R. H. Performance of disabled and normal readers on the Bender-Gestalt, auditory discrimination test and visual-motor matching. *Perception and Motor Skills*, 1969, 29, 154.

Lowder, R. G. A *perceptual training procedure for beginning school children: Manual*. Winter Haven, Florida: Winter Haven Lion's Club, 1963.

Lowe, A. J., & Follman, J. Comparison of the Dolch list with other word lists *Reading Teacher*, October 1974, 28 (1), 40–45.

Mackworth, J. A. Cited in S. G. Sapir and A. C. Nitzburg, *Children with learning problems*. New York: Brunner/Mazel, 1973, 487–491.

Mackworth, J. F. Some models of the reading process: Learners and skilled readers. *Reading Research Quarterly*, Summer 1972, 7, 701–733.

Makita, K. The rarity of reading disability in Japanese children. *American Journal of Orthopsychiatry*, July 1968, *38*, 599–613.

Malley, J. D. The measurement of reading skills. *Journal of Learning Disabilities*, July 1975, *8* (6), 376–381.

Mangieri, J. N., & Kahn, M. S. Is the Dolch list of 220 basic sight words irrelevant? *Reading Teacher*, March 1977, *30* (6), 649–650.

Marshall, J. D. & Newcombe, F. Patterns of paralexia: A psycholinguistic approach. *Journal of Psycholinguistic Research*, 1973, *2*, 175–199.

Martin, E. A. *Mental capacity and learning behavior hypothesis: Nutrition in action*. New York: Holt, Rinehart & Winston, 1971.

Maryland State Department of Education. *Functional Reading Resource Manual for Teachers, Vol. I, Vol. II*. Baltimore: Maryland State Department of Education, 1975.

Matthes, C. *How children are taught to read*. Lincoln, Nebraska: Professional Educators Publications, 1972.

Mattis, S.; French, J. H.; & Rapin, I. Dyslexia in children and young adults: Three independent neurological syndromes. *Development Medicine and Child Neurology*, April 1975, *17* (2), 150–163.

Mauser, A. Learning disabilities and delinquent youth. *Academic Therapy*, 1974, *9*, 389–402.

McCarthy, D. *McCarthy scales of children's abilities*. New York: The Psychological Corporation, 1972.

McCroskey, R. L., & Thompson, N. W. Comprehension of rate controlled speech by children with specific learning disabilities. *Journal of Learning Disabilities*, December 1973, *6* (10), 621–627.

McCullough, C. Emphasize how to read. *Reading Improvement*, Spring 1976, *13*, 26–28.

_____. *The literature sampler*. Chicago: Learning Materials, (no date).

McGhee, P. E. Development of the humor response: A review of the literature. *Psychological Bulletin*, Winter 1971, *76*, 328–348.

McGinnis, M. A. *Aphasic children*. Washington, D.C.: Alexander Graham Bell Association, 1963a.

_____. *Aphasic children*. Washington, D.C.: Volta Bureau, 1963b.

McGinnis, M. A.; Kleffner, F.; & Goldstein, R. *Teaching aphasic children*. Washington, D.C.: The Voltar Bureau, 1963.

McGlannan, F. K. When film is flim. *Newsweek*, July 31, 1967, *69*, 48.

McLeod, J. *Dyslexia in young children: A factorial study with special reference to the ITPA*. University of Illinois IREC Papers in Education, 1966.

_____. Reading expectancies from disabled readers. *Journal of Learning Disabilities*, February 1968, *1* (2), 97–105.

Menyuk, P., & Looney, P. Relationship between components of the grammar in language disorders. *Journal of Speech and Hearing Research*, June 1972, *15*, 395–406.

Messing, E. S. Auditory perception: What is it? Selected papers on learning disabilities. San Rafael: Association of Children with Learning Disabilities, 1969.

Miller, W. H. *Identifying and correcting reading difficulties in children*. New York: The Center for Applied Research in Education, 1971, 137–152.

_____. *Reading diagnostic kit*. New York: The Center for Applied Research in Education, 1974.

_____. *Reading correction kit*. New York: The Center for Applied Research in Education, 1975, sections 6, 10, 12.

Mills, R. E. *Learning methods test*. Fort Lauderdale, Florida: Mills Center, 1955.

Minskoff, E.; Wiseman, D. E.; & Minskoff, J. G. *The MWM program for developing language abilities.* Ridgefield, N.J.: Educational Performance Association, 1972.

Mohr, J. P. Evaluation of the deficit in total aphasia. *Neurology,* 1973, 23, 1302–1312.

Money, J. *Reading disability: Progress and research needs in dyslexia.* Baltimore: Johns Hopkins Press, 1962.

———. *The disabled reader: Education of the dyslexic child.* Baltimore: Johns Hopkins Press, 1966, 148–151.

Monroe, M. *Diagnostic reading examination.* Pittsburgh, Pa.: C. V. Nevins, 1932a.

———. *Children who cannot read.* Chicago: University of Chicago Press, 1932b.

Montessori, M. *Dr. Montessori's own handbook.* New York: Shocken Books, 1965 Edition (original 1914).

———. *The Montessori method.* Cambridge, Mass.: Robert Bentley, 1967.

Morency, A. Auditory modality: Research and practice. In H. K. Smith (Ed.), *Perception and reading.* Proceedings of the 12th Annual Convention, International Reading Association, Newark, Del., 1968, 17–21.

Morgan, W. P. A case of congenital word-blindness. *British Medical Journal* 1896, 2, 1378.

Morris, J. M. Television and reading. Paper presented at the International Reading Association Convention, New Orleans, 1974.

Murphy, J. F. Learning by listening: A public school approach learning disabilities. *Academic Therapy,* Winter 1972, 8 (2), 167.

Mutti, M.; Spalding, N. V.; Sterling, H. M.; & Crawford, C. S. *Quick neurological screen test.* San Rafael: Calif.: Academic Therapy Publications, 1974.

Myklebust, H. R. *Auditory disorders in children.* New York: Grune & Stratton, 1954.

———. Aphasia in children. In L. Travis (Ed.), *Handbook of speech pathology.* New York: Appleton-Century-Crofts, 1957.

———. Learning disorders: Psychoneurological disturbances in childhood. *Rehabilitation Literature,* December 1964, 25, 354–359.

———. *Picture story language tests.* New York: Grune & Stratton, 1965.

Naidoo, S. Specific development dyslexia. *British Journal of Educational Psychology,* 1971, 41, 19–21.

Neisser, U. *Cognitive psychology.* New York: Appleton-Century-Crofts, 1967.

Newborough, J. R., & Kelley, J. G. A study of reading achievement in a population of school children. In J. Money, *Reading disability.* Baltimore: Johns Hopkins Press, 1962.

Newcombe, N. J. The good start program: Reading readiness in action. *Library Journal,* February 15, 1974, 99, 541.

Newcomer, P., & Magee, P. The performance of learning (reading) disabled children on a test of spoken language. *Reading Teacher,* May 1977, 30 (8), 896–980.

Newcomer, P.; Hare, B.; Hammill, D.; & McGettigan, J. Construct validity of the Illinois test of psychologistic abilities. *Journal of Learning Disabilities,* April 1975, 8 (4), 221–231.

Nielson, J. M. *Agnosia, agnoxia, aphasia* (2nd ed.). New York: Hafner Publishing Co., 1965.

Oakland, T., & Williams, F. *Auditory perception.* Seattle, Washington: Special Child Publications, Inc., 1971, 15.

Oettenger, L. The use of Deanol in the treatment of disorders of behavior in children. *Journal of Pediatrics,* Spring 1958, 53, 671–675.

Ogden, C. K. *The system of basic English.* New York: Harcourt Brace, 1934.

Orton, S. T., *Reading, writing and speech problems in children.* New York: Horton, 1937.

Osgood, C. E. *Method and theory in experimental psychology.* New York: Oxford University Press, 1953.

Osgood, C. E., & Miron, M. (Eds.). *Approaches to the study of aphasia.* Urbana, Illinois: University of Illinois Press, 1963.

Otto, A. A guide to helping children with learning problems. *The Clearing House,* October 1965, *40* (2), 000.

Otto, W.; Chester, R.; McNeil, J.; & Myers, S. *Focused reading instruction.* Reading, Mass.: Addison-Wesley, 1974.

Paine, C. A. Comics for fun and profits. *Learning,* January 1974, *3,* 86–89.

Park, G. E. Nuture and/or nature cause reading difficulties? *Archives of Pediatrics,* November 1952, *64,* 432–444.

Pasamanick, B., & Knoblock, H. The epidemiology of reproductive causality. In S. Sapir and A. Nitzburg (Eds.), *Children with learning problems.* New York: Brunner/Mazel, 1973, 193–199.

Paul, G. T. The relationship between parental and perinatal stress and cognitive functioning in preschool children. Speech presented at Eastern Psychological Association, Philadelphia, Pa., April 10, 1969.

Joint statement of the Academy of Pediatrics, the American Academy of Ophthalmology and Otolaryngology and the American Association of Ophthalmology. *Pediatric News,* February 1972, *1,* 63–66.

Peterson, R. (Ed.), *Project read.* Washington, D.C.: Right to Read, 1975.

Piaget, J. *The origins of intelligence in children.* New York: W. W. Norton, 1952.

_____. Piaget's ideas have been updated in *The mechanisms of perception.* New York: Basic Books, 1969; and *Structuralism.* New York: Basic Books, 1970.

Pick, A. S. Improvement of visual and tactual form discrimination. *Journal of Experimental Psychology,* 1965, *65,* 331–339.

Pine, M. *Revolution in learning: The years from birth to six.* New York: Harper, Row, 1967.

Pope, L. Sight words for the seventies. *Academic Therapy,* Spring 1975, *10* (3), 285–289.

Porch, B. *Porch index of communicative ability.* Palo Alto, California: Consulting Psychologists Press, 1971.

Potter, T. C., & Rae, G. *Informal reading diagnosis: A practical guide for the classroom teacher.* Englewood Cliffs, N.J.: Prentice-Hall, 1973, 81–87.

Price, L. D. The trouble with poor auditory perception. *Academic Therapy,* Spring 1973, *8* (3), 331–337.

Pronovost, W., & Dumbleton, C. A picture type speech sound discrimination test. *Journal of Speech and Hearing Disorders,* 1953, *18,* 258–266.

Quant, I. Investing in word banks—a practice for any approach. *Reading Teacher,* November 1973, *27* (2), 171–173.

Rabin, A. I. Diagnostic use of intelligence tests. In B. B. Wolman, *Handbook of clinical psychology.* New York: McGraw-Hill, 1965.

Rabinovitch, R. D. Reading and learning disabilities, Vol. 2, In S. Arieti (Ed.), *American handbook of psychiatry.* New York: Basic Books, 1959, 857–870.

_____. Reading problems in children: Definitions and classifications. In A. H. Keeney and V. T. Keeney, *Dyslexia.* St. Louis: C. V. Mosby, 1968.

Rabinovitch, R. D., & Ingram, W. Neuropsychiatric considerations in reading retardation. *Reading Teacher*, May 1962, 433–438. Reprinted with permission of the International Reading Association and the authors.

Rabinovitch, R. D.; Drew, A. C.; DeJones, M.; Ingram, W.; & Witbey, L. A research approach to reading retardation in neurology and psychiatry in childhood. *Research Publications of the Association for Research in Nervous and Mental Diseases*, 1954, 34, 363–396.

Rappaport, S. R. *Childhood aphasia and brain damage*. Narberth, Pennsylvania: Livingston Publishing Co., 1964.

————. *Child aphasia and brain damage* (Vol. II). Narberth, Pennsylvania: Pathway School, 1965.

Rawson, M. B. Developmental dyslexia: Educational treatment and results. In D. D. Duane and M. B. Rawson, *Reading, perception and language*. Baltimore: The Orton Society, 1975.

Renshaw, D. C. *The hyperactive child*. Chicago: Nelson Hall, 1974.

Richardson, S. W. *Learning disabilities–An introduction, international approach to learning disabilities of children and youth*. Pittsburgh, Pennsylvania: Association for Children with Learning Disabilities, 1966.

Richman, V.; Rosner, J.; & Scott, R. H. A study of perceptual-motor dysfunction among emotionally disturbed, educable mentally retarded and normal children in the Pittsburgh schools. In the Manual for the Rosner-Richman Perceptual Survey (RRPS). Pittsburgh: Division of Mental Health, Pittsburgh Public Schools (Pa.), July 1968.

Rigg, P. Getting the message, decoding the message. *Reading Teacher*, April 1977, 30 (7), 745–749.

Right to Read '77. Newark, Del.: International Reading Association, April 1977, 3 (4).

Roach, E. C., & Kephart, N. C. *The Purdue perceptual-motor survey*. Columbus: Charles E. Merrill, 1966.

Robbins, M. P. A study of the validity of Delacato's theory of neurological organization. *Exceptional Children*, April 1966, 32 (8), 517–524.

Robinson, F. P. *Effective reading*. New York: Harper, Row, 1962.

Robinson, H. M. *Why pupils fail in reading*. Chicago: University of Chicago Press, 1946.

————. *Why children fail in reading*. Supplementary Monograph #79, Chicago: University of Chicago Press, 1953.

————. Visual and auditory modalities related to methods for beginning reading. *Reading Research Quarterly*, Fall 1972, 8 (1), 7.

Roeder, H. H., & Lee, N. Twenty-five teacher-tested ways to encourage voluntary reading. *Reading Teacher*, October 1973, 27 (1), 48–50.

Rosner, J. Language arts and arithmetic skills, and specifically related perceptual skills. American Educational Research Journal, Winter 1973, 10 (1), 59–68.

Ross, A. O. *Psychological aspects of learning disabilities and reading disorders*. New York: McGraw-Hill, 1976.

Rubin, R. A.; Rosenblatt, C.; & Barlow, B. Psychological and educational sequelae of prematurity. *Pediatrics*, 1973, 52, 352–363.

Rude, R. T. Readiness tests: Implications for early childhood education. *Reading Teacher*, March 1973, 26 (6), 572–580.

Rugel, R. P. WISC Subtest scores of disabled readers: A review with respect to Bannatyne's recategorization. *Journal of Learning Disabilities*, January 1974, 7 (1), 48–55.

Rychener, R., & Robinson, J. Reading disabilities and the ophthalmologist. *American Academy of Ophthalmology and Otolaryngology*. November-December 1958, 62.

Sabatino, D. A., & Streissguth, W. O. Word form configuration training of visual perceptual strengths with learning disabled learners. *Journal of Learning Disabilities*, August-September 1972, 5 (7), 435–441.

Samuels, S. J. Automatic decoding and reading comprehension. *Language Arts*, March 1976, 53, 323–325.

Sartain, H. W.; Larsen, S. C.; Steck, S.; & Wallace, G. Symposium: Who shall teach the learning disabled child? *Journal of Learning Disabilities*, October 1976, 9 (8), 488–532.

Schiffman, G. Dyslexia as an educational phenomenon: Its treatment and recognition. In J. Money, *Reading disability*. Baltimore: John Hopkins Press, 1962.

Schoolfield, L. D., & Timberlake, J. B. *The phonovisual method*. Washington, D.C.: Phonovisual Products, 1960.

———. *The phonovisual method* (Rev. ed.). Rockville, Md.: Phonovisual Products, 1974.

Schrag, P., & Divoky, D. *The myth of the hyperactive child*. New York: Pantheon Books, a Division of Random House, 1975.

Schuell, H. A short examination for aphasia. *Neurology*, 1957, 7 (9), 625–634.

———. *Minnesota test for differential diagnosis of aphasia*. Minneapolis, Minnesota: University of Minnesota Press, 1965.

Serio, M. Readiness training: Myth or reality in this space age? *Academic Therapy*, Summer 1973, 8 (4), 447–460.

Shearer, R. V. Eye findings in children with reading difficulties. *Journal of Pediatric Ophthalmology*, November 1966, 4, 47–53.

Shephard, D. L. *Effective reading in social studies*. Evanston, Illinois: Row Peterson, 1960a.

Shepherd, D. L. *Effective reading in science*. Evanston, Illinois: Row Peterson, 1960b.

Shirley, M. M. *The first two years* (2 Vols). Minneapolis: University of Minnesota Press, 1933.

Shoreline School District #412, Phonics Committee. *Phonics handbook*. Shoreline, Washington: Shoreline School District #412, 1970.

Silberberg, N. E., & Silberberg, M. C. A note on reading tests and their role in defining reading difficulties. *Journal of Reading Disabilities*, February 1977, N (2), 100–104.

Silvaroli, N. *Classroom reading inventory*. Dubuque, Iowa: William C. Brown, 1972.

Silver, A. A., & Hagin, R. A. Specific reading disability, an approach to diagnosis and treatment. *Journal of Special Education*, December 1976, 2, 109–118.

Silver, A. A.; Hagin, R. A.; & Hersch, M. F. Specific reading disability: Teaching through stimulation of deficit perceptual area. Paper read at the Annual Meeting of the American Orthopsychiatric Association, New York, 1965.

Silverton, R. A., & Deichmann, J. W. Sense modality research and the acquisition of reading skills. *Review of Educational Research*, Winter 1975, 45 (1), 149–172.

Simons, H. D. Linguistic skills and reading comprehension. In H. A. Klein (Ed.), *The quest for competency in teaching reading*. Newark, Del.: International Reading Association, 1972, 165–170.

Skydgaards, H. B. *Dyslexiens prognose*. Skolshygiejnisk, Tedskrift, 1944.

Slingerland, B. H. A *multi-sensory approach to language arts for specific language disability: A guide for primary teachers*. Cambridge, Massachusetts: Educators Publishing Service, 1971.

Sloan, W. *Lincoln-Oseretsky motor development scale*. Chicago: C. H. Stoelting Co., 1955.

Slosson, R. *Slosson intelligence test*. East Aurora, N.Y.: Slosson Educational Publications, 1963.

Small, M. W. Just what is dyslexia? *The Instructor*, August–September 1967, 77, 54–57.

Smedslund, J. The acquisition of conservation of substance and weight in children. *Scandinavian Journal of Psychology*, 1961, 2, 71–87.

Smith, D. E. *The Michigan successive discrimination reading program*. Ann Arbor, Michigan: Ann Arbor Publishing Co., 1966.

Smith, D. E., & Carrigan, P. *The nature of reading disability*. New York: Harcourt, Brace & World, 1960.

Smith, N. B. The many faces of reading comprehension. *Reading Teacher*, December 1969, 23 (3), 249–259.

———. *The role of the teacher, parent, reading specialist and administrator in developing successful reading programs*. Newark, Del.: International Reading Association, 1974.

Smith, P. A., & Marx, R. W. The factor structure of the revised edition of the ITPA. *Psychology in the Schools*, July 1971, 8, 349–356.

Smith, R. J. The physiology of reading. *The Journal of Educational Research*, May-June 1974, 67 (9), 400.

Snyder, R. T. et al. Reading readiness and its relation to maturational unreadiness as measured by the spiral after-effect and other visual perceptual techniques. *Perception and Motor Skills*, December 1967, 25, 854.

Spache, G. D., & Spache, E. B. *Reading in the elementary school* (2nd ed.). Boston: Allyn & Bacon, 1969.

Spache, G. D. *Binocular reading test*. Davenport, Iowa: Mast/Keystone View Co., 1961.

———. *Diagnostic reading scales*. Monterey: California Test Bureau, 1972.

———. *Investigating the issues of reading disabilities*. Boston: Allyn & Bacon, 1976.

Spalding, R. B., & Spalding, W. T. *The writing road to reading*. New York: Whiteside, and William R. R. Morrow & Co., 1957.

Spradlin, J. E. Parsons 'language sample. *Journal of Speech and Hearing Disabilities Monograph Supplement*, January 1963, 10, 8–31, 81–91.

Stanger, M. A., & Donohue, E. K. *Prediction and prevention of reading difficulties*. New York: Oxford University Press, 1958.

Stauffer, R. G. Do sex differences affect reading? *The Instructor*, May 1968, 77, 25.

———. *The language-experience approach to the teaching of reading*. New York: Harper, Row, 1970.

Stephenson, W. *The study of behavior: Q-Technique and its methodology*. Chicago: University of Chicago Press, 1953.

Strang, R.; McCullough, G. M.; & Traxler, A. E. *The improvement of reading* (4th ed.). New York: McGraw-Hill, 1967.

Strauss, A. A., & Lehtinen, L. E. *Psychopathology and education of the brain injured child*. New York: Grune & Stratton, 1947.

Street, R. F. *A Gestalt completion test*. New York: Teacher's College Press, Contributions to Education #481, 1931.

Sutphin, F. F. *A perceptual testing-training handbook for first grade teachers*, Winter Haven, Florida: Winter Haven Lions Club, 1964.

Taylor, S. E.; Frackenpohl, H.; & Pettee, J. L. Grade Level norms for the components of the fundamental reading skill. Huntington, New York: Educational Development Laboratories, 1960, Bull. No. 3, 12.

Teaching Reading Skills (Vol. II). *Comprehension, critical reading/thinking skills, K–12*. Montgomery County Public Schools, Rockville, Maryland, Bulletin No. 246, 1974.

Templin, M. C., & Darley, F. L. *Templin-Darley screening and diagnostic tests of articulation.* Iowa City, Iowa: Bureau of Educational Research & Service, University of Iowa, 1960.

Terman, L. M., & Merrill, M. A. *Revised Stanford-Binet scale.* Boston: Houghton Mifflin, 1960.

Terman, L. M., & Merrill, M. A. *Stanford-Binet Intelligence Scale* (3rd ed.) Form L-M. Boston: Houghton Mifflin, 1960.

Thomas, C. J. Congenital word-blindness and its treatment. *Ophthalmoscope,* 1905, *3,* 380.

Thorpe, L. P.; Clark, W. W.; & Tiegs, E. W. *California test of personality.* New York: Psychological Corporation/CTB, 1953.

Thorson, G. An alternative for judging confusability of visual letters. *Perceptual and Motor Skills,* 1976, *42,* 116–118.

Thurstone, L. L., & Thurstone, T. G. Factoral studies of intelligence. *Psychometric Monographs,* 1941, no. 2.

Tinker, M. A., & McCullough, C. M. *Teaching elementary reading.* New York: Meredith, 1968.

Tjosseim, T. D.; Hansen, T. J.; & Ripley, H. S. An investigation of reading difficulties in young children. *American Journal of Psychiatry,* 1962, *118,* 1104–1113.

Tovey, D. R. Improving children's comprehension ability. *Reading Teacher,* December 1976, 30:3, 288–292.

Tredgold, A. F. *Mental deficiency.* London: Bailliere, 1908.

Treichel, J. A. School lights and problem children. *Science News,* April 20, 1974, *105,* 258.

Trzcinski, B. *All about me, myself and I.* San Rafael, California: Academic Therapy Publications, 1972.

U.S. Department, HEW. *The anchor test study* (No. 1780–01312). Washington, D.C.: U.S. Govt. Printing Office, 1975.

Van Allan, R. *Language experiences in communication.* Boston: Houghton Mifflin, 1976, 5–8, 257–273.

Vande Voort, L.; Senf, G. M.; & Benton, A. L. Development of audiovisual integration in normal and retarded readers. *Child Development,* 1972, *43,* 1260–1272.

Van Witsen, B. *Perceptual training activities handbook.* New York: Teachers College Press, 1967.

Vogel, S. A. Syntactic abilities in normal and dyslexic children. *Journal of Learning Disabilities,* February 1974, 7 (2), 103–109.

Walcott, C. C., & McCracken, G. *Basic reading.* Philadelphia: Lippincott, 1963.

Walker, S. We're too cavalier about hyperactivity. *Psychology Today,* December 1974, 8, 43 ff.

Wallace, G., & Kauffman, J. M. *Teaching children with learning disabilities.* Columbus: Charles E. Merrill, 1973.

Wallace, P. Complex environment: Effects on brain development. *Science,* September 20, 1974, *185,* 1035–1037.

Wallach, G. P., & Goldsmith, S. C. Language-based learning disabilities: Reading is language, too. *Journal of Learning Disabilities,* March 1977, *10* (3), 178–182.

Wallach, L., & Wallach, M. A. *Teaching all children to read.* Chicago: University of Chicago Press, 1976.

Wallach, L.; Wallach, M. A.; Dozier, M. G.; & Kaplan, N. E. Poor children learning to read do not have trouble with auditory discrimination but do have trouble with phoneme recognition. *Journal of Educational Psychology,* February 1977, *69* (1), 36–39.

Wallen, C. J. *Competency in teaching reading.* Chicago: Science Research Associates, 1972.

Walter, W. G. *The living brain.* New York: Norton, 1953.

———. Intrinsic rhythms of the brain. In J. Field (Ed.). *Handbook of neurophysiology.* Washington, D.C.: American Physiological Association, 1959, 279–298.

Walton, H. Vision and rapid reading. *American Journal of Optometry and Archives of the American Academy of Optometry, Monograph,* February 1957, 208.

Wardhaugh, R. The teaching of phonics and reading comprehension: A linguistic evaluation. In K. S. Goodman and J. T. Fleming (eds.), *Psycholinguistics and the teaching of reading.* Newark, Del.: international Reading Association, 1969, 79–90.

Wechsler, D. *Wechsler adult intelligence scale.* New York: Psychological Corporation, 1955.

———. *Wechsler preschool and primary scale of intelligence.* New York: The Psychological Corporation, 1967.

———. *Wechsler intelligence scale for children* (Rev. ed). New York: Psychological Corporation, 1974.

Weintraub, S. Eye-hand preference and reading. *Reading Teacher,* January 1968, 21 (3), 369–373.

Wepman, J. M. *Auditory discrimination test.* Chicago: Language Research Associates, 1958.

———. Dyslexia: Its relationship to language acquisition and concept formation. In J. Money *Reading disability: Progress and research needs in dyslexia.* Baltimore: Johns Hopkins Press, 1962.

———. The perceptual basis for learning in meeting individual differences, H. Robinson (Ed.). Supplementary Educational Monograph, No. 94, Chicago: University of Chicago Press, 1964, 25–33.

Wepman, J. M., & Jones, L. *Studies in aphasia: An approach to testing.* Chicago: Language Research Associates, 1961.

Whaley, W. J. Closing the blending gap. *Reading World,* December 1975, 15 (2), 97–100.

Whisler, N. G. The newspaper: Resource for teaching study skills. *Reading Teacher,* April 1972, 25 (7), 652–656.

Whorf, B. L. Linguistics as an exact science. In J. B. Carroll (Ed.), *Language, thought and reality.* Cambridge, Mass.: MIT Press, 1956.

Wiig, E. H., & Semel, E. M. *Language disabilities in children and adolescents.* Columbus: Charles E. Merrill, 1976.

Wilson, R. M. *Diagnostic and remedial reading for classroom and clinic* (2nd ed.). Columbus: Charles E. Merrill, 1972.

Wilson, R. M., & Hall, M. A. *Reading and the elementary school child.* New York: Van Nostrand Reinhold, 1972, 172–175.

Witelson, S. Abnormal right-hemisphere specialization in developmental dyslexia. In R. Knights and D. Baker (Eds.), *The neuropsychology of learning disorders: Theoretical approaches.* Baltimore: University Park Press, 1976a.

———. Sex and the single hemisphere. *Science,* 1976b, 193: 425–427.

Witkin, B. R. Auditory perception—implications for language development. *Journal of Research and Development in Education,* Fall 1969, 3, 53–71.

Wold, R. Vision and learning disabilities. *The Journal of the American Optometric Association,* February 1972, 43 (2).

Wolf, A. Hyperactive children give food for thought. *Times Education Supplement,* January 17, 1975, 3112, 17.

Woodcock, R. W. *Peabody rebus reading program.* Circle Pines, Minnesota: American Guidance Service, 1967.

Wunderlich, R. C. Treatment of the hyperactive child. *Academic Therapy,* Summer 1973, 8 (4), 375–390.

Yoakam, G. A. *Basal reading instruction*. Englewood Cliffs: Prentice-Hall, 1955.

Young, V., & Scrimshaw, N. The physiology of starvation. *Scientific American*, October 1971, 225, 14–21.

Zangwill, O. L. *Cerebral dominance and its relation to psychological function*. London: Oliver & Boyd, 1960.

Zeidel, E. Auditory vocabulary of the right hemisphere following brain bisection or hemidecortication. *Cortex*, September 1976, 12, 3, 191–211.

———. Unilateral auditory language comprehension on the token test following cerebral commissurotomy, and hemispherectomy. *Neuropychologia*, 1977, 15 (1), 1–18.

Zeman, S. S. Word analysis skills are not reading skills. *Academic Therapy*, Summer 1964, 9 (6), 465–467.

Zigmond, N. K. Auditory processes in children with learning disabilities. In L. Tarnapoli (Ed.), *Learning disabilities: Introduction to education and medical management*. Springfield, Illinois: Charles C. Thomas, 1969.

Zigmond, N. K., & Cicci, R. Auditory learning. Belmont, Calif.: Fearon, 1968.

Zirbes, Laura. *Comparative studies of current practice in reading with techniques for the improvement of teaching*, New York: AMS Press, 1928 (reprint 1964).

INDEX